ISBN 978-0-331-00268-3
PIBN 11000923

FB &c Ltd, Dalton House, 60 Windsor Avenue, London, SW19 2RR.
Company number 08720141. Registered in England and Wales.

For support please visit www.forgottenbooks.com

VOL. XIV., No. 1. OCTOBER, 1903.

THE MONIST

A QUARTERLY MAGAZINE

Devoted to the Philosophy of Science

Editor: Dr. Paul Carus. *Associates* { E. C. Hegeler. Mary Carus.

CONTENTS:

CHICAGO:

THE OPEN COURT PUBLISHING CO.

Price, 50 cts.; Yearly, $2.00.

LONDON: Kegan Paul, Trench, Trübner & Company, Limited.

In England and U. P. U., half a crown; Yearly, 9s 6d.

 Entered at the Chicago Post Office as Second-Class Matter.

THE MONIST

A QUARTERLY MAGAZINE

DEVOTED TO THE PHILOSOPHY OF SCIENCE

VOLUME XIV

CHICAGO
THE OPEN COURT PUBLISHING COMPANY
LONDON AGENTS:
Kegan Paul, Trench, Trübner & Co., Ltd.
1904

CONTENTS OF VOLUME XIV.

ARTICLES AND AUTHORS.

BOOK REVIEWS AND NOTES.

VOL. XIV. No. 1. OCTOBER, 1903.

THE MONIST

A QUARTERLY MAGAZINE

Devoted to the Philosophy of Science

Editor: DR. PAUL CARUS. *Associates:* { E. C. HEGELER. MARY CARUS.

CONTENTS:

CHICAGO:

THE OPEN COURT PUBLISHING COMPANY.

1903.

VOL. XIV. OCTOBER, 1903. NO. 1.

THE MONIST

SPACE AND GEOMETRY FROM THE POINT OF VIEW OF PHYSICAL INQUIRY.[1]

OUR notions of space are rooted in our *physiological* constitution. Geometric concepts are the product of the idealisation of *physical* experiences of space. Systems of geometry, finally, originate in the logical classification of the conceptual materials so gathered. All three factors have left their indubitable traces in modern geometry. Epistemological inquiries regarding space and geometry accordingly concern the physiologist, the psychologist, the physicist, the mathematician, the philosopher, and the logician alike, and they can be gradually carried to their definitive solution only by the consideration of the widely disparate points of view which are here offered.

Awakening in early youth to full consciousness, we find ourselves in possession of the notion of a *space* surrounding and encompassing our body, in which space move various *bodies*, partly altering and partly retaining their size and shape. It is impossible for us to ascertain how this notion has been begotten. Only the most thoroughgoing analysis of experiments purposefully and me-

[1] The present article is intended to supplement the two preceding papers which I wrote on similar subjects in *The Monist*, Vol. XI., page 321, and Vol. XII., page 481. I am endeavoring in this essay to define my attitude as a physicist toward the subject of metageometry so called. Detailed geometric developments will have to be sought in the sources. I trust, however, that by the employment of illustrations which are familiar to every one I have made my expositions as popular as the subject permitted. [Translated from Professor Mach's manuscript by T. J. McCormack.]

thodically planned has enabled us to conjecture that inborn idiosyncracies of the body have coöperated to this end with simple and crude experiences of a purely physical character.

An object seen or touched is distinguished not only by a *sensational quality* (as "red," "rough," "cold," etc.), but also by a *locative quality* (as "to the left," "above," "before," etc.). The sensational quality may remain the same, while the locative quality continuously changes; that is, the same sensuous object may move in space. Phenomena of this kind being again and again induced by physico-physiological circumstances, it is found that however varied the accidental sensational qualities may be, the same order of locative qualities invariably occurs, so that the latter appear perforce as a fixed and permanent system or register in which the sensational qualities are entered and classified. Now, although these qualities of sensation and locality can be excited only in conjunction with one another, and can make their appearance only concomitantly, the impression nevertheless easily arises that the more familiar system of locative qualities is given antecedently to the sensational qualities (Kant).

Extended objects of vision and of touch consist of more or less distinguishable sensational qualities, conjoined with adjacent distinguishable, continuously graduated locative qualities. If such objects move, particularly in the domain of our hands, we perceive them to shrink or swell (in whole or in part), or we perceive them to remain the same; in other words, the contrasts characterising their bounding locative qualities change or remain constant. In the latter instance, we call the objects rigid. By the recognition of permanency as coincident with spatial displacement, the various constituents of our intuition of space are rendered *comparable* with one another,—at first in the *physiological* sense. By the comparison of different bodies with one another, by the introduction of *physical* measures, this comparability is rendered quantitative and more exact, and so transcends the limitations of individuality. Thus, in the place of an individual and non-transmittable intuition of space are substituted the universal concepts of geometry, which hold good for all men. Each person has his own individual intuitive space; geometric space is common to all. Between the space of intuition and *metric* space, which contains physical experiences, we must sharply distinguish.

II.

The need of a thoroughgoing epistemological elucidation of the foundations of geometry induced Riemann,[1] about the middle of the century just closed, to propound the question of the nature of space; the attention of Gauss, Lobachévski, and Bolyai having before been drawn to the empirically hypothetical character of certain of the fundamental assumptions of geometry. In characterising space as a special case of a multiply-extended "magnitude," Riemann had doubtless in mind certain geometric constructs which may similarly be imagined to fill all space,—for example, the system of Cartesian co-ordinates. Riemann further asserts that "the propositions of geometry cannot be deduced from general conceptions of magnitude, but that the peculiar properties by which space is distinguished from other conceivable triply-extended magnitudes can be derived from experience only.... These facts, like all facts, are in no wise necessary, but possess empirical certitude only,—they are hypotheses." Like the fundamental assumptions of every natural science, so also, on Riemann's theory, the fundamental assumptions of geometry, to which experience has led us, are merely *idealisations* of experience.

In this physical conception of geometry, Riemann takes his stand on the same ground as his master Gauss, who once expressed the conviction that it was impossible to establish the foundations of geometry entirely *a priori*,[2] and who further asserted that "we must in humility confess that if number is exclusively a product of the mind, space possesses in addition a reality outside of our mind, of which reality we cannot fully dictate *a priori* the laws.[3]

---

[1] *Ueber die Hypothesen, welche der Geometrie zu Grunde liegen.* Göttingen, 1867.

[2] *Brief von Gauss an Bessel*, 27. Januar 1829.

[3] *Brief von Gauss an Bessel*, 9. April 1830.—The phrase "Number is a product or creation of the mind" has since been repeatedly used by mathematicians.

Every inquirer knows that the knowledge of an object he is investigating is materially augmented by *comparing* it with related objects. Quite naturally therefore Riemann looks about him for objects which offer some analogy to space. Geometric space is defined by him as a triply-extended continuous manifold, the elements of which are the points determined by every possible three co-ordinate values. He finds that "the places of objects of sense and colors are probably the only concepts [*sic*] whose modes of determination form a multiply-extended manifold." To this analogy others were added by Riemann's successors and elaborated by them, but not always, I think, felicitously.[1]

Comparing *sensation* of space with *sensation* of color, we discover that to the continuous series "above and below," "right and left," "near and far," correspond the three sensational series of mixed colors, black-white, red-green, blue-yellow. The system of sensed (seen) places is a triple continuous manifold like the system of color-sensations. The objection which is raised against this analogy, viz., that in the first instance the three variations (dimensions) are homogeneous and interchangeable with one another, while in the second instance they are heterogeneous and not interchangeable, does not hold when space-*sensation* is compared with color-*sensation*. For from the psycho-physiological point of view "right and left" as little permit of being interchanged with "above and below" as do red and green with black and white. It is only when we compare *geometric* space with the system of colors that the objection is apparently justified. But there is still a great deal lacking to the establishment of a complete analogy between the space of intuition and the system of color-sensation. Whereas

---

Unbiassed psychological observation informs us, however, that the formation of the concept of number is just as much initiated by experience as the formation of geometric concepts. We must at least know that virtually *equivalent* objects exist in multiple and unalterable form before concepts of number can originate. Experiments in counting also play an important part in the development of arithmetic.

[1] When acoustic pitch, intensity, and *timbre*, when chromatic tone, saturation, and luminous intensity are proposed as analogies of the three dimensions of space, few persons will be satisfied. *Timbre*, like chromatic tone, is dependent on several variables. Hence, if the analogy has any meaning whatever, several dimensions will be found to correspond to *timbre* and chromatic tone.

nearly equal distances in sensuous space are immediately recognised as such, a like remark cannot be made of differences of colors, and in this latter province it is not possible to compare physiologically the different portions with one another. And, furthermore, even if there be no difficulty, by resorting to physical experience, in characterising every color of a system by three numbers, just as the places of geometric space are characterised, and so in creating a metric system similar to the latter, it will nevertheless be difficult to find something which corresponds to distance or volume and which has an analogous physical significance for the system of colors.

There is always an *arbitrary* element in analogies, for they are concerned with the coincidences to which the attention is directed. But between space and time doubtless the analogy is fully conceded, whether we use the word in its physiological or its physical sense. In both meanings of the term, space is a triple, and time a simple, continuous manifold. A physical event, precisely determined by its conditions, of moderate, not too long or too short duration, seems to us physiologically *now and at any other time* as having the same duration. Physical events which at any time are temporarily coincident are likewise temporarily coincident at any other time. Temporal congruence exists, therefore, just as much as does spatial congruence. Unalterable physical temporal objects exist, therefore, as much as unalterable physical spatial objects (rigid bodies). There is not only spatial but there is also temporal substantiality. Galileo employed corporeal phenomena, like the beats of the pulse and breathing, for the determination of time, just as anciently the hands and the feet were employed for the estimation of space.

The simple manifold of *tonal sensations* is likewise analogous to the triple manifold of space-sensations.[1] The comparability of the different parts of the system of tonal sensations is given by the possibility of directly sensing the musical *interval*. A metric

[1] My attention was drawn to this analogy in 1863 by my study of the organ of hearing, and I have since then further developed the subject. See my *Analysis of the Sensations*, etc.

system corresponding to geometric space is most easily obtained by expressing tonal pitch in terms of the logarithm of the rate of vibration. For the constant musical interval we have here the expression,

$$\log \frac{n'}{n} = \log n' - \log n = \log \tau - \log \tau' = \text{const.},$$

where n', n denote the rates, and τ', τ the periods of vibration of the higher and the lower note respectively. The difference between the logarithms here represents the constancy of the length on displacement. The unalterable, substantial physical object which we sense as an interval is for the ear *temporally* determined, whereas the analogous object for the senses of sight and touch is spatially determined. Spatial measure seems to us simpler solely because we have chosen for the fundamental measure of geometry distance *itself*, which remains unalterable for sensation, whereas in the province of tones we have reached our measure only by a long and circuitous physical route.

Having dwelt on the coincidences of our analogised constructs, it now remains for us to emphasise their *differences*. Conceiving time and space as sensational manifolds, the objects whose motions are made perceptible by the alteration of temporal and spatial qualities are characterised by other sensational qualities, as colors, tactual sensations, tones, etc. If the system of tonal sensations is regarded as analogous to the optical space of sense, the curious fact results that in the first province the spatial qualities occur *alone*, unaccompanied by sensational qualities corresponding to the objects, just as if one could see a place or motion without seeing the object which occupied this place or executed this motion. Conceiving spatial qualities as organic sensations which can be excited only *concomitantly* with sensational qualities,[1] the analogy in question does not appear particularly attractive. For the manifold-mathematician, essentially the same case is presented whether an object of definite color moves continuously in optical space, or whether an object spatially fixed passes continuously through the

[1] Compare *The Monist*, Vol. XI., p. 326.

manifold of colors. But for the physiologist and psychologist the two cases are widely different, not only because of what was above adduced, but also, and specifically, because of the fact that the system of spatial qualities is very familiar to us, whereas we can represent to ourselves a system of color-sensations only laboriously and artificially, by means of scientific devices. Color appears to us as an excerpted member of a manifold the arrangement of which is in no wise familiar to us.

The manifolds here analogised with space are, like the color system, also threefold, or they represent a *smaller* number of variations. Space contains surfaces as twofold and lines as onefold manifolds, to which the mathematician, generalising, might also add points as zero-fold manifolds. There is also no difficulty in conceiving analytical mechanics, with Lagrange, as an analytical geometry of four dimensions, time being considered the fourth co-ordinate. In fact, the equations of analytical geometry, in their conformity to the co-ordinates, suggest very clearly to the mathematician the extension of these considerations to an unlimited *larger* number of dimensions. Similarly, physics would be justified in considering an extended material continuum, to each point of which a temperature, a magnetic, electric, and gravitational potential were ascribed, as a portion or section of a multiple manifold. Employment with such symbolic representations must, as the history of science shows us, by no means be regarded as entirely unfruitful. Symbols which initially appear to have no meaning whatever, acquire gradually, after subjection to what might be called intellectual experimentation, a lucid and precise significance. Think only of the negative, fractional, and variable exponents of algebra, or of the cases in which important and vital extensions of ideas have taken place which otherwise would have been totally lost or have made their appearance at a much later date. Think only of the so-called imaginary quantities with which mathematicians long operated, and from which they even obtained important results ere they were in a position to assign to them a perfectly determinate and withal visualisable meaning. But symbolic representation has likewise the disadvantage that the object represented is very easily lost sight of, and that operations are continued with the symbols to which frequently no object whatever corresponds.[1]

It is easy to rise to Riemann's conception of an n-fold continuous manifold, and it is even possible to realise and visualise portions of such a manifold. Let $a_1, a_2, a_3, a_4 \ldots . a_{n+1}$ be any elements whatsoever (sensational qualities, substances, etc.). If we conceive these elements intermingled in all their possible relations, then each single mixture will be represented by the expression

$$\alpha_1 a_1 + \alpha_2 a_2 + \alpha_3 a_3 + \ldots \ldots \alpha_{n+1} a_{n+1} = 1,$$

where the coefficients α satisfy the equation

$$\alpha_1 + \alpha_2 + \alpha_3 + \ldots \ldots \alpha_{n+1} = 1.$$

Inasmuch, therefore, as n of these coefficients α may be selected at pleasure, the totality of the mixtures of $n+1$ elements will represent an n-fold continuous manifold.[2] As co-ordinates of a point of this manifold, we may regard expressions of the form

$$\frac{\alpha_m}{\alpha_1}, \text{ or } f\left(\frac{\alpha_m}{\alpha_1}\right), \text{ for example, } \log\left(\frac{\alpha_m}{\alpha_1}\right).$$

But in choosing a definition of distance, or of any other notion

---

[1] I confess that as a young student I was always incensed with symbolic deductions of which the meaning was not perfectly clear and palpable. But historical studies are well adapted to eradicating the tendency to mysticism which is so easily fostered and bred by the somnolent employment of these methods, in that they clearly show the heuristic function of them and at the same time elucidate epistemologically the points wherein they furnish their essential assistance. A symbolical representation of a method of calculation has the same significance for a mathematician as a model or a visualisable working hypothesis has for the physicist. The symbol, the model, the hypothesis runs parallel with the thing to be represented. But the parallelism may extend farther, or be extended farther, than was originally intended on the adoption of the symbol. Since the thing represented and the device representing are after all *different*, what would be concealed in the one is apparent in the other. It is scarcely possible to light directly on an operation like $a^{\frac{1}{2}}$. But operating with such symbols leads us to attribute to them an intelligible meaning. Mathematicians calculated for many decades with expressions like $\cos x + \sqrt{-1} \sin x$ and with exponentials having imaginary exponents until in the struggle for adapting concept and symbol to each other the idea that had been germinating for a century finally found expression in 1806 in Argand, viz., that a relationship could be conceived between magnitude and *direction* by which $\sqrt{-1}$ was represented as a mean direction-proportional between $+1$ and -1.

[2] If the six fundamental color-sensations were totally independent of one another, the system of color-sensations would represent a five-fold manifold. Since they are contrasted in pairs, the system corresponds to a three-fold manifold.

analogous to geometrical concepts, we shall have to proceed very arbitrarily unless *experiences* of the manifold in question inform us that certain metric concepts have a real meaning, and are therefore to be preferred, as is the case for geometric space with the definition[1] derived from the voluminal constancy of bodies for the element of distance $ds^2 = dx^2 + dy^2 + dz^2$, and as is likewise the case for sensations of tone with the logarithmic expression mentioned above. In the majority of cases where such an artificial construction is involved, fixed points of this sort are wanting, and the entire consideration is therefore an ideal one. The analogy to space loses thereby in completeness, fruitfulness, and stimulating power.

In still another direction Riemann elaborated ideas of Gauss; beginning with the latter's investigations concerning curved surfaces. Gauss's measure of the curvature[2] of a surface at any point is given by the expression $k = \frac{d\sigma}{ds}$, where ds is an element of the surface and $d\sigma$ is the superficial element of the unit-sphere, the limiting radii of which are parallel to the limiting normals of the element ds. This measure of curvature may also be expressed in the form $k = \frac{1}{\rho_1\rho_2}$, where $\rho_1\rho_2$ are the principal radii of curvature of the surface at the point in question. Of special interest are the surfaces whose measure of curvature for all points has the same value,—the surfaces of *constant* curvature. Conceiving the surfaces as infinitely thin, non-distensible, but flexible bodies, it will be found that surfaces of like curvature may be made to coincide by bending,—as for example a plane sheet of paper wrapped round a cylinder or cone,—but cannot be made to coincide with the surface of a sphere. During such deformation, nay, even on crumpling, the proportional parts of figures drawn *in the surface* remain invariable as to lengths and angles, provided we do not go out of the two dimensions of the surface in our measurements. Conversely, likewise, the curvature of the surface does not depend on its conformation in the third dimension of space, but solely upon its *interior proportionalities*. Riemann, now, conceived the idea of gen-

[1] Comp. *The Monist*, Vol. XII., pp. 502–503.

[2] *Disquisitiones generales circa superficies curvas*, 1827.

eralising the notion of measure of curvature and applying it to spaces of three or more dimensions. Conformably thereto, he assumes that finite unbounded spaces of constant positive curvature are possible, corresponding to the unbounded but finite two-dimensional surface of the sphere, while what we commonly take to be infinite space would correspond to the unlimited plane of curvature zero, and similarly a third species of space would correspond to surfaces of negative curvature. Just as the figures drawn upon a surface of determinate constant curvature can be displaced without distortion upon this surface only (for example, a spherical figure on the surface of its sphere only, or a plane figure in its plane only), so should analogous conditions necessarily hold for spatial figures and rigid bodies. The latter are capable of free motion only in spaces of constant curvature, as Helmholtz[1] has shown at length. Just as the shortest lines of a plane are infinite, but on the surface of a sphere occur as great circles of definite finite length, closed and reverting into themselves, so Riemann conceived in the three-dimensional space of positive curvature analogues of the straight line and the plane as finite but unbounded. But there is a difficulty here. If we possessed the notion of a measure of curvature for a four-dimensional space, the transition to the special case of three-dimensional space could be easily and rationally executed; but the passage from the special to the more general case involves a certain arbitrariness, and, as is natural, different inquirers have adopted here different courses[2] (Riemann and Kronecker). The very fact that for a one-dimensional space (a curved line of any sort) a measure of curvature does not exist having the significance of an interior measure, and that such a measure first occurs in connection with two-dimensional figures, forces upon us the question whether and to what extent something analogous has any meaning for three-dimensional figures. Are we not subject here to an illusion, in that we operate with symbols to which perhaps nothing

---

[1] *Ueber die Thatsachen, welche der Geometrie zu Grunde liegen*, *Göttinger Nachrichten*, 1868, June 3.

[2] Compare, for example, Kronecker, "Ueber Systeme von Functionen mehrerer Variablen." *Ber. d. Berliner Akademie*, 1869.

real corresponds, or at least nothing representable to the senses, by means of which we can verify and rectify our ideas?

Thus were reached the highest and most universal notions regarding space and its relations to analogous manifolds which resulted from the conviction of Gauss concerning the empirical foundations of geometry. But the genesis of this conviction has a preliminary history of two thousand years, the chief phenomena of which we can perhaps better survey from the height which we have now gained.

III.

The unsophisticated men, who, rule in hand, acquired our first geometric knowledge, held to the simplest bodily objects (figures): the straight line, the plane, the circle, etc., and investigated, by means of forms which could be conceived as combinations of these simple figures, the connection of their measurements. It could not have escaped them that the mobility of a body is restricted when one and then two of its points are fixed, and that finally it is altogether checked by fixing three of its points. Granting that rotation about an axis (two points), or rotation about a point in a plane, as likewise displacement with constant contact of two points with a straight line and of a third point with a fixed plane laid through that straight line,—granting that these facts were *separately observed*, it would be known how to distinguish between *pure* rotation, *pure* displacement, and the motion compounded of these two independent motions. The first geometry was of course not based on purely metric notions, but made many considerable concessions to the physiological factors of sense.[1] Thus the appearance is explained of two different fundamental measures: (the straight) length and the angle (circular measure). The straight line was conceived as a rigid mobile body (measuring-rod), and the angle as the rotation of a straight line with respect to another (measured by the arc so described). Doubtless no one ever demanded special proof for the equality of angles at the origin described by the same rota-

[1] Comp. *The Monist*, Vol. XII., p. 509.

tion. Additional propositions concerning angles resulted quite easily. Turning the line *b* about its intersection with *c* so as to describe the angle α (Fig. 1), and after coincidence with *c* turning it again about its intersection with *a* till it coincides with *a* and so describes the angle β, we shall have rotated *b* from its initial to its final position *a* through the angle μ in the same sense.[1] Therefore the exterior angle $\mu = \alpha + \beta$, and since $\mu + \gamma = 2R$, also $\alpha + \beta + \gamma = 2R$. Displacing (Fig. 2) the rigid system of lines *a*, *b*, *c* which intersect at 1 within their plane to the position 2, the line *a* always remaining within itself, no alteration of angles will be caused by the mere motion. The sum of the interior angles of the triangle 1 2 3 so produced is evidently 2 *R*. The same consideration also throws into relief the properties of parallel lines. Doubts as to whether successive rotation about several points is equivalent to rotation about *one* point, whether *pure* displacement is at all possible,—which are justified when a surface of curvature differing

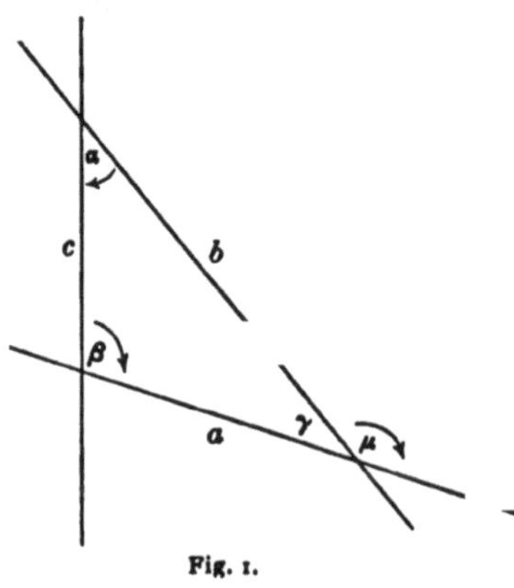

Fig. 1.

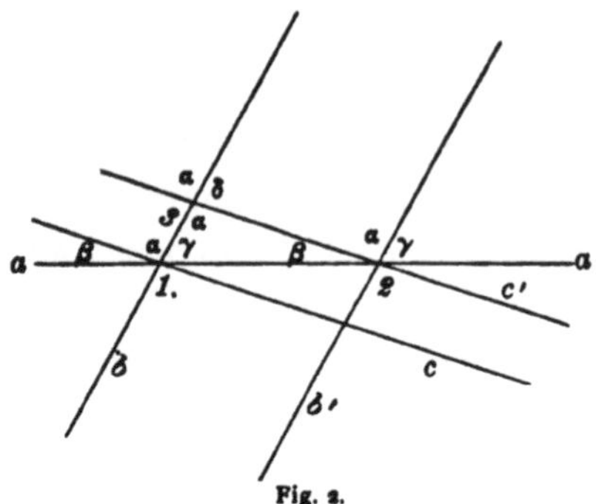

Fig. 2.

[1] C. R. Kosack, *Beiträge zu einer systematischen Entwickelung der Geometrie aus der Anschauung*, Nordhausen, 1852. I was able to see this programme through the kindness of Prof. F. Pietzker of Nordhausen. Similar simple deductions are found in Bernhard Becker's *Leitfaden für den ersten Unterricht in der Geometrie*, Frankfort on the Main, 1845, and in the same author's treatise *Ueber die Methoden des geometrischen Unterrichts*, Frankfort, 1845. I gained access to the first-named book through the kindness of Dr. M. Schuster of Oldenburg.

from zero is substituted for the Euclidean plane,—could never have arisen in the mind of the ingenuous and delighted *discoverer* of these relations at the period we are considering. The study of the movement of rigid bodies, which Euclid studiously avoids and only covertly introduces in his principle of congruence, is to this day the device best adapted to elementary instruction in geometry. An idea is best made the possession of the learner by the method by which it has been found.

This sound and naïve conception of things vanished and the treatment of geometry underwent essential modifications when it became the subject of *professional* and *scholarly* contemplation. The object now was to systematise the knowledge of this province for purposes of individual survey, to separate what was directly cognisable from what was deducible and deduced, and to throw into distinct relief the thread of the deduction. For the purpose of instruction the simplest principles, those most easily gained and apparently free from doubt and contradiction, are placed at the beginning, and the remainder based upon them. Efforts were made to reduce these initial principles to the utmost, as may be observed in the system of Euclid. Through this endeavor to support every notion by another, and to leave to direct knowledge the least possible scope, geometry was gradually detached from the empirical soil out of which it had sprung. People accustomed themselves to regard the derived truths more highly than the directly perceived truths, and ultimately came to demand proofs for propositions which no one ever seriously doubted. Thus arose,—as tradition would have it, to check the onslaughts of the Sophists,—the system of Euclid with its logical perfection and finish. Yet not only were the ways of research designedly concealed by this artificial method of stringing propositions on an arbitrarily chosen thread of deduction, but the varied organic connection between the principles of geometry was quite lost sight of.[1] This system was more fitted to produce nar-

[1] Euclid's system fascinated thinkers by its logical excellences, and its drawbacks were overlooked amid this admiration. Great inquirers, even in recent times, have been misled into following Euclid's example in the presentation of the results of their inquiries, and so into actually concealing their methods of investi-

row-minded and sterile pedants than fruitful, productive investigators. And these conditions were not improved when scholasticism, with its preference for slavish comment on the intellectual products of others, cultivated in thinkers scarcely any sensitiveness for the rationality of their fundamental assumptions and by way of compensation fostered in them an exaggerated respect for the logical form of deductions. The entire period from Euclid to Gauss suffered more or less from this affection of mind.

Among the propositions on which Euclid based his system is found the so-called Fifth Postulate (also called the Eleventh Axiom and by some the Twelfth): "If a straight line meet two straight lines, so as to make the two interior angles on the same side of it taken together less than two right angles, these straight lines being continually produced, shall at length meet upon that side on which are the angles which are less than two right angles." Euclid easily proves that if a straight line falling on two other straight lines makes the alternate angles equal to each other, the two straight lines will *not* meet but are *parallel*. But for the proof of the converse, that parallels make equal alternate angles with *every* straight line falling on them, he is obliged to resort to the Fifth Postulate. This converse is equivalent to the proposition that *only one* parallel to a straight line can be drawn through a point. Further, by the fact that with the aid of this converse it can be proved that the sum of the angles of a triangle is equal to two right angles and that from this last theorem again the first follows, the relationship between the propositions in question is rendered distinct and the fundamental significance of the Fifth Postulate for Euclidean geometry is made plain.

The intersection of slowly converging lines lies without the

---

gation, to the great detriment of science. But science is not a feat of legal casuistry. Scientific presentation aims so to expound all the grounds of an idea that it can at any time be thoroughly examined as to its tenability and power. The learner is not to be led half-blindfolded. There therefore arose in Germany among philosophers and educationists a healthy reaction, which proceeded mainly from Herbart, Schopenhauer, and Trendelenburg. The effort was made to introduce greater perspicuity, more genetic methods, and logically more lucid demonstrations into geometry.

province of construction and observation. It is therefore intelligible that in view of the great importance of the assertion contained in the Fifth Postulate the successors of Euclid, habituated by him to rigor, should, even in ancient times, have strained every nerve to demonstrate this postulate, or to replace it by some immediately obvious proposition. Numberless futile efforts were made from Euclid to Gauss, to deduce this Fifth Postulate from the other Euclidean assumptions. It is a sublime spectacle which these men offer: laboring for centuries, from a sheer thirst for scientific elucidation, in quest of the hidden sources of a truth which no person of theory or of practice ever really doubted! With eager curiosity we follow the pertinacious utterances of the ethical power resident in this human search for knowledge, and with gratification we note how the inquirers gradually are led by their failures to the perception that the true basis of geometry is experience. We shall content ourselves with a few examples.

Among the inquirers notable for their contributions to the theory of parallels are the Italian Saccheri and the German mathematician Lambert. In order to render their mode of attack intelligible, we will remark first that the existence of rectangles and squares, which we fancy we constantly observe, cannot be demonstrated without the aid of the Fifth Postulate. Let us consider, for example, two congruent isosceles triangles *ABC*, *DBC*, having right angles at *A* and *D* (Fig. 3), and let them be laid together at their hypothenuses *BC* so as to form the equilateral quadrilateral *ABCD*; the first twenty-seven propositions of Euclid do not suffice to determine the character and magnitude of the two equal

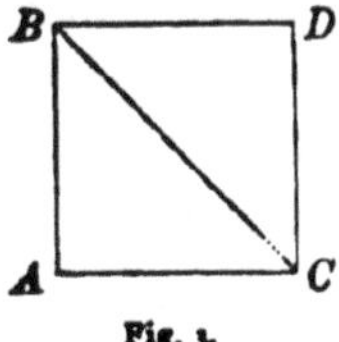

Fig. 3.

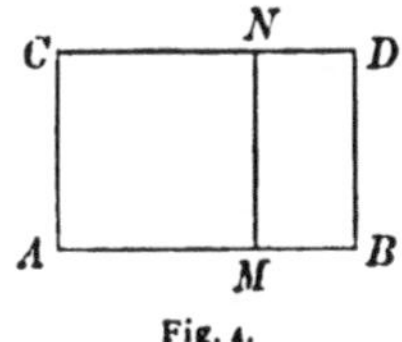

Fig. 4.

(right) angles at *B* and *C*. For measure of length and measure of angle are fundamentally different and directly not comparable; hence the first propositions regarding the connection of sides and angles are *qualitative* only, and hence the imperative necessity of a *quantitative* theorem regarding angles, like that of the angle-sum. Be it further remarked that theorems analogous to the twenty-seven planimetric propositions of Euclid may be set up for the surface of a sphere and for surfaces of constant negative curvature, and that in these cases the analogous construction gives respectively obtuse and acute angles at B and C.

Saccheri's cardinal achievement was his form of stating the problem.[1] If the Fifth Postulate is involved in the remaining assumptions of Euclid, then it will be possible to prove without its aid that in the quadrilateral $ABCD$ (Fig. 4) having right angles at A and B and $AC=BD$, the angles at C and D likewise are right angles. And, on the other hand, in this event, the assumption that C and D are either obtuse or acute will lead to contradictions. Saccheri, in other words, seeks to draw conclusions from the hypothesis of the right, the obtuse, or the acute angle. He shows that each of these hypotheses will hold in all cases if it be proved to hold in one. It is needful to have only one triangle with its angles $\lesseqgtr 2R$ in order to demonstrate the universal validity of the hypothesis of the acute, the right, or the obtuse angle. Notable is the fact that Saccheri also adverts to *physico-geometrical* experiments which support the hypothesis of the right angle. If a line CD (Fig. 4) join the two extremities of the equal perpendiculars erected on a straight line AB, and the perpendicular dropped on AB from any point N of the first line, viz., NM, be equal to $CA=DB$, then is the hypothesis of the right angle demonstrated to be correct. Saccheri rightly does not regard it as self-evident that the line which is equidistant from another straight line is itself a straight line. Think only of a circle parallel to a great circle on a sphere which does not represent a shortest line on a sphere and the two faces of which cannot be made congruent.

Other experimental proofs of the correctness of the hypothesis of the right angle are the following. If the angle in a semicircle

---

[1] *Euclides ab omni naevo vindicatus.* Milan, 1733. German translation in Engel and Staeckel's *Die Theorie der Parallellinien.* Leipsic, 1895.

(Fig. 5) is shown to be a right angle, $\alpha+\beta=R$, then is $2\alpha+2\beta=2R$, the sum of the angles of the triangle ABC. If the radius be subtended thrice in a semicircle and the line joining the first and the fourth extremity pass through the center, we shall have at C

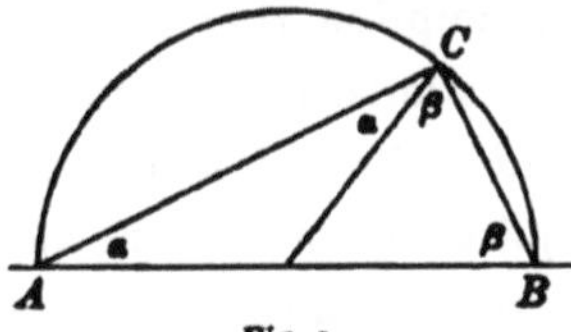

Fig. 5.

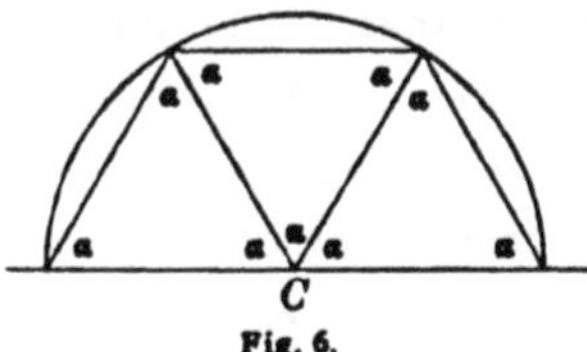

Fig. 6.

(Fig. 6) $3\alpha=2R$, and consequently each of the three triangles will have the angle-sum $2R$. The existence of equiangular triangles of different sizes (similar triangles) is likewise subject to experimental proof. For (Fig. 7) if the angles at B and C give $\beta+\delta+\gamma+\epsilon=4R$, so also is $4R$ the angle-sum of the quadrilateral $BCB'C'$. Even Wallis[1] (1663) based his proof of the Fifth Postulate on the assumption of the existence of similar triangles, and a modern geometer, Delbœuf, deduced from the assumption of similitude the entire Euclidean geometry.

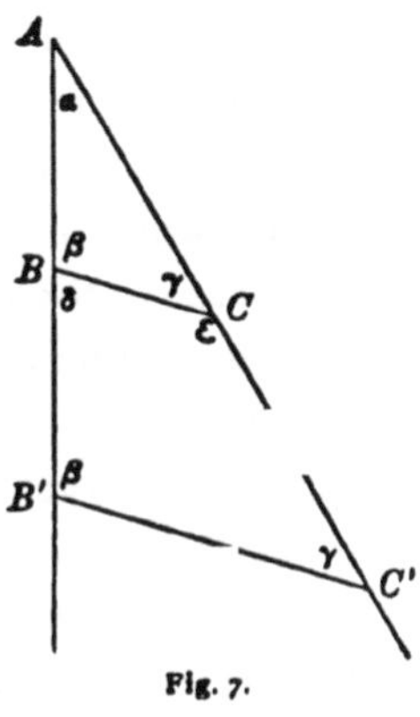

Fig. 7.

The hypothesis of the obtuse angle, Saccheri fancied he could easily refute. But the hypothesis of the acute angle presented to him difficulties, and in his quest for the expected contradictions he was carried to the most far-reaching conclusions, which Lobachévski and Bolyai subsequently rediscovered by methods of their own. Ultimately he felt compelled to reject the last-named hypothesis as incompatible with the nature of the straight line; for it led to the assumption of different kinds of straight lines, which met at infinity, that is, had there a common perpendicular. Saccheri did much in anticipation and promotion of the labors that were subsequently to elucidate these matters, but exhibited withal toward the traditional views a certain bias.

[1] Engel and Staeckel, *loc. cit.*, p. 21 et seq.

Lambert's treatise[1] is allied in method to that of Saccheri, but it proceeds farther in its conclusions, and gives evidence of a less constrained vision. Lambert starts from the consideration of a quadrilateral with three right angles, and examines the consequences that would follow from the assumption that the fourth angle was right, obtuse, or acute. The similarity of figures he finds to be incompatible with the second and third assumptions. The case of the obtuse angle, which requires the sum of the angles of a triangle to exceed $2R$, he discovers to be realised in the *geometry of spherical surfaces*, in which the difficulty of parallel lines entirely vanishes. This leads him to the conjecture that the case of the acute angle, where the sum of the angles of a triangle is less than $2R$, might be realised on the surface of a sphere of imaginary radius. The amount of the departure of the angle-sum from $2R$ is in both cases proportional to the area of the triangle, as may be demonstrated by appropriately dividing large triangles into small triangles, which on diminution may be made to approach as near as we please to the angle-sum $2R$. Lambert advanced very closely in this conception to the point of view of modern geometers. Admittedly a sphere of imaginary radius, $r\sqrt{-1}$ is not a visualisable geometric construct, but analytically it is a surface having a negative constant Gaussian measure of curvature. It is evident again from this example how experimenting with *symbols* also may direct inquiry to the right path, in periods where other points of support are entirely lacking and where every helpful device must be esteemed at its worth.[2] Even Gauss appears to have thought of a sphere of imaginary radius, as is obvious from his formula for the circumference of a circle (*Letter to Schumacher*, July 12, 1831). Yet in spite of all, Lambert actually fancied he had approached so near to the proof of the Fifth Postulate that what was lacking could be easily supplied.

We may turn now to the investigators whose views possess a most radical significance for our conception of geometry, but who announced their opinion only briefly, by word of mouth or letter.

---

[1] Engel and Staeckel, *loc. cit.*, p. 152 et seq.

[2] See note, p. 8.

"Gauss regarded geometry merely as a logically consistent system of constructs, with the theory of parallels placed at the pinnacle as an axiom; yet he had reached the conviction that this proposition could not be proved, though it was known from *experience*,—for example, from the angles of the triangle joining the Brocken, Hohenhagen, and Inselsberg,—that it was approximately correct. But if this axiom be not conceded, then, he contends, there results from its non-acceptance a different and entirely independent geometry, which he had once investigated and called by the name of the Anti-Euclidean geometry." Such, according to Sartorius von Waltershausen, was the view of Gauss.[1]

Starting at this point, O. Stolz, in a small but very instructive pamphlet,[2] sought to deduce the principal propositions of the Euclidean geometry from the purely observable facts of experience. We shall reproduce here the most important point of Stolz's brochure. Let there be given (Fig. 8) *one* large triangle ABC having the angle-sum $2R$. We draw the perpendicular AD on BC, complete the figure by $BAE \cong ABD$ and $CAF \cong ACD$, and add to the figure $BCFAE$ the congruent figure $CBHA'G$. We obtain thus a

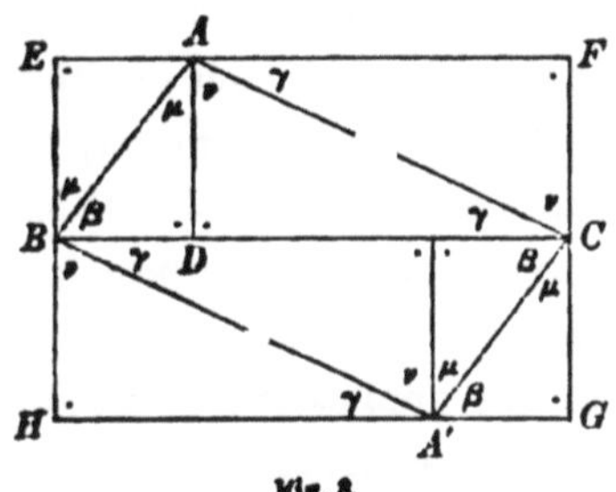

Fig. 8.

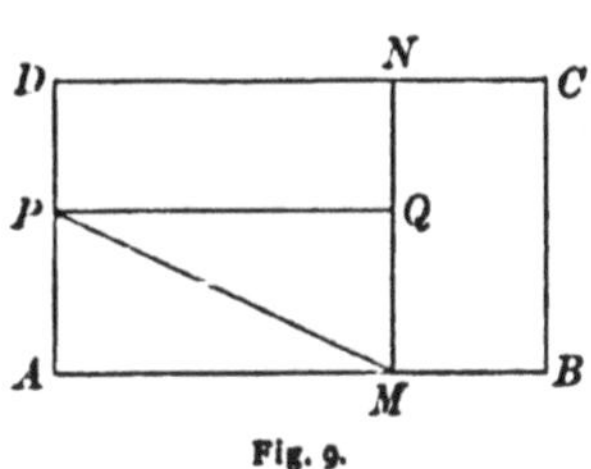

Fig. 9.

single rectangle, for the angles at E, F, G, H are right angles and those at A, C, A', B are straight angles (equal to $2R$), the boundary lines therefore straight lines and the opposite angles equal. A rectangle can be divided into two congruent rectangles by a perpendicular erected at the middle point of one of its sides, and by

[1] *Gauss zum Gedächtniss*, Leipsic, 1856.

[2] *Das letzte Axiom der Geometrie. Berichte des naturw.-medicin. Vereins zu Innsbruck*, 1886, pp. 25–34.

continuing this procedure the line of division may be brought to any point we please in the divided side. And the same holds true of the other two opposite sides. It is possible, therefore, from a given rectangle $ABCD$ (Fig. 9) to cut out a smaller $AMPQ$ having sides bearing any proportion to one another. The diagonal of this last divides it into two congruent *right-angled* triangles, of which each, independently of the ratio of the sides, has the angle-sum $2R$. Every oblique-angled triangle can by the drawing of a perpendicular be decomposed into right-angled triangles, each of which can again be decomposed into right-angled triangles having still smaller sides,—so that $2R$, therefore, results for the angle-sum of *every* triangle if it holds true exactly of *one*. By the aid of these propositions which repose on observation we *conclude* easily that the two opposite sides of a rectangle (or of any so-called parallelogram) are everywhere, no matter how far prolonged, the same distance apart, that is, never intersect. They have the properties of the Euclidean *parallels*, and may be called and *defined* as such. It likewise *follows*, now, from the properties of triangles and rectangles, that two straight lines which are cut by a third straight line so as to make the sum of the interior angles on the same side of them less than two right angles will meet on that side, but in either direction from their point of intersection will move indefinitely far away from each other. The straight line therefore is *infinite*. What was a *groundless* assertion stated as an axiom or an initial principle may as *inference* have a sound meaning.

Geometry, accordingly, consists of the application of mathematics to experiences concerning space. Like mathematical physics, it can become an exact deductive science only on the condition of its representing the objects of experience by means of schematising and idealising concepts. Just as mechanics can assert the constancy of masses or reduce the interactions between bodies to *simple* accelerations *only within the limits of errors of observation*, so likewise the existence of straight lines, planes, the amount of the angle-sum, etc., can be maintained only on a similar restriction. But just as physics sometimes finds itself constrained to replace its ideal assumptions by other more general ones, viz., to put in the place of a constant acceleration of falling bodies one dependent on the distance, instead of a constant quantity of heat a variable quantity,—so a similar procedure is permissible in geometry, when it is demanded by the facts or is necessary temporarily for scientific elucidation. And now the endeavors of Legendre, Lobachévski, and the two Bolyai's, the younger of whom was probably indirectly inspired by Gauss, will appear in their right light.

Of the labors of Schweickart and Taurinus, also contemporaries of Gauss, we will not speak. Lobachévski's works became first known to the world of thinkers and so productive of results (1829). Very soon afterward the publication of the younger Bolyai appeared (1833), which agreed in all essential points with Lobachévski's, departing from it only in the form of its developments. According to the originals which have been made almost completely accessible to us in the beautiful editions of Engel and Staeckel,[1] it is permissible to assume that Lobachévski also undertook his investigations in the hope of becoming involved in contradictions by the rejection of the Euclidean axiom. But after he found himself mistaken in this expectation, he had the *intellectual courage* to draw all the consequences from this fact. Lobachévski gives his conclusions in synthetic form. But we can fairly well imagine the general analysing considerations that paved the way for the construction of his geometry.

From a point lying outside a straight line *g* (Fig. 10) a perpendicular *p* is dropped and through the same point in the plane

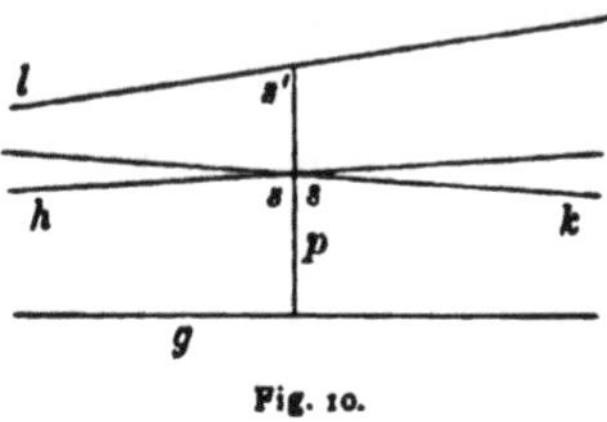

Fig. 10.

pg a straight line *h* is drawn, making with the perpendicular an acute angle *s*. Making tentatively the assumption that *g* and *h* do

[1] *Urkunden zur Geschichte der nichteuklidischen Geometrie.* L. N. I. Lobatschefskij. Leipzig, 1899.

not meet but that on the slightest diminution of the angle *s* they would meet, we are at once forced by the homogeneity of space to the conclusion that a *second* line *k* having the same angle *s* similarly deports itself on the other side of the perpendicular. Hence all non-intersecting lines drawn through the same point are situate between *h* and *k*. The latter form the *boundaries* between the intersecting and non-intersecting lines and are called by Lobachévski *parallels*.

In the Introduction to his *New Elements of Geometry* (1835) Lobachévski proves himself a thorough natural inquirer. No one would think of attributing even to an ordinary man of sense the crude view that the "parallel-angle" was very much less than a right angle, when on slight prolongation it could be distinctly seen that they would intersect. The relations here considered admit of representation only in drawings that distort the true proportions, and we have on the contrary to picture to ourselves that with the dimensions of the cut the variation of *s* from a right angle is so small that *h* and *k* are to the eye undistinguishably coincident. Prolonging, now, the perpendicular *p* to a point beyond its intersection with *h*, and drawing through its extremity a new line *l* parallel to *h* and therefore parallel also to *g*, it follows that the parallel-angle *s'* must necessarily be less than *s*, if *h* and *l* are not again to fulfil the conditions of the Euclidean case. Continuing in the same manner, the prolongation of the perpendicular and the drawing of parallels, we obtain a parallel-angle that constantly decreases. Considering, now, parallels which are more remote and consequently converge more rapidly on the side of convergence, we shall logically be compelled to assume, not to be at variance with the preceding supposition, that on approach or on the decrease of the length of the perpendicular the parallel-angle will again increase. The angle of parallelism, therefore, is an inverse function of the perpendicular *p*, and has been designated by Lobachévski by $\Pi(p)$. A group of parallels in a plane has the arrangement shown schematically in Figure 11. They all approach one another asymptotically toward the side of their convergence. The homogeneity of space requires that every "strip" between two parallels can be made to coincide with every other strip provided it be displaced the requisite distance in a longitudinal direction.

If a circle be imagined to increase indefinitely, its radii will cease to intersect the moment the increasing arcs reach the point where their convergence corresponds to parallelism. The circle then passes over into the so-called "*boundary-line.*" Similarly the surface of a sphere, if it indefinitely increase, will pass into what Lobachévski calls a "*boundary-surface.*" The boundary-lines bear a relation to the boundary-surface analogous to that which a great circle bears to the surface of a sphere. The geometry of the surface of a sphere is independent of the axiom of parallels. But

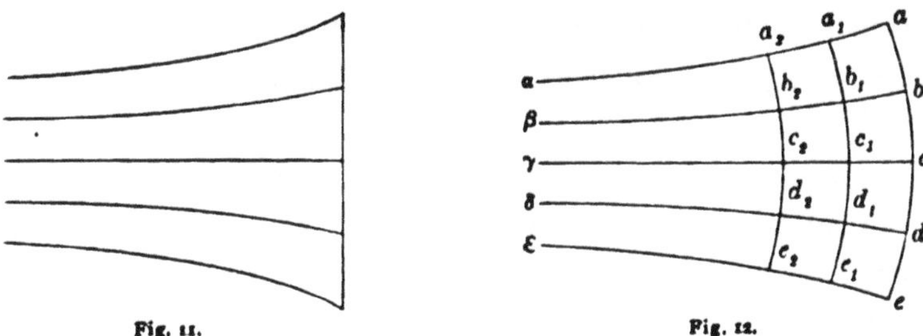

Fig. 11. Fig. 12.

since it can be demonstrated that triangles formed from boundary-lines on a boundary-surface no more exhibit an excess of angle-sum than do finite triangles on a sphere of infinite radius, therefore the rules of the Euclidean geometry also hold good for these boundary-triangles. To find points of the boundary-line, we determine in a bundle of parallels $a\alpha$, $b\beta$, $c\gamma$, $d\delta$.... lying in a plane points a, b, c, d in each of these parallels so situated with respect to the point a in $a\alpha$ that $\angle \alpha ab = \angle \beta ba$, $\angle \alpha ac = \angle \gamma ca$, $\angle \alpha ad = \angle \delta da$...... Owing to the sameness of the entire construction, each of the parallels may be regarded as the "*axis*" of the boundary line, which will generate, when revolved about this axis, the boundary-surface. Likewise each of the parallels may be regarded as the axis of the boundary-surface. For the same reason all boundary-lines and all boundary-surfaces are *congruent.* The intersection of every plane with the boundary-surface is a *circle*; it is a boundary-line only when the cutting plane contains the axis. In the Euclidean geometry there is no boundary-line, nor boundary-surface. The analogues of them are here the straight line and the plane. If no boundary-line exists, then necessarily must any three points not in a straight line lie on a circle. Hence the younger Bolyai was able to replace the Euclidean axiom by this last postulate.

Let $a\alpha$, $b\beta$, $c\gamma$ be a system of parallels, and $a\epsilon$, $a_1\epsilon_1$, $a_2\epsilon_2 \ldots\ldots$ a system of boundary-lines, each of which systems divides the other into equal parts. The ratio to each other of any two boundary-arcs between the same parallels, e. g., the arcs $a\epsilon = u$ and $a_2\epsilon_2 = u'$, is dependent therefore solely on their distance apart $aa_2 = x$. We may put generally $\frac{u}{u'} = \epsilon^{\frac{x}{k}}$, where k is so chosen that ϵ shall be the base of the Naperian system of logarithms. In this manner exponentials and by means of these hyperbolic functions are introduced. For the angle of parallelism we obtain $s = cot\frac{1}{2}\Pi(p) = \epsilon^{\frac{p}{k}}$. If $p = o$, $s = \frac{\pi}{2}$; if $p = \infty$, $s = 0$.

An example will illustrate the relation of the Lobachévskian to the Euclidean and spherical geometries. For a rectilinear Lobachévskian triangle having the sides a, b, c, and the angles A, B, C, we obtain, when C is a right angle,

$$\sinh\frac{a}{k} = \sinh\frac{c}{k} A.$$

Here *sinh* stands for the hyperbolic sine, $\sinh x = \frac{\epsilon^x - \epsilon^{-x}}{2}$,

whereas $\sin x = \frac{\epsilon^{xi} - \epsilon^{-xi}}{2i}$,

or, $\sinh x = \frac{x}{1!} + \frac{x^3}{3!} + \frac{x^5}{5!} + \frac{x^7}{7!} + \cdots\cdots$,

and $\sin x = \frac{x}{1!} - \frac{x^3}{3!} + \frac{x^5}{5!} - \frac{x^7}{7} + \cdots\cdots$

Considering the relations $\sin(xi) = i(\sinh x)$, or $\sinh(xi) = i \sin x$, involved in the foregoing formulæ, it will be seen that the above-given formula for the Lobachévskian triangle passes over into the formula holding for the *spherical* triangle, viz., $\sin\frac{a}{k} = \sin\frac{c}{k}\sin A$, when ki is put in the place of k in the former and k is considered

[1] F. Engel, *N. I. Lobatschefskji, Zwei geometrische Abhandlungen*, Leipsic, 1899.

as the radius of the sphere, which in the usual formulæ assumes the value unity. The re-transformation of the spherical formula into the Lobachévskian by the same method is obvious. If k be very great in comparison with a and c, we may restrict ourselves to the first member of the series for sinh or sin, obtaining in both cases, $\frac{a}{k}=\frac{c}{k}\sin A$ or $a=c\sin A$, the formulæ of *plane Euclidean* geometry, which we may regard as a limiting case of both the Lobachévskian and spherical geometries for very large values of k, or for $k=\infty$. It is likewise permissible to say that all three geometries coincide in the domain of the infinitely small.

As we see, it is possible to construct a self-consistent, non-contradictory system of geometry solely on the assumption of the convergence of parallel lines. True, there is not a single observation of the geometrical facts accessible to us that speaks in favor of this assumption, and admittedly the hypothesis is at so great variance with our geometrical instinct as easily to explain the attitude toward it of the earlier inquirers like Saccheri and Lambert. Our imagination, dominated as it is by our modes of visualising and by the familiar Euclidean concepts, is competent to grasp only piecemeal and gradually Lobachévski's views. We must suffer ourselves to be led here rather by mathematical *concepts* than by *sensuous images* derived from a single narrow portion of space. But we must grant, nevertheless, that the quantitative mathematical concepts by which we through our own initiative and within a certain arbitrary scope represent the facts of geometrical experience, do not reproduce the latter with absolute exactitude. Different ideas can express the facts with the same exactness in the domain accessible to observation. The *facts* must hence be carefully distinguished from the *intellectual* constructs the formation of which they suggested. The latter—the concepts—must be *consistent* with observation, and must in addition be *logically* in accord with one another. Now these two requirements can be fulfilled in *more than one* manner, and hence the different systems of geometry.

Manifestly the labors of Lobachévski were the outcome of protracted and intense mental effort, and it may be surmised that he first gained a clear conception of his system from general considerations and by analytic (algebraic) methods before he was able to present it synthetically. Expositions in this cumbersome Euclidean form are by no means alluring, and it is possibly due mainly to this fact that the significance of Lobachévski's and Bolyai's labors received such tardy recognition.

Lobachévski developed only the consequences of the modification of Euclid's Fifth Postulate. But if we abandon the Euclidean assertion that "two straight lines cannot enclose a space," we shall obtain a companion-piece to the Lobachévskian geometry. Restricted to a surface, it is the geometry of the surface of a sphere. In place of the Euclidean straight lines we have great circles, all of which intersect twice and of which each pair encloses two spherical lunes. There are therefore no parallels. Riemann first intimated the possibility of an analogous geometry for three-dimensional space (of positive curvature),—a conception that does not appear to have occurred even to Gauss, possibly owing to his predilection for infinity. And Helmholtz,[1] who continued the researches of Riemann physically, neglected in his turn, in his first publication, the development of the Lobachévskian case of a space of negative curvature (with an imaginary parameter k). The consideration of this case is in point of fact more obvious to the mathematician than it is to the physicist. Helmholtz treats in the publication mentioned only the Euclidean case of the curvature zero and Riemann's space of positive curvature.

IV.

We are able, therefore, to represent the facts of spatial observation with all possible precision by both the Euclidean geometry and the geometries of Lobachévski and Riemann, provided in the two latter cases we take the parameter k large enough. Physicists have as yet found no reason for starting from the assumption $k=\infty$ of the Euclidean geometry. It has been their practice, the result of long and tried experience, to adhere steadfastly to the *simplest*

[1] "Ueber die thatsächlichen Grundlagen der Geometrie," 1866. *Wissensch. Abhandl.*, II., p. 610 et seq.

assumptions until the facts forced their complication or modification. This accords likewise with the attitude of all great mathematicians toward *applied* geometry. The deportment of physicists and mathematicians toward these questions is in the main different, but this is explained by the circumstance that for the former class of inquirers the physical facts are of most significance, geometry being for them merely a convenient implement of investigation, while for the latter class these very questions are the main material of research, and of greatest technical and particularly epistemological interest. Supposing a mathematician to have modified tentatively the simplest and most immediate assumptions of our geometrical experience, and supposing his attempt to have been productive of fresh insight, certainly nothing is more natural than that these researches should be further prosecuted, in a purely mathematical interest. Analogues of the geometry we are familiar with, are constructed on broader and more general assumptions for any number of dimensions, with no pretention to being regarded as more than intellectual scientific experiments and with no idea of being applied to reality. In support of my remark it will be sufficient to advert to the advances made in mathematics by Clifford, Klein, Lie, and others. Seldom have thinkers become so steeped in revery, or so far estranged from reality, as to imagine for our space a number of dimensions *exceeding the three of the given space of sense*, or to conceive of representing that space by any geometry that appreciably departs from the Euclidean. Gauss, Lobachévski, Bolyai, and Riemann were perfectly clear on this point, and cannot certainly be held responsible for the grotesque fictions which subsequently arose in this field.

It little accords with the principles of a physicist to make suppositions regarding the deportment of geometrical constructs in infinity and non-accessible places, then subsequently to compare them with our immediate experience and adapt them to it. He prefers, like Stolz, to regard what is directly given as the source of his ideas, which he considers applicable also to what is inaccessible until obliged to change them. But he too may be extremely grateful for the discovery that there exist *several* sufficing geometries, that we can manage also with a *finite* space, etc.,—grateful, in short, for the abolition of certain *conventional barriers* of thought.

If we lived on the surface of a planet with a turbid, opaque atmosphere, and, on the supposition that the surface of the earth was a plane and our only instruments were square and chain, we undertook measurements, the increase in the excess of the angle-sum of large triangles would soon compel us to substitute a spherometry for our planimetry. The *possibility* of analogous experiences in three-dimensional space the physicist cannot as a matter of *principle* reject, although the phenomena that would compel the acceptance of a Lobachévskian or a Riemannian geometry would present so odd a contrast with that to which we have been hitherto accustomed, that no one will regard their actual occurrence as *probable*.

The question whether a given *physical* object is a straight line or the arc of a circle is not properly formulated. A stretched chord or a ray of light is certainly neither the one nor the other. The question is simply whether the object so spatially reacts that it conforms better to the one concept than to the other, and whether with the exactitude which is sufficient for us and obtainable by us it conforms at all to any geometric concept. Excluding the latter case, the question arises, whether we can practically remove, or at least determine in thought and make allowance for, the *deviation* from the straight line or circle, in other words, *correct* the result of the measurement. But we are dependent always, in practical measurements, on the comparison of *physical* objects. If on direct investigation these coincided with the geometric concepts to the highest attainable point of accuracy, but the indirect results of the measurement deviated more from the theory than the consideration of all possible errors permitted, then certainly we should be obliged to *change* our physico-metric notions. The physicist will do well to await the occurrence of such a situation, while the mathematician will always have free scope for his speculations.

Of all the concepts which the natural inquirer employs, the *simplest* are the concepts of space and time. Spatial and temporal objects conforming to his conceptual constructs can be framed with great *exactness.* Nearly every observable *deviation* can be eliminated. We can imagine any spatial or temporal construct realised without doing violence to a fact. The remaining physical properties of bodies are so intimately connected that here arbitrary fictions are subjected to narrow restrictions by the facts. A perfect gas, a perfect fluid, a perfectly elastic body does not exist; the physicist knows that his fictions conform only approximately and by arbitrary simplifications to the facts; he is perfectly aware of the deviation, which cannot be removed. We can conceive a sphere, a plane, etc., constructed *with unlimited exactness,* without running counter to any fact. Hence, if any new physical fact happens to render a modification of our concepts necessary, the physicist will prefer to sacrifice the less perfect concepts of physics rather than to give up the simpler, more perfect, and more lasting concepts of geometry, which forms the solidest foundation of all his theories.

But from another direction the physicist can derive substantial assistance from the labors of geometers. Our geometry refers always to objects of sensuous experience. But the moment we begin to operate with mere things of thought like atoms and molecules, which from their very nature *can never be made the objects of sensuous contemplation,* we are under no obligation whatever to think of them as standing in spatial relationships which are peculiar to the Euclidean three-dimensional space of our sensuous experience. This may be recommended to the special attention of thinkers who deem atomistic speculations indispensable.[1]

Let us go back in thought to the origin of geometry in the practical needs of life. The recognition of the spatial substantial-

[1] While still an upholder of the atomic theory, I sought to explain the line-spectra of gases by the vibrations of the atomic constituents of a gas-molecule with respect to another. The difficulties which I here encountered suggested to me (1863) the idea that non-sensuous things did not necessarily have to be pictured in our sensuous space of three dimensions. In this way I also lighted upon analogues of spaces of different numbers of dimensions. The collateral study of various physiological manifolds (see footnote on page 4 of this article) led me to the problems discussed in the conclusion of this paper. The notion of finite spaces, converging parallels, etc., which can come only from a historical study of geometry, was at that time remote from me. I believe that my critics would have done well had they not overlooked the italicised paragraph. For details see the notes to my *Erhaltung der Arbeit,* Prague, 1872.

ity and spatial invariability of spatial objects in spite of their movements is a biological necessity for human beings, for spatial quantity is related directly to the quantitative satisfaction of our needs. When knowledge of this sort is not sufficiently provided for by our physiological organisation, we employ our hands and feet for comparison with the spatial object. When we begin to compare *bodies* with one another, we enter the domain of physics, whether we employ our hands or an artificial measure. All *physical* determinations are *relative*. Therefore, all *geometrical* determinations likewise possess validity *relatively* to the measure. The concept of measurement is a concept of relation, which contains nothing not contained in the measure. In geometry we simply assume that the measure will always and everywhere coincide with that with which it has at some other time and some other place coincided. But this assumption is determinative of nothing concerning the measure. In place of spatial *physiological* equality is substituted an altogether differently defined *physical* equality, which must not be confounded with the former, no more than the indications of a thermometer are to be identified with the sensation of heat. The practical geometer, it is true, determines the dilatation of a heated measure, by means of a measure kept at a constant temperature, and takes account of the fact that the relation of congruence in question is disturbed by this non-spatial physical circumstance. But to the pure theory of space all assumptions regarding the measure are foreign. Simply the physiologically created habit of regarding the measure as invariable is tacitly but unjustifiably retained. It would be quite superfluous and meaningless to assume that the measure, and therefore bodies generally, suffered alterations on displacement in space or that they remained unchanged on such displacement,—a fact which in its turn could only be determined by the use of a new measure. The *relativity* of all spatial relations is made manifest by these considerations.

If the criterion of spatial equality is substantially modified by the introduction of measure, it is subjected to a still further modification, or intensification, by the introduction of the notion of *number* into geometry. There is nicety of distinction gained by this introduction which the idea of congruence alone could never have attained. The application of arithmetic to geometry leads to the notion of *incommensurability* and *irrationality*. Our geometric concepts therefore contain adscititious elements not intrinsic to space; they represent space with a certain latitude, and arbitrarily also with greater precision than spatial observation could possibly realise. This imperfect contact between fact and concept explains the possibility of different systems of geometry.[1]

V.

The entire movement which led to the transformation of our ideas of geometry must be characterised as a sound and healthful one. This movement, which began centuries ago but is now greatly intensified, is not to be looked upon as having terminated. On the contrary, we are quite justified in the expectation that it will redound not only to the great advancement of mathematics and geometry, especially in an epistemological regard, but also to that of the other sciences. This movement was, it is true, powerfully stimulated by a few eminent men, but it sprang, nevertheless, not from an individual, but from a general need. This will be seen from the difference in the professions of the men who have taken part in it. Not only the mathematician, but also the philosopher and the educationist, have made large contributions to it. So, too, the methods pursued by the different inquirers are not unrelated. Ideas which Leibnitz[2] uttered recur in slightly altered form in Fourier,[3] Lobachévski, Bolyai, and H. Erb.[4] The philosopher Ueberweg,[5] closely approaching in his opposition to Kant

---

[1] It would be too much to expect of matter that it should realise all the atomistic fantasies of the physicist. So, too, space, as an object of experience, can hardly be expected to satisfy all the ideas of the mathematician, though there be no doubt whatever as to the general value of their investigations.

[2] See *The Monist*, Vol. XII., pp. 488, 498, and 499.

[3] *Séances de l'École Normale. Débats.* Vol. I., 1800, p. 28.

[4] H. Erb, Grossherzoglich Badischer Finanzrath, *Die Probleme der geraden Linie, des Winkels und der ebenen Fläche*, Heidelberg, 1846.

[5] "Die Principien der Geometrie wissenschaftlich dargestellt." *Archiv für Philologie und Pädagogik*. 1851. Reprinted in Brasch's *Welt- und Lebensanschauung F. Ueberwegs*, Leipzig, 1889, pp. 263-317.

the views of the psychologist Beneke,[1] and in his geometrical ideas starting from Erb (which later writer mentions K. A. Erb[2] as his predecessor) anticipates a goodly portion of Helmholtz's labors.

The results to which the preceding discussion has led, may be summarised as follows:

1. The source of our geometric concepts has been found to be experience.

2. The multiplicity of the concepts satisfying the same geometrical facts has been revealed.

3. By the comparison of space with other manifolds, more general concepts were reached, of which the geometric represented a special case. Geometric thought was thus freed from conventional limitations, heretofore imagined insuperable.

4. By the demonstration of the existence of manifolds allied to but different from space, entirely new questions were suggested. What is space physiologically, physically, geometrically? To what are its specific properties to be attributed, since others are also conceivable? Why is space three-dimensional, etc.?

With questions such as these, though we must not expect the answer to-day or to-morrow, we stand before the entire profundity of the domain to be investigated. We shall say nothing of the inept strictures of the Bœotians, whose coming Gauss predicted, and whose attitude determined him to reserve. But what shall we say to the acrid and captious criticisms to which Gauss, Riemann and their associates have been subjected by men of high standing in the scientific world. Have they never experienced in their own persons the truth that inquirers at the outermost boundaries of knowledge discover many things that do not slip smoothly into all heads, but which are not on that account nonsense? True, such inquirers are liable to error, but even the errors of some men are often more fruitful in their consequences than the discoveries of others.

VIENNA, February, 1903. ERNST MACH.

---

[1] *Logik als Kunstlehre des Denkens*, Berlin, 1842, Vol. II., pp. 51–55.

[2] *Zur Mathematik und Logik*, Heidelberg, 1821. I was unable to examine this work.

ANTS AND SOME OTHER INSECTS.[1]

AN INQUIRY INTO THE PSYCHIC POWERS OF THESE ANIMALS WITH AN APPENDIX ON THE PECULIARITIES OF THEIR OLFACTORY SENSE.

WHEN discussing the ant-mind, we must consider that these small animals, on the one hand, differ very widely from ourselves in organisation, but on the other hand, have come, through so-called convergence, to possess in the form of a social commonwealth a peculiar relationship to us. My subject, however, requires the discussion of so many complicated questions that I am compelled to assume acquaintance with the work of others, especially the elements of psychology, and in addition the works of P. Huber, Wasmann, von Buttel-Reepen, Darwin, Romanes, Lubbock, my *Fourmis de la Suisse*, and many others. Since the functions of the sense-organs constitute the basis of comparative psychology, I must also refer to a series of articles entitled "Sensations des Insects" which I have recently published (1900–1901) in the *Rivista de Biologia Generale*, edited by Dr. P. Celesia. In these papers I have defined my position with respect to various authors, especially Plateau and Bethe.

Very recently Bethe, Uexkull, and others have denied the existence of psychic powers in invertebrate animals. They explain the latter as reflex-machines, and take their stand on the ground of the so-called psycho-physical parallelism for the purpose of demon-

---

[1] Lectures delivered in Berlin, August 13, 1901, before the Fifth International Congress of Zoölogists. Published by Ernst Reinhard, Munich, 1901. Translated from the German by William Morton Wheeler.

strating our inability to recognise mental qualities in these animals. They believe, however, that they can prove the mechanical regularity of behavior, but assume unknown forces whenever they are left in the lurch in their explanations. They regard the mind as first making its appearance in the vertebrates, whereas the old Cartesians regarded all animals, in contradistinction to man, as mindless (unconscious) machines.

The Jesuit father E. Wasmann and von Buttel-Reepen are willing, on the other hand, to accept the inductive inference from analogy as a valid scientific method. Like Lubbock, the lecturer and others, they advocate a comparative psychology of the invertebrates and convincingly demonstrate the existence of psychic faculties in these animals. Wasmann, however, puts a very low estimate on the mental powers of the higher vertebrates and, in my opinion, improperly, denies to them any ability of drawing inferences from experience when in the presence of new conditions (this alone he designates as intelligence); he believes that man alone possesses an immortal soul (independent of natural laws?) in addition to the animal mind.

It is necessary, first of all, to arrive at some common understanding concerning the obscure notion "psychic" in order that we may avoid logomachy, and carrying on theology in the sense of Goethe's Mephistopheles. Two concepts are confounded in an obscure manner in the word "psychic": first, the abstract concept of introspection, or subjectivism, i. e., observation from within, which every person knows only, and can know only, in and by himself. For this let us reserve the term "consciousness." Second, the "activity" of the mind or that which determines the contents of the field of consciousness. This has been included without further ado with consciousness in the wider sense, and thence has arisen the confusion of regarding consciousness as an attribute of the mind. In another place I have designated the molecular wave of activity of the neural elements as "neurocyme."

We cannot speak of the consciousness of human beings other than ourselves without drawing an inference from analogy; quite as little ought we to speak of a consciousness of forgotten things.

The field of our consciousness is constantly changing. Things appear in it and disappear from it. Memory, through association, enables us to recall, more or less directly and with more or less difficulty, things which appear to be momentarily absent from consciousness. Moreover, both the experience of self-observation and the phenomena of hypnotism teach us experimentally that many things of which we seem to be unconscious, are nevertheless present in consciousness or have been. Indeed, certain sense-impressions remain, at the moment of their occurrence, unconscious so far as our ordinary consciousness or superconsciousness is concerned, although they can be subsequently recalled into consciousness by suggestion. Whole chains of brain-activities, (dreams, somnambulism, or secondary consciousness) seem ordinarily to be excluded from the superconsciousness, but may subsequently be associated by suggestion with the remembered contents of consciousness. In all these cases, therefore, what seems to be unconscious is after all proved to be conscious. The above-mentioned phenomena have frequently led to mystical interpretations, but they are explainable on a very simple assumption. Let us assume —and this is quite in harmony with observation—that the fields of the introspectively conscious brain-activities are limited by so-called association or dissociation processes, i. e., that we are unable actively to bring them all into connection at the same time, and that therefore all that seems to us unconscious has also in reality a consciousness, in other words, a subjective reflex, then the following results: Our ordinary waking consciousness or superconsciousness is merely an inner subjective reflex of those activities of attention which are most intimately connected with one another, i. e., of the more intensively concentrated maxima of our cerebral activities during waking. There exist, however, other consciousnesses, partly forgotten, partly only loosely or indirectly connected with the contents of the superconsciousness, in contradistinction to which these may be designated as subconsciousness. They correspond to other less concentrated or otherwise associated cerebral activities. We are bound to assume the existence of still more remotely interconnected subconsciousnesses for the infra-cortical (lower) brain-centers, and so on.

It is easy to establish the fact that the maximum of our psychic activity, namely, attention, passes every moment from one perception or thought to another. These objects of attention, as visual or auditory images, will-impulses, feelings or abstract thoughts, come into play—and of this there is no doubt—in different brain-regions or neuron-complexes. We can therefore compare attention to a functional *macula lutea* wandering in the brain, or with a wandering maximal intensity of neurocymic activity. But it is quite as satisfactorily established that other psychic phenomena external to attention are likewise present in consciousness, though in a feebler condition. Finally, it is well known that all that has been in consciousness—even that which is now more, now less, forgotten—is included in the psychic, i. e., in the contents of consciousness. On superficial consideration this appears to satisfy theoretical requirements. But in fact and in truth there are innumerable processes of which we are feebly conscious for only a scarcely appreciable instant and which anon disappear from consciousness. Here and not in the strong and repeated "psychomes"—I beg your indulgence for this word, with which I would for the sake of brevity designate each and every psychic unit—are we to seek the transition from the conscious to the apparently unconscious. Even in this case, however, the feeble condition of consciousness is only apparent, because the inner reflex of these processes can merely echo-faintly in the field of a strongly diverted attention. This, therefore, in no wise proves that such half conscious processes are in and for themselves so feebly represented in consciousness, since a flash of attention is sufficient subsequently to give them definite shape in consciousness. Only in consequence of the diversion of the attention do they lose more and more their connection with the chain of intensity-maxima which, under ordinary circumstances, constitute the remembered contents of our superconsciousness. The more feebly, however, they are bound to the latter, with the more difficulty are such half-conscious processes later associated anew through memory with the dominant chain. Of such a nature are all dreams, all the subordinate circumstances of our lives, all automatised habits, all instincts. But if there exists between the clearly conscious and the unconscious, a half-conscious brain-life, whose consciousness appears to us so feeble merely on account of the deviation of our ordinary train of memories, this is an unequivocal indication that a step further on the remaining connection would be completely severed, so that we should no longer have the right to say that the brain-activities thus fading away nebulously from our superconsciousness do not have consciousness in and for themselves. For the sake of brevity and simplicity we will ascribe subconsciousness to these so-called unconscious brain-processes.

If this assumption is correct—and all things point in this direction—we are not further concerned with consciousness. It does not at all exist as such, but only through the brain-activity of which it is the inner reflex. With the disappearance of this activity, consciousness disappears. When the one is complicated, the other, too, is complicated. When the one is simple, the other is correspondingly simple. If the brain-activity be dissociated, consciousness also becomes dissociated. Consciousness is only an abstract concept, which loses all its substance with the falling away of "conscious" brain-activity. The brain-activity reflected in the mirror of consciousness appears therein subjectively as a summary synthesis, and the synthetical summation grows with the higher complications and abstractions acquired through habit and practice, so that details previously conscious (e. g., those involved in the act of reading) later become subconscious, and the whole takes on the semblance of a psychical unit.

Psychology, therefore, cannot restrict itself merely to a study of the phenomena of our superconsciousness by means of introspection, for the science would be impossible under such circumstances. Everybody would have only his own subjective psychology, after the manner of the old scholastic spiritualists, and would therefore be compelled to doubt the very existence of the external world and his fellow-men. Inference from analogy, scientific induction, the comparison of the experiences of our five senses, prove to us the existence of the outer world, our fellow-men and the psychology of the latter. They also prove to us that there is such a thing as comparative psychology, a psychology of animals. Finally our own psychology, without reference to our brain-activity, is an incomprehensible patchwork full of contradictions, a patchwork which above all things seems to contradict the law of the conservation of energy.

It follows, furthermore, from these really very simple reflections that a psychology that would ignore brain-activity, is a monstrous impossibility. The contents of our superconsciousness are continually influenced and conditioned by subconscious brain-activities. Without these latter it can never be understood. On the other hand, we understand the full value and the ground of the complex organisation of our brain only when we observe it in the inner light of consciousness, and when this observation is supplemented by a comparison of the consciousness of our fellow-men as this is rendered possible for us through spoken and written language by means of very detailed inferences from analogy. The mind must therefore be studied simultaneously from within and from without. Outside ourselves the mind can, to be sure, be studied only through analogy, but we are compelled to make use of this the only method which we possess.

Some one has said that language was given to man not so much for the expression as for the concealment of his thoughts. It is also well known that different men in all honesty attribute very different meanings to the same words. A savant, an artist, a peasant, a woman, a wild Wedda from Ceylon, interpret the same words very differently. Even the same individual interprets them differently according to his moods and their context. Hence it follows that to the psychologist and especially to the psychiatrist—and as such I am here speaking—the mimetic expression, glances and acts of a man often betray his true inner being better than his spoken language. Hence also the attitudes and behavior of animals have for us the value of a "language," the psychological importance of which must not be underestimated. Moreover, the anatomy, physiology and pathology of the animal and human brain have yielded irrefutable proof that our mental faculties depend on the quality, quantity, and integrity of the living brain and are one with the same. It is just as impossible that there should exist a human brain without a mind, as a mind without a brain, and to every normal or pathological change in the mental activity, there corresponds a normal or pathological change of the neurocymic activity of the brain, i. e., of its nervous elements. Hence what we perceive introspectively in consciousness is cerebral activity.

As regards the relation of pure psychology (introspection) to the physiology of the brain (observation of brain-activity from without), we shall take the theory of identity for granted so long as it is in harmony with the facts. The word identity, or monism, implies that every psychic phenomenon is the same real thing as the molecular or neurocymic activity of the brain-cortex coinciding with it, but that this may be viewed from two standpoints. The phenomenon alone is dualistic, the thing itself is monistic. If this were otherwise there would result from the accession of the purely psychical to the physical, or cerebral, an excess of energy which would necessarily contradict the law of the conservation of energy. Such a contradiction, however, has never been demonstrated and would hold up to derision all scientific experience. In the manifestations of our brain-life, wonderful as they undoubtedly are, there is absolutely nothing which contradicts natural laws and justifies us in postulating the existence of a mythical, supernatural "psyche."

On this account I speak of monistic identity and not of psychophysical parallelism. A thing cannot be parallel with itself. Of course, psychologists of the modern school, when they make use of this term, desire merely to designate a supposed parallelism of phenomena without prejudice either to monism or dualism. Since, however, many central nervous processes are accessible neither to physiological nor to psychological observation, the phenomena accessible to us through these two methods of investigation are not in the least parallel, but separated from one another very unequally by intermediate processes. Moreover, inasmuch as the dualistic hypothesis is scientifically untenable, it is altogether proper to start out from the hypothesis of identity.

brum, however, all three regions merge together in many neurons of the cortex.

Within ourselves, moreover, we are able to observe in the three above-mentioned regions all varieties and degrees of so-called psychic dignity, from the simplest reflex to the highest mental manifestations. The feelings and impulses connected with self-preservation (hunger, thirst, fear) and with reproduction (sexual love and its concomitants) represent within us the region of long-inherited, profoundly phyletic, fixed, instinct-life. These instincts are nevertheless partially modified and partly kept within due bounds through the interference of the higher cerebral activities. The enormous mass of brain-substance, which in man stands in no direct relation to the senses and musculature, admits not only of an enormous storing up of impressions and of an infinite variety of motor innervations, but above all, of prodigious combinations of these energies among themselves through their reciprocal activities and the awakening of old, so-called memory images through the agency of new impressions. In contradistinction to the compulsory, regular activities of the profoundly phyletic automatisms, I have used the term "plastic" to designate those combinations and individual adaptations which depend on actual interaction in the activities of the cerebrum. Its loftiest and finest expression is the plastic imagination, both in the province of cognition and in the province of feeling, or in both combined. In the province of the will the finest plastic adaptability, wedded to perseverance and firmness, and especially when united with the imagination, yields that loftiest mental condition which gradually brings to a conclusion during the course of many years decisions that have been long and carefully planned and deeply contemplated. Hence the plastic gift of combination peculiar to genius ranks much higher than any simpler plastic adaptability.

The distinction between automatism and plasticity in brain-activity is, however, only a relative one and one of degree. In the most different instincts which we are able to influence through our cerebrum, i. e., more or less voluntarily, like deglutition, respiration, eating, drinking, the sexual impulse, maternal affection, jeal-

the physiological method, because it alone is exact and restricts itself to what can be weighed and measured. This, too, is an error which has been refuted from time immemorial. Only pure mathematics is exact, because in its operations it makes use solely of equations of abstract numbers. The concrete natural sciences can never be exact and are as unable to subsist without the inductive method of inference from analogy as a tree without its roots. Bethe and Uexkull do not seem to know that knowledge is merely relative. They demand absolute exactitude and cannot understand that such a thing is impossible. Besides, physiology has no reason to pride itself upon the peculiar exactitude of its methods and results.

Although we know that our whole psychology appears as the activity of our cerebrum in connection with the activities of more subordinate nerve-centers, the senses and the muscles, nevertheless for didactic purposes it may be divided into the psychology of cognition, of feeling and volition. Relatively speaking, this subdivision has an anatomico-physiological basis. Cognition depends, in the first instance, on the elaboration of sense-impressions by the brain; the will represents the psycho- or cerebrofugal resultants of cognition and the feelings together with their final transmission to the muscles. The feelings represent general conditions of excitation of a central nature united with elements of cognition and with cerebrofugal impulses, which are relatively differentiated and refined by the former, but have profound hereditary and phylogenetic origins and are relatively independent. There is a continual interaction of these three groups of brain-activities upon one another. Sense-impressions arouse the attention; this necessitates movements; the latter produce new sense-impressions and call for an active selection among themselves. Both occasion feelings of pleasure and pain and these again call forth movements of defense, flight, or desire, and bring about fresh sense-impressions, etc. Anatomically, at least, the sensory pathways to the brain and their cortical centers are sharply separated from the centers belonging to the volitional pathways to the muscles. Further on in the cere-

quired culture by his own impulse. Even the impulse to do this is entirely lacking. Nevertheless, every brain that is trained by man is capable of learning and profiting much from the experience of its own individual life. And one discovers on closer examination that even lower animals may become accustomed to some extent to one thing or another, and hence trained, although this does not amount to an understanding of conventional symbols.

In general we may say, therefore, that the central nervous system operates in two ways: *automatically* and *plastically*.

The so-called reflexes and their temporary, purposefully adaptive, but hereditarily stereotyped combinations, which respond always more or less in the same manner to the same stimuli, constitute the paradigm of automatic activities. These have the deceptive appearance of a "machine" owing to the regularity of their operations. But a machine which maintains, constructs, and reproduces itself is not a machine. In order to build such a machine we should have to possess the key of life, i. e., the understanding of the supposed, but by no means demonstrated, mechanics of living protoplasm. Everything points to the conclusion that the instinctive automatisms have been gradually acquired and hereditarily fixed by natural selection and other factors of inheritance. But there are also secondary automatisms or habits which arise through the frequent repetition of plastic activities and are therefore especially characteristic of man's enormous brain-development.

In all the psychic provinces of intellect, feeling, and will, habits follow the constant law of perfection through repetition. Through practice every repeated plastic brain-activity gradually becomes automatic, becomes "second nature," i. e., similar to instinct. Nevertheless instinct is not inherited habit, but phylogenetically inherited intelligence which has gradually become adapted and crystalised by natural selection or by some other means.

Plastic activity manifests itself, in general, in the ability of the nervous system to conform or adapt itself to new and unexpected conditions and also through its faculty of bringing about internally new combinations of neurocyme. Bethe calls this the power of modification. But since, notwithstanding his pretended issue with anthropomorphism, he himself continually proceeds in an anthropomorphic spirit and demands human ratiocination of animals, if they are to be credited with plasticity (power of modification),—he naturally overlooks the fact that the beginnings of plasticity are primordial, that they are in fact already present in the Amœba, which adapts itself to its environment. Nor is this fact to be conjured out of the world by Loeb's word "tropisms."

Automatic and plastic activities, whether simple or complex, are merely relative antitheses. They grade over into each other, e. g., in the formation of habits but also in instincts. In their extreme forms they resemble two terminal branches of a tree, but they may lead to similar results through so-called convergence of the conditions of life (slavery and cattle-keeping among ants and men). The automatic may be more easily derived from the plastic activities than *vice versa*. One thing is established, however: since a tolerably complicated plastic activity admits of many possibilities of adaptation in the individual brain, it requires much more nervous substance, many more neurons, but has more resistances to overcome in order to attain a complicated result. The activities of an Amœba belong therefore rather to the plasticity of living molecules, but not as yet to that of coöperating nerve-elements; as cell-plasticity it should really be designated as "undifferentiated."[1] There are formed in certain animals specially complex automatisms, or instincts, which require relatively little plasticity and few neurons. In others, on the contrary, there remains relatively considerable nerve-substance for individual plasticity, while the instincts are less complicated. Other animals, again, have little besides the lower reflex centers and are extremely poor in both kinds of complex activities. Still others, finally, are rich in both. Strong so-called "hereditary predispositions" or unfinished instincts consti-

[1] If I expressly refrain from accepting the premature and unjustifiable identification of cell-life with a "machine," I nevertheless do not share the so-called vitalistic views. It is quite possible that science may sometime be able to produce living protoplasm from inorganic matter. The vital forces have undoubtedly originated from physico-chemical forces. But the ultimate nature of the latter and of the assumed material atoms is, of course, metaphysical, i. e., unknowable.

tute the phylogenetic transitions between both kinds of activity and are of extraordinarily high development in man.

Spoken and especially written language, moreover, enable man to exploit his brain to a wonderful extent. This leads us to underestimate animals. Both in animals and man the true value of the brain is falsified by training, i. e., artificially heightened. We overestimate the powers of the educated negro and the trained dog and underestimate the powers of the illiterate individual and the wild animal.

I beg your indulgence for this lengthy introduction to my subject, but it seemed necessary that we should come to some understanding concerning the validity of comparative psychology. My further task now consists in demonstrating to you what manner of psychical faculties may be detected in insects. Of course, I shall select in the first place the ants as the insects with which I am most familiar. Let us first examine the brain of these animals.

In order to determine the psychical value of a central nervous system it is necessary, first, to eliminate all the nerve-centers which subserve the lower functions, above the immediate innervation of the muscles and sense-organs as first centers. The volume of such neuron-complexes does not depend on the intricacy of mental work but on the number of muscle-fibres concerned in it, the sensory surfaces, and the reflex apparatus, hence above all things on the size of the animals. Complex instincts already require the intervention of much more plastic work and for this purpose such nerve-centers alone would be inadequate.

A beautiful example of the fact that complex mental combinations require a large nerve-center dominating the sensory and muscular centers is furnished by the brain of the ant. The ant-colony commonly consists of three kinds of individuals: the queen, or female (largest), the workers which are smaller, and the males which are usually larger than the workers. The workers excel in complex instincts and in clearly demonstrable mental powers (memory, plasticity, etc.). These are much less developed in the queens. The males are incredibly stupid, unable to distinguish friends from enemies and incapable of finding their way back to their nest. Nevertheless the latter have very highly developed eyes and antennae, i. e., the two sense-organs which alone are connected with the brain, or supra-oesophageal ganglion and enable them to possess themselves of the females during the nuptial flight. No muscles are innervated by the supra-oesophageal ganglion. These conditions greatly facilitate the comparison of the perceptive organs, i. e., of the brain (*corpora pedunculata*) in the three sexes. This is very large in the worker, much smaller in the female, and almost vestigial in the male, whereas the optic and olfactory lobes are very large in the latter. The cortical portion of the large worker brain is, moreover, extremely rich in cellular elements. In this connection I would request you to glance at the figures and their explanation.

Very recently, to be sure, it has come to be the fashion to underestimate the importance of brain-morphology in psychology and even in nerve-physiology. But fashions, especially such absurd ones as this, should have no influence on true investigation. Of course, we should not expect anatomy to say what it was never intended to say.

In ants, injury to the cerebrum leads to the same results as injury to the brain of the pigeon.

In this place I would refer you for a fuller account of the details of sensation and the psychic peculiarities of insects to my more extended work above mentioned: *Sensations des Insects.*

It can be demonstrated that insects possess the senses of sight, smell, taste, and touch. The auditory sense is doubtful. Perhaps a sense of touch modified for the perception of delicate vibrations may bear a deceptive resemblance to hearing. A sixth sense has nowhere been shown to occur. A photodermatic sense, modified for light-sensation, must be regarded as a form of the tactile sense. It occurs in many insects. This sense is in no respect of an optic nature. In aquatic insects the olfactory and gustatory senses perhaps grade over into each other somewhat (Nagel), since both perceive chemical substances dissolved in the water.

The visual sense of the facetted eyes is especially adapted for seeing movements, i. e., for perceiving relative changes of position

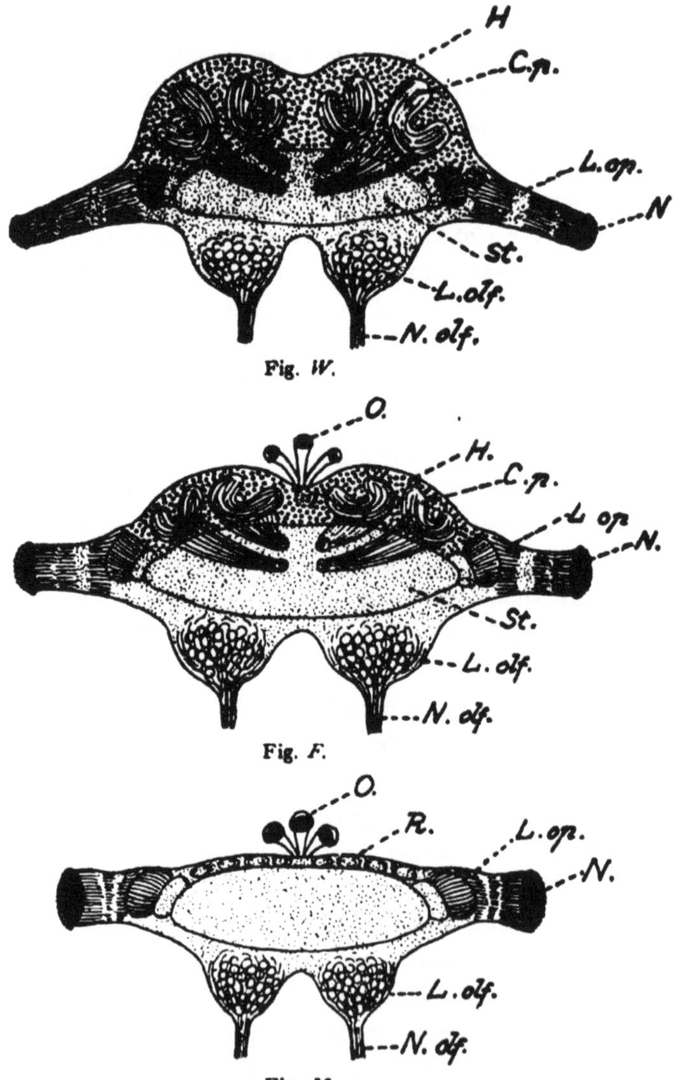

Fig. *W*.

Fig. *F*.

Fig. *M*.

EXPLANATION OF THE FIGURES.

Brain (supra-œsophageal ganglion) of an ant (*Lasius fuliginosus*), magnified 60 diameters, seen from above.

Fig. *W*. Brain of the Worker.

Fig. *F*. Brain of the Queen (Female).

Fig. *M*. Brain of the Male.

St. = Brain trunk. *L. op.* = Lobus opticus (optic lobe). *L. olf.* = Lobus olfactorius sive antennalis (olfactory lobe). *N.* = Facetted eye. *N. olf.* = Nervus olfactorius sive antennalis (olfactory nerve). *O.* = Ocelli, or simple eyes with their nerves (present only in the male and queen). *H.* = Cellular brain cortex (developed only in the worker and queen). *C. p.* = Corpora pedunculata, or fungiform bodies (developed only in the worker and queen). *R.* = Rudimental cortex of male.

The length of the whole ant is:

in the worker 4.5 mm;
in the queen 6.0 mm;
in the male 4.5 mm.

N. B. The striatim of the corpora pedunculata and their stems is represented diagrammatically, for the purpose of indicating rather coarsely their extremely delicate fibrillar structure.

in the retinal image. In flight it is able to localise large spatial areas admirably, but must show less definite contours of the objects than our eyes. The compound eye yields only a single upright image (Exner), the clearness of which increases with the number of facets and the convexity of the eye. Exner succeeded in photographing this image in the fire-fly (Lampyris). As the eyes are immovable the sight of resting objects soon disappears so far as the resting insect is concerned. For this reason resting insects are easily captured when very slowly approached. In flight insects orient themselves in space by means of their compound eyes. Odor, when perceived, merely draws these animals in a particular direction. When the compound eyes are covered, all powers of orientation in the air are lost. Many insects can adapt their eyes for the day or night by a shifting of the pigment. Ants see the ultra-violet with their eyes. Honey-bees and humble-bees can distinguish colors, but obviously in other tones than we do, since they cannot be deceived by artificial flowers of the most skilful workmanship. This may be due to admixtures of the ultra-violet rays which are invisible to our eyes.

The ocelli (simple eyes) play a subordinate rôle, and probably serve as organs of sight for objects situated in the immediate vicinity and in dark cavities.

The olfactory sense has its seat in the antennæ, usually in the club-shaped flagellum, or rather in the pore-plates and olfactory rods of these portions of the antennæ. On account of its external and moveable position at the tip of the antenna, the olfactory organ possesses two properties which are lacking in the vertebrates, and particularly in man. These are:

1. The power of perceiving the chemical nature of a body by direct contact (contact-odor);

2. The power of space-perception and of perceiving the form of objects and that of the animal's own trail by means of odor, and the additional property of leaving associated memories.

The olfactory sense of insects, therefore, gives these animals definite and clear-cut perceptions of space-relations, and enables the animal while moving on the surface of the ground to orient itself with facility. I have designated this sense, which is thus qualitatively, i. e., in its specific energy, very different from our olfactory sense, as the topochemical (olfactory) sense. Probably the pore-plates are used for perceiving odor at a distance and the olfactory rods for contact-odor, but this is pure conjecture. Extirpation of the antennæ destroys the power of distinguishing friends from enemies and deprives the ant of the faculty of orienting itself on the ground and of finding its way, whereas it is possible to cut off three legs and an antenna without seriously impairing these powers. The topochemical sense always permits the ant to distinguish between the directions of its trail, a faculty which Bethe attributes to a mysterious polarisation. The ability to sense different odors varies enormously in different insects. An object possessing odor for one species is often odorless for other species (and for ourselves) and *vice versa*.

The gustatory organs are situated on the mouth-parts. Among insects the reactions of this sense are very similar to our own. Will accustomed some wasps to look in a particular place for honey, which he afterwards mixed with quinine. The wasps detected the substance at once, made gestures of disgust, and never returned to the honey. Mixing the honey with alum had the same result. At first they returned, but after the disagreeable gustatory experience they failed to reappear. Incidentally this is also a proof of their gustatory memory and of their powers of association.

Several organs have been found and described as auditory. But after their removal the supposed reaction to sounds persists.

This would seem to indicate that a deceptive resemblance to hearing may be produced by the perception of delicate vibrations through the tactile sense (Dugès).

The tactile sense is everywhere represented by tactile hairs and papillæ. It reacts more especially to delicate tremors of the atmosphere or soil. Certain arthropods, especially the spiders, orient themselves mainly by means of this sense.

It may be demonstrated that insects, according to the species and conditions of life, use their different senses in combination for purposes of orienting themselves and for perceiving the external world. Many species lack eyes and hence also the sense of sight. In others, again, the olfactory sense is obtuse; certain other forms lack the contact-odor sense (e. g., most Diptera).

It has been shown that the superb powers of orientation exhibited by certain aerial animals, like birds (carrier-pigeons), bees, etc., depend on vision and its memories. Movement in the air gives this sense enormous and manifold values. The semi-circular canals of the auditory organ are an apparatus of equilibrium in vertebrates and mediate sensations of acceleration and rotation (Mach-Breuer), but do not give external orientation. For the demonstration of these matters I must refer you to my work above-cited. A specific, magnetic, or other mode of orientation, independent of the known senses, does not exist.

The facts above presented constitute the basis of insect psychology. The social insects are especially favorable objects for study on account of their manifold reciprocal relationships. If in speaking of the bahavior of these animals I use terms borrowed from human psychology, I would request you, once for all, to bear in mind that these are not to be interpreted in an anthropomorphic but in an analogous sense.

The Realm of Cognition.—In the first place it can be shown that at least many insects (perhaps all, in a more rudimental condition) possess memory, i. e., they are able to store up sense-impressions in their brains for subsequent use. Insects are not merely attracted directly by sensory stimuli, as Bethe imagines. Huber, myself, Fabre, Lubbock, Wasmann, Von Buttel-Reepen, have demonstrated this fact experimentally. That bees, wasps, etc., can find their way in flight through the air, notwithstanding wind and rain (and hence under circumstances precluding the existence of any possible odoriferous trail), and even after the antennæ have been cut off, to a concealed place where they have found what they desired, though this place may be quite invisible from their nest, and this even after the expiration of days and weeks, is a fact of special importance as proof of the above assertion. It can be shown that these insects recognise objects by means of their colors, their forms, and especially by their position in space. Position they perceive through the mutual relations and succession of the large objects in space, as these are revealed to them in their rapid change of place during flight in their compound eyes (shifting of retinal images). Especially the experiments performed by Von Buttel-Reepen and myself leave no doubt concerning this fact. Additional proof of a different nature is furnished by Von Buttel, who found that ether or chloroform narcosis deprives bees of all memory. By this means enemies can be converted into friends. Under these circumstances, too, all memory of locality is lost and must be reacquired by means of a new flight of orientation. An animal, however, certainly cannot forget without having remembered.

The topochemical antennal sense also furnishes splendid proofs of memory in ants, bees, etc. An ant may perform an arduous journey of thirty meters from her ruined nest, there find a place suitable for building another nest, return, orienting herself by means of her antennæ, seize a companion who forthwith rolls herself about her abductrix, and is carried to the newly selected spot. The latter then also finds her way to the original nest, and both each carry back another companion, etc. The memory of the suitable nature of the locality for establishing a new nest must exist in the brain of the first ant or she would not return, laden with a companion, to this very spot. The slave-making ants (*Polyergus*) undertake predatory expeditions, led by a few workers, who for days and weeks previously have been searching the neighborhood for nests of *Formica fusca*. The ants often lose their way, remain standing and hunt about for a long time till one or the other finds the topochemical trail and indicates to the others the direction to be followed by rapidly pushing ahead. Then the pupæ of the *Formica fusca* nest, which they have found, are brought up from the depths of the galleries, appropriated and dragged home, often a distance of forty meters or more. If the plundered nest still contains pupæ, the robbers return on the same or following days and carry off the remainder, but if there are no pupæ left they do not return. How do the Polyergus know whether there are pupæ remaining? It can be demonstrated that smell could not attract them from such a distance, and this is even less possible for sight or any other sense. Memory alone, i. e., the recollection that many pupæ still remain behind in the plundered nest can induce them to return. I have carefully followed a great number of these predatory expeditions.

While Formica species follow their topochemical trail with great difficulty over new roads, they nevertheless know the immediate surroundings of their nest so well that even shovelling away the earth can scarcely disconcert them, and they find their way at once, as Wasmann emphatically states and as I myself have often observed. That this cannot be due to smelling at long range can be demonstrated in another manner, for the olfactory powers of the genus Formica, like those of honey-bees, are not sufficiently acute for this purpose, as has been shown in innumerable experiments by all connoisseurs of these animals. Certain ants can recognise friends even after the expiration of months. In ants and bees there are very complex combinations and mixtures of odors, which Von Buttel has very aptly distinguished as nest-odor, colony- (family-) odor, and individual odor. In ants we have in addition a species-odor, while the queen-odor does not play the same rôle as among bees.

It follows from these and many other considerations that the social Hymenoptera can store up in their brains visual images and topochemical odor-images and combine these to form perceptions or something of a similar nature, and that they can associate such perceptions, even those of different senses, especially sight, odor, and taste, with one another and thereby acquire spatial images.

Huber as well as Von Buttel, Wasmann, and myself have

always found that these animals, through frequent repetition of an activity, journey, etc., gain in the certainty and rapidity of the execution of their instincts. Hence they form, very rapidly to be sure, habits. Von Buttel gives splendid examples of these in the robber-bees, i. e., in some of the common honey-bees that have acquired the habit of stealing the honey from the hives of strangers. At first the robbers display some hesitation, though later they become more and more impudent. But he who uses the term habit, must imply secondary automatism and a pre-existing plastic adaptability. Von Buttel adduces an admirable proof of this whole matter and at the same time one of the clearest and simplest refutations of Bethe's innumerable blunders, when he shows that bees that have never flown from the hive, even though they may be older than others that have already flown, are unable to find their way back even from a distance of a few meters, when they are unable to see the hive, whereas old bees know the whole environment, often to a distance of six or seven kilometers.

It results, therefore, from the unanimous observations of all the connoisseurs that sensation, perception, and association, inference, memory and habit follow in the social insects on the whole the same fundamental laws as in the vertebrates and ourselves. Furthermore, attention is surprisingly developed in insects, often taking on an obsessional character and being difficult to divert.

On the other hand, inherited automatism exhibits a colossal preponderance. The above-mentioned faculties are manifested only in an extremely feeble form beyond the confines of the instinct-automatism stereotyped in the species.

An insect is extraordinarily stupid and inadaptable to all things not related to its instincts. Nevertheless I succeeded in teaching a water-beetle (*Dytiscus marginalis*) which in nature feeds only in the water, to eat on my table. While thus feeding, it always executed a clumsy flexor-movement with its fore-legs which brought it over on its back. The insect learned to keep on feeding while on its back, but it would not dispense with this movement, which is adapted to feeding in the water. On the other hand, it always attempted to leap out of the water (no longer fleeing to the bottom of the vessel) when I entered the room, and nibbled at the tip of my finger in the most familiar manner. Now these are certainly plastic variations of instinct. In a similar manner some large Algerian ants which I transplanted to Zurich, learned during the course of the summer months to close the entrance of their nest with pellets of earth, because they were being persecuted and annoyed by our little *Lasius niger*. In Algiers I always saw the nest-opening wide open. There are many similar examples which go to show that these tiny animals can utilise some few of their experiences even when this requires a departure from the usual instincts.

That ants, bees, and wasps are able to exchange communications that are understood, and that they do not merely titillate one another with their antennæ as Bethe maintains, has been demonstrated in so many hundred instances, that it is unnecessary to waste many words on this subject. The observations of a single predatory expedition of Polyergus, with a standing still of the whole army and a seeking for the lost trail, is proof sufficient of the above statement. But, of course, this is not language in the human sense! There are no abstract concepts corresponding to the signs. We are here concerned only with hereditary, instinctively automatic signs. The same is true of their comprehension (pushing with the head, rushing at one another with wide-open mandibles, titillation with the antennæ, stridulatory movement of the abdomen, etc.). Moreover, imitation plays a great rôle. Ants, bees, etc., imitate and follow their companions. Hence it is decidedly erroneous (and in this matter Wasmann, Von Buttel, and myself are of but one opinion) to inject human thought-conception and human ratiocination into this instinct-language, as has been done to some extent, at least, even by Pierre Huber, not to mention others. It is even very doubtful whether a so-called general sensory idea (i. e., a general idea of an object, like the idea "ant," "enemy," "nest," "pupa") can arise in the emmet brain. This is hardly capable of demonstration. Undoubtedly perception and association can be carried on in a very simple way, after the manner of insects, without ever rising to such complex results. At any rate proofs of such an assumption are lacking. But what exists is surely in itself-sufficiently interesting and important. It gives us at least an insight into the brain-life of these animals.

Better than any generalisations, a good example will show what I mean.

Plateau had maintained that when Dahlia blossoms are covered with green leaves, bees nevertheless return to them at once. At first he concealed his Dahlias incompletely (i. e., only their ray-florets), afterwards completely, but still in an unsatisfactory manner, and inferred from the results that bees are attracted by odor and not by sight.

a. In a Dahlia bed visited by many bees and comprising about forty-three floral heads of different colors, I covered first seventeen and then eight at 2.15 P. M., September 10th, with grape-leaves bent around them and fastened with pins.

b. Of four I covered only the yellow disc;

c. Of one, on the other hand, I covered only the outer ray-florets, leaving the disc visible.

So many bees were visiting the Dahlias that at times there were two or three to a flower.

Result: Immediately all the completely covered flowers ceased to be visited by the bees. Dahlia (*c*) continued to be visited like those completely visible. The bees often flew to Dahlias (*b*) but at once abandoned them; a few, however, succeeded in finding the disc beneath the leaves.

Then as soon as I removed the covering from a red Dahlia the bees at once flew to it; and soon a poorly concealed specimen was detected and visited. Later an inquisitive bee discovered the entrance to a covered Dahlia from the side or from below. Thenceforth this bee, but only this one, returned to this same covered flower.

Nevertheless several bees seemed to be seeking the Dahlias which had so suddenly disappeared. Towards 5.30 o'clock some of them had detected the covered flowers. Thenceforth these insects were rapidly imitated by the other bees, and in a short time the hidden flowers were again being visited. As soon as a bee had discovered my imposition and found the entrance to a hidden flower, she flew in her subsequent journeys, without hesitation to the concealed opening of the grape-leaf. As long as a bee had merely made the discovery by herself, she remained unnoticed by the others. When this was accomplished by several, however, (usually by four or five,) the others followed their example.

Plateau, therefore, conducted his experiments in a faulty manner and obtained erroneous results. The bees still saw the Dahlias which he at first incompletely concealed. Then, by the time he had covered them up completely, but only from above, they had already detected the fraud and saw the Dahlias also from the side. Plateau had failed to take into consideration the bee's memory and attention.

September 13th I made some crude imitations of Dahlias by sticking the yellow heads of Hieracium (hawkweed) each in a Petunia flower, and placed them among the Dahlias. Neither the Petunias nor the Hieracium had been visited by the bees. Nevertheless many of the honey and humble-bees flew at first to the artefacts in almost as great numbers as to the Dahlias, but at once abandoned the flowers when they had detected the error, obviously by means of their sense of smell. The same results were produced by a Dahlia, the disc of which had been replaced by the disc of a Hieracium.

As a control experiment I had placed a beautiful, odorous Dahlia disc among the white and yellow Chrysanthemums which had been neglected by the bees. For a whole half hour the bees flew by only a few centimeters above the disc without noticing it; not till then was it visited by a bee that happened to be followed by a second. From this moment the Dahlia disc which lay in the path of flight was visited like the others, whereas on the other hand the Petunia-Hieracium artefacts, now known to be fraudulent, were no longer noticed.

Plateau has demonstrated that artificial flowers, no matter how carefully copied from the human standpoint, are not noticed by insects. I placed artefacts of this description among the Dahlias. They remained in fact entirely neglected. Perhaps, as above suggested, the bees are able to distinguish the chlorophyll colors from other artificial hues, owing to admixtures of the ultra-violet rays, or by some other means. But since Plateau imagines that the artificial flowers repel insects, I cut out, Sept. 19th, the following rather crude paper-flowers:

α. A red flower;

β. A white flower;

γ. A blue flower;

δ. A blue flower, with a yellow center made from a dead leaf;

ε. A rose-colored piece of paper with a dry Dahlia disc;

ζ. A green Dahlia leaf (unchanged).

It was nine o'clock in the morning. I placed a drop of honey on each of the six artefacts mounted among the Dahlias. For a quarter of an hour many bees flew past, very close to my artefacts but without perceiving and hence without smelling the honey. I went away for an hour. On my return artefact δ was without honey, and must therefore have been discovered by the bees. All the others had remained quite untouched and unnoticed.

With some difficulty I next undertook to bring artefact α very close to a bee resting on a Dahlia. But the attention of the bee was so deeply engrossed by the Dahlia that I had to repeat the experiment four or five times till I succeeded in bringing the honey within reach of her proboscis. The insect at once began to suck up the honey from the paper-flower. I marked the bee's back with blue paint so that I might be able to recognise her, and repeated the experiment with β and ε. In these cases one of the bees was painted yellow, the other white.

Soon the blue bee, which had in the meantime gone to the hive, returned, flew at once to α, first hovering about it dubiously, then to δ, where she fed, then again to α, but not to the Dahlias. Later the yellow bee returned to β and fed, and flew to α and δ where she again fed, but gave as little heed to the Dahlias as did the blue bee.

Thereupon the white bee returned seeking ε, but failing to find it, at once went to feeding on some of the Dahlias. But she tarried only a moment on each Dahlia as if tortured by the *idée fixe* of honey. She returned to the artefacts, the perception of which, however, she was not quite able to associate with the memory of the honey flavor. At last she found a separate piece of ε, which happened to be turned down somewhat behind, and began lapping up the honey.

Thenceforth the three painted bees, and these alone, returned regularly to the artefacts and no longer visited the Dahlias. The fact is of great importance that the painted bees entirely of their own accord, undoubtedly through an instinctive inference from analogy, discovered the other artefacts as soon as their attention had been attracted by the honey on one of them, notwithstanding the fact that the artefacts were some distance from one another and of different colors. For were not the Dahlias, too, which they had previously visited, of different colors? Thus the blue bee flew to α, β, γ, and δ, the yellow to β, α, δ, and γ, the white ε, α, β, and δ. Matters continued thus for half an hour. The hidden green ζ was not found, evidently because it was indistinguishable from the green foliage.

Finally one bee, by herself, having had in all probability her attention attracted by the three others, came to δ and fed. I marked her with carmine. Thereupon she flew to α and drove the blue bee away. Another bee was attracted to ε of her own accord and was painted with cinnobar. Still another bee came by herself to β and was painted green. It was now 12.30 o'clock. The experiment had therefore lasted more than three hours, and during this time only six bees had come to know the artefacts, while the great majority still kept on visiting the Dahlias. But now the other bees began to have their attention attracted by the visitors to the artefacts. One, then two, then three, and finally more new ones followed, and I had not sufficient colors with which to mark them. Every moment I was obliged to replenish the honey. Then I went to dinner and returned at 1.25. At this moment seven bees were feeding on β, two on α, one on γ, three on δ, the white one alone on ε. More than half of all these were new, unpainted followers. Now a veritable swarm of bees threw themselves on the artefacts and licked up the last traces of the honey. Then for the first time, after more than four hours, a bee from the swarm discovered the honey on the artefact ζ, which on account of its color had remained concealed up to this time!

As a pack of hounds throws itself on an empty skeleton, the swarm of bees, now completely diverted from the Dahlias, cast themselves on the completely empty artefacts and vainly searched every corner of them for honey. It was 1.55 P. M. The bees began to scatter and return to the Dahlias. Then I replaced α and β by a red and white paper respectively, which had never come in contact with honey and could not therefore smell of the substance. These pieces of paper, nevertheless, were visited and examined by various bees, whose brains were still possessed with the fixed idea of the flavor of honey. The white bee, e. g., investigated the white paper very carefully for a period of three to four minutes. There could, of course, be no such thing as an unknown force or attraction of odor, or brilliancy of floral colors. This fact can only be explained by an association of space, form, and color memories with memories of taste.

Thereupon I took all the artefacts in my left hand for the purpose of carrying them away. Two or three bees followed me, hovering about my left hand, and tried to alight on the empty artefacts. The space-image had changed and only the color and form could any longer be of service to the bees in their recognition of these objects.

This experiment is so clear and unequivocal that I mention it here among many others. It demonstrates:

1. The space, form, and color perceptions of the honey-bee. That these are possible only through the agency of the compound eyes is proved by other experiments (varnishing the eyes, extirpation of the antennæ, mouth-parts, etc.).

2. The memory of the honey-bee, in particular her visual and gustatory memory.

3. Her power of associating gustatory with visual memories.

4. Her ability instinctively to draw inferences from analogy: If she has once been offered honey in an artefact, she will investigate others, even those of a different color and hitherto unnoticed.

These she compares by means of the visual sense, since they are relatively similar, and recognises them as similar though such objects are most unusual in the bee's experience.

5. Her poor olfactory sense, which is useful only at very close range.

6. The onesidedness and narrow circle of her attention.

7. The rapid formation of habits.

8. The limits of imitation of bees by one another.

Of course, I should not allow myself to draw these conclusions from a single experiment, if they had not been confirmed by innumerable observations by the ablest investigators in this field. Lubbock showed clearly that it is necessary to train a bee for some time to go to a particular color if one wishes to compel her to pay no attention to other colors. This is the only way in which it is possible to demonstrate her ability to distinguish colors. My bees, on the contrary, had been trained on differently colored objects (Dahlias and artefacts) and therefore paid no attention to differences in color. It would be a fallacy to conclude from this that they do not distinguish colors. On the contrary, by means of other experiments I have fully confirmed Lubbock's results.

By 2.20 P. M. all of my bees, even the painted ones, had returned to the Dahlias.

On September 27, a week later, I wished to perform a fresh experiment with the same bees. I intended to make them distinguish between differently colored discs, placed at different points on a long scale, representing on a great sheet of paper, varying intensities of light from white through gray to black. First, I wished to train a bee to a single color. But I had calculated without the bee's memory, which rendered the whole experiment impracticable. Scarcely had I placed my paper with the discs on the lawn near the Dahlia bed, and placed one or two bees on the blue discs and marked them with colors, when they began to investigate all the red, blue, white, black and other discs with or without honey. After a few moments had elapsed, other bees came from the Dahlia bed and in a short time a whole swarm threw itself on the paper discs. Of course, those that had been provided with honey were most visited, because they detained the bees, but even the discs without honey were stormed and scrutinised by bees following one another in their flight. The bees besieged even the paint-box. Among these there was one that I had previously deprived of her antennæ. She had previously partaken of the honey on the blue discs and had returned to the hive. This bee examined the blue piece of paint in the color-box.

In brief, my experiment was impossible, because all the bees still remembered from a former occasion the many-colored artefacts provided with honey, and therefore examined all the paper discs no matter of what color. The association between the taste of the honey and the paper discs had been again aroused by the sight-perception of the latter, and had acquired both consistency and rapid and powerful imitation, because honey happened to be actually found on some of the discs.

Together with the perceptive and associative powers, the power of drawing simple, instinctive inferences from analogy is also apparent. Without this, indeed, the operation of perception and memory would be inconceivable! We have just given an example. I have shown on a former occasion that humble-bees, whose nest I had transferred to my window, when they returned home often confounded other windows of the same façade and examined them for a long time before they discovered the right one. Lubbock reports similar facts. Von Buttel shows that bees that are accustomed to rooms and windows, learn to examine the rooms and windows in other places, i. e., other houses. When Pissot suspended wire netting with meshes twenty-two mm. in diameter in front of a wasp nest, the wasps hesitated at first, then went around the netting by crawling along the ground or avoided it in some other way. But they soon learned to fly directly through the meshes. The sense of sight, observed during flight, is particularly well adapted to experiments of this kind, which cannot therefore be performed with ants. But the latter undoubtedly draw similar inferences from the data derived from their topochemical antennal sense. The discovery of prey or other food on a plant or an object induces these insects to examine similar plants or objects and to perform other actions of a like nature.

There are, on the other hand, certain very stupid insects, like the males of ants, the Diptera and may-flies (Ephemerids) with rudimental brains, incapable of learning anything or of combining sense-impressions to any higher degree than as simple automatisms, and without any demonstrable retention of memory-images. Such insects lead a life almost exclusively dominated by sensory stimuli; but their lives are adapted to extremely simple conditions. In these very instances the difference is most striking, and they demonstrate most clearly through comparison and contrast the *plus* possessed by more intelligent insects.

The Realm of the Will. The notion of volition, in contradistinction to the notion of reflex action, presupposes the expiration of a certain time interval and the operation of mediating and complex brain-activities between the sense-impression and the movement which it conditions. In the operation of the purposeful automatisms of instinct which arouse one another into activity in certain sequences, there is also a time interval, filled out by internal, dynamic brain-processes as in the case of the will. Hence these are not pure reflexes. They may for a time suffer interruption and then be again continued. But their operation is brought about in great measure by a concatenation of complicated reflexes which follow one another in a compulsory order. On this account the term automatism or instinct is justifiable.

If we are to speak of will in the narrower sense, we must be able to establish the existence of individual decisions, which can be directed according to circumstances, i. e., are modifiable, and may, for a certain period, remain dormant in the brain to be still performed notwithstanding. Such volition may be very different from the complex volition of man, which consists of the resultants of prodigiously manifold components that have been long preparing and combining. The ants exhibit positive and negative volitional phenomena, which cannot be mistaken. The ants of the genus Formica Linné are particularly brilliant in this respect, and they also illustrate the individual psychical activities most clearly. The above-mentioned migrations from nest to nest show very beautifully the individual plans of single workers carried out with great tenacity. For hours at a time an ant may try to overcome a multitude of difficulties for the purpose of attaining an aim which she has set herself. This aim is not accurately prescribed by instinct, as the insect may be confronted with several possibilities, so that it often happens that two ants may be working in opposition to each other. This looks like stupidity to the superficial observer. But it is just here that the ant's plasticity reveals itself. For a time the two little animals interfere with each other, but finally they notice the fact, and one of them gives in, goes away, or assists the other.

These conditions are best observed during the building of nests or roads, e. g., in the horse-ant (*Formica rufa*) and still better in *F. pratensis*. It is necessary, however, to follow the behavior of a few ants for hours, if one would have a clear conception of this matter, and for this much patience and much time are necessary. The combats between ants, too, show certain very consistent aims of behavior, especially the struggles which I have called chronic combats (*combats à froid*). After two parties (two colonies brought together) have made peace with each other, one often sees a few individuals persecuting and maltreating certain individuals of the opposite party. They often carry their victims a long distance off, for the purpose of excluding them from the nest. If the ant that has been borne away returns to the nest and is found by her persecutrix, she is again seized and carried away to a still greater distance. In one such case in an artificial nest of a small species of Leptothorax, the persecuting ant succeeded in dragging her victim to the edge of my table. She then stretched out her head and allowed her burden to fall on the floor. This was not chance, for she repeated the performance twice in succession after I had again placed the victim on the table. Among the different individuals of the previously hostile, but now pacified opposition, she had concentrated her antipathy on this particular ant and had tried to make her return to the nest impossible. One must have very strong preconceived opinions if in such and many similar cases one would maintain that ants are lacking in individual decision and execution. Of course, all these things happen within the confines of the instinct-precincts of the species, and the different stages in the exetion of a project are instinctive. Moreover, I expressly defend myself against the imputation that I am importing human reflection and abstract concepts into this volition of the ant, though we must honestly admit, nevertheless, that in the accomplishment of our human decisions both hereditary and secondary automatisms are permitted to pass unnoticed. While I am writing these words, my eyes operate with partially hereditary, and my hand with secondary automatisms. But it goes without saying that only a human brain is capable of carrying out my complex innervations and my concomitant abstract reflections. But the ant must, nevertheless, associate and consider somewhat in a concrete way after the manner of an ant, when it pursues one of the above-mentioned aims and combines its instincts with this special object in view. While, however, the instinct of the ant can be combined for only a few slightly different purposes, by means of a small number of plastic adaptations or associations, individually interrupted in their concatenation or *vice versa*, in the thinking human being both inherited and secondary automatisms are only fragments or instruments in the service of an overwhelming, all-controlling, plastic brain-activity. It may be said incidentally that the relative independence of the spinal chord and of subordinate brain-centers in the lower animals (and even in the lower mammals) as compared with the cerebrum, may be explained in a similar manner if they are compared with the profound dependence of these organs and their functions on the massive cerebrum in man and even to some extent in the apes. The cerebrum splits up and controls its automatisms (*divide et impera*).

While success visibly heightens both the audacity and tenacity of the ant-will, it is possible to observe after repeated failure or in consequence of the sudden and unexpected attacks of powerful enemies a form of abulic dejection, which may lead to a neglect of the most important instincts, to cowardly flight, to the devouring or casting away of offspring, to neglect of work, and similar conditions. There is a chronically cumulative discouragement in degenerate ant-colonies and an acute discouragement when a combat is lost. In the latter case one may see troops of large powerful ants fleeing before a single enemy, without even attempting to defend themselves, whereas the latter a few moments previously would have been killed by a few bites from the fleeing individuals. It is remarkable how soon the victor notices and utilises this abulic discouragement. The dejected ants usually rally after the flight and soon take heart and initiative again. But they offer but feeble resistance, e. g., to a renewed attack from the same enemy on the following day. Even an ant's brain does not so soon forget the defeats which it has suffered.

In bitter conflicts between two colonies of nearly equal strength the tenacity of the struggle and with it the will to conquer increases till one of the parties is definitively overpowered. In the realm of will imitation plays a great rôle. Even among ants protervity and dejection are singularly contagious.

(TO BE CONCLUDED.)

AUGUST FOREL.

ZURICH, SWITZERLAND.

BEL, THE CHRIST OF ANCIENT TIMES.

IT is admitted by every one who has studied the religion of the Babylonians, that it is from the first to the last *polytheistic*. If we were to take the trouble of counting together the Babylonian divinities occurring in the inscriptions and especially in the several "lists of gods," we would get nearly as many as 500–1000 different gods. This state of affairs is indeed annoying for one who tries to understand such a "theological system." The difficulty is, however, still more increased, not only by the various *identifications* of one god with another, but especially by the so-called different *genealogies* of one and the same divinity. Take, e. g., the goddess ISHTAR! She appears in one inscription as the daughter of the moon-god, *Sin*;[1] in another as that of the god *Anu*,[2] in a third as a child of *Anshar* or *Ashshur*,[3] in a fourth as that of *Bel*,[4] in a fifth as a child of *Nin-ib*,[5] thus being considered not only as a daughter of Bel, but also

---

[1] [ilu] *Ishtar* (SUCH) *mârat* (dumu-sal) [ilu] *Sin* (ESH), Ishtar's descent, *Keilinschriftliche Bibliothek* (= K. B.) VI[1]. p. 80, 2 *et passim*.

[2] *illik mârat Anim ana pân Bêl abîsha* = the daughter of Anu went to Bêl her father. IV. R. 65, col. II. 32; Jensen, *Kosmologie*, p. 273.

[3] *Anshar* (= Ashshur)....*ba-nu-ú ilâni*[pl] *mu-al-lid* [ilu] *Ish-tar* = Anshar, the creator of the gods, the begetter of Ishtar. Craig, *Religious Texts*, Vol. I. p. 32, 16.

[4] See note 2 above.

[5] As such she is known under the name *É-gi-a*, which means, according to Haupt, S. A. K. T. p. 214, 11 = *kal-la-a-tu* = "bride." *É-gi-a dumu-sag* [dingir] *IB-A*: Reisner, *Hymnen*, pp. 132, 44; 79, 14; 56, 10; IV. R. 21, No. 2, Rev. 54; Craig, R. T., I. p. 20, 28 is therefore translated by: *kal-lat mar-tum resh-ti-tum sha* [ilu] *Nin*-[*ib*], i. e., "the bride, the principal daughter of Ninib," Reisner, *loc. cit.*, p. 65, 13. This latter passage proves also [dingir] *IB-A* is = [ilu] *Nin-ib*, who changes again with [dingir] *IB* in Zimmern, *Ritualtafeln*, No. 26, col. III. 48, 49, where [dingir] *IB* is called the *gash-ru bu-kur* [ilu] *Bêl* ([dingir] *BE*), i. e., "the mighty,

as a daughter of the first-born of Bel, for *Ninib* himself is a son of Bel.[1] Furthermore, the divinity ilu *SUCH* is not only = Ishtar,[2] but also = Ninib himself,[3] nay, even = dingir *Lugal-banda*,[4] the god of Eshnunna, and husband of dingir *Nun-sun*, his wife. Ishtar is also = *An-tum*, the wife of Anu,[5] and as such = ilu *Nin-shar*,[6] who again is the "thunderbolt carrier of *Nin-Girsu*,"[7] or of the *É-kur*.[8] Yes, Ishtar has become even a common name for "goddess," and suffered to have a plural form "Ishtarâte" = goddesses.[9] Not very much better is it with god NUSKU (PA+KU). In one and the same sentence, he is called: "The one begotten by Anu," the "firstborn of Enlil," the "sprout of the ocean," the "creature of the lord of heaven and earth.[10]

In another inscription he appears as the "son of É-kur," the great one, who like Nannar (the moon-god)....busies himself with

---

the first-born of Bel." The title *kallâtu*, "bride," is not only borne by (*a*) *Ishtar* but also by (*b*) ilu *A-a*, the *é-gi-a rabîtu*, V. R. 65, 19*b*, who as such is identified not only with the Ishtar Annunit of Sippar, the wife of Shamash, the sun-god: V. R. 61, 5*b*; 40*b*; 65, 35*a*, etc., but even with Shamash himself: II. R. 57, 15*a*; (*c*) by *Tashmetum*, the wife of Nabû; IV. R. 59, 41*b*; Zimmern, *Shurpu*, II. 157: *kal-la-tum rabî-tum*, "the great bride." Here Tashmetum is mentioned in close connection with ilu *Na-na-a*, who in *loc. cit.* l. 156 is directly coupled with Nabû, while in l. 197 it is Tashmetum again who is mentioned with Nabû. Hence Tashmetum = Nanâ! (*d*) *Tsarpanitum*: ilu *Tsar-pa-ni-tum be-el-tum rabî-tum chirat* ilu *En-bi-lu-lu ka-lat* ilu *Nu-[gim-mut]*, i. e., the great mistress, the wife of Enbilulu (= Marduk, see Reisner, *Hymnen*, pp. 53, 19; 46, 10: *umun* dingir *En-bi-lu-lu dumu-sag* dingir *En-ki-ge*; cf. also Reisner, *loc. cit.*, 138, 118), the kallat of Nugimmut, Craig, R. T., I. p. 31, 22, cf. l. 16.

[1] See preceding note.

[2] See above note 1.

[3] II. R. 57*b*, Rev. 35: dingir(ti-ish-chu) *SUCH* = dito (i. e., ilu *Nin-ib*) *sha ra-am-ku-ti*, i. e., dingir *SUCH*, when pronounced Tishchu, is the god Ninib of "the pouring out," or better of "the washing, cleansing, himself" (Jensen, K. B. VI[1]. p. 365).

[4] See my forthcoming article on Jahveh.

[5] Hence his daughter *and* his wife!

[6] II. R. 54, No. 3, l. 19.

[7] See my *Creation Story*, (= C. S.) p. 44, note 1, and p. 46.

[8] Reisner, *Hymnen*, pp. 137, 44; 134, col. I. 31.

[9] See Delitzsch, *Handwörterbuch*, p. 154*a*. This is the reason why Ishtar may signify almost any goddess.

[10] *Nusku shurbû ilidti* ilu *A[nim] tamshil abi bukur* ilu *Bêl* (= *Enlil*) *tarbît apsî binût* ilu *En-an-ki*: IV. R[2]. 49 [56], 15*b*, ff. See Jensen, *Kosmologie*, p. 273.

the command of the "Enlilship," who guardeth the mystery.[1] In a third he is called the "son of the thirtieth day of the month.[2] In a fourth he is designated "the great one, the one begotten by *Dur-an-ki*."[3] He is identified not only with Nergal,[4] the god of the nether world, whose "day of death" was celebrated on the twenty-eighth of a month,[5] but also with [dingir]*BIL-GI*, resp. [dingir]*GISH-BAR*, etc., etc.

Provoking as such genealogies might seem at the first glance, yet, we will have to admit, that they had, yes, must have had and still have a *reason*. If, therefore, we want to bring light into this chaos, we cannot do it by ridiculing[6] these genealogies, nor by building up, first of all, a theory of our own and then try to fit and force the different gods into our theory,[7] but we always and under all circumstances must maintain the accuracy of these "contradictory" genealogies and explain them by other passages of the Cuneiform Literature, which may help us to the right understanding of

---

[1] *Mâr* (*dumu-ush*) *É-kur shur-bu-û sha ki-ma* [ilu]*URU-KI-ri* (= Nannar-ri!) ....*mut-tab-bil pa-ra-ats* [ilu]*EN-LIL-û-ti na-tsir pi-r*[*is-ti*]. Craig, *Religious Texts*, I., p. 35. obv. 7. 8. Zimmern, *Keilinschriften und das Alte Testament* (= K. A. T.[3]), p. 416, note 3. wants to find in this inscription the statement that Nusku is also the son of Sin! The reading *âlidishu*, which he finds in the Rev. l. 6 f., is—at least according to Craig's copy—not justified!

[2] IV. R[2]. 23, 3 f.

[3] K. 3285, Bezold, *Catalogue*, p. 520: [ilu]*PA+KU shur-bu-û i-lid-ti Dur-an-ki*.

[4] See *Cossæan Vocabulary*.

[5] IV. R. 33. 33. From these latter three references Jensen (K. B. VI[1]. pp. 413 and 466) concludes that Nusku = Nergal, the former being the *Neumondsichel*, the latter the *abnehmender Mond*,—a conclusion which I am willing to accept with the following reserve: Nusku = Nergal is = SIN or Nin-Girsu. As Nin-Girsu was the chief messenger of Enlil, so [dingir]*Nusku lugh-magh* [dingir]*En-lil-lal* (E. B. H. 223, 3), i. e., "the exalted ambassador of Enlil," originally = Nin-Girsu, became, when Sin was made the highest god of the Babylonian pantheon, thus being identified with Enlil (*Creation Story*, p. 50), his (Sin's) messenger. And as the מלאך יהוה was identified with יהוה, so was Nin-Girsu with Enlil, and Nusku or Nergal with Sin,—hence Nusku's worship in the temple of the moon-god at Harran, Inscript. of Nabû-nâ'id, K. B. III[2]. p. 101, col. II. 18, 42. But the messenger of a god is always his son! Hence Nusku or Nergal, the messenger of Sin, *had* to become also his (Sin's) son. The son of Sin (or ZU) is Shamash (or UD), thus it happened that Nergal (= Nusku) was said to be = Shamash, see Sp. I. 131 (*Zeitschrift für Assyriologie*, VI. p. 241) l. 52 ff.; Zimmern, K. A. T[3]. p. 388.

[6] As Jensen, K. B. VI[1]. 319, 320; *Kosm.* 273 does it.

[7] As is done by Barton, *Sketch of Semitic Origins*.

the nature of the god in question. If in course of such an investigation we come to understand his nature and his essence correctly, we also will and must be able to account for his genealogy, even if it were the most contradictory.

That so many different genealogies of one and the same god do exist in the religious doctrines of the Babylonians, is, no doubt, due to the various elements to be found in the Babylonian population. The little valley between the Tigris and the Euphrates was since the "dawn of history" the land which, on account of its fertility, almost all the nations of the ancient world tried to possess and actually did possess. In the inscriptions discovered in this valley we find mentioned, besides the specific Semitic-Babylonian, also Persian, Aramæan, Arabic, Hittite, Elamitic, Cossæan, Canaanitish, and Sumerian gods. A religion of the Babylonians must, therefore, be primarily a *history* of their religion; and if the investigator ignores such a historic development, his results must be pronounced, from the very first, a failure.

It is not my intention to give such a history of the Babylonian religion here—the material so far accessible to scholars would prevent me from doing this—but I want to show by a few examples that we are still able to bring some light into the chaos, if we study the religion historically.

To put it briefly, we may say that the religion of the Babylonians may be divided into three epochs:

I. *The Sumerian*, embodying in it the oldest so-called "Semitic-Babylonian" religious elements. What these latter are or were, we cannot tell as yet. It would seem; however, that the oldest Semitic religious ideas, as expressed in the inscriptions, were in all essentials and particulars the same as those of the Sumerians, i. e., the so-called Semitic-Babylonians seem to have adopted the Sumerian pantheon "in toto" without any perceptable admixture of their own.

II. The *Canaanitish* epoch. This began at about 3000 B. C.[1]

---

[1] Shortly before the "kings of Ur and of the four quarters of the world." The inscriptions of these kings distinguish very often between the "*Nippurian* Enlil or Bel" and another, i. e., probably Marduk or possibly Dagan.

when the Canaanites invaded Babylonia. At the time of Hammurabi, at about 2200 B. C., they are masters of the whole of Babylonia. Their own specific god has become the god κατ' ἐξοχήν. These Canaanites made Babylon their capital. Their god became thus the city-god of Babylon, and when, in course of time the whole of Babylonia had been subjugated, the city-god of Babylon became the "god of Babylonia." We may call, therefore, this epoch, also the *Babylonian* epoch.

III. The *Assyrian*. During this time we find nearly all the characteristics, not only of the Sumerian but also of the Babylonian period, with this exception, however, that the specific god of the Assyrians is put at the head of the pantheon and worshipped in the royal capital of the Assyrian kings.

The god of the first epoch was *Enlil*, that of the second *Amar-ud or Marduk*, that of the third *An-shar*, which name was read at this time *Ashshur*. As Marduk displaced Enlil, so did Anshar displace Marduk. Such a "*displacing*," however, was only one in "*name*,"[1] not in essence, i. e., simply the name of the new victorious god was substituted for that of the old conquered god. Thus it happened that the attributes, genealogy, court, servants, etc., etc., of the conquered god were added to those of the victorious god, to whose glory, power, and honor they were thought to contribute greatly. Thus we get the strange phenomenon, that one and the same god may have *two* genealogies, two different kinds of servants, etc. In a historic investigation, such a phenomenon will always have to be kept in mind, and the question will have to be asked and answered: What genealogy belongs to the god *originally*, and what was *transferred* to him? That such questions can be answered only by taking into consideration the *historic development* of the Babylonian religion, is, of course, self-evident. As times went on, the attempt was made to harmonise or better identify such two originally very different genealogies. The result of such harmonising or identification was that, e. g., the father of the conquered god was made to be the same as the father of the victorious, at that

[1] See also my remarks with regard to the change of the name of El-shaddai into that of Jahveh, *Creation-Story*, p. 58.

time reigning, god, and so on. The outcome of such an attempt was finally not merely henotheism but an almost pure monotheism.

Not only, however, were the attributes of the Sumerian Enlil transferred to Marduk resp. Anshar or Ashshur, but even the very name "Enlil" became a title of these latter gods—a title, which, is generally transcribed and read bêl, i. e., "lord," but which still betrays to us the fact that Marduk[1] as well as Anshar played the rôle of Enlil, nay, were in all particulars—even with regard to their respective genealogies—identified with him. In a hymn, written at the time of Ashshur-bân-apal, King of Assyria, Ashshur is addressed as follows:[2]

1. "The great one, the hero of the gods, the omniscient,
2. "The esteemed one, the glorious one, the *En-lil-lal* of the gods, he who determines the fates,
3. "An-shar (=Ashshur), the great lord, the omniscient,
4. "The esteemed one, the glorious one, the *En-lil-lal* of the gods, he who determines the fates
5. "[ ] An-shar, the powerful one, the hero of the gods, the *lord of the lands*."

In the very same hymn we further learn, that Ashshur has his abode in *É-char-sag-gal-kur-kur-ra*,[3] i. e., in the "house of the great mounain of the lands, or in the *É-shar-ra*, i. e., "the house of the totality."[4] He is "the creator of AN-NA, the builder of the forests,"[5] "the creator of the gods, the one who begot Ishtar."[6] His lordship is glorified by Anu, Enlil, Ea, Bêlit-ilî, the Igigi, and the Anunnaki in the Ubshugina, i. e., the place or room of the assem-

---

[1] C. S. p. 69.

[2] 1. *shur-bu-ù e-til ilâni*[mesh] *mu-du-ù ka-la-ma*
2. *kab-tu shù-tu-qu* [ilu] *EN-LIL-LAL ilâni*[mesh] *mu-shim shi-ma-a-ti*
3. *An-shar bêlu shur-bu-ù mu-du-ù ka-la-ma*
4. *kab-tu shù-tu-qu* [ilu] *EN-LIL-LAL ilâni*[mesh] *mu-shim shi-ma-a-ti*
5. [ ]*-bi An-shar dan-dan-nu e-til ilâni*[mesh] *be-el ma-ta-a-ti*.
Craig, *Rel. Texts.*, I. p. 32, 1–5.

[3] [*ilu a*]*-shib É-char-sag-gal-kur-kur-ra*, Craig, *loc. cit.*, l. 8.

[4] [*ilu a*]*-shib É-shar-ra An-shar mu-shim shîmâti*[mesh]. Craig, *loc. cit.*, l. 10.

[5] [*ilu*] *ba-nu-ú shu-ut AN-*[*N*]*A* (!) *pa-ti-qu chur-sha-a-ni*. Craig, *loc. cit.*, l. 15. For AN-NA see below!

[6] [*ilu*] *ba-nu-ú ilâni* [*me*]*sh mu-al-lid* [ilu] *Ish-tar*. Craig, *loc. cit.*, l. 16.

bling hand."[1] Similar are Anshar's titles in a prayer of Sinacherib (?), where we read:[2]

1. "To Ashshur, the king of the totality of the gods, to him who begot himself,[3] the father of the gods.
2. Who prosper by his hand in the abyss,[4] the *king of heaven and earth*,
3. The lord of all the gods, to him who begot[5] the Igigi and the Anunnaki,
4. Who built the heaven of Anu and the "great place," who made all men,[6]
5. Who inhabiteth the bright heavens, the *Enlil of the gods*, who determines the fates,
6. Who dwelleth in É-shar-ra, which is in Ashshur, the great lord, his lord."

Not satisfied with this, the Assyrians went still a step farther. If Anshar be equal to Enlil, be indeed identical with him, then, it was quite natural for them that they should consider Ninlil, the wife of Enlil, to be also Anshar's wife. Sinacherib, when praying to Anshar, includes in his supplication also an address to the wife of Anshar, whom he calls:

"Nin-lil, queen of É-shar-ra, wife of Anshar, who created the great gods."[7]

These passages will suffice to prove that Anshar or Ashshur is in all respects the same as Enlil, whose name he even received.

---

[1] [*ilu A*]-*nu* *ilu EN-LIL* *ilu É-a* *ilu Be-lit-ili mesh u* *ilu* [*Igigi u* *ilu Anunnaki*] *shá An-shar ina Ub-shú-ka(!)-na-ki it-ta-a'-i-du bêlu* (=*en*)-*us-su*. Craig, *loc. cit.*, p. 34, 6, 7.

[2] 1. *a-na An-shar shar kish-shat ilâni mesh ba-nu-u ram-ni-shu ab(=ad) ilâni mesh*.

2. *shá ina apsî ish-mu-chu qat-tu-ush shar shamê e u irtsitim ti* [*m*]
3. *bêl ilâni mesh ka-la-ma sha-pi-ik* *ilu Igigi* (= *V* + *II.*) *u* *ilu A-nun-na-*[*ki*].
4. *pa-ti-iq sa-mi* *ilu A-nim u ki-gal-li e-pish kul-lat da-ad-me*
5. *a-shib bu-ru-mu ellûti mesh* *ilu EN-LIL ilâni mesh mu-shim shîmâti mesh*.
6. *a-shib É-shar-ra sha ki-rib Ashshur* (=*BAL-BAT*) *ki bêli rabî e bêli-shu*.

—Craig, *loc. cit.*, I., p. 83, 1–6.

[3] Ashur is here without father and mother, the self-existing god.

[4] I. e., the Anunnaki.

[5] Lit. = "poured out" = *rûchû*. The Igigi and the Anunnaki are repeatedly called the *richût* *ilu Anim*, i. e., "the outpouring" = seed of Anu. For this signification of *rachû* see Jensen, K. B. VI[1]. pp. 365 ff. 513.

[6] Or human habitations.

[7] *ilu NIN-LIL shar-rat É-shar-ra chi-rat An-shar ba-nit ilâni mesh rabûti mesh*, Craig, *Rel. Texts*, I., p. 77, 10.

Both are "the father and god of the gods,"[1] the "king of the gods," "the king of heaven and earth," the "creator of all mankind";[2] both have the same wife: Nin-lil.[3] We may make therefore the equation:

Anshar = Enlil = Ashshur
Ninlil = Bêlit = Ishtar.

Anshar has his abode in É-char-sag-gal-kur-kur-ra or in É-shar-ra; Ninlil, his wife, dwells in É-shar-ra; Enlil of the Sumerians dwells in É-kur. If Anshar and his wife be the same as Enlil and his wife, it would follow that their respective habitations—their temples, which here, as in all other cases, stand for a certain definite cosmic quantity—are also the same, i. e., that the cosmic É-char-sag-gal-kur-kur-ra or É-shar-ra be = the cosmic É-kur. If É-kur, "the mountain-house," be the realm of Enlil, and if Enlil be the king of "heaven and earth," then É-kur = É-shar-ra = É-char-sag-gal-kur-kur-ra must be = "heaven and earth" too![4]

When making the equation Anshar (Ashshur) = Enlil, we would seem to be in straight contradiction not only to Damascius, but also to the Babylonian Creation Epic.

Damascius[5] informs us that Tauthe (= Tiâmat), the mother of the gods, and Apason (= Apsû) begot 1. Moümis (= Mummu); 2. Lache (= Lachamu) and Lachos (= Lachmu); and 3. Kissare (= Kishar) and Assoros (= *Anshar*). By the latter two were born Anos (= Anu), Illinos (= Enlil), and Aos (= Ea). Damascius's authority for this statement is generally supposed to be the first tablet of the Babylonian Creation Epic, from which we learn, that Tiâmat and Apsû, "when their waters in one joined themselves totogether," brought forth Lach-mu and La-cha-mu, and later on

---

[1] Thus the *ab-ba dingir dingir-ru-ne* in E. B. H. p. 97, and C. S. p. 19, 9, ought to be translated.

[2] For these attributes in connection with Enlil see my *Creation Story*, p. 19 f.

[3] Just as Enlil became a title, viz., *bêl* = lord, so Ninlil became at this time = *bêlit* = mistress —an attribute borne chiefly by Ishtar, who therefore appears in most cases as the wife of Ashshur.

[4] This against Jensen, *Kosm.*, p. 194; K. B. VI[1]. pp. 50, 41; 369, who thinks that E-kur, etc., be = earth!

[5] Zimmern, K. A. T.[3] p. 490; Carus, *Monist*, XI., p. 405.

also (?) An-shar and Ki-shar. A long time after these latter two there were born also Anu, Enlil, and Nugimmut (= Ea). If we compare these two accounts we find, that Moûmis (= Mummu[1]) is not mentioned at all in the beginning of the Babylonian Creation Epic. Later on he is introduced quite abruptly and seems to have been a "son of Apsû."[2] In the newly-discovered fragments of this very same Epic[3] Mummu appears as a messenger (!)[4] of Apsû, which latter, together with his wife, Tiâmat, and Mummu enters into a conspiracy against the newly-created gods, who had by their "action" disturbed him. Ea hears of this conspiracy and puts—it would seem—an end to Apsû and Mummu.[5]

But how could Damascius possibly put Mummu before Lachmu and Lachamu, seeing that the first tablet of the Creation Epic cannot have been in this respect his authority?

In order to explain this we shall have to consider somewhat more fully Damascius's statement as well as that of the first tablet of the Babylonian Creation Epic.

We begin with:

A. MUMMU.

The Babylonian Mummu was correctly recognised to be the prototype of the Greek Μωυμις (Moûmis)—an attribute not only of Tiâmat,[6] but also of god Ea.[7] The god Ea is the Sumerian En-KI,

---

[1] Mummu appears there only as an attribute of Tiâmat, K. B. VI[1]. p. 2, 4.

[2] K. B. VI[1]. p. 4. 17. According to Damascius, however, he is undoubtedly a son of Apsû and Tiâmat: *ἐξ ὧν μονογενῆ* (!) *παῖδα γεννηθῆναι τὸν Μωϋμίν.* K. A. T.[3] p. 490. Notice the *μονογενῆ* (!) = only begotten!

[3] King, *The Seven Tablets of Creation*, Vols. I. and II.

[4] I. e., the son! Cf. Nin-Girsu and Enlil, Nusku or Nergal and Sin, etc.

[5] According to these new facts, brought out by Mr. King's book, we would have to distinguish two "*fights*" in the Creation Epic: (1) That of Ea against Apsû and Mummu. (2) That of Marduk against Tiâmat. The result of both these "fights" is the same: Apsû and Mummu as well as Tiâmat are done away with, are conquered and killed. And because Apsû and Mummu were killed by Ea before Marduk entered the field of battle, we may see in this the reason why Qingu, who takes the place of Apsû, plays such a significant rôle in the Epic, and why Mummu is not mentioned at all in the first tablet.

[6] K. B. VI[1]. p. 2, 4; Carus, *loc. cit.*, p. 409: *mu-um-mu ti-amat mu-al-li-da-at gi-im-ri-shu-un.*

[7] Merodach-Baladan-stone (*Beiträge zur Assyriologie*, II. p. 261), col. III. 5:

i. e., "Mr."[1] KI, and as such the "god of the terrestrial ocean." On another place[2] I have shown that "Mr." KI was a brother of AN, "the heavenly ocean." Mr. KI's mother is said to have been ^{dingir}*GUR* = the primeval ocean or Tiâmat; hence, if ^{dingir}*GUR* be the mother of Mr. KI, she also must have been the mother of Mr. AN. At the time when I wrote my *Creation-Story*, I was not aware of the fact that there was to be found in the cuneiform literature an excellent corroboration of this statement. While studying Jensen's *Kosmologie* I found that he already had mentioned two passages[3] in which ^{dingir}*Gur* is called the ^{dingir}*âm-ù-tu-AN-KI*, which name can be translated, however, only by "the mother that brings forth AN and KI," and not, as Jensen does, "the mother that brings forth heaven and earth," for if ^{dingir}*GUR* be the mother of Mr. KI, and if Mr. KI be "the terrestrial ocean," it follows, that KI in the name ^{dingir}*âm-ù-tu-AN-KI* cannot mean "earth." And if KI means "the terrestrial ocean," then AN must mean "the heavenly ocean," who is a brother (achu) and as such opposed to (an achû) the terrestrial one. This name also proves that according to the Sumerian conception, upon which Genesis i. is based, the world was not *created* but *generated*, that we have to see indeed in Genesis i. a תולדות (Toledoth), a "*generation*" of heaven and earth, a *cosmogony*, which *cosmogony* in Sumerian is at the same time a *theogony*!

Mr. KI or Ea, the god of the terrestrial ocean, was considered to be the father not only of the "produce of the sea," but also of the "produce of the earth,"[4]—he, therefore, is called the *mummu* or *ocean*,[5] that builds, creates, produces (*ba-an*) everything (*ka-la*).[6]

(^{ilu}*E-a....*) *mu-um-mu ba-an ka-la.* Marduk, the son of Ea, is called (Craig, *Rel. Texts*, I. p. 31, 23) = *mâr mu-um-me*, i. e., the son of *mumme*.

[1] "Mr." = *en* is used here in opposition to "Mrs." = *nin*, i. e., *en* is the husband and *nin* is the wife. The translation "lord" for *en* and "mistress" for *nin* does not give in this particular case the correct and *intended* meaning. In other words: en = lord is the *sensus litteræ*, while en = Mr. is the *sensus litteralis*.

[2] *Creation-Story*, p. 33 ff.; *Monist*, XII. p. 600.

[3] II. R. 54, No. 3, 18; III. R. No. 1, 25–26.

[4] *Creation-Story*, p. 37; *Monist*, XII. p. 604.

[5] Sic! Against, Jensen, K. B. VI[1]. p. 303: "Form." See also Delitzsch, *Handwörterbuch*, p. 415*b*. Marduk, the *mâr mu-um-me* is therefore the same as Marduk *mâr apsî*.

[6] See above, p. 75, note 7.

Damascius, when explaining the name Moûmis, calls him a *νοητὸς κόσμος*, which is generally translated by "intelligible world."[1] The word for "cosmos" in Sumerian is AN-KI. Hence Moûmis = Mummu = ocean must have consisted of an AN and a KI., i. e., of something that is "above" and "below." Moûmis, then, was the ocean that was "above and below"—but this he was not as yet in *fact*, in *reality*, but only *in mind* (*νοητὸς* !). Hence Mummu = Moûmis must have been the "heavenly and the terrestrial ocean" before the *actual* separation or better *differentiation* took place, i. e., before he was considered by the Babylonians as consisting of two brothers (*achu*), who at the same time were opposed to each other (*achû*).[2] Furthermore, Damascius calls Moûmis the "*μονογενῆ*(!) *παῖδα*," the *only begotten* son of Apason and Tauthe! If, therefore, Moûmis be a *νοητὸς κόσμος*, an ocean consisting "in mind" of an AN and a KI, of an "upper and lower" part, and if *dingir GUR* be "the mother that brought forth the upper (*an*) and the lower (*ki*) ocean," and if the upper part became god AN and the lower part god KI, then Moûmis must be the common name for god AN and god KI before they had been differentiated. This god An and this god KI were—before their differentiation—"the *only begotten*" of Apsû and Tiâmat, hence if Damascius says,[3] that out of Tauthe and Apason be born also "another" generation, viz., Lache and Lachos, he *contradicts himself!* This contradictory statement of Damascius, has led, it is strange to notice, nearly all translators, even Professor Jensen, to translate lines 9–10 of the first tablet of the Epic as follows: (When Apsû and Tiâmat their waters in one had joined together) 9 "da wurden die Götter gebildet [— — —], 10, da entstanden [*zuerst*] Lachmu und Lachamu."[4] Having recognised the contradiction in Damascius's statement, we have to separate line 10 from line 9 by a "period" and begin a new sentence! Translate: "When....then the gods were created. Lachmu and Lach-

---

[1] Zimmern, K. A. T[3]. p. 490; Carus, *Monist*, XI. p. 406 f.

[2] See *Creation-Story*, pp. 34, 64; *Monist*, XII. p. 601.

[3] K. A. T[3]. p. 490: *ἐκ δὲ τῶν αὐτῶν* (i. e., Tauthe and Apason) *ἄλλην γενεὰν προελθεῖν, Λαχην καὶ Λαχον.*

[4] Jensen, K. B. VI[1]. pp. 2, 9, 10.

amu came into existence, etc." By this translation we are left in doubt with regard to the parents of Lachmu and Lachamu, who otherwise are mentioned quite frequently in the Babylonian Creation Epic. What else we learn about Lachmu and Lachamu may be classified under the following heads:

B. LACHMU AND LACHAMU.

1. They are the *parents of An-shar*, who therefore is the son of Lachmu and Lachamu.[1]

2. They are the *parents of Marduk*. Marduk becomes thus, together with Anshar, a son of Lachmu and Lachamu.[2]

3. *Tiâmat* appears as the *enemy* of Lachmu and Lachamu.[3]

4. Lachmu and Lachamu are *creators*, and those whom they had created are to be found at the side of Tiâmat.[4]

5. *ilu*La-cha-mi is one of the eleven helpers of and created by Tiâmat.[5]

Summing up these facts we would have to distinguish—it seems—between at least the following Lachmus and Lachamus:

a. the parents of Anshar and Marduk, Nos. 1, 2.

b. the enemies of Tiâmat and creators, Nos. 3, 4.

c. and Lachami as one of the eleven helpers of Tiâmat.

This confusion is increased, if we take into consideration two lists of gods,[6] where *iluLach-ma* and *iluLa-cha-ma* form one pair

---

[1] K. B. VI[1]. p. 12, l. 11 ff.: 11. "Go, Gaga, present thyself to them," 12. "The command which I gave thee, make known unto them": 13. "An-shar, your (i. e., L. and L.'s) son hath sent me." Conf. *loc. cit.*, p. 16, 67; Carus, *Monist*, *loc. cit.*, p. 414, where it is recorded that Gaga did go to L. and L., and, when he appeared before them, said unto them: "An-shar *ma-ru-ku-nu u-ma-'i-ir-an-ni*," i. e., "Anshar, your son hath sent me." See, however, below sub C. 1.

[2] K. B. VI[1]. p. 14, 55: Carus, *loc. cit.*, p. 414. Anshar dispatches his messenger Gaga to inform L. and L. that Anu and Nugimmut had been sent out already by him (i. e., Anshar) against Tiâmat—but with no result. "Whereupon I (i. e., Anshar) commanded Marduk, the wise one among the gods, *your son* (to go against Tiâmat)."

[3] K. B. VI[1]. pp. 16, 65; 20, 124, 125; cf. p. 12, 4. and see below, C. 3.

[4] K. B. VI[1]. p. 4, 4 below; cf. pp. 12, 17–18; 17, 76.

[5] K. B. VI[1]. pp. 6, 17 (=Carus, *loc. cit.*, p. 411); 18, 89.

[6] II. R. 54, No. 3, 9, and III. R. 69, No. 1, obv. *l. l.* 14, 15.

among the "twenty-one who have An-na for their parent"[1] and where they are identified with ^{ilu}*A-nu-um* and *An-tum*. In a third list[2] appears ^{ilu}*Lach-ma* even as the "^{ilu}*A-nu* of the totality of heaven and earth."[3]

The same confusion is met with

C. ANSHAR AND KISHAR.

1. The first tablet of the Babylonian Creation Epic mentions Anshar and Kishar after Lachmu and Lachamu, as children of whom? of Tiâmat and Apsû? or of Lachmu and Lachamu?[4] Later on, however, appears Anshar as the *son of Lachmu and Lachamu.*[5]

2. Anshar is the *father of* ^{ilu}*A-ni(u)m.*[6]

3. Anshar[7] sends out Anu and Nugimmut against Tiâmat after he had been informed of her rebellion by Ea.[8] Anshar appears here evidently as the *chief opponent, chief enemy of Tiâmat.*[9]

4. Marduk, after having overcome Tiâmat, put into prison her helpers, taken the tablets of fate from Qingu, had, by doing all this, "completely established Anshar's supremacy over the enemy."[10]

---

[1] See below.

[2] II. R. 54. No. 4. 7.

[3] *sha kish-shat AN-KI*, see below! For still other occurrences of ^{ilu}*Lachmu* see, besides the places quoted by Jensen, *Kosm.*, p. 275, also Craig, R. T. I. p. 8, Rev. 1: ^{ilu}*Lach*(= Tsab!)*-mu*, Craig, *loc. cit.*, p. 30, 37: ^{ilu}*Lach-me*; Zimmern, Shurpu, VIII. 19: ^{ilu}*La-ach-mu*.

[4] See K. B. VI^1. p. 2, 12; Carus, *loc. cit.*, p. 410. According to this passage, then, we are left in doubt as to the parents of Anshar and Kishar! According to Damascius, however, (see K. A. T^3. p. 490: *εἶτα αὖ τρίτην ἐκ τῶν αὐτῶν* i.e., Tauthe and Apason, *Κισσαρη καὶ Ἀσσωρον*), were Anshar and Kishar, the sons of Tiâmat and Apsû. If this be true, then Damascius would contradict himself here again, for he expressly told us that Mummu = Moûmis was the "only begotten" son of Tauthe and Apason!

[5] K. B. VI^1. pp. 12, 13; (= Carus, *loc. cit.*, p. 413); 16, 68 (= Carus, *loc. cit.*, p. 414). See already above, sub B. 1. Also these passages show quite clearly that Damascius's statement cannot be true.

[6] K. B. VI^1. p. 10, 1, 8, 10, 12.

[7] K. B. VI^1. p. 14, 53, 54.

[8] King, Tablet II.

[9] Cf. above, B. 3, where Lachmu and Lachamu are opposed to Tiâmat.

[10] K. B. VI^1. p. 28, 125; Carus, *loc. cit.*, 418.

Marduk apparently is here the *champion of Anshar*, the enemy of Tiâmat.[1]

5. Anshar and Kishar are likewise to be found among the "twenty-one who have An-na for their parent," and as such again either $=$ ^{ilu}*A-nu-um* and *An-tum*, or $=$ ^{ilu}*An-num* "of the totality of heaven and earth."[2]

6. An-shar is the builder of *É-shar-ra*;[3] according to the fourth tablet of the Babylonian Creation Epic it is Marduk who builds it.[4]

7. An-shar is, as we have seen above, the common ideographic writing of the chief-god of the Assyrians: Ashshur.

This confusion throws a striking light upon the literary character of the Babylonian Creation Epic. Taking the above-given peculiarities into account, we would have to distinguish at least the following different sources—each source being represented by its own specific god, who at one time or another was the opponent of Tiâmat:

1. Lachmu (and Lachamu): B. 3.
2. Anshar: C. 3, 4.
3. Marduk: the whole of the Creation Epic as we have it now.
4. Ashshur, whose name is only the Assyrian equivalent of the Sumerian Anshar.

From this it would also follow, that these four gods were the same—at least in "essence," if not in name:

I. Anshar is = Lachmu[5] (and Lachamu), because both appear

[1] See No. 3 and cf. B., No. 3.

[2] II. R. 54, No. 3, 6; III. R. 69, No. 1, obv. 8, 9; II. R. 54, No. 4, 4.

[3] K. 3445 + Rm. 396, published in *Cuneiform Texts*, XIII. 24 f. See also Delitzsch, *Weltschöpfungsepos*, No. 20, p. 51 ff.

[4] "After the lord (i. e., Marduk) had measured the form (?) of the ocean
He erected "a great house" (*esh-gal-la*) like unto it; (i. e., like unto the ocean), viz., É-shar-ra,
'The great house,' viz., *É-shar-ra*, which he had built as a (or: to be a) *sha-ma-mu*
He caused ^{ilu}*A-num*, ^{ilu}*En-lil*, and ^{ilu}*Éa* to inhabit as their city."
K. B. VI^1. p. 30, 144–146 (Carus, *loc. cit.*, p. 419).

[5] Just as Nin-Girsu, the son of Enlil, was identified with his father, cf. among other arguments also the name: É-ninnû-*dingir* Im-gig-ghu-bar-bar (ninnu = Enlil!), and as the "angel of the Lord" with the "Lord," so was Anshar, the son of L. and L. (B. i.), with Lachmu.

a. as the enemy of Tiâmat: C. 3, 4; B. 3;

b. among the "twenty-one who have Anna for their parent";

c. are identified (α) either with *ilu A-nu-um* (and *An-tum*), (β) or with *ilu A-num* "of the totality of heaven and earth."

II. Anshar = Marduk:

a. both are the sons of Lachmu (and Lachamu): B. 1; B. 2.; C. 1.

b. both are the builders of *É-shar-ra*: C. 6.

c. both are the enemies of Tiâmat; Anshar: C. 3. 4; Marduk: the whole Creation Epic in its present literary form.

III. Anshar = Ashshur: C. 7.

The rôle of Ashshur as creator was derived from Anshar, or better: "Ashshur the creator" can also be read "Anshar the creator." Marduk the creator derived his power from Enlil, whom he displaced and whose name and attributes he received. Above we have seen, that even Anshar = Ashshur was completely identified with, and even called, Enlil. If therefore Anshar be = Enlil, and if Anshar be also = Lachmu, then Lachmu must be = Enlil too!

Enlil is the "king" of "heaven and earth," Anshar as well as Lachmu are = *ilu A-num* "of (the totality of) heaven and earth"—hence if our identification, Enlil = Anshar = Lachmu, be correct, then Enlil the "king of heaven and earth" *must* be = *ilu Anum* "of (the totality of) heaven and earth," i. e., Enlil = Anum!

This result sheds a new and unexpected light upon the hitherto completely misunderstood[1] three lists of gods, mentioned above.

For the sake of completeness and on account of their importance I may be permitted to give them here in transcription.

List I.: II. R. 54, No. 3.

This list arranges the "twenty-one who have Anna for their parent," in *pairs*. These pairs are husband and wife. The first three lines, which are separated from the rest, must contain only one out of the twenty-one names. This *one* name is explained according to its different meanings, which it may have when brought into relation to the following ten pairs. It reads:

[1] Jensen, *Kosm.*, pp. 192 f., 272 f.; Zimmern, K. A. T[3], p. 506.

I. 1.[1]	*AN*	[ilu]*A*(!)[2]-*nu*(!)[2]-[*um*]
2. *AN*, i. e.,[3] *An-tum*[4] =[5]		*irtsitim*[6] [*tim*]
3. *AN-KI*[7]		[ilu]*A-nu* ù [*An-tum*]
II. 4. [dingir]	*IB*[8]	[dingir]*Nin*-[*IB*[8]]
III. 5. *An-shar-gal*[9]		[dingir]*Ki-shar*-[*gal*][10]
IV. 6. *An-shar*[11]		[dingir]*Ki*-[*shar*][12]

[1] The Roman numbers indicate the "*pairs*." The Arabic numbers give the lines of the inscription.

[2] Copy gives for A-nu = ZI, but wrongly.

[3] Sign GUR: S[c] 239 = Brünnow, *List*, No. 7315.

[4] The sign for god is wanting in order to avoid a possible misreading: *ilâni* (= gods of) *Tum*. See also note to Anshargal!

[5] The common "sign of separation," Brünnow, *List*, No. 7757.

[6] Written KI[ ]. Notice here that AN = KI!

[7] If *KI* = *irtsitu* = *Antum* = *AN*, and if [ilu]*A-nu-um* be also = *AN*, then we have to see in this *AN* = the first *pair!*

[8] According to II. R. 54. No. 4 (see below!) *IB* has the gloss: *ú-ra-ash*, and according to II. R. 57. obv. C. l. 31, that of *ú-ra-âsh*, as such he is identical with [ilu]*NIN-IB sha ud-da-zal-li*. This latter passage shows that we should read in each and every instance the god [dingir]*IB* resp. [dingir]*NIN-IB* = [dingir]*Urash* resp. [dingir]*Nin-urash*. Zimmern, *Babylonische Busspsalmen*, p. 50, thinks that *urash* be a Semitism, it being derived from *erêshu* = "entscheiden." Not from *erêshu* = "entscheiden," however, but from *erêshu* = "to irrigate" (!). Delitzsch, H. W. B. p. 140*b*, has *urash* "to be derived." This holds true not only of the [ilu]*Ir-resh* = *êrish* in IV. R. 34. 51*b*, and the [ilu]*Ir-ri-esh* UR-SAG in Reisner, *Hymnen*, pp. 86, 8; 134. 25, 26, but also of the "*Eresh*" in the name of the goddess *Eresh-ki-gal*, against Jensen, K. B. VI[1]. p. 388, who takes *eresh* here in the sense of "gewaltig." Hence [dingir]*Nin-IB*(= *urash*) is also called [dingir]*Engar*(= *erêshu*) = "the irrigator," as such he is the god of the "farmers" = *ikkaru* = *engar!* Cf. also *Ur*-[dingir]*Nin-Girsu* = *ikkaru* = farmer (Č. S. p. 66, note). This also proves that [dingir]*Nin-Girsu* is = [dingir]*Engar* = [dingir]*Nin-IB* (= *urash*) which latter, originally masculine, was identified not only with [dingir]*IB* but even with [dingir]*Nin-IB*, the *wife* of [dingir]*IB!*

[9] *Shar* = *CHI* = *kishshatu* = totality. The sign for "god" = *an* is wanting before this name, because, if it had been written, one might read "*dingir-dingir shar-gal*" and translate "the gods of the great totality." In order to avoid such a possible reading and translation, the sign for "god" was omitted. Cf. also Antum and An-shar. The name signifies: "the great upper totality."

[10] "The great lower totality"—as such opposed to the upper one!

[11] For this writing instead of [dingir]*An-shar*, see sub An-shar-gal. The name means = "the upper totality."

[12] The lower totality."

V.	7. *dingir En-shar*[1]	*dingir Nin-[shar]*.[2]
VI.	8. *dingir Du-uru*	*dingir Da-[uru]*[3]
VII.	9. *dingir Lach-ma*[4]	*dingir La-cha-m[a]*[5]
VIII.	10. *dingir É-kur*[6]	*dingir Gá-r[a]*[7]
IX.	11. *dingir A-la-la*	*dingir Be-li-l[i]*[8]
X.	12. *dingir* ditto(= *A-la-la*)-*alan*	*dingir* ditto(= *Be-li-li*)-*alan*
XI.	13. *dingir En-uru-ul-la*	*dingir Nin-uru-ul-la*[9]
	14. *zi en ám-*	*a-a An-na-ge*(!)[10]

[1] Either Mr. Shar (= totality) or "lord of the totality."

[2] Mrs. Shar, or mistress of the totality. These two names as well as those in l. 13 show, that these *pairs* are husband and wife!

[3] Both these names have to be translated by "Eternal (one)" = Hebr. דור, and are as such Semitic names. Cf. also l. 13.

[4] Sign *lach* = *LUCH*, so generally. For other writings, see besides note 3 above p. 79, also *dingir Lach-mu*, K. B. VI[1]. pp. 2, 10 [12, 4]; 16, 68; *dingir Lach-cha*, K. B. VI[1]. p. 20, 125, and Λαχος.

[5] Also written *dingir La-cha-mu*, K. B. VI[1]. pp. 2, 10; [12, 4]; 20, 125. *dingir La-cha-me*, *loc. cit.*, p. 16, 68, (In *loc. cit.*, p. 18, 89 appears this name among the eleven helpers of Tiâmat); Λαχη. What these names mean, is not yet apparent, but cf. at the present the note of Houtsma, *Zeitschrift für alttestamentliche Wissenschaft*, 1902, p. 329 ff., on לָחֶם, לְחוּם, and מִלְחָמָה.

[6] "The god of E-kur." *É-kur* is the temple of *dingir En-lil* in Nippur. Hence *dingir É-kur* = *dingir En-lil!*

[7] *dingir Gá-ra* for *Gar-ra* = *Gál-la* = Assyrian *Muallidtu* = "the one who brings forth." For *gá* = *gal* see Jensen, Z. A. I. 192; Strassmaier, *Syll.* 154. This pair is left out in the list III. R. 69, No. 1, obv., where instead of it the pair *AN* + *KI* is added.

[8] For this reading see Jensen, *Kosm.*, 272, 2. She appears as the sister of Tammuz, who is "her only brother" (*a-chi e-du*) as well as "the paramour (Buhle) of her youth" (*cha-mer tsi-ich-ru-[ti-sha]*): K. B. VI[1]. p. 90, 51, 55, 47. Jensen, *loc. cit.*, p. 404, thinks it not impossible that *Belili* be = *Bulala*, the queen of *PA-AN*, mentioned in II. R. 60, 27*a* and 26*b*. *PA-AN* he takes to be a name for "the nether world." An identification of *Belili* with the Elamitic divinity *Belala* or *Bilala* he does not venture to maintain.

[9] "Lord resp. Mistress of the eternal city." Cf. l. 8.

[10] III. R. 69, No. 1, obv. 22 has: *zi en ám-a-a An-na-ge-ne*. *Am-a-a* is translated in IV. R. 25 f. by *a-bi um-mi*:

25. *zi dingir En ám-a-a dingir En-lil-lal-ge ghe-pad*
26. *nish be-el a-bi um-mi sha ilu EN-LIL lu-u ta-ma-a-ta.*
27. *zi dingir Nin ám-a-a dingir Nin-lil-lal-ge ghe-pad*
28. *nish be-el-ti a-bi um-mi sha ilu* ditto(= *NIN-LIL*) *lu-u ta-ma-a-ta*,

i. e., "by Bel resp. Belit the *ám-a-a* of Enlil resp. Ninlil mayest thou swear." This shows that *ám-a-a* may be applied to a male or a female god. *Am-a-a* lit. translated is = "*mother-father*," the Assyrian translates it by "*father-mother*"

Similar to the preceding is

LIST II.: III. R. 69, No. 1, OBV.,

where the names of the single pairs are arranged—with the exception of the second—not side by side, but one below the other. This list reads:

I. 1.	*AN*	^{ilu}*A-nu-um*
2.	*AN*	*An-tum*
3. *AN-KI*[1]		^{ilu}*A-nu-um u* (i. e., and) *An-tum*
III. 4. ^{dingir}*IB*(=*urash*)		ditto (i. e., ^{ilu}*A-nu-um u An-tum*)[2]
5. ^{dingir}*Nin-IB* (=*urash*)		ditto
IV. 6. *An-shar-gal*		ditto
7. ^{dingir}*Ki-shar-gal*		ditto
V. 8. *An-shar*		ditto
9. ^{dingir}*Ki-shar*		ditto
IV. 10. ^{dingir}*En-shar*		ditto
11. ^{dingir}*Nin-shar*		ditto
VII. 12. ^{dingir}*Du-uru*		ditto
13. ^{dingir}*Da-uru*		ditto
VIII. 14. ^{dingir}*Lach-ma*		ditto
15. ^{dingir}*La-cha-ma*		ditto
IX. 16. ^{dingir}*A-la-la*		ditto
17. ^{dingir}*Be-li-li*		ditto

(conf. also II. R. 62, 21*c*: *AM-TU* [which has the gloss *a-ga-ri-in* in V. R. 29, 67*g*] =*a-bu um-mu*). It is a shorter form for *âm tu-ud-da* and *a-a tu-ud-da*: IV. R. 10, Rev. 51, and corresponds to our word "*parent*." The line in question may therefore be translated: "twenty-one of (*ge*) the lord (*en*), the parent (*âm-a-a*) *An-na* they are (*ne*)," i. e., twenty-one who are of the lord, the parent Anna or who have Anna for their parent. If this translation be accepted, then AN-NA-ge would be a genetivus *objectivus*. It *may* be, however, also a genetivus *subjectivus*. In this latter case the twenty-one would be=the "parent AN-NA"—thus leaving us in doubt with regard to the "parentship" of these twenty-one gods. If the AN-NA-ge be construed as a gent. subj., the translation would be: twenty-one (sc. names) of (=for) the lord, the parent AN-NA (they are). But whatever translation we accept—the result remains the same!

[1] This pair is not found in the above-given list, for there *an-ki* is used as a kind of introductory explanation not only to all the following pairs, but also to the pair *AN!* *An-ki* here takes the place of ^{dingir}*É-kur* and ^{dingir}*Gá-ra* of the preceding list.

[2] We would expect that ^{dingir}*IB* would be=^{ilu}*An-nu-um only*, but not so here. Cf. for the present here ^{dingir}*En-lil*=king of heaven and earth, and ^{dingir}*Nin-lil* also=queen of heaven and earth, and see below!

X. 18. *dingir*ditto (= *A-la-la*)[1]*-alan*	ditto
19. *dingir*ditto (= *Be-li-li*)*-alan*	ditto
XI. 20. *dingir En-uru-ul-la*	ditto
21. *dingir Nin-uru-ul-la*	ditto
22. *21* (!) *en âm-a-a*	*An-na-ge-ne*

List III.: II. R. 54, No. 4,

gives us the names of the "husbands" only. It reads:

1. [ ] *AN*	*uu A-nu-um*
2. [*dingir*] (*u-ra-ash*)[2] *IB*	*uu* ditto (= *A-nu-um*) *sha ish-shim ik-ri-bi*[3]
3. [*A*]*n-shar-gal*	*uu* ditto (= *A-nu-um*) *sha kish-shat AN-KI*[4]
4. [*A*]*n-shar*	*uu A-nu* (*chi-bi*)[5] ditto (= *sha kish-shat AN-KI*)
5. [*din*]*gir En-shar*	*uu* ditto
6. *dingir Du-uru*	*uu* ditto
7. *dingir Lach-ma*	*uu* ditto
8. *dingir É-kur*	*uu* ditto
9. *dingir A-la-la*	*uu* [ditto
10. *dingir*ditto (= *A-la-la*)*-alan*	*uu* [ditto
11. *dingir En-uru-ul-la*	*uu* [ditto

Looking over these three lists we will have to admit that the "*husbands*" as well as the "*wives*" are the same "*among themselves*," for they are identified either with *Anum* resp. *Antum* or with *Anum* "*of the totality of heaven and earth*." If we succeed in identifying one husband resp. wife correctly—we *ipso facto* did it with all.

A good starting-point is, no doubt, *dingir É-kur*, i. e., "the god

[1] This writing shows that we have here also an arrangement according to *pairs*—or else the "ditto" in lines 18 and 19 would have to be referred to line 17—an hypothesis which is forbidden by the first list! Cf. List I., lines 11 and 12.

[2] *u-ra-ash* is the gloss to *IB*, giving its pronunciation. See above, note to *dingir IB*.

[3] I. e., "Anu who hears prayers." See also Jensen, *Kosm.*, p. 194 and note 1.

[4] I. e., Anu of the totality of heaven and earth.

[5] *chi-bi* = "is broken, damaged"—shows that the original from which this copy has been made, was unreadable here—the sign "*um*" probably having been broken away.

of É-kur." É-kur is the temple of Enlil—hence "the god of É-kur" can be only Enlil. And if *dingir É-kur* be = *dingir Enlil*, then his wife *dingir Gá-ra* must be *dingir Ninlil*. We are justified in saying:

The "*twenty-one who have Anna for their parent*" are nothing more nor less than *twenty-one different names* (!) *of god LIL* "*the king of heaveu and earth*,"[1] the son of AN or "heavenly ocean"—of god LIL considered either

a. as a whole = *AN*[2] = *LIL* = רקיע (firmament) = "heaven and earth" = *an* + *an* or *an* + *ki* = *Anum* + *Antum*.

b. or as consisting of a male or female, i. e., of *husband* and *wife*: *En*-lil + *Nin*-lil = *En*-shar + *Nin*-shar = *En*-shar-gal + *Nin*-shar-gal = *En*-uru-ul-la + *Nin*-uru-ul-la = *Anum* + *Antum*.[3]

c. or as "brother and sister" (i. e., *achu* + *achatu*): En-*lil* + Nin-*lil* = En-*shar* + Nin-*shar* = En-*shar-gal* + Nin-*shar-gal* = En-*uru-ul-la* + Nin-*uru-ul-la*.[4]

d. or as "opposed to each other" (i. e., as *achû* and *achitu*):[5] *AN* + *KI* = *An*-shar + *Ki*-shar = *An*-shar-gal + *Ki*-shar-gal.

Although we have only *twenty-one* (!) names, yet we are supposed to have, according to the arrangement of the lists, eleven (!) pairs. This difficulty would require a few words of explanation.

AN is the first *name*, but also the first *pair*, for *AN* is not only explained by Anum and Antum,[6] but also by *an* = *Anum* and *an* = *Antum* = *KI*, i. e., = *irtsitim* or earth.[7] If *Antum*, the *wife*, be the "*earth*," then *Anum*, the *husband*, must be the *heaven*. Hence the

---

[1] C. S. p. 19, 4; *Monist*, XIII. p. 586.

[2] See below!

[3] From this it follows that *lil* = *shar* = *shar-gal* = *uru-ul-la* = (Anum + Antum *sha kish-shat*) *AN-KI*, i. e., "*the totality of heaven and earth*." Hence the *shar* = *kishshatu* = totality in Enlil's and Anshar's temple É-shar is = the totality of heaven *and* earth—and the cosmic É-shar must be = *heaven and earth*!

[4] Does our modern custom of the wife's taking the "name" of her husband go back to this oldest of historic times, when the wife was the *sister*—thus also of *one flesh*—of her husband? Has anyone made this point the subject of a special investigation?

[5] C. S. p. 34 = *Monist*, XII. p. 601.

[6] See second list!

[7] See first list.

name AN reveals to us the remarkable fact that it is a *pair*, consisting out of *husband* and *wife:*

Anum + Antum, that the husband and wife are also brother and sister:
an + an, and that the husband is opposed to the wife:
an + ki = heaven + earth—the husband being "above" and the wife being "below."

Thus we find here a welcome corroboration of our statement[1] that "*heaven and earth*" were considered to be *one*. This one cosmic quantity was called not only LIL, but also AN. AN when translated into Semitic-Babylonian becomes = *shamê*. *Shamê*, therefore, *must* stand for "*heaven and earth*" too! "Heaven and earth" are the Sumerian as well as Semitic-Babylonian and Hebrew *terminus technicus* for "*cosmos*"—hence *shamê* must be = *cosmos!* Now we understand Hesychius's remarkable statement quoted, but misunderstood, by Jensen in his *Kosm.*, p. 3: Σαvη (read Σαvη) ὁ κόσμος Βαβυλώνιος, i. e., "shamê is the Babylonian cosmos," and Hesychius's gloss to Βῆλος (= Marduk): οὐρανὸς καὶ Ζεῦς καὶ Ποσειδῶνος υἱός, i. e., Bel or Marduk (originally = Enlil!) is not only the οὐρανός (= shamê = AN = an + ki = heaven + earth), but also (our) Zeus, and a son of (our) Poseidon, the terrestrial ocean = EN-KI or Ea (originally AN, the heavenly ocean!).[2] The Sumerian AN, thus, is indeed a word for *cosmos* and stands as such for the first "pair," i. e., either for an + an, or for an + ki = Anum + Antum, the personifications of "heaven and earth."[3]

In Craig, *Religious Texts*,[4] we learn of "a house in Nippur" called *Dur-an-ki*[5]—a name which is translated by "band of heaven

---

[1] C. S. p. 52; *Monist*, XII. p. 619.

[2] All this against Jensen, *Kosm.*, p. 391.

[3] Against Jensen, *Kosm.*, p. 3.

[4] Vol. I. p. 19, l. 9: *esh En-lil-ki Dur-an-ki*.

[5] Hilprecht, *Excavations*, p. 462, mentions this *Dur-an-ki* in such a way, as if *he* only knew anything about the existence of this "house," saying: "A fourth name (viz., of the zigurrat of Nippur), *to state this distinctly here*, occurs in another *unpublished* text....belonging to the results of *our latest* excavations at Nuffar." The passage cited from Craig will show Hilprecht that the name *Dur-an-ki* of the zigurrat of Nippur was known *eight years* before *he* discovered (!) it!

and earth."[1] According to *Zeitschrift für Assyriologie*, Vol. X., p. 294, l. 1, it is the *É-char-sag-kur-kur-ra*, which is called "the band of heaven and earth"—hence *É-char-sag-kur-kur-ra* = *Dur-an-ki*. Above[2] we have seen that *É-char-sag(-gal)-kur-kur-ra* is not only = *É-shar-ra* but also = *É-kur* "the mountain house," hence also this latter must be = "band of heaven and earth." But the god of *É-kur*, the *dingir*É-kur*, is one of the "twenty-one who have Anna for their parent," hence the "god of É-kur" must also be the "god of the band of heaven and earth." The god of Ékur being Enlil, Enlil becomes thus the "god of the band of heaven and earth."

Furthermore, just as the "band of the sill" is = sill,[3] and as the "firmament of heaven" is = heaven,[4] so is the "band of heaven and earth" = "heaven and earth"[5]—hence *DUR* = רקיע, and *dur-an-ki* = firmament of heaven and earth = heaven and earth. The god of Dur-an-ki, Enlil, is therefore again the god of "heaven and earth" or of the "firmament of heaven and earth"!

Above we saw that *AN* is = heaven and earth = cosmos, hence the *dingir*Dur-an*,[6] who is said to be = *ilu*BE* (= Bêl = Enlil!), is not only a corroboration that our conclusions be correct, but this name also shows, that *dingir*Dur-an* is not an abbreviation of *dingir*Dur-an-ki*,[7] but a *correct* and *justified* writing. *dingir*Dur-an* means the "god of the band of the *shamê*" = Σαυη, which is the "*Babylonian cosmos*," i. e., heaven and earth = an + ki!

These considerations put us into a position to explain also the following peculiarities:

a. The god *IM*, whom we identified with *Nin-Girsu* or *Im-gig-ghu bar-bar* is called "*the son of Anna*,"[8] instead of—as in case of Nin-Girsu—the son of Enlil. Anna being here only

---

[1] *Rikis shamê u itsirtim*, from *rakâsu* to bind.

[2] P. 74.

[3] K. 8665, Meissner, *Suppl.*, p. 14, hinten: *rikis sippi* = *sippi*.

[4] רקיע השמים = שמים, Gen. i. 8.

[5] *Dur-an-ki* = *an-ki*.

[6] II. R. 54, 4*a*.

[7] As Hilprecht, *Excavations*, p. 463, 2, thinks.

[8] Reisner, *Hymnen*, p. 120, 10, 15.

another name for Enlil, the "king of heaven and earth," must stand here likewise for "cosmos."[1]

b. Very often we read of the "*hosts of A-nim*"[2] as well as of the "*warriors of A-num, i. e., (sic!) Da-gan.*"[3]

That Anum be here = Enlil is apparent from the following reasons:

a. The *tsa-ab* resp. *qi-its-ri Anim* was rightly recognised[4] to correspond to the Hebrew יהוה צבאות—hence Anim = Jahveh!

β. According to Gen. ii. 1, the "hosts" belong to "the heaven and the earth"[5]—hence the "hosts of Jahveh" are those of "heaven and earth," i. e., Jahveh = cosmos.

γ. "Heaven and earth" or the cosmos are in Hebrew as well as in Babylonian the respective domains of Enlil or Jahveh. The former has therefore the title "king of heaven and earth,"[6] and the latter "god of heaven and earth"[7]—hence Jahveh = cosmos = Enlil.

δ. Anum is one of the "twenty-one who have Anna for their parent" and corresponds not only to the Sumerian *an* + *an* or *an* + *ki*, but also to *AN*, i. e., the Σαυη, and to the AN in *dingir**Dur-AN*, i. e., he is the personified *cosmos*, as such also called *dingir**É-kur* who is the *Enlil*. Hence *Anim* = *Enlil*. But if Anim be here = Enlil, then the *hosts* can be only the *children* resp. *grandchildren* of Enlil, i. e., *ZU* or the moon, *Nin-Girsu* or the thundering dark cloud, *UD* or the sun, *Innanna* or the morning- resp. evening-star, etc. These children are *gods* and *stars*

---

[1] See also the different genealogies of Ninib in my forthcoming article on Jahveh, and also the genealogies of Nusku, the son of Anu = Enlil = lord of heaven and earth = É-kur = Dur-an-ki, who again were identified with Ea = ocean and with Sin.

[2] See e. g. K. B. VI[1]. pp. 122, 4; 134, 31 *et passim*: *qi-its-ri sha ilu A-nim*.

[3] Sargon, *Bronce-Inscript.*, 14: *tsa-ab ilu A-num u* (*Var. ù*) *ilu Da-gan*.

[4] Jensen, K. B. VI[1]. 431.

[5] ויכלו השמים והארץ וכל צבאם.

[6] lugal an-ki.

[7] יהוה אלהי השמים והארץ.

—even Nin-Girsu = Adad was considered to be a star: VR. 46, 44*ab* = *mul nu-mush-da* = *ilu Sha-gi-mu* and K. 263: [ ] *nu-mush-da* = *namashshû* = *ilu Adad*. *Shâgimu* is a name of Adad and signifies: "the one that roars or thunders." See also Jensen, *Kosm.*, p. 140. Hence the בני אלהים mentioned together with Jahveh in Psalm xxix. 1 ff., can be only = the children of Enlil, as such also *gods* and *stars* and the *powers of nature*—for even according to Hebrew conception the stars belong to the רקיע (Gen. i. 14; C. S. p. 53), which רקיע again is = *Dur-an-ki*, the habitation of *dingir Dur-an* or Enlil! The יהוה צבאות corresponds, therefore, exactly to the title of Enlil "king of the gods" (*lugal dingir-ri-ne*) or to the *tsa-ab* resp. *qi-its-ri Anim*.

c. Above, p. 72, we heard that Anshar = Ashshur is said to have been the "creator of An-na"[1]—an expression which signifies the same as that on p. 73, above, where Anshar = Ashshur appears as the "builder of the heaven of Anim."[2] Anu is in our three lists a name for "the god of É-kur," i. e., for Enlil. AN or AN-NA, we saw, means = Σαvη = Assyr shamê—hence "the builder of AN-NA" can mean only the "builder or creator of the *cosmos*," as such it is parallel to the "builder of the *sa-mi* (i. e., Σαvη = cosmos) of *ilu A-nim* = Enlil. The "heaven(s) of Anu" therefore are not the abode of god AN, the heavenly ocean, but are in each and every case the *cosmos*, "heaven and earth" the abode of Enlil, or more especially, the "firmament of heaven" or "heaven" as opposed to the "firmament of the earth" or "earth," the specific domain of Ninlil. "The great gods that inhabit the shamê of Anim" are therefore the moon, sun, the stars, and the powers of nature (=Adad), etc. Hence we cannot find in this phrase the idea—as Jeremias, *Vorstellungen vom Leben nach dem Tode*, p. 60, wants it —that the "Wohnsitz der Götter in verschiedene abgegrenzte Himmel geteilt ist." See also Jensen, *Kosm.*, p. 11.

---

[1] *ba-nu-û shu-ut AN-[N]A*.

[2] *pa-ti-iq sa-mi ilu A-nim*.

d. In the sentence "the daughter of Anu (= Ishtar) went to Bel her father," above p. 67, Anu and Bel signify the *same god.* Ishtar is the daughter of Bel because she is the *wife* (as such called *Bau*) of *Nin-Girsu.* But Nin-Girsu being the son of Enlil or Bel, his wife *had* to become *also* a daughter of Bel—because a wife is always the *sister* of her husband.

e. As already said, the "heaven and earth," originally one, were later on differentiated and considered as husband and wife: Enlil + Ninlil = Enshar + Ninshar, etc.,—the wife being not only the sister but also "opposed" to her brother or husband. Thus it happed that there corresponds to the Enshar, the husband, an An-shar, and to the Ninshar, the wife, a *Ki-shar,* in other words: the husband was considered to be "above" = an, and the wife to be "below" = ki. The "heaven" becomes thus the husband of the "earth." This "heaven and earth" had two sons: the "moon (ZU) and the "thundering, lightning, dark cloud" (Nin-Girsu or Im-gig-ghu-bar-bar), who by means of his nature was the "mighty hero or prime minister" of his father. The "moon" had for his son the sun (UD). Exactly the same genealogy we find again in *Orac. Sib.*, III. 110 ff., where *Kronos, Titan,* and *Japetos* are called the sons of *Ouranos* (= heaven) and *Gaia* (the earth). Now, there cannot be any doubt that Kronos was *originally* the moon, who had become at the time when this genealogy was imported from the Babylonians, the "sun."[1] This change took place at a time when the people began to reckon according to "sun-years." We would like, therefore, to identify *Kronos* with UD the *sun* (originally the moon), *Titan* with *Nin-Girsu, "the mighty hero,"* and *Japetos* with the *moon* (originally the sun).[2]

These identifications explain also correctly the hitherto mis-

---

[1] An analogy of this we find also in the Old Testament, Gen. i. 16, where the sun is likewise put before the moon and called "the greater light." See C. S., p. 65.

[2] This against Zimmern, K. A. T[3]. p. 351, who thinks that they are "genau entsprechend der babylonischen Trias Anu-Bel-Ea als Söhnen des Paares Anshar-Kishar.

understood statement of Berosus,[1] according to which *Kronos* warns Chisouthros (= *Ut-napishtim*), while according to the Babylonian flood-story it is Ea. On account of this peculiarity Jensen[2] identified Kronos with Ea; but wrongly! Ea is = Poseidon. Marduk is in the *theological* system the son of Ea or Poseidon. But Marduk is the AMAR-UD, i. e., the son of UD—according to his *name*—and UD is = Kronos, hence Markuk, the AMAR-UD, may quite correctly be called the "son of Kronos." If Kronos was the father of Marduk, the chief-god of the Babylonians, then Ahuramazda *had to have* likewise Kronos for his father! Hence the gloss to Belos in the Arm. Vers. of Euseb. Chron., *loc. cit.*, p. 19: *κρόνον, quem patrem nuncupant Aramazdi.*[3]

Returning once more to our three lists we will have to distinguish between

a. AN = "heavenly ocean," who is called in two of our lists "the lord, the parent AN-NA," and is as such the *father* of those twenty-one gods—or better of one god under twenty-one different names. In Assyrian this god is called Anum, and is a brother of Ea. Anu and Ea again are sons of the "mother that brought forth AN and KI = "heavenly and terrestrial ocean," i. e., of *dingir GUR*.

b. AN = cosmos. As such it stands either for an = Anum + an = Antum or for an = Anum + ki (i. e., earth) = Antum. *Anum[4] resp. Antum is here only another name for Enlil resp.*

---

[1] *Liber chron.*, edit. Schoene, p. 19–20.

[2] *Kosm.*, p. 391.

[3] This statement is very important. It shows that Ahuramazda was considered to be the same as Marduk—had therefore to have the same father. Ahriman and Ahuramazda is Marduk differentiated into the Marduk of the winter = darkness, and the Marduk of the summer = light. The Marduk of the winter is = Nebo, and the Marduk of the summer = AMAR-UD. Cf. the important passage Isaiah xlv. 7: "I am the lord....I form the light, and create darkness." Here the prophet expressly denies that light and darkness have two different sources. Both have *one* god for their author,—a very correct Babylonian idea.

[4] This name Anum was even applied to the moon-god, Sin! See IV. R. 9, 6*a*, and K. 155, quoted by Jensen, *Kosm.*, p. 191, note 1. This is not strange. We know that in Ur as well as in Harran the god Sin was considered to be the highest god, hence—if he were—he *had* to receive all the attributes, names, etc., of Enlil. Yes, even Nin-Girsu the "mighty hero" of Enlil became Sin's messenger and this under the name of Nusku resp. Nergal, see above, page 69, note 5.

Ninlil, the king resp. queen of "heaven and earth"! This AN is the Σαυη or κόσμος Βαβυλώνιος of Hesychius.[1]

c. AN either = *shamû*, i. e., "heaven" or = KI., i. e., "earth." The former, when personified may also be called *Anum* or *Enlil*, and the latter *Antum* or *Ninlil*. That *KI* = *earth* was called *Antum* follows also from different other passages in the cuneiform literature, as, e. g., Reisner, *Hymnen*, p. 133,

---

[1] Here belongs beside the *dingir Dur-an*, and the expressions: "the creator of *AN-NA*," "the shamê of Anim," mentioned above, also

a. *dingir Si* = *dingir En-lil*: V. R. 44, 35, because *Si* is = *shamû* = Σαυη! See II. R. 50, 25*c*, cf. II. R. 39, 47 f. (Against Jensen, *Kosm*., p. 24.)

b. *dingir BE* = *dingir En-lil*: I. R. 15, 51; V. R. 4, 111 etc., for *BE* is again = *shamû*: II. R. 7, 26*a*; V. R. 39, 45*c*.

c. *dingir NAB*. The sign NAB is expressed by two *an*'s, one put above the other. NAB has according to Delitzsch, *Assyrische Lesestücke*, No. 90, the meaning *shamû*. This NAB is again (because = an + an = heaven + earth) = Cosmos. The *dingir NAB* is not only identified with *dingir En-lil* in V. R. 44, 46*c*., but he is called—like the "twenty-one who have AN-NA for their parent"—the *dumu sag AN-NA*, i. e., the first-born or principal son of AN-NA (= heavenly ocean): Reisner, *Hymnen*, pp. 140, 194; 135, col. IV. 1; 88, 7. And when this *dingir NAB* is called in II. R. 54, 10*a*, *b*, the "Bel of the *shamû*," he does not, as Jensen, *Kosmologie*, p. 25, cf. K. B. VI[1]. p. 347 wants, stand for "den Punkt am Himmel, wo die verschiedenen Teilungslinien zusammenlaufen," but for the Bel of the Σαυη! [NAB is also = Tiâmat: 83-1-18, 1332 obv. II. 22, published in *Proceedings of the Society of Biblical Arch*., Dec., 1888, plate V. But Tiâmat is = *dingir GUR*, "the mother of AN and KI." *GUR* again is not only = *apsû*, "ocean," but also, if pronounced *zikum*, = *shamû*. Hence NAB signifies Tiâmat as the mother of the *apsû* or ocean considered as a cosmos or *shamû* or *AN* + *KI*, i. e., of the ocean as consisting of an upper and of a lower one!]

d. Possibly even *AN-SHAR*, who might be read also *dingir SHAR*. *SHAR*, when pronounced "*du*," is also = *shamû*; hence *dingir SHAR* (= *du*) might be translated "the god of the Σαυη, i. e., cosmos! *É-shar* would accordingly become not so much "the house of the totality (= *kishshatu*)" as "the *world-house*. See also above, p. 80, where it is said of Marduk that he had build *É-shar-ra* as (or: to be) a *sha-ma-mu*, i. e., a Σαυη or cosmos! This sha-ma-mu here, because it is the habitation of Anu, Bel (= Enlil), and Ea, *must* include the *two oceans*—the heavenly and the terrestrial—*also*. This peculiarity is even adopted by the Priestcode. P.'s expression for "*cosmos*" is generally = "heaven and earth": Gen. i. 1, ii. 1, Ex. xxxi. 17; but also "heaven and earth and the ים," i. e., ocean: Ex. xx. 2! The É-shar-ra, the world-house, is thus made = heaven and earth and ocean—a, no doubt, late conception, thus showing a tendency towards henotheism, resp. monotheism.

No. III. (sic!), ll. 10–13,[1] where Antum is expressed in the Sumerian line by KI, the ideograph for *irtsitu* = earth. Again on another place[2] this AN-NA is directly translated by *shamê* or "heaven," and the KI (or KI-a) directly by *irtsitim* or "earth"—thus proving beyond a shadow of doubt that *Anum* = *AN* is = heaven and *Antum* = *KI* is = earth. AN thus means indeed either *heaven* or (!) *earth.*.[3]

---

[1] ^{dingir}*A-nun-na AN-NA a-ri-a-ne*
^{ilu}ditto *sha ri-chu-ut* ^{ilu}*A-nim ri-chu-u*
^{dingir}*A-nun-na KI* (sic!) *a-ri-a-ne*
^{ilu}ditto *sha ri-chu-ut An-tum ri-chu-u.*

Instead of KI we have the correcter writing KI-*a* in Reisner, *loc. cit.*, pp. 132, 19, 20; 78, 12, 13. Cf. also IV. R. 21, No. 2, rev. 1. For *richûti* see Jensen, K. B. VI[1]. p. 365, 6.

[2] ^{dingir}*A-nun-na AN-NA mu-ush V-bi*
^{ilu}*A-nun-na-ki sha shamê*^{e} *V shu-shi*
^{dingir}*A-nun-na KI-a mu-ush X-bi*
^{ilu}*A-nun-na-ki sha irtsitim*^{tim} *ni-e-ir-shu.*

Reisner, *Hymnen*, p. 139, 155–158.

See also Reisner, *loc. cit.*, pp. 92, 24, 25; 135, col. III. 30. With regard to the 300 (= 5 soss!) "Anunna of heaven," and with regard to the 600 (1 *nêr*) "A-nunna of the earth," see Zimmern, K. A. T[3]. p. 453; Jensen, K. B. VI[1]. p. 587. The passages cited in this and the preceding note are important. (1) We have here the Anunna of *heaven*, i. e., the Igigi and the Anunna of the *earth*, i. e., the Anunnaki, as they are generally called in the Assyrian inscriptions. Both classes are said to be the richût, i. e., lit. "the pouring out" = *seed* or *sons* of Anu and Antum. (2) We have seen (C. S. p. 49) that the *king* of the storm-flood is Enlil, while the storm-flood itself is Nin-Girsu or Imgigghubarbar, the *son* of Enlil. Hence, when we read, that either Bêl, i. e., the old Enlil, be the "lord, the *king* of all Anunnaki" (Tiglat-Pileser I. = K. B. I. p. 14, col. I. 3), or that Anu be "the *king* of the Igigi and the Anunnaki" (Shalmanassar II., Obelisk = K. B[1]. p. 128, l. 2), or that Ashshur (= Anshar) be termed "the *king* of the Igigi" (Adad-nirâri III. = K. B[1]. p. 188, No. 2, ll. 2, 3), we must understand these statements as above, i. e., that these *kings* of the Igigi and the Anunnaki are at the same time their *fathers*, and if so, then Enlil is = Anu = Anshar. See here also above, p. 73, where it is expressly said that Anshar is he "who begot (*shâpik* = *râchû*!) the Igigi and the Anunnaki"! Where the moon-god Sin was considered to be the highest god, it is, of course, natural to find that these very same Igigi and Anunnaki should be assigned to his court, as is done in the celebrated hymn to Sin: IV. R. 9.

[3] That one and the same ideograph should have two diametrically opposed significations is not by any means uncommon—it is simply a corroboration of Winckler's maxim: "Jedes Ding schlägt schliesslich in sein Gegentheil um, wie es der Kreislauf der Natur vorschreibt und bedingt: Wir haben die unzertrennlichen und doch getrennten Dioskuren, Mond und Sonne = Tag und Nacht = Licht und Finsterniss = Winter und Sommer, die beiden Sonnen- und Naturhälften" (M. V. A. G., 1901, IV., Part I., p. 15, note 1), and I may add the "two halves of the world":

If we would sum up our results so far obtained they would be the following:

Out of the primeval ocean, Apsû and Tiâmat, the Sumerian GUR, is born mummu or Moûmis, *νοητὸς κόσμος*—which was only a "world," i. e., an AN and a KI in *mind*, but not in fact. It became a world in fact, when AN begot LIL, who took his place between AN and KI, thus not only separating the AN from the KI, but forming with them the first *triad*. This LIL, the son of AN, appears in the lists above mentioned under twenty-one different names among which are also to be found Anshar and Lachmu. These names are arranged in pairs of husband and wife—the husband being considered the *upper* and the wife the *lower* part. The upper part is the heaven and the lower part the earth. This gives us the most important fact of our whole investigation, which is: heaven and earth are husband and wife, as such called Anum and Antum who again are only two other names for Enlil and Ninlil—Enlil is the heaven and Ninlil is the earth when considered as husband and wife, but when considered as "one flesh" Enlil resp. Ninlil is the "heaven and earth" or "cosmos," hence may be called "king resp. queen of heaven and earth."[1]

---

heaven and earth. Among the different ideographs that may stand either for "heaven" or for "earth," I mention besides AN only the two following:

a. *IM*=*heaven*, Sc. 288; =*earth*, *ibidem*. A double IM, Brünnow, List, No. 12241, cf. No. 8502, is translated in II. R. 50, 28*c*; II. R. 48, 26*a-b*, by *shamû*, which latter can mean here only=cosmos=heaven + earth. Hence the *dingir*IM + *IM* in III. R. 67, 45*c*; III. R. 67, 42*c*, cannot signify originally the god Adad (or Rammân) but Enlil or Bêl, the god of "heaven and earth." Cf. here also "the gods who are above (*eli*) the IM and below (shapal) the IM" (Pinches, P. S. B. A., 1882, p. 164, 10–11), i. e., beyond the firmament or "heaven and earth," which in the passage cited, p. 163, l. 10, is called the *Char-sag-kalam-ma*=mountain of the world!

b. *U*=*shamû* "heaven": V. R. 36, 45*b*; *U*, also read *buru*, =*irtsitu*: V. R. 36, 46*b* and *U* is the ideograph for *dingir*En-lil: V. R. 36, 5*a*. This ideograph therefore signifies Enlil as the god of "heaven and earth"—and just as in later times Enlil became an ideographic writing for *bêl* or lord, so *U* was used as an ideograph for *bêl*. Conf. here also V. R. 37, 4*d*, *e*, *f*: buru or A-buru=*shamû ruqûtum* "the *far* away heaven," and l. 5: *buru*=*shamû shaplûtum* "the low(er) heaven," which latter does not speak so much in favor of the "different" heavens, as it proves that the "lower heaven" be the *earth*!

[1] Therefore Anu is called also "(the one) of the totality of heaven and earth."

It was not without some very definite reason that we had to linger so very long over this preliminary investigation, for here we are in direct opposition to all other Assyriologists, who either take Enlil to be the "god of the earth" or the "god of the air."

Our result is of the highest importance, not only for a right understanding of the Babylonian religion as such, but also for the religion both of the Old and the New Testament. In the latter it is especially the *doctrine of the Resurrection* which from our investigation receives a new and welcome light.

The doctrine of the Resurrection, because so closely connected with the personality of Christ, is the *central doctrine* of the Christian religion. It is the *pillar* upon which the Christian Church is built. With it Christianity stands and falls. Says St. Paul:

> "If Christ be not raised, then is our preaching vain, our faith also is vain" (1 Cor. xv. 14.)

And again, v. 17:

> "If Christ hath not been raised, your faith is vain."

It is, however, here of special interest to notice what *philosophic proofs* St. Paul is able to adduce for the resurrection of Christ. His proofs are:

> "Now if Christ is preached that he hath been raised from the dead, how say some among you that there is no resurrection of the dead? But if there is no resurrection of the dead, neither hath Christ been raised."[1]

The same argument is to be found also in verses 15, 16:

> "We witnessed of God that he raised up Christ: whom he raised not up, if so be that the dead are not raised. For if the dead are not raised, neither hath Christ been raised."

Notice, St. Paul does not say: "because Christ rose, therefore the dead rise," but *vice versa*: "If there be no resurrection of the dead, then Christ did not rise;" he wants us, however, to draw the last conclusion: "there *is* a resurrection of the dead, and if there be, then did Christ rise!" Paul, then, takes it for an indisputable fact that the dead *can* and *do* rise, and because *they* can

---

[1] 1 Cor. xv. 12, 13.

and do rise therefore *Christ* also *could* and *did* rise. Hence with the resurrection of the dead, the resurrection of Christ is given. The fact of Christ's resurrection is thus based, according to St. Paul's argumentation, upon the fact of the resurrection of the dead as such. If you deny the latter, you *ipso facto* deny the former. Everything depends upon our belief in the resurrection of the dead. If we do not believe in this, we do not and cannot believe in Christ's resurrection! Hence, it is quite natural, that St. Paul, when adducing the arguments in favor of the resurrection of Christ, should bring in also those proofs which establish the truth of the resurrection of the dead! And what are these?

> "But some one will say, how are the dead raised? and with what manner of body do they come? Thou foolish one, that which thou thyself sowest is not quickened, except it die: and that which thou sowest, thou sowest not the body that shall be, but a bare grain, it may chance of wheat, or of some other kind."[1]

The proof in favor of the resurrection of the dead is taken from *nature*! He compares the human bodies to "*grain*, it may chance of wheat, or of some other kind." The grain is put into the earth not to die and remain there, but to die and be quickened again, and thus sprout anew, rise to new life, and bear fruit. But this the grain does only in the *spring*! St. Paul's argument then is this: As in the spring nature or mother earth brings forth new life, quickens the "grain," makes it sprout again, so also the "dead" will be quickened, be raised to new life on that great morning when the eternal spring begins! *Nature* demonstrates the *fact* of the resurrection. This "resurrection," because a fact in nature, was *transferred* to "men" also—because they too are a part of nature! Men, as a part of nature, could not make an exception, could not upset the laws of nature, hence had to rise. But if men, as a part of nature, do rise, then Christ also had to rise,—for he belongs to "man." That is the argument of St. Paul.

Having made this clear, we may now pass to the details in

---

[1] 1 Cor. xv. 25.

connection with Christ's resurrection. These are probably enumerated best in the well-known, but most difficult, passage of 1 St. Peter iii. 18 ff., where we read:

> "Christ also suffered for sins once.... being put to death in the flesh, but quickened in the spirit, in which also he went and preached unto the spirits in prison, which aforetime were disobedient....the resurrection of Jesus Christ, who is on the right hand of God, having gone into heaven; angels and authorities and powers being made subject unto him."[1]

According to this passage the specific historic facts connected with the resurrection of Christ occurred in the following sequence:

1. suffering, 2. death, 3. quickening, 4. (*a*) going and (*b*) preaching unto the spirits in prison, 5. resurrection.

As Christ's suffering has nothing to do with our investigation here, we confine ourselves to facts Nos. 2–5.

"Death" according to N. T. *usus loquendi* is the separation of the "life-principle" or "soul" from the "body." The body is put into the grave while the soul continues to live as a "spirit." To such spirits, i. e., souls separated from the body[2] Christ went and preached.

If "*death*" be a *separation* of the soul from the body, then the "*quickening*" must be a *joining* together, a reuniting of the soul and body. Christ had to be dead, according to Scripture, for three days. During these three days, then, body and soul were separated. After these three days—or as the varient gives it: on the third day—he had to rise, hence his "being quickened" and his resurrection had to fall on the same day! Christ is said to have risen on early Easter-morning, hence his quickening or the re-

---

[1] *ὅτι καὶ Χριστὸς ἅπαξ περὶ ἁμαρτιῶν ἔπαθε....θανατωθεὶς μὲν σαρκί, ζωοποιηθεὶς δὲ τῷ πνεύματι ἐν ᾧ καὶ τοῖς ἐν φυλακῇ πνεύμασι πορευθεὶς ἐκήρυξεν ἀπειθήσασί ποτε....δι' ἀναστάσεως Ἰησοῦ Χριστοῦ ὅς ἐστιν ἐν δεξιᾷ τοῦ θεοῦ, πορευθεὶς εἰς οὐρανόν, ὑποταγέντων αὐτῷ ἀγγέλων καὶ ἐξουσιῶν καὶ δυνάμεων.*

[2] Also according to Babylonian conception the death consists in a separation of the *napishtu* or life-principle from the body. This *napishtu* continues to live after death as a so-called *ekimmu* or *utukku*, see also jensen, K. B. VI[1]. pp. 406,

uniting of soul and body must have taken place on early Easter-morning too! As soon as this "quickening" had become a fact "he went and preached." If, therefore, the question be asked: "When did Christ go and preach?" the correct answer can be only this: "On early Easter-morning, immediately after his being 'quickened in spirit'!" In this (ἐν ᾧ) "being quickened in spirit" he went. Hence Christ's going and preaching did not take place during those three days, while his body was lying in the grave, nor did his *soul* only go down to the prison, but "his soul reunited to the body"—for he was *quickened*! Christ's journey to prison, then, falls between his being quickened and his resurrection, i. e., *likewise* on early Easter-morning. As such a "quickened one in spirit," i. e., as one having acquired new life—a spiritual life[1]—he went and preached, or better: "he going preached" (πορευθεὶς ἐκήρυξεν). And what did he preach? The "contents" of Christ's preaching is not given here. We are therefore obliged to determine the exact nature of this ἐκήρυξεν from the context. The word κηρύσσειν expresses simply the idea that Christ "was a herald," or "officiated as a herald," or "proclaimed something after the manner of a herald." A herald always acts in the name and upon the command of a *higher person*—hence whatever Christ proclaimed or heralded must have been something which he had received from someone else, something to which he was authorised. That this "something" cannot have been the "gospel" follows from the following consideration.

1. "To preach the gospel" is expressed in the New Testament *always* by εὐαγγελίζειν.

2. The verse in 1 Peter iv. 6: "*For unto this end was the gospel preached even unto the dead*" does not help us very much either, for "the dead" are those who were *alive* when the preaching took place, but who died in the meantime. Besides that, we have for the "dead" the word νεκροῖς,[2] and for to preach not κηρύσσειν but εὐηγγελίσθη.

---

[1] This is the common explanation of the phrase, which, however, does *not* explain the difficulties involved, see my article on Jahveh!

[2] And not πνεύμασι or the "souls separated from the body"!

3. Whenever the contents of the proclaiming or heralding are given, this is expressed by an *object* which follows the verb *κηρύσσειν*. Thus we have to preach: "Moses," Acts xv. 21; "circumcision," Gal. v. 11; "the word," Mark i. 45; "the gospel (of the kingdom)," Matth. iv. 23; Mark xvi. 15; "baptism," Mark i. 4; "repentance and remission of sins," Luke xxiv. 47; "Christ," Acts viii. 5, and it is used of "*an angel* as God's herald" in Rev. v. 12.

4. Suppose, for the sake of argument, that Christ indeed *preached the gospel* unto the spirits in prison in order to give them a last chance to get out of it—but then we would be again in straight contradiction to the parable of the "rich man and poor Lazarus." What this parable wants to teach us is this: the "*time of salvation*" is *here upon earth*, not after death: "*They have Moses and the prophets, let them hear them.*" If they hear them and do accordingly, they will be saved, if they do not listen to them they lose all chances of their salvation! Hence there was not and could not be offered to the "spirits that are in prison" a *last chance*!

This last consideration leads us over to the next point of our inquiry, viz., to the question with regard to the meaning of the "prison," φυλακή.

This prison appears here as a kind of "keeping-place," a place where the "spirits," the "souls separated from their bodies," the *ekimmu* or *utukku* are to be found. The *ekimmu* and *utukku* have, according to Babylonian ideas, their abode in the "nether world"—a place which was considered to be (within) the "*earth.*" It would therefore be natural to suppose that this place, the nether world, Hades, place of departed spirits, be also meant here. If it be, then it has to be subdivided again—according to the parable of the "rich man and poor Lazarus"—into two subdivisions: (1) a seemingly *comfortable* place, which is called in that parable: Abraham's bosom (κόλπος 'Αβραάμ); (2) an *uncomfortable* one or Hades proper. In the former we find Lazarus, in the latter the rich man. Both of these men arrive in their respective abodes as soon as they die:

> "And the beggar died, and....was carried away by the angels into Abraham's bosom, and the rich man also died, and was buried....and in Hades he lifted up his eyes, being

in torments, and seeth Abraham afar off, and Lazarus in his bosom!"

If the "prison" of St. Peter be the same as the Hades with its two subdivisions, the question may be asked: Did Christ go to the "uncomfortable" or the "comfortable" part of Hades in order to preach? According to St. Peter Christ preached "unto the spirits in prison, which aforetime were *disobedient.*" The assumption, therefore, might seem to favor the view that he went to Hades proper, the uncomfortable place, the abode of the rich man. Granted he went to this place, and granted also that he preached the gospel to the spirits in this "place of torment" in order to give them a last chance to secure their salvation, then again we would be in contradiction to Christ's express statements, who quotes Abraham as saying:

> "And beside all this, between us and you there is a great gulf (χάσμα μέγα) fixed, that they who would pass from hence to you may not be able, and that none may cross over from thence to us."

In other words: there is "no getting out" any more—those that are in Abraham's bosom remain there for ever, and those that are in Hades proper cannot be transferred any more to Abraham's bosom! Hence if Christ had indeed preached the "gospel to the spirits in Hades proper" he would have done something which was —to say the least—useless, for he knew that he could not help them! From this it follows that Christ did not and could not have preached the *gospel*, nor did he or could he have gone to Hades proper, the uncomfortable place!

Above we saw that the verb κηρύσσειν simply expresses the idea that Christ as the messenger of a higher person, heralded or proclaimed something. This he did immediately after his "being quickened in the spirit"—after having acquired a new (spiritual) life. With his being quickened Christ's battle against the powers of darkness: death and grave comes to an end. It is the assurance that he has become the victor, the king not only over death but also over life. As such a king over life and death it behoves him to sit in judgment over the life and death of the spirits in prison—and not only over these, but also over that of all mankind. Christ's heralding—because it cannot be a preaching of the gospel—must therefore express the idea that He as king over life and death has now also the fates with regard to the life and death of the whole of mankind and in particular of the spirits in prison in his hand. He instantly exercises the powers that belong to him: he sits in judgment over the fates of the spirits—he becomes what the Babylonians would call a *mushîm shîmâti*, i. e., "one that determines (and destines and seals) the fates." As such a *mushîm shîmâti* he is a herald—one that acts for another person. This "other person" is, as we shall see shortly, "the great gods," or in New Testament language "God the Father."

Judgment, however, is not passed except in a place especially set aside for this purpose. This place is called here "prison"; as such it is a house, a room in which the spirits are "kept" to await their judgment, and has, therefore, nothing to do with *Hades*. We shall hear more about this room when we come to speak of the Babylonian Ubshugina.

If we sum up our results they would be the following: Christ died: body and soul were separated, this separation lasted for three days! On the third day his body and soul were reunited again: he was quickened in the spirit—acquired a new spiritual (?) life. This took place on early Easter-morning. But not only the quickening occured at this time but also his "showing or his proclaiming himself as the victor," and his resurrection. The proclaiming himself as victor took place in a room called "prison," where the departed spirits were kept, held for judgment. By this heralding the *fates* of the spirits were sealed or determined,—Christ becomes thus a Babylonian mushîm shîmâti, i. e., "one who determines the fates," as such he acts again as "herald," i, e., as one commissioned by a higher authority, which latter are the gods. After Christ had "determined the fates" of the spirits in prison, he rises. He could and did rise, because he was man. Man again can and does rise because he is part of "nature," and nature demonstrates to us every year in the spring that "the dead do rise to new life"

—hence as there is a resurrection of *nature*, so there is and was also a Resurrection of Christ!

That this doctrine of the Resurrection cannot have its source in the Old Testament is now admitted by all who made this the subject of a special investigation; see here especially Professor Gunkel's article in *The Monist* for April, 1903, pp. 417–419 and 439–440, where he considers the resurrection of Christ and his descent into Hades, inclining to the belief that these doctrines were brought to Judaism from "a stellar religion in which it was the ideal of the faithful to be snatched away from the transitoriness of the earth and to become like unto the ever-beaming divine stars." And a little further below he says (p. 419): "It is well known that the belief in life after death has long been present in a number of Oriental religions, for example, the Egyptian and the Persian, and that the whole Orient was filled with it at the time of which we are speaking. It is not remarkable that Judaism also finally adopts this belief, but rather is it strange that it resisted the belief so long." Indeed, it is strange that Judaism did resist this belief so long, seeing that the belief in the resurrection existed among the Babylonians as early as the time of Gudea, patesi of Shirpula, at about 3200 B. C.

But some one may say that there are several passages in the Old Testament which *do* show that the Hebrews did believe in a resurrection, quoting especially the familiar passage in Job xix. 25: "I know that my redeemer liveth, etc." Professor Gunkel, when speaking of this passage, remarks quite rightly, all we can gather from this passage is that "Job thinks for a moment of the possibility that God may justify him even after death" (*loc. cit.*, p. 417). On account of the importance of this doctrine it would seem advisable to examine the several passages of the Old Testament more closely and see whether we cannot detect in them at least *some* traces of a belief in a resurrection and a life after death.

The several passages of the Old Testament with regard to a life after death and a possible resurrection may be divided into three classes:[1]

[1] Conf. for the first two classes especially Cheyne in his *Encyclopædia Biblica* sub "Eschatology," Vol. II., pp. 1340, 1341.

1. Those according to which the "state" after death is a continuation of the life upon the earth. According to this view the dead possess a certain degree of self-consciousness, retain their power of speech and movement,[1] have knowledge, are therefore called ידענים = "knowing ones";[2] they not only know what happens upon the earth, but they also take an interest in the fortunes of their living brethren: "Rachel weeps for her children,"[3]—as if she knew what had happened to the Jews during the time of their captivity; they know the future,[4] whence they were consulted about it by the living. And because this life after death is simply a continuation of the life upon the earth, therefore it is natural to expect that the prophet should wear his garb of distinction, the mantle, even in Sheol.[5] Kings appear here with crowns and sit upon thrones,[6] the uncircumcised retain their foreskin, nations their national garb and customs,[7] old people their gray hair,[8] and those slain with the sword bear forever the tokens of a violent death.[9] Cheyne, no doubt, is right when he calls this view "*the older.*" Of a resurrection we hear in these passages not a single word, although they clearly prove that with death life has *not* come to an end.

2. Those that express a *later* idea and are as such *diametrically opposed* to the former. According to these, death is destruction,[10] and destruction is Sheol,[11] or also called (the place of) *violence*,[12] a place out of which "*he that goeth down shall come up no more*,"[13] a place not only where "kings," "counsellors of the earth," and "princes" are to be found, but also where "*the wicked cease from troubling*, and where "*the weary are at rest*," where "*prisoners are at ease together*," "*the small and great are there, and the servant is free from his master.*"[14] It is indeed a place for all classes and conditions of men! There "*Abraham knoweth us not, and Israel doth not acknowledge us*,"[15]—the dead therefore have absolutely no knowledge of what is happening or going on upon the earth!

---

[1] Isaiah 14. [2] Lev. xix. 31. [3] Jerem. xxxi. 15.
[4] 1 Sam. xxviii. 13–20: Saul and the witch of Endor.
[5] 1 Sam. xxviii. 14. [6] Is. xiv. [7] Ezek. xxxii.
[8] Gen. xlii. 38. [9] Ezek. xxxii. 25. [10] Job xxviii. 22. [11] Job xxvi. 6.
[12] ψ cxv. 17. [13] Job vii. 9. [14] Job. iii. 14 ff. [15] Is. lxiii. 16.

Especially important is here the passage in Job xiv. 7:

"For there is hope of a tree, if it be cut down, that it will
sprout again,
And that the tender branch thereof will not cease.
Though the root thereof was old in the earth
And the stock thereof die in the ground,
Yet through the scent of water it will bud
And put forth boughs like a plant.
But man dieth, and wasteth away:
Yea, man giveth up the ghost, and where is he?
As the waters fail from the sea
And the river decayeth and drieth up,
So man lieth down and riseth not:
Till the heavens be no more, they shall not awake,
[Nor be roused out of their sleep.]

What a difference between Job and St. Paul! Both employ the same method of reasoning,—but how different are the conclusions reached. For St. Paul it is just the nature which proves conclusively that there is a resurrection, but alas! for Job the tree, though the root thereof was old, and the stock thereof die, will bud again, but man when he dieth will never rise again! Two arguments, though both based upon the phenomena of nature, lead to two diametrically opposed conclusions! And because there is absolutely no hope for man after death, therefore argues Ecclesiastes (ix. 5 ff.) in his pessimistic spirit:

> "Eat thy bread with joy, and drink thy wine with a merry heart; for God hath already accepted thy works.....Live joyfully with the wife whom thou lovest all the days of the life of thy vanity, which he hath given thee under the sun, all the days of thy vanity: for that is thy portion in life, and in thy labor wherein thou laborest under the sun. Whatsoever thy hand findeth to do, do it with thy might; for there is no work, nor device, nor knowledge, nor wisdom, in the grave, whither thou goeth."

Dark, very dark is the outlook indeed, which men have according to this view! No life, no joy, no resurrection after death! With the death everything comes to an end.

3. And yet, there are some passages in the Old Testament which do indeed betray to us a belief in a deliverance out of the grave! All these passages, however, belong to the very latest portions of the whole Old Testament writings. Now it is not necessary to construe with Professor Gunkel (*Monist*, April, 1903, p. 487) such sayings as meaning that "the faithful expects in this connection not the resurrection from the dead, but rather something very different, namely that God will save him in *present danger* and not permit his soul to go down into Sheol (the grave). This explanation might possibly hold good of such passages as:

> "God will redeem my soul from the power of Sheol" (ψ ixl. 15).
>
> "For thou wilt not leave my soul to Sheol" (ψ xvi. 18).

But it never could be applied to ψ xxxvii. 28:

> "For the Lord knoweth judgment
> And forsaketh not the saints
> They are preserved *for ever*
> But the seed of the wicked shall be cut off."

This "for ever" clearly shows that the psalmist not only believed that God could and would preserve the soul of the saints in *present danger* but *continually*, always and always, for ever and ever, unto all eternity.

Meagre and few as these passages are, yet they help us to follow up the path that leads us to the source whence such a view possibly might have been important. These passages, belonging to the latest portions of Hebrew literature, and as such having been written *after* the *Babylonian* captivity, point thus to *Babylonia* as their source.

Quite recently Zimmern, in his K. A. T³. p. 638 *et passim*, saw fit to make the statement, "von einer Auferstehungslehre ist bis jetzt wenigstens keine sichere Spur in der babylonischen Litteratur zu finden." That this cannot be maintained any more now I hope to be able to show.

We have seen above[1] that Enlil, the husband of Ninlil, was the "heaven," while his wife was "the earth." This "wife" had in the three lists, transcribed above, different names, among which there was to be found one, viz., *dingir Gá-ra*, i. e., *Muallidtu* or "the one who brings forth,"—a name which is even found in Herodotus i. 131, 199 under the form Μύλιττα.[2] In our *Creation-Story*, p. 19, we heard that the wife of Enlil had several names even in the oldest Sumerian inscriptions—such as: (*a*) *dingir Nin-tu*, i. e., the divine mistress of the TU or "*bringing forth*" (= *alâdu*), therefore she is also called "the *mother* of the gods"; (*b*) *dingir Nin-in-si-na*, "the *mother* of the world (or people), who created the creatures of the world," but especially (*c*) *dingir Ba-ú*, who as the wife of Enlil becomes thus the *earth*. Now it happens that we read in several inscriptions of Gudea, the patesi of Shirpurla, who lived at about 3200 B. C., of a "wedding" of Nin-Girsu, the god of rain, thunders, and lightnings, and *dingir Ba-ú*.[3] This wedding was celebrated on the *New-Years-day* of the month called *Ezen-dingir Ba-ú*, i. e., "the festival of Bau." The significance of this wedding-celebration becomes at once plain! *It is the fructification of the earth by the rain in consequence of which the earth is made pregnant and brings forth new life. Ba-ú* becomes thus not only an *AM* or mother, a *muallidtu*, one "that brings forth," but also a *dingir Nin-din-dug*,[4] a Sumerian name, which when translated into Assyrian would be = *muballitat miti*,[5] i. e., "*the one who quickens the dead.*" That which she quickens, restores to new life, are "*the green things of the earth*"

---

[1] See also C. S. p. 52.

[2] See also Jensen, *Kosm.*, pp. 294, 515. Zimmern, K. A. T[3]. pp. 423, 7; 428, 4.

[3] Gudea, Statue G. II. 1–7; III. 6 *v. u*: *Ud-zag-mu ezen dingir Ba-ú ni(g)-gal-gish-as ag-da*; IV. 18.

[4] If Ba-u is able to quicken the *dead*, then, of course, she has the power to "restore to health the sick" also. Cf. Craig, *Relig. Texts*, I. p. 18, 5–6: *dingir Ba-ú mà nam-ti-la shub-ba shag-gig-ga-ge = ilu ditto na-da-at shi-pat ba-la(l)-di ana qi-its lib-bi*, i. e., "Bau who giveth the salvina of life to the sick heart."

[5] This name is also given to the goddess Gula—a name which was originally only an attribute of Ba-ú, and meaning as such "the great one," *rabîtu*, *shurbûtu*. In the oldest texts Gula appears still used as an attribute, has therefore not the sign for god prefixed to it, see E. B. H. p. 443.

—hence the name *Ba-ú*, i. e., "the giver (*ba*) of *u*=green things.[1] Such a fructification and vivification of the earth can only take place in the spring. Hence during that time which precedes the spring *the earth*[2] as well as *Nin-Girsu must be fruitless, barren, or dead.* The time that precedes the spring is the winter. In *winter* then both "the earth" and the "god of rain and thunder and lightning," must be dead, must lie in the grave. Now we understand why Gudea records repeatedly in his inscriptions that he built for Nin-Girsu in the temple *É-ninnû-dingir Im-gig-ghu-bar-bar* also a so-called Gi-gunu[3] out of cedar-wood. This Gi-gunu appears in IV. R. 24, 4*b*[4] not only in parallelism with É-kur and with Arallû, i.e., the "nether world," but is called there even the *ashar la naplusi*, i. e., "*the place of the not-seeing*, i. e., where one does not and cannot see=the place of darkness. Nin-Girsu then dies every year and goes to the Gi-gunu. Here he is during the winter. In winter he is dead: there are no rains, thunders, and lightnings at this time! But in *spring* he is quickened and rises again, this he indicates by his first lightnings and thunders that even at our present times take place in the early spring. As soon as he is quickened, he rises and marries the *mother* earth, i. e,, Ba-ú: the warm rains of the spring unite themselves with the earth, who becomes pregnant: in consequence of this pregnancy the dead things of the earth are quickened, they rise and new life sprouts! If this wedding could take place in the spring *only*, and if this was at the same time "the New Year's day," it follows that already at Gudea's time or about

---

[1] *ú* in this signification has according to the syllabaries (see Br. List, 6019, 6027) probably the pronunciation SHAM; we ought to read therefore Ba-sham. This latter reading seems to be implied also in Reisner, *Hymnen*, p. 89, 12; 83, 9 (cf. l. 28): *ugun-mu dingir Ba-ú-MU*, where the MU can hardly be taken as a pronoun (="my"), but where it seems to contain the overhanging vowel=*Ba-sham-mu*.

[2] See here especially the drastic description of the "deadness" of nature while Ishtar (=Innanna, another name for Ba-ú, C. S. p. 20) is in the nether world, i. e., while she is dead, barren, while it is winter: Ishtar's descent, K. B. VI[1]. p. 86, Rev. 6 ff.

[3] See E. B. H., Index, *sub* buildings, and Gudea, Statue B, V. 15–19; Statue D, II. 7–III. 1.

[4] See Jensen, *Kosm.*, p. 185.

3200 B. C. the year began with the spring, with the first of Nisan, the vernal equinox,[1] and that the wedding of Nin-Girsu and Ba-ú is nothing but a spring festival celebrating the *resurrection of nature to new life!* It is a *Resurrection-festival.*

In view of this fact we now understand why Nin-Girsu should have become the "*god of vegetation*": he it is, who by his fructification of the earth produces vegetation, he is therefore the "god of the farmers." That Nin-Girsu was = Ninib has been recognised long ere this. Our investigations,[2] however, force us to abandon the erroneous idea that Ninib was either the South or Summer sun[3] or the East sun.[4] Ninib (because = Nin-Girsu) is the god of storm, rain, lightnings, etc., as such also a god of vegetation,[5] and a god of the farmers.[6] And just as Nin-Girsu quickens the dead, so it is said of Ninib: "Who has been brought down into the nether world, his body thou bringest back again."[7]

Nin-Girsu was the *ur-sag*, i. e., prime minister of Enlil, and as in the Old Testament the "angel of the lord" was in course of time identified with "the lord," so was Nin-Girsu, resp. Ninib, with Enlil! So it happened that when the Canaanites had invaded Babylonia and made themselves masters over it, Marduk displaced not only Enlil but also his "prime minister,"—both of whose attributes and functions were now attributed to him (i. e., Marduk).

Marduk's wife was Tsarpanitum, i. e., "the one who shines (like silver)," as such she was again identified with Ishtar (= Innanna, another name for the wife of Enlil). Now, it is strange to notice that the name Tsarpanitum should have become, according to the folk-etymology, Zêr-bânîtu, i. e., "the one who creates, pro-

---

[1] This is the answer to Zimmer, K. A. T.[3] p. 514.

[2] See also my forthcoming article on Jahveh.

[3] Winckler, *Geschichte Israels*, II., 79.

[4] Jensen, *Kosm.*, p. 457 f.

[5] K. 133 Rev. 20 (A. S. K. T. p. 81): mit-cha-rish shumi-shu im-bu-u sham-mu (= ú-mu) ana shar-ru-ti-shu-nu = with one consent the plants called his (i. e., Ninib's) name to a kingship over them.

[6] Cf. here Engar = ikkaru = farmer; and ^{dingir} Engar = ^{ilu} Ninib. See also above!

[7] King, *Magic*, No. 2, 21: *sha ana arallê shûrudu pagarshu tuterra!*

duces, seed!" That this must have had a reason is, of course, evident! And what is the reason?

The spring-festival of the resurrection of nature, which was conceived to be (at the time of Gudea) a wedding of Nin-Girsu and Ba-ú, was transferred to Marduk who now took the highest place in the Babylonian pantheon,—it became a wedding[1] of Marduk and Tsarpanitu, which wedding likewise took place in the spring, in Nisan. This event was also considered to be a *tabû*[2] or *resurrection* of Marduk and the *beginning* of his "*kingship*"[3] upon earth. These facts alone help us considerably to explain more fully the nature of god Marduk. Marduk begins his *reign*, his *kingship* in the *spring*. What precedes the spring is again the winter. In winter, then, Marduk has no kingship,—he is *powerless*. In the *spring* he *rises*, during the *winter* he must be in the *grave*, must be *dead*. In the spring he "hastens to the brideship," i. e., he weds, he unites himself with Tsarpanitu. The result of this is again that Tsarpanitu becomes a *mother*, is fructified and vivified,—hence the Tsarpanitu becomes a Zêr-bânîtu, as such she *brings forth seed*. This she does because she takes the place of Ba-ú or Ishtar (= Innanna), the *earth*! The earth by wedding Marduk is made to produce the "green things of nature," and Marduk, who causes all this, is therefore called sha mîti bulluṭa irammu,[4] i. e., he "who delights in quickening the dead,"—therefore he has the name bêl balâṭi,[5] "the lord of life." These "*dead*," whom Marduk quickens can therefore be primarily only = "the *dead things of nature*,"[6] but came to include, because man is a part of nature, "mankind" also.

---

[1] I-chi-ish ana cha-da-ash-shú-tu, i. e., he [*sc.* Marduk] hastened to the brideship. Reisner, *Hymnen*, p. 145, 8.

[2] Neb. VII. 24; Nerigl. I. 35; Jensen, K. B. VI.[1] p. 306; Zimmern, K. A. T.[3] p. 371.

[3] Ir-mu-ú ana sharru-ú-tu, i. e., he sat down for the kingship. Reisner, *loc. cit.*, l. 9.

[4] Zimmern, *Shurpu*, VII. 84.

[5] Zimmern, *Shurpu*, VIII. 71.

[6] Against Zimmern, K. A. T.[3] pp. 373, 639, who thinks that mîti here = Totkranke, Schwerkranke. But the √ מות never means sick, but *dead only*!

In another place[1] I have shown that Marduk was the god of *light*, —the light considered, however, not as an illuminating power, but as a *life-giving* principle. Marduk, the AMAR-UD, i. e., "the son of the sun," if he were an illuminator *only*, could never be called "dead" or "powerless" during the winter. The "*rays of the sun*" —for these are Marduk—are *dead* or *powerless* in the winter, because they do not give *warmth*.[2] Marduk, the god of light, becomes thus the god of the *warmth of the spring*,[3] because in the spring, when he is quickened again and rises, when he begins his "kingship" and enters into a wedlock with mother earth, the *rays of the sun become to be felt*,[4]—his power begins, the earth is fructified, brings forth fruit: the *dead things* of the earth are quickened, rise to new life. The fight of Marduk against Tiâmat appears thus as a fight of the light, i. e., the *warmth* (the summer beginning with the spring) against the darkness, i. e., the cold (the winter, chaos, when everything is barren, dead), which fight took place not only "in the beginning" on "the first spring," but which repeats itself every year and which will go on *ach-ra-tash nishi la-ba-rish ûme*[me],[5] —for all eternity, for ever and ever. After having overcome his enemy, the winter, and thus made the creation possible, Marduk receives the highest honor which a god can or may receive: he is henceforth called by the *name* of that ancient Sumerian god, viz., *En-lil*, the "king and father of the gods," the "king of the lands,"[6] as such a "king" he also has the life and death of his people in his hands. He can now determine their fates, he is a mushîm shîmâti.

---

[1] C. S. p. 5 f. = *Monist*, XII., 572; see also Jensen, K. B. VI.[1] p. 563, cf. *ibid.*, p. 562, and Jastrow, *Jewish Quarterly Review*, 1901, p. 638,—both these scholars have drawn my attention to these places.

[2] This against Jensen, K. B. VI.[1] p. 563.

[3] The idea that Marduk be the god of the early sun either of the day, or of the spring, or "at the beginning" when the world was created, ought now to be given up once for all, seeing that even the originator of the same, Professor Jensen, has himself abandoned it.

[4] In the winter they are *not* felt, although the sun is shining: Marduk is in the grave, is powerless, is dead, and is as such called Nabû! Marduk and Nabû represent thus the two halves of the year: summer and winter!

[5] K. B. VI.[1] p. 36, 10 f.

[6] K. B. VI.[1] p. 36, 13.

This latter point leads us over to another important event which took place in connection with this New Year's festival.

The resurrection of Marduk was celebrated by the people in this way:

Just as Marduk left the nether world—a place within the earth—so his statue left or went out (*atsû*) of the temple Esagil and was wheeled around on a ship[1] in solemn procession (*mashdachu*). This "wheeling around" took place on the most celebrated street in Babylon, the street Ai-ibur-shabum, i. e., probably, "not shall the dark one gain victory."[2] Especially sacred during this festival were the eighth to the tenth day, on which Marduk as the highest and as the spokesman of all the other great gods "determines the fates" of mankind in a place called *Du-azag*, which again was in another called *Ubshugina*. See here especially K. B. III. 2 p. 15 ff. (=Neb. II. 54.):

Du-azag, the "place of the destiners of fate," which is (in) Ub-shu-gin-na, the chamber of fates (=the room where judgment is given!), where at (the time of) the ZAG-MU-KU, the "New-Year," on the eighth (to the) eleventh day the "king of the gods of heaven and earth," the "lord of the gods," takes his abode (=sits down sc. for judgment), and where he, while the gods of heaven and earth reverently listen (?) and stand, doing homage to him, determines a fate of eternal days (to be) the fate of my life.[3]

---

[1] That is: the ceremonies connected with this festival were such that went against "the common order of things,"—it was a festival "der ausgelassensten Freude," where everything went "upside down."

[2] Shâbû not = "enemy" as Del. H. W. B. p. 637 wants, see Jensen, K. B. VI.[1] 335. The "dark one" is the "death," "winter," "chaos," "darkness," Tiâmat, etc.

[3] *Du-azag ki-nam-tar-tar-e-ne*
sha Ub-shu-(u)gin-na parak shi-ma-a-ti
sha ina ZAG-MU-KU ri-esh sha-at-ti
ûmu VIII[kam] ûmu XI[kam]
[ilu]Lugal-dim-me-ir-an-ki-a bêl ili
i-ra-am-mu-u ki-ri-ib-shu
ilâni shu-ut shamê irtsiti
pa-al-chi-ish u-ta-ak-ku-shu
ka-am-su in-za-zu mach-ru-ush-shu
shi-ma-at û-um da-er-u-tim

Du-azag means "bright or holy hill," and *Ubshugina* the "room of the assembling hand"[1]—we have, then, here a larger place within which there is a "hill." On this hill the great gods are assembled and determine under the presidency of Marduk the fates of mankind. Whatever may be the outcome of this *shimtu shimu*, this "determining of fates," Marduk declares it; he appears thus as a "herald" who although the highest god acts only with the consent of the other great gods!

Taking all these facts into consideration, the sequence of the events, connected with this New-Year's festival, has probably to be conceived of as follows:

1. During the winter Marduk is powerless, i. e., dead.

2. In the spring or in Nisan, which is the beginning of the New Year, Marduk enters upon his kingship again, i. e., he acquires new power, *new life*; is *quickened.*

3. As soon as he is quickened he rises—his quickening and his resurrection practically fall together.

4. Having thus been quickened and having risen, he unites himself with mother earth.

5. This union makes the earth "give up her dead"—the resurrection of nature is thus conditioned by Marduk's resurrection—if Markuk had not risen, nature (vegetation) could not rise to new life!

6. Marduk as the victor and conqueror of darkness enters in solemn procession the "holy hill" within the "room of the assembling hand" and determines here in the name of all the other great gods the fates of mankind.

This festival of the resurrection of Marduk and that of nature was celebrated every Nisan while the Jews were in the Babylonian captivity. Surely we must suppose that this spring-festival was known to the returning Jews, if we do not want to maintain that they were dead, absolutely dead, to their surroundings. We saw

---

shi-ma-at ba-la-ti-ia
i-shi-im-mu i-na ki-ir-bi.

[1] Jensen, *Kosm.*, p. 240, translates this name by "Raum der Versammlung," but in this translation the *shu* is not accounted for.

above that we could detect in the Old Testament at least some meagre relics of a doctrine of the resurrection, which doctrine, however, in the New Testament holds almost the same place as it did in ancient Babylonia.

As Marduk had displaced old Enlil and his messenger, so Christ displaced Marduk. Marduk is the god of light—and Christ is the "light of the world," he was therefore made to have been born on the 25th of December—the festival of light—when the days begin to lengthen again and thus save the world from falling into utter darkness. Marduk was the light as a "life-giving principle," he died, and was in the grave during *three* double-months,[1] but rose again in the spring, on the first of Nisan, when he acquired new life, new strength, new power, and entered into a wedlock with mother earth, his wife, i. e., with Tsarpanitum or Ishtar. Christ, too, died, and was put into the grave, where he was for *three* days, but had to rise again on *Easter*—the festival of Ishtar.[2] By his resurrection he demonstrated that he, like Marduk, had overcome the powers of darkness (= the old dragon, the serpent!) and had entered upon his kingly rulership, and thus became the bêl balâṭi, "the lord of life." Marduk, however, not only rose himself, but *forced* by entering into wedlock with mother earth, this latter *to give up her dead.* Thus also Christ, if he really wanted to show that there began with *his* resurrection also *his kingly rulership* upon earth, *had* to force the earth to give up her dead—therefore it is said[3]:

> "And behold, the veil of the temple was rent in twain from the top to the bottom, and the earth did quake; and the rocks were rent; and the tombs were opened; and many

---

[1] I. e., during the six months of the winter.

[2] Easter and Ishtar are one and the same word. It has come into the English language from the Germans, who worshipped the goddess *Ostara.* This Ostara was brought to the Germans from the Greeks, among whom the goddess Aphrodite, = Astarte, plays the same rôle as does among the Germans the goddess Ostara. This Aphrodite was called by Herodotus (see above) Μύλιττα and thus identified with the Hebrew Ashtoreh, who again is the Semitic-Babylonian Ishtar, and this the Tsarpanitu resp. Innanna or Bau!

[3] Matth. xxvii. 53.

> *bodies of the saints* that had fallen asleep *were raised*, and *coming forth out of the tombs* AFTER HIS RESURRECTION[1] they entered into the holy city and appeared unto many!"

This passage proves, more than anything else, that there was transferred to Christ all that originally belonged to Marduk! Although we hear in these verses of all the circumstances connected with the death of Christ yet it said that "many bodies of the saints were raised, and coming forth out of the tombs *after his resurrection* they entered the holy city! According to Babylonian ideas there never could come forth the dead out of the earth at the death of Marduk. Matthew wanting to record the terrible earthquake in connection with Christ's death—an earthquake so terrible that even the graves were opened—feels that it was impossible to say that the "saints" rose while their life-giver was dead—hence he makes the addition "*after his resurrection.*" With Marduk's resurrection the resurrection of the dead was given, the dead could not rise if Marduk had not risen first—hence Matthew's statement: the dead rose after *his*, i. e., Christ's resurrection! Christ had to rise *first*—if Christ did not rise, then the dead could not rise. Neither could Christ rise alone, the *earth* had to give up her dead! And what a difference there is between this statement of Matthew and the reasoning of St. Paul! According to Paul, Christ did rise, because the dead rise, and the dead rise because nature proves it that there is a resurrection every spring. Matthew's conception of the resurrection of Christ is more in accord with the teachings of the Babylonian religion.

Marduk after his quickening and resurrection enters in solemn *procession* the "holy hill" within the Ubshugina and "determines the fates of mankind." Christ, too, after his being quickened sets out on a journey to the so-called φυλακή, the great "keeping-place." That this latter cannot be the "nether world" as such, but must be =the Ubshugina, the "room of the assembling hand," seems evident enough. Christ as well as Marduk were in the nether world while they were *dead*, while lying in the grave, i. e., during the three

[1] καὶ ἐξελθόντες ἐκ τῶν μνημείων μετὰ τὴν ἔγερσιν αὐτοῦ εἰσῆλθον εἰς τὴν ἁγίαν πόλιν.

double-months of the winter, resp. the *three* days that preceded Christ's quickening. During these days Christ's body was separated from the soul,—the former being in the tomb, the latter continuing to live as an *utukku*, resp. *ekimmu*, i. e.—according to the New Testament *usus loquendi*—as a "spirit." *After* these three days, i. e., *after* the time of Christ's being in the lower world, he goes to the "prison" not only as a "spirit" but as a "spirit reunited to its body," i. e., as a *quickened one*. If this "prison" were the "nether world," we would necessarily have to postulate *two* descents to Hades,—one while he was dead, the other while he was *alive*, quickened. Besides this, if Christ went to the "prison" as a quickened one, and if this latter (the prison) was the nether world, then the question would have to be answered, where was Christ's body, where was his soul during the three days of his death? We see, these difficulties force us to maintain the identity of the "keeping-place" or "prison" with the "room of the assembling hand." Marduk "determines here the fates of mankind," and Christ "heralds" something,—that this heralding or preaching could not have been a "proclamation of the *Gospel*," we saw above; hence the heralding can be only a proclamation of the fates of the "spirits" in prison. Christ appears here like Marduk as one "who determines the fates." If this be true, then we may also venture to decide the exact nature of the Ubshugina, resp. the prison. The Ubshugina is never identified, as far as I know, with the Babylonian Hades. Taking all the places in consideration where we hear something about the Ubshugina, we may say at the present[1] this much: It is a room in the temple of Marduk. This temple of Marduk called Esagila represents as each and every temple does "the world" or "cosmos," hence Ubshugina must represent also a cosmic quantity and as such be situated in the Cosmos. In the Ubshugina the Anunnaki are said to live. The Anunnaki, however, play an important rôle in the "judgment" of the departed souls. Hence the Ubshugina is the "place or room in which the souls of the departed are assembled" and where judgment is passed upon

[1] See also my forthcoming article on jahveh, and cf. Jensen, *Kosmologie*, p. 239 ff.

them. This "judgment" is given by the great gods under the presidency of Marduk, who are therefore likewise assembled in the Ubshugina. While the gods thus "determine" what shall be done with this or that soul, they sit on the Du-azag[1] or "holy hill" which likewise is to be found in the Ubshugina. After the judgment has been passed, the "souls" are dismissed to the nether world proper, where they enjoy, resp. do not enjoy their fates. The Ubshugina, therefore, as well as the "prison," is the *judgment hall* for the departed spirits, and is as such situated likewise in the cosmos, more especially in the earth, and clearly distinct from the nether world.

Christ as well as Marduk, after having overcome the powers of darkness, and thus shown that they have power over life and death, take upon themselves instantly the functions of the *highest judge*, by "determining the fates." But not only this is their only reward: Marduk was made the highest god and called "*En-lil of the gods*," thus practically put at the head of all the other gods, so also Christ,—he was seated

> "on the right hand of God, having gone into heaven; angels and authorities and powers—i. e., the whole heavenly world—being made subject unto him" (1 Peter iii. 21).

Our investigations will have shown us, I hope, the following: The doctrine of the Resurrection was known in Babylonia as early as 3200 B. C., at which time there was celebrated a spring-festival. This spring-festival was a marriage between "the rains of the spring" and "mother earth." In consequence of this marriage the earth became a *mother* and brought forth in due time "the green things of the earth": the vegetation. These "green things of the earth" as well as mother earth and the god of rain were also considered to be "*dead during the winter*,"—Nin-Girsu therefore had a *tomb* or *burial-place, the Gi-gunu*, for his abode during the time of his "death." This was again based upon the common phenomena of nature: during the winter there are *no* rains, no thunders, no lightnings,—hence Nin-Girsu must be dead. In the spring, however, with the first rolling of the thunders,[2] the

[1] See Jensen, *Kosmologie*, p. 234 ff.

[2] Mathew's statement about the earthquake in connection with the death of

people gathered that Nin-Girsu has been quickened again! Very soon there appeared also the first rains of the spring, who fructified the earth. As Nin-Girsu is not only the god of the thunder and lightning, but also that of the rain, this "raining upon the earth" was considered to be a marriage between the "god of the rain" and the "goddess of the earth." The resurrection of nature has thus two causes: the vivification or quickening of the god of rain (and mother earth) and the marriage relation between Nin-Girsu and Ba-ú. No wonder, then, that even at our present times this latter aspect should play such an important rôle at Easter, the festival of the Ishtar, i. e., the goddess of *love*!

At the time when Marduk was introduced into the Babylonian pantheon, these two aspects, i. e., the quickening and the marriage —were retained, only the *names* of the parties concerned were changed: Nin-Girsu, the god of rain, became Marduk, the god of light, and Ba-ú became Tsarpanitum or Ishtar. Besides these two ancient features there was introduced a *third* one. The new life of the nature was not merely considered to be the result of a *quickening* and a *marriage*, but they were made dependent also upon a *preceding fight*. The Canaanites before they could think of mastering the whole of Babylonia had first of all to *fight*, subdue their enemies. Marduk being their god, becomes thus the god who subdues his enemies. And as he subdued them once, so he always has and will continue to subdue them for all eternity. Marduk subdued Babylonia, conquered his enemies who lived there before him. With this subjugation the "new life," the new forms and governments of Babylonia were made possible. For these conquering Canaanites, Babylonia became the "world," κατ' ἐξοχήν, and Marduk their god, κατ' ἐξοχήν. Just as Marduk conquered the enemies of Babylonia, so he also *must* have conquered the old, old enemy of the "world,"—the Tiâmat, or chaos; just as with the subjugation of his Babylonian enemies the new life and development of "Babylonia" were made possible, so also was with his conquering Tiâmat the life and development of the "world." Mar-

Christ *ought to have* occurred at his (Christ's) resurrection! Cf. the remarkable addition "*after* his resurrection"!

duk means according to his name AMAR-UD = "son of the sun," and is, therefore, a god of light, hence if he be the *light*, then his enemy can be only the *darkness*. Marduk's fight becomes thus a fight of the *light* against the *darkness*,—after having overcome the darkness the creation of the world is possible. But Marduk is not a "light" because it *illuminates* but because it *warms*, gives *life*, hence his enemy, the darkness, must be the winter! The fight of Marduk and Tiâmat thus repeats itself yearly: it is the fight of the "*rays of the sun*" in the *spring* against the *cold*! The "rays of the sun" gain in this fight the victory: the cold, the darkness is overcome, a new order of things is now initiated, the earth is forced to give up her dead, new life sprouts, the resurrection takes place!

Again a change of *names* takes place—but *only* of *names*! Marduk becomes *Christ*, Tiâmat = "*the old serpent, the dragon*," and Tsarpanitum or Ishtar = who? According to analogy, Christ also ought to marry—an idea almost obliterated, but still preserved in allusions to the bride of the lamb, the personification of the Church.

Just as Marduk conquered the primeval dragon, Tiâmat, and created the world, so Christ *had* to create the world; just as Marduk rose as the god of light every spring, and married Ishtar or the earth, and fructified and vivified her, by means of which she *begat children* or *produced* new *life*, so did Christ because he too is the light. He *did* rise because he was = Marduk. Marduk is the *author* not only of the first creation but of every *new* creation, so is Christ: only *in* and *through* Christ men do rise. Marduk in consequence of his victory over the dragon was exalted, and received the *name* of *Enlil*, the "*father and god of the gods*," the "*god of heaven and earth*," the *Bêl* or *Lord*, *κατ' ἐξοχήν*, so Christ was taken up into the heavens and enthroned on "the right hand of God," for "God highly exalted him, and gave unto him the *name which is above every name* (!); that in the name of Jesus every knee should bow, of things in heaven and things on earth, and things under the earth, and that every tongue should confess that Jesus Christ is the *Lord*![1]

Our Easter-festival is the old, old spring-festival, celebrating the resurrection of nature, made possible by the victory of the spring over the winter. Nature does indeed rise, man is a part of nature, Christ is man, therefore Christ did rise! And the risen Christ is the Bêl, the *Lord*!

HUGO RADAU.

CHICAGO.

---

[1] Phil. ii. 9 ff.

CHRISTIANITY AS THE PLEROMA.

THE HISTORICAL SIGNIFICANCE OF CHRISTIANITY.

HISTORIANS divide the development of mankind into two periods, which are separated by the appearance of Christ, and this method of chronology, counting the years backward and forward from Christ, as A. D. (*anno domini*) or B. C. (before Christ), is not limited to Church history, but is also universally used in profane history. No doubt it was introduced in Christian countries and at a time when Christianity was commonly accepted as the only universal religion. The division has once only been objected to and replaced by a new calendar—viz., during the time of the French revolution; but the old conservative powers overruled this innovation, and at present even the non-Christian countries have accepted the Christian chronology, not so much in recognition of Christianity as for the reason that they prefer to use a universal standard of reckoning events.

And is not, after all, this division justified? Does not the origin of Christianity with its universalistic tendencies, its ethical ideals, and its rapid spread over the historical nations of the old world, establish a new period in the history of mankind? Certainly we have to deal with a phenomenon that may be paralleled in other countries, but which on the soil of the Mediterranean civilisation was unprecedented. It is true that Buddhism in India is an historical phenomenon which in many respects furnishes significant analogies in the East to the development of Christianity in the West, but this parallelism only proves that the development of Christianity is not an accident, but took place according to a law of nature, nature to be understood in the most general sense,—a law of the psychological development of mankind, a law that would find its application also in other worlds where different conditions may prevail.

No doubt wherever sentiency appears on any planet, animal life will in the progress of its evolution develop rationality, and the hearts of rational beings will be filled with cosmic emotions, taking shape in a belief in supernatural beings, that finally will result in monotheism. At the same time all creatures pine under the incessant sufferings of life; they will tremble at death; they will yearn for life immortal; and finding the body decay, and noticing that in sleep they appear to move about with an etherial body woven of the stuff that dreams are made on, they believe in a soul and they will long for an immortality of the soul. There is no doubt that human life on earth is only one instance of all sentient life in the universe, and though the conditions on other planets may be widely different, we may be sure that the inhabitants of other worlds will have the same geometry, the same arithmetic, (though it may not be based on the decimal system which is purely accidental, depending on the numbers of our fingers), the same moral ideals, the same social development, and also similar religions. Their whole progress, including their beliefs and dogmas and religious institutions, will be on the same line with ours.

Now in the course of the religious development there will appear after the long night of ignorance and wild struggles, the promising dawn of a glorious day of a general goodwill on earth. The religious longings and hopes, the prophetic promises, the moral ideals, first faintly foreshadowed in dark oracular utterance, will find their fulfilment. The world in former days was swayed by brute force, and cunning, egotism, greed, and ill will seemed to be the only factors that promised success. But in the time of fulfilment a religion appears that upsets the old order of things and proclaims the new ideal of benevolence, charity, and love.

Christ was hailed by the Apostle St. Paul as this fulfilment of the times (*πλήρωμα τοῦ χρόνου*, Gal. iv. 4; or *πλήρωμα τῶν καιρῶν*, Eph. i. 10) for in Christ was revealed the fulness of the godhead bodily (*πλήρωμα τῆς θεότητος*, Col. ii. 9).

The religion of fulfilment in India was Buddhism, in Palestine Christianity. And Christianity became the religion of the West; first of western Asia, then of northern Africa, then it spread over the whole Roman empire, whence it was carried to northern Europe and to all the European nations. Thus to them the appearance of Christianity is the pleroma of the times, the fulfilment of their religious ideals, the turning point of their history.

Christianity, not unlike Buddhism, its noble precursor and sister-religion of the East, is characterised by a spirit of universality. It ushers in a period of international ideals, international ethics, international religious truth, the main doctrine of which is expressed in the sentence, "Have we not all one Father?" And truly, are we not all brothers? Have we not all common duties, and should we not love one another, help one another, live for one another?

The dogmatic side of Christianity is of great importance, but the universality of its ethical ideals is more significant.

While we recognise that Christianity is something new in the history of the Mediterranean nations, we cannot be blind to the fact that the elements from which it is compounded are old. The contents of Christianity, its several dogmas, the forms of its institutions, and even its ideals, are old. They are new only in so far as they receive a new setting, being systematised and universalised. There is not one idea in Christianity which cannot be traced back to pre-Christian ages, or which has not been recorded here or there, or which has not been uttered by religious prophets and poets and philosophers of Jewish, Greek, Egyptian, Babylonian or other nationality. Christianity in fact is like the concentration of many scattered rays in one focus. The light of the past is gathered to one and the same point and shines now in undivided brightness. Thus Christianity, even if considered from a secular standpoint, is truly the pleroma of the religious history of the pre-Christian world. It necessarily became in the very form which it assumed, the fulfilment of the historical development of pre-Christian thought and, naturally enough, it appeared to the generations that lived in the third and fourth centuries as absolute truth, as the fulness of God's revelation, and the solution of the deepest problems of life.

THREE ESSENTIAL DOCTRINES OF CHRISTIANITY.

The substance of the doctrines of Christianity was upon the whole fore-determined by historical conditions, but the way in which they were systematised depended mainly upon the center round which these ideas had crystallised, and this center was the personality of Jesus of Nazareth. A new religion was needed, and Christianity grew and spread over the whole western world; but Christianity was not the only applicant to fill the vacant place. Christianity had its rivals. History witnessed a short but bitter contest between several competitors, and it would not have been impossible that some other figure than Jesus had taken the central place in the new religion that was then in the process of formation. At one time the most powerful rival of Christ was Apollonius of Tyana, a noble personality, of whom legend and tradition told similar stories as of Jesus of Nazareth. He healed the sick; he comforted the poor; he raised the dead; he travelled from country to country preaching the belief in one god,—the universal god of all mankind, a god who was not in need of sacrifices; and Apollonius set an example to the world by his unassuming modesty, his renunciation and the purity of his life. At another time, Mithraism came dangerously near to being accepted as the state religion of the Roman empire. The Mithraists worshipped Mithra, the son of God, of Ahura Mazda, the Lord Omniscient, as the virgin-born, divine Saviour, as the Word, as righteousness incarnate, as the mediator between God and man, and as the king of the kingdom to come, who on the day of the resurrection will judge the quick and the dead. There were many other rival religions of a similar nature, and we may be sure that if a faith other than Christianity had gained supremacy, the religion of the world would in its main contents have become the same as Christianity. Even if the reformed paganism of Julian the Apostate had gained the day, the theology of the new religion would finally have become very similar to the theology of the Christian Church. Christians of later generations were not reluctant in recognising the "Christian spirit" of Seneca, of Epictetus, of Marcus Antoninus, and even of Julian the Apostate, —so that Seneca could be believed to be a personal friend and disciple of Paul, that Epictetus and Marcus Antonius were said to be unconsciously influenced by Christianity, and that Julian the Apostate in his antagonism to the Church could be said to have adopted many good qualities from Christianity. Whatever the new religion that was needed might have been, one thing is sure, that it would have developed the doctrines of the trinity, of the god-man and god-incarnation, of the fatherhood of God and the sonship of man, of original sin, of the remission of sin by vicarious atonement, of the immortality of the soul, of the resurrection of the dead, of a day of judgment, of divine bliss in Heaven, of a punishment of the unamenable in Hell, and of the establishment of the kingdom of God on earth. All these notions were in the air and would have come out one way or another. They might have become somewhat different in detail in Mithraism, in a reformed classical religion, such as Julian tried to establish, or in the philosophical faith of Apollonius of Tyana, or in any Neoplatonic or Gnostic system, or in a reformed Egyptian religion in which Hermes-Trismegistos would have taken the place of Christ, but the general result would have been the same.

We will not investigate here why the belief in Jesus of Nazareth gained the day, nor will we underrate the importance of Jesus after he had become the centre of the new religion. We will only indicate that the belief in Jesus as given in the Gospel accounts and the Epistles of St. Paul offered views that were more human and humane, more practical, more ethical, more appealing to the hearts of the great multitudes in the Roman empire than those of other religions which competed with Christianity, and we do not hesitate to say that in the struggle for existence Christianity necessarily remained victorious; it was the strongest, the best adapted to conditions, the fittest for survival.

If Mithraism had become universally accepted, our theologians of to-day would study the Zendavesta and the Gathas; if Buddhism had reached the West, they would study the Pali books; if Apollonius had been worshipped as the saviour of mankind, they would look up to Plato and Socrates as their prophets, but since the western nations are Christians, their theologians accept the Jewish Canon and the New Testament Scriptures as the highest authorities of God's revelation.

Leaving aside those features of Christianity which characterise it as different from its rivals, especially the personality of Jesus and the central position of Hebrew traditions, we will now limit our discussion to the most important general tenets that from the beginning, down to the modern days have been considered as characteristically Christian.

Christianity is the religion which recognises in Jesus, the Christ; meaning thereby that Jesus is God incarnate, that as such he is the mediator between God and man, that he is the King in the Kingdom of Heaven that is to come, the realisation of all ideals, that he is in one person, the priest and the sacrificial lamb offered for the forgiveness of sins, and finally that Jesus, having died on the cross, rose from the dead, and, having assumed a transfigured body which is no more subject to decay, is sitting now on the right hand of God, whence he will come at the end of the world to judge the living and the dead. Such is Christianity as accepted by all sects, with the exceptions perhaps of the Unitarians and similar Churches of later-born generations, and no one who does not accept these ideas will be accepted as an orthodox Christian.

Now when we consider one Christian doctrine after another, we shall find that none of them are absolutely new, and all of them were held, not by the Jews, but by the Gentiles as religious truths of great importance. It is true that among a few educated people of Greece and Rome the idea of vicarious atonement lost its hold; that religious thinkers, such as Plato and Apollonius of Tyana, repudiated sacrifices as not desired by the gods. Nevertheless, the large masses of mankind clung to them, which is best seen from the fact that the last pagan emperor, Julian Apostate, would not drop them from his worship of the gods. The practice of sacrifices had become offensive to the better educated class of people but the idea was not yet overcome. The belief in the efficiency of blood atonement still lingered with the great masses, and even in Christian times we meet occasionally with relics of ancient superstitions, of burying people alive under foundation stones and other human sacrifices.

When we systematise the main Christian dogmas, we will find them to be:

1. A belief in an immortality of the soul, which was originally a hope of a resurrection of the body.

2. The consciousness of sin, and a yearning for its expiation, finding peace in the assurance of forgiveness through the bloody sacrifice of Jesus Christ on the Cross, based upon the conception of vicarious atonement; and

3. The idea of God-incarnation, viz., that Jesus Christ is at once true God and real man, that in him, the sinless man, the innocent sufferer, the ideal of human perfection, dwelleth all the fulness of the God-head bodily.

The three notions of immortality, vicarious atonement, and god-incarnation were deeply rooted in the minds of the people by a development of many thousands of years, for these ideas had been the very essence of pre-Christian beliefs, and unless they were satisfied, a religion would not have been deemed a pleroma, a fulfilment and realisation of the religious longing of the heart.

These three points are the essentials of all religion according to the notions of the people who lived shortly before and shortly after the beginning of the Christian era. At that time men longed for salvation from evil and death; they were anxious to remove the curse of sin, not by undergoing punishment themselves but by making a sacrifice that would appease the wrath of God or the gods, in a word, by vicarious atonement; and as they felt the need of supernatural assistance, they hoped for some god that would appear on earth and be a mediator between God and mankind. Hence the legends of the heroes, the saviours, the sons of Zeus or of other gods, Æsculapius, Theseus, Jason, Perseus, etc., Hor the god-child and avenger, Shamash, the sun-god and his labors, humanised in the Hebrew Sampson and the Greek Heracles, the ten incarnations of Krishna, Hiawatha among the North American Indians, etc., etc.

Historians have again and again proved that Christianity is the product of either the Egyptian religion, or of the Babylonian religion, or of the Persian religion, or of some other Oriental faith, Brahmanism, Buddhism, etc.; and there is a truth in every one of these attempts. No one of these theories, however, is in itself alone sufficient and satisfactory, no one of them is complete. The truth is that all these religions contain the general elements from which Christianity has developed and the essential ideas can be traced in all religions with the exception perhaps of Judaism.

Judaism is a religion that stands unique among the religions of the old world. All religions have a tendency towards universalism. There is no god but its devotees declare him to be the creator and the ruler of the universe, the highest of the most powerful among the gods, and in the final course of religious development, other gods are identified with him so as to leave him the only one, the all-sustaining, all-pervading deity of the world. But here the Jews differed from the pagans: when their Yahveh had become the universal god, they regarded other gods as enemies of their own deity. It is true that every nation regards itself as the chosen people, so did the Egyptians, so the Greek, so the Babylonians, and Assyrians, but by and by this narrowness widens into a respect for others, resulting in cosmopolitanism. Among the jews, however, the idea that they are the chosen people of God became a fundamental doctrine that would not yield. Yahveh though universalised into the creator and the ruler of the entire world remained the particular god of the Jews; and in Ezra we are assured that he created the whole world solely for the benefit of the Jews.[1]

A most characteristic feature of Judaism is its neglect of a belief in the immortality of the soul. The immortality of the soul is not specially denied but all vestiges of an official recognition of it

[1] See, for instance, 2 Esdras vi. 55. "All this have I spoken before thee, O Lord, because thou madest the world for our sakes"; and further down, vii. 10–11, "Even so is Israel's portion. Because for their sakes I made the world."

are carefully removed from the canonical scriptures of the Old Testament.[1] Judaism originated as a protest against the religion of the Gentiles. The Jews established a rigorous monotheism, which as a matter of principle rejected the idea of god-incarnation that filled all the religious stories and mythologies of the pagan world.[2] It rejected idolatry also as based upon a belief in god-incarnation, god being represented in a statue, the idol, to which as a symbol of his god the worshipper addressed himself. It rejected myth and mythology, and with it also the legends of the dying and resurrected god, the Thamuz of Babylonia, the Osiris of the Egyptians, the Adonis of the Greeek. No doubt the objections of the Jewish reformers were justified from their standpoint, for these legends were full of superstitious notions and led to practices that were little recommendable, but we cannot deny that the underlying ideas of paganism, the hope for an immortality of the soul and for a resurrection of the dead is fundamentally and essentially the same as in Christianity. The main difference between paganism and Christianity lies not in the single elements and doctrines, but in the setting of them. In place of many contradictory legends filled with erratic ideas and irrational notions, there is one simple story of a reformer who died a martyr's death on the cross. We have here the substitution of a realistic human life for the rambling romances of mythology, yet the general background remains the same with the sole exception that polytheism yields to monotheism; otherwise the events in the life of Jesus are interpreted in the light of the current religious traditions of the Gentiles—not of one nation, but of all.

Leaving out here a discussion of the doctrine of immortality we shall devote our special attention to the doctrines of the God-man as the Saviour and the vicarious atonement by blood.

---

[1] For details see the authors article "The Babylonian and Hebrew Views of Man's Fate After Death," in *The Open Court*, Vol. XV., pp. 346–366.

[2] Mohammed, endorsing the strict monotheism of the Jews, declares, not without an unconcealed criticism of the Christian faith, "Allah is neither begotten nor a begetter." To him, as to any rigorous monotheist, the very idea that God can have a son is a symptom of paganism, of superstition, of heresy, and the utterance of it sounds like blasphemy.

THE GOD-MAN AS SAVIOUR.

The classical book which sums up the matured Christian idea of God-incarnation is *Cur Deus Homo*, by Anselm of Canterbury, a treatise which is recognised as an authority by all Christian Churches.[1]

It has always been praised as a masterpiece of clearness and logic, and we cannot help but admire the ability with which the good Bishop argues in favor of his belief. But all his arguments presuppose the old pagan notions of resurrection, vicarious atonement by blood and God-incarnation, and anyone who does not accept these three ideas as fundamental truths will naturally remain unaffected by Anselm's demonstrations.

Anselm's faith is ultimately derived not from the Gospels but by *a priori* reasoning from the three fundamental ideas above mentioned, and this greatest among great ecclesiastics, this leader in the realm of Christian thought and philosophy, expresses himself plainly in the preface. He declares of his treatise that it meets the objection of infidels as well as replies to the question of believers, saying:

> "Leaving Christ out of view (as if nothing had ever been known of him), it proves, by absolute reasons, the impossibility that any man should be saved without him," and "likewise, as if nothing were known of Christ, it is moreover shown by plain reasoning and fact that human nature was ordained for this purpose, viz., that every man should enjoy a happy immortality, both in body and in soul; and that it was necessary that this design for which man was made should be fulfilled; but that it could not be fulfilled unless God became man, and unless all things were to take place which we hold with regard to Christ."

Anselm here lays the philosophical foundations of Christianity, which are independent of the Gospel, but will help to explain them and set the historical facts related therein into a proper light. Thus as stated in the quotation, he leaves Christ (that is to say, the Gos-

[1] A new edition of Anselm's main works containing the "Proslogium" and the "Monologium," both translated for the first time by Mr. Sidney Norton Deane, and "Cur Deus Homo," translated by james Gardiner Vose, has just been published by The Open Court Publishing Co.

pel narrative of Jesus) out of view, and relies upon "absolute reason," presupposing all the time the general notions of his time and the pre-Christian ages.

Man is a sinner, and so an atonement must be made for sin which of course must be in proportion to man's guilt. Sin is disobedience to God and is as such "the most heinous offence which not even God, on account of His justice, can forego." Divine justice for the sake of preserving its own dignity demands a punishment which in consideration of the heinousness of the offence can only be death. The sinner is doomed to eternal torments, and humanly considered, there is no way of escape. Man can be helped only by some supernatural power; and God in his infinite compassion has devised a means to help man. Humanity is one great family, one great organic unity, and as by one's man's guilt all become guilty, so by one man's virtue all may become ransomed. This idea, which is an application of the law of heredity to the domain of moral responsibility, furnishes a basis to the juridical theories of all primitive societies, and accepting it as a self-evident truth, Anselm declares that mankind can be saved only if God himself becomes man and pays the debt of mankind. The God-man is at once real God and real man. If he were not man, his sacrifice would avail nothing. If he were not God, he could not have accomplished the task. In this way, Anselm argues, God remains consistent. He remains all-just and all-good. Man's guilt is paid with blood, and the sinner may be ransomed from the power of evil.[1]

Man's nature is not intrinsically corrupt. He was created potentially good and potentially immortal. He is not necessarily subject to death (p. 241), the fall of man and his sin made him subject to death, but God will complete the work which he has begun (p. 242–244), but to accomplish his aim he must become a man of Adam's race (p. 247).[2]

Anselm's argument, that the second person of the trinity, God

---

[1] Page 232.

[2] We omit all details that are mere side issues, e. g., that God should be born of a virgin, and that man was created to make up for the fallen angels.

the Son, should take upon himself the task of incarnation, moves in a circle and may be considered as naïve, but here again we are confronted with his *a priori* method of reasoning, based upon the assumption that the second person of the trinity is God the Son. "If one of the other persons be incarnated," Anselm argues, "there will be two sons in the Trinity, viz., the Son of God, who is the Son before the incarnation, and he also who, by the incarnation, will be the son of the virgin." He comes to the conclusion that "it is more fitting for the son to be incarnated than the other persons" (p. 251). God becomes in Christ a real man, who, though made of a sensual substance, yet remains free from sin. If angels do not sin, they are without merit, but if a real man is free from sin, he deserves praise for his holiness. Thus God in order to deserve the glory of his victory over the devil, would have to become a real man with all the shortcomings and weaknesses of humanity.

The death of the God-man outweighs the number and the greatness of the sins of mankind (Chapter XIV., p. 261 ff.), and thus the ransom has been paid by the sacrificial death of Christ on the cross. It is a complete fulfilment of all the yearnings of pre-Christian religions, and Boso, the interlocutor of Anselm, the fictitious person who puts questions and raises objections, having listened to the arguments of the Bishop concerning the work of salvation accomplished by God the Son, exclaims:

> "The universe can hear of nothing more reasonable, more sweet, more desirable. And I receive such confidence from this that I cannot describe the joy with which my heart exults. For it seems to me that God can reject none who come to him in his [i. e., Christ's] name."

Such, in brief, is the Christian argument as summed up at the time of its highest development by a representative member of the clergy. It is the high flight of a prophetic soul, but as we analyse its sentiments, we find the same views prevalent in Egypt, Babylonia, and Greece. Osiris was dear to the Egyptian, because he had lived among them as a man, and he had passed through the same ordeal of death through which every mortal must go. His soul went down to the land of shades in the far West, and with the help of the arts of Anubis he was resurrected and attained to immortality. Every Egyptian based in his dying-hour his hopes on the god. He identified his own fate after death with the fate of Osiris. Osiris died with him and he with Osiris. With Osiris he travelled to the Western abode; the divinity of Osiris protected him on the long and dreary journey. His body was mummified like the body of Osiris; and finally he regained life and vitality in the same way as did Osiris. Osiris had opened the way, and his faithful devotees can now follow him through the valley of death to a glorious resurrection, in which they shall be endowed with a new and shining body, and attain a state of glory or saintedness. Osiris was to the Egyptians, as Christ is to the Christians, according to St. Paul, the first fruits of resurrection.[1]

The idea of a god that lived as a man among men on earth, that died, and, having passed through the shadow of death, was resurrected, is not limited to Egypt. In its main outlines the same myth is repeated among almost all the nations of the world. Yea, the same nation tells the same story in different forms, and the same hero reappears under many different names. In Babylonia, we know of Thammuz, who is mentioned by Ezekiel (viii. 14)[2] as the god for whom the women were weeping on the festival of lamentation, and we know that his return to life was celebrated with a great rejoicing,—a Babylonian Easter.

The hope of the Babylonians for salvation was further expressed in the tale of Ishtar's descent to and her return from Hades. Bel Marduk also conquered the gates of hell and set free the prisoners so as to allow the dead to come out of the grave and rise to new life.[3]

In Asia Minor, Attis[4] took the place of the Babylonian Tham-

---

[1] The only complete source of the story of Osiris is found in Plutarch's *De Iside et Osiri*, but there are innumerable allusions to the myth in the Egyptian monuments and papyri to indicate that Plutarch's account is upon the whole correct.

[2] See also Baruch vi. 30. Ammianus (Mark xxii. 9) mentions Thammuz worship in Antioch, Theocritus (III. 28) in Egypt, Pausanies (IX. 41) in Cyprus. Cp. Strabo, XVI. 755, and Lucian, *De dea Syr.* 6.

[3] See Dr. Hugo Radau's article "Bel, the Christ of Ancient Times," in the present number of *The Monist*, pp. 113 ff.

[4] Aronobius, *adv. gentes* V. 4; Diodorus, III. 158; Servius, *ad Æn.* IX. 116,

muz, and in Greece he was called Adonis, a Hellenised form of the Semitic word אדון (Adon), i. e., "Lord."

Orpheus, Dionysus, Jason, Hercules, Odysseus, and many other gods, demigods, and heroes are one and the same figure, are god-incarnations of the same type.

The underlying idea is the spiritualisation of natural events due to a change of winter and summer. The hero is the sun or vegetation, or as is the case with Osiris, the Nile.

The form of the myth is different in different countries, but everywhere we can trace the same underlying idea of the god that dies and is resurrected.

Some myths travel, and if they are twice told in two different versions, we scarcely recognise their common origin. Shamash, the Babylonian sun-god, the Hebrew Sampson and the Greek Heracles, is also Odysseus who roams over the whole earth, descends to Hades, and comes again to the world of the living.

The birthday of the sun-god is celebrated at the winter solstice, while its death is placed at the summer solstice on the day of St. John the Baptist.

In some religions, the growing god and the waning god are two different persons. Sometimes they are represented as male and female. Sometimes the god is said to lose his power by having his hair cut off (Sampson), the hair representing the rays of the sun; sometimes he is supposed to be torn to pieces (Dionysos Zagreus); and sometimes the head is cut off (Orpheus).

Reminiscences of these religions are still preserved in Christianity, and the selection of Christian festivals has been made with special consideration of such pagan traditions. John the Baptist's festival was celebrated on the summer solstice, because it is the day of the sun's decrease, and Christ's birthday was fixed at the winter solstice, the day of the sun's increase.[1]

Thus the origin of Christianity is ultimately based upon the natural conditions of our planet. It originates with man's observ-

---

Pausanias, VII. 17. 5. Cf. also Lucian, *De dea Syr.*, 51; Eusebius, *præp. Evang.* VI. 279.

[1] John iii. 30: "He must increase, but I must decrease."

ance of the laws of nature, of decay and growth, of inundation and drought, of winter and summer, of the course of the sun, its decline, its death and regeneration, and thus the constant reappearance of life in nature suggests to man the immortality of his own being.

The development of all these doctrines upon the basis of the Gospel narrative of the life of Jesus, and their systematisation into a system of theology was the task of the fourth and fifth centuries of the Christian era. The material of religious notions was given by pagan traditions, but these pagan views were purified in the furnace of Jewish monotheism. At the same time they were filled with ethical contents, for the ethical ideas of a general good-will or love and self-sacrifice had also spread over the Roman empire and were preached by many philosophers and moralists.

Pagan philosophers, such as Seneca, speak of Hercules and of other hero saviours in the same tone as Christians did of Christ. We read:

> "Hercules never conquered for himself. He wandered over the earth not as a conqueror, but as a guardian angel. What indeed should the enemy of the bad, the protector of the good, the restorer of peace, conquer for himself on sea or on land?"—*De Ben.*, I., 13.

And the ethics of Greek and Roman philoshers do no not differ much from the injunction "Love your enemies."[1] Seneca taught:

> "One should show the way to those that are erring, and with him that is ahungered one should divide one's bread."—*Ep.*, 95, 51.

And again he teaches to be:

> "Towards friend pleasant, toward enemies mild and yielding." *De vit. beat.*, 20, 5.

Seneca's idea of moral perfection is expressed in his consideration of the death of Hercules on Mount Oeta. Only he can lift up mankind who has conquered the terror of death, and the good man must remain good even if goodness is rewarded with suffering.

---

[1] See the author's article "On Greek Religion and Mythology," especially the chapters "The Fatherhood of Zeus" and "The Ethics of Returning Good for Evil," in *The Open Court*, 1901, January, Vol. XV., pp. 1-16.

This idea is expressed in many of his letters,[1] from which we quote the following sentences:

"If the good one perceives that true faithfulness is persecuted with the penalties of faithlessness, he will not descend from his height but will rise above the punishment, and say 'I have attained what I wanted, what I sought. I do not regret and never will regret.' By no misfortune shall fate compel me to express myself thus, 'What did I do for my own benefit? Of what use is now my good will?' Indeed this good will is still useful at the martyr's stake. It is useful even in the heat of the flame. When the fire touches the several limbs and gradually surrounds the living body, the heart which is filled with a good conscience may indeed melt, but such a fire by which genuine faith is illumined, will be pleasing to a man." (*De ben*, IV., 21–26.)

In one of his letters Seneca makes the ideal man say:

"I am burning but I remain unconquered. Why should that not be a desirable fate? Desirable it is, not that the fire burns, but that it does not conquer. Nothing is more glorious, nothing more beautiful than virtue; and good and desirable is everything which is achieved at virtue's request."

The good man considers his conscience alone; he is not afraid of contumely. Virtue rewarded is not yet put to the test, but virtue in infamy (*virtus cum infamia*) is sublime. Seneca says:

"I shall pursue with greatest equanimity an honest policy in the midst of infamy.. No one seems to show a higher respect for virtue than he who loses the repute of being a good man without losing his conscience."[2] (*Ep.*, XXXI., 20.)

This is the same idea which Plato expresses in his description of the "perfectly just man" who remains good even though his eyes were burned out and he suffer the cruel death of impalement —crucifixion on the pointed pole.

In reading pagan sentences, we are apt to consider the events narrated in their mythology as fables, and we are apt to pity these heathens for taking comfort in illusions, but we forget that the myths of antiquity were as real, as genuine, and as true to the pagan as the narrative of Christ is to the Christian. We cannot doubt

---

[1] Michael Baumgarten, L. A., *Seneca und das Christenthum*, p. 82.

[2] See also *Ep.*, XII., 1, and CXIII., 32, and CXV., 6. Seneca praises the constancy of those who act according to this principle, Marcus Cato "*quo nemo altior*" (*Ep.*, XCV., 70, *de tranq.*, VII., 3. and XIV., 1) the philosopher Diogenes (*de ira*, III., 38, 1), Aristides, (*Ad Helv.*, XIII., 7. *De const.*, I., 3. *Ep.*, XIV., 13, *Ad Helv.*, XIII., 7. *De const.*, XIV., 3).

that the Egyptian derived a genuine comfort from his belief in Osiris. We cannot doubt that the Babylonian when putting his trust in Bel Marduk was perfectly serious, and the need of a new religion was only felt when in the general progress of civilisation, the several myths ceased to be believed. Since the time of Alexander the Great, the different nations led no longer isolated existences. They became acquainted each one with the other, they broadened; they lost thereby the implicit faith in their own traditions without at the same time gaining a higher view. The thinkers of the several local centers of the world compared the several religions and began to search after the truth that would hold good universally. They searched for a religion that would be the religion of all mankind. A fermentation spread over the religious world, resulting in the formation of religious societies seeking the light, searching for truth. Hence the rise of Gnosticism which is pre-Christian, and its finding utterance in many places and among men of different nationalities; and it is not to be wondered that the several religious movements, of the Therapeutæ in Egypt, of the Essenes and Sabians in Palestine, of the Mandæans in Syria, of the Ophites and other Gnostics, etc., etc., were quite similar, in spirit, in their institutions and doctrines.

The same spirit which animated Christianity had spread over the Roman empire shortly before the time of Christ. The formation of the Roman empire as a universal state under one government with one ruler paved the way for the one universal church. The idea of Cæsar as the representative of order and law, his deification as a living god, drove home to the people the idea of a godman to whom is given all power on earth as it is in heaven. It seemed so natural to a Roman subject that there should be a vicar of god, resident in the capital of the world; and the idea was retained even among the Protestant nations where the king rules "by the grace of God." It is interesting to see how secular history shaped the mould from which the Church institutions were cast; but it is more noteworthy that the spirit of the new religion could be felt long before it assumed its definite shape, and thus we learn to understand why, for instance, the philosopher Seneca, who lived and wrote before Christianity was heard of in Rome, and who died under Nero and was thus a contemporary of St. Paul,[1] could even in ancient times be regarded as a Christian author and the idea spread among the Christians that he must have derived his philosophy from Christian sources. The belief was current in the fourth century of the Christian era, that Seneca had exchanged letters with St. Paul. At any rate St. Augustine and St. Jerome make allusions to it, and a scribler of the Middle Ages made an attempt to construct such letters and palm them off on the world as genuine; but the imposition was too bold and they are regarded as unequivocally apocryphal.

Christian historians and philologists find traces of Christianity not only in Seneca,[2] Tacitus,[3] and Epictetus, but also in pre-Christian authors,[4] thus establishing the doctrine of God's educational plan, according to which mankind is being prepared for the advent of Christ not only by the Hebrew prophets but also by pagan sages.

Christianity was born among the Nazarenes, a sect which must have been closely allied to, if not identical with, the Essenes, and it passed at first as one Gnostic sect among the others; but the life history of Jesus, so impressed the people and appealed so powerfully to the great masses of the population, who were among all most eager for religious comfort and ready to accept a Gospel of the poor, that the new faith became popular at once and quickly overshadowed all other Gnostic sects.

The history of dogma proves how much theology dominated the Gospels, and not *vice versa*, the Gospels, theology. Gospels

---

[1] The persecution of Christians under Nero seems to have been a persecution of Oriental religions which Tacitus wrongly identified with Christianity. It seems pretty sure that the name Christian was not coined before the end of the first century, and it took the Romans some time to distinguish Christians from Jews and other Orientals. See Dr. R. A. Lopsius *Ueber den Ursprung und den ältesten Gebrauch des Chrislennamens*, a memorial published by the theological faculty Jena in bonor of Dr. Carl August Hase, 1873.

[2] Michael Baumgarten, *Seneca und das Christenthum*. Johannes Kreyher, *L. Annæus Seneca u. s. Bez. z. Urchristenthum*. Amédée Fleury, *St. Paul et. Sénèque*.

[3] Bötticher, *Das Christliche in Tacitus*.

[4] R. Schneider, *Christliche Anklänge aus den gr. und Lat. Klassikern*.

were accepted or rejected according to their theology; they were worked over and changed, omissions were made and additions inserted until they suited the demand and became acceptable. Yet even in their final shape, they are far from justifying the theology of the several self-styled orthodox Churches.

THE GOSPELS HISTORICAL.

The Gospels are in their bulk genuine. The nucleus of the narrative embodies a tradition which dates back to the generation of Christ and we may assume that the original text was written in Aramæic not later than the latter half of the first century. This theory is proved by such statements of the Gospel as would not have been received into the text by Gentile Christians. Jesus says for instance that his second coming shall take place before the present generation shall pass away[1] and he declares in unmistakeable words, "There are some standing here," meaning among the audience of the people whom he addressed, "who shall not taste of death till they see the son of man coming in his kingdom."[2]

This prophecy of the second advent of Christ which, it was most vigorously insisted upon, should take place during the time of the generation then living, was a most essential doctrine of primitive Christianity. The Apostle St. Paul is as unequivocal as Jesus in his statement that even he and his converts, or at least some of them, will not "sleep," but "be alive and remain" to be "caught up together with them [the resurrected dead], in the clouds to meet the Lord in the air."[3] The most critical doubter will concede that these passages must have been written when people still believed that the prophecy could be fulfilled.

Theologians have tried to restore the original Gospel, which is commonly called by German scholars *Ur-Markus*,[4] because the

---

[1] Matt. xxiv. 34; Mark xiii. 30; Luke xxi. 32.

[2] Matt. xvi. 27–28. The passage refers to the second advent of Christ and admits of no other interpretation.

[3] 1 Thess. iv. 15–18, and 1 Cor. xv. 51.

[4] The method of reconstruction is well explained in Rev. Edwin A. Abbot's article on the Gospels in the *Encyclopædia Britannica*, Vol. X., esp. p. 793.

Gospel according to Mark contains most of that primitive narrative, and this original Mark is undoubtedly based upon facts, although we will have to grant that the historical Jesus is somewhat different from the Christ such as he is commonly represented to be.

The historical Jesus was a Jew to the backbone, and we have the statement from his own mouth that he believes in the absolute divinity of the law. He says, Matt. v. 18:

"Verily, I say unto you, till heaven and earth pass, one jot or one title shall in no wise pass from the law."

This passage stands in flat contradiction to the declaration of St. Paul, that the law has been fulfilled and is therefore no longer binding, that circumcision is a means of education only in the religious development of mankind and must be considered as abolished because fulfilled in Christ. Thus Christ's word was a puzzle to the Gentile Christians who looked upon the Jewish law as only of temporary and local significance, and so a copyist added to Christ's words the clause "till all be fulfilled," a clause that is missing in the best manuscripts and, moreover, is grammatically out of place because Jesus says expressly, "Till heaven and earth pass away," which is quite different from the other "till all be fulfilled."

The same spirit of a narrow Judaistic spirit crops out in other passages, and we may look upon these traits which Gentile Christians would not have superadded to the original text of the Gospel as most primitive and historically true. Jesus declares most unequivocally:

"I am not sent but unto the lost sheep of the house of Israel." Matthew xv. 24.

And when sending out his disciples, he expressly warns them not to go to the Gentiles, saying:

"Go not into the way of the Gentiles, and into any city of the Samaritans enter ye not.

"But go rather to the lost sheep of the house of Israel."

Jesus calls the Israelites "children" and the Gentiles "dogs," and heals a Canaanite woman's daughter, only making an exception for once from his rules, on account of her persistence and strong faith.

The passages Matt. xxviii. 19–20, and Mark xvi. 15, in which Jesus proclaims the universality of Christianity, were spoken not by Jesus in his lifetime but after the resurrection, and are even by the most orthodox critics conceded to be very late additions.

There is, further, not a word in the Gospels which teaches the doctrine of Christ's sacrificial death and vicarious atonement. This conception of the crucifixion is entirely due to St. Paul's interpretation.

Moreover, the doctrine of the trinity was so universal that the Christians accepted it without much argument; nor did they find any special and unequivocal statement of it in the Scriptures; but it would not be wrong to say that it is presupposed in the New Testament. The idea that God must be trinitarian was common among all the nations of the East, nay, of the world. In every Egyptian temple God was worshipped in a trinitarian form. Even the local divinities in the valley of the Nile appeared as triple personalities or as families of three, e. g., Osiris, Isis, Hor; and the same is true of Babylonia where every religious system adopts the trinitarian theory, e. g., Ea, Anu, and Bel; nay, even in India and in China the same tendency prevails. The Brahmans worship Brahma, Vishnu, and Shiva; and the Buddhists the three gems, the Buddha, the Dharma, and the Sangha. Taoist temples form no exception; they erect altars to the three Holy Ones. In fact, the trinitarian idea of the Godhead is almost universal, and we can understand, therefore, how the trinitarian dogma was accepted by the Christians even without the special endorsement of Scriptural authority, almost as a self-evident truth.

The New Testament contains no theory of the soul, nor any specified doctrine of immortality. But it is noteworthy that immortality is conceived as a resurrection of the body, and even the apostolic confession of faith emphasises this materialistic belief in the resurrection of the flesh. The custom of burial has been adopted in preference to the method of burning the dead, solely because the idea prevailed that the very body of the deceased will rise on the day of judgment from the grave and be reanimated to new life. In fact, the hope that the second coming of Christ would take place during the lifetime of the first generation after Christ, and that the flesh and blood should be transfigured into an immortal body without seeing death, was one of the favorite doctrines of St. Paul himself. Yet after all, Christianity established the theory of the immortality of the soul (or rather a resurrection of the body) not because Christ taught it, but because the belief was generally accepted in the Gentile world.

The influence of the pre-Christian notions upon the history of the Christian Church is noticeable in almost all the dogmas, but most especially in the doctrines of incarnation that Christ is God and man in one person, and of vicarious atonement by the blood of Christ.

HUMAN SACRIFICE AND VICARIOUS ATONEMENT.

It is frequently claimed that the dogma of vicarious atonement as well as the deep consciousness of man's guilt (the theological conception of sin) is an exclusively Christian idea, but such is not the case. On the contrary, the idea that all evil, disease, pain and all great misfortunes are due to sin, and that sin is whatever gives offence to God, or the gods, and that their favor must be bought by supplication, prayer, penance, or sacrifice, was wide-spread. The greatness of man's guilt demanded a severe punishment, and people thought that nothing but blood, the most precious thing on earth, would be acceptable to the gods.

The Ancient Babylonians have penitential psalms which compare favorably with the same productions of Hebrew literature.

The Babylonian psalmist when suffering under a visitation without being conscious of guilt, exclaims:

> "The sin that I have committed, I know not."

And in the same strain, the Hebrew poet exclaims:

> "Who can understand his errors? Cleanse thou me from my secret faults" (Ps. xix. 12).

A Babylonian hymn expresses the penitential sentiment in these lines:

"O Lord, do not cast aside thy servant
Overflowing with tears.[1] Take him by thy hand.
. . . .
The sin I have committed, change to mercy.
The wrong I have done, may the wind carry off!
Tear asunder my many transgressions as a garment,
My God, my sins are seven times seven, forgive me my sins."[2]

Man in his penitential disposition clamors for atonement, and the atonement is mostly made in blood. The prophet Isaiah opposes the festivals of his people, speaking in the name of the Lord.

"To what purpose is the multitude of your sacrifices unto me? saith the Lord: I am full of the burnt offerings of rams, and the fat of fed beasts; and I delight not in the blood of bullocks, or of lambs, or of he goats" (i. 11).

Similar opinions are now and then voiced in Hebrew literature,[3] but they are not intended to suppress bloody sacrifices, they only insist on righteousness as a condition without which God is not pleased with offerings. Says the Psalmist:

"Then shalt thou be pleased with the sacrifices of righteousness, with burnt offering and whole burnt offering: then shall they offer bullocks upon thine altar."

Bloody sacrifices continued at Jerusalem until 70 A. D., and at the time of Christ the temple was more like a slaughter house than a holy place. Innumerable sacrifices were offered upon its altar almost daily, and the blood of rams and bullocks reeked to heaven.

According to the Jewish law, sacrifices could be made only in the temple and not in the synagogues. The synagogue was merely a meeting house in which pious Jews assembled for prayer, Scripture-reading, and sermons.

The destruction of the temple made an end of bloody sacrifices among the Jews, and now even if the temple of Jerusalem would be built up again,—which is by no means an impossibility, considering the obstacles to be overcome and the cost, —yet even if the temble were rebuilt, it is pretty certain that bloody sacrifices would not be renewed for the simple reason that mankind, according to

[1] Literally "rushing water."

[2] Jastrow, *Religion of Babylonia and Assyria*, p. 321.

[3] Jer. vi. 20; Hos. vi. 6; Ps. li. 16 and Ps. xl. 6.

the law of religious evolution, has outgrown the idea, and has reached a higher state of civilisation in which the efficacy of blood is no longer maintained.

Everywhere we notice a progress from human sacrifices to the immolation of animal substitutes, and finally the abandonment of bloody sacrifices of any kind. The law of evolution is the same throughout, but the idea that man's guilt is so great and divine mercy so dear, still lingers with Christianity, and while the practice of bloody sacrifices is abandoned, the underlying belief is still retained in the doctrine of the sacrificial significance of the death of Christ. The orthodox conception of Christ's crucifixion and vicarious atonement bears many striking similarities to the most prevalent religious notions among the inhabitants not only of the Orient, but also of India and America.

Élie Reclus, in his interesting book, *Primitive Folk*, which is one of the best of basic treatises on comparative ethnology, speaks of religion among primitive people, saying:

"Sacrifice, under its varied forms, in its manifold acceptations, sacrifice is the fundamental doctrine of religion!"

Among all savages, the motto is, he says, "Slay! Slay!" for blood is made to propitiate the gods, to satisfy their demands, to gain their favors. M. Reclus continues (p. 304–305):

"Blood, the element pre-eminently plastic, the constituent principle of nutritive milk and generative sperm, blood was looked upon as the very soul of living organisms. But there is blood and blood; the blood of man was held most precious of all, richest in force and vitality. It was believed that water was concentrated in blood, especially in human blood, which could sublimate itself into divine blood Blood, they said, conserved life throughout nature, even in plants and in spirits. Blood was shed to the Manes to restore their intelligence and sensibility, was served out to the Olympians to keep them in health and vigor, and to the earth, genetrix of harvests, to fertilise her."

As an instance representing human sacrifice, M. Reclus speaks of the Khond tribe in a remote corner of India, who have but a short time ago compromised with the progressive spirit of the age, represented by the British invaders, and have substituted animals for their human victims. M. Reclus describes their cruel religious custom as follows (pp. 305–307):

"The Khonds, a tribe forgotten behind their ramparts of forest and marsh, have preserved in its primitive integrity the ancient belief, according to which the most potent virtue resides in blood given without repugnance or regret. They believe that no act is more meritorious than to immolate oneself for the benefit of the community. Nevertheless such acts of devotion have always been rare..... and the Khond even prefers to sacrifice the life of others rather than his own; his fellow-citizens still praise his generosity when he buys human creatures wherewith to regale the gods. He who desires to make himself popular and deserve the favor of heaven, announces that on such a day he will have one or several victims butchered....Theoretically male sufferers are preferred to female, and the more beautiful those presented, the more costly the offering....

"No victim could be sacrificed if his price had not been liquidated in full. This condition was indispensable. The liturgy insisted upon the fact that there was no sin in slaying the man, provided he had been bought for ready money."

There is no need of entering into details as to how the Khonds treated their victims with great consideration. The person to be sacrificed, the "meriah" or "poussiah," is regarded as the incarnation of the god or goddess in whose honor the feast is given. After having enjoyed a good time, the victim is decorated, tied to a May-pole, covered with flowers, and slaughtered or killed in some way or other as an offering of vicarious atonement. M. Reclus describes a sacrifice in which the officiating priest explains the ceremony on ancient mythological grounds, that blood was needed to give stability to the earth, and that human blood must be spilled to propitiate the gods. It is not sufficient to have the sacrifice performed once, it must be continually repeated. A page in the liturgy, addressed to the goddess Pennou, runs thus (p. 317):

"If we immolate thee once for all, the virtue of thy sacrifice will grow weaker day by day. It will be better to sacrifice thee every year, and each time that there shall be need. For this cause, O Pennou shalt thou enter into the bodies of meriahs at the season of seed-time, or when evil spirits shall lay waste the earth, puffing forth the empoisoned winds of drought, the miasms of sterility and pestilence. Then shalt thou be sacrificed for the good of all."

The liturgy ends with a prayer which, according to Élie Reclus, is addressed to the goddess incarnated in the meriah, as follows (p. 319):

"'All living things suffer, and thou, wouldest thou be exempt from the common anguish? Know that blood is needful to give life to the world, and to the gods: blood to sustain the whole creation and to perpetuate the species. Were not blood spilt, neither peoples nor nations nor kingdoms could remain in existence. Thy blood poured forth, O Meriah! will slake the thirst of the earth; she will be animated with fresh vigor. In thee has Pennou been born again to suffer; but thou, Goddess in thy turn, shalt be born again into her glory. Then, Meriah, remember thy Khond people, remember the village where we reared thee, where we cared for thee! O Tari Meriah! deliver us from the tiger, deliver us from the snake! O Pennou Meriah! grant that which our soul desireth!" (P. 321.)

M. Reclus adds:

"Our ancestors, the Kelts also had their meriahs; they bought slaves, treated them liberally, and when the year had run its course, led them with great pomp to the sacrifice. Each twelve months the Scythian tribe of the Albanes fattened a betaira and killed her with spear thrusts before the altar of Artemis.[1] When the fitting moment returned, hierodules, who had been fed with dainty meats, were sacrificed to the Syrian Goddess. 'The spirits of the earth thirst for blood,' said Athenagorus. At the Thargelia, the Athenians splendidly adorned a man and woman, who had been entertained at the expense of the State, and led them forth in procession to be burnt at the confines of the open country. At the festivals of Patræ in Achia, wild beasts were thrown upon a flaming pile; amongst the Tyrians, sheep and goats; the worship of Demeter and that of Moloch are scarcely distinguishable from each other."

No doubt the Semitic nations clung to human sacrifice longer than others, and the passage of Silius Italicus in his poem *Punica* is certainly based on fact, for it agrees with the Moloch worship as we know it otherwise, both from the Bible and Phœnician history. The lines run as follows:

"Mos fuit in populis, quos condidit advena Dido,
Poscere caede Deos veniam, ac flagrantibus aris,
Infadum dictu, parvos imponere natos;
Urna reducebat miserandos annua casus!"[2]

This means:

"There was a custom among the people whom Dido on her arrival settled [in the city of Carthage] to ask the gods for forgiveness by means of murder, and to place upon the burning altar (it is horrible to relate!) little children, and the yearly lottery repeated these horrible events."

---

[1] Strabo.

[2] Silius Italicus, *Punica*. Cf. the statements of Thomas Herbert; Paul Lucas, *Voyage au Levant*; Pietro della Valle, *Viaggi*.

How deep-seated is man's consciousness of guilt and his yearning for a remission of his sins! And if we consider that the ideas of expiation by blood and vicarious atonement, still prevalent among savage peoples and traceable among the traditions of the Orient, were very common in the days of the first century of the Christian era, we can appreciate how the Gospel account dwells with great emphasis on certain features in the report of Chrrist's death. We learn that Christ was sold and paid for (just as the Meriah among the Khonds had to be), that his death was voluntary and that he freely consented to die for mankind; (his withdrawal from Jerusalem for the sake of hiding on the Mount of Olives is obviously obliterated), further even the need of a repetition of the sacrifice is insisted on in the Roman Catholic Church by an interpretation of the Mass as a renewal of Christ's sacrificial death, which we must understand involves the continued passion of the Saviour. There is a continued need of redemption. Mankind continues to commit sin and still deserves the wrath of God; thus necessitating the continuation of the sacrifice of vicarious atonement that takes away the sin of the world.

What a comfort it was to the pagan mind that his guilt could be washed away with the blood of a sacrifice by vicarious atonement; what a consolation it was to a bereaved family to know that the fate of the deceased was determined by divine interference, by a god who lived as a man among men, that Osiris, or Bel Marduk, or Thammuz, or Ishtar, or Orpheus, had passed through the same ordeal, had descended into the domain of death and thence returned safely, that thereby the way had been prepared and resurrection or immortality in some form or other was assured. And so the hope of the Christian is based upon the innocent death of Jesus who was offered up for sinful mankind on the cross. How similar are the underlying ideas; yet here is the great progress of Christianity over paganism. The old idea of sin and atonement by blood remains the same, but Christianity abolished for good any further sacrifices on the ground that Christ's sacrifice was sufficient for all times to come, and the condition by which alone we can partake of the blessings is repentance of our sins and a renewal of our heart.

CONCLUSION.

When we interpret the rites of savage sacrifices in the light of Christian dogmas, we shall better appreciate the sentiments of those poor deluded pagans, who by the shedding of blood, even of human blood, expected or still expect to gain salvation. Certainly they are mistaken in their religion, but subjectively considered, they are as honest and serious in their faith as are the Christians in theirs. They believe in the efficacy of blood and vicarious atonement, and they live up to their conviction according to the letter. The underlying system is the same in both paganism and Christianity. Both, pagan sacrifices and the Christian dogma of Christ's death on the cross for the remission of sin, are based upon the ideas of the efficacy of blood and vicarious atonement, a theory which is deeply rooted in the history of our race. In both, paganism and Christianity, it is based upon tradition and sanctified by long usage from generation to generation. In both it is vouched for by inspired prophets as a divine revelation. It is a mysterious echo of man's misinterpreted longings for deliverance from evil, a relic of the childhood of our race, a wrong answer to the questions of an anxious heart, yet at the same time it indicates the rise of religious ideals that at bottom are noble and elevating, a yearning for purity from sin, for peace of soul and the blessings of a good conscience.

The rapid growth of Christianity is easily explained if we consider that the fundamental ideas, the belief in resurrection, and immortality, in a God-man as our saviour, and in a vicarious atonement of blood were commonly accepted among all the nations of the Roman empire. The old religions had broken down; the old myths had become fables; yet the old religious yearning still remained and found a new setting in the touching story of Jesus of Nazareth. The old legends were too closely connected with polytheism; the Gospels had grown up on the Jewish soil of a rigorous monotheism, and when thus the old Gentile ideas appeared in their new form, they appealed at once to the hearts of the people as a new and a true divine revelation.

St. Augustine meant what he said when he declared that Christianity is a most ancient institution of the human race, that only the name is new, for it was called Christianity only since Christ appeared in the flesh.[1]

Christianity accordingly can rightly be regarded as the fulfilment of the religious yearnings of the Gentiles. The elements of the Christian faith were believed in by almost all of the nations. That the external forms of the Roman Catholic ritual, the use of candles, sacred water, rosaries, etc., the reading of masses for the benefit of the dead, processions, responsaries, hymns, etc., are practically the same as the ceremonies of pagan religions is interesting but not important. The main thing remains, that the essential doctrines are not Jewish but Gentile, hence the animosity of the Jews against the Christians, and the Christians against the Jews, is ultimately based upon an instinctive recognition of a deep difference. The Nazarenes were not yet true Christians, nor did they ever flourish. They were heretics in the opinion of both Jews and and Christians; and Jerome (in his epistle to Augustine, 79) says of them): "Desiring to be both Jews and Christians, they were neither the one nor the other." According to Epiphanius (*Pan.* XXIX., 7) they were neither more nor less than Jews pure and simple, but they recognised the new covenant as well as the old, believed in one God and in Jesus Christ.[2] Being too Jewish in their habits and having not accepted the general traits and beliefs which characterise the Gentiles, the Church never recognised them as orthodox Christians.

If we ask who prepared this combination of Judaism with an idealised conception of Gentile notions, there can be but one answer: it was St. Paul. St. Paul was born at Tarsus of orthodox Jewish parents. Living in the diaspora among Gentiles, he imbibed

[1] Ipsa res quae nunc Christiana religio nuncupatur, erat apud antiquos nec defuit ab initio generis humani, quousque ipse Christus veniret in carne, unde vera religio quae jam erat, coepit appellari Christiana." *Retr.*, I., 13.

[2] *Enc. Brit.*, Vol. XVII., p. 302.

from his early childhood Gentile ideas which in the development of his life appear precipitated upon his Pharsaic philosophy. His conception of Christianity was gradually matured and he passed through a complicated process of religious growth. He showed his zeal in the persecution of the Nazarenes, and when he witnessed the enthusiasm of this new sect he became converted to a belief in the crucified and resurrected Christ, in the vicarious atonement of Christ's blood and the fulfilment of all religious hopes of mankind in him, the unique incarnation of God.

In recognising that these elements of Christianity possess a close kinship to pagan beliefs, we do not mean to degrade Christianity but rather to recognise the relative dignity of paganism as a stage in the development of Christianity. We are apt to judge the Gentiles after the fashion of the ancient Jews, as idolators and children of wickedness. We are inclined to condemn their superstitions, and to brand their idolatry; and of course, if we are severe we are entitled to do so, but we ought to say that they cherished fundamentally the same ideals, and although Christianity ranges higher, being greatly purified, we should not be blind to the fact that pagans in their errors were not less serious, were not less devout, were not less religious than the Israelites or Christians. Human sacrifices are unquestionably a grievous mistake of the human mind, but we should know that wherever and whenever Gentiles fall into this gross aberration, they are only misguided. Their motives are ultimately as religious as was Jepthah's when he offered his daughter to the God of Israel.

While we recognise that pagan devotion is or may be just as fervid as Christian devotion, and that there is much in common between these two successive stages of religious development, we must at the same time understand that Christianity being the fulfilment of the religious development at a certain period of humanity is not as yet, as it appeared at that time, the realisation of absolute truth but only the solution of the problem as it recommended itself at that period. It was not as yet the final realisation of universal truth and it contains still many notions which are still pagan, that is to say, immature, erroneous, superstitious. And in truth Christianity has not remained stationary; it developed higher and nobler conceptions, discarding the childish notions of mediævalism. Nor is the religious evolution of mankind as yet at an end. New vistas open before our eyes and there are still higher goals that must and will be attained.

Religious institutions are and have always been over-conservative. They cling to the letter of a dogma, they retain the traditional form of vestments, they use for sacrificial meals the primitive food or drink, and cling to the old conceptions even though they may have become antiquated, simply because all these things have become sanctified by sacred usage. In the beginning of the Christian era and during the growth of Christianity, however, the leaders of the Church were bold: while they unconsciously retained traditional ideas which had become part of their very souls, they were iconoclastic in rejecting the forms of paganism and, at the same time, they were bold as well as positive in their constructive work. Thus it happened that the most powerful leaders who by their influence, oratory, and impressive personality swayed the majority of bishops in the oecumenical councils, as innovators, reformers, and organisers are apt to do, formulated the theology of the new religion in very emphatic terms condemning every one that did not subscribe to the dogmas as they formulated it.[1] No doubt they did great service for the cause of religion, but we are apt to overrate the significance of their work. They have passed away and are now sainted in the memory of later generations, but if we could rouse them from their graves, they themselves would have modified their views if they could have revised them in the new light that in the course of human development throughout the intervening centuries had come to them; they would in the present age have expressed themselves differently. Their credos are the interpretation of Christianity from their own standpoint as seen in the light they had at that age; but it is our duty, the duty of the present generation, to work out our own salvation, and these sainted leaders of past ages would, if we could call them back and imbue them

[1] Hence the expression "*Qui cunque vult salvus esse*," the opening words of the Athanasian creed.

with the results of our more advanced science, justify our course of action.

Listen to St. Anselm whose writings have been accepted by the Church as an authority that is regarded as canonical or indeed little short of infallible. He says concerning his exposition *Cur Deus Homo:*

> "It is not to be received with any further confidence than as so appearing *to me for the time*, until God in some way make a clearer revelation to me."

The clearer revelation has come in the development of modern science, astronomy, physics, physiology, psychology, anthropology, text criticism, and above all a clearer philosophical conception of the universe. While we may remain conservative in letting the old dogmas stand as the interpretations of religion, held by the leading men of past ages, and while we may preserve the continuity of Church traditions, we are yet free to infuse new life into our Church institutions by giving them a new interpretation such as is warranted by the maturest science of to-day. For science in its unequivocal and definite results is as truly and surely a divine revelation as the voice of conscience in a pure-hearted soul, and indeed it is superior and more reliable than the verdicts of oecumenical councils, the opinions of Church-fathers, and bishops, and archbishops, and popes, and even of the prophets and apostles whose revelations were mostly in dreams and visions and ecstacies.

The practical problem for our Christian Churches of the present century will be whether or not they can adapt themselves to the new conditions. Will they exclude the new light that science sheds on the religious problem, or will then open their doors and windows to let the rays of truth in. The probability is that most of our Churches will hail reform and will, as soon as they see their way, adapt themselves to the new conditions. They will broaden more and more until they have actualised the new ideals. Instead of being a brake on the wheel of progress, they can become leaders of people in the new dispensation that is dawning now upon mankind.

EDITOR.

BOOK REVIEWS.

Eleusinia. De quelques problèmes relatifs aux Mystères d'Eleusis. Par le Comte *Goblet d'Alviella*, Professeur a l'Université de Bruxelles, Membre du Sénat et de l'Académie Royale de Belgique. Paris: Ernest Leroux. 1903. Pp., viii, 154.

Count Goblet d'Alviella, well known in the literary world as an anthropologist and historian, sketches in an interesting pamphlet of about 150 pages the significance of the Eleusinian Mysteries. He describes the initiation as it took place in the first century of our era (Chapter I.); investigates the origin of the grand mysteries (Chapt. II.); explains the eschatology of the rite, the descent to Hades, and the belief in a future life (Chapt. III.); points out the changes which the mysteries of Orphism, the belief in the Dionysus Zagreus and the philosophy of time made upon the traditional festival of Demeter and Kore (Chapt. IV.); and finally the survival of the Mysteries, albeit in a changed form, in Gnosticism and Christianity.

Alviella distinguishes seven epochs in the history of Eleusinian Mysteries:

(1) The prehistoric times when families of the village Eleusis, devotees of the goddess Demeter and her daughter, Kore, practised magical rites for the sake of invoking the divine blessing upon their crops.

(2) After the annexation of Eleusis to Athens, outsiders were admitted to the ceremony. Their initiation was assumed to renew the life of the neophyte, and comprised a descent to the other world. In this stage the mystic drama forms an important part of the traditional rites.

(3) In the eighth century before our era, the main aim of the ceremony is sought in the regeneration of the initiated persons, and the main use of the Mysteries is expected to be attained in their beneficent influence upon man's life after death.

(4) The next period is characterised by a development of the ceremonial which is now divided into the greater and smaller mysteries.

(5) A new epoch beginning with the fifth century B. C. witnesses the addition of the Epopty, the sacred vision, a rite which is superimposed upon the traditional ceremonies, embodying a deeper conception of the soul, such as was taught by the priests of Orpheus, containing a cosmogonic system and ethical doctrines. Henceforth Dionysus plays a most prominent part in the Mysteries.

(6) A general syncretism characterises the sixth period in which the light of paganism flickers up for the last time, finally meeting its doom.

(7) The last period witnesses the rise of Christianity. Certain forms of the mysteries are transmitted to the new faith, and thus some of the Eleusinian ceremonies are perpetuated in the rituals of the victorious Church. P. C.

THE STUDY OF RELIGION. By *Morris Jastrow, Jun., Ph. D.*, Professor in the University of Pennsylvania. London: The Walter Scott Publishing Co., Ltd.; New York: Charles Scribner's Sons. 1902. Pages, xi, 451.

Morris Jastrow, Professor in the University of Pennsylvania, well known through his works on Assyriology and the religion of the Assyrians, presents the public with a stately volume of 451 pages on *The Study of Religion*, in which he employs throughout the historical method, beginning with a delineation of the history of the study of religion itself. He shows in the first chapter how utterly lacking the ancients were in their appreciation of the religion of others; for instance, Tacitus cannot learn anything from the religion of the Germans who to him are barbarians, and Lucretius sees the sublime monotheism of the Jews merely in the light of a superstition. The introduction of Christianity changed the situation by replacing the standpoint of indifference for one of onesidedness. One religion was regarded as absolute truth, all the others as mere idolatries, and here we have "the glaring inconsistency of a religion preaching love, and everlastingly brandishing the sword." Even a man like Voltaire saw in Mohammed merely "a deceiver and a monster of cruelty," and to Luther, the Pope and the Turk in their position represented Antichrist. Spinoza was the first to appreciate the historical development of religion. In his *Tractatus Theologico-Politicus* he makes an attempt to show how "certain leading principles....passing on from age to age, are modified and elaborated until they reach their culmination in Christianity." Spinoza, however, knows nothing as yet of other religions, and has as yet to hear of Buddhism and Zoroastrianism, and thus the historical attitude is still lacking in the comparative method. Broader tendencies were introduced by Alexander Ross, who published his work on *The Religions of the World*, in 1653, and by Picart and Bernard, whose illustrated work on the *Ceremonies and Religious Customs of the World* tried to be fair toward non-Christians. Bernard shows "a marked desire to be accurate in the information he furnishes, and has recourse to the best sources at his disposal." The progress is now rapid, and we may mention next in order Herder in his *Ideas for a Philosophy of the History of Mankind*. He sees in the religious development a great "movement forward and upwards....the golden chain of culture." "Since I have come to recognise thee, Oh golden chain

the Wise" contains the famous parable of the three rings, is no less significant. Still they all share with Samuel Reimarus, the author of *Wolfenbütteler Fragmente*, "a strong feeling of hostility towards priests and the clergy in general." The scope widens in Hegel, and becomes truly historical when we come down to the present age, when the late F. Max Müller of Oxford is mentioned, C. P. Tiele of Leyden, Ernest Renan, Albert Réville of Paris, E. B. Tylor of Oxford, and many more, nor does our author overlook the influence of museums, among which the Musée Guimet is specially mentioned.

In the second chapter, on *The Classification of Religions*, Professor Jastrow makes an incidental remark when speaking on Monotheism and Henotheism: "The popular notion which makes the Hebrews the originators of monotheism is erroneous. The distinctive contribution of the Hebrews to religion is not the belief in one God, but the investing of that God with ethical attributes which separated him gradually from the deities in which the other nations believed, and eventually brought about his triumphant survival in the great crash which befell the ancient world and swept away the faiths of Egypt, Babylonia, Phœnicia, Greece, and Rome." (Pp. 77–78.)

"Among the Hebrews, the prophetical movement of the eighth century definitely gave an ethical flavor to the conception of the national deity, and thus paved the way for a distinctive form of monotheism." (P. 79.) While entering into the classification of others, among whom Eduard v. Hartmann and Raoul de la Grasserie are specially discussed, Professor Jastrow states his own views as follows (p. 117):

"The classification which we would thus propose for religion is fourfold, corresponding to four stages of intellectual culture and moral development:

"1. The Religions of Savages.

"2. The Religions of Primitive Culture.

"3. The Religions of Advanced Culture.

"4. The Religions which emphasise as an ideal the coextensiveness of religion with life, and which aim at a consistent accord between religious doctrine and religious practice."

In the descriptions of the character and definitions of religion, our author goes over the field from Cicero to Tiele, discussing the philosophy of fear as the cause of religion, proposed by the ancient ones and held by more modern authors like Hobbes. He quotes Cicero's definition from "*re*-legere," and that of Lactantius from "*re*-ligare," the latter having been accepted throughout the Middle Ages through the influence of Augustine. He discusses the religion of rationalism of the deists and rationalists of the eighteenth century, a movement which culminated in Kant. As to *The Origin of Religion* (Chapt. IV.) we are again specially referred to F. Max Müller, Tiele, and Réville. Spencer's proposition to trace religion to ancestor-worship and the theory of totemism is regarded as insufficient, and it seems that our author is inclined to accept Prof. Max Müller's theory of religion (pp. 195, 197–198):

"In this theory of the origin of religion there are involved three factors: (1) the desire to satisfy one's wishes, irrespective of the fact whether this desire is looked upon as the ambition to attain the goal of human life, or as a hopeless longing for unrealisable happiness; (2) the impulse to seek external help in overcoming obstacles or in avoiding dangers; (3) the spiritual influence of the perception of the Infinite, involving the idealisation of the powers of nature, and furnishing man with a thought capable of exercising a lasting influence upon him and of stirring the emotional side of his being.

"The religious instinct, aroused by the perception of the Infinite, abides amidst all changes in the kaleidoscope of mankind's history. It is a permanent element in the chequered career of humanity,—in a certain sense, indeed, the only permanent element."

The second part of the book (Chapters V. to XI.) is devoted to special aspects treated: first, the factors involved in the study of religion; secondly, religion and ethics; thirdly, religion and philosophy, religion and mythology, religion and psychology, religion and history, religion and culture. In all of them the modern scientific standpoint is taken, especially so in the discussion of psychology, where the new psychology is relied upon and where Professor Jastrow finds one of his sources, Eduard v. Hartmann, lacking and replaces him by Professor Starbuck, relying on his book *The Psychology of Religion*, 1899.

The third and last part is devoted to the practical aspects of the study of religion and the teaching of the history of religion. Chapter XII. recommends strongly the sympathetic attitude to be taken as the only one that is fair and which will prove at the same time successful. Our author then passes in review the study of the sources of the historical study of religion: the colleges, universities, seminaries and generally the museums as an aid to the study of religion. Here again he calls attention to the Musée Guimet. Emile Guimet's entire life has been devoted to a single purpose, the furtherance of research into religious history. His own personal interest lay in the religions of China and Japan, by reason of which the collection is somewhat onesided. In the Musée Guimet the classification is geographical, but Professor Jastrow proposes as a more scientific plan to place religions in groups according to a scheme of classification which might be: first, the religions of savages; second, of primitive culture; third, of advanced culture; and, finally, all those that emphasise the coextensiveness of religion with life. Further, the visitor should be enabled to follow with ease the plan of religious development underlying the arrangements. "A prominent feature in each section would be a large map, or series of maps, illustrating the distribution of the religions belonging to the group....The objects collected will serve as illustrations of the traits and features, as well as the objects used in the cults, models of primitive altars and temples, images of the gods and spirits worshipped, and either models or photographs illustrative of religious worship, of religious dances and processions, of incantations and magic ceremonies, as well as of marriage and burial customs. Particular stress should be laid upon the latter, as furnishing in most instances a key to the most significant of a people's religious beliefs."

Professor Jastrow further insists: "The museum of religious history would form a bond between the public and the investigators It would be the means of rendering generally accessible the results of research; and, in return, the consciousness of thus directly contributing towards the education and liberalising of the masses will give the scholar that courage and cheer which constitutes the chief reward of his labors." κ

L'IDÉE D'ÉVOLUTION DANS LA NATURE ET L'HISTOIRE. Par *Gaston Richard*, Agrégé de philosophie, docteur ès lettres, chargé du cours de sociologie à l'Université de Bordeaux. Paris: Félix Alcan. 1903. Pages, iv, 406. Price, 7 fr. 50.

M. Gaston Richard presented this book under the form of a memoir to the French Academy of the Moral and Political Sciences, which awarded him the prize "*Crouzet*" in the year 1901. It is here republished in book form, embodying only such additional observations as were written by the author in reply to M. Theodule Ribot's references to the book in his capacity as President of the Academy at the meeting, October, 26, 1901.

We are informed by the author that "the idea of evolution may be considered as the summary of a doctrine which formulates the law of the origin and of the development of the world, as the directing principle of a method which should lay the basis of a cosmogony. But a discussion of the doctrine of evolution should be preceded by a study of the relation between the idea of evolution and the method which applies to the origin of the great processes into which the whole world may be analysed. This problem of method should take precedence over the question of the doctrine itself. The critical philosophy and the philosophy of the sciences divide themselves in the work of a study of the idea of evolution in both nature and history, but the critical philosophy will have to pronounce the final verdict. It is to the examination of this law that Monsieur Gaston Richard has devoted his book, which has been introduced by so high an authority as the French Academy.

The first part starts with a consideration of "simple evolution" and of "complex evolution"; it discusses the origin of the earth and the origin of organic life, organisation and vitalism, including a discussion of transformism. Next in question is the problem of adaptation, the origin of the brain, the cerebral functions, and generally the law of retrogression compared with the law of adaptation.

While the first part is devoted to biological problems, the second part discusses evolution in the domains of psychology and sociology. The nature of accident [illegible] history is set forth and the fact itself as such eliminated. With the historical method, a social psychology is established in which the unconscious plays an important part, while sociality is pointed out as the factor that produces rational [illegible] ings. The concrete data of social psychology are enumerated, and the significance of instinct is insisted on. The law of the division of labor is introduced, and finally a parallel is drawn between social retrogression and biological retrogression.

The third part discusses consciousness, and the part which it plays in the gradual development of life. For the appendices, some topics are reserved which did not find room in the body of the book: A Discussion of the Genetic Method and Teleology, Segregation and the Geography of Zoölogy, The Brain of Woman and the Theory of Selection, The Science of Historical Criticism After the Criticists' School, The History of Sects and Social Psychology, The Law of Localisation and Survival in the Division of Social Labor, Judiciary Discussion and Progress of the Law, and finally, The Rôle of the Malcontent and the Utopian Imagination. Σ.

MORALE. Essai sur les principes théoriques et leur application aux circonstances particulières de la vie. Par le *Dr. Harald Höffding*, Professeur à l'Université de Copenhague. Traduit d'après la deuxième édition allemande par *Léon Poitevin*, Professeur de philosophie au collège de Menton. Paris: C. Reinwald. 1903. Pages, xv, 578. Price, 10 fr.

We have discussed Dr. Harald Höffding's work on ethics in *The Monist* for October, 1890, Vol. I., No. 1, p. 139 ff., and need not enter into a detailed exposition of his theories, especially as no essential changes of the contents have been made in the French translation which has been made with great fidelity to the original, and, as it seems, under the superintendence of Dr. H. Höffding himself. It has been amplified only by articles of the author which appeared in the *International Journal of Ethics*, in *The Monist*, in *Ethical Investigations*, and other publications, all of which are written from the original standpoint of Professor Höffding. The book contains a thorough review of the principles of morality, individual as well as social, including family life, education, philanthropy, and politics. A good index is attached to the book. *ρ*.

EINLEITUNG IN DIE PHILOSOPHIE, Von *Hans Cornelius*. Leipzig: B. G. Teubner. 1903. Pages, xiv, 357.

Cornelius lays down in the present volume his views of philosophy under the title of "Introduction Into Philosophy." Philosophy according to him is due to the aspiration for clearness. He analyses "the mechanism of thought" of its "equilibrium" upset by doubt in our search for cognition. Philosophy in distinction from other provinces of thought is an explanation for *final* clearness, that is clearness as to final questions, the demand of a philosophical inquisition for our longing for a unitary explanation of the entirety of the world. This is practically all that is meant by metaphysics, but it is necessary for us to investigate the nature of the materials from which we construct our "world-conception" and also the methods. The latter is called "Epistemology." Most of the failures of philosophy are due to the lack of a proper analysis of comprehension.

Cornelius passes in review, the several philosophical conceptions, first, the natural picture of the world, body and spirit, the ego and our fellow beings, the desire for cognition, the unscientific explanations, the question of causality.

Our author then continues to investigate the scientific methods of dogmatism, the nature of hypotheses, and knowledge as a picture of reality. Here he falls back on Mach and Kirchhoff, who regard knowledge as a reconstruction of facts. The ultimate aim of philosophy consists in finding the psychological foundations of epistemology, a reconstruction of the development of pre-scientific notions and an epistemological solution of the metaphysical problems. In the first part of the special argument, Cornelius discusses the metaphysical phases of dualism, idealism, materialism, sensualism in ethics, eudemonism, utilitarianism, etc., etc., coming down to an explanation why consequent scepticism is impossible.

The second part treats of the epistemological phase of philosophy. Cornelius analyses the elements of experience, explains the doctrine of the association-psychology, criticising its atomistic tendency for overlooking the factor of connection in experience, and enters into the details of Kant's categories, paying special attention to the law of causation and its universality and necessity in spite of its subjective source.

The concluding chapters touch on the belief of immortality, which according to our author lies beyond the province of scientific inquiry, on the antinomies, the latter being illegitimate problems, and the notion of value (*Wert Begriff*), which depends upon the nature of our personality. He concludes with an appreciation of the two determinants of the will, happiness and fear, the former Eudemonistic and the latter Timetic, bringing out the demand of self-education. Σ

Essai sur la psycho-physiologie des monstres humains. Un anencéphale—un xipho[illegible]. Par *N. Vaschide*, Chef des Travaux du Laboratoire de Psychologie expérimentale de l'École des Hautes-Études (Asile de Villejuif), et *Cl. Vurpas*, Interne des Asiles de la Seine (Asile de Villejuif). Paris: F. R. de Rudeval. 1892. Pages, 287.

France seems to be the country which contributes most to the solution of the psychological problem; M. Ribot has condensed the psychology of double personality, of the diseases of the will, and other valuable topics; M. Richet has studied the psychology of micro-organisms, and also the phenomena of telepathy and kindred subjects, and now the Doctors, N. Vaschide and Cl. Vurpas, present us with an interesting essay on the psycho-physiology of human monsters, devoting the one half of their investigations to a brainless creature, the other half to xiphopagous twins. The first case is a sad production of a brute formation in human form, which, however, gives us important information on several problems of the nervous anatomy of the human system, a condition which justifies our authors to speak of it as *ce cas heureux*, "this happy instance" being a rare case from which we can derive important information.

Nothing could be said about the mental life of the monster, for there is none. The individual under observation used to show its displeasure by ejecting cries which were sometimes sharp, feeble, rather prolonged, monotonous, now spontaneous, and now expressions of resentment made in response to disagreeable impressions. The case in question which has been studied in the living individual as well as the post-mortem obduction, proves that the cerebral hemispheres, which were utterly missing cannot be the seat of pain or of the feeling of temperature, or of other well co-ordinated reactions, which are sometimes regarded as having their seat in the cortex. All these phenomena are purely physiological, and have their seat in the lower regions, viz., the upper portions of the medulla.

The cerebrum, which for all mental activity is the most important organ, is after all dispensable for the purely physical, the barely psychological and biological life. It must be regarded as the organ of co-ordination between the higher psychodynamic and properly mental activities, but life and even sentiency can be maintained without it.

Less unpleasant than the study of the anencephalic monster is the exposition of the biology and the psychology of xiphopagous twins. Our authors pass in review two special cases which came under their observation, viz.: a description of Chinese twins called Liou Tang Sen and Liou Seng Sen; and the Hindu twins, the sisters Radica and Doodica. In addition they give a summary of similar cases, among them the Siamese twins and the sisters Rita-Christina, animal monsters, a man with a double head, etc. Close observation of the Chinese twins proves that in their psychical life, one was superior to the other, being the initiator of most actions. As a rule they went to sleep at the same time, but not always, a fact which proves that the chemical theory of sleep is not tenable. The case of Radica and Doodica is more interesting because for the sake of saving the life of one, they had to be separated by an operation. The weaker one, Doodica, died after the operation, the cause of death being peritoneal tuberculosis. The operation was made just in time to save the life of Radica.

The operation was not without difficulty and revealed a very strange state of affairs. There were three great arteries communicating between the twins. Radica drew constantly and daily upon the blood of Doodica, giving back venous blood, an inequality which in the long run could only be detrimental for both. Radica was the stronger one and she was upon the whole of better temperament. Doodica used to torment her twin sister constantly. The latter, however, showed a great patience and considerable endurance with the pranks of her twin sister.

The lessons of these strange cases as presented by our authors are very instructive, and must be studied by specialists in the original communications. Abhorrent though the subject naturally may be to the lay reader, we cannot help recognising the great significance which a close investigation of the physique as well as the psychology of monsters possess for the specialist, and we take pleasure in calling attention to this unique work. The book is sufficiently illustrated with seventy photographs, plates, and diagrams in the text.

FRIEDRICH NIETZSCHE, SEIN LEBEN UND SEIN WERK. By *Raoul Richter.* Verlag der Dürr'schen Buchhandlung. Leipzig, 1903. Pages, vi, 288. Price, 4 Marks.

It is a sign of the times that a young *Privatdocent* in the University of Leipzig lectures on the philosophy of Nietzsche. Herr Raoul Richter is an enthusiastic admirer of this most modern thinker whom he regards, not as Nietzsche regarded himself as a Slav, but as a typical Teuton.

Herr Richter delineates in the first part the biography of Friedrich Nietzsche, the events in the life of the learner and then of the teacher, explaining his death and quoting the diagnosis of Dr. Moebius.

The most important part of the book is devoted to the work of Nietzsche in which Herr Richter condenses the several writings of his hero, adding to it his criticism and an appreciation of the significance of Nietzsche's philosophy in the history of mankind.

LES GRANDS PHILOSOPHES. ARISTOTE. Par *Clodius Piat*, Agrégé de philosophie, Docteur ès Lettres, professeur a l'école des carmes. Paris: Félix Alcan. 1903. Pages, viii, 396.

M. Clodius Piat, a French savant, convinced of the immortal merits of Aristotle has undertaken to write a monograph of the Aristotelian system, in which he sets forth in a systematic review, the doctrines of the great Stagirite thinker, making his work a welcome handbook for students, and bringing it up to date by comparing it with other systems, mainly that of St. Thomas Aquinas, who is of especial importance for Aristotle, because his interpretation of the Greek thinker was practically accepted throughout the Middle Ages as authentic, and the genuine Aristotle has only been recovered in the times of the Renaissance with the revival of classical studies and a renewed acquaintance with the Greek original.

Professor Piat has done his work well and English scholars who are in the same line would do well to take notice of the labors of their French colleague.

LORD ROSEBERY

OUR FIELD

ARE REPRESENTED IN ITS PAGES

All of the writers whose portraits appear in the margin of this page were represented in last year's numbers of THE LIVING AGE; and with them **Katharine Tynan, Maxwell Gray, George Meredith, Fiona Macleod, Maurice Mæterlinck, Hilaire Belloc,** Sir **Rowland Blennerhassett, Eugene Melchior de Vogue, Paul Bourget, Henry Lawson, Arthur Christopher Benson, Max Beerbohm, Pierre de Coubertin, William Watson, Maxime Gorky, G. M. Trevelyan, Emily Lawless, Theophile Gautier, Prince Kropotkin,** and many others.

THE LIVING AGE

AS IT ENTERS UPON ITS

SIXTIETH YEAR AND 236TH QUARTERLY VOLUME

still maintains the high standard of literary excellence which has characterized it from the beginning. It presents in an inexpensive form, considering its great amount of matter, with freshness, owing to its weekly issue, and with a **satisfactory completeness** equalled by no other publication, the best **Essays, Reviews, Criticisms, Serial and Short Stories, Sketches of Travel and Discovery, Poetry, Scientific, Biographical, Historical and Political Information,** from the vast field of Foreign Periodical Literature.

TO INTRODUCE THE MAGAZINE

To readers who are not now familiar with it, the publishers of **THE LIVING AGE** will send it by mail, postpaid, to any name not already on the subscription lists, for

THREE MONTHS, Thirteen Weeks, FOR ONE DOLLAR.

These thirteen issues will aggregate about eight hundred and fifty octavo pages of the **World's Best Current Literature**. Subscriptions may begin with any desired date.

Published every Saturday, and giving about **3,300 pages** a year. Popular, yet of permanent value.

Subscription Price, $6.00 a Year **Single Number, 15 Cents**

THE LIVING AGE COMPANY

P. O. Box 5206 **13½ BROMFIELD STREET, BOSTON**

$100.00
$125.00
The Jewett
"THE TYPEWRITER
WITH HANGERS THAT DON'T WEAR OUT."
For ELEGANT Work. Jewett RESULTS
PERMANENTLY
E. A. BANSCHBACH, Genl. Mgr.
150 La Salle St. Main 1422 CHICAGO
(Employment Department)
$150.00
$175.00
Jewett

L. XIV., No. 2. JANUARY, 1904.

A QUARTERLY MAGAZINE

Devoted to the Philosophy of Science

r: Dr. Paul Carus. Associates { E. C. Hegeler. Mary Carus.

CONTENTS:

CHICAGO:

THE OPEN COURT PUBLISHING CO.

Price, 50 cts.; Yearly, $2.00.

LONDON: Kegan Paul, Trench, Trübner & Company, Limited.

In England and U. P. U., half a crown; Yearly, 9s 6d.

MESHA'S INSCRIPTION.

Reproduced from the article "Mesha's Declaration of Independence" in *The Open Court* September, 1903, page 520 ff., containing transcription, translation, Bible references and other explanations of this famous monument of Biblical history.

Articles on kindred subjects will be published in eventual numbers of *The Open Court*.

VOL. XIV. No. 2 JANUARY, 1904.

THE MONIST

A QUARTERLY MAGAZINE

Devoted to the Philosophy of Science

Editor: DR. PAUL CARUS. *Associates:* { E. C. HEGELER. MARY CARUS.

CONTENTS:

CHICAGO:

THE OPEN COURT PUBLISHING COMPANY.

1904.

VOL. XVI. JANUARY, 1904. NO. 2.

THE MONIST

PRIMITIVE ROME.[1]

PHILOSOPHERS endeavor to discover the origin of things, anthropologists the origin of man, and all naturalists the origin of living beings. So archæologists delve into the sites of ancient cities to find the origin of civilisation, or the humble birth of a city which has been distinguished for its magnificence or its power.

Man is not satisfied to know merely how things are, especially the noteworthy, nor is he content to know merely the great works of man. He wishes to know also how these things have been produced, and how the greatness of man has developed. Consequently he searches for origins with an anxious curiosity, and notices the least phases of increase and development with a religious zeal. All this explains, in part at least, the almost instinctive love of antiquity, even in men who are unable to estimate its value and significance.

Rome has been venerated on account of its historical greatness, its immense power, and the great and numerous monuments it has left in all parts of the world into which its dominion has extended. It has always been a center of attraction to all cultivated men, and visitors to its ruins have been innumerable—the too many ruins which are scattered all over the city. In the presence of these ruins, which bring to mind a world destroyed, the imagination rises and, leaping through space and time, calls forth a religious sentiment which makes a ruin a sacred relic to be adored, and in-

[1] Translated from the author's manuscript by Prof. Ira W. Howerth, of The University of Chicago.

vests with a halo every stone, every inscription, and every little piece of sculpture, which frequently are of no value in comparison with the creations of modern art.

A few years ago we admired the Coliseum, the Arch of Septimius Severus, the Basilica Julia, the almost irrecognisable ruins of the Palatine, the Cloaca Maxima, which by the way is by no means primitive, the *Meta sudante*, etc. We admired the artistic remains of the Roman and the Trajan Forums, the two celebrated columns, the Antonine and the Trajan, all imperial and relatively recent constructions. We entered with sacred horror the labyrinthine sepulchre of Scipio, excavated in the Tufa, and we visited the tomb of Cecilia Metella, or the Pyramid of Cestus. But now our attention is turned to a difficult investigation, and yet one which rouses greater curiosity, namely, an inquiry into the origin of Rome.

When the engineer Boni, who directed the excavations in the Forum and who investigated indefatigably this center of ancient Roman life, first applied the pick to discover what was hidden under these ruins, all the fetich worshippers, archæologists, and dilettante raised a howl of protest against the profaner who would remove a single stone of the Forum and dig a trench to explore it. But now, after some discoveries of great value, the horror has diminished, but is by no means ended, for it is still desired that many parts of the surface which are already known, and that part which really forms the alphabet of Roman archæology, namely, that of the Imperial epoch, be left undisturbed.

No one will be astonished to learn that the place of the Roman Forum, and which bears that name, although the Forum occupies only a part of it, has to-day an altitude above the sea which it did not have at various times from the origin of Rome to the Empire. At present its altitude is from fourteen to fifteen metres, and its slope is less than what it must have been in primitive times. And so the two neighboring hills, the Palatine and the Capitoline, must have had a higher elevation in relation to the valley in which were founded the Forum and other monuments.

If at its present level the Forum is flooded when the Tiber is out of its banks and remains submerged like the Pantheon and some parts of the lower city, in primitive times the lowest part of the valley between the Palatine and the Capitoline must have been a swamp, as recent excavations plainly show, and must have been uninhabitable. During the various epochs of the city there was a gradual and continuous rise in elevation which continued down to the Imperial epoch. The excavations of to-day reveal a series of strata which are, so to speak, the sediment which has modified the area of that center of Roman life where transpired the great popular events, and from which departed the legions for the conquest of the world. For more than seven centuries that small bit of ground witnessed the destruction and reconstruction of houses, temples, sewers, prisons, and political edifices. So that to-day there are found one above the other the remains of old buildings which have been destroyed or modified, sometimes the ruins of one palace above those of another. All this appears chaotic enough, but it is the expression of the life of the successive periods of the city from its origin to its final destruction by the barbarians.

If one did not know that for seven hundred years at least, except during the temporary occupation of the Gauls, the dominion of Rome was not changed, and that the same people dwelt there, one might believe that various invasions and transfers of power had transformed the city. And yet it is a well-known fact that the invaders of a state do not change the places occupied by their predecessors, at least only in exceptional cases, because they find already established what they could create only at great expense and with much labor. The sudden changes which have taken place in the city of Rome during the long period of its existence are due, then, to the many and grave vicissitudes to which it was subjected in about seven centuries of its most active public life. But to know the construction and reconstruction of the city in the valley where the Forum stands is not to know its origin, that humble origin from which arose its grandeur and which contained the germs of its immense vitality, on account of which Rome was superior to other contemporaneous cities. But now the exploring (by some thought to be the devastating) hand of Boni discovers now something which tradition had handed down in historical works, now something which no one knew anything about. Among many things I shall speak only of two; one of which occasioned grave disputes between the archæologists and the philologists of all nations; the other a surprise to many, even to those who confidently believed themselves able to foretell in accordance with ideas now held something about the origin of Rome and of the Latin civilisation.

STELE WITH AN ARCHAIC LATIN INSCRIPTION.

The *Lapis Niger*, which is an area paved with ancient black marble, about twelve Roman feet in width, about a foot thick, and enclosed, was discovered in the center of the Comitium. It is rumored that at the depth of one and forty hundredth metres they covered an esplanade of yellow tufa (from the Palatine or from the upper strata of the Capitoline underneath the clay) supporting two oblong quadrilateral pedestals decorated with magnificent Etruscan *gola*, with the face turned to the north, that is, toward the Curia Hostilia.

Passages from ancient authors referring to this place include the well-known passage from Festus which refers to the *Niger Lapis* almost as the mark of the funeral place in the Comitium; that of Varro which places the Rostra in front of the Curia, and another from Varro which places the sepulchre of Romulus behind the Rostra: *ubi etiam in huius rei memoriam duos leones erectos fuisse constat.* The tradition of the sepulchre and of a lion (stone) has been gathered also from Dionysius of Halicarnasus. Passing beyond a large house at the west, the esplanade of tufa is transformed, bends to the left and supports a plinth slightly curvilinear which in turn supports the trunk of a monolithic cone of yellow tufa .48 metres in height and with a diameter of .773 metres at the base, and .695 metres at the top. Behind the trunk of the cone, at a distance of .171 metres from the front, rises a half column of tufa in the form of a truncated quadrangular pyramid, with smooth corners, .47 metres by .518 metres at the base, and broken off at a height from .455 metres to .610 metres, not counting the part encased in the paved surface. On the four sides and upon the corner at the southwest angle of the half column, which is .053 metres in size, is the inscription.[1]

The inscription begins from right to left and is folded back on the second line from left to right and so on successively in the manner called boustrophedon. The lines are therefore not horizontal but vertical, so that the words begin at the base and run toward the top and then re-descend in boustrophedon, as it is called.

This method of writing recalls the most ancient of Greek inscriptions. There is no example of it in Etruscan, Umbrian, Oscian or archaic Latin inscriptions. Some epigraphs of Picenus and of Marsi preserve the old style. Since in Greece the boustrophedon appeared between the seventh and the sixth century, it is held by some that the inscription of the Stele must belong at least to the sixth century. According to others it is more recent, but I need not discuss this, for the matter is still *sub judice* and is related to the discussion of types of writing and to that of the archaic language itself. (Fig. 1.)

Fig. 1.

The inscription, according to the reading of Gamurrini, is as follows:

Quoi hoi..../ sakros: es / edsorm..../ .....eiasias / necei:

[1] From *Notizie degli scavi di antichità*, 1899. Boni relatore.

lo..../.....evam / quos: ri..../....m: kalato / rem: hap. ....ciod: iovxmen / ta: kapia: dotav.... / m: i: te: ri: i:. ....m: quoi ha / velod: ne qu.... / ....od: iovestod..../ i viod....

The inscription is thus disposed upon the sides of the S and begins at the bottom of the western side. (Fig. 2.)

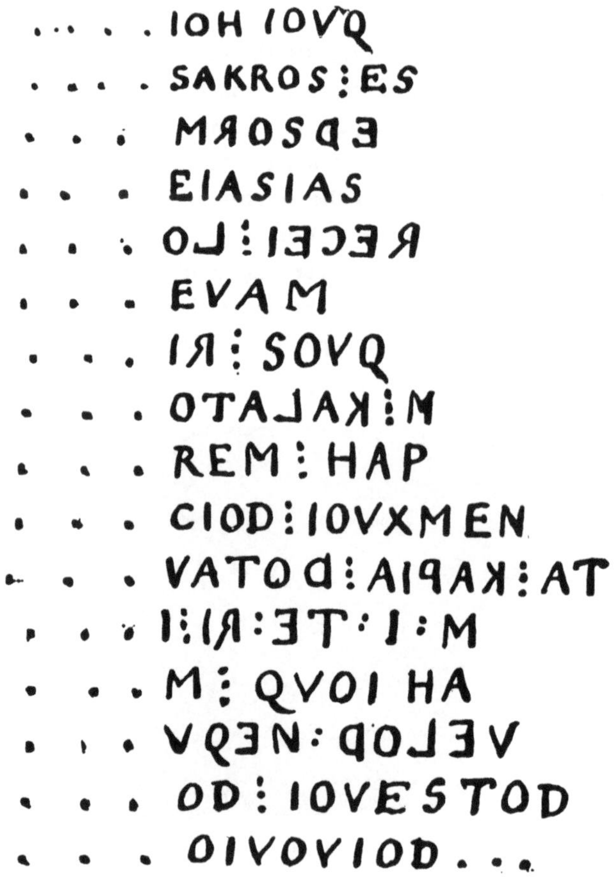

..... IOH IOVQ
.... SAKROS : ES
... MЯOSqƎ
... EIASIAS
... O⅃ : IƎƆƎЯ
... EVAM
... IЯ : SOVQ
... OTA⅃Aꓘ : M
... REM : HAP
... CIOD : IOVXMEN
... VATOd : AIqAꓘ : AT
... I : IЯ : ƎT : I : M
... M : QVOI HA
... VQƎN : qO⅃ƎV
... OD : IOVESTOD
... OIVOVIOD ...

Fig. 2.

Others have transcribed the inscription with some variat but this is not the place to speak of these, because every vari implies a different interpretation, and therefore the problem t solve is the interpretation. I make no pretension to being a philologist by profession, but I may say that the philologists of many nations have encountered insuperable difficulties, and are still engaged in lively disputes without coming, it seems to me, to any definite results.

The principal difficulties are two: The inscription is incomplete because the Stela is broken and the upper part is wanting, and it is cut longitudinally, so that the continuity of the lines is broken. If it had been cut horizontally, we should have the lower part of the inscription entire and might read the last part of it without interruption. But there is another difficulty, it appears to me, and that is this: the inscription does not contain the Latin as we know it, but a language spoken by the people in that epoch. This language was not at that time completely formed, and doubtless contained many parts of the vocabulary of a language anterior to that with the Aryan inflection, that is, of a language spoken by the indigenous Italians. The effort to interpret all the words by comparing them with the Aryan languages, while overlooking what might be indigenous, produces greater obscurity and prevents any complete interpretation.

I have many times expressed the opinion, an opinion based upon observed facts, that the Italian languages were formed upon the soil of Italy itself; hence, all the linguistic elements of the languages spoken prior to the Aryan invasions could not have been lost. Even to-day we find the relics of these languages in the vocabulary and the inflection of every language of the Aryan type. In a recent work I have shown this conclusively.[1] If this is true, it is not possible to interpret the fragmentary words of the archaic inscription of the Roman Stele with the Latin vocabulary alone. Possibly the Stele will remain undeciphered, like many other inscriptions of Latium! But this does not diminish the importance and the value of the discovery. Perhaps it even increases it, because it shows once more that the Latin language and the Roman

---

[1] Compare my works: *Arii e Italici*, Turin, 1898; *The Mediterranean Race*, *The Origin of the European Peoples*, London, 1901; *Gli Arii in Europa e in Asia*, Turin, 1902 (bearing the date 1903).

people which speak it were horn of many elements, and it represents an obscure fringe of primitive Rome.

AN ARCHAIC SEPULCHRE.

A discovery not less important than the preceding is that of an archaic sepulchre with tombs for two different funeral ceremonies, incineration and inhumation.

The engineer Boni, testing in various places the depth of the area between the Palatine and the Capitoline which contained Republican and Imperial Rome, that is to say, the valley where the Roman Forum, the temples and the other monuments are found, discovered near the foundations of the Temple of Faustina a tomb for incineration (April, 1902). By an exploration of the foundation of the Temple, and from the depth of the Tomb, it is easily seen that the architect who erected the temple not only ignored the existence of a very ancient sepulchre, but having discovered it cared so little for it that he destroyed that part which served him in laying the foundation of the temple.

Fig. 3.

The tomb is situated at a depth of 4.50 metres below the present level of the Forum and 10.63 metres above the level of the sea. It consists of a dolium containing a vase with charred bones, a cinerary urn, and other smaller vases, among which is one with a half-moon shaped handle characteristic and common in the Terremare of the valley of the Po. The dolium was packed in a ditch or sink which was .60 metres in diameter and .45 metres in depth. In the

Fig 4.

cinerary urn were found the charred remains of a human skeleton crumbled by a fire which must have been very hot, and some remains of the bones of other animals; no trace of metal. (3, 4.)

Some months afterward another tomb was discovered at almost the same level as the first, but of a different character. It consisted in a kind of box formed by blocks of tufa placed about .50 metres from the sink containing the dolium with the cinerary urn, and contained an inhumed, but not burned, skeleton. This skeleton is still in place (Aug. 18, 1902), for only the upper part of it has been uncovered, the cranium and the upper part of the thorax. The remainder of the skeleton is still covered with earth. The place contiguous to this tomb gives indications of other neighboring tombs, but it cannot be easily explored without destroying or damaging the constructions which stand above it and which belong to the

Republican period. At a distance of a few metres, however, in freer ground, another exploration has succeeded in discovering new tombs for incineration, of which some contain cottage urns, well known by their forms, because other similar urns have been found in Latium and elsewhere. The discovery of these few tombs is sufficient to demonstrate the existence of a very ancient sepulchre in the valley which contains the Forum and the other remains of Republican and Imperial monuments lying at the foot of the Palatine and the Capitoline.[1]

It is no new thing to discover in Rome tombs for cremation mingled with those for inhumation. About twenty years ago such tombs were discovered not far from the church of Santa Maria Maggiore in the Via dello Statuto. I myself possess a skull from these tombs, and many other skulls, also studied by me, are preserved in the Capitoline Museum.[2] In Latium several burying-grounds with tombs for incineration have been explored, and a year ago one near Grottaferrata in the villa Cavalletti, a kilometre and a half from Frascati, was brought to light.[3]

In the judgment of the explorers of these burying-grounds, Colini and Mengarelli, it seems that this tomb belongs to the same epoch as that of the Roman Forum, that is, to the first period of Latium. Both show intimate connection with other sepulchres of Latium, commencing with those discovered at the beginning of the past century. Few differences of any importance are found. They are not sufficient to place them in different periods or to indicate diverse influences. All have substantially common fundamental characteristics which show a single civilisation. The discovery of a burying-ground in the Roman Forum ought not, therefore, to occasion surprise, for Latium and even places in the city of Rome itself are covered with burying grounds of the same type. About a year ago when I wrote on this question, I pointed out that a people which practiced burning the dead had occupied Latium,

---

[1]After that time new tombs have been discovered.

[2] "Studi di anthropologia laziale." *Boll. Accademia-Medica*, Rome, 1895.

[3]*Notizie degli scavi di antichita*, 1902, *cit.*

at least to the Tiber, as it had already occupied the Valley of the Po and the territories of this valley as far as Latium. This people, which invaded Italy from the North, had found a population which practiced inhumation and possessed a neolithic civilisation highly developed and with the use of copper, whence the name *eneolithic*, given by Italian archæologists to this epoch.[1]

Where the invaders were most numerous the funeral custom was almost altogether changed, even the primitive inhabitants adopting incineration. But where they were less numerous the indigenous inhabitants preserved in part the earlier custom of inhumation. Consequently, in parts of Italy, and especially in Latium, both rites are found together. In the Roman Forum, where the new burying-ground was discovered, a tomb with a cinerary urn was found near a tomb for inhumation, as has already been seen. Probably others might be found if the excavations were extended.

From my own investigations and studies I have come to the conclusion that the invaders with the rite of incineration were the Aryans, and that those who inhumed were the indigenous inhabitants, whose differences in physical characteristics from the former were especially in the form of the head. The Aryans had a large, short (brachicephalic) skull with forms spheroidal platycephalic and cuneiform. The indigenous inhabitants had a long and narrow head (dolicho- and mesocephalic) with ellipsoidal forms, and they belong to the great Mediterranean variety whose existence I have shown, and which I have many times described.[2]

The skull of the inhumed body in the tomb in the Roman Forum, near the tomb of the body which has been burned, is of the Mediterranean type, ellipsoidal and dolichocephalic. Hence that tomb is one of an indigenous inhabitant, which I call *Italico*, while the others for cremation are tombs of the Aryans, and also of the Italians who accepted the Aryan custom.[3] This agrees exactly

---

[1] See *Arii e Italici*, Turin, Rome, 1897.

[2] *The Mediterranean Race. A Study of the Origin of the European Peoples.* London, Walter Scott, 1901.

[3] On this question compare *Arii e Italici, cit.*, and *Arii in Europa e in Asia*, Turin, 1902.

with the result of another study which I have made of the oldest skulls of ancient Rome, skulls antedating the walls of Servius Tullius,[1] and which for the most part belong to the Mediterranean type.

The problem which now presents itself is to determine who were the founders of Rome, to ascertain whether they were Aryans or Italians, that is, whether they burned their dead or buried them, or in other words, whether they were Asiatic Aryans or the Mediterraneans.

All those who with the philologists admit the Italicity of the Aryans, notwithstanding the great confusion of the facts, and who consider the Aryans as the bearers of the Hellenic and Latin civilisation, believe that Rome was founded by the Aryans; and hence they find some confirmation of their opinion in the discovery of the burying-ground in the Roman Forum. This burying-ground, according to their opinion, must have been one of those belonging to the founders of the four square city on the Palatine. Some even say that the body inhumed near the tomb of the incinerated one was a client or a dependent of the latter, a patrician!

To be sure, it is difficult to establish any exact chronology by means of burying-grounds alone, but approximately it seems that the burying-grounds of Latium belong to about the eighth century B. C., as does also that of the Roman Forum. This was the epoch of the Etruscan colonisation, which is undoubtedly of Oriental origin, and which carried into the Occident the twilight of the Mycenean civilisation. This colonisation, it appears, interrupted the continuity of the invasion and dominion of the Aryans, who at that time extended from the valley of the Po to the Tiber.

From the number of burying-grounds scattered through Latium and over the Roman territory itself, and in the place where rises the most ancient city, we must conclude that there was a large community of a mixed population, the indigenous (Mediterranean) and the foreign (Aryan). This community adopted a mixed funeral custom, the ancient and primitive practice of burying their

---

[1] See *Studi di antropologia laziale, cit.*

dead, and the recent one peculiar to the Aryans, that of incinerating them. As it is on the Esquiline (Via dello Statuto), so also in the Roman Forum. In the necropolis of the Esquiline a few hundred metres from the Forum, most of the Tombs are for incineration, only a few being found for inhumation. And we must admit the fact that it is natural in the domination of one people by another, especially when it is severe, for the conquered and subject race to imitate the customs of their masters. Hence all the tombs of a necropolis never represent a single type of population. Many of the indigenous inhabitants followed the custom of their masters, the Aryans, in burning their dead, and this custom was never completely abolished. In Rome even in recent epochs funeral pyres were sometimes constructed for the dead, especially for illustrious persons. And the same thing happened also in Etruria, where today the visitor may find recent Etruscan tombs with the funeral custom of cremation.

In Latium and in the Roman territory the number of foreign Aryans must have been very great. In confirmation of this I may present two arguments: First, the study which I have made of the skulls from the necropolis of the Esquiline, and from which it appears that the majority belong to the Mediterranean type, and a few to the Aryan type;[1] and second, the composition of the modern population outside of the walls of Rome, which in spite of the mingling undergone at various times belongs chiefly to the Mediterranean type.

The community, which on account of its ethnical components is called the Ario-Mediterranean, dwelt in cottages, never in walled houses. Their cities were not different from the villages which are found among other indigenous populations, savage or semi-savage. The city surrounded by walls, with its regular life and all that belongs to it, did not exist in the eighth century B. C. We know that construction in stone was very ancient in the eastern Mediterranean where the art was taught by Egypt and the Mycenean civilisation. In Etruria, since the remains of the Pelasgian civilisation

---

[1] See *Studi di antropologia Laziale*, *cit*.

are not found anterior to the advent of the Etruscans, stone architecture must have owed its origin to them. In upper Italy buildings of stone, the result of the Etruscan invasion and dominion, have been found, as for instance at Marzabotto, near Bologna.

We may ask, then, how did it happen that with so many Ario-Mediterranean communities in Latium and in the Roman territory, no city was built except by that community which dwelt upon the Palatine and the Capitoline or between these two hills? A year ago, writing on the origin of Rome, I attributed the principal cause to the Etruscan colonisation, which on the one hand broke the relations of the Aryan invasion between Latium and the north, and on the other hand threatened to take possession of the territory of the Tiber and had already founded, a few kilometres from the Tiber, the city of Veio. If Latium wished to remain independent, it was compelled to fortify itself against its new enemy, which was not only more powerful in arms, but also of a more advanced civilisation, and hence could have easily conquered a tribe little more than half savage, as were the people of Latium in general and the Latins especially.[1]

But this could not have been accomplished suddenly without some change taking place within the tribes of Latium, and especially in those nearest the sea and the Etruscan territory, which now lay between Ceres and Veio on the right bank of the Tiber. This change took place through the acquisition of a part of the Mediterranean civilisation, which for a few centuries had advanced from the Orient and infiltrated itself in the riverain populations of the Occident. The Etruscans, late Pelasgians, as I have called them,[2] being continually near them, contributed more than commerce with the Orient to change the inferior conditions of the Latin tribe near the Tiber. We find great difficulty to-day, however, in distinguishing and separating the primitive culture of Rome from the Etruscan. Indeed, there are those who believe there is no difference between them.

---

[1] See *Arii e Italici, cit.*, last chapter.

[2] Sergi, *The Mediterranean Race, cit.*

What they taught the Romans was stone architecture, the orientation of the city, and the construction of walled fortifications. Hence arose the citadel on the Capitoline, and the city on the Palatine, two hills already inhabited by two tribes, and separated in part by the swampy valley now occupied by the Forum.

With this first nucleus of a type of city until then unknown were united a few neighboring tribes who dwelt on the surrounding hills and were independent communities with their own orderly arrangements and also with their own burying-grounds, as we have seen. Nor is this all that happened. There must have been much commerce with the people of other communities, and therefore an influx into the new and strong city constituted with new arrangements and fortified against the nearest dangerous enemies, namely, the Etruscans.

A little later this city, which may be called the daughter of the Etruscan civilisation, measured its strength with the Etruscans themselves, but was constrained by them to allow the Etruscans to participate in the State and in part also in the colonisation: a concession necessary to allow it to live in peace and without danger. But finally their emancipation was complete, and many communities of Latium having been conquered, there was a great increase of power.

In all this profound change the Aryan elements, which formed a part of the communities of Latium, together with the Mediterranean elements, lost all their distinction and value. The populations were fused so as to be no longer distinguishable, as we saw with reference to the burying-grounds in which inhumation, which was preserved by the conquered, exists along with those for cremation, which were introduced by the Aryans. And the increasing power of the new city began to level the ethnic differences so that in time they completely disappeared, even from tradition. Aryanism dominates in one thing only, namely, language, for now that domination is complete. The inflected language has destroyed the primitive language of the indigenous population.

When the fusion of the tribes of the Seven Hills began, and the Capitoline was united more closely with the Palatine, the valley which separated them began to fill up and to be occupied by houses and temples, and the Forum was established. Then it was forgotten by the Romans that in that swampy valley there existed a primitive cemetery which contained the remains, sometimes burned, sometimes buried, of the Ario-Mediterranean tribe which dwelt on the top of the Palatine and built there the structures which are now uncovered.

My firm conviction, therefore, is that primitive Rome was founded under the influence of the Mediterranean civilisation and especially of the Etruscan, which was almost the model in its construction, and of ethnic elements already mingled, the Mediterranean the larger, and the Aryan the lesser, as is shown by a study of the ancient and modern populations of Latium. The Aryans were incapable of constructing a city like Rome, because when they emigrated into Europe and into Italy their civilisation was inferior to the Mediterranean, and they were ignorant of the art of building in stone;[1] they gave only the language.

G. Sergi.

Rome, Italy.

[1] Cf. *Gli Arii in Europa e in Asia, cit.*

ANTS AND SOME OTHER INSECTS.[1]

AN INQUIRY INTO THE PSYCHIC POWERS OF THESE ANIMALS, WITH AN APPENDIX ON THE PECULIARITIES OF THEIR OLFACTORY SENSE.

[CONCLUDED.]

THE REALM OF FEELING.

IT may perhaps sound ludicrous to speak of feelings in insects. But when we stop to consider how profoundly instinctive and fixed is our human life of feeling, how pronounced are the emotions in our domestic animals, and how closely interwoven with the impulses, we should expect to encounter emotions and feelings in animal psychology. And these may indeed be recognised so clearly that even Uexkuell would have to capitulate if he should come to know them more accurately. We find them already interwoven with the will as we have described it. Most of the emotions of insects are profoundly united to the instincts. Of such a nature is the jealousy of the queen bee when she kills the rival princesses, and the terror of the latter while they are still within their cells; such is the rage of fighting ants, wasps, and bees, the above-mentioned discouragement, the love of the brood, the self-devotion of the worker honey-bees, when they die of hunger while feeding their queen, and many other cases of a similar description. But there are also individual emotions that are not compelled altogether by instinct, e. g., the above-mentioned mania of certain ants for maltreating some of their antagonists. On the other hand, as I have

[1] Lectures delivered in Berlin, August 13, 1901, before the Fifth International Congress of Zoölogists. Published by Ernst Reinhard, Munich, 1901. Translated from the German by William Morton Wheeler.

shown, friendly services (feeding), under exceptional circumstances, may call forth feelings of sympathy and finally of partnership, even between ants of differents species. Further than this, feelings of sympathy, antipathy, and anger among ants may be intensified by repetition and by the corresponding activities, just as in other animals and man.

The social sense of duty is instinctive in ants, though they exbibit great individual, temporary, and occasional deviations, which betray a certain amount of plasticity.

PSYCHIC CORRELATIONS.

I have rapidly reviewed the three main realms of ant-psychology. It is self-evident that in this matter they no more admit of sharp demarcation from one another than elsewhere. The will consists of centrifugal resultants of sense-impressions and feelings and in turn reacts powerfully on both of these.

It is of considerable interest to observe the antagonism between different perceptions, feelings, and volitions in ants and bees, and the manner in which in these animals the intensely fixed (obsessional) attention may be finally diverted from one thing to another. Here experiment is able to teach us much. While bees are busy foraging on only one species of flower, they overlook everything else, even other flowers. If their attention is diverted by honey offered them directly, although previously overlooked, they have eyes only for the honey. An intense emotion, like the swarming of honey-bees (von Buttel) compells these insects to forget all animosities and even the old maternal hive to which they no longer return. But if the latter happens to be painted blue, and if the swarming is interrupted by taking away the queen, the bees recollect the blue color of their old hive and fly to hives that are painted blue. Two feelings often struggle with each other in bees that are "crying" and without a queen: that of animosity towards strange bees and the desire for a queen. Now if they be given a strange queen by artificial means, they kill or maltreat her, because the former feeling at first predominates. For this reason the apiarist encloses the strange queen in a wire cage. Then the foreign odor annoys the bees less because it is further away and they are unable to persecute the queen. Still they recognise the specific queen-odor and are able to feed her through the bars of the cage. This suffices to pacify the hive. Then the second feeling quickly comes to the front; the workers become rapidly inured to the new odor and after three or four days have elapsed, the queen may be liberated without peril.

It is possible in ants to make the love of sweets struggle with the sense of duty, when enemies are made to attack a colony and honey is placed before the ants streaming forth to defend their nest. I have done this with *Formica pratensis*. At first the ants partook of the honey, but only for an instant. The sense of duty conquered and all of them without exception, hurried forth to battle and most of them to death. In this case a higher decision of instinct was victorious over the lower impulse.

In *résumé* I would lay stress on the following general conclusions:

1. From the standpoint of natural science we are bound to hold fast to the psychophysiological theory of identity (Monism) in contradistinction to dualism, because it alone is in harmony with the facts and with the law of the conservation of energy.

Our mind must be studied simultaneously both directly from within and indirectly from without, through biology and the conditions of its origin. Hence there is such a thing as comparative psychology of other individuals in addition to that of self, and in like manner we are led to a psychology of animals. Inference from analogy, applied with caution, is not only permissible in this science, but obligatory.

2. The senses of insects are our own. Only the auditory sense still remains doubtful, so far as its location and interpretation are concerned. A sixth sense has not yet been shown to exist, and a special sense of direction and orientation is certainly lacking. The vestibular apparatus of vertebrates is merely an organ of equilibration and mediates internal sensations of acceleration, but gives no orientation in space outside of the body. On the other hand the visual and olfactory senses of insects present varieties in the range

of their competency and in their specific energies (vision of ultra-violet, functional peculiarities of the facetted eye, topochemical antennal sense and contact-odor).

3. Reflexes, instincts, and plastic, individually adaptive, central nervous activities pass over into one another by gradations. Higher complications of these central or psychic functions correspond to a more complicated apparatus of superordinated neuron-complexes (cerebrum).

4. Without becoming antagonistic, the central nervous activity in the different groups and species of animals complicates itself in two directions: (*a*) through inheritance (natural selection, etc.) of the complex, purposeful automatisms, or instincts; (*b*) through the increasingly manifold possibilities of plastic, individually adaptive activities, in combination with the faculty of gradually developing secondary individual automatisms (habits).

The latter mode requires many more nerve-elements. Through heredity predispositions (imperfect instincts) of greater or less stability, it presents transitions to the former mode.

5. In social insects the correlation of more developed psychic powers with the volume of the brain may be directly observed.

6. In these animals it is possible to demonstrate the existence of memory, associations of sensory images, perceptions, attention, habits, simple powers of inference from analogy, the utilisation of individual experiences and hence distinct, though feeble, plastic, individual deliberations or adaptations.

7. It is also possible to detect a corresponding, simpler form of volition, i. e., the carrying out of individual decisions in a more or less protracted time-sequence, through different concatenations of instincts; furthermore different kinds of discomfort and pleasure emotions, as well as interactions and antagonisms between these diverse psychic powers.

8. In insect behavior the activity of the attention is one-sided and occupies a prominent place. It narrows the scope of behavior and renders the animal temporarily blind (inattentive) to other sense-impressions.

Thus, however different may be the development of the automatic and plastic, central neurocyme activities in the brains of different animals, it is surely possible, nevertheless, to recognise certain generally valid series of phenomena and their fundamental laws.

Even to-day I am compelled to uphold the seventh thesis which I established in 1877 in my habilitation as *privat-docent* in the University of Munich:

"All the properties of the human mind may be derived from the properties of the animal mind."

I would merely add to this:

"And all the mental attributes of higher animals may be derived from those of lower animals." In other words: The doctrine of evolution is quite as valid in the province of psychology as it is in all the other provinces of organic life. Notwithstanding all the differences presented by animal organisms and the conditions of their existence, the psychic functions of the nerve-elements seem nevertheless, everywhere to be in accord with certain fundamental laws, even in the cases where this would be least expected on account of the magnitude of the differences.

APPENDIX.

THE PECULIARITIES OF THE OLFACTORY SENSE IN INSECTS.

Our sense of smell, like our sense of taste, is a chemical sense. But while the latter reacts only to substances dissolved in liquids and with but few (about five) different principal qualities, the olfactory sense reacts with innumerable qualities to particles of the most diverse substances dissolved in the atmosphere. Even to our relatively degenerate human olfactories, the number of these odor-qualities seems to be almost infinite.

In insects that live in the air and on the earth the sense of taste seems to be located, not only like our own, in the mouth-parts, but also to exhibit the same qualities and the corresponding reactions. At any rate it is easy to show that these animals are usually very fond of sweet, and dislike bitter things, and that they perceive these two properties only after having tasted of the re-

[illegible] substances. F. Will, in particular, has published [illegible] on this subject.

In aquatic insects the conditions are more complicated. [illegible] studied them more closely, shows how difficult it is in [illegible] to distinguish smell from taste, since substances dissol[ved] [illegible] are more or less clearly perceived or discerned from [illegible] by both senses and sought or avoided in consequence. [illegible] succeeded in showing that the palpi, which are [illegible] in terrestrial insects, have an important funct[ion] [illegible] forms.

In this place we are concerned with an investigation [illegible] sense of smell in terrestrial insects. Its seat has been prove[d] [illegible] the antennæ. A less important adjunct to these organs is lo[cated] [illegible] Nagel and Wasmann have shown, in the palpi. In the an[tennæ] [illegible] usually the club or foliaceous or otherwise formed dila[tations] which accommodate the cellular ganglion of the antennary [illegible] shall not discuss the histological structure of the nerve-te[rminations] [illegible] but refer instead to Hicks, Leydig, Hauser, my own i[nvestigations] [illegible] and the other pertinent literature, especially to K. K[illegible] [illegible] excellent work. I would merely emphasise the foll[owing]:

All the olfactory papillæ of the antennæ are transfo[rmed] [illegible] pore-canals.

All of these present a cellular dilatation just in front [illegible] [illegible]ation.

Tactile hairs are found on the antennæ together wi[th] [illegible] papillæ.

The character and form of the nerve-terminations is [illegible] but they may be reduced to three principal types: [illegible] olfactory rods, and olfactory hairs. The two latt[er] [illegible] quite indistinguishable from each other. The [illegible] always covered with a cuticula which may be [illegible]

[illegible] organs of the Hymenopteran antenna describ[ed] [illegible] are still entirely obscure, so far as their fu[nction] [illegible] but they can have nothing to do with the se[nse] [illegible] smell, since they are absent in insects with a delicate sense of smell (wasps) and accur in great numbers in the honey-bees, which have obtuse olfactories.

That the antennæ and not the nerve-terminations of the mouth and palate functions are organs of smell, has been demonstrated by my control experiments, which leave absolutely no grounds for doubt and have, moreover, been corroborated on all sides. Terrestrial insects can discern chemical substances at a distance by means of their antennæ only. But in touch, too, these organs are most important and the palpi only to a subordinate extent, namely in mastication. The antennæ enable the insect to perceive the chemical nature of bodies and in particular, to recognise and distinguish plants, other animals and food, except in so far as the visual and gustatory senses are concerned in these activities. These two senses may be readily eliminated, however, since the latter functions only during feeding and the former can be removed by varnishing the eyes or by other means. Many insects, too, are blind and find their way about exclusively by means of their antennæ. This is the case, e. g., with many predatory ants of the genus Eciton.

But I will here assume these questions to be known and answered, nor will I indulge in polemics with Bethe and his associates concerning the propriety of designating the chemical antennal sense as "smell." I have discussed this matter elsewhere.[1] What I wish to investigate in this place is the psychological quality of the antennal olfactory sense, how it results in part from observation and in part from the too little heeded correlative laws of the psychological exploitation of each sense in accordance with its structure. I assume as known the doctrines of specific energies and adequate stimuli, together with the more recent investigations on the still undifferentiated senses, like photodermatism and the like, and would refer, moreover, to Helmholtz's *Die Thatsachen in der Wahrnehmung*, 1879. Hirschwald, Berlin.

[1] "Sensations des Insects," *Rivista di Biologia Generale*. Como, 1900–1901. For the remainder see also A. Forel, *Mitth. des Münchener entom. Vereins*, 1878, and *Recueil. Zool. Suisse*, 1886–1887.

When in our own human subjective psychology, which alone is known to us directly, we investigate the manner in which we interpret our sensations, we happen upon a peculiar fact to which especially Herbert Spencer has called attention. We find that so-called perceptions consist, as is well known, of sensations which are bound together sometimes firmly, sometimes more loosely. The more intimately the sensations are bound together to form a whole, the easier it is for us to recall in our memory the whole from a part. Thus, e. g., it is easy for me to form an idea from the thought of the head of an acquaintance as to the remainder of his body. In the same manner the first note of a melody or the first verse of a poem brings back the remainder of either. But the thought of an odor of violets, a sensation of hunger, or a stomach-ache, are incapable of recalling in me either simultaneous or subsequent odors or feelings.

These latter conditions call up in my consciousness much more easily certain associated visual, tactile, or auditory images (e. g., the visual image of a violet, a table set for a meal). As ideas they are commonly to be represented in consciousness only with considerable difficulty, and sometimes not at all, and they are scarcely capable of association among themselves. We readily observe, moreover, that visual images furnish us mainly with space recollections, auditory images with sequences in time, and tactile images with both, but less perfectly. These are indubitable and well-known facts.

But when we seek for the wherefore of these phenomena, we find the answer in the structure of the particular sense-organ and in its manner of functioning.

It is well known that the eye gives us a very accurate image of the external world on our retina. Colors and forms are there depicted in the most delicate detail, and both the convergence of our two eyes and their movement and accommodation gives us besides the dimensions of depth through stereoscopic vision. Whatever may be still lacking or disturbing is supplied by instinctive inferences acquired by practice, both in memory and direct perception (like the lacunæ of the visual field), or ignored (like the turbidity of the corpus vitreum). But the basis of the visual image is given in the coördinated *tout ensemble* of the retinal stimuli, namely the retinal image.[1] Hence, since the retina furnishes us with such spatial projections, and these in sharp details, or relations, definitely coördinated with one another, the sense of sight gives us knowledge of space. For this reason, also, and solely on this account, we find it so easy to supply through memory by association the missing remnant of a visual spatial image. For this reason, too, the visual sensations are preëminently associative or relational in space, to use Spencer's expression. For the same reason the insane person so readily exhibits halucinations of complicated spatial images in the visual sphere. This would be impossible in the case of the olfactory sense.

Similarly, the organ of Corti in the ear gives us tone or sound scales in accurate time-sequence, and hence also associations of sequence much more perfectly than the other senses. Its associations are thus in the main associations of sequence, because the end-apparatus registers time-sequences in time-intervals and not as space images.

The corresponding cortical receptive areas are capable, in the first instance, merely of registering what is brought to them by the sense-stimuli and these are mainly associated spatial images for sight and tone or sound-sequences for hearing.

Let us consider for a moment how odors strike the mucous membranes of our choanæ. They are wafted towards us as wild mixtures in an airy maelstrom, which brings them to the olfactory terminations without order in the inhaled air or in the mucous of the palate. They come in such a way that there cannot possibly be any spatial association of the different odors in definite relationships. In time they succeed one another slowly and without order, according to the law of the stronger element in the mixture, but

[1] It is well known that in this matter the movements of the eyes, the movements of the body and of external objects play an essential part, so that without these the eye would fail to give us any knowledge of space. But I need not discuss this further, since the antennæ of ants are at least quite as moveable and their olfactory sense is even more easily educated in unison with the tactile sense.

without any definite combination. If, after one has been inhaling the odor of violets, the atmosphere gradually becomes charged with more roast meat than violet particles, the odor of roast succeeds that of violet. But nowhere can we perceive anything like a definitely associated sequence, so that neither our ideas of time nor those of space comprise odors that revive one another through association. By much sniffing of the surface of objects we could at most finally succeed in forming a kind of spatial image, but this would be very difficult owing to man's upright posture. Nevertheless it is probable that dogs, hedge-hogs, and similar animals acquire a certain olfactory image by means of sniffing. The same conditions obtain in the sphere of taste and the visceral sensations for the same reasons. None of these senses furnish us with any sharply defined qualitative relations either in space or time. On this account they furnish by themselves no associations, no true perceptions, no memory images, but merely sensations, and these often as mixed sensations, which are vague and capable of being associated only with associative senses. The hallucinations of smell, taste, and of the splanchnic sensations, are not deceptive perceptions, since they cannot have a deceptive resemblance to objects. They are simply paræsthesias or hyperæsthesias, i. e., pathological sensations of an elementary character either without adequate stimulus or inadequate to the stimulus.

The tactile sense furnishes us with a gross perception of space and of definite relations, and may, therefore, give rise to hallucinations, or false perceptions of objects. By better training its associative powers in the blind may be intensified. The visual sensations are usually associated with tactile localisations.

Thus we see that there is a law according to which the psychology of a sense depends not only on its specific energy but also on the manner in which it is able to transmit to the brain the relations of its qualities in space and time. On this depends the knowledge we acquire concerning time and space relations through a particular sense and hence also its ability to form perceptions and associations in the brain. More or less experience is, of course, to be added or subtracted, but this is merely capable of enriching the knowledge of its possessor according to the measure of the relations of the particular sense-stimuli in space and time.

I would beg you to hold fast to what I have said and then to picture to yourselves an olfactory sense, i. e., a chemical sense effective at a distance and like our sense of smell, capable of receiving impressions from particles of the most diverse substances diffused through the atmosphere, located not in your nostrils, but on your hands. For of such a nature is the position of the olfactory sense on the antennal club of the ant.

Now imagine your olfactory hands in continual vibration, touching all objects to the right and to the left as you walk along, thereby rapidly locating the position of all odoriferous objects as you approach or recede from them, and perceiving the surfaces both simultaneously and successively as parts of objects differing in odor and position. It is clear from the very outset that such sense-organs would enable you to construct a veritable odor-chart of the path you had traversed and one of double significance:

1. A clear contact-odor chart, restricted, to be sure, to the immediate environment and giving the accurate odor-form of the objects touched (round odors, rectangular odors, elongate odors, etc.) and further hard and soft odors in combination with the tactile sensations.

2. A less definite chart which, however, has orienting value for a certain distance, and produces emanations which we may picture to ourselves like the red gas of bromine which we can actually see.

If we have demonstrated that ants perceive chemical qualities through their antennæ both from contact and from a distance, then the antennæ must give them knowledge of space, if the above formulated law is true, and concerning this there can be little doubt. This must be true even from the fact that the two antennæ simultaneously perceive different and differently odoriferous portions of space.[1]

[1] It is not without interest to compare these facts with Condillac's discussion (*Treatise on the Sensations*) concerning his hypothetical statue. Condillac shows that our sense of smell is of itself incapable of giving us space knowledge. But it

They must therefore also transmit perceptions and topographically associated memories concerning a path thus touched and smelled. Both the trail of the ants themselves and the surrounding objects must leave in their brains a chemical (odor-) space-form with different, more or less definitely circumscribed qualities, i. e., an odor-image of immediate space, and this must render associated memories possible. Thus an ant must perceive the forms of its trail by means of smell. This is impossible, at least for the majority of the species, by means of the eyes. If this is true, an ant will always be able, no matter where she may be placed on her trail, to perceive what is to the right, left, behind or before her, and consequently what direction she is to take, according to whether she is bound for home, or in the opposite direction to a tree infested with Aphides, or the like.

Singularly enough, I had established this latter fact in my "Études Myrmeoologiques en 1886" (*Annales de la Societé Entomologique de Belgique*) before I had arrived at its theoretical interpretation. But I was at once led by this discovery in the same work to the interpretation just given. Without knowing of my work in this connection, A. Bethe has recently established (discovered, as he supposes) this same fact, and has designated it as "polarisation of the ant-trail." He regards this as the expression of a mysterious, inexplicable force, or polarisation. As we have seen, the matter is not only no enigma, but on the contrary, a necessary psychological postulate. We should rather find the absence of this faculty incomprehensible.

But everything I have just said presupposes a receptive brain. The formation of lasting perceptions and associations cannot take place without an organ capable of fixing the sense-impressions and of combining them among themselves. Experience shows that the immediate sensory centers are inadequate to the performance of this task. Though undoubtedly receptive, they are, nevertheless, incapable of utilising what has been received in the development

is different in the case of the topochemical sense of smell in combination with the antennary movements. Here Condillac's conditions of the gustatory sense are fulfilled.

of more complex instincts and can turn it to account only in the grosser, simpler reflexes and automatisms. To be sure, a male ant has better eyes than a worker ant, and probably quite as good antennæ, but he is unable to remember that he has seen and is especially incapable of associating it in the form of a trail-image, because he is almost devoid of a brain. For this reason he is unable to find his way back to the nest. On the other hand, it is well known that the brain of a man who has lost a limb or whose hearing is defective, will enable him to paint pictures with his foot, write with the stump of an arm or construct grand combinations from the images of defective senses.

I venture, therefore, to designate as topochemical the olfactory antennal sense of honey-bees, humble-bees, wasps, etc.

Can we generalise to such an extent as to apply this term without further investigation to all arthropods. To a considerable extent this must be denied.

In fact the multiformity in the structure and development of the arthropod sense-organs is enormous, and we must exercise caution in making premature generalisations.

It is certain that in some aerial insects the olfactory sense has dwindled to a minimum, e. g., in those species in which the male recognises and follows the female exclusively by means of the eyes, as in the Odonata (dragon-flies). To insects with such habits an olfactory sense would be almost superfluous. Here, too, the antennæ have dwindled to diminutive dimensions.

But there are insects whose antennæ are immovable and quite unable to touch objects. This is the case in most Diptera (flies). Still these antennæ are often highly developed and present striking dilatations densely beset with olfactory papillæ. By experiment I have demonstrated the existence of an olfactory sense in such Dipteran antennæ, and I have been able to show that, e. g., in *Sarcophaga vivipara* and other carrion flies, the egg-laying instinct is absolutely dependent on the sensation of the odor of carrion and the presence of the antennæ. In these cases the contact-odor sense is undoubtedly absent. More or less of a topochemical odor-sense at long range must, of course, be present, since the antennæ are external, but the precision of the spatial image must be very imperfect, owing to the immobility of the antennæ. Nevertheless, flies move about so rapidly in the air that they must be able by means of their antennæ to distinguish very quickly the direction from which odors are being wafted. These insects do, in fact, find the concealed source of odors with great assurance. But this is no great art, for even we ourselves are able to do the same by sniffing or going to and fro. But the flies find their way through the air with their eyes and not at all by means of their sense of smell. Hence their olfactory powers probably constitute a closer psychoogical approximation to those of mammals than to the topochemical odor-sense of ants, for they can hardly furnish any constant and definite space-relations.

Even in many insects with movable antennæ and of less ærial habits, e. g., the chafers and bombycid moths, the antennal olfactory sense is evidently much better adapted to function at a distance, i. e., to the perception of odors from distant objects, than to the perception of space and trails. Such insects find their way by means of their eyes, but fly in the direction whence their antennæ perceive an odor that is being sought.

A genuine topochemical antennal sense is, therefore, probably best developed in all arthropods, whose antennæ are not only movable in the atmosphere, but adapted to feeling of objects. In these cases the still imperfect topochemical oder-sense for distances can be momentarily controlled by the contact-odor-sense and definitively fixed topographically, i. e., topochemically, as we see so extensively practised in the ants.

It would be possible to meet this view with the objection that a contact-odor sense could not accomplish much more than the tactile sense. I have made this objection to myself. But in the first place it is necessary to reckon with the facts. Now it is a fact that insects in touching objects with their antennæ mainly perceive and distinguish the chemical constitution of the objects touched and heed these very much more than they do the mechanical impacts also perceived at the same time. Secondly, the tactile sense gives only resistance and through this, form. On the other hand, he multiplicity of odors is enormous, and it is possible to demonstrate, as I have done for the ants, and Von Buttel-Reepen for the bees, that these animals in distinguishing their different nest-mates and their enemies, betray nothing beyond the perception of extremely delicate and numerous gradations in the qualities of odors.

In combination with topochemical space-perception, these numerous odor-qualities must constitute a spatial sense which is vastly superior to the tactile sense. The whole biology of the social Hymenoptera furnishes the objective proof of this assertion.

It would certainly be well worth while to investigate this matter in other groups of arthropods which possess complex instincts.

In conclusion I will cite an example, which I have myself observed, for the purpose of illustrating the capacity of the topochemical olfactory sense.

The American genus Eciton comprises predatory ants that build temporary nests from which they undertake expeditions for the purpose of preying on all kinds of insects. The Ecitons follow one another in files, like geese, and are very quick to detect new hunting grounds. As "ants of visitation," like the Africo-Indian species of Dorylus, they often take possession of human dwellings, ferret about in all the crevices of the walls and rooms for spiders, roaches, mice, and even rats, attack and tear to pieces all such vermin in the course of a few hours and then carry the booty home. They can convert a mouse into a clean skeleton. They also attack other ants and plunder their nests.

Now all the workers of the African species of Dorylus and of many of the species of Eciton are totally blind, so that they must orient themselves exclusively by means of their antennal sense.

In 1899 at Faisons, North Carolina, I was fortunate enough to find a temporary nest of the totally blind little *Eciton carolinense* in a rotten log. I placed the ants in a bag and made them the subject of some observations. The Eciton workers carry their elongate larvæ in their jaws and extending back between their legs in such a position that the antennæ have full play in front.

Their ability to follow one another and to find their way about rapidly and unanimously in new territory without a single ant going astray, is incredible. I threw a handful of Ecitons with their young into a strange garden in Washington, i. e., after a long railway journey and far away from their nest. Without losing a moment's time, the little animals began to form in files which were fully organised in five minutes. Tapping the ground continually with their antennæ, they took up their larvæ and moved away in order, reconnoitering the territory in all directions. Not a pebble, not a crevice, not a plant was left unnoticed or overlooked. The place best suited for concealing their young was very soon found, whereas most of our European ants under such conditions, i. e., in a completely unknown locality, would probably have consumed at least an hour in accomplishing the same result. The order and dispatch with which such a procession is formed in the midst of a totally strange locality is almost fabulous. I repeated the experiment in two localities, both times with the same result. The antennæ of the Ecitons are highly developed, and it is obvious that their brain is instinctively adapted to such rapid orientation in strange places.

In Columbia, to be sure, I had had opportunities of observing, not the temporary nests, but the predatory expeditions of larger Ecitons (*E. Burchelli* and *hamatum*) possessing eyes. But these in no respect surpassed the completely blind *E. carolinense* in their power of orientation and of keeping together in files. As soon as an ant perceives that she is not being followed, she turns back and follows the others. But the marvellous fact is the certainty of this recognition, the quickness and readiness with which the animals recognise their topochemical trail without hesitation. There is none of the groping about and wandering to and fro exhibited by most of our ants. Our species of Tapinoma and Polyergus alone exhibit a similar but less perfect condition. It is especially interesting, however, to watch the *perpetuum mobile* of the antennæ of the Ecitons, the lively manner in which these are kept titillating the earth, all objects, and their companions.

All this could never be accomplished by a tactile sense alone. Nor could it be brought about by an olfactory sense which furnished no spatial associations. As soon as an Eciton is deprived of its wo antennæ it is utterly lost, like any other ant under the same circumstances. It is absolutely unable to orient itself further or to recognise its companions.

In combination with the powerful development of the cerebrum (*corpora pedunculata*) the topochemical olfactory sense of the antennæ constitutes the key to ant psychology. Feeling obliged to treat of the latter in the preceeding lecture, I found it necersary here to discuss in detail this particular matter which is so often misunderstood.[1]

---

[1]In his latest *Souvenirs entomologiques* (Seventh Series) J. H. Fabre has recorded a number of ingenious experiments showing the ability of the males of Saturnia and Bombyx to find their females at great distances and in concealment. He tried in vain (which was to have been foreseen) to conceal the female by odors which are strong even to our olfactories. The males came notwithstanding. He established the following facts: (1) Even an adverse wind does not prevent the males from finding their way; (2) if the box containing the female is loosely closed, the males come nevertheless; (3) if it is hermetically closed (e. g., with wadding or soldered) they no longer come; (4) the female must have settled for some time on a particular spot before the males come; (5) if the female is then suddenly placed under a wire netting or a bell-jar, though still clearly visible, *the males nevertheless do not fly to her, but pass on to the spot where she had previously rested and left her odor*; (6) the experiment of cutting off the antennæ proves very little. The males without antennæ do not, of course, come again; but even the other males usually come only once: their lives are too short and too soon exhausted.

At first Fabre did not wish to believe in smell, but he was compelled finally, as a result of his own experiments, to eliminate sight and hearing. Now he makes a bold hypothesis: the olfactory sense of insects has two energies, one (ours), which reacts to dissolved chemical particles, and another which receives "physical odor-waves," similar to the waves of light and sound. He already foresees how science will provide us with a "radiography of odors" (after the pattern of the Roentgen rays). But his own results, enumerated above under (4) and (5) contradict this view. The great distances from which the Bombyx males can discern their females is a proof to him that this cannot be due to dissolved chemical particles. And these same animals smell the female only after a certain time and smell the spot where she had rested, instead of the female when she is taken away! This, however, would be inconceivable on the theory of a physical wave-sense, while it agrees very well with that of an extremely delicate, chemical olfactory sense.

It is a fact that insects very frequently fail to notice odors which we perceive as intense, and even while these are present, detect odors which are imperceptible to our olfactories. We must explain this as due to the fact that the olfactory papillæ of different species of animals are especially adapted to perceiving very different substances. All biological observations favor this view, and our psycho-chemical theories will have to make due allowance for the fact.

ZURICH, SWITZERLAND. AUGUST FOREL.

THE STILL SMALL VOICE.

NEVER has there been a time in which the changes that took place in man's religious attitude were more significant than during the last decade, and yet the period of transition is so little marked by any ostentation, or noise, or excitement that the fact itself might easily be overlooked by a superficial observer.

When the Reformation set in we had a vigorous clashing of opinions; public debates were held that kept the world in suspense; œcumenical councils convened; the Diet of the German empire, then the centre of the world, legislated on the religious situation; Papal bulls and imperial decrees were issued; the boldest dissenters were burned at the stake—a method of enforcing uniformity of belief from which even Protestants did not shrink; the opposed parties rushed to arms, and most sanguinary wars were waged, accompanied by famines and epidemics. A period of the most terrible barbarism set in, in which all the powers of Hell seemed to be let loose; cities were demolished, villages burned down, and whole provinces laid waste, until by sheer exhaustion peace was restored.

Think of the millions of human lives sacrificed upon the altar of religious freedom, and yet, even at that price, the Reformation was not too dearly bought; for our present culture with all its blessings, our liberty of conscience, free investigation, scientific progress, and following in its trail invention and prosperity, are the glorious consequences which may all be traced back to the struggle for liberty, to the religious reform begun by Wyckliffe and Huss, culminating in Luther, defended by Gustavus Adolphus, and victoriously maintained after the terrible Thirty Years' War.

It is no accident that the Protestant countries are marching in the van of civilisation. It is among them, more than in Roman Catholic or Greek Catholic countries, that science has slowly but surely laid the foundation of a higher civilisation built upon the ruins of the past, and here in the United States we feel its blessings more than in any other country.

There is at present another reform going on, which in its intrinsic tendency and main import is nothing but the consequence of Luther's demand for the freedom of the Children of God. Liberty of conscience, as demanded by Luther, includes free investigation; and the quiet reformation that is going on now is due to the influence of science upon religion.

Reactionary historians, however, claim that we are on the high road to ruin. They tell us that the reformers clamored for freedom but established license, and that the final result will be political and religious anarchy. The reformed churches, it is claimed by Roman Catholic critics, (and there is some truth in it,) stand on a slanting platform. Their position is inconsistent. Having cast off the authority of the established Church they are driven by inexorable logic to deny all authority in both religion and government. They called for a free Bible and now they suffer from the cancer of the higher criticism; they granted the liberty of theological investigation, and now one dogma after another is condemned before the tribunal of science. While the Roman Church, built upon the rock of St. Peter, remains the same and shows a strong united front, Protestantism has from time to time to change its position and is divided into as many sects as there are different opinions.

There is a truth in this censure of the Protestant position, yet the question is whether the stability of Roman Catholicism is so very desirable. Are not these changes symptoms of life and indispensable accompaniments of progress?

The change in our religious attitude that is coming on slowly and surely, that is taking place under our very eyes, is of a peculiar kind. It is the power of thought within, which comes as a still small voice, a silent power that brooks no violence, a spiritual movement that is not in need of swords or guns to assert its principles. It is the influence of science upon the minds of the thoughtful, the honest, the truth-loving, and it comes about by the gradual establishment of a scientific world-conception.

The Reformation of Luther was a moral reformation. It demanded a cleansing of the Church in head and limbs. It swept out the leaven of Roman paganism, with its saint-worship, reverence for relics, hierarchical institutions, indulgence sales and other abuses, and submission to papal authority. The present movement that is transforming our churches is above all an intellectual reform. It is the direct influence of science upon faith, and cleanses the Church of the paganism of dogma. After all it is merely the logical consequence of the recognition of a free science. Its ideal is radical honesty of thought.

The influence of science upon religion is a reformation that (like the kingdom of heaven in the time of Christ, indeed like all spiritual movements) works from within. It is taking place in the hearts of the theologians who teach it to the growing generation of clergymen; it spreads with the spread of science and is imperceptibly purifying Christianity, giving it a higher, broader and deeper interpretation.

There are thousands and millions who are not aware of the change; yet the transformation is most radical and will, when it has become a matter of history, be recognised as such. It affects to some extent even the Roman Catholic Church and the result is that Protestants take more kindly to their old adversary and begin to set aside the old grudges against it.

But, is the influence of science not antagonistic to religion? Is it not destroying the Christian faith? Does it not take away the fond illusions of our dearest hopes? Philosophy offers us nothing but empty abstractions, and higher criticism invades the Bible and destroys its sanctity!

Allow me to protest against the popular phrase, "empty abstraction." Abstractions would be empty if they were meaningless. Mathematical formulæ, for instance Kepler's laws, are abstract but they are empty only to the uneducated who do not know their importance. They are freighted with meaning to those who understand their universal application and appreciate their significance for a scientific comprehension of the world.

Call the philosopher's definition of God an "abstraction," but do not forget that all abstractions represent realities. No one speaks of gravitation as an "empty abstraction," because we know too well that gravity is real. The same is true of the abstractions of the moral factors that build up our life. If the philosopher defines God as the world-order, or as the sum-total of law, or the unity of law, or specifically as the authority of moral conduct, as that which leads living creatures to develop the ideal of justice and love and good-will, or the *raison d'être* of man's spirituality, viz., that which produces man and leads him higher; we have abstractions which cover facts of experiences and these facts, the spiritual features of existence, the moral factors of life, are not less real than is the gravity of stones.

Even Christ speaks of God in abstract terms as "love" and as "spirit," not as "a loving being" nor as "a spirit," and shall we denounce his definitions as empty abstractions?

The spiritual and moral factors of life, the power that makes for righteousness, are a part of the general world-order, but they are its most significant part which gives character to the rest; and it is most important to remember that all the factors which shape the world are not mere words but living presences.

The scientist formulates the uniformities of the world as a multiplicity of natural laws, but there is unity in variety. All of them constitute one great system, one organic whole. They are the eternal in the transient and the universal in the particular. They positively possess qualities which are attributed to God alone. They are as intrinsically necessary as mathematical truths are rigorous. Therefore they are absolutely true. They are true of any possible kind of existence, and would remain true even if the world were annihilated. They apply not only to nature as it is, but to any possible nature. In other words, they are supernatural or hyperphysical in the literal sense of the word.

The supernatural in nature is not corporeal; it is neither concrete nor individual, but universal and non-material. It is comparable to a great personality, but I hesitate to call it a personality, because these creative factors in their totality are higher than the highest personality; they are the prototype of all human personality. Man becomes man by acquiring reason, and reason is nothing but the vision of the eternal, a comprehension of the absolute, an appreciation of the universal. If we speak of the supernatural as a personality, we must know that it is not a human personality but a divine personality, and thus the scientific view of God (Nomotheism, as we might call it), which sees in the laws of nature the eternal thoughts of God, does not declare either a personal or an impersonal God, but a superpersonal God.

Sensual natures need sensual allegories, and mythology is required in the period of the childhood of the race, but mature minds will take no offence at the more exact methods of scientific conceptions.

Everyone's God-conception is the measure of his own stature. A sensual man, incapable of abstract thought, should have a mythological and anthropomorphic God-conception, otherwise he would look upon God as an empty phrase. A philosophical definition would not impress him as describing a reality; and though his mythological belief would in details be subject to error, he would in the main act rightly, for mythology, though not the truth, can very well serve as a surrogate for the truth and will retain its poetical value even when its fairy-tale character is beginning to be understood.

Our notions of a heaven above the clouds, and a brimstone hell, and many other religious conceptions, have become mythological, but they have not lost their meaning. The curse of sin and the bliss of righteousness remain as real as they ever were, and if there are people who still believe in a brimstone hell, we may be sure that they still stand in need of a sensual imagery. A purer conception would be an empty abstraction to them, for every one's religion ought to keep pace with his mental growth; and as a rule, every one has the religion which he deserves.

The destructive character of science appears to special disadvantage in the field of Bible literature. Our religious traditions, no longer assured facts of history, are changed into legends and myths. The first chapter of Genesis has been degraded into the mere echo of a pagan cosmology. Samson is the Babylonian Shamash, a Hebrew Hercules, the sun-god on his migration, who performs his twelve labors and loses all strength when his hair, the solar rays, is cut off. The Book of Esther is the myth of Ishtar and Marduk. The stories of Abraham and Lot have become Hebrew folklore, and the very name, "Jehovah," endeared to us through church hymns, has become a philological monstrosity, while the Hebrew "Yahveh," which now takes its place, signifies a tribal deity, which, closely considered, is not very different from the Phœnician Baal and the Moabite Chemosh. The monotheistic conception appears now as the result, not so much of a direct revelation, as of a long historical development. In a word, the inroads which science made from all sides are so formidable that nothing worth speaking of seems to be left.

The uniqueness of the Hebrew revelation too is gone. Moses is now paralleled by Hammurabi, and Isaiah by Zarathushtra, the golden rule was pronounced more than half a millennium before Christ by Confucius, and love of enemies has been preached by Buddha and Lao-Tze. Obviously the uniqueness of our revelation is unique to *us* because it is *ours*. The Egyptians, too, considered themselves the chosen people; so did the Brahmans, so the Chinese, so does every nation on earth in a stage of immaturity. Greek cosmopolitanism is the first symptom of a higher civilisation with broad humanitarian ideals.

Yet, suppose that *our* civilisation should finally conquer all others, (which can be done by absorbing them, by accepting their good features,) the uniqueness of *our* religion would become a universal uniqueness, but it would be developed by the breadth of a genuine catholicity. Man's religious conceptions too are subject to the laws of a survival of the fittest, and in the long run truth alone will prove strong.

The aim of the religious development of mankind is determined by truth, and objectively determined truth is, in a word, called science; but the course of evolution might have run over different paths. If the prophets of monotheism had not risen among the Jews, or if the monotheistic reformers had not formulated their faith and incorporated it in their redaction of the Hebrew scriptures, monotheism would after all have risen; but it would have come to the front in another place and through some other medium perhaps in Persia, where a very pure conception of the Deity was dawning.

In fact we know that the Persian religion exercised an enormous influence upon the Jews in Babylon, and Mazdaism is as elevating and noble as the prophetic movement in Israel. If Persian monotheism had met with universal acceptance, the place of Moses would have been taken by Zarathushtra and the place of David by Cyrus, the great founder of the Persian empire, whom Isaiah called "the anointed one of the Lord," "the Messiah of Yahveh."

There is no need of ventilating the question whether our religious development would have been better if it had taken a different course, but it is well to know what might have been. If we had received our monotheism from the Persians, our theologians would quote from the Avesta; if we had learned the ethics of "love of enemies" from Buddha, they would study the Dhammapâda and other Pâli scriptures. In either case these other Bibles would have become canonical and held a unique place in our literature, but the great outlines of our religious growth would have remained the same.

Having learned that in several countries the same, or a similar, evolution is taking place according to an intrinsic law of nature, the idea has been proposed that all religion is purely human—and truly it is. All religious evolution is purely human, just as the present movement, the influence of science upon our belief is purely human. Yet in spite of the purely human character of scientific investigation, we find that science itself is possessed of an element that is superhuman.

Science is not a product of man's fancy. Man can neither make nor mar scientific truth. He cannot manufacture it to suit his pleasure. Scientific truths are eternal verities. Man does not invent them; man discovers them. Science is nothing but the tracing of those features of nature which are eternal. It is the disovery of the laws that shape the universe and guide the evolution of the world. Science accordingly is purely human only in its subjective aspect; the objective norm of science and its results are beyond human interference. There is a deep truth in the old doctrine of the God-man, for the ideal of perfect humanity is a theophany—an incarnation of the Deity. The human element of the scientist's labors does not exclude the divinity of science. The truths discovered by science are the eternal laws of being which cannot be made or unmade, changed or altered by any mortal, be he ever so powerful and grand, be he king or emperor or pope.

Verily and truly, science, if it but be genuine science, is a divine revelation, and the spread of a scientific world-conception is the coming of the Holy Ghost, the Spirit of God who will guide us into all truth. (John xvii. 13.)

Whenever a scientist discovers a truth, he receives a revelation from on high; whenever he comprehends a law, he deciphers the hieroglyphs of a thought of God; whenever he gains a new insight into the constitution of the world either in its general significance or its special reference to man's duties, he should in reverence take off his shoes, for he is in the presence of God.

Yet while science is divine and applicable to the whole range of life, including the domain of religious belief, while science should not be twisted to suit the purposes of dogmas of an established religion, we must bear in mind the difference between religion and science.

The clergyman is appointed to spread religion; his first duty is his pastoral work; he is sent out as an adviser and counselor to the members of his congregation, to comfort them in affliction, to stablish them in the love of truth and honesty, to strengthen them in temptation, to elevate their minds and consecrate their lives to a higher purpose than transient pleasures. He is not expected to deliver scientific discourses, be it on physics or bacteriology or the Higher Criticism. He should address himself to the heart, not to the head. Even in a scientific age the maxim remains true, *pectus facit theologum*, "it is the heart that makes the clergyman." But the progress of the age demands that the clergyman should have a scientific training, otherwise he runs the risk that the members of his congregation stand above him and he will in consequence lose his hold on their minds.

A clergyman should be familiar with the scientific method, its exactness and its rigor; he should have imbibed the spirit of science, and it would be well if he had devoted some time to the study of some specialty, mathematics, mechanics, physics, or physiology; but at the same time, while becoming scientific, he should not be changed into a scientist. He should bear in mind the purpose of his profession. He should be a teacher, an adviser, a pastor, a guide through the labyrinth of life.

But if the main burden of pastoral work lies in the moral field, why should we not abandon religion and preach pure morality? In reply I would say that religion as I conceive it is the basis of all morality. Religion implies a world-conception and morality is nothing but the application of a man's belief as to his destiny in life to practical problems; for religion is conviction, specifically that conviction which refers to the entirety of existence. Conviction is a power which dominates the will. Conviction is the motive, which determines the action of man; conviction is that which gives character to his personality. There is no such thing as non-religious ethics.

Religion consists in sentiment, but the nature of sentiment depends upon the idea by which it is inspired. There is no sentiment which is nothing but sentiment; all real sentiment possesses definite contents. Sentiments are directed toward an aim and the contents of religious sentiments are formulated in doctrines. Doctrines naturally constitute the backbone of religion and doctrines may either be right or wrong. They may be mere assumptions (commonly called dogmas) based on insufficient knowledge, or they may be sound truths which can stand the test of science and will pass through the furnace of critique unscathed.

In former ages belief (in the sense of insufficient knowledge) has been extolled but we know now that we can have a faith well founded,—a faith the application of which in the domain of conduct can be justified by inquiry and by experience.

Agnosticism is an untenable position which, though invented to stifle religion, chokes science. If agnosticism were true, science would have no right to interfere with blind belief, but superstition would be entitled to the same respect as any pure and noble faith. Agnosticism pretends to take an advanced position, but it is as reactionary as it is wrong. It is not true that the problems of God, his existence or non-existence, his nature and his dispensation, of the soul and immortality, of the destiny and duty of man, etc., lie outside the pale of investigation. We can in all these questions as much as in mathematics, or physics, or chemistry, find out the truth and distinguish between right and wrong, between orthodoxy and error, between good and evil. Agnosticism falls like a blight on the spirit of enquiry; it makes one blasé and disheartens the thinker, the inventor, the student. What our young men need is belief in science, not this pernicious and unjustifiable awe of nescience.[1]

But would not science thus reintroduce the antiquated horrors of dogmatic orthodoxy? Scarcely! For the new orthodoxy of provable truth will not brook violence and will be a blessing to all those who love clearness and definiteness.

The old venerable word "orthodoxy" has been greatly misused in past ages, and has thus rightly acquired a savor of narrowness. Nevertheless, the ideal of seeking and having the right doctrine is not only legitimate but indispensable and should not be abandoned.

Only let us substitute the orthodoxy of sound doctrine for the old ideal of an orthodoxy of dogma.[2]

The old orthodoxy clung to certain dogmas established by tradition and sanctioned by œcumenical councils. Dogmas, as a rule, are symbols, i. e., formulations of the faith in allegorical language; they are collected in the symbolical books. The upholders of ancient orthodoxy were narrow-minded and scorned every one who used other allegories or other rituals, even if the meaning was the

---

[1] For a discussion of Agnosticism see the author's pamphlet *Kant and Spencer*.

[2] See the author's article "The New Orthodoxy" in *The Monist*, Vol. VI., No. 1, pp. 91–98, republished in *The Dawn of a New Religious Era*, pp. 21–30. Chicago: The Open Court Publishing Co.

same. The new orthodoxy would not be a stickler for words and similies but would insist on essentials.

You notice that I make a difference between dogma and doctrine, between belief and faith: I discard the former, I retain the latter; and at the same time I cling to the old ideals of catholicity and orthodoxy. But I insist that our catholicity be catholic, not Roman, or Greek, or Anglican; but as universal as is science. I insist that orthodoxy be genuine rightness of opinion, not an orthodoxy of dogma, of belief based upon insufficient knowledge, but an orthodoxy of doctrine, of objectively provable truths.

The essentials of a religion may be classified under the heads of God, Soul, and World as follows:

First, there must be a standard of right and wrong, which can be discovered by experience and finds in man's conscience an instinctive expression. The ultimate authority of conduct is commonly called "God."

Secondly, if religion shall regulate man's conduct, he must be shown that he is responsible for his actions and their consequences. He has the choice between good and evil, and the very idea that he is held responsible will become an important factor in his decision. Hence the importance of the dogma of free will.

Finally, we are concrete beings, and all concrete existence involves temporal and spatial limitations. In other words, we are limited parts of an unlimited whole, and we should have a clear conception toward our beyond as to both time and space. As to time, we should know our relation: (1) toward the past, viz., our pre-existence, our indebtedness to former generations, and (2) our post-existence, i. e., our mode of life after death, viz., our immortality in times to come. As to space, we must comprehend our kinship to other sentient beings, especially to our fellow-men.

We do not mean here to enter into further details, especially as we have repeatedly discussed the several problems of God, freedom, immortality, the sonship of man, and the brotherhood of mankind, etc.; and trust that a philosophy of religion such as that outlined here will be needed by our theologians in the measure that people begin to feel the want of a philosophical and tenable explanation of the true significance of the old dogmas.

There is much objection to theology and even pulpiteers sometimes denounce it. Some would-be reformers imagine that all trouble in the churches comes from theology, from the intrusion of scientific thought into the domain of religious feeling. The truth is the very reverse. We need not less but more theology, and by "theology" I understand simply, the science of religion. We need a radical theology reverent toward the past, respectful in tone, considerate of the faith of others, even if it be erroneous, yet unshrinking and uncompromising as to the essentials of truth. If the present reformation is a reformation of the intellect, rather than the heart, salvation can come alone from the science of religion, from theology.[1]

The idea prevails within and without the churches that the liberal thought which is at present invading the study of the Bible, comes from the circles of Freethinkers or infidels. That is a strange error. The scientific interpretation of the Scriptures comes exclusively from theologians. Ingersoll has written the *Mistakes of Moses*, but his criticism of the Pentateuch is on the surface. He really could have made his onslaught on the Scriptures much more formidable, if he had been acquainted with the labors of modern theologians. Avowedly irreligious people sometimes utilise chips from the theological work-shop, but, as a rule, they do not study, they do not search and investigate, they do no plodding. The plodding has been done and is still being done in theological schools, at the seminaries and universities in this country as well as abroad, and especially in Germany. All the so-called "destructive critics" are theologians. With very few exceptions they are professors of theology in good standing; Harnack, who wrote *The History of the Dogma*, Holzmann, our greatest authority on the New Testament,

[1] To characterise the New Theology which to the Old Theology bears the same relation as astronomy bears to astrology, the author proposed the term "Theonomy." See the editorials on "Theology as a Science" in *The Monist*, Vol. XII., No. 4, and Vol. XIII., No. 1. See also the author's articles "God," "Unmateriality of God and Soul," "The Personality of God" in *The Monist*, Vol. IX., No. 2, and "The Personality of God" in *The Open Court*, Vol. XI., No. 10.

De Wet, Kuenen, Wellhausen, Cornill, Delitzsch, Gunkel, and other Old Testament scholars are not only theologians themselves but descendants from theological families, and their very fathers are known as great lights in the orthodox circles of Protestant Christendom.

And there is no frivolity in the destructive side of the higher criticism. Most of our higher critics have reached their conclusions in spite of themselves, in spite of their beliefs, and though the destructive side is perhaps as yet the most assured part of their work, it will prove wholesome in the end. The higher criticism destroys not the Scriptures, not theology, not religion, but only a wrong interpretation of the Scriptures, a narrow conception of theology, the pagan features of religion.

Science is never destructive except of illusions. It does not destroy truth, it destroys error. Its destruction will soon prove to be a mere clearing for a new and better construction, and this is true as well of the higher criticism, as of the philosophical foundation of theology. In place of a narrow belief, we shall have a wider and yet not less definite faith with higher ideals and a broader outlook.

M. Guyau, an unusually gifted thinker, a representative of modern science in France, wrote a book on *The Irreligion of the Future*; but his judgment was limited to a consideration of the situation in his own country. In the clash of party strife he rejected the religion of ecclesiastical dogmatism and espoused the cause of irreligious science. He saw no middle-ground. He was sufficiently familiar with science to know that scientific truth must in the end gain the victory; but he did not understand its religious meaning. Had he listened to its less obvious but not less significant message, he would have appreciated the divinity of science, he would have learned that there is a higher God-conception than the anthropomorphism of dogma and that all truth is holy; and science, the revealer of truth, is the still small voice of divine revelation.

EDITOR.

A BUDDHIST GENESIS.[1]

THIS document is translated from the twenty-seventh Dialogue of the Long Collection (*Dîgha-Nikâyo*). It occurs in a discussion on the caste question; but that it is a book in itself is clear from the fact that a rival recension of the Scriptures has transmitted it in a different connection, and with a different title. This rival recension is that of the Sublime Story (*Mahâvastu*), an expanded portion of the Book of Discipline belonging to the sect called the Transcendentalists or Docetists (*Lokottaravâdino*), which is a branch of the Great Council School (*Mahâsaṁghiko*). Now the Great Council was the rival sect of the School of the Elders (*Theravâdo*) who have preserved the Scriptures in Pâli. The Great Council preserved them in some kind of Prâkrit, which has since been partially Sanskritised. We have therefore this old Buddhist Genesis in two different Indian languages (to say nothing of a fifth-century translation into Chinese); transmitted by two different sects which parted company in the pre-Christian period of Buddhism; and in two different portions of the Canon: viz., the Book of Dialogues (*Sutta-Piṭakam*) and the Book of Discipline (*Vinaya-Piṭakam*). In the former (in Pâli) it is entitled the Dialogue Primeval (*Aggañña-suttam*) and in the latter, The History of Kings. These two ancient recensions agree in the main, but are verbally different. When an old document has such a transmission, its antiquity is well established.

The Buddhist Genesis was epitomised by Robert Spence Hardy in his *Manual of Budhism* (*sic*) published at London in 1853. But

[1] Translated from the Pâli by Albert J. Edmunds, Philadelphia.

Hardy translated not from the Pâli texts, but from mediæval Singhalese commentaries, which in turn are based upon Pâli texts and commentaries combined. Therefore we can never be sure, when reading Spence Hardy, how much of a narrative is from the primitive text and how much has been expanded or exaggerated from commentaries in Pâli and Singhalese.

An account of the Great Council version has been given in French by Émile Senart, in the Introduction to Vol. I. of his splendid edition of the Mahâvastu (Paris, 1882). So corrupt and difficult is the text that even this learned Prâkrit scholar shrank from giving a verbal translation, but contented himself with an epitome.

A brief account in English, based upon the Pâli recension, has been given by Rhys Davids, in his *Dialogues of the Buddha* (London, 1899, p. 105). Samuel Beal translates two versions from the Chinese, the second one being from the Long Collection. (*Four Lectures*: London, 1882, pp. 151–155.)

The present is the first translation of the text itself, and is made from the King-of-Siam's edition, printed in Siamese characters, in Vol. XI. of his thirty-nine volumes of the Pâli Canon, which was published at his capital in 1894, and in 1895 distributed throughout the world to universities and libraries. There are two copies in Philadelphia: viz., at the University of Pennsylvania and the Mercantile Library. In 1905 it is expected that the Pâli Text Society of London will print our present Genesis text in Roman letters, when it will be much easier to read.

We cannot here discuss the many questions raised by this ancient book. Suffice it to say that the idea of Genesis as a fall is ancient, and the interpretation of Paradise as a spiritual state instead of a material one is now regarded by a high authority to be the original conception of Eden in the Babylonian mythology.[1] The Christian student will be aware that such an interpretation was given to the Hebrew Genesis by Philo the Jew of Alexandria, at the time of Christ; by Origen of Alexandria, in the third cen-

[1] *Babylonian and Hebrew Genesis*. By Heinrich Zimmern. London, 1901, p. 33.

tury; by Jacob Boehme of Görlitz in the sixteenth, and by Emanuel Swedenborg of Stockholm, in the eighteenth.

The exact date of our document cannot be fixed, but after years of research I am satisfied that the Pâli Canon existed, in its main constituents, if not in its present form, at the Council of Vaṭṭagâmini, about B. C. 40,[1] in the ancient capital of Ceylon. At this Council the sacred lore, which had hitherto been oral, was committed to writing, say the Ceylon Chronicles; and a number of facts, which cannot be detailed here, give probability to the statement. Even if only the older parts of the Canon existed then, the Genesis document was certainly among them, because transmitted by a branch of the rival sect which had split off from the sect of Ceylon (the School of the Elders) some centuries before. The Buddhist tradition maintains that this document, together with most of the Dialogues and Discipline, was fixed in its present form by the Council of Râjagaha, upon Buddha's decease in the fifth century before Christ. But while criticism allows that something was settled then, it cannot admit so early a redaction for a literature bearing all the marks of long development. We may safely say, then, that the Buddhist Genesis was composed between the fifth and the first centuries before Christ.

How far the main idea of our document can be regarded as compatible with the underlying philosophy of the teachings of Buddha himself, does not fall within the scope of our investigation.

ALBERT J. EDMUNDS.

EASTER, 1902.

THE DIALOGUE PRIMEVAL (AGGAÑÑA-SUTTAM).[2]

O Vâseṭṭhâ,[3] there is a season, at vast intervals in the lapse of time, when this world is dissolved; and upon the world's dissolution, the inhabitants are mostly brought together in the heaven of

---

[1] Kern's corrected date.

[2] The discussion on caste, which precedes, is omitted, being no part of the Genesis document.

[3] The plural name of two Brahmin disciples, to whom Gotamo addresses the account. Hereafter we omit it: it occurs in every paragraph.

men are touched by some divine catastrophe, they say the same: "Alas for us! Alas, it has failed us!" They recall the very letter of the ancient primeval men, but know not the meaning thereof.

Now, when the sweet creeper had gone from those people, a delicate rice appeared, without coating or husk, pure, sweet-scented, and with the fruit already winnowed. They fetched food at evening for supper, and in the morning it was ripe and grown again. They fetched food in the morning for breakfast, and at evening it was ripe and grown again. It was not known to fail. Then the people lived a long, long time, enjoying the delicate rice for their food and support; and so long as they did thus, mere coarseness entered more and more into their bodies and differences of caste arose.

Then the organ of womanhood appeared in the woman and the organ of manhood in the man. And the woman offered to the man strong drink in excess, and the man unto the woman. And as they did so, passion arose, and suffering entered into their bodies. By reason of the suffering they indulged in the act of sex. Then, when people saw them in those days, indulging thus, some threw dust and others ashes, and others cow-dung, saying: "Perish, vile wench! Perish, vile wench!" And again: "How can one being do such a thing unto another?" Even now, in some country places, when a murderess is being executed, some people throw dust, others ashes, and others cow-dung.[1] They recall the very letter of the ancient primeval men, but know not the meaning thereof.

O Vâseṭṭhâ! that was an impious practice in those days, but now it is a pious one. People who, in those days, indulged in the act of sex, were not allowed to return to town or village for two months and three. When those people had fallen into exceeding mischief in that impiety, they began to make houses, in order to hide the impiety. Then it occurred to some idle person: "Why should I be troubled to bring rice at evening for supper and at morning for breakfast? Suppose I now bring it only once every

[1] The Sanskrit here reads: "Monks, just as now, when a maiden is being married, they throw a stick or a clod," etc. This is doubtless the true sense, and the Pâli is probably corrupt.

evening for breakfast." He accordingly did so, and then some one approached him and said:

"Come, fellow-being! let us go and bring some rice."

"Enough, O fellow-being! I only fetch rice once every evening for breakfast."

Thereupon that other, following his example, said: "It would be good indeed to bring the rice only once in two days." Just then some one else approached that person and asked him likewise to go for rice, and he gave the same answer as the first, whereupon the other, following his example, said: "It would be good indeed to bring the rice only once in four days." When another person invited the last one to bring some, he was told about the four-day plan, and forthwith suggested once in eight days as enough. So soon as those people began to eat stored-up rice, then was the grain enveloped by the red coating and the husk; no harvest was reaped; failure ensued, and there were groves on groves of standing rice.

Then the people met together and lamented, saying: "Alas! Evil things have appeared among beings; for of yore we were mind-made, feeders on joy, self-radiant, traversing the sky and abiding in goodness, and so did we long remain. Then, after a vast period, arose the savory earth upon the water, and we ate thereof and lost our splendor, till moon and sun came forth, and stars and starry forms. So night and day, month and half-month and seasons yearly rolled, and we enjoyed the savory earth for long, until by the appearance among us of things wicked and demeritorious the savory earth did fail. Then the fine moss came round, and we lost it likewise; and the sweet creeper and the huskless rice. The rice we gathered morn and even for our meals, a daily harvest; failure was unknown; and so we stayed for long, till for wicked and demeritorious things a coating and a husk did wrap the grain; no harvest was there reaped; failure ensued, and groves on groves are standing. Let us now divide the rice and set a boundary."

So they divided the rice and a boundary did they set.

Now a certain greedy person, while keeping his own share, took a share not given him, and enjoyed it. They arrested him and said: "Alas! O being, thou hast done a wicked thing, in th thou hast, while keeping thine own share, taken and enjoyed share ungiven. O being, thou shouldest not do thus."

"Be it so," replied that being to the others. But a secon time he stole likewise, and a third; whereupon, after the same r proof, some struck him with their hands, some with clods, an others with staves. And so theft came first to be known, and u braiding, and lying, and violence.

Then the best people met together, and lamented, sayin "Alas! Evil things have appeared among beings, in that theft h come to be known, and upbraiding, and lying, and violence. Su pose we now elect one being and tell him: 'Do thou rebuke who soever is rightly deserving of rebuke, and upbraid or expel who soever is rightly deserving thereof; but we will provide for t share of the rice.'"

Thereupon the people approached a person who was fin handsomer, pleasanter, and more commanding than the rest, a said: "Come, fellow-being! Rebuke whomsoever is rightly d serving of rebuke, and upbraid or expel whomsoever is rightly d serving thereof; but we will provide for your share of the rice."

"Be it so," replied that person to the rest; and so he r buked, upbraided, or expelled those rightly deserving thereof, wh they provided for his share of the rice.

Now because he was the great man elected by the race, the arose the first title[1] of "Great Elect." And because he was lo of the fields,[2] there arose the second title of "Nobleman." A because he reconciles others by justice, there arose the third ti of "King." Such was the origin of this circle of Nobles by an a cient primeval title; yea, and of those very people who, thou different, are alike and not dissimilar, by virtue of justice, not injustice. Justice, O Vâseṭṭhâ! is best for the human race in th world and the next.[3]

[End of the Genesis document common to the Pâli Aggañña-suttam and the S krit Mahâvastu.]

---

[1] "Title" is *akkharam*, the regular word for a letter of the alphabet. literal meaning is "imperishable."

[2] There is here, and also in the words "reconcile" and "king," a punning e mology: "field" is *khettam*, and "nobleman" is *Khattiyo*.

[3] The closing passage about justice (or religion) is not in the Mahâvastu, bu part of the discussion about caste which is now resumed in the Pâli dialogue. like manner there is frequent divergence of words and sentences between the recensions, but agreement in the main story.

THE HIGHER CRITICISM.

AN INAUGURAL.

MATTHEW ARNOLD, in his *God and the Bible*, uses with telling effect a line from Homer: "Wide is the range of words! Words may make this way or that way!" Of nothing could that line be more true than of the phrase "Higher Criticism." To some it conveys the idea of sober, honest investigation conducted in reverent spirit with the purpose of reaching the truth; to others it is a synonym for high-sounding dogmatism, starting from preconceived notions and having for its object the overthrow of Christian faith; while to other some it is nothing but a scholarly "fad," which indeed has had a longer run than most fads but will soon have finished its course. Like most things good or bad, higher criticism has had its friends and its enemies; and in company with many a different cause, it has suffered from both. Its enemies often misunderstand its purpose, caricature its methods, and misstate its results; its friends, on the other hand, depend too implicitly on its deductions, exaggerate the reach of its conclusions, and refuse soberly to submit them to the thorough tests which are imperative.

It is the purpose of this paper to attempt to correct some current misrepresentations of its objects and methods, and to set forth its aim, its limitations, and its advantages.

It is an old saying that no antagonism is so violent as that engendered by the odium theologicum. This is quite natural. Matters which have to do with man's eternal relations arouse the strongest passions, give rise to the intensest convictions. And so "wide is the range of words" that from the same phrase, through conflicting interpretations, conclusions the most opposite are reached.

I have spoken of "current misrepresentations" of the higher criticism. It should be no cause for surprise that these exist. Had that not been the case, if there had been no opposition to the application of the Bible of the methods of critical research, we should have a new thing in the annals of science and of the world. The growth of science, the attainment of results contrary to the conceived order of things, have always occasioned apprehension, have ever persuaded to charges and recriminations. Says Freeman:

> "Nothing is more morally certain than....that every worthy movement, be it on behalf of learning or of higher objects than learning, on behalf of freedom or humanity or right in any shape, will have to go through much opposition, much ridicule, that it will have to live through many adverse votes, through many scornful articles in newspapers, but that if its promoters bear up stoutly, it will win in the end."

We find Christians in doubt and full of fear because of the half-truths expressed by those supposed to be opponents of the Christian faith. These half-truths are often the results of a one-sided, incomplete application of principles which are legitimate when *thoroughly* applied, and which when thoroughly applied complete the statements of half-truths and furnish material to fortify the wavering faith of the faint-hearted. A good example of this class of objections are the anachronisms in the Pentateuch which yield at once upon the basis of the documentary hypothesis. An examination of the grounds upon which faith rests is sometimes as necessary to confirm believers as it is at other times to induce belief.

A fair statement of one of the difficulties encountered is that by Dr. Aiken as follows:

> "We cannot take many steps in exegesis without finding that before we are aware of it we were grappling with some of the most complex and representative problems of historical criticism—and of the (so-called) 'higher criticism': who said this, when, where, why? For the who, when, where, why, seriously affect our interpretation of that which is surely something more than a mere colorless formula of words."

In the kindred science of textual criticism the same experience was had. "The first collections of various readings excited great alarm." The earliest critics of the text had to meet the accusation of infidelity. The conception that the traditional view of the verbal and literal accuracy of the Bible was the teaching of the Bible itself was in possession of the field—to question this was to assail the Bible itself. So the scholarly Geddes was called a "would-be corrector of the Holy Ghost." This citadel of traditionalism had to be carried under a hot and often not harmless fire of scorn, invective, and even excommunication. Within the eighth decade of the last century Dean Burgon led an almost virulent attack upon the cautious revisers of the New Testament for omitting unsanctioned passages from their Greek basis of the Revised Version, and he found an energetic follower on this side of the Atlantic.

These experiences, therefore, are not peculiar in investigations of a purely Biblical character. Rather, it should be said, the Bible is only just ceasing to be regarded the court of last resort, whose pronouncements, as formerly interpreted by the Church, on all subjects,—cosmology, astronomy, geology, geography, chronology, anthropology, sociology, and what not—decide what may be believed and known. It is on record, for instance, that "on Feb. 24, 1616, the consulting theologians of the Holy Office characterised the two propositions—that the sun is immovable in the centre of the world, and that the earth has a diurnal motion of rotation—the first as 'absurd in philosophy, and formally heretical, because expressly contrary to Holy Scripture,' and the second as 'open to the same censure in philosophy, and at least erroneous as to faith.'" Galileo himself, apropos of whose discoveries these deliverances had been made, was admonished "not to 'hold, teach, or defend' the condemned doctrine."

There are those living who remember the great outburst of religious horror which attended the projection into the world of Darwin's application of the theory of evolution to the origin of man. It seemed as if the whole Christian world was aroused, and a pestilence of satire and invective assailed the daring innovator. Within only a very few years have theologians—indeed, not yet all theologians—become reconciled to that to which once the only possible reply was—*horribile dictu*; says Mr. Gladstone:

"In 1698 an ordinance was passed in the Long Parliament by which it was actually made an offence punishable by death to deny that which is manifestly only a question of historical inquiry—the authenticity of any one book contained in the Canon of Scripture."[1]

If the prosecution of research has thus suffered in branches which had so remote a connection with theological science, we need hardly wonder that the application of scientific processes to the Bible itself has caused great burning of heart. It is necessary that we look for a few minutes at current representations, for only thus perhaps will it be seen that our investigation is not entirely a work of supererogation. The examples I adduce come down to within a few weeks of the present.

It is a curious fact that the misrepresentations of the higher criticism are most frequently found in the religious press, and particularly in those papers that are the "organs" of the denominations they represent. These misstatements consist most often of unfounded assumptions as to the purposes of the critics. Writers assume dishonesty and hostility to the word of God as the motive of these same critics, they discount the reverence and impugn the veracity of the students who employ this method of research.

A few examples only from many that might be adduced.—One editorial, treating of the sale of the English Bible, says that:

"Neither hard times, nor higher criticism, nor infidelity....has any effect upon the sale of the divine Scriptures."

A sandwich composed of an upper crust of hard times, a lower crust of infidelity, and a filling of higher criticism must indeed be an *indigesta moles*. But what can we say of either the intelligence or the honesty of the writer who threats these three things as equally vicious or destructive. A reviewer in the *Lutheran Standard* informs us that:

"The so-called Higher Critics, *it is well known*, are constantly *trying to*

---

[1] W. E. Gladstone in debate on Dissenter's Chapel Bill, *Westm. Rev.*, Oct., 1889, p. 395.

shake the faith of the Christian by telling him that the books of the Bible were not written by the men whose names are usually given as the human authors."

That is, when a higher critic tells the people that say, the title —"The Epistle of Paul the Apostle to the Hebrews" is not found in the best manuscripts, and is, by the common consent of scholars, the addition in great part of an age long after the time of the composition of the book to which it is prefixed, and is moreover untrustworthy,—when a critic does this, stating a fact no scholar disputes, his object is "to shake the faith of the Christian."

The question at once arises, are we debarred from stating the truth?

Still another reviewer tells us that a certain book:

"....Is a most telling arraignment of the so-called higher criticism and an unmasking of its pretensions."

We hear from still a different source that one of the causes for the "Bible's being the best abused of books" is:

"....Its treatment by the higher critics, alleging (*sic*) that it is the offspring of incompetence and fraud."

One of the most influential papers of a large denomination assumes a slightly different tone and thus reassures its readers:

"That sort of criticism which, by a curious anomaly, goes by the name of the 'higher' criticism, is one of those scholarly 'fads' which have broken out at intervals ever since the revival of learning. But nobody need be seriously disturbed by it. It isn't going to destroy the Bible, nor lessen its authority, nor diminish the faith of the great body of Christian people in its divine authorship."

The examples I have given are what may be called impersonal. They are uttered behind the shield of the editorial "we." These are not the only instances of false estimates of the higher criticism. It often happens that men of eminence in the ranks of the Christian ministry lend their influence and name to the attack on this method of research. For example, one of the most prominent of Baptist clergymen was recently quoted as follows:

"Higher Criticism tends inevitably, whether its teachers realise the fact or not, to absolute rationalism and the discrediting of inspiration. If dates are erroneous, if scientific statements are wrong, if historical representations are misleading, if Jesus only fell in with popular views when he seemed to attribute the Pentateuch to Moses, is it possible to believe that the Almighty had much to do with the preparation of such a book?"

It has doubtless not escaped notice that one object of the attack in the preceding citations is the name *higher* criticism. This makes it necessary to remove a possible prejudice before we proceed farther in the discussion. It is constantly assumed by those who should know better that the adjective *higher* demonstrates the arrogance of those who use it, who claim thereby an unwarranted importance and precedence for their method. It *is* unfortunate that this name has been given. But all scholars know and other people are fast learning that the adjective is used to distinguish this process from the *lower* or textual criticism which has for its province the examination of manuscripts and versions and for its object the settlement of the text, the attainment of the *ipsissima verba*—the true reading, the very letters of the original documents—and which is therefore preparatory to the application of the processes of the higher criticism.

Arguments against the method on the ground that it is called the *higher* criticism and that it involves an arrogation of superior authority to other methods of research are inspired either by ignorance or by deliberate intent to deceive or to instill prejudice. We trust that the time is at hand when arguments of this character shall entirely cease.

The meaning of all this disparagement can be nothing if it is not to show that the higher criticism as applied to the Bible is utterly and essentially faulty. It is time then that we ask—What is this method of study that is causing so much animosity in the Christian world? Is higher criticism "a synonym for rationalism" ("rationalism" in the sense of "irreverence"), and are "the higher critics all 'infidels'"? Is it impossible for a higher critic to be honest and reverent, and can his conclusions escape being destructive? In other words, is the principle in itself essentially vicious[1] and must the reverent student be debarred its use? Or is it, like

[1] Professor Sayce says in so many words: "The 'critical' method is thus essentially vicious."

most things on earth, something which may be used or abused, the employment of which may therefore be allowed under proper safeguards and with a true apprehension of its powers and limitations?

What is this higher criticism? I offer as a tentative definition the following: *A method* of investigation scientifically applied to any given document or documents for ascertainment of truth, particularly the truth as to "the authorship, construction, unity, time, and place of composition, literary form," "credibility as history, or authority as ethics or religion," the results of which investigation may be used either destructively or constructively of present opinions.

It will be noticed that into this definition of the higher criticism the word "Bible" does not enter. The omission was designed. For the method of research under discussion is not confined to the Bible, does not deal solely with religious documents. We are, indeed, led to the further remark that it is not even a modern science. It dates far back of the Christian era, when the objects of its application were the poems of Homer and the events of Grecian history. Dr. Thomas Arnold, in his edition of *Thucydides*, has informed us that that historian was fully aware of the mythical character of many of the accounts which in his time passed as history. In fact, the great master of Rugby makes it perfectly clear that the historian of the Peloponnesian war employed at least some of the tests of our method. We may make the further assertion that the application of the principles of historical criticism to the Scriptures of the Old Testament began in the days of the Christian Apologists. Perhaps the best examples of the use of these principles are those most commonly given—the cases of the Letters of Phalaris, the Isidorian Decretals, and the Donation of Constantine.

The Letters of Phalaris are a series, one hundred and forty-eight in number, formerly supposed to have been written in the sixth century B. C. This date and the assumed authorship were commonly taken for granted as correct until Dr. Richard Bentley, in his controversy with Chas. Boyle, proved from the mention, in the Letters, of towns that did not exist till long after the time of Phalaris, from reference to tragedies that were not written till centuries after, and from imitations of authors of a later age,—in other words, by internal evidence as compared with established facts, that these letters could not have been written till quite late in the Christian era.

This example, it will be noted, is taken from the history of purely secular literature.

The Donation of Constantine was the basis of the Papal claim to the temporal dominion of the West. The document embodying the claim contained the legend that Constantine was healed of leprosy in the waters of baptism by St. Silvester the Bishop of Rome. In gratitude the royal proselyte withdrew from Rome to found a new capital in the East and "resigned to the popes the perpetual sovereignty of Rome, Italy, and the West." This document was first adduced during Charlemagne's reign in the ninth century, and was written probably in the latter half of the preceding century. A single word betrayed the character of the composition and its origination at a time when the limits of empire had greatly shrunk, by an author who did not know what regions were within Constantine's dominion.

The history of the Isidorian Decretals furnishes another example of the application of the principles of the higher criticism. These decretals consist of a series of edicts and letters supposed to have been written by the popes, some of them dating back to Clement of Rome. On them many of the claims of the Roman Catholic hierarchy in the Middle Ages were founded. The literary criticism of these documents conclusively showed that they were forged in the ninth century, and that therefore they lose their authority.

These examples and others that might be cited by the score demonstrate that this method of examining documents has not been invented for use merely in a religious direction and against or upon the Bible, but actually grew up in connection with other than religious literature. It is at the present day applied in every field of research involving the use of documents. Every discovery of a manuscript or document, whether secular or sacred, is the signal for employing the tests, for using the processes, of this science.

The rigor with which this method is applied in other than Biblical fields is illustrated in the following extract from Lord Acton's inaugural lecture on taking the chair of History at Oxford:

"The critic is one who, when he lights on an interesting statement, begins by suspicion. He remains in suspense until he has subjected his authority to three operations. First, he asks whether he has read the passage as the author wrote it. For the transcriber and the editor and the official or officious censor on the top of the editor have played strange tricks and have much to answer for. And if they are not to blame it may turn out that the author wrote his book twice over, that you can discover the first jet, the progressive variations, things added, and things struck out.[1] Next is the question where the writer got his information. If from a previous writer, it can be ascertained, and the inquiry has to be repeated. If from unpublished papers, they must be traced; and when the fountain-head is reached, or the track disappears, the question of veracity arises. The responsible writer's character, his position, antecedents, and probable motives have to be examined into; and this is what, in a different and adapted sense of the word, may be called the higher criticism in comparison with the servile and almost mechanical work of pursuing statements to their root. For a historian has to be treated as a witness, and not believed until his sincerity is ascertained. The maxim that a man must be assumed to be honest until the contrary is proved *was not made for him*.

The main thing to learn is not the art of accumulating material, but the sublimer art of investigating it, of discerning truth from falsehood, and certainty from doubt. It is by solidity of criticism, more than by the plenitude of erudition, that the study of history strengthens, and straightens, and extends the mind."

All this, to some people, sounds like the sheerest rationalism. Of its applicability to ordinary history no one feels a doubt, but to the Bible—ah, that is a different thing! The awful irreverence of it in that connection makes the blood run cold! It may therefore be a surprise to know that the late Dr. Aiken speaks as follows from the very citadel of conservatism in America:

"There is a measure of truth in what Renan says with a frankness and force that are almost brutal: 'Criticism knows no reverence; it judges gods and men. For it, there is neither prestige nor mystery; it breaks all charms; it tears aside all veils. This irreverent power, turning upon everything a firm and scrutinising look, is by its very essence guilty of treason towards God and man.'"

And yet, the question at once confronts us, can the application of these principles be excluded from the Bible? Is it possible in

---

[1] *The very case with the Acts of the Apostles as represented in two sets of manuscripts*, according to some of the foremost critics of our times.

the first place, is it desirable in the second place, that the Bible should be exempted? To which question the answer comes from a certain school,—"This exemption is imperative, for *the Bible is different from other books; the Bible is the word of God.*" To question or cross-examine the Bible is "consciously to test the credibility of the Holy Ghost, to dispute the veracity of God Himself," an awful sin, a fearful irreverence!

The answers to this objection must be postponed till we come to the consideration of the *necessity for the employment of critical processes in the study of the Bible.* All I am concerned to show now is that this method of study is not an engine of war expressly invented to batter down the walls of Christian faith and to assault the fortress of Biblical truth. The genesis of the science lies far back of the Christian era, its scope is as extensive as literature itself, while its principal field of practice has been the domain of general history.

The exercise of its principles in *Biblical* study is indeed for the most part modern; but that was as inevitable as the march of science, as necessary as the succession of the seasons. It is not anti-Biblical any more than astronomy or geology is anti-Biblical. If it be said that this is drawing the long bow, my reply is that what I have claimed in my last statement is supported by the late veteran Dr. Wm. Henry Green, the late leader of the conservative hosts in this country.

While we have defined positively that which is the subject of our discussion, it may be well to borrow the substance of an article by Professor Zenos that we may see the negative side of our theme. For while many do not know what the higher criticism really is, they imagine it to be several things it is not. A few of these shall be noted.

1. "It is not the criticism of the literary characteristics of the Bible." That is to say, while it observes the difference in style displayed in the separate books of the Bible or even in the different parts of the same book, while it takes cognisance of a greater or less degree of grammatical or syntactic or lexicographic purity, of

the agreement or disagreement with models that are assumed as classic, it does not do this *for the style itself.*

When it marks a peculiarity in style, a difference in vocabulary, a habitual felicity in expression, it does so because they are data for use in the solution of a problem.

2. "It is not a philosophical principle or mode of viewing the Bible and its contents." To illustrate: the Tübingen school used as their guide in Biblical criticism the Hegelian principle of thesis, antithesis, and synthesis. They read all the New Testament Scriptures in the light of this philosophical lantern. That was not higher criticism! Yet the results of just such work as theirs is continually set forth as the fruitage of higher criticism, as higher criticism itself. We are therefore compelled to make the distinction and emphasise it that a method like the Tübingen school's is not the scientific procedure of the higher criticism, nor is it the higher criticism itself.

3. "It is not a theory of inspiration." Perhaps the most common error concerning our method is the one negatived by the proposition just enunciated. The results given by the exercise of the critical processes belonging to our method may lead to or suggest a theory of inspiration. But that theory when formulated is not to be identified with the critical procedure which gave the data for the formula.

4. "It is not a set of views as to the books of the Bible." The higher criticism bears the same relation to a set of views concerning the Bible as the tools and machinery in a saw-mill, a stone-quarry, and a blacksmith-shop to a house. All these shape the material of which the house is built, but they are not the house. The comparison may be carried still farther. The materials turned out by the machinery may be perfectly sound and well worked. Yet the house constructed from them may be a monstrosity, neither substantial, convenient, nor sightly, all because the material has not been employed in fit proportions and in a suitable manner.

The confusion hinted at in the statement "It is not a set of views as to the Bible" has led to an identification of all sorts of vagaries, of real attacks upon the Bible, of infidelity itself, with the higher criticism. Any mad hypothesis, any untenable theory, is charged at once to the higher critic. "The critics have a *mania*," says one paper, "for forming hypotheses." These same critics are not only infidels, they are madmen. In consequence, the caveat at the head of this section—"It is not a set of views of.... the Bible" is one most necessary to bear in mind.

We are therefore thrown back to the first clause of one definition which contains the essence of it: "*a method of investigation scientifically applied.*" This is what it is—a method. It is not denunciation of the Bible, not an engine of war erected to undermine or batter down its truths, not a philosophical principle or prepossession which forbids a man to come out of the woods at a place different from that where he entered, not a theory of inspiration (even though the result of its processes be to make certain theories of inspiration untenable), not even a set of views about the Bible. It is just "a method of investigation *scientifically applied.*" Scientifically, not erratically, not blindly, not capriciously, not even inflexibly without regard to circumstance and fitness. And this should lead us to see at once how misleading are the statements that the higher critics are "taking away the Bible," are "robbing Christians of their guide." To take away is not the function of the *higher* criticism. If any branch of Biblical study takes away aught from the Word of God, it is the *lower* or Textual criticism. That with which we are concerned is simply a method of investigation scientifically applied to the Bible *as* it is, to discover *what* it is.

This brings us to the next point of importance—the *material* with which *Biblical* higher criticism deals. We have here to bring into consideration a fact which is obscured in the common mind, no doubt largely through the influence of the title of our book—"The Bible." The truth thus obscured is that the Bible is a collection or library of books. The name "Bible" carries with it as a noun in the singular a truth the importance of which should by no means be minimised. But in this connection we are compelled to notice not the unity so much as the diversity which appears. The Bible is not one book as we use the term nowadays, in the sense of being the production of a single individual. Even if it be referred on the very highest and most mechanical theory of inspiration to God as the ultimate author, the fact remains that its parts were given at different times during a period of over a thousand years. Upon the basis of the traditional authorship of its component parts, it reflects the conditions and modes of thought and of expression of widely separated ages.

It is a question at least open to debate whether this notion of the unity of the Bible is not extra-Biblical if not indeed anti-Biblical. Bp. Westcott has noted that in the New Testament the Old is called "The Law, Prophets, and Psalms," "The Law and the Prophets," "The Writings," "The Scriptures," etc.,—names which recognise the complexity of the book. When the singular "The Scripture" is used, a special passage or book is meant and not the whole collection. It is doubtful whether a singular term is found in the New Testament to express the collective of all the books of the Old Testament. 2 Cor. iii. 14 has been applied in this association, but v. 6 of the same chapter makes it more than doubtful whether the phrase "Old Testament" refers to what we mean when we use the expression. By the beginning of the third century the terms "Old Testament" and "New Testament" were probably in common use. "The first collective title" appears "in Jerome in the fourth century 'The Divine Library.'" The term "The Books" came to be used by Greek writers, and "in the thirteenth century," says Bp. Westcott, "by a happy solecism, the neuter plural came to be regarded as a feminine singular, and 'The Books' became by common consent 'The Book' (Biblia), our 'Bible.'" So it has come about that the composite character of the Bible, as made up of many books, has been largely forgotten. To the clergy and to scholars, of course, the truth I state is trite, but in the mind of the people the common thought is not *e pluribus*, but *unum*.

For the higher criticism then the Bible is a library, a collection of books. Consequently the problem of the origin of the Bible becomes a very complex one. The inquiry cannot lead us by a single step to a definite conclusion enunciated in a simple sentence. The same questions must be asked respecting every one of its sixty-six component parts. And after the comparatively easy problems of the origin and character and meaning and historical situation of each of these parts has been worked out, there remains the infinitely more delicate task of combining all these results into one conception, which shall do all justice and no injustice to the library so grandly opened with the stately words "In the beginning God created the Heavens and the Earth" and so propitiously closed with the benediction "The grace of the Lord Jesus be with the saints. Amen."

Were the Bible only divine, were there no human elements interwoven into its fabric, many of the tasks set for the higher criticism would not exist. To change the figure, "We have this treasure in earthen vessels." Granting the divine origin of Scripture, this Scripture came through human channels. It reflects the influence of the age which produced it, of the civilisation in which it arose, the circumstances of the people to whom it came and of the place where it was written, it mirrors the soul of the man who indited it. Each of these can but have left some impress on the product. The vocabulary, the style, the philosophy and theology, the matter itself, each has earmarks of its origin. The writer and his environment inevitably reappear in his work—necessarily so as he writes in entire conformity with the laws of his being and without attempt at imposture.

It follows therefore that to the trained student a literature will tell its own story of its origin, time of writing and purpose. Somewhat as the expert in English literature can tell almost at a glance the age to which a production belongs, locating it in the Early English, Middle English, Elizabethan, or some later period; so the expert Hebraist or Græcist detects in a given document signs of the golden age of early Hebrew or Greek, or signs of a decadence. A book which should tell of the trolley car or the ironclad, or should know the massacre of St. Bartholomew or the Monroe doctrine, could not be placed in the Middle Ages. Similarly a document which speaks of the subjection of the Canaanites from the standpoint of accomplished fact, which knows of kings over Israel, cannot be the product of a Moses who lived centuries before.

The higher criticism, let me repeat, deals primarily with the *components* of the Bible. It comes to them with certain questions. It interrogates the documents themselves. It desires to know the testimony of the books to themselves and to each other. To this end it cross-examines them. Its questions are directed as suggested in the definition we give. It makes such inquiries as: Is the book a unit or is it composite? the work of one author, of several, or of a school of writers? Is it as the author left it or has it been edited? Does the book claim or appear to claim authorship for itself? Is this claim consistent with the contents? Does the subject-matter mirror the known characteristics of the assumed author and his age? Does it, viewed from that standpoint, contain anachronisms, and if so, how are they to be accounted for? What is its literary form? Is it prose or poetry, drama or song, literal history, didactic allegory, or philosophical investigation? If history, what are its sources? How near was the author to them and how has he used them? Is ecclesiastical or other bias discoverable? From what standpoint did the author view his material? What is its philosophic background? Do its teachings accord with well-ascertained facts and is it therefore authoritative?

It will be seen that these questions simply expand the compound query: What is the origin, what the literary form, and what the historicity and credibility and therefore authority of the book?

In all this the higher criticism does not come with antagonism to any known or accepted theories. Says Zenos:

> "Its relation to the old and [the] new views respectively is one of indifference. It may result in the confirmation of the old as well as [*sic*] in the substitution of the new for the old."

The common supposition is that our method is fundamentally opposed to tradition. This is a grave mistake. The higher criticism acknowledges the presumption in favor of that which exists until reasons appear against such a presumption. It does not necessarily begin by doubting tradition unless the tradition is palpably indefensible.

August Böckh, one of the most noted of German philologists, is quoted with approval by the late Dr. Aiken of Princeton, although the original author was speaking of classical work and Dr. Aiken of Biblical criticism:

"We should be in the negative criticism more circumspect than the ancients. We must always start with the tradition, and try whether the unsuspected positive testimonies for the origin of a written work do not admit of being confirmed and completed by 'combinatory' criticism.

"Where the judgment is in any degree uncertain, the principle holds: any *book whatsoever is presumed genuine until the contrary is proved.*"

True, Dr. Aiken shows that "criticism must be suspicious rather than indolently credulous. It tests all traditions. It is in part negative in its first aim and its earliest working."

And yet we are justified in maintaining that it may accept the correctness of accepted views *as a working hypothesis* until facts antagonistic to those views transpire. But when once facts which discredit the received opinions are clearly established, regard for that which is in error, be the error hoary with antiquity, is no longer manifested and the discredited theory is repudiated. If then in answer to the searching questions of criticism results opposed to those given by tradition appear, and if repeated attempts to reconcile the newer results of research with the commonly accepted views fail, the blame must rest not with the newly applied method of study but with the older tradition, the deposit of an earlier, a less critical, a less completely equipped period of scholarship.

It seems a fit place here to insert a few words in answer to the question: "Who are higher critics?" They are usually supposed to be a few scholars, mostly professors in German universities or teachers in other than German schools who have adopted the views of the Germans, and whose claim to distinction is that they hold views subversive of traditional theories concerning the Bible. But the term is far more inclusive than this would allow.

The pastor who instructs his people about the plagues of drought and locusts which form the background of Joel's prophecy and so gives them the historical occasion for that prophecy, is a higher critic and makes his people such as far as they follow him. The Sunday School teacher who calls the attention of his scholars to the burning of the roll of Jeremiah and the issuing of a second edition of the prophecies as the narrative relates in Jer. xxxvi., is a higher critic and those scholars are *quoad hoc* also critics. The student of the Bible, who notes the characteristics which the author of the third gospel claims for his production in the preface, and who tests them by the light of facts ascertained from other sources, has joined the great army of critics. The teacher of history, who compares with the help of a harmony or without it the accounts of the four gospels to discover what their words authorise him to assert concerning Jesus of Nazareth, is a higher critic. The cursory reader of the last eight verses of Deuteronomy, which give the account of the death of Moses, and which tell of the absence of his equal up to some indefinite time,—the reader of those verses who says to himself, "Moses could not have written this," is putting into practice the methods of a higher critic. In fact, as soon as a person asks of a Biblical passage, "What does this mean, and why?" he has entered the ranks of these bold bad men!

Higher criticism is not at all a question of degree, it is wholly a matter of fact. That our statement in this paragraph is correct, is shown by the following from Dr. Chalmers as quoted by the late Dr. Aiken who, be it remembered, was of Princeton Seminary, neither of whom will be charged with neology. Dr. Chalmers' words are as follows:

"Without (this criticism) there could have been no interpretation at all of the sacred writings, and so no access to the mind and will of God as expressed by a revelation from Heaven."

Artists who picture the sphinx are wont to show on it some object, the approximate height of which is known, in order that the magnitude of that colossal monument may appear. So the study of a document is almost always relative to some other document or set of documents or array of facts. Some established standard by which measurements may be governed, some test-stone, comparison with which will afford ground for a conclusion, are prime necessities. Hence the higher criticism seeks criteria by which to guide its procedure and check its results, and it finds them in the assured conclusions of every department of study. Geography, history, chronology, archæology, philology, hermeneutics, philosophy,—in fact, all the sciences are its handmaidens. The stock in trade of the critic is not, as so often declared, subjective hypothesis and conjectural theory. The spade of the archæologist, the reading glass of the assyriologist, the basket of the fellah of the Nile, furnish him tests. He must ever bear in mind that the theodolite of the surveyor and the sextant of the explorer of the tels of Babylonia are brought to bear on his conclusions. His results must tally with the findings of the philologist. His interpretations are scrutinised by the trained exegete.

For ease of comprehension we may divide the criteria used by our system of investigation as applied to the Bible into three types or classes:

1. Those furnished by the study of a book itself, or to put it in another way, those purely internal.
2. Those which are internal to the Bible, the data given by comparison of the book under study with other books of the Bible.
3. Those afforded by the assured conclusions in the more general branches of knowledge. These are—known facts
    1. In History, particularly as given by Archæology in all its branches: Ancient Geography, Ethnology, Assyriology, Egyptology; indeed the science of Antiquities in its widest and most comprehensive domain as well as in its most highly specialised departments. Known facts
    2. In Comparative Philology,
    3. In Comparative Religion,
    4. In Hermeneutics, and
    5. In History of Theology or of Doctrine and of Philosophy.

It must ever be kept in mind that it is the certified results in these different domains of knowledge that the higher criticism applies to the solution of the problems it attacks.

How does it use them? Let me take them in order and illlustrate as best I can.

First, *the study of a book in and by itself.* In this criticism is almost entirely limited to a canvas of the literary qualities of diction, style, and rhetorical form. Considering the last first, we notice that the bearing, value, and use of an investigation of rhetorical form is to give a clue to the interpretation. We do not construe the statements of a poetical book as we do those of a prose narrative, an apologue will not bear the interpretation we give to a chronicle. Thus a contribution to the solution of the problem of Jonah was made when the suggestion first came that it is parable and not history. The fact, now firmly maintained, that the two accounts of the creation, the narrative of the fall, and that of the flood are poetry, is a help to the interpretation of those passages, though not the entire solution of the difficulties. What is the form of Ezekiel xl–xlviii? Is it a programme, or is it the first draft ever made of a Utopia, an ideal never to be realised? To the solution of these problems the higher criticism addresses itself. It asks: prose or poetry, fiction or history? It investigates the language used, whether figurative or literal; the method of arrangement, rhythmical or broken; the mood of discourse, imperative or persuasive or narrative. In this way it determines the character of the hermeneutic to be applied.

It is true, there is in all this an implicit reference to external standards. This simply raises the question whether there is any criterion that is purely internal.

Two other criteria, the diction and the style, are employed to determine the unity or integrity of a document.

It is conceivable that a book should be a composite, the result of uniting the productions of two or more writers. The parts would be likely to present a differing vocabulary and divergent styles. The phenomenon here outlined is presented prominently in at least three parts of the Old Testament, in the Pentateuch, in Isaiah, and in Zechariah, as well as in the New Testament in the Synoptic Gospels. In two of these, linguistic data play a most important part. In the Pentateuch this was the feature that led to the investigations which have continued for over a century and a half, and which have conducted with ever-increasing certainty and even inevitably to what is to-day a postulate in the larger part of the scholarly world,—thc composite character of the Pentateuch and the combination of its parts into a whole in a period long subse-

quent to Moses. In the book of Isaiah it is an argument of
force in supporting conclusions reached from other data.

I must ask indulgence if I dwell on this part of our
longer than I otherwise would, for it is a feature of the high
cism which greatly provokes the wrath of the enemy. T
constituent parts of a document can be distinguished al
word, is by one scholar pronounced a "preposterous ass
and that in the face of the accomplishment of the task in
of the book of Genesis and of the growing, almost comp
sensus of authorities in the other parts of the Pentateu
scholar just referred to makes an attempt to prejudge t
bility by stating that criticism of this character "can
grounded only when it has a greater amount of literatur
accessible in Hebrew." I could show that an English doc
composite make-up far less extensive than the book of Ge
been analysed into its components in the face of those w
have denied the analysis if they could, and by a man wh
no pretence to expert scholarship in English.

It is a well-known fact that an author becomes habitu
more or less limited vocabulary, acquires a habit of usin
methods of expression, may come to exhibit well-defined a
recognisable peculiarities. The classical scholar is in no d
confounding the style of Cæsar with that of Sallust, or Li
that of Tacitus. "The style is the man" is a literary ax
is true in any developed language, particularly true of the
This arises from a peculiarity which the Hebrew shares wi
ably no other tongue, its wealth of synonyms. Think of
guage that has 55 words for 'destroy,' 60 for 'break,' a
'take'!" A Hebrew writer cannot run the gamut of expr
which the speech is capable. His vocabulary becomes

the divine names Jehovah and Elohim). These parts, differentiated tentatively on the basis of the difference that has appeared, may or may not reveal upon examination other dictional individualities. If such further peculiar phrasical characteristics do appear, more minute and careful investigation is suggested, till the literary character of the parts is thoroughly set forth. This takes in the use of single words, of phrases or combinations of words, the employment of literal or figurative language, and discrimination of the *kinds* of figures used, thus advancing to the higher qualities of rhetorical style. If exhaustive scrutiny along these lines develops in each of the supposed components literary traits peculiar to itself, a *prima facie* case is made out; but the verdict is not yet rendered, an advance has to be made to other tests which it will be our business to describe a little later.

I shall make but two remarks here. (1) The process is thoroughly scientific. But one thing is assumed to start with, and that is a principle well known in literature, "sufficiently pronounced difference in style betokens difference of authorship." And the security of this method is becoming greater as the advance of learning makes more exact and discriminating knowledge of the languages. As Professor Sayce remarks: "A philological fact once ascertained is a fact that cannot be overturned or explained away." (2) This process is only preliminary. The case for the critics does not rest upon its results; more crucial and advanced tests are applied. The unity or diversity of the historical point of view, the theology of the assumed parts, the philosophy underlying the conceptions, the ethnographical and geographical indications are all taken into account. If the outcome as determined by these tests does not support the theory suggested by the exclusively literary or linguistic method, the discrepancy indicates a fault in either the reasoning or the application of the tests. It is in the convergence of the different lines of testimony, in the consensus of results reached by the various critical steps, that the great strength of the higher criticism lies.

We come now to the second class of tests spoken of: comparison of one or more books with others in the Bible.

These are used in two ways and for two purposes. The first brings to light the periods of a language and affinities in time. The second exhibits use of one book by another and therefore relative priority of the one to the other. The first is used with fine effect in Pentateuchal analysis, where it is shown that one of the documents, that of the priestly writer—presumed on other than linguistic grounds to be the latest—has many affinities with the late writers Jeremiah, Ezekiel, the latter half of Isaiah, the Chronicler, Daniel, and late Psalms. It therefore supports conclusions reached from the consideration of other data.

The second argument, that from citation, is one which, by itself, must be used with great caution, and its results are not always indisputable. For, when an identical passage appears in two books, the question has to be asked, which is the original? Even this does not exhaust the possibilities, for both may have borrowed from a third which has been lost. Thus that Is. ii. and Mic. iv embody a short prophecy by a third writer is more probable than that either has borrowed from the other. On the other hand, the question whether Jude has borrowed from 2 Peter or Peter from Jude is much debated in spite of the fact that Jude professes to quote "the Apostles of our Lord Jesus." If, however, it can be established that one author quotes another, the relative priority of the one is established, and an approach is made to the solution of the problem of the origin of the writings in question. Says Sayce:

> [While] "literary analysis" [of a book] "is independent of the facts of history so called,.....the higher critic is also required to determine the authenticity of the historical narratives which the documents contain....He must compare their statements with those of other ancient records, and ascertain how far they are in accord with the testimony derived from elsewhere." (Sayce, H. C. etc., p. 8.)

Hence "he must seek the aid of archæology, and test the results at which he may arrive by the testimony of the ancient monuments" and remains. The knowledge gained from these other sources enables him often to locate the origin in time and place of the document he is examining.

The date before which a book could not have been written, is often determinable from the book itself by the mention of an event, the time of which, either relative or absolute, is known. Thus we should know the earliest date to which we could refer a passage speaking of the opening of the Kiel canal. Similarly, a passage that informs us that "there arose not a prophet *since in Israel* like unto Moses," could not have been written by Moses, and a statement to the effect that "these are the kings of Edom before there dwelt any king over the Children of Israel," is hardly to be placed before the establishment of the kingdom under Saul. In like manner Professor Sayce shows that Gen. x., which mentions Gomer and Magog, could not have arisen earlier than Ezekiel; for the Assyrian inscriptions prove that not till the seventh century "did Gomer or the Kimmerians emerge from their primitive homes and come within the geographical horizon of the civilised nations of Western Asia."

In connection with such passages as these, there is sometimes possible the explanation of interpolation or of re-editing in later times. If evidence of this exists, it may sufficiently account for the facts. But the difficulty increases not in direct but in geometrical ratio with the number of interpolations that are required to explain the anachronisms. If *evidence* of interpolation is lacking and the explanation by interpolation is a theory propounded to get rid of a difficulty in a theory, the validity of the explanation is seriously in question.

Events whose time and order is established, are useful not only in determining the date of a document, they are employed also in fixing the credibility and authority of the same.

Thus, Belshazzar is represented in the Book of Daniel as sole king ol Babylon, as son of Nebuchadnezzar, and as succeeded by Darius the Mede. But it is regarded as proved by Assyriologists that Belshazzar was never king, that he was the son of Nabonidus who was a usurper not related to Nebuchadnezzar, and that Nabonidus was succeeded by Cyrus.

These and other facts are regarded as invalidating the Book of Daniel as history, and led even the apologetic Sayce to conclude that "it is with good reason that the Book of Daniel has been excluded from the historical books of the Old Testament in the Jewish Canon and classed along with the Hagiographa." As Professor Driver, building upon the conclusions of Professor Sayce, says:

"The aim of the author was not to write history, in the proper sense of the word, but to construct upon a historical basis, though regardless of the facts as they actually occurred, edifying religious narratives. 'This is the kind of history which the Jewish mind in the age of the Talmud loved to adapt to moral and religious purposes. This kind of history thus becomes as it were a parable, and under the name of Haggadah serves to illustrate the teaching of the Law.'"

In what precedes a hint has been given of the value of archæology in its various branches. Considerable use has been made of the subdivision of Assyriology. The vast libraries already unearthed, of which only a tithe has been read, and which await the application of those expert in the cuneiform writings, are continually furnishing data with which on the one hand we prove the general trustworthiness of the Old Testament history; or on the other compel the modification of conclusions respecting books and parts of books.

Some acknowledgement is due also to the services rendered by the science of ethnology. Professor Sayce has contributed to our knowledge in this respect no little amount, and has taught us to apply it to the elucidation of Scripture and the settlement of problems that arise there. Thus, on the basis of the mention of the tribes mentioned in Gen. x., as compared with facts gleaned from other sources, he has made clear that the "chart of the Pentateuch presents us with a picture of the Jewish world as it existed in the seventh century B.C." The citation already made from this scholar, covering the rise of the Gomer of Genesis and the connection therewith of the Gog and Magog of Ezekiel, is additional evidence of the value of ethnological tests.

No less useful and sometimes equally convincing are the premises furnished by philology. To quote Professor Sayce once more:

"A philological fact once ascertained is a fact which cannot be overturned or explained away."

Thus, the doubts raised concerning the historicity of the Book of Daniel are increased, when we find (1) that the word "Chaldæans" as used in that book dates from a period after the fall of the Babylonian empire; (2) that Persian words occur which certainly belong to a period later than the rise of the Persian empire; and (3) Greek words of such a type that they could not have been found in a Hebrew work till long "after the dissemination of Greek influences in Asia through the conquests of Alexander the Great."

But philological evidence is not all of this decisive character. The English scholar is aware that in the rural districts of both England and America he may find in current use forms which are survivals from the times of Chaucer. Literature composed on the border in early times may show the characteristics of a later time, when one language has superseded another, as Aramaic supplanted the Hebrew. Provincialisms may lead to a miscalculation of the age of a document unless the critic is on his guard. A fine example of the indecisiveness of this type of philological testimony is presented by the Book of Job. This book has been placed, on the testimony its language affords, all the way from the times of Moses to the times of the Maccabees. And, let me say in passing, some historic data possess this character of indefiniteness. Thus the stone age is not a definite period the limits of which can be fixed for a certain century for all parts of the world. The age of flint continued for the North American Indians centuries after the introduction of fire-arms in Europe. Similarly, the patriarchal period has not yet passed by, for on the steppes of Northern Asia and in the deserts of Arabia that form of life still exists. Hence the historical evidence of the Book of Job is in this respect indecisive. The patriarchal mode of life reflected in the surroundings of the "most patient of men" has been taken to mirror the times of Moses or earlier. But place that sufferer on the edge of the desert or in one of its oases, and the conditions given might exist in the Roman period.

This brings us to another criterion of value—the signs of philosophical and theological development. Thus, the age of the book to which we have been referring is probably to be placed by its stage of thought. The "age of unquestioning faith has passed.... the laws of providence [even]....are made the subject of doubt." There is "a struggle between a traditional creed which taught that all suffering was a penalty for sin, all prosperity a reward for goodness, and the spectacle of undeserved suffering afforded by more complex social conditions." (Driver, p. 406.)

A like problem arises in connection with the Epistle to the Colossians, the Pastoral Epistles, and the Fourth Gospel. When was the form of gnosticism which each of these combated, and when did it arise? Is the origin of this heresy *in its Christian form* to be put back into the fifth decade of the first Christian century of our era, or must it be deferred? If it did not rise till the second century, those books are second century publications.

Similarly in the Old Testament the question arises concerning the origin of the doctrine of the resurrection and of angels. Can this be placed behind the contact of the mass of the Jewish people with Babylonian and Persian forms of belief? These problems take us back into the history of doctrine and of theology. In fact they lead us to the last set of tests which we may mention—those furnished by the still youthful science of Comparative Religion. We are here brought face to face with the most determined opposition to the methods of historical study on the part of the traditionalists. The emphasis they lay upon the uniqueness of Judaism and of Christianity is most firm. Comparison with other religions is scouted. Between these two religions and the ethnic beliefs there is a gulf fixed which no bridge may span.

And yet, light is thrown by the study of ethnic religions upon Christianity and its predecessor. And as a consequence, just as students may put darkening blinds in the windows of their own studies, but cannot enclose in a darkened room the glorious sun, nor prevent his shining upon the rest of the world; so they cannot hinder the light of research from throwing into high relief the facts resulting from such comparison. By using this newly-risen branch of science, the thesis tnat Hebrew and Christian records are composite is made at least hypothetically tenable by the discovery of this character in Veda and Shastra and Avesta. The miraculous conception is no exclusive possession of Christianity. It appears in the religions of Buddha, Brahma, and Zoroaster.

In like fashion, the story of Moses is not unexampled. The

essentials of the fabric, "his exposure in the basket of rushes, his rescue and subsequent greatness" are told of Sargon who lived (say) 3800 B. C., and "of other great personages in the ancient world." The source of "The Early Narratives of Genesis" is no longer hidden, but exists uncovered in Babylonian libraries. The ten tables of Genesis are put alongside similar tens in Egypt, Chaldæa, Armenia, and Persia. And the background of the New Testament, the philosophy and theology of the times as revealed in the literature of Greece, Palestine, and Egypt, give comparative data of no little worth.

If we have thus cursorily glanced at the touchstones called into use by Biblical criticism, we have yet to see how they are to be employed. Certain qualifications must exist in the critic. The telescope pointed at a star is ready to tell of that star's glory to any observer. But there is a vast difference in what the instrument says to the ordinary beholder and to the trained astronomer.

A prime requisite in the Biblical critic is a profound common sense fortified by a varied and exact knowledge. And we wish to specify as belonging here and a part of this common sense what is known as the "historic imagination." The critic may not judge the workings of the Oriental mind by the psychological experiences of the Occidental; the patient pursuit of a train of reasoning by the Aryan differs much from the Semite's intuitional leap to a conclusion and his externalising of a subjective affection. This critic may not read into the life of three thousand years ago the experiences of the present. While his inductions must be no less complete and no less carefully followed out than those of the investigator of what are called natural phenomena, while he must balance with most exact justice external testimony and internal evidence, he must ever remember that the facts he is investigating, the literature he studies, are those of a different race, the fruitage of another civilisation, the outcome of a dissimilar environment. Before he can correctly estimate their value and apply his tests, he must have projected himself into the situation of the writers, have lived their life, thought their thoughts, experienced their emotions, felt their aspirations, breathed their hopes, sympathised with their disappointments; he must have danced to their pipings and have wept to the accompaniment of their mourning.

A second requisite in the critic is divorcement from theological or other presuppositions. The chances are many to one that if a scholar enters upon the study of the Bible with a theory to support, he will find plenty of props in its declarations. "Wide is the range of words; words may make this way or that way." If Arminianism and Calvinism, Episcopacy and Congregationalism, Quakerism and lusty rousing Methodism can each find its support in the "written Word," why despair of support for any theory? In how many ways during the last fifty years has Gen. i. been twisted by apologists to fit the varying forms of philosophic cosmogonies? "Words may make this way or that way."

In demanding freedom from bias in the critic, we acknowledge to running counter to all prejudice. Perhaps we are asking something impossible of accomplishment. But we "hitch our wagon to a star." And this much must be admitted, that no basis short of this will give us the ultimate truth.

This demand does not mean that the mind shall come a blank to the study of the Bible. It does not mean, for example, that the investigator shall at the outset cast aside all tradition as fundamentally useless. Nor does it ask that he come with the belief that no results but those tradition gives can be truthful. What is meant is that he shall be thoroughly candid, entirely open to the force of all evidence. Perhaps one presupposition may be allowed, viz., that "all evidence has some value direct or indirect." The "supernatural" in literature is not to be ruled out nor assumed. The word must first be defined. The miraculous is a matter of evidence. Criticism can progress only on solid ground. It requires an adamantine standing-place. It has neither wings nor fins nor skates. It neither cleaves the atmosphere, nor cuts the liquid waste, nor skims over thin ice. Its movements are slow, not always graceful. Like the elephant, it tests the bridge by which it crosses a problem. And as with that huge beast, successfully to oppose it requires keenest weapon sped by unerring hand. The ideal criticism will have not even the vulnerable heel of Achilles.

The third and last requisite of a critic that I shall mention is that he regard truth alone as an end. To repeat the quotation used by the venerable Dr. Green of Princeton:

"Let the truth be told though the heavens fall."

The use of criticism to support a creed is a perversion of its functions. A writer in the *Quarterly Review* (Oct., 1895) has the following:

"The Church historian [and equally the higher critic,—indeed the Church historian is above all a higher critic] must not ask what relation the early Christian books bear to the thirty-nine articles or the decrees of the Council of Trent or the Shorter Catechism or to the Andover Creed; he must not ask a great many questions which were not in the writers' minds, but he must ask what were the problems of their day, and how did they answer them.

"The New Testament does not for him contain a collection of texts proving or not proving certain scholastic theses, but a body of documents moulded by the personality of their writers, bearing witness to different aspects of a common belief held in different ways by different temperaments."

It may be that the conclusions fortify a dogmatic position. That is one thing. But to set out with that end in view is not criticism.

On the other hand, advice is sometimes given which is as wrong in principle as dogmatic search for proof-texts:

"A man must pursue his method no matter where it leads him."

It may often happen that a course of argumentation points to a palpable absurdity. He would rightly be reckoned a fool who should persist in that course. The very tendencies of a line of argument may, as judged by current belief, indicate fallacy in inference or falsity in premise. When such results appear, it is time to scan the whole process that seems to lead astray. Each step must undergo scrutiny. The premises must be scanned for material error, the deductive operations carefully examined; if then the result is still contrary to received opinion, that opinion must be challenged whatever the cost.

To illustrate by a crucial test. The majority of Christians hold the Bible to be, not to contain, the Word of God. It is therefore inerrant. That is current opinion. Doubtless the majority of Christians would be shocked at the thought of a mistake in God's word. This popular belief is borne out by syllogistic reasoning thus: The Bible is from God; Whatever is from God is perfect; Ergo, the Bible is perfect. Now whatever contains a mistake is imperfect; the Bible is not imperfect; therefore the Bible does not contain a mistake.

So much for current opinion and deductive reasoning!

Let us study a little of the reign of Jehoshaphat as given by the Chronicler. 2 Chr. xvii. 6 informs us that the king "took away the high places and the Asherim out of Judah." But according to 2 Chr. xx. 33 "the high places were not taken away," and 1 King xxii. 43 agrees with this. Here is an evident contradiction, and so far as has yet been discovered there is no way of reconcilement. What shall we do? Luther could take off his hat and acknowledge that the Holy Spirit was wiser than he. Will that satisfy us? Or shall we exclude the Chronicler from the Canon? But that is impossible! What then? There is but one thing to do—we must face the fact without subterfuge; current opinion is wrong, the Bible is not inerrant in matters of history. If our opponents insist, as does an essayist in one of our great denominations, "No other revelation than an inerrant one is worthy the confidence of the race," if they force upon us the dilemma—"Either an errorless Bible or none" and allow us no other horn, the answer of candor and of scholarship must be—"You persist in this to your own confusion." And no less than Professor Sayce has said "in the end the opinion of the scholars will always prevail." Here then as elsewhere the old maxim must hold: "Be sure, be *sure* you're right, then *go ahead*." No matter what the consequence, you *must* go ahead!

With such a method of study and with students so qualified, what are likely to be the results? In stating these it is not my intention to go into minutiæ, to detail the consequences which affect individual books or even groups of books of the Bible. We cannot linger here to state the views now so widely received concerning the Pentateuch, Isaiah, Solomon's Song, the Synoptic Gospels, the Apocalypse, etc.

I propose to give the effects of the new method as bearing upon the general study of the Bible.

It may be remembered that in the definition I gave it was stated that consequences destructive and constructive might appear.

And first, the destructive results. We have already attempted to show that the higher criticism does not destroy the Bible itself. That is left entire. But its character as literature, as history, as religious teaching, is made clear. The methods of the writers of those early days is in many cases laid open. There is no attack, open or covert, upon the book. But false estimates of it and unfounded teachings about it are shown to be supportless. The way is cleared for a true apprehension of its beauties, its truth, and its true function. This wonderful book has been made for centuries a pack-horse to carry the theories of pseudo-scientists and visionaries upon the functions of a book of religious teaching. The higher criticism makes this use of the Bible no longer possible.

The *inspiration* of the Bible is not destroyed. That is unassailable. No mine is driven against its truth. In fact, its true nature is exhibited in the results of critical research. But false notions about the inspiration of the Bible are by the processes of criticism shown to be baseless. Our tests reveal how untenable are such positions as, for example, that of Dr. Hodge, who tells us that "(inspiration) is not confined to moral and religious truths, but extends to the statements of facts, whether scientific, historical, or geographical." Persistence in that position necessitates the abandonment of all inspiration.

Biblical criticism has made impossible reliance upon *a priori* methods of reasoning about the Bible, its origin and nature. And it is destroying the wall of tradition built on deductive reasoning that kept the Bible from being "understanded of the people."

These are but a few of the services rendered by the iconoclastic tendencies of the newer method. But its destructive tendencies are not its only virtue. It would be deserving of support if it did no more than clear the ground of the underbrush which has grown up and almost hidden the Bible from men's eyes. But, as Professor Menzies says in the *Contemporary* for April, 1895:

"The ultimate aim of criticism is not to deny, but to build up; and the ve negations with which it sets out tend, by awakening inquiry and showing the tra tional view of a subject, to bring about in time a positive and scientific constr tion, every part of which has been well tested, and may therefore be regarded wi confidence "

Indeed, it can be affirmed with assurance that it has alrea produced positive results of the highest value.

It has rendered hermeneutics or the science of interpretati great benefits. It has done no small duty in putting the parts the Bible in their true historical setting. The interpretation many an obscure passage is at once cleared up, when the historic background and the immediate occasion for its utterance is know

The "fourfold fetters" of the Council of Trent—conformati to the rule of faith, the practice of the Church, the consent of t fathers, and the decisions of the councils—no longer bind the Bo of Books. Criticism has reinstated the principle of Luther:

"Every word [of Scripture] should be allowed to stand in its natural mea ing."

Investigation of the word of Scripture in all the light shed b philology and history and archæology and all the kindred inducti sciences, makes clearer the "natural meaning" and therefore th content of "revelation" as given in the Bible. It is all the tim making less and less possible false and distorted and warped an allegorical views of Scripture as a whole and of individual passage "The historical sense first and above all" is the newer principle o exegesis.

In this way great advantage accrues to the pulpit. There i gained a firmer foothold, a more rational basis upon which to res appeals to duty. Says one scholar known favorably to all school of thought in two hemispheres:

"I owe any joy, any confidence, any power I have in preaching the Old Te tament to the higher criticism."

The almost unanimous testimony of those who have bee pressed onward by the procedure is that the Bible becomes deepe in intent and richer in content through the application of the new research.

Speaking of the view of the Hebrew literature which relates to the origins of the nation and holds that they are idealised history, Professor Flint has the following:

"This view of their formation—of which Reuss and Kuenen, Wellhausen and Stade, have been among the most prominent advocates—does not deprive them of any of those rare merits either of contents or form for which they justly claim our admiration. The unity, consistency, naturalness, moral elevation, and spiritual instructiveness of the presentation of history given in the ancient Hebrew literature, are facts which cannot be denied, however they may have been attained.

"It reflected with wonderful faithfulness and completeness the theocratic life of Israel, of which it was an outcome. It was pervaded by a profound sense of a supernatural presence and of an eternal law making for righteousness. All events were exhibited in it from the religious point of view, God being set forth as the supreme factor of history, His will as the historical standard of judgment, and His kingdom as the goal of historical development. Yet human nature is also skilfully and truthfully delineated, in a style almost always simple and natural, and at times pathetic and sublime.

". . . . Man appears nowhere more man than where God is represented as miraculously (?) at his side."[1]

Another of the services rendered by the subject of our consideration is that done to apologetics. The bitterness manifested against Spinoza and Hobbes and Tom Paine and other "infidels" was due probably in great part to the fact that no small portion of the declaration of those men was truth and could not be gainsayed. Men usually feel good-natured toward opponents whom they have whipped. But the apologetic of those times could not answer completely the arguments of the "infidels"; and consequently what refutation could not compass, invective was expected to accomplish.

Upon the Bible as read in these days the arrows of the early skeptics fall blunted and shattered. Now newer and more subtle objections are raised. To rebut these, keener and more discerning study by the faithful must follow, until the last arrow has been shot, the last bolt sped, and the Word of God remains unassailed and unassailable.

One great gain flowing from the work of the critics is the dis-

---

[1] *Philosophy of History*, pp. 48–49.

closure of the reason why to many Christian souls some parts of the Bible are infinitely more precious than others.

How many qualms of conscience have been raised, how many baseless fears for his salvation aroused in a humble believer by the consciousness that to him the Song of Songs did not appeal as did John xiv., that the answer of God out of the whirlwind of Job was not as beloved as the Twenty-third Psalm, nor the prayer of Hezekiah as 1 Cor. xv! Such a one often wondered why the pessimism of Koheleth did not come home as did the glorious optimism of Rom. viii.

The Bible to the Bible student no longer appears a level of Dead Sea waters with neither ebb nor flow. It is a stream whose origin in the mountains of antiquity is as obscure as that of the four rivers of Eden, but it emerges in history a river of salvation now flowing deep and strong as the current of God's love, here it glides peacefully by banks of restful green where trees of healing arch their boughs and make refreshing shade, now it rushes a mighty torrent of impetuosity as the "kings of the earth set themselves, and the rulers take counsel together, against the Lord and against His Messiah," again it murmurs in sorrow as the wind of anguish sweeps its waters, and we hear in the throbbings of its tender music, "How shall I give thee up, Ephraim? Shall I deliver thee over, O Israel?" And so it goes sweeping on, its waters carrying refreshing to the nations and becoming a broad sea of deliverance heaving in the hand of the Almighty.

No less important for us to notice is the recovery by the higher criticism of the human element in the Bible.

In this it has done a service like that the newer theology is performing for the life of Jesus. One of Chas. Gore's Essays on Subjects connected with the Incarnation traces the gradual obscuration in theological dogma of the humanity of Christ, until He became unapproachable, was pure and sheer Deity, and then came as a necessity in Catholic ritual the invocation of the Virgin, for man must have a mediator! So the Bible had been removed and laid upon an unapproachable altar, and what followed was not reverent use but *bibliolatry*. This rock of offence criticism has drilled and shattered, and has in the truest sense restored to the people the Bible, written by men, holy men indeed, but thoroughly human. And now the Book of Books comes throbbing through and through in response to the heartbeat of humanity, soothing sorrows, inspiring hope, giving comfort, revealing the great love of God for His creation, making known His yearning for His wayward children, and assuring men of His will that not one sinner should be lost, but that all should turn from their wickedness and live.

A question of the highest importance is the *necessity* of applying the processes of the higher criticism to the Bible.

We have asked whether it is possible in the first place and desirable in the second place that the Bible should be exempted. The reply is that it is neither possible nor desirable. We can do no other, therefore, than oppose firmly the school which insists on the irreverence of such treatment of the Bible. The plea of this school is, "The Bible is different from other Books for it is the Word of God." To question or cross-examine the Bible is "consciously to test the credibility of the Holy Ghost, to dispute the veracity of God Himself."

The reply to this is at least twofold: first theoretically. Yes, such is the claim! But something more than the assertion of a claim is needed. Moreover the claim itself cannot be set up as a bar to an examination of the grounds of the claim. Every pretension is not only subject to investigation, *it is of itself a challenge to investigate*. Besides, the usual statement of those who insist upon the exemption of the Bible from the processes of critical study is a perfectly correct one, that the Bible testifies to itself. Why then not examine it? But in the second place the theoretic answer to the objection issues practically in the phenomena of Christianity's contact with the world. Christianity aspires to be a world-religion, to embrace within its protecting arms the whole of humanity. It is distinctively a missionary religion if not *the* missionary religion. In fulfilment of its mission it comes into contact and conflict with the other religions which also have claims to be divine. The documents on which those religions rest are regarded by the possessors as God-given. Claims are in conflict. How shall the dispute l settled? Mere vociferation, loud shouting of bare pretensions, w not secure the victory Christianity desires. And even if Christi scholars should desire it, they may not scrutinise the claims of no Christian religions and documents while imposing upon all othe the dilemma—"Believe (without evidence) or be condemned Can a higher imperative be shown for Christianity's claims th for those of other beliefs? Then why oppose an examination?

Moreover, whoever discerns the condition of things in Christe dom to-day sees that the Bible is assailed on historic grounds. Tl question is principally whether the defenders of the Bible shall l allowed to use in its defence the principles and methods used l the assailants so far as they are legitimate. As Dr. Aiken has e pressed it:

"Neither unbelief nor the proudest and strictest science is more concerned expose any unfounded claim that may have been made in or by the Church in 1 gard to those Scriptures than the Church is to know precisely what it possesses and with its sacred books."

Once more, the Bible appeals to our moral and mental fa ulties. As the astronomer in "The Poet at the Breakfast Tabl has it:

"I claim the right of knowing whom I serve,
Else is my service idle; He that asks
My homage asks it from a reasoning soul."

And now, finally, we have to ask whether there are *limitatio* to this process. The answer must be, that if revelation itself w gradual, if there was a progress in the knowledge of Himself a of man which God conveyed to the race, we must expect develo ment in this human process. We cannot look for a human produ to transcend that of the divine mind. We may not count upon Minerva springing full-armed from the brain of the critic. W may hope for the growth of a sturdy oak, to outlast the centurie or rather the course of events is to resemble the deposition, as l a stream, of particles which harden through the ages into eve lasting rock—fit foundation for firm faith.

What are some of these limitations?

First, much still depends on the interpretation of passag

upon which conclusions are founded. To illustrate, there are those who find evidences of totemism among the Hebrews. They point to researches among kindred races, as the Arabs, the results of which seem to indicate the existence of totemistic customs. By this means they think to establish a probability that it is a Semitic institution. They then find in the Old Testament such passages as the Ebenezer text, 1 Sam. vii. 12, the references to the serpent as an object of worship, such names as Oreb and Zeeb—raven and wolf—Caleb (dog), Nahash (serpent), and regard these as evidences of totemism among Hebrews and their neighbors. The theory is a very fascinating one, but the data are wholly dependent upon interpretations that do not necessarily commend themselves to the scholar. Till the *meaning* of passages like these is definitely settled, such questions must wait.

A second limitation is that the critic must perforce depend for his criteria upon specialists in many various departments. In the growing volume and complexity of knowledge no man can be an expert in more than a very narrow field. The man who uses results attained by others in any department of research, must therefore wait till those results have the sanction of scholars in those departments. Impatience may in no case enter into the make-up of the critic. "The product of each new source of knowledge," says Prof. Fr. Brown, "is apprehended only by degrees. A long time is needed to exhaust it." He has, moreover, on his hands the delicate task of judging how vital to the problem which possesses him any fact or set of facts really is. The principle of proportion is no easy one to master. The proper adjustment of the elements of an answer is a task requiring not only nicety but firmness of touch. Indeed the qualifications of a critic differ from those of a poet, he must be both born and made; born with a fine mental and moral and spiritual endowment, and made in the workshop of the purest scholarship, the frankest candor, and the most reverent devotion.

A third limitation is the character of the phenomena which underlie the Bible, which are its cause. As Dr. George A. Gordon has said:

"The Bible transcends the mere historian. So far as it is outward fact, i falls within his domain; but so far as it is a body of ethical and spiritual truth, i falls within the concern of humanity. The revelation of God as a record belong to learning; but as a moral and spiritual content it belongs to all prophetic souls.

What can criticism do with such facts as that embodied in th statement of Samuel, "Behold, to obey is better than sacrifice, t hearken than the fat of rams"? Whether the story of Samuel an Saul be history or legend, this teaching commends itself to the sou with an emphasis unmistakable. How can criticism treat the state ment of the Master: "If a man keep my word he shall never se death; but it shall be in him a fount of water, springing up int everlasting life"? In a word, after criticism has done its best, com pleted its studies of words and style and mythologies and historie and what not, it comes to the question of Zophar: "Canst thou b searching find out *God*?"

As Professor Menzies has said:

"It may be maintained that the seed-plot of religion must always be sought i the ideal rather than the real."

What is therefore the attitude to be assumed by the critic? I is recognised in what has been said that an approach only to fina ity can be expected. The goal, like the goal of prophecy, recede ever into the infinite. Results, like knowledge, must long remai partial, though approximating completeness. In the face of a this, the critic can least of men afford to be dogmatic. He mus leave that to those who must be dogmatic to maintain their pos tions. He must recognise that conclusions reached now, whi obligatory with present knowledge, are only tentative; that upo the *ruins* of what may seem to him an eternal structure may b erected the ultimate temple of truth. And he must be content he be privileged to hew and shape some humble blocks which th great Architect may deem not unworthy of being built into th walls of the City of God.

GEO. W. GILMORE.

MEADVILLE, PA.

THE FIRST BUDDHIST COUNCIL.

PREFATORY NOTE.

TEITARO SUZUKI has made, in the present translations, the most valuable contribution to our knowledge of the First Buddhist Council, which has appeared in Western nations since Samuel Beal's translation from the Chinese Dharmagupta document presented by that scholar to the Oriental Congress at Berlin in 1881, and reprinted in his *Abstract of Four Lectures* (1882). It is well known to students of the *Sacred Books of the East* that there is, in the twentieth volume of that series, an account of the first two Councils of the Buddhist Order, translated from the Pâli. The account is a later addition to the Minor Section on Discipline, and we may call it the Council Appendix. It proceeds from the orthodox and aristocratic School of the Elders, the great rival of whom was the School of the Great Council (*Mahâsamghika*) who, says the Pilgrim Hsüan-Tsang, admitted to their deliberations the common people, the foolish and the wise.[1] This being so, it is important for us to know both sides of the story, indeed as many sides as possible; and this we can do, to some extent, by reading the different sectarian statements translated by Suzuki. It is very satisfactory to me, on comparing the one document which he has in common with Beal (viz., the Dharmagupta) to find that the two Sinologues substantially agree in their list of the Canonical books.[2]

[1] The Ceylon Chronicles do not admit this sect's existence until the Second Council.

[2] The only real disagreement is Suzuki's *Itivrittaka* and *Nidâna* in place of Beal's "good *Nidâna Sûtra*." I sincerely hope Suzuki is right, for the Pâli *Itivuttaka* is one of the jewels of the Canon.

Hermann Oldenberg, in his pioneer essay on the Canon (1879), threw grave doubts upon the historicity of the First Council, as Suzuki now reminds us. Rhys Davids, while admitting the doubt, subtracted from its cogency. (*S. B. E.*, XI., Introd., 1881.) For that doubt is based upon the argument from silence, viz: the silence of the *Decease Book* upon any convocation, while yet reporting the very speech of Subhadra which, according to the Council Appendix, gave rise to the Council. But there is another speech in the *Decease Book* which really requires a Council, or at least a discussion which would inevitably be decided by authority. It is the speech of Buddha to Ânanda: "If the Order should so desire, Ânanda, after my demise, let them abrogate the lesser and minor precepts."

Now, according to the Council document of the Great Council School, here translated by Suzuki, this speech did raise a vehement debate, as indeed how could it fail to? The document agrees with the Pâli account of the rival sect, that the objectors were overruled by Kassapa the Great.

Again, the *Decease Book* also tells us that not only monks and nuns, but laymen and laywomen, were, at the time of the Master's death, *bahussutâ*, *dhammadharâ*, full of learning and repositories of the Dhamma. In the Numerical Collection we find the names of the chief ones who were thus expert. This ancient list of disciples holds a place in the Pâli Canon like that of the Christian list in the Third of Mark. Now the list in the Numerical Collection tells us that *Kaccâna was the foremost among those who could accurately expand an utterance of the Master's which had been spoken concisely.* (*Anguttara* I., 14). The Middling Collection adds that Buddha complimented Kaccâna upon his ability to do this. (*Majjhima*, No. 18.) The same Nikâya (No. 84) tells us that Kaccâna converted the King of Avanti after Buddha's decease, and the monarch was ready to take him for his master. Besides this learned Kaccâna, there was Ânanda learned in the Suttas, Upâli in the Vinaya; while others, both clerical and lay, were preachers of the Dhamma, or otherwise expert in points of the great religion.

So obviously does this great list of disciples bear upon the First Council, that the oldest Chronicler of Ceylon gives a poetic abridgment thereof in his two accounts;[1] for, like the Hebrew compilers of the Old Testament, the Ceylon Chronicler is not content with a composition of his own, but transmits two separate documents concerning each of the three Councils. These documents probably emanate from the Great Minster and some other monastery in the ancient capital of Ceylon.

There is, in the Pâli Canon, an archaic work, the *Itivuttaka*, which I venture to call the Buddhist Logia-Book. Each paragraph in this venerable Gospel-source is attested by the solemn words: "Exactly this is the meaning of what the Blessed One said, and thus it was heard by me."[2]

Though no names are given, this formula implies that ear-witnesses made depositions as to what they had heard from the Master.

Another ancient document, the Great Section on Discipline, exhibits a charming picture of the monks reciting the Master's words even during his lifetime: on the last night of the yearly residence during the rains, the reciters sat up late comparing notes and fixing in their minds the discourses they had chanted together. Another document of the Discipline, the Minor Section, tells us how the famous disciple Dabba the Mallian (who could light the monks to bed by emitting magnetic flames from his fingers) allotted apartments to the different reciters: the Sutta-reciters and the Vinaya-reciters were housed together. Another ancient Discipline document, the *Pârâjika*, enumerates Nine Divisions into which the sacred lore was divided. Three of these divisions, *Jâtaka*, *Udâna*, *Itivuttaka*, are names of leading books of the Canon to this day; a fourth one, *Sutta*, is the name of the great fivefold collection; while three other names enter into the titles of books or discourses.

Thus we have reason to believe, from the Canon itself, even in its oldest documents, that a Council to fix it after Buddha's decease was inevitable. The monks had been used to hold just such a council every year through the long decades of his life-work, and

[1] *Dîpavamsa* 4 and 5.

[2] Cf. "Gospel Parallels from Pâli Texts," in *The Open Court* for January, 1901.

they could not have done without one when he was no more. Agai does the *Decease Book* come to our aid: "Ânanda, the Doctrine an Discipline set forth and laid down by me must, after my departure be your Master." And again: "These four great References, monks, will I set forth," viz.: that when a monk maintains a give doctrine to be that of the Buddha, of the Order, of the reciters, of some Elder learned in the Âgamas, the Dhamma, the Vinay and the Summaries (*Mâtikâ*), it must be compared with the established Doctrine and Discipline, *line by line and letter by letter* (*padavyañjanâni*). This implies, according to Western ideas, a written standard whereto appeal could be made; but many facts brought forward by Max Müller and Rhys Davids prevent our believing this. The appeal could only be, therefore, to some established form of the Sacred Lore *as held by the reciters in their collective capacity*: for, says the text of the Great References, a monk may be misled by a numerous company of Elders who are learned in the Âgamas (and so forth, as above). There must therefore have been *a standing Council on Doctrine and Discipline during Buddha's lifetime.*

The later testimony of the Council Appendix affirms that the Elders of the First Council *revised corruptions of the text*,[1] because Buddha had commended it. It had therefore been done before, doubtless at the yearly meetings aforesaid. The Council Appendix also gives a hint that more than one recension was compiled. For, just as Papias, when Peter and John were no more, said that he preferred the living voice of those who remained who had heard the Apostles, rather than written records; so, when the monk Purâṇa was informed that the Elders had recited and fixed the Canon, whereto he was asked to bow, he politely replied: "Gentlemen, the Doctrine and Discipline have been beautifully chanted in chorus by the Elders; but, all the same, I shall maintain what I heard and received from the mouth of the Blessed One exactly as I heard it."

Now Purâṇa was the leader of a party of five hundred—a sym

[1] Thus do I translate *khandaphullam patisamkharimsu*, rendered in *S. B. E.* XX., p. 373, "they repaired dilapidation."

bolical number, meaning a large body; and the same number is attached to the orthodox party. Therefore, from the moment of Buddha's death, there were at least two recensions of the Canon maintained by parties of equal strength. The documents here set before us by Suzuki plainly proclaim the existence of rival recensions, agreeing in fundamentals, but differing in arrangement and extent. We may gather from the Island Chronicle that a favorite bone of contention was the question: What is text and what is commentary? Accordingly we find that sharp divergences prevail in those portions of the Canon which embody commentary: the Short Collection and the Higher Doctrine (*Khuddaka Nikâya* and *Abhidhamma*).

Of course, the Canons here given as fixed at the Master's death are taken by each school from its own recension as it existed when the account was written; but this does not upset the fact that at least two such recensions existed from the first, viz., an aristocratic and a democratic. The first is the School of the Elders and the second the Great Council. It is true that the latter (the Mahâsamghika) did not formally secede until the second council, at the end of the first Buddhist century; but it has long been clear to me that its germ is to be found in the words of Purâṇo.

Suzuki's documents are valuable, if nothing else, as lists of the contents of the different sectarian Canons. It is just such fundamental documents as these that are in crying need of translation, from Sanskrit, Chinese, and Tibetan. We want to compare the statements of the conservative school, transmitted to us through the Pâli, with those of other sects who had other and rival recensions. (Unless we are very orthodox Theravâdins, we may even call them Canons, in the plural, just as we should speak of the Greek, Armenian, and Abyssinian Canons of the Old and New Testaments, which accept or reject the Apocalypses of Enoch and John.) According to the Tibetans (*teste* Csoma) the Confessional (and presumably the Scriptures generally) were recited in four different dialects: Sanskrit, Pâli,[1] and two more.

[1] The name *Pâli* is not used, but from the names of the Ceylon sects who used the dialect called "the vernacular," we know that Pâli is meant.

Let us hope that Teitaro Suzuki will go on adding to knowledge in the same useful way.

ALBERT J. EDMUNDS.

Historical Society of Pennsylvania, August, 1901.

THE FIRST CONVOCATION OF BUDDHISM.

The purpose of the present article is not to enter into an hi torical or critical examination of the First Convocation of th Buddhist Order, which is generally admitted by all the schools c Buddhism to have taken place immediately after the death of th Master. Though, some critics, for instance, Oldenberg, doubts it historical reality, it is apparently natural that the pious disciple of Buddha wished to rescue all his teachings from oblivion as soo as an opportunity presented itself. It may not, of course, hav taken place in all its details as told by different sects, but eve then those records possess an important historical significance o account of the light which they throw on the later development o Buddhism. Having this in view, I have collected and compare as many materials as available from the Chinese sources, but hav refrained from giving an entire translation of them, which, howeve interesting to the specialist, cannot be presented in a limited space The following summarised notes may serve in giving some insigh into the nature of the First Convocation as well as into the attitud assumed towards it by different schools of Buddhism.

SOURCES.

The Chinese sources relating to the First Convocation of Bu dhism are as follow:

1. The *Sudarçana-vinaya-vibhâshâ* (right-comprehension-vinay analysis): Case *Han*,[1] fas. VIII., pp. 1–4. (Translated by San ghabhadra, A. D. 489. 18 fasciculi.)

2. The *Mahîçâsaka-nikâya-pañcavarga-vinaya* (the Vinaya-te of the Mahîçâsaka school in five divisions): Case *Chang*, fas. II

[1] This refers to the japanese edition of the Chinese Tripiṭaka, 1883, commo known as the Kôkyô Shoin Edition.

pp. 68–69. (Translated by Buddhajîva with the assistance of some native Chinese Buddhists, A. D. 423–424. 30 fasciculi.)

3. The *Caturvarga-vinaya* (the Vinaya-text of the Dharmagupta school in four divisions): Case *Lieh*, fas. VI., pp. 49–51. (Translated by Buddhayaças and Chu Fo-nien, A. D. 405. 60 fasciculi.)

4. The *Mahâsanghika-vinaya* (the Vinaya-text of the Mahâsanghika school): Case *Lieh*, fas. X., 32–35. (Translated by Buddhabhadra and Fâ-hsien, A. D. 416. 46 fasciculi.)

5. The *Mûlasarvâstivâda-nikâya-vinaya-samyuktavastu* (the miscellaneous part of the Vinaya-text of the Sarvâstivâda school): Case *Han*, fas. II., pp. 87–93. (Translated by I-tsing, A. D. 710. 40 fasciculi.)

6. The *Vinaya-mâtrikâ Sûtra* (the Sûtra of the Vinaya-summaries): Case *Han*, fas. IX., pp. 15–16. (The translator's name is lost, but the work is considered to have been done under the Chin dynasty, A. D. 350–431. 8 fasciculi.)

7. The *Mahâ-prajñâ-pâramitâ Çâstra* (a treatise on the great wisdom-perfection): Case *Wang*, fas. I., pp. 15–17. (The work is ascribed to Nâgârjuna. A commentary on the *Mahâ-prajñâ-pâramitâ Sûtra*. Translated by Kumârajîva, A. D. 402–405. 100 fasciculi. The original is said to have been thrice as large as the present translation.)

8. The *Life of King Açoka*: Case *Tsang*, fas. X., pp. 13–14. (Translated by An Fa-chin, between A. D. 281–306. 5 or 6 fasciculi.)

9. The *Record of the Compilation of the Three Pitakas and the Miscellaneous Pitaka*: Case *Tsang*, fas. VIII., pp. 32–35. (The translator's name is lost, but the work is said to be a production of the Eastern Chin dynasty, A. D., 317–420.)

10. The *Sûtra on Kâçyapa's Compilation*: Case *Tsang*, fas. VIII., pp. 35–37. (Translated by Ân Shih-kao, a monk from Parthia, A. D. 148–170. The above two works are very short and consist of a few pages only.)

11. *The Accounts of the Transmission of the Dharmapitaka*: Case *Tsang*, fas. IX., p. 92. (Translated by Chi-chia-yeh [Kiṃkâra?], A. D. 472. 6 fasciculi.)

Besides the above works we may consult Fâ-hsien and Hsüan-tsang as well, but I have refrained from making extracts from their works, because good English and French translations are accessible to the students of Buddhism.

CIRCUMSTANCES WHICH LED KÂÇAYAPA TO SUMMON THE FIRST CONVOCATION.

That Mahâkâçyapa, the first Buddhist patriarch, was the originator of the first assembly for compiling the Pitakas, is a matter of general acceptance by all schools of Buddhism. His motive, according to the Ceylon tradition, is ascribed to the imprudent utterance of a certain Bhikshu Subhadra[1] who, hearing of Buddha's entrance into Nirvâna, unreservedly gave vent to his feeling of relief, for he thought the religious discipline demanded by his Master was too rigorous. This tradition agrees with the records in the Vinaya texts of the Mahîçâsaka, the Mahâsaṇghika, and the Dharmagupta schools, and also with those in the Vinaya-mâtrikâ-Sûtra and the Sudarçana-Vinaya-vibhâshâ,[2] whereas in the Vinaya text of the Dharmagupta an additional reason why the Pitaka should be rehearsed immediately after Buddha's death is given by Kâçyapa thus: "We should now compile[3] the Dharma and the Vinaya, in order that heretics (tîrthakas) shall not make us [the subject of] superfluous comments and censures, saying that the discipline of the Çrâmaṇa Gautama is like smoke; that when the World-honored One was living, all [his disciples] observed the precepts, but now, after his disappearance, there are none who observe them."

But the Vinaya text of the Sarvâstivâda, Transmission of the Dharmapitaka and the Mahâprajñâpâramitâ Çâstra do not make any allusion to the unwise Bhikshu. The Sarvâstivâda-vinaya, the Mahâprajñâpâramitâ Çâstra, and the Life of Açoka, on the other

[1] This monk Subhadra should not be confounded with Buddha's last convert, who happens to bear the same name.

[2] The name of the imprudent Bhikshu is Bhânanda in the Mahîçâsaka, the Dharmagupta, and the Vinaya-mâtrikâ; Mahallaka in the Mahâsanghika; Subhadra-Mahallaka in the Sudarçana-vibhâshâ-Vinaya.

[3] *Chieh chi*. Literally, *chieh* means to tie, to join, or to unite, and *chi* to gather, to collect, to compile, and the like. The term is apparently an equivalent of *samgîti*, but I have retained its Chinese sense by translating it "compilation."

hand, state that Mahâkâçyapa was requested or instigated by devas who deeply lamented the possibility of the future loss of the Pitakas, if not compiled in due time. The Transmission of the Dharmapitaka, however, says nothing about the superhuman suggestion. To quote the Sarvâstivâda-vinaya: "Those devas whose long life extends over many kalpas were greatly afflicted at witnessing the Nirvâna of Buddha. But when they came to observe that many a sage had also entered into Nirvâna, they at last began to blame [the disciples], saying: 'The Sûtra, Vinaya, and Mâtrikâ [which constitute] the genuine Dharmapitaka taught by the World-honored One are left uncompiled; but surely [the disciples] are not going to have the right doctrine turned into ashes?'"

Surmising the wish of those devas, Mahâkâçyapa said to all Bhikshus: "You know that the venerable Çâriputra and the venerable Mahâmaudgalyâyana, each with a large number of great Bbikshus who could not bear witnessing Buddha's entrance into Mahânirvâna, had already reverted to a state of perfect tranquillity; and now the World-honored One himself, in turn with 18,000 Bhikshus, has also entered into Parinirvâna. All those devas who are living innumerable kalpas, however, come forth to express their deep grief, and blame us, saying: 'Why do you not have the holy teachings of the Tripitaka compiled? Are you going to have the deepest spiritual doctrine of the Tathâgata turned into ashes?' So I declare to you all that the greatest thing we can do now is the compilation of the Pitaka. All then responded: 'Well, let us do the work.'"

In the Transmission of the Dharmapitaka, Mahâkâçyapa is stated to have told all Bhikshus, as follows: "Buddha is now cremated, but we have no concern with the relics (çârîra) of the World-honored One, for kings, the rich, ministers of state, and lay-believers who desire the most excellent bliss will, of their own accord, make offerings [to them]. What we have to do is the collection of the Dharmacakshu [literally, the eye of the law], whereby to prevent an untimely extinction of the torch of the law. In order that it may illuminate the future generation, let a prosperous perpetuation of the Triratna be not interrupted."

The Record of the Collection of the Tripitaka and the Samyuktapitaka, which was translated during the Eastern Tsin dynasty, A. D. 317–420, agrees with the above-mentioned work in referring neither to the imprudent Bhikshu nor to the suggestion of devas.

THE EXCLUSION OF ÂNANDA.

It is almost[1] unanimously recorded in all the Chinese books that Ânanda was not admitted to membership in the Convocation, until he attained to the state of mastery, through the reprimand of Mahâkâçyapa, which successfully awakened in his heart the feelings of deep remorse and shame. There is, however, no agreement of statements as to how Ânanda was instigated by him in obtaining final emancipation.

According to The Sudarçana-vibhâshâ-vinaya, Mahâkâçyapa insisted on the exclusion of Ânanda from the Convocation in order to protect it against all the reprehension that might arise from admitting one who was still in the stage of training; but the rest of the congregation thought it impossible to compile the Sûtras without Ânanda, so they admonished him to exert all his spiritual powers for the attainment of Arhatship.

The Life of Açoka, the Caturvarga-vinaya of the Dharmagupta school, and the Pañcavarga-vinaya of the Mahîçâsaka school, these three works generally agree in this connection. Ânanda was preaching the Law to a large crowd of people, not knowing anything about Mahâkâçyapa's determination to exclude him from the meeting. A certain Bhikshu named Po-she,[2] who perceived through his supernatural insight that Ânanda was not yet free from attachment, felt pity for him, and told him the following in verse:

"Calmly sitting under a tree, contemplate Nirvâna.
Be not indolent, but exercise Dhyâna.
For what good would there be in chattering?"

---

[1] Except the Transmission of the Dharmapitaka, where no mention is made of this incident.

[2] So in the Caturvarga-vinaya, but Po-ch'i in the Pañcavarga-vinaya, and Po-shê-fu-to, as a disciple of Ânanda, in the Life of Açoka. It is very difficult to find the Sanskrit equivalents of those names when their meanings are not given, for there is a tendency among the so-called "old translators" to simplify long Sanskrit terms in such a manner as to make them appear like native Chinese names.

Thereupon Ânanda made up his mind to obtain final emancipation, etc., etc.

In the Sarvâstivâda-vinaya, a verse slightly different in meaning from the above is also mentioned, but it was given by a mysterious boy who served him as an attendant, instead of by a Bbikshu. This incident occurred after a severe censure by Mahâkâçyapa of eight misdemeanors committed by Ânanda. The Vinaya text states that Mahâkâçyapa at first considered what would be the proper way of treating Ânanda, whether with a severe reprehension or with a gentle encouragement. When he had determined to take the first course, Ânanda was brought before the congregation. Mahâkâçyapa said: "You must leave this place. [It is not proper for] this congregation of worthy [Bhikshus] to be associated with you in their work." Hearing this, Ânanda felt as if his heart were being pierced with arrows, and, trembling all over his body, he pleaded with Mahâkâçyapa not to exclude him from the congregation, as he was not conscious of any faults [which would justify this severe punishment]. Mahâkâçyapa now enumerated his eight misdemeanors, which caused Ânanda at last to retire from the assembly and to train himself for the attainment of Arhatship.

In the Mahâsanghika-vinaya, Ânanda is stated to have received a very humiliating treatment from Mahâkâçyapa. When Mahâkâçyapa was requested by Bhikshus to admit the former to their assembly, he said: "No, if such a one [who is still in the stage] of training should be admitted into a congregation of those who are above training and are perfect in their meritorious powers, he would appear like a leprous fox (?) in an assemblage of lions." When this ignominious comparison was communicated by a deva to Ânanda, who was travelling towards Râjagriha, it did not please him at all. But he thought that Mahâkâçyapa who well knew to what family he belonged, would not have referred to him in such a way, if he were free from prejudices. But in the meantime having attained final deliverance, Ânanda hastened through the air to the Convocation. Mahâkâçyapa, it is stated, then explained to him that he used such a vigorous expression, only as he wished to encourage him to reach the stage of Arhatship.

In the Mahâ-prajñâ-pâramitâ-Çâstra, the episode is described somewhat in a similar way to that in the Sarvâstivâda-vinaya. Ânanda is brought before the congregation by Mahâkâçyapa, and is reproached first for his not being yet qualified to rejoin it, and then for his six (not eight) misdemeanors. When Ânanda is expelled from the assembly, Mahâkâçyapa closes the gate behind him, and begins to compile the Vinaya with the remaining Bhikshus. Exceedingly mortified, Ânanda during the night exercised all his spiritual powers to reach the Path, and when at last he attained to the state of freedom from all prejudices, he rushed at midnight to Mahâkâçyapa's gates. Being told there to come inside through the keyhole, he did so by his supernatural power. Mahâkâçyapa consoled him, saying that the severe reproach had been inflicted upon him simply because he wished to see him enter into the state of Arhatship.

In the Sûtra on Kâçyapa's Compilation [of the Tripitaka] Ânanda is said to have been expelled from the congregation after he was censured by Mahâkâçyapa for his nine misdemeanors in the presence of the Samgha.

ÂNANDA'S MISDEMEANORS.

When Ânanda said to Mahâkâçyapa that he was not conscious of any faults, and that therefore there was no reason to exclude him from the assembly, Mahâkâçyapa enumerated several of his (duskrita), which were considered by him to be the proof that Ânanda was still in the stage of training. This incident is said to have occurred, according to some, before the compilation, but according to others, after it. To the former belong the Sarvâstivâda-vinaya, the Sûtra on Kâçyapa's compilation, the Mahâ-prajñâ-pâramitâ-Çâstra, and the Caturvarga-vinaya of the Dharmagupta school; to the latter belong the Vinayamâtrikâ Sûtra, the Pañca-varga-vinaya of the Mahîçâsaka, the Life of Açoka, and the Mahâ samghika-vinaya. But in the Caturvarga-vinaya, the Mahâsamghika-vinaya,[1] the Life of Açoka, the Pañcavarga-vinaya, the faults

[1] Here the accuser is not Mahâkâçyapa, but Upâli.

of Ânanda are simply enumerated without any reference to his qualification as a member of the Convocation.

The number of his faults as censured by Mahâkâçyapa or Upâli is variously estimated at six, seven, eight, and nine. The following sums up all that was charged against him:

1. Ânanda asked Buddha for the admittance of women into the Samgha, in spite of Buddha's prediction that if women were admitted, the Law of the Tathâgata would not long abide on earth.[1]

2. Ânanda did not ask Buddha for the prolongation of his life, when the latter expressly suggested this to him, by saying that those who were trained in the four supernatural powers could either prolong or shorten their life for the period of one kalpa.

3. When Buddha preached in parables, Ânanda made, in spite of his presence, some superfluous remark on them.

4. Ânanda trod on Buddha's golden-colored robe while trying to wash it (*a*), or while trying to sew it (*b*).

5. Being asked by Buddha to give him some water when he was going to enter into Nirvâna, Ânanda gave him muddy water (*a*), or he did not give him any, even when thrice asked (*b*).

6. When Buddha told Ânanda that Bhikshus might dispense with minor precepts, he did not make any inquiry as to what precepts should be regarded minor.[2]

7. Ânanda exposed the secret parts of Buddha in the presence of women, thinking that the act would tend to the cessation of their passions, but how could he know this when he had not yet attained to the stage of Arhatship?

8. Ânanda showed the gold-colored body of Buddha to a multitude of women, allowing them to defile it with their tears.

9. Ânanda first allowed women to worship the remains of Buddha.

10. When Ânanda was one time reproached by Buddha, he secretly cherished ill-will, and was mischievous to others.

---

[1] Most of the Chinese books here referred to give all the reasons by which Ânanda justified himself for having committed those alleged misdemeanors, but from want of space, no mention here is made of them.

[2] This naturally caused a vehement demonstration among the Samgha later.

11. Ânanda was not yet free from the three evil passions: lust, malice, and ignorance, while all the other Bhikshus assembled in the Convocation were free therefrom.

12. Buddha asked Ânanda three times to serve him as one who offers things (?) to Buddha, but he declined it.[1]

The number and the order of these faults committed by Ânanda are different in different works.

In the Sarvâstivâda-vinaya eight faults are counted in the following order: 1, 2, 3, 4*a*, 5*a*, 6, 7, 8.

The Pañcavarga-vinaya counts six in this order: 6, 4*b*, 1, 2, 5*b*, 9.

The Life of Açoka, six: 6, 5*b*, 4 (simply stepping on Buddha's robe), 2, 7 (the reason given by Ânanda is that he wished to awake in the minds of women the desire to be born as men in their future life), 1.

The Sûtra on Kâçyapa's Compilation has nine: 1, 2, 10, 4 (simply stepping over the golden robe of Buddha), 5*b*, 6, 7, 8, 11.

The Caturvarga-vinaya states seven: 1, 12, 4*b*, 2, 5*b*, 6, 8.

The Mahâsamghika-vinaya describes seven, thus: 1, 2, 4*b*, 5*b*, 6, 7, 8.

The Mahâ-prajñâ-pâramitâ Çâstra has six: 1, 5*b*,[2] 2, 4 (when folding), 7.

The Vinaya-mâtrikâ Sûtra merely states that Mahâkâçyapa accused Ânanda for his seven faults, but does not particularise any of them: on the other hand it relates nine disadvantages arising from the admittance of women into the Samgha.

It is significant that the Sudarçana-vinaya does not make any reference to Ânanda's misdemeanors.

THE INCIDENT OF GAVÂMPATI.

The incident of Gavâmpati in connection with the First Convocation is stated in all the Mahâyâna literature and also in some[3]

---

[1] Note how trifling all these accusations are.

[2] The fault is viewed here from two points: (1) not giving any water, (2) not knowing the fact that Buddha is able to cleanse any kind of water.

[3] That is, the Sarvâstivâda-vinaya and the Mahâsamghika-vinaya.

of the Hînayâna. In the Mahâyâna literature we have the following works: The Life of Açoka, the Mahâ-prajñâ-pâramitâ Çâstra, the Sûtra concerning Kâçyapa's Compilation, the Record of the Transmission of the Dharmapitaka, and the Record of the Compilation of the Tripitaka and the Samyuktapitaka. On the other hand, the Vinaya-mâtrikâ Sûtra, the Caturvarga-vinaya, the Pañcavarga-vinaya, and the Sudarçana-vinaya, all of which belong to documents of the Hînayâna class, make no statement about the Gavâmpati incident.

The incident of Gavâmpati, though it is more or less differently recorded as to its details in different works, is briefly this. Hearing the great bell rung by Mahâkâçyapa, the five hundred Bhikshus[1] hastened to the place of meeting, but when Mahâkâçyapa found that one of them[2] called Gavâmpati[3] had not yet joined them, he asked Anuruddha of the whereabouts of the missing Bhikshu. Being told that he was enjoying a peaceful life in one of the Heavens,[4] he sent a message thither to invite him to the convocation presided over by Mahâkâçyapa. Gavâmpati, who knew nothing about the late events relating to Buddha and his disciples, scrutinisingly asked the messenger why Mahâkâçyapa, instead of the Blessed One himself, stood at the head of the congregation: what was the object of such a grand religious convention, and some other questions.[5] When he was informed of all that had been going on below, he was so greatly afflicted that he said he had now no inclination to descend to the earth, which was made entirely desolate by the eternal departure of Buddha. So saying, Gavâmpati entered into a state of deep meditation, suddenly rose in the air

---

[1] The number of the Bhikshus who took part in the First Convocation is generally estimated at five hundred, but according to the Mahâ-prajñâ-pâramitâ Çâstra, the Convocation consisted of one thousand Bhikshus.

[2] According to the Mahâsamghika, two Bhikshus were missing when the members were counted by Kâçyapa, but one of them, Anuruddha, soon joined them.

[3] The Mahâ-prajñâ-pâramitâ Çâstra makes him a disciple of Çâriputra.

[4] According to some, the Çrîvriksha (?) palace, but according to others the Çrîdeva palace.

[5] So in the Sarvâstivâda-vinaya.

shining with supernatural brilliancy, and then consumed himself in a heavenly fire.[1]

The Mahâ-prajñâ-pâramitâ Çâstra says that Gavâmpati having been fully familiar with the Vinaya and the Sûtra, his presence was necessary to the assembly.

According to the Mahâsamghika-vinaya, Mahâkâçyapa sent several messages to Heaven to summon those Bhikshus who were abiding there, but all of them, having learned that Buddha had already entered into Parinirvâna, were so exceedingly mortified that they disappeared one after another in the same manner. Mahâkâçyapa then declared that no more messages would be despatched to Heaven, nor should those Bhikshus who were living on earth enter into Nirvâna until their work of great importance had been completed.

THE PROCEEDINGS.

What was done by the Convocation? Were the Vinayapitaka and the Sûtrapitaka alone compiled? Did a compilation of the Abhidharmapitaka also take place? Did any dissension occur in the assembly? These questions constitute the most important part of the First Convocation, and the following abstracts from various Chinese translations are calculated to throw some light on them.

A. The Vinaya in Four Divisions (*Caturvarga-vinaya*).—When the cremation ceremony of Buddha was over, all the five hundred Bhikshus went from Vaiçâli to Râjagriha, where Mahâkâçyapa intended to summon the assembly. First, Ânanda was blamed for his seven faults, as already mentioned; then Upâli was requested to recite the Vinaya, beginning with the first of the Principal Sins (Pârâjika), as to the individual, the circumstance, and the nature of the crime. Rules concerning the Bhikshu and the Bhikshuni, the Prâṭimoshka, the Poshadha, the Residing Season, the Wandering Season, the use of leather, the robes, medicaments, the Kaṭhina ceremonies,—all these regulations were incorporated in the Vinaya

[1] The Sarvâstivâda-vinaya, the Mahâprajñâ-pâramitâ Çâstra, and the Sûtra on Kâçyapa's Compilation relate, in addition, that four streams ran out of his transfigured body, each murmuring a gâthâ which proclaimed the transiency of life and the lamentable departure of the Lord.

Ânanda was next asked to compile the Sûtrapitaka. Such Sûtras as the Brahma-jâla (translated Brahma-moving), the Ekottara (increasing by one), the Daçottara (increasing by ten), the Formation and Destruction of the World, the Saṇgîti (chorus), the Mahânidâna (great cause), the Questions of the Çakradeva (Indra), were included in the Longer Âgama (Pâli, Dîgha Nikâyo); those Sûtras of middle length were called the Middling Âgama (Pâli, Majjhima Nikâyo); those in which the subjects were arranged numerically from one to eleven were called the Âgama Increasing by One (Aṇguttara Nikâyo); those which were miscellaneously preached for (?) the Bhikshus, Bhikshunis, Upâsakas, Upâsikâs, Devas, Çakra, Mâras, and Brâhmarâjas, were called the Miscellaneous Âgama (Samyutta Nikâyo); and lastly such Sûtras as the Jâtaka, Itivrittika,[1] Nidâna, Vaipulya, Adbhûta, Avadâna, Upadeça, the Explanation of Aphorisms (Nirdeça?), Dharmapada, Pârâyana,[2] Miscellaneous Discussions and several Gâthâs, were comprised in the Miscellaneous Pitaka, (Pâli, Khuddaka Nikâyo, with other matter). The Discursive [Book] (Kathâ Vatthu),[3] the Non-discursive [Book] (Vibhaṇga or Puggala paññati?), the Yoking (Dhamma Sangaṇi?), the Correlating (Yamaka?), and the Place of Birth (Paṭṭhâna?) made up the Abhidharmapitaka.[4]

B. The Vinaya in Five Divisions (*Pañcavarga-vinaya*).—When the five hundred Bhikshus were assembled in Râjagriha, Mahâkâçyapa inquired of Upâli in due formulary of the four Principal Precepts (Pârâjika) as to the place where they were occasioned, as to the individual with whom they were concerned, and as to the matter with which they dealt. All the Vinaya, for the Bhikshus as well as for the Bhikshunis, was compiled in this way.

Mahâkâçyapa then asked Ânanda where Buddha taught the Ekôttara Sûtra, the Daçôttara Sûtra, the Mahânidâna Sûtra, the

---

[1] Not given by Beal.

[2] Beal gives the Anâgata-Bhayâni and Munigâthâ.

[3] This and following four titles are so concisely given in the text that it is very difficult to make out what they are, and the translation and the reference to the Pâli Abhidharma works here presented are merely tentative.

[4] The text is reticent about the author of the compilation of this Pitaka.

Samgîti Sûtra, the Çrâmañaphala Sûtra, the Brahmajâla (translated Brahmâ-moving), as well as those Sûtras which were preached to Bhikshus, Bhikshunis, Upâsakas, Upâsikâs, Devapûtras, and Devîs. When all the Sûtras were thus recited, Mahâkâçyapa declared to the Samgha: "Those longer Sûtras which are now compiled in one group shall be called the Longer Âgama; those Sûtras which are neither long nor short, and are now compiled in one group, shall be called the Middling Âgama; those which are miscellaneously preached to Bhikshus, Bhikshunîs, Upâsakas, Upâsikâs, Devapûtras, and Devîs, and are now compiled in one group, shall be called the Miscellaneous Âgama; those Sûtras which start with one dharma and increase by one, up to eleven dharmas, and are now compiled in one group, shall be called the Âgama Increasing by One; while the remainder, all consisting of miscellaneous teaching, and now compiled in one group, shall be called the Miscellaneous Pitaka. And to them all shall be given a collective name, Sûtrapitaka. We have now finished compiling the Law, and henceforth let us not put any unnecessary restraint on what was not restrained by Buddha; let us not violate what has already been restrained by Buddha; let us sincerely train ourselves according to the teachings of Buddha."

C. The Vinaya-mâtrikâ Sûtra.—Ânanda being admitted to join the assembly, and the five hundred Arhats having taken their seats, they began to compile the Tripitaka out of the materials which consisted of Sûtras in five or five hundred[1] divisions. Rules for the Bhikshu and Bhikshuni, and the Skandhas (divisions) relating to the Kaṭhina and other things composed the Vinayapitaka. The four Âgamas, (1) Long, (2) Middling, (3) Increasing by One, and (4) Miscellaneous—the last one consisting of those Sûtras which relate to Bhikshus, Bhikshunis, the Çakrendra, devas, and Brâhma-râjâs, as well as (5) the sundry collection which comprised the Dharmapada, the Exposition, the Pârâyana, the Upadeça and others,—these five groups of the Sûtras were classified under the Sûtrapitaka. The Discursive (or Dialogical) Treatise (Kathâ va-

[1] According to other editions.

thu ?), the Non-discursive (or Non-dialogical) Treatise (Vibhanga?), the Mutual Enclosing (Dharma Sangaṇi?), the Correlating (Yamaka?), and the Regions (Dhâtu Kathâ or Paṭṭhâna?)[1] made up the Abhidharmapitaka. And the general name Tripitaka was given to them all.

D. The Vinaya Text of the Sarvâstivâda School.—Mahâkâçyapa and the five hundred Bhikshus kept the assembly in the Pippâla Cave. He announced that as Bhikshus in coming generations would be inferior in their natural endowment (literally, root, mûla?) and lacking in the power of concentration, the assembly would first compile, for the sake of such, the Gâthâs (verses)[2] in which the Sûtra, Vinaya and Abhidharma[3] were treated in comprehensive brevity. This was done before the meal. They then proceeded to compile the Sûtras. Ânanda was requested by Mahâkâçyapa as well as by the Samgha to select and compile them. Having gone through due formality and having reflected on the impermanence of things, he thought: "Among those Sûtras which I heard personally from Buddha, some are traditional,[4] some are preachings in the Nâga (Serpent) Palace,[5] others are preachings in the heavens.

[1] Those five titles of the books contained in the Abhidharmapitaka closely agree, though the translation is a little different, with those above referred to in the Vinaya in Five Divisions, but the terms being too concise, we cannot give anything more than a mere conjecture as to their correspondence to the Pâli works.

[2] Was the Gâthâ already existing side by side with the prose at the time of the First Convocation? Did Buddha himself put some most important tenets of his doctrine into a rhythmical form, that his disciples might learn them by heart? (Yes: See *S. B. E.*, XIII., p. 151.—Edmunds.)

[3] Were some parts of the Abhidharma also versified?

[4] Does this mean that Buddha preached on some traditional subjects, or that some Sûtras deal with traditions, or that the first sermons of Buddha, such as were delivered for the five Bhikshus in Vârânasî before the conversion of Ânanda, were heard by him afterwards from Buddha's own mouth, or from those who were then present, in which case the term tradition would be used in the sense of hearsay? Judging from similar passages in some other works, the last sense seems to be most preferable.

[5] This statement is most significant, for many Mahâyâna texts are said to have been taken from the Nâga Palace where they were long preserved in secret. The Vinaya text of the Sarvâstivâda is generally considered to belong to the Hînayâna work, and this fact makes the above statement much more mysterious. Is the Nâga Palace an ideal creation of later Buddhists? or is it some yet unknown region in the Himâlaya? [Buddha converted several yakkhas, nâgas, etc.—Edmunds.]

As I keep them all in memory and do not forget any of them, shall now recite them." All Devas expressed their willingness to listen, and Mahâkâçyapa praised the words of Buddha as the foremost of all doctrines.

Ânanda then recited the first Sûtra, the Dharmaçakrapravartana (Revolution of the Law-wheel), which was taught in Benâres for the five Bhikshus, one of whom, Ajñâta Kauṇḍiṇya, being present in the assembly, told Mahâkâçyapa how at that time he gained the eye of the Law. Hearing this, devas as well as those Bhikshus who were not yet freed from attachment,[1] uttered a pitiful cry as if their hearts were being pierced with thousands of arrows, and lamented that they could not hear those words of Buddha any more from his own mouth. In this lamentation the Bhikshus of the assembly also joined. When they recovered from the shock of deep feeling, Mahâkâçyapa declared that this first Sûtra, taught by the Blessed One, having been accepted by all, should be recognised as the genuine doctrine of Buddha.

The second Sûtra, Ânanda now went on, which was also preached in Benâres for the sake of the five Bhikshus, consisted in the elucidation of the Four Noble Truths and the Eight Right Paths. Kauṇḍiṇya's confirmation and Mahâkâçyapa's conclusion were declared as before.

The occasion which induced Buddha to preach the third Sûtra was also in Benâres for the sake of the five Bhikshus. He taught that the five Skandhas (aggregates) have no Âtman, that they are subject to transformation, that they cause misery, that one can save oneself from misery through a right comprehension of the nature of things. The conclusion of Mahâkâçyapa was the same as before.

---

[1] This is very strange, considering that those who were admitted to the assembly were all free from attachment, that is, they were all Arhats; but in spite of this were many other Bhikshus also admitted as the audience, though not actually partaking in the work of the compilation of the Tripitaka? In the Mahâyâna work a statement is sometimes made to the effect that the followers of the Mahâyâna Buddhism had their own convocation somewhere in the neighborhood. Does the present text refer to this, or to the council of the Mahâsanghika school as it is mentioned in Hsüan-Tsang?

In this way all the other Sûtras taught by Buddha in several places were recited by Ânanda and confirmed by the Arhats of the assembly. They were all classified in proper forms according to the subject: for example, Sûtras which treated the five Skandhas were grouped under the heading of Skandha, those which treated the six Âyatanas or the eighteen Dhâtus were classified under the Âyatana or Dhâtu; and so on with the (twelve) Chains of Causation, the (four) Noble Truths, the speeches of Çrâvakas, the speeches of Buddha, the (four) subjects of Recollection, the (four kinds of) Right Effort, the (four) Supernatural Powers, the (five) Indriyas, the (five) Balas, and the (eight) Bodhyangas.[1]

Those Sûtras which are in coincidence with the Gâthâs (verse parts), were called the Coincidence[2] Âgama; those which consist of lengthy teachings, the Longer Âgama: those which are of medium length, the Middling Âgama; those in which the subjects are numerically arranged, the Âgama Increasing by One. "There are," says Mahâkâçyapa, "no other Âgamas than these" now compiled.

Next, the Convocation proceeded to compile the Vinaya, led by Upâli, who was considered by Buddha to be the first of the Vinaya-dharâ.[3] Being asked by Mahâkâçyapa where, to whom, and on what the first rule of propriety, (Çikshâ)[4] was announced by Buddha, Upâli said that it was in Vârâṇasi (Benâres) and for the five Bhikshus, and that the matter related to the arrangement of

[1] These subjects also appear in the Abhidharmapitaka, as we see below. Do the statements mean that those subjects as taught by Buddha were classified with the Sûtrapitaka, while a further exposition of the same by his disciples was included in the Abhidharma?

[2] Samyukta in Sanskrit. *Coincidence* is a literal translation of it, which is commonly rendered *miscellaneous*, according to its derived meaning—so says the text.

[3] Literally, those who carry the Vinaya, i. e., know it by heart.

[4] It is very strange that Mahâkâçyapa did not first ask Upâli about the four Principal Sins (Pârâjika), instead of about such insignificant regulations as the Çikshâ rules. Why does the Sarvâstivâda school attach such importance to the latter, while other schools invariably give the first place to the Pârâjika, as is naturally expected? Noticing, however, the inconsistent statement which is made immediately below, I am inclined to think that some spurious elements have crept later into the body of the original text.

natural Powers (Riddhi), the five Indriyas (lit. root), the five Powers (Bala), the seven Bodhyangas (constituent parts of enlightenment), the Eightfold Noble Path, the four Abhayas (fearlessness), the four Pratisamvids (unimpeded knowledge), the four Çrâmanaphala (obtainment of Çramaṇaship), the four Dharmapadas, the Ârañya (solitude), Wish, Knowledge, the Dhyâna of Boundary (the fourth Dhyâna?), Emptiness (Çûnyatâ), Unconditionality (Animitta), Freedom from Desire (Apraṇihita), miscellaneous Disciplines, various Meditations, the Right Entering, Presentation (or perception), Knowledge of Phenomena, Çamatha (tranquilisation), Vipaçyana (insight), the Dharmasamgraha, and the Dharmaskandha.[1]

When the compilation of the Sûtra, the Vinaya, and the Abhidharma was thus done, the heaven and the earth resounded with the praise of the devas.

E. The Vinaya text of the Mahâsanghika school.—Having reached at last the state of Arhatship, Ânanda was permitted to join the assembly, which unanimously acknowledged him as the disciple of best memory. They requested him to compile the Dharmapitaka.[2] When Ânanda began to recite, "Thus have I heard: 'Buddha was at one time in the Bodhimaṇḍara by the river Nairañjanâ,'" the five hundred Bhikshus showed their deep feeling, which, however, soon passed to the calm reflection that all things which originate from a combination of causes are necessarily subject to ruin and transformation.

The Dharmapitaka thus compiled by Ânanda consisted of the Longer Âgama; the Middling Âgama; the Miscellaneous Âgama,

---

[1] Observe that some of those subjects also appear in the Sûtrapitaka, while the identity of others cannot be determined, owing to the brevity of the statement.

[2] According to some the Dharmapitaka is identified with the Sûtrapitaka, as in the present text; while, according to others, it is a general name given to the entire collection of the sacred writings. This disagreement among the records of different Buddhist schools apparently shows that at the earlier stage of development of Buddhist literature there was no definite name for the Pitaka compiled by the First Convocation, which had probably been known by the simple designation, Buddhavâcâ (Words of Buddha). Therefore we shall not run much risk in considering those terms which are now currently used by Buddhists themselves, as well as by Buddhist scholars, (to-wit, Vinayapitaka, Sûtrapitaka, Abhidharma, Tripitaka or Dvipitaka), as the elaboration of later Buddhists.

which was so called because of its dealing with miscellaneous subjects concerning predisposition (lit. root, *mûla*), power (*bala*), enlightenment (*bodhi*), and the path (*mârga*); and the Âgama Increasing by one, which was so called because of a numerical arrangement of subjects from one up to one hundred:[1] while the Miscellaneous Pitaka comprised the Udâna (narratives), Itivrittika (incidents), and Nidâna (circumstantial notes), relating to Pratyekabuddhas and Arhats, which are written in verses (Gâthâ).[2]

Upâli, who was announced by Buddha as well as by the Sangha as the first of the Vinaya-dharâ, was asked next to compile the Vinaya text. He first told the Convocation that there were five sorts of purity, and then proceeded to censure Ânanda for having committed the seven faults as stated elsewhere, two of which, however, Ânanda refused to acknowledge.[3]

Upâli is said to have then recited the nine divisions of the Vinaya, to wit, (1) Pârâjika, (2) Samghâvaçesa, (3) two Aniyatas, (4) thirty Naissargika, (5) ninety-two Prâyaçcittika, (6) four Pratideçanîya, (7) Çikshâ, (8) seven Adhikaranaçamathas, and (9) rules conforming to the Doctrine. He also explained in addition various meanings of the Vinaya: for example, as to the distinctions between the dreadful sins (pârâjika) and serious offences (sthûlâtyaya), or as to a different classification of the Vinaya-text. When thus they had finished compiling the Pitaka, the ten hundred Bhikshus staying outside[4] were called in and informed of the work of the Convocation.

[1] The reader will observe that the number of the subjects contained in the "Âgama increasing by one" differs in different texts.

[2] This statement is very valuable. The Mahâsanghika quarreled with the Theravâda about the contents of the Khuddaka Nikâya, where these books belong, and the very treatises which the Dîpavamsa says they omitted, are wanting here. —Edmunds.

[3] It is noteworthy that according to the Mahâsamghika school the man who blamed Ânanda before the assembly was not Mahâkâçyapa, but Upâli, the first of the Vinaya-dharâ.

[4] What does the statement here refer to, which says one thousand Bhikshus staying outside were summoned in? Hsüan-tsang mentions that the Mahâsanghika school, being excluded from the assembly of the Sthavira school, had their own compilation, meeting to the west of Mahâkâçyapa's convocation. Does the present text refer to that?

A vehement discussion now arose in the assembly as to what was meant by Buddha when he said to Ânanda that the precepts of minor importance could be dispensed with. A certain group of six Bhikshus went so far to the extreme as to say that "if the World-Honored One were still living, he would have everything at once abolished." Mahâkâçyapa, whose majestic dignity and authority were equal to those of Buddha, then sternly ordered them to keep silence, and made a declaration that all which had ever been forbidden should be forbidden, and what had not been forbidden should not be forbidden, and that they should not give any chance to the heretics who were willing to blame the congregation at all costs.

The text concludes with a list of the venerable masters through whom this knowledge of the First Convocation was lineally transmitted down to the venerable Tao-lih (Bodhibala?).[1]

F. The Sudarçana-vinaya.—When the five hundred Bhikshus were seated, Mahâkâçyapa asked them what they would first compile, the Dharmapitaka or the Vinayapitaka, and to this they answered: "Venerable Sir, the Vinayapitaka is the life of Buddhism, and so long as the Vinayapitaka exists, Buddhism will also exist. Therefore, let us first produce the Vinayapitaka."

The next question was who should be the principal compiler of it: Upâli suggested that Ânanda could be chosen for the position, but it was not accepted by the assembly. Being recognised by Buddha as the first of the Vinaya-dharâ, Upâli himself was prevailed upon to recite the Vinaya by a general vote. After due formulary he produced all parts of the Vinaya which consisted of the Prâtimoksha of Bhikshu and Bhikshuni, and Skandhaka, and the Parivâra.

Mahâkâçyapa then nominated Ânanda, according to a general wish of the Sangha, to compile the Dharmapitaka. The Brâhmajâla and the Çrâmaña-phala were first recited, and then all the five divisions of the Sûtra, which consist of the Longer Âgama Sûtra, the Middling Âgama Sûtra, the Samyukta Sûtra, the Anguttara

[1] Why not give names, so as to compare with Theravâda list in Mahâvamsa?—Edmunds.

Sûtra, and the Khuddhaka Sûtra, the last one containing all the words of Buddha (Buddha-vâcâ) not included in the first four Âgamas.[1]

The speeches of Buddha, the text goes on to say, are of one taste, have two functions, and are divisible into three periods: that is, they all teach the means of deliverance (moksha) which consist in morality, meditation, and understanding; they are composed of the Dharmapitaka and the Vinayapitaka; they are divisible into the first speech, the last speech, and those speeches which were delivered between them. The text then raises the question: What is the Tripitaka? to which is given the answer that it consists of Vinayapitaka, Sûtrapitaka, and Abhidharmapitaka, together with their analytic explanation.[2] The contents of the Tripitaka given in this way agree with those of the Pâli collection.[3]

G. *Mahâprajñâpâramitâ Çâstra.*[4]—Mahâkâçyapa in a friendly way requests Ânanda to compile the Dharmapitaka, saying: "Though there were many great disciples of the Buddha to whom the guarding of Dharmapitaka was entrusted, they are now all gone except you. Therefore, out of the compassion for all beings and in accordance with the spirit of Buddha, you shall compile the Buddhadharmapitaka." Thus requested, Ânanda ascends the lion-seat, and reverentially turning towards the place where Buddha's Nirvâna took place, says: "Though I did not personally hear the first preaching of Buddha, I have learned it by hearsay. When Buddha was in Vârâṇasî, he first opened the gate of nectar for the five Bhikshus and preached the Four Noble Truths of Suffering,

---

[1] The Pâli commentaries say the same.—A. J. E.

[2] This is very strange, because the text has before said that the First Convocation compiled the Vinaya and Sûtra only. I am inclined to think that these additional statements, as well as the succeeding detailed explanation of such terms as Sûtra, Abhidharma, Pitaka, and Âgama, are later interpolations put down here by way of commentary, but which in the course of time have been mixed up with the text.

[3] The Chinese characters for transliteration in the present text, so far as they have come under my notice, strongly suggest that the text is a translation of the Pâli original, though I have retained the Sanskrit terms for the sake of uniformity.

[4] The present text belongs to the Mahâyâna literature, and it will be very interesting to contrast its accounts of the First Convocation with those of the preceding ones, which all belong to the Hînayâna Buddhism.

Amassing, Cessation, and the Path. Ajñâta Kauṇḍinya was the first to perceive the Path, and 80,000 devas also all entered upon the Path."

When the one thousand Arhats assembled in the Convocation heard the words of Buddha as recited by Ânanda, they were greatly afflicted with the thought that they could no more hear Buddha's personal address. The Sthaviras Anuruddha and Mahâkâçyapa expressed in verses their deep feelings about the impermanence of things.

Mahâkâçyapa told Ânanda that all the teachings of Buddha, from the Dharma-cakra-pravartana Sûtra down to the Mahâparinirvâna Sûtra, should be classified in four divisions, each being called an Âgama, viz.: the Âgama Increasing by One, the Middling Âgama, the Longer Âgama, and the Coincidence Âgama.[1] And to them all was given a general name: Sûtradharmapitaka.

Upâli, who was recognised by the Samgha to be the first of the Vinaya-dharâ among the five hundred Arhats,[2] was then asked to recite the Vinaya consisting of eighty divisions.[3]

Lastly, Ananda was again requested to recite the first Abbidharma taught by Buddha, as he was acknowledged among the five hundred Arhats to be most conversant with the exposition of the Sûtra. He addressed the Sangha: "Thus have I heard: Buddha was at one time in Çrâvasti, when he told the Bhikshus that those who neither removed nor exterminated the five dreadful [sins], the five misdemeanors, and the five sorts of malice, would suffer in consequence innumerable misfortunes in this life, bodily as well as spiritual, and in the future would fall down into the evil paths; that those, however, who were free from these five dreadful [sins], five misdemeanors, and five sorts of malice, would enjoy in consequence various blessings in this life, bodily as well as spiritual, and in the future be born in a pleasant heavenly abode. What

[1] A literal translation of Samyuktâgama.

[2] Here, as well as further on, five hundred Arhats are mentioned. Is this the number of the Arhats assembled in the Convocation? If so, it is in direct contradiction to the above statement that there were a thousand.

[3] One edition reads eight thousand, which is probably a misprint.

are those five dreadful [sins] which are to be kept away? They are: (1) killing, (2) stealing, (3) unlawful lust, (4) lying, and (5) drinking spirits."

All such matters were comprised under the Abhidharmapitaka. Thus ended the compilation of the three Dharmapitakas.

INCIDENT OF PURÂNA.

Tbree[1] out of the eleven Chinese translations which contain accounts of the First Convocation refer to the episode of Purâṇa, who was in the south[2] when Mahâkâçyapa and five hundred Bhikshus were working on the compilation of the Pitaka. According to the Caturvarga-vinaya, the event occurred in the following manner:

Having heard that the Convocation was taking place in Râjagriha, Sthavira Purâṇa hastened thither, accompanied by his party, which consisted of five hundred Bhikshus. He went to Mahâkâçyapa and asked if he also might be allowed to learn all that had happened. Mahâkâçyapa thereupon again summoned the assembly, requested Upâli to rehearse what he had recited, and had other things repeated as they had been done before. Purâṇa expressed his satisfaction with the general proceedings of the Convocation, except as to the insertion of the following eight indulgences, which had been plainly approved by Buddha, and unmistakably kept in memory by himself. The eight things were: (1) Keeping food indoors; (2) Cooking indoors; (3) Cooking of one's own accord; (4) Taking food of one's own accord; (5) Receiving food when rising early in the morning; (6) Carrying food home according to the wish of a giver; (7) Having miscellaneous fruits; (8) Eating things grown in (or by?) a pond.

These indulgences, said he, were not against the rule that forbids the taking of the remnant of food. Mahâkâçyapa told him that he was correct in saying so, but that Buddha permitted them only on account of a scarcity of food, when the Bhikshus could not

---

[1] The Pañcavarga-vinaya, the Caturvarga-vinaya, and the Vinaya-mâtrikâ.

[2] According to the Pañcavarga-vinaya, agreeing with the Pâli.

get a sufficient supply of it by going their rounds, and that therefore when this circumstance was removed, Buddha again bade them to abstain from these eight indulgences. Purâṇa, however, protested, declaring that Buddha, who was all-wise, would not permit what otherwise was forbidden, nor would he forbid what otherwise was permitted. To this Mahâkâçyapa replied: "The very reason of his being all-wise has enabled him to permit what otherwise was forbidden, and to forbid what otherwise was permitted. Purâṇa, we will now make this decision: That whatever Buddha did not forbid shall not be forbidden, and whatever Buddha forbade shall not be disregarded. Let us train ourselves in accordance with the disciplinary rules established by Buddha."

The Pañcavarga-Vinaya mentions, instead of the eight above enumerated, seven indulgences which, however, may be taken for eight, according to how we punctuate the passage, though the text apparently states "these seven things." They are slightly different from those in the Caturvarga-vinaya, to-wit: (1) Keeping food indoors; (2) Cooking indoors; (3) Cooking of one's own accord; (4) Receiving food in compliance with the wish of another; (5) Taking fruit of one's own accord; (6) Receiving things coming out of a pond; (7) Eating fruit with its seeds (or stone) removed, when received from one who is not a regular attendant in the Samgha.[1]

According to the Vinaya-mâtrikâ Sûtra, the first of the eight indulgences is the keeping of food indoors, and the last is the eating of sundry grasses and roots (or roots of grass) growing by a pond, but the six intermediate ones are not mentioned.

Mahâkâçyapa is said to have told Purâṇa about the eight excellent qualities of Buddha, by virtue of which he could, when deemed fit, establish or abolish the rules for the benefit of the Samgha.

PLACE AND TIME.

All the Chinese works, already referred to, agree in stating that the First Convocation took place in Râjagriha, though they

[1] The last passage is not clear, and we may consider it either as forming an independent statement or as an appendix to the sixth.

differ as to the special locality of the city. The Saptaparṇa Cav the Pippala Rock, the Kshatrya Cave, and the Gridhrakûta are t places thus mentioned in them.

As to the time, they unanimously say that the event happen immediately after the demise of Buddha, though they in no w agree regarding the exact date.

TEITARO SUZUKI.

LA SALLE, ILL.

LITERARY CORRESPONDENCE.

FRANCE.[1]

THE philosophy of the sciences is tending to-day clearly in two directions,—toward psychic monism on the one hand and materialistic monism on the other. One may choose as one likes, either the dynamic or the static aspect of phenomena. We may subordinate quality to quantity or *vice versa*. M. LE DANTEC, in a volume composed of different articles, *Les limites du connaissable*, *La vie et les phénomènes naturels*, affirms anew and with force the second thesis. Without quitting the ground of transformism, especially as Lamarck understood it, he is ambitious, as I have already had occasion to remark to your readers, to reduce the phenomena of life to the laws of physics and chemistry. Animals, he says, are the transformers and not the creators of motion. All the manifestations of life are, in the end, derived from the chemical phenomena of "assimilation." A modification of the properties of an organism is nothing else than a modification of the living molecules of which it is composed. So, in short, vital activity, the evolution of organised beings, is a phenomenon of the chemical order; and hence the facts of consciousness, as well as life itself, are ranged under the formula of a monism of which the movement of matter is everywhere the essential and fundamental principle.

I am far from contradicting this thesis, in so far as it signifies in the first place a methodical position, and since it serves as a directive hypothesis. Biology has already profited too much from researches undertaken in this direction for savants not to push

---

[1]Translated by Prof. Ira W. Howerth, The University of Chicago.

them as far as possible. We should not conceal the fact, however, that this point of view, in the eyes of many biologists who are not metaphysicians, does not exclude the validity of dynamism. M. Le Dantec himself is led to suppose, when there is a question of explaining the genesis and the nature of consciousness, that "the material elements of which our organism is composed contain *the elements of consciousness*," and it then seems legitimate to him to ask whether these latter elements—belonging to the atom just as life belongs to it—may not in biological phenomena take a directive rôle, so that considerations of *finality* would have their necessary employment in the study of these phenomena.

Such in effect is the position taken by M. GASTON RICHARD in his work, somewhat rambling but interesting, *L'idée d'évolution dans la nature et l'histoire.* He deliberately opposes Spencerian evolutionism and rejects its pretention, which is, in short, to submit all scientific disciplines to a mathematical theory of the universe. The metaphysic of Spencer, he says, is only a last form of the ancient doctrines, according to which consciousness is only an epiphenomenon, and qualitative diversity is reduced to the homogeneous, that is to say, to quantity. It pretends to sum up and unify without contradiction the "relative," to place necessity where there is causality, mechanism where there is life and action, to govern experience and the genetic method in the name of a purely rational law.

It might be, avows M. Richard, that Descartes and Spinoza were right as against Bacon, Hume, and Kant; that is to say, that a static knowledge of the universe answers fully only to our logical aptitudes, and that the rôle of experience is simply judgments pronounced upon the value of the details of a mathematical construction quite *a priori*. But, for himself, he does not think so. He is opposed to reducing the complex to the simple, to impoverishing the representation of the universe with the hope of rendering it intelligible. Vital spontaneity is denied, he declares, in order that one may not be led to affirm that, far from being an epiphenomenon, consciousness is the very basis of phenomena, connecting the parts of the universe, the conditions of its diversity and of its unity; and, moreover, the evolutionist is obliged to recognise that it is everywhere and always inseparable from the evolution of an apparatus, the brain, which reacts upon the whole animal organisation.

Either evolution signifies the development of conditions implicit in a primitive condition, in which case the rôle of science would be limited to discovering the law or the order of this development, and the absolute would contain in itself and govern all the future: or it signifies the appearance and history of autonomous processes (whatever may be their connection with other anterior or concomitant processes), in which case the rôle of science would be to describe and compare these processes, and it would be necessary to admit the intervention of spontaneities which would produce them, and which would determine the realisation of possible contingencies within limits difficult to point out.

Here appears once more the metaphysical question of a law anterior to contingencies, of a general law common to all processes.

If the genetic method is incompatible with the idea of an arbitrary creation, it is not incompatible, according to M. Richard, with the idea of a plan which is realised as a plastic or poetic construction. It is not illegitimate to posit in the interior of the world itself this creative power whose nature is regularly manifested and which is found and is concentrated in the personal reflection of each human individual.

* *

The work of M. Renouvier, *Le personalisme, suivi d'une étude sur la perception externe et sur la force*, falls naturally into this place. The same questions which divide biologists and sociologists are here debated and solved according to the idea of the liberty and spontaneity of the person. M. Renouvier takes up and fully develops what he calls the metaphysics, the sociology, and the eschatology of personalism; the notion of a divine, creative personality; the general conditions of a perfect world; the perfect society and the possibility of the fall; the ruin of the primitive world; the conservation and the reproduction of the human organism under new laws; and finally the possibility of a restoration of immortal beings.

Those of your readers who are not acquainted with the doctrines of this dean of our philosophers may find in this volume a new exposition of them, rich in scientific and historic views.

M. Renouvier is willing that the decisive argument in favor of the thesis of a beginning, a thesis which he knows is contradicted in the order of experience, may be furnished by "the principle of contradiction," this principle implying, he says, the logical impossibility of an actual whole of parts without end, of an actually infinite series of successive phenomena, real and discontinuous. So the order of experience ought to be distinct from the question concerning the origin and the cause of the phenomena which are subjected to that order. Here is evidently a difficult point, and I have already indicated some reservations in regard to the signification of the logical principles of contradiction, which I shall have further occasion to reproduce.

* * *

From M. Fouillée we have two considerable works. His *Esquisse psychologique des peuples européens* covers a field which may seem pretty large, but it is one which, from his wide information drawn from conversations and reading, if not from travel and a large personal acquaintance, he was prepared to traverse. A book of this kind cannot well be epitomised. It must suffice to show how M. Fouillée undertakes to lay the foundation of the psychology of peoples and what conclusions he draws in the present study.

M. Fouillée distinguishes from the very first, the inborn character from the acquired character. One is psycho-physiological and results from the component races; the other is especially psycho-sociological and is produced by the action and reaction of individuals upon each other. If race "conditions" development, it does not, according to him, "determine" it. We may judge of races, moreover, only by their effects upon history, which is full of speculative considerations. There is a "sociological determinism" which truly characterises each people and defines it. He even permits us to lay down as a law the progressive predominance of the psychological and sociological factors over race and habitat,— which are more important at the beginning.

The influence of these latter factors, in my opinion, cannot be set aside, and the mingling of races exerts an influence upon the destiny of national groups. It is true, however, that races in mingling tend to unite, and that the habitat, up to a certain point, is also transformed. I have no decisive objection to oppose to the method of M. Fouillée. As to his conclusions, they bear the general characteristic of the neo-Latin peoples, or of people of Latin education,—opposite to the Anglo-Saxons. The prognostications which may be made concerning the future of a people involves many uncertainties. They are founded upon actual but always modifiable facts. Actual events may themselves result in historical movements whose manifold causes it is impossible to analyse and estimate exactly enough to affirm with certainty that they will all remain in play, or will continue to act in the same way. The future, in fact, opens up a long perspective in which we can see no further than to-morrow.

Nietzsche et l'immoralisme is the title of the second work of M. Fouillée. He criticises the doctrine of Nietzsche with the *finesse* which he knows how to put into this kind of a work. He compares it with the doctrine of Guyau, with which he is certain that Nietzsche had been very much struck, and undertakes to show the superiority of the latter. It is to be desired that we shall have an end in France of the literature of Nietzsche after such a historian as Lichtenberger has given us an excellent outline of his philosophy, and such writers as M. Fouillée and M. de Roberty[1] have shown its signification in modern thought. I admit that I have always felt a certain impatience in reading his so celebrated works. The excellence of his style cannot hide from my eyes the incoherence and the contradictions of his thought, the vanity and the excess of his pretensions. How can we repress a smile, moreover, at the ambition of the speculative moralists to change the course of the world, and even the heart of man, according as they shall attach such or such importance to moral factors, or as they shall invoke the principle of altruism or of egoism, the desire for power or ben-

---

[1] *Frédéric Nietzsche*, par E. de Roberty, éditeur Alcan.

evolence, the categorical imperative or happiness, the intensity of life or abnegation. All our doctrines remain in the abstract; real life, life as it is lived, knows nothing of them. No matter how pleasing it is to us closet philosophers to seek the sources and laws of moral activity in duty or desire, in pleasure or pain, or in the will to be,—whether we wish to establish obligation by present or future sanctions,—the human individual is not changed by it, and the necessities of existence continue to exercise upon him the same restraint. This is why the great religions themselves, which are certainly the most powerful of moral systems, have not modified human nature appreciably, so that they have sometimes been accused of exercising no influence upon conduct. Their effectiveness consists less in doctrine than in discipline, and it must be said that their morality, although remaining the same in its general principles, has been a continual compromise with the actual and variable interests of each society. The great religions, in a word, have mutilated man much less than the philosophers have done; they have known him better, they have known him as he is, with his good and bad tendencies, the weaknesses of the flesh and the noble aspirations of the heart.

What do we find, then, beyond the general precepts established by the experience of all peoples, in the great religious movements which are known as Buddhism, Christianity, and Mahometanism? We find these two principles: the duty of mutual assistance and the sanction of conduct by a superior power. And what do we find in contemporary socialism, or in nihilism, even as it is in Russia? Still these two principles. It is only necessary to transform the duty of assistance into positive law (an eleemosynary tax is not levied in Islamism), and to find a sanction in present reality, in a law affirmed as a higher law of life. Save these two points, the speculative moralists might arrange things to suit their own fancy, and the world in general would not be profoundly affected. The sources of activity, passions, needs, the connection between causes and effects, these things are for all times and places. Only ways and means are subject to change.

Here are some truths, I think, which it is well not to lose sight of if we do not wish to become the dupes of our own speculations, as did Nietzsche in his foolish pride.

* * *

M. Jean Philippe gives us, in his *L'image mentale*, a very good psychological study. He endeavors to consider the *image*, apart from *memory* and *invention*, in the state of *simple representation*. He understands it as "a sort of living cell which preserves its own life through manifold and diverse transformations." In its elementary form, he tells us, this psychic cell, the representative image, is in reality as complex as the physiological cell. Each perception or representation is at once connected with and the outgrowth of all our previous and analogous representations. Furthermore, each has its history. Continually reconstructed, they increase on the one side, are diminished on the other, by effacement, by fusion, or by synthesis. Hence the object of the two first chapters of his volume; one giving us an analysis of the image, the other expounding the necessary reductions of it. A third chapter shows us why and how this mental compound is so unstable and subject to variations. Some *observations* clear up these delicate analyses and support the conclusions drawn from them.

Perhaps there should be some reservation in regard to the subject of the separation of the image, and in regard to memory. The remembrance of *having seen* is one thing; the remembrance of *what has been seen* is another. The memory I have of the Cathedral of Mayence, for example, varies according as the images upon which it is established vary. It remains attached to them, and it is in this sense that we speak so readily of the alterations of memory when we mean only the alteration of images.

Dr. Philippe describes with precision the fusion of successive images of the same object, which results in giving only a schema of that object. It would be easy to show the fertility of this operation in the technique of the artist. And this is what I indicated myself when I spoke of "general picturesque ideas," which are schema, but schema elaborate and flexible, while ordinarily they are dry and unproductive.

Under the title *Vus du dehors*, M. MAX NORDAU publishes a continuation of his studies on the novelists, the poets, and the modern French dramatists, studies which originally appeared in German periodicals and were translated into our language by M. Dietrich. They are not the studies of a common critic. There are few pages of Nordau, with his qualities as a writer, upon which may not be found a wide knowledge of man and things, which renders them instructive. In this volume the reader will find some important subjects discussed, such as the importance of observation in the literary art, the national value of history, the esthetic character of all religion, etc.

The volume of M. J. NOVICOW, *L'expansion de la nationalité francaise*,[1] is also a book "*vu du dehors*." M. Novicow looks upon the future as quite favorable to the French language and spirit. He perhaps neglects certain unfavorable factors, but it would be in bad taste to reproach him for it, and besides this is not the place to do so.

From M. G. L. DUPRAT we have a study in "pathological and normal psycho-sociology," *The Lie* (*Le mensonge*), which may be recommended to the attention of teachers, and from M. EMILE TARDIEU, a trenchant "psychological study" of ennui (*L'ennui*).

M. A. CRESSON in his *La morale de la raison theorique* supposes, rather hastily, that the doctrine of evolution may be accepted with all its consequences as a "universal law," and as the sole method. A bit hastily he departs from the way of idealism. He takes up the question where Guyau left it, but he treats it with less originality and does not distinguish himself very clearly from the numerous authors who have proposed the same solution of a morality purely rational and experimental.

M. G. DUMAS publishes the Theory of Emotion (*Théorie de l'émotion*) by W. JAMES, introducing it with a preface which sets forth this difficult, and not yet decided, question whether emotion

---

[1]Armand Colin, publisher. When no publisher is mentioned, the volume is issued by Felix Alcan.

is of peripheral or partially cerebral origin, and he shows very clearly the differences between the theory of James and that of Lange.

M. LOMBROSO gives us a new edition of *The Man of Genius* (*L'homme de génie*, Schleicher, publisher) a work which belongs among the best of the author.

One of the most interesting facts of modern thought is assuredly the change which is taking place, I will not say at the very heart of the Christian faith, but in its form, its methods, its criticism and exegesis; the appearance of a disposition rather rational than mystic. On this point may be consulted a brief and substantial article by M. G. SOREL, entitled *The Crisis of Catholic Thought* (*La crise de la pensée catholique*, Jacques, publisher), reprinted from the *Revue de métaphysique et de morale*. I have just read it, and with great profit. M. Sorel thinks that the Church will doubtless find an advantage in the tendency of contemporary science to establish itself upon the "fact of consciousness," and he indicates the different sources which it will be useful to consult.

On mysticism, I may recall a work already cited here, a work by P. JULES PACHEU entitled *An Introduction to the Psychology of the Mystics* (*Introduction à la psychologie des mystiques*, Oudin, publisher), in which is expounded correctly the method which must be employed in the study of matters of this kind. I may mention also an excellent brochure by M. EMILE BOUTROUX, the *Psychology of Mysticism* (*La psychologie du mysticisme*, Bureaux de la Revue Bleue).

Interest may be found also in reading HENRI BRÉMOND'S *Ames religieuses* (Perrin, publisher), six studies, of which three are devoted to Protestants (John Keble, Edward Hering, and Sheldon) and three to Catholics. A collection of articles by the Father ROURE entitled *Moral Anarchy and the Social Crisis* (*Anarchie morale et crise sociale*, Beauchesne, publisher) is worthy of mention. Finally I call attention to the study of the ABBÉ HOUTIN, *The Biblical Question Among the Catholics of France in the Nineteenth Century* (*La question biblique chez les catholiques de France au XIXe siècle*, Picard, publisher), a history of the debates occasioned by the Biblical question, from which it appears that Biblical criticism is taking on more and more, even in the eyes of the best of Catholic priests, the acter of a positive science independent of confessional beliefs

* * *

M. L'ABBÉ CLODIUS PIAT publishes his *Aristote* in the "C tion of Great Philosophers." He has the excellent thought c ing us simply a monograph on the Aristotelian system. monograph, based upon the text itself and upon the best so is very well done, and adapted to serve as a valuable help student. The same collection is enriched with *Gasali*, by the I CARRA DE VAUX, one of the members of the Council of the A Society.

M. MAURICE BOUCHER has written an essay entitled *Ess l'hyperespace*, in which I recognise an amplification of some much more precise, which may be found in the *Récréations blèmes mathematiques* of Rouse Ball, a work which is cited Boucher. He appears to have in view the founding on met metric considerations some metaphysical inductions. But clear that we cannot pass from a mathematical fiction, ho fruitful it may be for the material sciences, to the notions gether or partially involved in the problems of God and the

There remains a volume of which I should like to speak extensively. It is that of M. H. POINCARÉ, *La science et l thèse* (E. Flammarion, publisher). Readers of *The Monist* already been made acquainted with one of its most inter chapters. A critic has said, with some show of reason, th personal doctrine of the author, in regard to the principles of g etry and mechanics, is a sort of "symbolism," almost as fi moved from Kantian rationalism as from vulgar empiricism. Poincaré sees in ordinary geometry a "convenient language,' this is why it appears to him idle to ask whether all geomet Euclidean is false. It is all quite as legitimate, though not ad to the conditions imposed by sensibility. The great and ult problem considered in these studies is that of the *possibil* science, that is to say, what we really may know about things Poincaré places himself at the strict viewpoint of positive k edge.

I received, at the last moment, a volume by M. Lévy-Bruhl, *La morale et la science des meurs*. The author possesses considerable merit, but I wish to defer reading his book, and I merely mention it here. The task is all the more agreeable, since I agree with him on the debated question of morality. I accept entirely what he says of morality as a "function of the social organisation" and a "part of the existing social reality"; of the "apparent universality of principles," and the "real particularity of precepts." Without repeating what I said two pages above, I may say that I have insisted frequently on the necessity of making a distinction between the psychological mechanism and the social aspect of moral phenomena.[1] The questions comprised under the name science of ethics are distributed between psychology on the one hand, and hygiene on the other. The mechanism of obligation does not vary, but the objects of duty change. Obligation follows the laws. General principles are the empty forms which each society fills in its own fashion. This is why the real revolutionaries in morals are not the theorists but the men of action. The work of M. Lévy-Bruhl is to be recommended not only because of the justness of his ideas, but also because of the richness of the considerations by which he supports them, and the comprehensive breadth of his exposition. Henceforth this book must be taken account of.

It remains to mention the *Année philosophique*, which has arrived at its thirteenth year (1902). This volume contains four studies: Brochard's "Lois de Platon et la théorie des idées;" Hamelin's "Du raisonnement par analogie"; Pillon's "La critique de Bayle," "Critique des attributs de Dieu," and Dauriac's "Essai sur la notion d'absolu dans la metaphysique immanente." It contains also a bibliography of French philosophy for the past year, pp. 135–306, followed by the *comptes-rendus*, always from the point of view of the critical school.

I should notice in conclusion a book by M. E. Boutmy on the *Political Psychology of the American People* (*Psychologie politique du peuple americain*), which, however, I shall refrain from judging. In his study of the English people, M. Boutmy appears to me to attach too much importance to the qualities due to the influence of the climate of Great Britain. The psychological method of Taine presents the great danger of conducting sometimes to explanations a bit puerile, and to simplifications wholly unacceptable.

Paris. Lucien Arréat.

[1] Most recently in *Dix années de philosophie*.

CRITICISMS AND DISCUSSIONS.

PHYSICS AND METAPHYSICS.

Sir Oliver joseph Lodge (knighted for proficiency in physics) assert "life can generate no trace of energy, it can only guide it"; from which he that life is immaterial or hyperphysical. The answer to his assertion, I say, is what the lawyers call a demurrer. The assertion is true; but the in which he draws from it does not follow. Life cannot generate energy, to t Nor can energy itself. Nor can anything else. The total energy of the u is constant, admitting of neither generation nor destruction, as fixed by the the conservation of energy; a law, by the way, not generalised from expe but a necessity of thought, to which all experience is subject, and which quently is as little liable in the future to have a "question mark" placed ag by competent thinkers as the law of identity or the law of contradiction other part of the organic law of mind. In general, it may be said, the unifo of mind, not excepting the absolute uniformities, answer to uniformities of a subjective necessity being the obverse of an objective impossibility. Th is the outer, transformed, not transnatured. Resuming, the point to be pe this discussion is not that life cannot generate energy, but that life canno form energy—is not a link in the endless chain of physical transformations. fessor Lodge is guilty of what the logicians know as *ignoratio elenchi*. mistaken the question in dispute. Energy is not generated, but is trans and life indisputably transforms energy—generates not energy but forms of Life does nothing more or less than generate forms of energy. It consists erating them—subsists by generating them. The distinction between ener forms of energy, constituting the basis of physics, the distinguished physicist seem to have overlooked, probably because the content obscured it. When Doodle came to town he could not see it for the houses.

How can life guide energy without itself having energy, one may ask seriousness? The deserved prominence of Sir Oliver Lodge among scientific will excuse an examination of the mode in which he works out his fallacy. G implies changing the direction of motion, which, if we may accept the law tion accepted by physicists from Newton to Lodge or next to Lodge, can b only by force in the sense of something active. "Guidance," he nevertheless insists, "is a passive exertion of force without doing work; as a quiescent rail may guide a train to its destination, provided an active engine propels it"—a nondescript force, which he may be pardoned for not describing intelligibly—a sort of *tertium quid*, we may suppose, like St. Augustine's "light and air," part physical, part hyperphysical.

What is work, in the scientific conception of it? Moving through space against resistance, the scientists say; and the definition holds intrinsically no matter how small the space or how slight the resistance, applying in principle (nothing but principle concerns us here) equally to molecules and to the bodies which they compose. The work done in moving a train to its destination is, first, making the train move through space, and, secondly, making it move in the direction of its destination; of which factors the "active engine" supplies the one, the "quiescent rail" the other. Both are necessary. In the absence of either the train could not reach its destination—the work could not be done. Not the "red devils" of Paris or Narragansett Pier could reach their destination (were it anything but smash), unless directed by force homogeneous with the force that propels them.

As for the passivity of the guiding force, since the reaction of the rail on the engine equals the action of the engine on the rail, the two forces are equally passive, equally active. A force in equilibrium is not a passive force, but a force whose activity is balanced by that of a counter force. The resultant of forces in equilibrium is zero, but their activity is quantitative, and may be the maximum of one or both. The conception itself of equilibrium presupposes forces acting against one another. A body even in sensible motion, if the motion be uniform, is in equilibrium. Indeed, the forces acting upon a moving body at any instant, as the principle of d'Alembert affirms, may be resolved into a state of equilibrium. Equilibrium is thus kinetic as well as statical. "Statics," as a physicist of note remarks, "is but a special case of kinetics."

It is a static or equilibrated force which Sir Oliver Lodge pronounces "purely passive"—not "anything active"; and, as he uses these expressions in a philosophical inquiry, and rests his conclusion upon them, he may be held to use them in their absolute sense. In any other sense, for that matter, they are self-evidently of no use in his argument, which is employed to support the assumption that "life" and "energy" differ so radically as not to be interconvertible—as to have no common ground. A relative instance cannot illustrate, much less prove, an absolute distinction. Force at bottom is matter in motion; whether the motion is molar or molecular, sensible or insensible, is fundamentally indifferent. A force not "anything active" is a contradiction in terms. A "passive exertion of force" is a topping contradiction—Pelion upon Ossa piled.

Molecular activity may seem compatible with molar passivity, but molar passivity is seeming only, for, moved by gravitation, masses individually as well as particles act unceasingly, the tendency to act, comprehended in the law of gravitation, being a stage or phase of action. Activity belongs to matter in all its forms, respectively—to each combination as a whole no less than to its simplest constituent. When a stone falls to the earth, the earth, taking into account both velocity and mass, does as much falling as the stone, and shares equally in the stress of the resultant equilibrium. No aggregate, as no aggregant, is "purely passive." On the ground floor of physics there is no room for the word "passive." The universe is of activity "all compact." This is commonplace to Professor Lodge, yet in the paper in hand he reasons as if he rejected it or had never heard of it.

A particle of the rail, to recur to his illustrative case (if I may dwell a moment longer on the point), which changes its position with reference to another particle without changing its distance, exerts essentially the same kind of force as the rail or as the engine that wheels upon the rail—a force not only active, but entirely physical, and, moreover, consisting exclusively in the change in the direction of the particle. This is the force to which, in a discussion of ultimate principles, life is gravely compared by a scientist of the first distinction, for the purpose of showing that life is hyperphysical—void of physical energy, and incapable of giving rise to any form of it.

The maze of technicalities in which mathematical physicists have enveloped physics, either for their own convenience or to render their science "caviare to the general," has no place in discussions so fundamental as the one under notice. He who should seek to escape from the pressure of unsophisticated reason, by taking refuge in the windings of this labyrinth, would add nothing to the sum of human knowledge, and might subtract something from whatever just fame he had achieved. What the world asks from science is not superstition or prejudice adorned with refinements; but truth unadorned. If the gem is not given, the setting may be spared.

To speak literally, does Professor Lodge, trained and accomplished physicist as he is, really mean that the direction of a body moving against resistance can be changed not simply without doing work, but without activity at all? If he does, what, in his opinion, has become of the law of motion formulated in its threefold aspect by Newton? If he does not, what becomes of his contention?

Continuing, our physicist or metaphysicist illustrates his position as follows:

"Scribbling on a piece of paper results in a certain distribution of fluid and production of a modicum of heat; so far as energy is concerned, it is the same whether we sign Andrew Carnegie or Alexander Coppersmith, yet the one effort may land us in twelve month's imprisonment or may build a library, according to circumstances, while the other achieves no result at all. John Stuart Mill used to say that our sole power over nature was to *move* things; but strictly speaking we cannot do even that; we can only arrange that things shall move each other, and can determine by suitably preconceived plans the kind and direction of the motion that shall ensue at a given time and place Provided always that we include in this category of 'things' our undoubtedly material bodies, muscles and nerves."

In arranging that things shall move each other, do we not move "our undoubtedly material bodies, muscles and nerves," without moving which, indeed we cannot so much as plan or even think, be the movement duplicated hyperphysically or not? That one cannot exert his mind, without moving his body as the organ of his mind, if nothing more, is incontestable. But if we move our bodies we move the things which our bodies move. *Facit per alium facit per se* is a maxim as sound in philosophy as in law. Arranging for whatever purpose, therefore, whether to explode a mine, forge a name, operate a railroad, or take advantage of the forces of nature in any other way, involves not only moving the things arranged or pertaining to the arrangement, and moving them against resistance, but moving, first of all, the things that we call "our bodies, muscles and nerves." If we can move these "undoubtedly material" things, which stand at the head of the "category," why not the whole "category"? Is this eminent physicist one of the "blind guides which strain out the gnat and swallow the camel?" He says that, "so far as energy is concerned, it is the same whether we sign Andrew Carnegie or Alexander Coppersmith," which latter name has five letters more than the former. Whence comes the energy to scribble these letters, expressing the difference between the two signatures? If energy takes no account of this difference, something else must produce the letters that make it—life, perhaps, or some other force of the metaphysical or preternatural kind to which he refers that of life; but, if life can supply the energy to scribble the difference, why not the energy to scribble the sum? Besides, hyperphysical guidance is as indispensable in forming the several letters of these names, and arranging the letters into the names, relatively unimportant though the task may be, as in planning a forgery, donating a library, or arranging an explosion—directed activities all. If energy may dispense with immaterial guidance in the former operations, which he treats as material purely, why not also in the latter, which he considers a mixture of the material and the immaterial? Why this mixture? Supposing the immaterial to be anything more than the negation of the material, what is it? How can we represent it in thought? How can it express itself or get itself expressed in action? What is the use of it? Can that explain anything else which is inexplicable itself, and inconceivable, to boot? Is not the immaterial, so far at any rate as concerns life and mind, a fifth wheel, to say the least? What is mind, one may reverently ask, but matter not understood—matter of which radium is a clod?

When the author of the hypothesis in question wrote the article which sets it forth, where did the energy given out by his pen come from? Proximately, he will admit, from his muscles, which received it from his nerve-fibres, which in turn received it from his nerve-centers, interacting with each other, and with external things—a form of the physical whose interaction with a physical excitant, be it noted, not only gives rise to forms of energy distinctively physical, but, at the same indivisible instant and inseparably, gives rise to what we name the psychical, which, as conceived from this point of view, is neither of these interacting forms, singly, nor both together, integrally, but simply and purely their mutual ac with the transformations it sets up in the physical energy stored by such actio memorially in the structure of the more evolved form. The psychical, as viewed, is the interplay of the organism and its stimuli, registered organicall tained, and susceptible, under laws solely physical, of reproduction, separa reconstruction, and, in general, of the processes described collectively as cer tion or mentation, according as they are regarded from the viewpoint of the st or of the organism. But this, as we have seen, is not the author's view. merely scribal element of the writing he would assign to the physical alone. his philosophy, it appears, scribing is not directive, and hence is physical; scribing, on the contrary, is directive and hence hyperphysical. In consider of the pregnant fact, however, that, while the physical exists independently o psychical (witness the so-called inorganic world), the psychical confessedly dep on the physical, is conditioned by it, forms the counterpart (the phantom do of its labyrinthine coursings point for point, what warrant has he, in scienc philosophy, for concluding that the thoughts which his written characters shaped to signify, and which guided his hand in shaping and arranging them long not to the physical at all, but to the hyperphysical alone? Where ar facts of experience—where the canons of reason—which I do not say neces but which permit this conclusion? I am using the term *psychical*, let me parenthetically, in its ordinary sense of relating only to the human mind. Wi Oliver Lodge pretend that the physical has been proved incompetent to acc for the psychical? Will he contend, that, before this has been done, we are ranted in turning down the physical, whose existence is known, but whose p tialities are unknown, and calling up an agency the very existence of which is merely unknown, but unimaginable? Does he fancy that trampling on the la parsimony is consistent with legitimate philosophising?

The supposed activity of the hyperphysical, no one denies, is identical in with the known activity of the physical. What distinctive function, then, can hyperphysical perform, supposing it to exist? Can the entity derive effici from a non-entity, which, if it were anything, would be debarred by hypot from interacting with the entity? Does the physical become hyperphysica evolution, increase of degree culminating in subversion of kind, something dev ing into nothing? Is a fact difficult of comprehension made easier by an unt able explanation? But one need not beat about the bush. When an effe alleged to arise from two agencies, whereof the one is physical, the other not hyperphysical, but in the production of the effect admittedly incapable eith acting on the physical or of acting apart from it, what is the unavoidable i ence? As the hyperphysical cannot act apart from the physical, it cannot of i produce the effect or any part of the effect; and, since the hyperphysical ca neither on nor apart from the physical, it cannot co-operate with the physic producing the effect: so that the hyperphysical, unable itself to produce the e or to aid the physical in producing it, can exert in the case no influence, auxiliary or principal, and the physical unaided must produce the effect, as on a lower range of development it produces the cloud, the rain, the rainbow. From this conclusion there seems logically no escape. The doctrine which imports a hyperphysical element into the origination of life and mind is demonstrably a delusion. The hypothesis, if thinkable, would be self-destructive. Unless I mistake, it has fallen in the rear of the procession—is antiquescent, if not antiquated. Soon its surviving friends will be likely to have the melancholy privilege of inscribing on its headstone: "Gone to meet Occasional Causes, and Pre-established Harmony."

Professor Lodge sums up his speculation in these words:

"My contention, then, is that whereas life cannot generate energy, it can exer- guiding force, using the term force in its accurate mechanical sense; not 'power' or anything active, but purely passive, directing—perpendicular to the direction of motion; the same kind of force which can constrain a stone to revolve in a circle instead of in a straight line; a force like that of a groove or slot or channel or 'guide'."

He adds that "life" appears to him "to be something the full significance of which lies in another scheme of things." This undoubtedly is the thought which inspired his "contention," and to which apparently his physics is accommodated. Hence possibly these liberties with the elements of a science in which he is an acknowledged proficient. If so, the less credit to him. A theory may be very well; but, when a theory is used as an altar whereon to sacrifice elementary truths of science, and the sacrifice is performed, the priests of the altar must not complain if profane hands are laid on them.

His recapitulation suggests a word or two. Universally, and philosophically, force is matter in motion (energy); specifically, and scientifically, it is the impulse which changes the velocity or direction (the condition) of matter in motion—a mode of energy. Such as I understand it is "force in its accurate mechanical sense" —the strict acceptation of the term in physics. If life can exert force in this sense, it can "move things" with a vengeance, and is, according to his own showing, everything which he contends that it is not. If life can exert mechanical force in any sense, it is certainly not immaterial, but is as "undoubtedly material" as the body which it animates, and of whose forces it is in fact the moving equilibrium. We have all heard of the bungler who chopped off the tail of his dog just behind the ears. Professor Lodge would appear to have curtailed his argument with much the same maladroit completeness. He has done for it, anyway. His conclusion and the premises from which he has severed it, may be united "in another scheme of things"—but not in this world.

He exemplifies a guiding force without activity by citing the force which constrains a stone to revolve in a circle. That is to say, he assumes that the force which makes a moving body move in a curved path, continually changing its own direction in the process, is passive, although the circling body reacting against it is active—that the deflected body exerts activity, the deflecting body none—that though the action and the reaction are equal, the reaction alone is active, the action "purely passive." An example nobler than a stone, and not less familiar, though even more conspicuously irrelevant, stood at his beck. The sun, above all other things in our region of the universe, exerts a guiding force of the kind cited. In guiding his planetary system, is he "purely passive," while only the planets which he holds in their orbits are active? Is gravitation active only in the circumference, passive at the center? In a binary star, for further example, which of the members is active, which is passive? Which is the guiding force? Which the guided? Will he kindly draw the line between them, and tell us which is which, and in particular exactly what either is as distinguished inherently from the other?

Attentive readers will probably observe that in this connection our theorist asserts by implication, syntactically speaking, that a stone can be made to "revolve" in "a straight line." This is a slip of the pen. But judicious readers may think that in point of rationality, not to say conceivability, there is little to choose between this slip, and the movement of his pen in the "groove" which (by "passive exertion of force") he took pains to "arrange" for it. They may be tempted at least to pronounce his "contention" bad science and worse philosophy.

PAUL R. SHIPMAN.

EDGEWATER PARK, NEW JERSEY.

BOOK REVIEWS.

THE SILESIAN HORSEHERD. Questions of the Hour Answered by *Friedrich Max Müller*. Translated from the German by *Oscar A. Fechter*. With a Preface by *J. Estlin Carpenter, M. A.* New York, London, and Bombay Longmans, Green, and Co. 1903. Pages, ix, 220. Price, $1.20.

Our readers may remember an editorial essay which appeared in *The Monist*, Vol. 8, No. 1, page 123, October, 1897, under the title "Prof. Max Müller's Theory of the Self." It was a discussion of the Brahman theory of the atman with which Prof. Max Müller became acquainted in his study of the Upanishads and which he adopted as the corner-stone of his own philosophy. It is what may be briefly described as a theory of a soul in itself. The atman or the self is the real doer. Not the eyes see, but the atman through the eyes, not the feet walk, but the atman utilises the feet, not the hands work but the atman through the hands, not the mind thinks but the atman behind the mind. This atman is immutable and eternal. It is the real soul, and such an atman is supposed to reside in all things. Not the sun shines, but the atman behind the sun,—in a word it is the personification of things as things-in-themselves, and they are supposed to be the real thing.

Max Müller had written an essay on "Celsus" the well-known critic of the early Christians, a learned pagan whose books are known only through the Church-father Origen. This essay was written in a liberal spirit and elicited a reply in a private letter from a German-American farmer who signed himself "Das Pferdebauerle," which means the "horse-farmer." The writer declares that he had enjoyed the essay on Celsus and shows a great admiration for the professor's scholarship; yet he expresses at the same time regret (and he does it not without fine humor), that the learned Professor had not worked his way out to freedom but was still under the sway of some unscientific belief. Max Müller took great pains to answer his American countryman, and this answer is the most popular and most direct exposition of the belief in the atman that can be had. Prof. Max Müller here omits all learned by-work and goes directly to the point. At the same time he unconsciously exposes his weak spots and the untenability of his Brahman belief, for while we may believe in an atman of man it is difficult to understand what that atman will be in things. We know, for example, that the tree consists of root-stem, branches, and foliage, but we have no room for a tree in itself.

Prof. Max Müller had some further correspondence with his admirer in America, whose real name is Fritz Menzel, of Pittsburgh, Pa., where his temporary address was care of the Monongahela Hotel.

Prof. Max Müller's philosophy is philological to the core. Scholars who are dealing with words, not with concrete things, are apt to take the word as the reality and then treat all the realities which constitute the real thing as mere properties of their hypostasation. This reification of abstract nouns, so natural in a philologist who exaggerates the significance of words, is the basis of Prof. F. Max Müller's theory of the Self and of things-in-themselves, which is set forth in his essay *Language and Mind* (pages 105–153): but, as might have been expected, he failed to convince his correspondent, the horse-farmer.

Prof. Max Müller wrote a second answer to the "Pferdebürla" under the title of "The Reasonableness of Religion," which is a justification of his former position, containing many noteworthy passages and fine thoughts; but the impartial reader will feel that the most important points which the Pennsylvania farmer makes remain unanswered.

All these essays were written in German, and it was desirable that Professor Max Müller's views should be had in English. His widow, accordingly, prepared the whole series of essays for publication: (1) The "True History" of Celsus (2) The Horseherd. (3) Concerning the Horseherd. (4) Language and Mind (5) The Reasonableness of Religion. The whole was translated by an American admirer of the Professor, Oscar A. Fechter of North Yakima, Wash., U. S. A and edited by J. Estlin Carpenter, the accomplished Pâli scholar, an English Unitarian minister, well known among Orientalists through his editions of Pâli texts and among Unitarians as a liberal theologian. Mr. Carpenter naturally sympathises strongly with Prof. Max Müller's position.[1]

The book as it lies before us is well edited and well translated, although it very difficult to bring out in English an adequate expression of the Pferdebürla humor. We may add that at the time of its first appearance we corresponded with Prof. Max Müller on the subject and invited him to write an answer to our criticism of his atman theory, but he never did.

P. C.

Sectarianism and Religious Persecution in China. A Page in the History of Religions. By *J. J. M. de Groot.* Vol. I. (With three Plates.) Amsterdam: Johannes Müller. 1903.

Professor De Groot, the same who wrote a treatise on the non-existence of religious liberty in China, as reviewed in *The Monist* for April, 1903, page 478, here describes in a stately volume of 259 pages the conditions of the sects in China.

---

[1] We need scarcely mention that the translation "Horseherd" for *Pferdebürla* is a mistake. The foot-note on the first page of the Preface indicates that Professor Carpenter mistook the German word *Bürla*, which means *Bauer*, for *Bursche*; but the *Pferdebürla* himself explains the word as "a *farmer* who uses horses."

He dedicates the volume "to all missionaries of every Christian creed laboring in China," and collects a number of documents proving that the suppression of non-Confucian thought is deemed a basic principle of the Chinese government. This spirit is characterised in the Confucian dictum quoted by De Groot as a motto on the title-page, "The cultivation of heresy is so injurious!"

De Groot is one of the best-informed Sinologues, and the present volume is brimfull of valuable facts. He explains in the first chapter the fundamental principles of Confucianism regarding heresy, implying the request of its suppression. The second chapter contains a historical survey of religious persecution in China up to the seventeenth century. Persecution is not limited to non-Chinese religions but involves also Buddhist and Taoist sects. Chapter III. offers the documents containing the original text and faithful translations of the laws on convents and religious life. It is astonishing that, under these restrictions, it was at all possible for Buddhism to flourish; but the need of a religious faith and the satisfaction of a hope beyond the present life, such as Buddhism offers to the yearnings of the heart, overruled all obstacles and forced Buddhism again and again to the front, so that even in court circles and for the private religious wants of the emperor and his family Buddhist ceremonies proved indispensable. Chapter IV. contains the law against heresy and sects; Chapter V. discusses sectarianism, especially the power of the White Lotus Sect; Chapter VI. is devoted to the Sien T'ien, an important sect of Taoism; Chapter VII. characterises the Lun Hwa sect, its deities, its meeting places, the degrees of its devotees, initiation ceremonies and higher consecrations, its festivals, its influence in Chinese home life, and the observances in honor of the dead. The supplementary notices on sectarianism and heresy are relegated to the eighth chapter.

No one who wishes to be fully informed concerning the sad state of affairs in the religious life of China can afford to disregard Professor De Groot's book. P. C.

Chinas Religionen. Zweiter Teil: Lao-tsï und seine Lehre. Von *Dr. Rudolf Dvorák*, ord. Professor der oriental. Philologie an der k. k. böhm. Universität in Prag. Münster, i. W.: Aschendorff. 1903. Pages, viii, 216.

Aschendorff of Münster is a Roman Catholic publishing house which brings out quite a number of valuable publications, the general aim and tendency of which is to reconcile faith and revelation. The present work by Dr. Rudolf Dvorák is one volume in a series of contributions to an exposition of non-Christian religions. The author, who is Professor of Oriental Philology at the Bohemian University of Prague (an institution which is distinct from the German University in the same city), takes special interest in Chinese studies and is the author of a volume on Confucius and his doctrine[1] which appeared several years ago in the same series

[1] *Confucius und seine Lehre*. (Chinas Religionen. Erster Teil.) Münster i. W. 1895. Aschendorffsche Buchhandlung.

as the first volume of *China's Religions*, a book distinguished by careful study of the subject and the collection of all the material that is apt to be of interest to European readers.

While the first volume of Dvorák's book on *China's Religions* treats of the life and doctrines of the man who shaped the destiny of the nation, the second volume is devoted to the second important man of China, the old philosopher Lao-Tsï.[1]

Dvorák briefly discusses in the first chapter, Lao-Tsï's Life, quoting the report of Ssï-ma-tshien (p. 1), the great Chinese historian and alluding to other reports in the Confucian Analects and Cuang-tsï's (p. 7) report.[2]

Speaking of the authenticity of Lao-Tsï's book *Tao-Teh-King*, our author (in Chap. II.) accepts the current Chinese tradition as reliable and rejects Giles's theory of its spuriousness.

The bulk of Dvorák's book contains an exposition of Lao-Tsï's doctrine. Chapter III. contains a general exposition of the author's conception of Lao-Tsï's philosophy. He declares that Lao-Tsï believed (1) in Tao as the supreme being, (2) in Tek as the manifestation of the Tao, (3) in Tao as the origin of the world, from which come first heaven and earth, then the world of spirits, and finally the ten thousand things, among which two must be specially mentioned; the water, on account of its prominent qualities, and man as the highest creature. As to Tek, Lao-Tsï lifts up the ideal of the saintly man as a prototype for other creatures, and he characterises the saint first as a private personality, secondly as a member of society, and finally exalts him in politics as the ideal of a ruler.

This general sketch is discussed in detail in the fourth chapter, which alone contains more than half of the whole book (pages 33 to 130). He discusses the ideas of Tao and Tek, Lao-Tsï's conception of creation through the Yin and Yang, his idea of the unity of the heaven and earth, of spirits and ghosts, of the ten thousand things (the entirety of the visible creation), the ideal of the superior man, and the idea of the saintly man, and finally Lao-Tsï's conception of immortality, which may be briefly characterised as a final return to the Tao. Our author adds rightly that the alchemistic tendencies of later Taoism only prove how much Lao-Tsï was misunderstood by his later followers.

Chapter V. is an interesting comparison between Lao-Tsï and Confucius, from which, however, it becomes apparent how much the two sages agreed in spite of all claimed differences.

The sixth chapter is a brief description of Lao-Tsï's influence upon China, and

---

[1] We purposely retain in this article the spelling of Dvorák, although we are used to a different transcription of the Chinese characters and deem his method misleading at least to English-speaking readers, but since no system is perfect, we allow every author the right to use his own and striving to accomodate ourselves to readers of his book, we accept for review his own method of transcription.

[2] For translation into English of the same account, see Carus's *Lao-Tze*.

the last chapter is a *resumé* of the literature on Lao-Tsi among Western thinkers and a short review of the several translations that have heretofore appeared.

The book is carefully prepared, and the opinions of the author are both just and well matured.

THE MENTAL TRAITS OF SEX. An Experimental Investigation of the Normal Mind in Men and Women. By *Helen Bradford Thompson, Ph. D.*, Sometime Fellow in the Department of Philosophy, the University of Chicago, Director of the Psychological Laboratory, Mount Holyoke College. Chicago: The University of Chicago Press. 1903. Pages, vii, 188. Price, $1.25.

This little work by Helen Bradford Thompson comes from the Psychological Laboratory of the University of Chicago which is under the direction of Professor James Rowland Angell, and may be taken as a sample of the work that is accomplished in this institution. The author's material consisted mainly of students of the University of Chicago, and she subjected them to experiments which fall into seven groups, "dealing respectively with motor ability, skin and muscle senses, taste and smell, hearing, vision, intellectual faculties, and affective processes. One chapter of this monograph is devoted to each group. A list of the experiments under each group will be found at the beginning of each chapter. At the end of each chapter there is a comparison of results with those of other investigators, and a general summary."

These seven chapters, II. to VIII., are illustrated by diagrams, and the result is summed up in tables which make it easy to judge at a glance what were the results of the experiments. The summary of the author's conclusions is set forth in the last chapter.

As to discriminative sensibility, our author says: "The number of cases in which the advantage is on the side of the women is greater than the number of cases in which it is on the side of the men. The thresholds are on the whole lower

keener senses and better memory. The assertion that the influence of emotion is greater in the life of women found no confirmation. Their greater tendency toward religious faith, however, and the greater number of superstitions among them, point toward their conservative nature—their function of preserving established beliefs and institutions."

As our author does not wish to enter into the question as to whether or not woman's position will be changed in the future, she is satisfied with the following hint:

"There are, as everyone must recognise, signs of a radical change in the social ideals of sex. The point to be emphasised as the outcome of this study is that, according to our present light, the psychological differences of sex seem to be largely due, not to difference of average capacity, nor to difference in type of mental activity, but to differences in the social influences brought to bear on the developing individual from early infancy to adult years. The question of the future development of the intellectual life of women is one of social necessities and ideals, rather than of the inborn psychological characteristics of sex."

ESSAIS DE PHILOSOPHIE GÉNÉRALE. Cours de philosophie par *Charles Dunan*, professeur de philosophie au Collège Stanislas, Docteur ès Lettres. Paris: Ch. Delagrave. 1902. Pages, vi, 838.

This book of 838 pages, modestly called an essay, is properly speaking a compendium of philosophy, representing a course of all its branches, such as a student at a French university will have to pass through. The author, Charles Dunan, is Professor of Philosophy at the College Stanislas, and the book in its present form is the second edition which has grown out of the lectures and other practical labors of its author.

The book opens with a complete psychology, discussing the psychological method, the nature of consciousness, including the different theories of conscious-

[illegible] sensibility, pleasure and pain, the inclinations and tendencies, sentiments, sensations and emotions. Our author then investigates the nature of intelligence, bodily impressions and the nature of sensation and perception, including the theories of nativism, empiricism, the association of ideas, imagination, attention, abstraction, generalisation, judgment, reason, and language.

A shorter but no less important part is the study of activity, will and habit, special attention being paid to the problems or freedom and the part which habit plays in mental life. An entire chapter is devoted to animal psychology in which Condillac, Lamarck, and Spencer and Darwin are quoted and criticised.

The chapter on art treats such subjects as the nature of art, the means employed by art, art and craft, the emotions roused by art, the realism of art, religious art, the beautiful and the sublime, the pretty and the ridiculous.

An entirely different field is covered in the second part of the book, pages 337 ff., which are devoted to logic, covering the field of formal logic and methodology, comprising the methods of the nature sciences, the nature of hypothesis, the methods of the moral sciences and sophisms.

Under the main head of Metaphysics, our author discusses the several psychological explanations, especially the materialistic, the spirittalistic, and after an elaborate investigation of the question of liberty, he gives an exposition of the contrast of determinism and fatalism. The second part of Metaphysics takes up a discussion of rational cosmology with its several solutions. A whole chapter entitled "Théodicée" enters into the several arguments of the existence of God, and contrasts theism with pantheism and atheism.

Professor Dunan's epistemology discusses the relativity of knowledge, the criterion of error, the proposition of scepticism, and concludes with the affirmation that a universal and necessary philosophy exists, and that this philosophy is the spiritaistic. Our author grants that there are difficulties, but spiritualism alone can explain the existence of intelligence.

The last part of Professor Dunan's book is devoted to ethics. He discusses the principles of ethics, the nature of conscience, the moral law, responsibility, the problem of the ought, personal duties and social duties.

The whole work is thoughtful, albeit in parts pedantical and although to some expositions, scientists, especially those who are devoted to what is commonly called the natural sciences, will make serious objections, it is, considering its standpoint, a fairly impartial elucidation of the several philosophical problems, the main aim being, as stated by the author in the preface to establish "the existence of a personal god, man's freedom of will and moral responsibility, and the existence of another life than the one which we have now in the sensible world.

P. C.

PRINCIPES DE GÉOMÉTRIE. Par *E. Delsol.* Paris: C. Naud. Pages, 97.

Monsieur Delsol, a civil and mining engineer of Paris, proposes in this little book on the principles of geometry a new system which in its general outlines is closely allied to the expositions on the foundation of geometry which have been set forth in *The Monist* during the last year.

Monsieur Delsol himself sums up his proposition in a summary of the introduction as follows: "Pure geometry is a science *a priori*, which admits neither of hypothesis, nor postulates, nor axioms," and we cannot but say that this maxim is heartily endorsed by the editor of *The Monist*.

M. Delsol continues: "If my reasoning *a priori* is susceptible of verification by experience, the conclusions to which it leads are naturally laws of the exterior world. The laws which the exterior world seems to obey are no others than those which govern our understanding. Man if transferred to another world would preserve the same ideas *a priori*."

M. Delsol's theory is based upon the principle of distinction which involves divisibility and makes it that the exterior world can be considered as consisting of parts. The result is the concept of series involving the idea of number, and here M. Delsol contemplates the notion infinite and continuous. He defines his view of equality, of number, of zero, of positive and negative numbers, addition, multiplication, etc. We cannot say that M. Delsol is happy in these important details and his definitions will scarcely prove satisfactory to mathematicians, least of all to those trained in the modern modes of thought. The definition of a point, for instance, seems to us artificial. It is given at the start of Chapter II. as the result of the series α, β, γ, ending in a last term which is characterised by the fact of being indivisible, and M. Delsol calls it "the geometrical point." The straight line is arrived at after a consideration of two intersecting circles, and he says: "The straight line is accordingly a line such as only one can pass through two given points. There is no other which would be equal to it, or to be short and use the usual way of speech, it is one of which only one passes through two points." Surface, line, and point are characterised in the usual way as boundaries, the surface as separating two parts of space, the line of a surface, and the point of a line, but here M. Delsol finds a new aspect. "Suppose the points *A* and *B* limit the arc *AB*, and this arc be considered in itself not as a partition of the rest of the circle." In that case the points do not separate, but are only the extremities of the arc, and thus he finds himself necessitated to invent a new name to distinguish this kind of a point from the one defined above. He calls it the "sous-point," saying, "accordingly, we call *sous-point* the end of a line that is not closed (*non-fermée*) and *sous-line* the boundary of a surface that is not closed, which is the locus of the extremities of lines in a surface that is not closed" (p. 48). Upon analogous modes of reason, M. Delsol introduces the idea of *sous-spheres* and *sous-straights* (Chapt. III.). M. Delsol arrives at the conclusion that the Euclidean geometry is the only possible *a priori*. Time, number, and space is the triple emanation of the principle of distinction applied to the exterior world. He points out in the appendix that the non-Euclidean geometries do not agree with experience, and he scorns the objections of their representatives. It is impossible to interpret experience by different geometries, for only one of them can be true.

While we confess that the underlying tendencies of M. Delsol's explanation of the principles of geometry have fundamental points of contact with the theory set forth in *The Monist*, we cannot regard the details of his exposition as a solution of the difficulties in question.

P. C.

AN INTRODUCTORY STUDY OF ETHICS. By *Warner Fite*. New York, London, and Bombay: Longmans, Green, and Co. 1903. Pages, xi, 383.

Prof. Warner Fite treats the subject of ethics mainly by contrasting hedonism with idealism, the ethics of happiness with the ethics of conscience and principle. He sides with neither party, but points out the necessity of a compromise. We may characterise his book by quoting the following passages:

"The moral problem is the expression of a conflict between our aspirations toward an ideally perfect and complete human life and the limiting conditions.

"The hedonist proposes to ignore the ideal considerations and to conform strictly to the conditions. For in these conditions, he claims, we discover the real ground of things. The world of which we are a part is a world of mechanical forces. It is therefore bound to work itself out in its own way and in its own time. No effort of ours will either accelerate the process or retard it. Therefore let us study its workings, conform to its movements, and be content with the comfort and happiness which it affords us. The idealist, on the other hand, urges us to ignore the conditions and to devote ourselves immediately to the pursuit of ideal ends. From his point of view, it is in the ideals, and not in the conditions, that we are to discover the real ground of things. The conditions by which we are hemmed in are after all mere negation. They represent nothing but the absence of self-consciousness,—or, in social terms, nothing but the absence of mutual sympathy and understanding. Therefore let us set out immediately and directly toward the attainment of the highest personal and social ideals.

"Though we cannot bring the two ends of our problem quite together, still it remains *a priori* conceivable that they may be brought together. In chapter xvi, it is pointed out that the conceptions of a world determined by mechanical forces and of a world determined by reason or consciousness, upon which the two sides of the problem rest, are not logically contradictory but only empirically irreconcilable.

"The practical significance of the moral situation may then be summarised as follows: Our human life is permanently problematic. We never reach a point either of complete realisation of ideals or of complete conformity to conditions. At every point of our existence we stand between two immediately contradictory demands, those of our ideals and those of our conditions. Theoretically, the two ought not to be ultimately incompatible, but practically they cannot be wholly reconciled; and our duty will not admit of an exclusive attention to either. It must lie, then, in the best possible mutual adjustment; and the best pos justment must be that which, since both demand satisfaction, affords the satisfaction to each.

"Since the requirements of a moral life include both progress and ha any course that we may take will be of necessity a compromise."

LEHRBUCH DER PSYCHOLOGIE. Von *Friedrich Jodl*, o. ö. Professor der Phi an der Universität zu Wien. Erster und zweiter Band. Stuttgart u lin: J. G. Cotta'sche Buchhandlung Nachfolger. 1903.

The appearance of the second edition of Professor Jodl's text-book of ogy proves the popularity of its author both as a psychologist and an teacher. The first edition, a stately volume of 767 pages, has been increa few hundred pages so as to make a division into two volumes advisable. ditions do not change the character of the original work, but only bring date by incorporating discussions of more recent developments.

The character of the book has practically remained the same, and we c our readers to our review of the first edition, which appeared in *The Mon* VII., pages 459-463.

Professor Jodl is an associationist, and he has here collected the vast of psychological research, discussing in the several chapters: I. The Provi Methods of Psychology. II. Body and Soul. III. A Description and An the Phenomena of Consciousness. This is one of the most important c Taking the ego as a basis, Jodl treats of the nature of consciousness as the object, and discusses the narrows (*Enge*) and the threshold (*Schwelle*) of co ness, its continuity, the main functions of consciousness, and finally its su stages. IV. Sensations, including the methods of measuring sensations psycho-physics. V. The Several Provinces of the Senses,—cœnæsthesis sensations, skin sensations, taste and smell, hearing, sensations of sight, i a discussion of the eye and the sensations of light and color. The second contains: VI. Primary Feelings, Sensory Feelings, and the Elementary of Æsthetics. VII. The Primary Phenomena of Will, Appetence, Mov Will Proper, and Attention. VIII. Secondary Phenomena, Memory, Re tion, Association, and Concentration. IX. Psychical Constructions of Re tion, Time, Space, the External World, the Me and the Not-Me. X. S and Thinking, the Origin of Language, Word and Concept, Judgment and gism. XI. Feelings of a Secondary and Tertiary Degree, Feelings of Person, the Dynamics of Feelings, Complex Æsthetic and Ethical Feeling Phenomena of Will, of a Secondary and Tertiary Degree, defining will psychical antecedents of will, conflicts of the will, psychical inhibition, d tion, decision; the nature of repentance, the illusion of the idea that on have willed otherwise, the problem of freedom of will, the significance of t of will, inherited and acquired character, and characterology and ethics.

While the table of contents is very helpful, it by no means replaces the missing index, the desirability of which is not yet sufficiently appreciated by German scholars. A valuable appendix of Jodl's book, however, is a careful list of the psychological literature, which will be found very useful to the professional psychologist (pp. 407–448).

P. C.

OUR BENEVOLENT FEUDALISM. By *W. J. Ghent*. New York: The Macmillan Company. 1902. Pages, vii, 202. Price, $1.25.

The expansion of Mr. Ghent's article in the *Independent*, April 3, 1902, into a book has given us the best piece of social satire since the appearance of Mr. Veblen's *Theory of the Leisure Class*. The word satire may not be altogether applicable in this case, for the main purpose of each book is scientific, i. e., to present and reason upon the facts. But sometimes facts are the most satirical of all things.

Mr. Ghent's book is an attempt to portray the drift of dominant social and industrial tendencies, to forecast the future social order by noting the direction of the current of industrial and social evolution. Modern tendencies as described here are toward great combinations in specific trades, coalescence of kindred industries and the integration of capital, an increase of farm tenantry, a stronger State, greater dependence of labor upon capital, etc., and the outcome is to be a "Feudalism which, though it differs in many forms from that of the time of Edward I., is yet based upon the same status of lord, agent, and underling." It is to be "a Feudalism somewhat graced by a sense of ethics and somewhat restrained by a fear of democracy." As "bondage to the land" was the basis of villeinage under the old *régime*, so "bondage to the job" will be the basis of villeinage under the new. These tendencies are pointed out and discussed with a wealth of illustrative material, which alone makes the book valuable to the student of socia, questions.

Apologists for the present order may criticise the book as a one-sided presentation of the facts, as ignoring or slurring opposite tendencies making for a true democracy, and there is some basis for this criticism. But the book is none the less valuable, for it takes a loud call to startle the complacent optimists who see nothing wrong with modern life, and, moreover, we cannot be sure that the author's forecast is not a true one, merely because he does not enumerate all tendencies. Those he does mention certainly exist, and no doubt the author hopes by presenting them forcibly to provoke thought that will lead to a strengthening of counteracting tendencies. At all events, he discloses incidentally that, while present tendencies make for a benevolent feudalism, his own sympathies are with a vastly different social *régime*. The fine vein of irony running through the book, its felicitous expression, its marshalling of facts, and its luminous exposition of modern social and industrial life make it peculiarly interesting and valuable.

IRA W. HOWERTH.

STUDIES IN LOGICAL THEORY. By *John Dewey*, Professor of Philosophy, with the Co-operation of Members and Fellows of the Department of Philosophy. Chicago: The University of Chicago Press. 1903. Pages, xiii, 388. Price, $2.50.

This book gives us a fair insight into the method and nature of philosophical instruction in the University of Chicago. It is edited by John Dewey, who himself contributes a series of four articles to its contents. As to the character of the book, the editor says in the Preface:

"This volume presents some results of the work done in the matter of logical theory in the Department of Philosophy of the University of Chicago in the first decade of its existence. The eleven Studies are the work of eight different hands.

"The various Studies present, the author believes, about the relative amount of agreement and disagreement that is natural in view of the conditions of their origin. The various writers have been in contact with one another in Seminaries and lecture courses in pursuit of the same topics, and have had to do with shaping one another's views. There are several others, not represented in this volume, who have also participated in the evolution of the point of view herein set forth, and to whom the writers acknowledge their indebtedness. The disagreements proceed from the diversity of interests with which the different writers approach the logical topic; and from the fact that the point of view in question is still (happily) developing and showing no signs of becoming a closed system."

The views commented on are those of Mill, Lotze, Bosanquet, and Bradley, and the editor with the courtesy of the modern scholar expresses to them his special indebtedness, and at the same time a pre-eminent obligation to William James of Harvard, to whom the book is tendered as an "unworthy token of regard and an admiration that are coequal."

Professor Dewey discusses thought and its subject matter in four articles, including the antecedents of thought, the datum of thinking, and the content and object of thought.

The other seven articles are as follows: "Bosanquet's Theory of Judgment," by Helen Bradford Thompson, Ph. D.; "Typical Stages in the Development of Judgment," by Simon Fraser McLennan, Ph. D.; "The Nature of Hypothesis," by Myron Lucius Ashley, Ph. D.; "Image and Idea in Logic," by Willard Clark Gore, Ph. D.; "The Logic of Pre-Socratic Philosophy," by William Arthur Heidel, Ph. D.; "Valuation as a Logical Process," by Henry Waldgrave Stuart, Ph.D., and "Some Logical Aspects of Purpose," by Addison Webster Moore, Ph. D.

LA MORALE ET LA SCIENCE DES MŒURS. Par *L. Lévy-Bruhl*, Chargé de cours à l'Université de Paris, Professeur à l'École libre des sciences politiques. Paris: Félix Alcan. 1903. Pages, 300. Price, 5 fr.

Prof. L. Lévy-Bruhl does not propose to inquire into the principle of morality nor to criticise the existent systems, but in agreement with the present tendency among the philosophers and sociologists, he applies the principle of the positive philosophy to the current ideas of moral science. He claims that it is illogical to regard it as at once normative and theoretical, for in morality as well as in other branches of thought it would be irrational thus to conceive the relations between theory and practice. Theoretical science studies the given realities, that is to say, in the present case moral facts, and moral facts are social facts. Then only a practical application may be deduced from the established sciences.

An important part of the work is devoted to a reply to the several objections made by those who hold the old views. There is, e. g., a postulate, that human nature has always been and always will remain the same, but Lévy-Bruhl holds this conception is not tenable if we study the changes which society has undergone. Further, it will not be sufficient to base our notions of morality upon a psychological analysis of human nature. We must study sociology and derive the general principles as well as detailed applications from man's social relations. According to another postulate, commonly held, the moral conscience forms a moral and organic unity, but how about the conflicts of duties, how about the obvious changes in moral standards, which we observe in history? The author holds that positive morality must first of all collect and collate the facts, and shows how the adherents of the old school do not apply the scientific method. We must analyse the given realities of morality and judge them in their connection as well as in their conditions. We gain a higher view by comparative morality which will render impossible the narrowness of taking our own conscience as the type of all morality. If thus a moral science were established, we could base a rational morality upon it, and modify our moral principles accordingly, but at present such an enterprise is premature. Our author is not sceptical as to its realisation in the future, for, says he, science is never sceptical, and we shall finally be able to determine the fundamental laws of social and moral growth.

THE RELATIONS OF PSYCHOLOGY TO PHILOSOPHY. By *James Rowland Angell*. Decennial Publications of the University of Chicago. Chicago: The University of Chicago Press. 1903. Pages, 21.

In discussing the points of contact of the several philosophical sciences, psychology, logic, ethics, and epistemology, Professor J. R. Angell touches upon the influence which biology of late has exercised upon psychology and hints at the possible solution of the problem of consciousness by the methods of a structural and, even more so, of a functional psychology. We can determine what consciousness is only by what it does. And this rule is applicable also in our investigation of the standards of value, especially of truth. Says Angell:

"Either we must suppress functional psychology, or else admit that the so-called ethical examination of the element of value in conduct—being in point of fact simply an examination of the condition of largest effectiveness in conduct—belongs in reality to the field of functional psychology; and we must admit, fur-

"If a center of gravity for the detached portions of philosophy be necessary, psychology possesses as a claimant for this honor the notable advantage over its rivals that it is explicitly devoted to the study of the individual as such, from whom all philosophical problems emanate and to whom all solutions of them revert. When this psychological study is interpreted in a functional, as well as in a structural, sense, the theoretical distinctions between psychology and philosophy have ceased to exist."

—*ς*.

Der kategorische Imperativ. Rede zur Feier des Geburtstages Sr. Majestät des deutschen Kaisers, Königs von Preussen, Wilhelm II. Von *Dr. Paul Deussen*, Professor der Philosophie an der Universität Kiel. Kiel und Leipzig: Verlag von Lipsius und Tischer. 1903. Pages, 29.

A discussion of Kant's categorical imperative was chosen by Professor Paul Deussen as an appropriate subject for a spirited address, delivered in honor of Emperor Wilhelm II., at the official academical celebration of his birthday, Jan. 27. The remarkable solution of the Kantian problem is, according to Professor Deussen's interpretation, the statement that "Nature is appearance, not thing-in-itself," and while we do not find the *summum bonum* in nature, we find it in the thing-in-itself. Kant teaches that the highest good is found in God, Immortality, and Freedom; none of them is possible in nature. The existence of God is not only not proved but is even excluded by the order of things in the expanse of objective reality; immortality is absolutely impossible, and the idea of freedom so far as the domain of empirical investigation reaches, is untenable. Yet all three are safe possessions of man as soon as we turn to the realm of the thing-in-itself. There the irrefragable law of causation no longer applies, and thus the highest good of mankind resides in the nimbus of inscrutability (pp. 18–20). The categorical imperative, however, is the law which man as thing-in-itself dictates unto man as appearance (p 21).

This is all pleasant news to those who believe in the gospel of things-in-themselves, but what shall become of the editor of *The Monist*, who in his latest book declares that things-in-themselves are mere hypostasisations, and that the idea is contradictory and untenable?

In consideration of the fact that the strength of the German army, the reliableness of the German bureaucracy and the general welfare of the Fatherland was due to the categorical imperative having become incarnate in Frederick the Great, William the Great, and also in the present ruler of Germany, Professor Deussen concluded his speech with an enthusiastic *Hoch* for Emperor William the Second.

—*a*—

A PHILOSOPHICAL ESSAY ON PROBABILITIES. By *Pierre Simon*, Marquis de Laplace. Translated from the Sixth French Edition by *Frederick Wilson Truscott, Ph. D.* and *Frederick Lincoln Emory, M. E.* New York: John Wiley & Sons. London: Chapman & Hall, Ltd. 1902. Pages, iv, 196.

The republication of the old classical books has become a demand, and we are glad to see the philosophical essays on Probability by Laplace translated into English and published in a good and readable edition. The calculus of probability was first laid down by Pascal who worked it out at the instigation of Chevalier de Meré, but Laplace gave the first exposition of the science as a whole, showing its applications in the several fields, its significance and its value. Laplace concludes his essay in these words:

"It is seen in this essay that the theory of probabilities is at bottom only common sense reduced to calculus; it makes us appreciate with exactitude that which exact minds feel by a sort of instinct without being able ofttimes to give a reason for it. It leaves no arbitrariness in the choice of opinions and sides to be taken; and by its use can always be determined the most advantageous choice. Thereby it supplements most happily the ignorance and the weakness of the human mind. If we consider the analytical methods to which this theory has given birth; the truth of the principles which serve as a basic; the fine and delicate logic which their employment in the solution of problems requires; the establishments of public utility which rest upon it; the extension which it has received and which it can still receive by its application to the most important questions of natural philosophy and the moral science; if we consider again that, even in the things which cannot be submitted to calculus, it gives the surest hints which can guide us in our judgments, and that it teaches us to avoid the illusions which ofttimes confuse us, then we shall see that there is no science more worthy of our meditations, and that no more useful one could be incorporated in the system of public instruction."

DIE WILLENSFREIHEIT. Eine neue Antwort auf eine alte Frage. Von *Dr. Adolf Bolliger*, Professor an der Universität Basel. Berlin: Druck und Verlag von Georg Reimer. 1903. Pages, iv, 125.

Dr. Adolf Bolliger undertook to answer the prize question proposed by "The Hague Association for the Defence of the Christian Religion" anent the theory of indeterminism, its tenability, and its significance in religion and ethics, the answer being an outright condemnation of determinism in any shape and the proposition of a theory of indeterminism based upon the idea of the reality of the will.

Will is not an unconscious being pushed, but a conscious and active pushing,—a truth which will be contradicted by few, if any. That form of determinism (so important for ethical considerations) which regards man's will and his character as the most important factor among the determining conditions is passed over in silence. In reply to the objection that an act of the will independent of any determining motives is incomprehensible, Bolliger quotes Lotze as authority that "comprehension means the reduction of special cases to a general law." A free act of the will, however, says Bolliger, is an ἀρχή, a new start, something aboriginal: accordingly it cannot be reduced to law and must necessarily be incomprehensible.

Bolliger's religious expositions of divine sonship, salvation, God's love, and man's sin, are very edifying pastoral effusions, and he praises God for his decisive victory over determinism which makes our souls swell higher with the consciousness that we are of divine origin and have a mission in life worthy of our station (page 107).

The Hague Association for the Defence of the Christian Religion did not grant the prize of 400 fl. to our author, but for some reasons not stated in the present pamphlet offered him a premium of 250 fl. with "an extremely restricted recognition" (*einer äusserst limitirten Anerkennung*). κ.

GESCHLECHT UND CHARAKTER. Eine prinzipielle Untersuchung von *Dr. Otto Weininger*. Wien und Leipzig: Wilhelm Braumüller. 1903. Pages, xxiii, 632.

This book is the work of an extremist. The first chapters are quite sensible, but very soon he shows himself a faithful adherent of Schopenhauer's views of woman. The present tendencies of woman's emancipation are to him nothing new. He claims that the same tendencies always existed, sometimes more or less pronounced, and that only manish representatives of the fair sex take to them. He regards woman as inferior to man. While man, in addition to his sexual life, may devote himself to art, science, or industrial labors, the existence of woman is limited to womanish interests. Herr Weininger maintains further that the psychology of woman is always written by men; he does not know that there are women psychologists in several colleges for women in the United States. We hope that he is unmarried and we wish that some writer of the fair sex might rise who would publish a similar book on man if only for the sake of parody. For some unknown reasons, the thirteenth chapter of the book is devoted to the Jewish question, in which the author shows himself as an outspoken anti-Semite.

L'ANNÉE PSYCHOLOGIQUE. Publiée par *Alfred Binet*, Docteur ès sciences, etc., avec la collaboration de MM. *H. Beaunis*, *V. Henri*, et *Th. Ribot*. Paris: G. Reinwald. 1903. Pages, 662. Price, 15 fr.

The French Psychological Annual, published by Alfred Binet with the assistance of Beaunis, Henri, and Ribot, contains a number of valuable original contributions. The first is by Malapert, an investigation of the sentiment of anger among children; the second, by Bourdon, on the difference of the sensitiveness of the two eyes; and the third by the editor himself, a series of investigations on handwriting, during the state of artificial excitement, on the measure of sensibility, on one-sidedness in both children and adults, on the state of distraction, on the influence of suggestion in determining the threshold of sensation. The last of the volume, pages 253 to 656, is devoted to bibliographical reviews in the domain of physiological psychology and anthropology, and essays on visions, audition, touch, taste and smell, perception, ideation, association, memory, reason, imagination, suggestibility, moral and religious sentiments, æsthetic emotions, the instincts, the will and movement, pedagogical, pathological psychology, comparative psychology and general questions.

OUTLINES OF PSYCHOLOGY. An Elementary Treatise with some Practical Applications. By *Josiah Royce, Ph. D., L.L. D.*, Professor of the History of Philosophy in Harvard University. New York: The Macmillan Company, London: Macmillan & Co., Ltd. 1903. Pages, xxvii, 392. Price, $1.00.

Professor Royce's *Psychology* is published as a volume in the Teachers' Professional Library, edited by Nicholas Murry Butler, President of Columbia University. The editor says in the Introduction:

"How and by what warrant do I pass from a knowledge of my own mental states to a knowledge and interpretation of the mental states of others? What are the primary evidences of mind? Into what and how few simplest units can my own complex mental states be broken up? What are the processes of mental growth and development, and what laws govern them?

"If the student of psychology gains clear and reasonable convictions on such points as these, he has not studied psychology in vain."

Professor Royce's book is an attempt to answer these questions. In it he discusses the definition of psychology, the physical signs of the presence of mind, its nervous conditions and general features, the sensory experience and mental imagery, the feelings, devoting several chapters to the consideration of docility. The concluding chapter discusses the will.

GRUNDZÜGE DER PHYSIOLOGISCHEN PSYCHOLOGIE. Von *Wilhelm Wundt*, Professor an der Universität zu Leipzig. Fünfte völlig umgearbeitete Auflage. Dritter Band mit 75 Abbildungen im Text. Leipzig: Wilhelm Engelmann. 1903. Pages, ix, 805.

Professor Wundt's third volume of the outlines of physiological psychology contains his investigations of our notions of time, pages 107–241; the phenomena of volition, 242–319; consciousness and the flux of concepts, 320–517; psychical associations, 518–641; anomalous states of consciousness, 642–677; general conclusion, 677–755; and a discussion of the principles of psychology, 756–793.

The chapters on detailed investigations give us a clear insight into the laboratory work of Professor Wundt, which is the prototype of all psychological laboratories in the world. All other German and also all the American laboratories have developed after the precedence of the work of Professor Wundt, who can rightly be styled "the father of the psychological laboratory."

Though the interest in Professor Wundt's books is great, it reaches a climax in the last two chapters, which discuss in a masterful manner the relation of psychology to the natural sciences and also questions of general importance. Here we have a careful discussion of the basis of all natural sciences, the principle of cognition, causation, teleology, mechanism and energism, materialism and vitalism, and the significance of the will in psychology.

The last chapter discusses the conception of the soul. In this discussion Professor Wundt substitutes the actuality of the soul for the idea of soul-substance. The soul is soul not because it consists of substance, but because it is active; and its immateriality does not lessen its significance in the domain of science.

L'ESPRIT SCIENTIFIQUE ET LA MÉTHODE SCIENTIFIQUE. Par *Louis Favre*, Directeur de la "Bibliothèque des Méthodes dans les Sciences expérimentales." Paris, Librairie C. Reinwald. 1903.

The author of this spirited pamphlet, Monsieur Louis Favre, the editor of a magazine entitled *Bibliothèque des Méthodes dans les Sciences expérimentales*, expresses his belief in the scientific method, finding the essence of science in the scientific spirit, which is a love of truth, and a truthful adherence to the results obtained. It is the scientific spirit that makes science, constituting its essence and unity. It causes the progress and the discovery of truth, and the rejection of error. When the truth is found, it insists on having its statement accompanied with the necessary evidence and proofs, and shows a desire to communicate it to others so as to make the truth known and loved and recognised. The scientific spirit should be and will be the most powerful factor of man's life, ruling all human affairs. The day will come when the scientific spirit will penetrate everything, and its dominion over the world will be established.

Such are the conclusions of Monsieur Favre, set forth in a series of chapters with laudable zeal and insistency.

WHAT IS MEANING? Studies in the Development of Significance. By *V. Welby*. New York and London: The Macmillan Company. 1903. Pages, xxxi, 35[illegible] Price, 6s.

Lady Victoria Welby has devoted years of study to the word and the importance of "meaning," and in the present work we have her views on the application of its science and philosophy. The first of it may be expressed in her own words as follows:

"We must, at least, look forward to the substitution of the Significian for th[illegible]

Metaphysician, ...and we shall attain to what has here been called binocular thinking; we shall not merely adopt or expound, we shall not even be content merely to develop, we shall *account for* the great systems or the typical formulas of ancient or modern philosophy....The true philosophy, like the true science, appeals to intelligence as intelligence....The true philosophy comes not to abstract, but to interpret; not to destroy, but to fulfil; not to give mere passive reflection but to prove itself the creative energy of mind,—a ray of that Light whereby we learn what beauty, what goodness, what love, in brief, what life in its highest sense may be."

UEBER DIE GRENZEN DER GEWISSHEIT. Von *Dr. Ernst Dürr*, Privatdocent in Würzburg. Leipzig: Dürr'schen Buchhandlung. 1903. Pages, vii, 157. Price, 3 Marks 50 Pfg.

This pamphlet on the boundaries of certitude, written by Dr. Ernst Dürr, Privatdocent in the University of Würzburg and a disciple of Prof. Oswald Külpe defines the limits of cognition for the purpose of justifying religious belief. The author investigates the relation of epistemology to the several sciences and finding that consistency or absence of contradiction is the criterion of possibility, he comes to the conclusion that there is no absolute criterion of truth. He justifies what he calls scientific belief (perhaps better, belief of science), and also what is well described as ethico-metaphysical faith. His argument centres in the idea that the unity of the world represents and verifies the belief in God, which appears first as belief in the development of that which possesses worth and secondly in the hope of immortality. This is not the way in which faith naturally originates, but the author cherishes the confidence that he has succeeded in justifying it.

A HISTORICAL AND CRITICAL DISCUSSION OF COLLEGE ADMISSION REQUIREMENTS. By *Edwin Cornelius Broome, Ph. D.*, Sometime Fellow in Teachers College. New York: The Macmillan Co. Berlin: Mayer and Müller. 1903. Pages, 159. Price, $1.00.

It is not only interesting but important to know the requirements for admission to the colleges of a country. This work has been done by Dr. Edwin Cornelius Broome in one of the Columbia University contributions, and we may say that this collection furnishes the means of watching the growth and the changes of university life of this country.

ESQUISSE D'UNE ÉVOLUTION DANS L'HISTOIRE DE LA PHILOSOPHIE. Essais par *Nicolas Kostyleff*. Paris: Félix Alcan, Editeur. 1903. Pages, 224. Price, 2 fr. 50.

The author characterises the evolution of mankind as being determined by an instinctive tendency towards a monotheistic conception of the universe,—a conception which finds its first great spokesman in Spinoza, to whose life and works the second part of this spirited little pamphlet is devoted.

THE SOUL. A Study and an Argument. By *David Syme*. London and New York: The Macmillan Company. 1903. Pages, xxxi, 234. Price, 4s. 6d. net.

The author discusses the nature of life, of reflex action, of consciousness, teleology, instinct, and transformation. He takes great pains to refute Darwin and defend Paley's *Natural Theology* against modern innovations. He is quite anxious not only to deny a materialistic conception of the soul but to insist on the doctrine of mind as a substance. He says that "mind is a real substance, and not a product, property or function of some other real or supposititious substance; that sensation and consciousness are not the accompaniments of nerve action in the brain only, but are concurrent with all nerve action whatsoever."

PHILOSOPHISCHE BIBLIOTHEK, BAND 45. IMMANUEL KANT, DIE RELIGION INNERHALB DER GRENZEN DER BLOSSEN VERNUNFT. Dritte Auflage. Herausgegeben und mit einer Einleitung sowie einem Personen- und Sachregister versehen. Von *Karl Vorländer*. Leipzig: Dürr. 1903. Pages, xcvi, 260. Price, 3.20 Mark.

The publishing house of Dürr of Leipzig announces a new edition of Immanuel Kant's "Religion within the Limits of Pure Reason" edited and prefaced by Karl Vorländer. Kant's work needs no praise or characterisation, for it is sufficiently well known and has had a great influence upon the development of theology not only in Germany but also in England and America. Vorländer's preface contains a sketch of Kant's religious development in some ninety pages.

ESSAI PHILOSOPHIQUE SUR LES GÉOMÉTRIES NON EUCLIDIENNES. Par *L.-J. Delaporte*, Docteur en philosophie de l'Université de Fribourg (Suisse), Licencié ès sciences mathématiques. Paris: C. Naud. 1903. Pages, 140. Price, 3 fs. 50.

We have in this book a brief but careful memoir on non-Euclidean geometry, containing in an appendix a recapitulation of the fundamental purposes of the several geometries and presenting in parallel columns the geometries of Lobatchevski, Euclid, and Riemann.

Announcement.

The Open Court Publishing Company announces for early publication an elaborate work in two volumes by E. A. Wallis Budge, entitled "The Gods of the Egyptians; or Studies in Egyptian Mythology." A description of the Egyptian Pantheon based upon original research, incorporating all that is known; methodical, thorough and up-to-date in every respect.

There is no other book on this subject, nor is it likely that one will appear in the near future to rival it. It is unique, and the probability is that the work will soon become rare. The edition is limited to 1500 copies, three hundred of which have been secured for America.

It is published in two volumes, containing 988 pages, and is richly illustrated with 98 colored plates, averaging eight impressions each, and 131 illustrations in the text.

Two volumes, royal octavo, library binding, price $20.00 net.

The Open Court Publishing Co.

324 Dearborn Street, Chicago

CHAPTER XVI

THE GREAT TRIAD OF MEMPHIS, PTAḤ, [hieroglyphs] SEKHET, [hieroglyphs], AND I-EM-HETEP, [hieroglyphs]

THE greatest of all the old gods of Memphis was undoubtedl PTAḤ, [hieroglyphs], or PTAḤ-NEB-ĀNKH, [hieroglyphs], and his worship, in one form or another, goes back to the earliest part of the dynastic period. He has usually been regarded as a form of the Sun-god, and as the personification of the rising sun, either at the time when it begins to rise above the horizon or immediately after it has risen. The name has often been explained to mean "Opener," and to be derived from a root which was cognate in meaning with the well-known Semitic root *pâthakh*, פָּתַח, in fact Ptaḥ was thought to be the "Opener" of the day just as Tem was considered to be the "Closer" of the day. The chief drawback, however, to the acceptance of this derivation is the fact that Ptaḥ never forms one of the groups of the chief forms of the Sun-god in the texts, and his attributes are entirely different from those of Kheperȧ, Tem, Ḥeru, and Rā. Moreover, although the word *ptaḥ*, [hieroglyphs], is found in Egyptian it never has the meaning "open," in the sense of opening a door, and the determinative which follows it,[1] [hieroglyph], proves conclusively that although it does m "to open" it is always in the sense of "to engrave, to carve, chisel," and the like; compare Heb. פִּתּוּחַ "engraving, sculpture. The meaning proposed for the name "Ptaḥ" by Dr. Brugsch "sculptor, engraver," and many passages in the texts of all periods make it plain that Ptaḥ was the chief god of all handicraftsmen

[1] Brugsch, *Wörterbuch*, p. 528.

Seker-Asår.

called "the great god, who came into being "in the beginning, he who resteth upon the "darkness," [hieroglyphs]. In the xviith Chapter of the *Book of the Dead* (line 113) occurs a petition in which the deceased begs to be delivered from the "great god who carrieth away "the soul, who eateth hearts, and who "feedeth upon offal, the guardian of the "darkness, the god who is in the Seker "boat, [hieroglyphs]," and in the explanation of the passage which is given in answer to the question, "Who is this?" the god who is in the Seker boat is said to be either SUTI, [hieroglyphs], or SMAM-UR, [hieroglyphs], the soul of Seb. Thus it is clear that Seker was an ancient spirit or god whose attributes were such that he might well be represented by Set, or Suti, the enemy of Rā, or by the soul of the earth-god Seb. In comparatively early dynastic times Seker was exalted to the position of god of that portion of the Underworld which was allotted to the souls of the inhabitants of Memphis and the neighbourhood, and it is tolerably certain that he was regarded as the tutelary deity of the necropolis of Ṣakkâra.

Ptolemy Euergetes and the Ḥennu Boat.

AMERICAN MAHA-BODHI SOCIETY

INDO-AMERICAN INDUSTRIAL EDUCATIONAL PROPOGANDA

RECEIPTS

Mrs. G. E. Vincent, $1.00—Miss Clara Stumcke, $1.00—Mrs. Moore, $1.00—Miss Lena Horn, $1.00—Miss ice Butterworth, $1.00—Card 111, $1.00—Card 113, $1.00—Card 114, $1.00—A. L. Williams, $1.00—T. B. Con-r, $1.00—Miss Farmer, $20.00—Miss Belle McFarland, $1.00—Miss Adelaide Johnson, $1.00—F. S. Green, —C. A. Lane, $1.00—Mrs. William McLain and Mrs. George Anderson, $1.00—Miss Nellie Auten, $1.00—s. Emma Thompson, $1.00—Charles Langham, $1.00—Alios C. Runte, $1.00—Card 1104, 25c—F. O. Claus-, $1.00—Mrs. Steward, $6.00—Mrs. Steward, $1.00—Miss G. Holm, 1.00—George C. Waters, $1.00—George Falcomer, $2.00—Mrs. C. Bergmeier, $2.00—Miss Laura Benedict, $5.10—M. H. Wadsworth, $70.00—Mr. d Mrs. C. H. Sterns, $2.00—E. R. Plumb, $2.00—H. Burkland, $1.00—Mrs. Bergmeier (Photos), $4.00—Mrs. orge Arnold, $1.00—C. A. Lay (Miss), $2.00—Josiah M. Kagan, $1.00—Mrs. Charles Bangs, $1.00—Miss S. thon, $1.00—Mr. Meinhold, $1.00—Mrs. Edward Atkinson, $100.00—Dr. T. E. Francis, $15.00—Francis I. rker, $1.00—A. H. Dharmapala, $27.50—Mrs. L. G. Burleigh, $1.00—Annie F. Cronin, $1.00—Henry V. B. nith, $1.00—Mrs. Seaton, $1.00—Miss Mary Bangs, $2.00—Gustav Martin, $1.00—Mr. Pressey, $1.00,—Miss ns, $1.00—Mrs. Curier, 85c—Mrs. Bakin, 10c—Sale of Books, $2.40—Mrs. C. Bergmeier (Nayan R. Mitter), 0—Mrs. W. R. Johnson, 50c—B. A. Keljiket, $1.00—C. W. G. Withee, $2.00—First Cong'l Church (Sharon), R. Hewins, $6.04—Mrs. Steward, $1.00—Alfred L. Leonard, $1.00—E. B. Beckwith (photos) $5.50—Wor-ster, Mass., Lecture, $12.00—Mr. and Mrs. J. E. Solley, $8.00—Mr. and Mrs. J. E. Solley (photos), $7.00—ss Kate Conklin, $1.00—Total, $357.89.

DISBURSEMENTS

Traveling expenses (A. H. Dharmapala), $13.40—Photographs of A. H. Dharmapala, $10.00—Printing, 6.72—Freight and packing shipment to India, $51.34—Postage, $25.50—Express, $1.58—Miscellaneous ex-nses (car fare, books), $7.42—Total, $165.96—Balance on hand, $191.93.

AMERICAN MAHA-BODHI SOCIETY

RECEIPTS

Cash on hand April 1st, 1903, $19.34—Miss Mattie Smith, 50c—Mrs. F. W. Bergmeier, $4.00—C. A. Lane, 0—A. A. Waterman, $5.00—Mr. William Colwell, $2.00—J. B. Hatch, $3.00—Agnes Anderson, $3.00—Mrs. lward Atkinson, $5.00—Miss Helen Bangs, $3.00—Mrs. Annie Freeland, $3.00—Mrs. David L. Gibb, $3.00—iss Gudrun Holm, $3.00—Miss Josephine Ingersoll, $3.00—Mrs. A. J. Jackson, $3.00—Mrs. J. M. Kagan, rs. Fillmore Moore, $3.00—Mrs. F. A. Russell, $3.00—John G. Turnbull, $3.00—Mrs. Oliver Wadsworth, 00—Mrs. A. G. Windsor, $2.00—Miss M. A. Mallory, $2.00—Total, 80.84.

DISBURSEMENTS

A. A. Dharmapala (excess baggage from Calif.), $7.80—A. H. Dharmapala (car fares), $2.60—Printing, 50—Postage, 79c—Total, $12.69—Balance on hand, $68.15.

Deposit in bank, $231.33—Check on hand, $15.00—Cash on hand, $13.75—Total, $260.08.

MONON ROUTE

Best Line from

CHICAGO

to

INDIANAPOLIS,

CINCINNATI,

LOUISVILLE

Parlor and Dining Cars by Day	Palace Sleeping Cars by Night

Only Line to the Famous Health Resort

West Baden and French Lick Springs

City Ticket Office: 232 Clark Street	Depot: Dearborn Station

CHICAGO, ILL.

Blickensderfer Typew

Two Models: { No. 5, $35.00. No. 7, $50.00.

Where it Excels.—The Blickensderfer i able machine, and having a small nu parts is necessarily strong and durabl visible writing; all your work being vi the time. It has interchangeable typ means that the style and size of the be changed at will, and different la written on the same machine.

What We Guarantee.—The Blickensde do anything and everything that any c chine can do, and many things that oth not do.

The Price is Low but the Quality is H

Every machine guaranteed for a period year. One week's trial granted. For ca terms, testimonials, etc., address, or call,

Blickensderfer Manufacturi

O. T. OWEN, Manager.

227 Dearborn St., (1st floor) CHICAG

"Sequel to the Fencing Girl."

Copyright, 1903, by Chicago & Alton Railway.

ART CALENDAR

Four graceful poses from life; figures ten inches high, reproduced in colors by a process far superior to last year's calendar. Highest example of lithographic art.

"THE ONLY WAY"

to own one of these beautiful calendars is to send twenty-five cents with name of publication in which you read this advertisement, to Geo. J. Charlton, Gen'l Passenger Agent, Chicago & Alton Railway, Chicago, Ill.

The best railway line between Chicago, St. Louis, Kansas City and Peoria. Take the "Alton" to the St. Louis World's Fair, 1904.

THE NEW WHITE HOUS CALENDAR

TRADE MARK

For 1904. Four sheets 9x12 inches. E and interior views, in colors, of the New House and grounds. Also pictures from li autographs of the President, Mrs. Roosevel Alice Roosevelt and the children. A Chr present or holiday card useful for a year.

FIFTY CENTS **NO ADVERTI**

Remit direct, in stamps or cash, to

The White House Calendar Com

[Incorporated]

1040 Fine Arts Building, Chicago, Ill

Liberal discounts to agents and canvass

L. XIV. No. 3. APRIL, 190

THE MONIST

A QUARTERLY MAGAZINE

Devoted to the Philosophy of Science

tor: Dr. Paul Carus. Associates: E. C. Hegeler, Mary Carus.

CONTENTS:

CHICAGO:

HE OPEN COURT PUBLISHING CO

Price, 50 cts.; Yearly, $2.00.

LONDON: Kegan Paul, Trench, Trübner & Company, Limited.

In England and U. P. U., half a crown; Yearly, 9s 6d.

)L. XIV. No. 3 APRIL, 1904

THE MONIST

A QUARTERLY MAGAZINE

Devoted to the Philosophy of Science

litor: DR. PAUL CARUS. Associates: E. C HEGELER. MARY CARUS.

CONTENTS:

CHICAGO:

THE OPEN COURT PUBLISHING COMPANY.

1904.

VOL. XIV. APRIL, 1904. NO. 3.

THE MONIST

THE CHRIST OF PRIMITIVE CHRISTIAN FAITH. IN THE LIGHT OF RELIGIO-HISTORICAL CRITICISM.[1]

INTRODUCTORY REMARKS.

THE JESUS OF HISTORY AND THE CHRIST OF FAITH.

IT is a great and lasting glory of nineteenth century scientific theology that it has taught the distinction between the Christ of faith and the Jesus of history, which are identified by ecclesiastical dogmatics. By careful and painstaking critical investigations it has shown how the dogma of the god-man came into existence, gradually, as the result of a process of combination in which religious ideas of various origin were blended with the recollections of the primitive Christian congregation respecting the life of their master. It has attempted further, by eliminating later elements and by going back to the oldest sources, to get as near as possible to the historical reality regarding the founder of our religion, and to make the understanding and the heart of the modern world more familiar with his figure, stripped of its veil of myths, in its purely human greatness as the worshipful portrait of a lofty religious and moral hero.

The value of this undertaking is incontestable, even though sober common sense cannot shut its eyes to the fact that there are also involved many illusions with reference to the significance of the results thus obtained.

[1]Translated from the original manuscript by Prof. W. H. Carruth, University of Kansas.

In glancing at the abundance of literature connected life of Jesus the question cannot be avoided, whether these to get at the bottom of the historical reality can ever yi than hypothetical conjectures, whether they do not, precise portion as they paint the life of the founder more concre from under their feet the firm ground of what is historicall ticated and soar into the regions of ideal fiction. One car avoid giving an affirmative answer to these questions wh serves the profound differences in the professedly histoı clusions of the authors of the various lives of Jesus.

Indeed, could anything else be expected when we coı fact that even the earliest accounts reveal the most unn evidence of the transfusion of the historical elements with motives of legend, with apologetic argumentation and speculation? Jewish prophetic expectations, rabbinical lore gnosis and Greek philosophy had already mixed their colors palette from which the portrait of Christ was painted in the of the New Testament.

All that we can derive as authentic from these writir Christ of the faith of the primitive Christian congrega teachers. To this portrait, which was so varied and co from the beginning, the recollections of the first disciples c the life and death of their master contributed an importan indeed, the center of crystallization of the whole, but yet portion alongside many others. But the question, How mu portrait of Christ in the New Testament is to be credited inely historical recollection and how much to other sour problem which can never be solved with absolute certainty.

CHRISTIANITY BASED ON THE CHRIST OF FAITH, NOT ON T OF HISTORY.

The fact that so many people continue to shut their e incontestable reality of this situation is doubtless connected assumption, which seems to pass almost universally as an our day, that the knowledge of the nature of Christianity falls with the exact knowledge of the historical person of its

But is not this assumption also an illusion? For surely it is evident that the Christian religion and the Christian church are founded upon the faith in Christ of primitive Christianity, as it is recorded in the New Testament, and in contemporary Christian literature. This and nothing more is the solid historical fact, which cannot be altered, however the answer may run to the inquiry regarding the origin of this faith in Christ. Whether historical recollection concerning Jesus of Nazareth contributed more or less and directly or indirectly to its development, or, indeed, in case, as is highly improbable, it contributed nothing at all, yet for all that, the content of this faith and accordingly the nature of Christianity would remain altogether the same.

Now it follows from these reflections that scientific theology cannot fulfill its mission of investigating the nature of Christianity, if, instead of searching thoroughly and without reserve into the entire content of this New Testament belief in Christ, it selects out only what seems agreeable to present-day thought, in order, by ignoring everything else and by injecting much of its own invention, to construct an ideal of Christ in accordance with modern taste. This method of procedure is widespread to-day and much commended—who is not familiar with the series of novels called lives of Jesus, which was begun by Renan? And who does not praise Harnack's *Wesen des Christentums?*

In fact, a certain practical merit must be conceded to these works, inasmuch as they can reawaken among the many indifferent an interest in religious ideas and an enthusiasm for ethical ideals. Only we should guard against the tremendous error of thinking that the portraits of Christ drawn in these works, differing with the personality of the author, yet in all cases touched up in more or less modern fashion, are the result of scientific historical research, or that they compare with the primitive portrait of Christ, as does truth with error. We should be sufficiently sober and honest to admit that both the modern and the primitive portraits are the creations of the common religious spirit of their times, sprung from the natural necessity of faith to fix and visualize its characteristic principle in a typical form. The difference between the two corresponds to the difference in the periods—in the earlier case a naive, mythical epic, in the later a sentimental, subjective romanticism.[1] Which of the two is truer is an utterly idle question, as idle, as, for instance, would be the question whether Homer's *Odyssey* or Milton's *Paradise Lost* and Klopstock's *Messias* were truer.

To the antique consciousness the portrait of Christ in modern garb would be unintelligible, and therefore untrue, while for the modern consciousness the naive faith in the antique mythical epic is no longer possible. But to consider the myth an empty illusion and superstition because we, being no longer so naive as the antique mode of thought, cannot regard it as historical reality, would be a gross blunder, pardonable in the eighteenth century, but which the historically disciplined thought of modern science ought to be finally above. Myths especially, and the religious ceremonies connected with them, in which the mythical material is dramatically presented, detached from transient forms and elevated into a perpetual phenomenon, are everywhere the most primitive and most vigorous expression of the characteristic genius of every religion, and have therefore the very greatest value for the historical student of religion. They are absolutely his fundamental source of knowledge.

But to be sure, in order to understand the sense and significance of the primitive Christian myths, one must not examine them in their traditional isolation, but must derive instruction from their kinship or connection with the myths and legends of the general history of religion. In my opinion there still lies a rich field of labor for the theology of the twentieth century in the realm of the comparative history of religion, in the cultivation of which we shall find the solution of many problems which Biblical exegesis and literary criticism have thus far attempted without great success. The realism of the ancient fashion of religious thought and speech, which we moderns think so strange that we are always inclined to dissipate it into symbolism, will become more intelligible and our sense for the psychological motives and the historical backgrounds of the legends will grow keener.

[1]Cp. Schiller's distinction between naive and sentimental poetry.

We are, indeed, but at the threshold of this extensive task to-day. And if I venture, despite this fact, to offer a trial specimen of it in the religio-historical illumination of the primitive notion of Christ, I do so, hoping for kind indulgence, and at the same time with the purpose of paying my tribute of gratitude to the learned investigators of Holland, who have rendered the most distinguished service to the science of comparative religion—as one, instead of many, I name our never-to-be-forgotten friend, Tiele.

I.—CHRIST AS THE SON OF GOD.

THREE VIEWS.

That Christ was the son of God was the belief of the Christian Church from the beginning, but, as to how far and in what sense he was the son of God, there was at first much difference of opinion. We can distinguish at least three meanings of the word, each of which has its parallels partly in Jewish and partly in extra-Jewish religions.

1. According to the earliest views, the man Jesus was elevated to the rank of son of God by an act of divine adoption, which was associated in the first place with the resurrection from the dead and the ascent into heaven, and afterward by the voice from heaven at the baptism and the accompanying conference of the miraculous Messianic power of the spirit. According to this view "son of God" did not yet imply a supernatural character in Jesus, but only the endowment with the function and power of the Messiah, the divinely appointed king of the chosen people.

2. Alongside this view, which prevailed in the earliest church, there was found in the congregations of gentile Christians at a very early period the conception taught by the Apostle Paul, namely, that Jesus was the son of God in the sense that a personal spiritual being, who had previously existed in heaven, had become incorporate in him. Paul had conceived of this Christ-spirit not precisely as a god, but as God's own and first begotten son, and image, and as the prototype of man, as the celestial ideal man (the second man from heaven, 1 Corinthians, xv, 47), who was appointed from the beginning to save mankind from the curse of sin, of the law, and of death, by his appearance in an earthly body.

Now the mediator of salvation must also needs be from the beginning the mediator of creation, wherefore he is called in the Epistle to the Hebrews the "impress of the substance of God, upholding all things by the word of his power (i, 3), and in Colossians "the first-born of all creation, in whom and through whom and for whom all things are created, and in whom all things consist" (i, 15 f.).

Now the Gospel of John condensed this chain of thought in the doctrine that in Jesus the "logos" had become flesh, having been in the beginning with God and himself a god, through whom all things had come to pass, in whom was the life and the light of men (i. 1 f.). According to this conception Christ is the son of God no longer by virtue of adoption and apotheosis, but by virtue of the incarnation of the divine being accomplished in his person, who, as the "logos," that is, the personal word, has been the mediator of all divine revelation from the beginning of the world.

3. A combination of these two conceptions, the incarnation of a god and the apotheosis of a man, is finally met in the tradition which arose among the gentile Christians in the second century and soon became the most popular theory of all, namely, that Christ was the son of God in the sense that he was supernaturally begotten by the Holy Ghost, without a human father, and was born of the Virgin Mary, being therefore on the maternal side, indeed, a human being, but on the paternal side a son of God in the most specific physical sense of the word.

PARALLELS TO CHRISTIAN NOTIONS IN JEWISH RELIGION.

For these various views of the divine sonship of Christ Jesus we find precise parallels partly in the religious history of Judaism and partly, and more completely, in that of gentile nations.

---

[1]Matt. i, 18, 25, and Luke i, 34f. Only in these two passages, the latter of which did not belong, perhaps, to the original text, is this tradition mentioned in the Old Testament; it is therefore one of the latest elements of the New Testament Christ.

[2]For fuller proofs and exposition of the sketches of the New Testament Christ presented here, and in the lectures that are to follow, I refer once for all to my book, *Das Urchristentum, seine Schriften und Lehren*, 2 edition, 1902.

The adoptive-theocratic divine sonship of the Messiah goes back, as is known, to the early Israelitic notion of the intimate union of the Davidic kingdom with the tribal God Jahveh. The prophetic author of the Books of Samuel has God say of David: "I will establish the throne unto his seed forever. I will be his father and he shall be my son, so that if he commit iniquity I will chasten him with the rod of men and with the stripes of the children of men; but my mercy shall not depart from him as I took it from thy predecessor, but thy house shall be made sure forever before me" (2 Samuel, vii, 13, ff.).

Having faith in this alliance of Jahveh and the Davidic royal house, the pious king comforts himself (Psalm ii), in the face of the hostile counsels of the rulers against Jahveh and his anointed, with the certainty that God has established his king upon Zion, and has said to him: "Thou art my son, this day have I begotten thee (that is, appointed king). Ask of me and I will give thee the nations for an inheritance and the ends of the earth for thy possession; with an iron scepter thou mayest destroy them and dash them to pieces like potters' vessels" (Psalm ii, 6 ff.).

In this sense the Jewish people hoped for the anointed one (Messiah) of the day of salvation, who, as the son of David, was also to be the "son" of God, that is, his chosen favorite, protégé and vassal.

But beside this adoptive conception, which still prevails in the Psalms of Solomon, coming from the time of Pompey, there is found in the apocalyptic literature of late Judaism another, according to which the Messiah appears not as an earthly man and son of David, but as a mysterious spiritual being issuing from celestial concealment. In the metaphors of the Book of Enoch, written in the last decades before the Christian Era, the Messiah is described as the "Chosen One," the "Son of Man," who was concealed from God before the world was created, whose glory will endure from eternity to eternity and his power from generation to generation, in whom dwells the spirit of wisdom and might, who will judge the things that be in secret, work vengeance upon kings and rulers, but save the just and holy (Enoch, chapters xlv-li).

Furthermore, in the Apocalypse of Ezra (chapter xiii) the see beholds something in the likeness of a man rising from the sea, fly ing on the clouds of heaven, destroying hostile armies with a strear of fire from his mouth, but saving and leading home from captivit the scattered Israelites. And this vision is then interpreted as fol lows: "The man rising from the depths of the sea is the one whon the Most High has been reserving for long years and through whon he purposes to redeem creation. As no one can learn what is in th depths of the sea, so no one of the dwellers upon earth can see my son and his attendants, save at the hour of his day" (i. e., of his revelation for the last judgment and the salvation of the world).

From this we perceive that the depths of the sea, from which the savior and son of God shall come forth, is only a symbol for his primeval concealment in a mysterious place. And while it is not indeed expressly said that this place is heaven, yet as much might be inferred from the savior's "lying on the clouds of heaven" (xiii, 3) and by the "attendants" who accompany his advent (verse 52), by whom we must understand either the angels or the righteous men of the first dispensation who were transported into beaven, and who according to xiv, 9, tarry with the son of God until the fulfillment of the times.

Clearly, therefore, both according to the Apocalypse of Ezra and to the metaphors of Enoch, the coming savior is that son of God, the man (son of man), who was to preëxist in heaven unto the time of his revelation. True, it is hard to say how this is to be reconciled with the utterances of xii, 32, that the Christ would come from the seed of David, and that after a rule of four hundred years he, with all other men, would perish. A solution of this conflict will scarcely be found, but its existence may be explained by the fact that the author of this apocalypse remained undecided between the later thought of the Messiah as a preëxistent celestial being and the earlier notion of him as an earthly man and son of David.

PARALLELS IN NON-JEWISH THOUGHT—THE LOGOS DOCTRINE.

The combination of these two views, which existed in late Jewish times side by side, through the assumption of an incarnation of the celestial son of God and of man in the body of an earthly man and son of David, was not accomplished within the Jewish fold, but was in its nature so plausible that we have no cause for surprise when we see it brought about very early under the Christian dispensation, from the time of Paul on.

The same importance that is held by the son of God and of man in the late Jewish apocalyptic writers is attributed in the Alexandrine-Jewish religious philosophy to that mediatorial being who is called now "wisdom," and now "logos" (reason and word). In the book of the Wisdom of Solomon, by a Hellenistic Jew of Alexandria, from the first century before Christ, "wisdom" is represented (vii, 22 ff.) as an independent spiritual being beside God, the (feminine) mediator of his revelation in creation, maintenance and government of the world, a semi-personal hypostasis, a semi-material fluid, ethereal and divisible, pervading all space, like the Stoic-Heraclitic world-spirit, which is partly reason of the universe, partly primordial matter (primordial fire), but akin also to the Zarathustrian archangel, Vohu mano ("good thought"), who is associated with Ahura as his chief agent.

This Hellenistic hypostasis of the divine wisdom is partly a metaphysico-cosmic principle of the creative process, partly the underlying essence and mediatorial agent of the historical revelation of God in the religion of Israel and in general in pious souls, making them friends and children of God and raising them up to eternal life in association with Him (Wisdom of Solomon, iii, 1 ff., v, 16 ff., vi, 12 ff.). In this hypostasis[1] the Hellenistic-Jewish author has attempted to combine the monistic speculations of Greek philosophy (in Heraclitus and the Stoics) and the positive belief in revelation held by Jewish theism.

He was followed in this attempt by the religious philosopher of Alexandria, Philo.[2] He conceived of the opposition between the infinitely lofty, unknowable and unnamable God and the sensual world as mediated by "powers," which he calls also "ideas" and

---

[1]Cp. Stave, *Einfluss des Parsismus auf das Judentum*, p. 205 ff.

[2]For details I refer to my treatment of Philo in *Urchristentum*, 2d ed., ii, 25-54, where all the passages here cited may be found.

"angels," among whom he distinguishes six chief ones, who surround the throne of God as his satellites, like the six Amschaspands of the Zarathustrian religion, and perform the work of the government of the world as his agents. Among these mediatorial "powers" the first place is held by the "logos," who appears to be the essence and source of all the others, and therefore to be the central mediator of all divine activity and revelation. Philo calls him "the eldest, first-born son of God, the eldest angel, the beginning, the word and the name of God, his image and the prototype of man." As the mediator of God's revelation he has a rôle at the very creation of the world, and this partly as the idea of ideas, in accordance with which the universe is formed, partly as the creative power by which everything is called into being.

The logos, therefore, is both the metaphysical ideal principle, like the Platonic "idea," and also, the real principle, like the Stoic logos. But in distinction from these philosophical principles the logos of Philo is at the same time an independent, semi-personal mediatorial being, the earliest creation of God, most closely akin to the Persian-Jewish archangels. In this latter function he is the agent of all the historical revelation of God in Israel, the real presence in all the Old Testament theophanies, for instance, in the stories of the patriarchs, and especially of the giving of the law through Moses, and he comes into a relation with the logos so intimate that it borders closely on incarnation, although this doctrine was not taught.

Furthermore, the heavenly manna in the wilderness, the miraculous flow of water from the rock and the fiery flames of the cloud that accompanied the people of Israel were all forms of the appearance of the logos, whose ultimate substratum in animistic popular metaphysics is thereby clearly betrayed.

Just as the Stoic worldly wisdom was personified in Hermes, the messenger of the gods, and as in the Egyptian Thot[1] the creative

---

[1]Thot was identified with Hermes by the Greeks, and the latter, in the Stoic theology, had been made into an apparition of the divine wisdom. The kinship of this Logos-Hermes with the Logos-Christ was recognized by the early Christian apologists, cp. Justin, *Apol.* 1, 21.

spell of Ammon-Ra received independent existence as divine mediatorial beings, and in Vohu mano the creative wisdom of Ahura, and Marduk's supreme decree in the Babylonian Nabu, so Philo's logos arose from the fact that the personified creative wisdom and the word of revelation of Jahveh are identified with the worldly wisdom of the Stoa. Thus it became a composite of metaphysico-rationalistic principle, religio-positive mediator of revelation, and ideal man. As son, image and messenger of God he is at the same time the high priest, intercessor and advocate (paraclete) of men.

DIVINE SONSHIP IN PAGAN HISTORY.

Among pagan nations belief in the existence of sons of gods was universal, and pertained not only to mythical beings, but also to historical personages of conspicuous importance, especially to rulers and sages. In Egypt, from the earliest times up to the last of the Pharaohs, the king was regarded as an incarnation of divinity,[1] he was called the great and good god, Horus; prayers and offerings were made to him, and it was believed that he either fulfilled these prayers himself or else transmitted them to the celestial gods, his fathers and mothers, with whom he was in constant communication. The Egyptian kings even worshiped themselves, that is to say, the divine being, called Ka, incarnated in themselves.

An illustration in point is an extant prayer addressed to King Cherenptah. It reads: "Thou art, O King, altogether like the image of thy father, the sun, that rises in the heavens. Thy beams penetrate even the caverns. No place lacks thy beneficence. Thy words are law in every land. When thou art resting in thy palace thou hearest the words of all countries. Thou hast millions of ears. Bright is thine eye above all the stars of heaven, seeing everything that is done in secret, O merciful Lord, Creator of the breath of life!"

In Babylonia,[2] too, the kings from the time of Sargon, the

---

[1] Wiedemann, *Die aegyptische Religion*, S. 92 ff.

[2] Radau, *Early History of Babyl*, p. 308 ff.

founder of the realm, were regarded as emanations of the Sargon's son, Naram Sin, called himself "God of Agade, L Heavenly Disk." Later this system of giving titles disapp a time, but was revived again by the kings of the fourth d Ur, all of whom prefixed to their names the character (Dingir), erected temples in their own honor, placed t statues in various sanctuaries, had offerings brought to t spirits and appointed the first and the fifteenth day of eve as sacred to themselves.

This belief in the divine origin of kings was so deeply oriental thought that it was extended even to foreign conqu rulers. When Alexander the Great had conquered the Pe Egyptian empires he had himself announced as the son Egyptian god Ammon-Ra, and among his successors the Egypt, and to some extent those of Syria, followed his exa

It was therefore natural that the eastern portion of th empire should precede the western in its cult of the empe in the former there was no hesitation about accepting t emperor as God, i. e., as an incarnation of divinity, or w him with public ceremonies, while in the Occident there reserve in the matter.[1]

To be sure, divine honor was paid in Rome to th (genius) of the emperor, even during his lifetime, begin Augustus, but the majority of the emperors during the turies did not venture to assume the title of "God" direc elevation to the rank of a god ("divus") was not confe an emperor until after death, and even then not upon all i nately, but only upon those whom the senate considered this apotheosis (consecratio). In the Occident, therefore, ity of the emperor was understood as an apotheosis or the of the deceased to equal rank with the gods, on account o merit; in the Orient, on the contrary, it was understood actual incarnation of the godhead in every living empero

---

[1]Beurlier, *Le culte impériale*, p. 52. Boissier, *La religion roma* Compare the hymns to Emperor Augustus recently found at Pri

THE IMMACULATE CONCEPTION IN PAGAN LEGENDS.

The most striking parallels to the story of the miraculous conception of Christ by the virgin, without a human father, are found in pagan legends.[1] Pythagoras was regarded by his disciples as an incarnation of Apollo, and even as his son.[2] Concerning Plato, the legend was current among the Athenians, during his lifetime even, as appears from the funeral oration delivered by his nephew, Speusippus, that his mother, Periktione, conceived him by the god Apollo before cohabitation with her husband. On this account the Academy celebrated the memory of its founder on the birthday of Apollo. Concerning Alexander the Great, it was believed that he was a son of Zeus, who appeared to his mother, Olympias, in the form of a serpent, before King Philip wedded her. Among the Romans, Scipio Africanus and Augustus were regarded as sons of Apollo. The Pythagorean teacher and worker of miracles, Apollonius of Tyana, was thought by his compatriots to be a son of Zeus. Simon Magus proclaimed himself to be a superhuman being, born of a virgin mother, without a human father.

The common motive in these legends, so frequently found in the Græco-Roman world, is correctly traced by Origen (*Contra Celsum* I, 37) to the belief that a man of greater wisdom and strength than ordinary men must owe his physical being to a superior, divine origin. In an age that had no comprehension of natural laws, and whose fancy had been fed by the various legends of mythology about sons of gods and demigods, the most plausible assumption concern-

---

[1]Compare Usener, *Das Weihnachtsfest*, p. 70, ff.

[2]Iamblichus, *De vita pythagorica*, chap. 2, mentions the old legend that Pythagoras was conceived of Apolla by Parthenis, the wife of Minesarchos, adding, however, that this is incredible, but that rather the soul of Pythagoras in its previous existence had stood in closest relationship to Apollo, and had been sent by him to mankind. But, according to chap. 19, Pythagoras regarded himself as the incorporation of the god Apollo, who had taken human form in order that men might not be confounded by the sight of divine majesty, and consequently afraid of being taught by him. Cp. John I, 14, and Barnabas v., 10.

ing extraordinary personal greatness was to ascribe it to miraculou birth and divine conception.

THE IMMACULATE CONCEPTION OF BUDDHA.

But the most remarkable parallel to the Christian legend i offered by the Buddhistic legend, since in the latter as well as i the former the notion of the incarnation of a preëxistent divine bein in the person of the historical founder of the religion is found com bined with that of his virgin birth.

The legendary biography of Buddha, *Lalita Vistara*,[1] whic was translated into Chinese in the year 65 A. D., and is therefor without doubt of pre-Christian origin, begins with the celestial pre existence of Buddha, where in the assembly of the gods he in structs them regarding the "law," that is, the eternal truth of salva tion, and then announces his intention of descending for the salvatio of the world, into the womb of a terrestrial woman in order to be bor as a human being. The sons of the gods embrace his feet, weeping and saying: "Noble man, if thou dost not remain here these abode will no longer shine." But he leaves to them a successor and for mally dedicates him as candidate for the future office of Buddha b taking his own tiara from his head and placing it upon the other's with the words: "Noble man, thou art the one who will be endowe after me with the intelligence of a Buddha" (Foucaux' translation 40, chap. 5).

Thus we see that the standing epithet for the celestial being o Buddha who is assumed to precede the various incarnations is "man (purusha) or "great man" (mahapurusha), and sometimes "victor ous lord" (Cakravartin). Whether there is involved in these ex pressions an allusion to the god Vishnu we may leave an open ques tion;[2] what interests us is the relation of this notion to the Apocaly tic Jewish appellation for the preëxistent heavenly Messiah as "so

---

[1]Foucaux, *Le Lalita Vistara*, translated from Sanscrit into French, i, vi The above quotations are taken from this translation, which is general recognized as the best.

[2]Senart, *Essai sur la legende du Buddah*, Chapters 1 and 2.

of man" or "man" (Daniel, vii, 13), (Enoch and Ezra) to the Pauline "second man from heaven," to the Gospel title for the Messiah, "son of man," to the doctrine of the gnostic Ophites of a threefold divinity, consisting of the first man, or father, the second man, or son, and the holy ghost, or mother of all the living (Irenaeus, *adv. hæreses*, I. 30), and finally and most vitally, to the doctrine of the gnostic Elcesaites, which is also the basis of the homilies of Clement, in accordance with which the heavenly spirit of Christ and king of the future world first became man in Adam, then in Enoch, Noah, Abraham, Isaac, Jacob, Moses, and finally, by a supernatural and virgin birth, in Jesus, but is to be expected in yet other incarnations whenever they shall need to save the darkened world by true prophecy (Hippolytus *Philsophumena*, 9, 10. Epiphanius *Hær.*, 30, 53).

How far there may be a historical connection between that Indian doctrine of the incarnations (avatars) of the "great men" in the illuminated teachers or Buddhas of the various epochs and these Jewish-Christian doctrines of the celestial man, cannot be determined just at present. But the Elcesaitic doctrine of Clement of Alexandria, of the various incarnations of the heavenly spirit in Adam, the patriarchs and Jesus seems to me to bear such a striking resemblance to the Indian doctrine that a direct connection can scarcely be doubted in this case. And this is the more probable from the facts that the Elcesaitic Gnosticism originated with a Syrian or Parthian about the year 100 A. D., and that there existed beyond doubt at that time a close intercourse between eastern Persia and India. How long before this Indian influence had been at work upon western Asia we do not, indeed, know, and must accordingly limit ourselves for the present to the actual parallels between those Buddhistic "great men" and the Jewish-Christian "son of man," without venturing to maintain the existence of a historical interdependence.

Proceeding further with the account of the Lalita Vistara, we are told how Queen Maya asked of her husband, King Shuddhodana of Kapilavastu, permission to abstain for a time from marital intercourse, in order to lead an ascetic life in quiet seclusion. During her last in the spring, while the constellation Puchya was dominant, it came to pass that she saw in a dream a white elephant without harming her. She told the dream to her questioned the oracles about it. They replied with the great joy was in store for them, for the queen would b should become either a mighty ruler or a perfect sa and world-savior. And ten months later, when she son without spot or blemish, the new-born child straight with lionlike voice: "I am the sublimest and best world! This is my last birth; I shall put an end to birt and death!" At this moment the earth quaked and a was heard, a supernatural light filled all the spaces of driving out darkness. All creatures were filled with were freed from all passion and ignorance. The suf sick were alleviated, hunger and thirst stilled, the intox sober, the insane regained their reason, the blind their their hearing, the cripples their strength; the poor bec captives were released and the sorrows of all creatures, in hell, ceased.

THE HOMAGE OF THE HEAVENLY HOSTS AND OF THE

Thereupon the hosts of the celestial gods and spi presented to the Buddha-child and his mother their hom gifts, precious ointments, garments and adornments. of the gods appeared in the form of youthful Brahmins hymn of praise: "Happy is the entire world, for in tru who shall bring salvation, who shall restore the world He has appeared who by the splendor of his merits both sun and moon and dispel all darkness. The blind, hear, the lunatics receive again their reason. Natural vi torment men, for in all the world good-will prevails. G can henceforth approach each other without hostility, f the leader of their pilgrimage." (*Lalita vistara*, I, 78,

At the same time there lived in the Himalayas a named Asita; he perceived from marvelous signs in the birth of a prince with a lofty destiny, either as a royal saint and savior. He came to the royal palace in Kapil

the new-born child and recognized in him the thirty-two signs of the "great man" (the incarnation of the celestial Buddha).

After he had seen this sign the seer Asita began to weep and to sigh deeply. To the king's question whether perchance he foreboded any danger for the young prince Siddhartha, he replied: "No, I am not weeping on his account, but on my own, for I am old and frail; but this young prince will be clothed with the perfect wisdom of a Buddha, and then he will teach for the salvation and joy of the world and of the gods as well, the law which has virtue for its beginning, middle and end, and portray it in its clearest and most perfect sense. After they have heard it from his mouth creatures, heeding the law of their development, will be entirely freed from birth and age, from disease, trouble, complaint, pain and suffering of every sort; those inflamed with the fire of passion he will cool with the water of the good law; those bound in darkness and those who wander in the evil way he will lead upon the right path of happiness (of Nirvana); those bound in the fetters of natural corruption he will free from such fetters; he will open the eyes of wisdom in the blind whose eyes are clouded by the deep darkness of ignorance; he will lead myriads of beings out of the sea of life that is surging on this side showing the way into immortality. And we! we shall not live to see the work of this precious savior! That is why I weep and sigh, for it is too late for me to receive salvation from sickness and passion" (*Lalita vistara*, I, 91-94).

JESUS AND SIDDHARTHA.

The resemblance of these Buddhistic legends to the evangelical story of the childhood of Jesus, especially according to the gospel of Luke, is self-evident. Moreover, there are several parallels to the account of the twelve-year-old Jesus in the temple, Luke ii, 41-52. When Prince Siddhartha was taken to school he surprised and shamed his teachers by his superior knowledge of all the 64 writings comprising the learning of the Hindu schools. Once, when he had gone into the country, in order to observe agriculture,[1] he became

[1]According to another version it was at the time of the spring festival, when the king used to draw the first furrows with a golden plow; impelled by curiosity to witness this festival, the nurse had left the young prince alone.

absorbed in pious meditation under the shadow of a tı
strangers, sages or saints (rishis), coming along that
nized by the majestic glory radiating from the future
he must be a son of God, if not the incarnation of the
self. In the meantime the prince was missed at home
could answer the king's question as to where he had g
began to search for him everywhere. At last he was
the tree, whose shadow had not moved the whole day,
in meditation, surrounded by the holy men, radiant wit
majesty, like the moon in the midst of the stars. Hi
startled by this sight, but the son addressed him with
Brahma, full of dignity: "Leave thy plowing,[1] O fatl
higher!" Thus he rebuked his father's lack of highe
aspiration, just as the twelve-year-old Jesus rebuked
Luke ii, 49. Thereupon he returned with his father to
remained there, conforming to the customs of the w
mind occupied wholly with the thought of going awa
become the perfectly pure being (Buddha). (*Lalita v*
118, 122.)

BABISM—A RECENT PARALLEL.

How deeply the notion of successive incarnations
spirit in historical personages is rooted in the mind o
tions was seen even in the nineteenth century in th
religion of Babism in Persia.[2] Its founder, Mirza Ali
had come forward in his youth as the enthusiastic ref
official Mohammedan religion and the passionate opp
degenerate hierarchy, and he soon had a large number
who were devoted to him with worshipful zeal, (in th
The founder claimed unconditional authority, and c
"the Bab," i. e., the gate, through which alone one c
knowledge of God. He believed himself to be the supr
ration of the divine breath or word, whose former re

---

[1]This presupposes that the ceremony of the plow at the spri
the occasion of the boy's being lost.

[2]Gobineau: *Les religions et les philospohies de l'Asie centr*

appeared in Abraham, Moses, Jesus, and Mohammed. All these divine representatives are in fact only different manifestations of the same divine being, and are all alike in having their immediate origin from God, and, being more closely united with God, return to him more quickly than other men. What distinguishes them from one another is merely the form of their manifestation, conditioned by their time. Just as Jesus was a reproduction of Moses adapted to his time, and Mohammed a reproduction of Jesus, so the Bab is a reproduction of Mohammed. But although he is in his time the supreme manifestation of the divine spirit, he is not the last, but will have successors just as he had predecessors. With this conviction the Bab went to his martyrdom with joyful serenity. He predicted that the spirit of God dwelling within him would immediately after his death pass over to one of his disciples. "The one whom God shall reveal" shall continue the work of the Bab and deliver the world from the injustice now prevailing. And, in fact, after the execution of the Bab at Tebriz (1850) his sect maintained itself under new leaders and has still many adherents. One of its later leaders, Behá (died at Acre, 1892) was regarded by the faithful as the incarnation of the godhead, and was actually called "God" and "King or Creator of Gods."[1] But a protest was made to these preposterous claims by another party, and thus arose occasion for the discussion of the old question: What is the relation of the divine being to his human manifestation?

II.—CHRIST AS THE CONQUEROR OF SATAN.

From the beginning it was the settled conviction of the Christian communion that Christ had come for the purpose of destroying the works of the Devil. This belief found expression in various forms.

1. Before entering upon his career as Messiah, Christ successfully withstood the temptations of Satan. According to the accounts in the gospel of Matthew (iv, 1-11) and of Luke (iv, 1-13) this

---

[1] Brown, *The new History of the Bab,* 1893, p. 395.

moral battle between Christ and the Devil was fought in passages, in each of which Christ gained the victory throu weapon of the Word of God. Finally, it is said, Satan le (according to Luke, for a season at least), and angels came and ministered unto him. (Matt. iv, 11; Like iv, 13; Mark

2. Christ triumphantly proved his superiority to the De casting out evil spirits from the possessed and the sick. iii, 22 ff.; Matt. xii, 24-29.)

3. In the future, at his second coming to judge the Christ will put an end to the power of Satan forever. Thi victory over the evil spirit is divided into two scenes in the R tion of St. John: The King of kings, coming down from h with his armies, smites the nations gathered to make war upo with the sharp sword proceeding out of his mouth, whereup Devil is bound and thrown into the abyss (of hell), wh remains a thousand years under lock and seal. When the th years of the reign of Christ and of the resurrected marty finished, Satan will be loosed from his prison, to lead astr nations of the earth, especially Gog and Magog, and to gathe together for war upon the saints, but his armies will be des by fire from heaven and Satan himself will be thrown into th of fire to be tormented for ever and ever. (Rev. xix, 11-2 1-10.)

Parallels to the gospel story of the temptation are found Buddhistic and Iranian legend. The Buddhistic story of the te tion is told in various versions; the detailed account of the *Vistara*, chapter 21, may be condensed as follows:

After Prince Siddhartha had left his father's palace, an spent five years in monkish asceticism, he betook himself to th of knowledge, in order that he might by deep meditation complete wisdom and the dignity of Buddha. Now when Ma lord of the air and of all evil, recognized that his dominion come to an end through Buddha, he called all the hosts of h spirits together to fight against this dangerous opponent. hurled against him as he sat under the tree of knowledge. tains and flames of fire and weapons of all kinds, but all missiles fell at his feet as flowers, or remained hanging as garlands in the tree above him.

Then the hostile demon, full of wrath and envy, spoke to Buddha: "Arise, Prince, and enjoy your kingdom, for by what merit have you gained the redemption (dignity of Buddha)?" Buddha referred to the countless sacrifices which he had made for the benefit of others in his former existences; and he called upon the earth as a witness. Whereupon an earthquake ensued, with fearful rumbling, and the goddess of Earth appeared, and spoke to him: "O great man, it is indeed as thou hast said, thou hast thyself become the supreme witness of the earth, including the gods." Therewith the demons fled as jackals do at the voice of the lion.

Now the wicked adversary called his daughters, and bade them tempt Buddha by the display of all their charms. But he remained unmoved by their allurements and instructed them with serious discourse concerning the perishable and harmful nature of deceitful lusts, so that they withdrew in shame, and acknowledged the invincibility of his virtue, and the sublimity of his perfect wisdom. Then the good spirits drew near to the tree of knowledge, and rejoiced in the victory of Buddha over the evil spirit.

Once more the fiend accosted Buddha with the demand that he give way to him, the lord of the air and of the visible world, since the aim of his striving was, after all, too difficult to be attained. But Buddha answered: "If you are the lord of the air and of the visible world, I am the lord of the law, and in spite of you, I shall gain the supreme knowledge." Thus the holy man resisted the temptations of the adversary; unshaken by threats or by allurements, he steadfastly kept the conviction of his higher vocation, and the resolve to follow it on the road of renunciation and of knowledge. And immediately afterward he attained complete enlightenment, under the tree of knowledge, and became "Buddha."

Iranian legend, too, tells of the temptation of the prophet Zarathustra by the evil spirit Ahriman, who made this proposition to him: "Renounce the good law of the worshipers of Mazda, and thou shalt have such power as was possessed by Zohak, the ruler of nations." But Zarathustra answered: "No, never will I renounce the good law of the worshipers of Mazda, even though my life, body and soul are sundered; the word taught by Mazda is my weapon, my best weapon."

But the Iranian religion looks for the final conquest of the diabolic realm of Ahriman by the future redeemer Soshyans. In him we may see a sort of miraculous return of Zarathustra since he is to be born of a virgin, who is supposed to receive, while bathing in a lake, the seed of Zarathustra there preserved.[1]

The Iranian religion expects the future coming of this "victorious savior" to bring about the resurrection and the restoration of the world. This will be preceded by insurrection and warfare in the spirit-world. The wicked dragon Dahak, whom the hero Feridan had once conquered and bound within the mountain Demavend, will break loose from his bonds and spread disaster over the world, but he will be slain by the hero Keresaspa, who will come to life again after long sleep. Then Soshyans will cause the resurrection of all men, and will bestow upon them their reward according to their works. The ungodly will be punished three days and nights in hell, then a general conflagration of the world will destroy all evil. In the last conflict, Ahura and his archangels will overcome Ahriman and his evil spirits, who will then be annihilated in the molten metal resulting from the conflagration of the world. But for the souls that have undergone purification Soshyans will prepare the draught of immortality.

Thus the course of events in the last days is described in chapter 30 of the Bundehesch, a theological tract of the time of the Sassanidae.[2] But even before this, an ancient song in the Avesta[3] celebrates Soshyans as the conqueror of the hostile demons and the restorer of the world: "Then the King in majesty will walk with Soshyans and his other friends, when the world is formed anew, when he shall release it from age, from death, from decay and

[1]Compare Hübschmann: "Parsische Lehr von Yenseits und jüngsten Gericht" in *Yahrbucher fur prot. Theol.*, 1879, p. 234. Böcklin: *Die Verwandtschaft der judisch-christlichen mit der parsischen Eschatologie*, p. 91 ff.

[2]*Sacred Books of the East*, V. 120 ff.

[3]*Sacred Books of the East.*—XXIII, 306.

corruption, so that it shall ever blossom and flourish, when all the dead shall arise, all that live shall become immortal, when the world shall be renewed according to the heart's desire, when that which is pure and good shall become changeless and permanent, when the spirit of lies shall also perish."

In the twelfth chapter of the Revelation of St. John there is handed down to us in a Christian transcription a Jewish legend of the persecution of the child-Messiah by the Devil, and the defeat of the latter by the archangel Michael. This legend has not parallels alone, but its direct source in a pagan myth of the conflict between the gods of light and of darkness. According to the Greek legend,[1] Leto, before the birth of Apollo, her son by Zeus, was persecuted by the earth-dragon, Python, who sought to destroy her expected son, because the oracle had predicted that the child would do him harm. But Boreas, the god of the wind, bore away the persecuted goddess, and brought her to Poseidon, who prepared a refuge for her on the island Ortygia, where the waves of the ocean hid her from the eyes of the pursuer. Here Leto gave birth to Apollo, who was so strong by the fourth day after his birth that he slew Python, the Dragon, upon Parnassus.

This myth, widely diffused in Asia Minor, as attested by coins bearing the image of Leto in flight, was first applied to the (future) Messiah in the Jewish-Hellenic syncretist circles, and accordingly underwent certain changes. To be sure, the chief features remain the same: The persecution of the heavenly child (the Messiah), and of his mother (idealized Israel), by the dragon (the Devil), and their rescue, by transportation on the wings of the wind (the eagle) to a sheltered place in the wilderness (instead of an island), bodies of water playing an important although different part in each version. But the defeat of the hostile dragon is ascribed, not to the Messianic child, which is caught up to God, but to the militant archangel Michael, who, as guardian angel of Israel, to a certain extent represents the Messiah in the world

[1] See Hyginus' *Fabulæ* (ed. Schmidt, p. 17). Deterich (Abraxas, p. 117 ff.) first called attention to this mythical basis of Rev. 12.

of spirits. But the result of this conflict of angels and dem in heaven is not yet the complete destruction of the drag but only his being cast down from heaven to earth, where fo time he continues his fierce hostility to the seed of the woman u his future defeat by the Messiah.

The simple pagan myth of the persecution and rescue of young sun-god and his speedily ensuing victory over the ho demon of darkness is the more complicated in the Jewish interp tation, because the complete defeat of the devil's dominion u earth is not looked for until the coming of the future Mess hence cannot be already ascribed to the Messianic child. Th fore this conflict had to be divided into two acts, the first of wh is put into the past, as a prologue in heaven, the hero of which Michael, while the second, the Messiah's final victory, is reser for the future. Thus the pagan-Jewish myth of the Messiah co be more easily adapted in the Apocalypse to Christ Jesus, since too, is not to manifest himself fully as the conqueror of Satan u his second coming (parusie) being meanwhile caught up to throne of God (by his ascension to heaven), and sheltered fr all attacks.

This same myth, which is the groundwork of the apocaly vision in Rev. xii, comes to light again in the legend of the perse tion and flight of the child Christ, as told in the gospel of Matth Here the mythical dragon, the Devil of the Apocalypse, is crafty Jewish King Herod, who seeks the life of the Messianic ch and orders the massacre of the children at Bethlehem. Here, the mother flees with her child, not into the wilderness, howe but to Egypt, because the young Messiah was to be called out the same land from which Israel had once gone forth, that word of the prophet, Hosea xi, 1, might be fulfilled.

This legend likewise has a number of prototypes in the lege of heroes: in the rescue of the child Moses, by the Egyptian pı cess (Exodus ii), likewise in that of the Assyrian prince, Sarg who, when his uncle sought his life, was placed in a basket of re in the Euphrates, and was rescued and reared by a water carri

[1]Smith, *Early History of Babylonia*, 46.

in the Hindu myth of the god-man Krishna (the incarnation of the god, Vishnu), whose life was sought by his uncle, King Kansa, who commanded that all boys of the same age in his dominion should be killed; by Krishna was hidden in the hut of a poor shepherd and brought up by him.[1] In the same way, the young Persian prince, Cyrus, was to be killed, by command of his grandfather, Astyages, but was spared by the shepherd commissioned to do the deed and was brought up by him as his own child.[2] There is a similar tradition about Augustus:[3] that before his birth, the Senate, impelled by an oracle, foretelling the birth of a Roman king, had issued an edict, ordering that all boys born in that year should be killed, but the parents of Augustus did not obey the decree.

All these legends doubtless have their source in nature-myths like the myth of Leto and Apollo, and they all have a common motive which is easily recognized. The value of the conspicuous life of a hero is to be enhanced by the fact that the powers of light and of darkness contend over his existence from the very beginning. The life of the child is to show in the prologue what is to be later the life-task of the hero; the divine principle of life and of light, of goodness and truth, is to gain the victory over the hostile forces of the universe.

III. CHRIST AS THE WONDER-WORKING SAVIOR.

Although Jesus himself spurned the suggestion that he should work startling wonders, and sharply rebuked such a desire as betokening of a perverse spirit (Mark viii, 11 ff.; Matthew xvi, 1-4) it was inevitable that faith should adorn the image of Christ with a rich wreath of miraculous stories. This was the natural consequence of belief in his Messiahship, for even according to Jewish expectation, the Messiah was to repeat and surpass the miracles of the holy men of the Old Testament, and of belief in his divine sonship, for it

---

[1]Wheeler, *History of India*, i., 462, ff.

[2]Herodotus, i, 108 ff.

[3]Seutonius, *Octavianus*, 94.

seemed a matter of course that the supernatural spirit with which he was filled or by which he was begotten should reveal itself even during Christ's earthly career, by supernatural powers. The miracles of the Gospels are partly those of knowledge, partly those of power.

1. Miracles of knowledge:
   a. Miraculous insight into the innermost thoughts of men. (John ii, 25.)
   b. Foreknowledge of future events (prophecy of the passion, the resurrection and second coming).
   c. Miraculous knowledge of past occurrences, as well as of those contemporaneous but far distant. (John i, 48; iv, 17; xi, 14.)
2. Miracles of power:
   a. Casting out of demons from those possessed.
   b. Healing of other sick people.
   c. Awakening of the dead.
   d. Miraculous power over matter and the forces of nature (multiplying the loaves, changing water into wine, calming the storm).
   e. Freedom from the limitations of space and matter (sudden disappearance and reappearance, passing through closed doors, walking upon the water, ascension to heaven). John vi, 19 ff.; Luke xxiv, 31, 36, 51; John xx, 19, 26.

Countless parallels to these marvelous stories are to be found in the legends of pagan heroes and Christian saints. It will suffice to mention a few examples.

In the Buddhistic legend the miracles of knowledge play an important part. Buddha knows not only his own previous births and careers in all their details, but he knows those of others that come into contact with him, their merits and their faults in former existences, and often explains conversion to the ranks of his disciples as the result of merit in a previous existence (the Hindu form of predestination). Moreover, he can penetrate the thoughts of all beings, from the very lowest up to great Brahma himself: "Whaever passes through your mind is revealed to me. Ye may deceive others, but me ye cannot deceive."[1]

But when, at the beginning of his active career, his opponents, at the instigation of the devil Mara, challenged him to manifest his superiority to the holy men, revered hitherto, by performing miracles in the presence of the King and the people, he replied: "I do not teach my disciples to go and work miracles before the Brahmins by supernatural power, but this is what I teach them: So live, ye pious men, as to conceal your good works, and to reveal your sins."[2] Nevertheless, in this very connection, the legend proceeds to relate how Buddha shamed and subdued his stubborn foes, by a succession of the most astonishing miracles.

When the King, listening to a false accusation against his innocent brother, ordered the hands and feet of the latter to be cut off, Buddha heard from afar the prayer of the unfortunate man, and immediately sent his favorite disciple with the commission to heal the maimed sufferer by pronouncing the sacred formulas of the Buddhistic law. Scarcely were these words spoken, when the body of the prince resumed its former shape, and he, being healed by the power of Buddha, at once manifested supernatural powers, and entered the ranks of the master's followers. Further we are told that fire broke out in the house where Buddha was lodging, but it was quenched of its own accord without doing any damage; that Buddha, by stamping on the ground, produced a fearful earthquake that shook all parts of the earth; that the spirits of the air caused a shower of flowers to fall upon him, and heavenly music to resound; that Buddha, while absorbed in deep meditation, lifted himself up in the air, and that while hovering in the bright atmosphere, wondrous flames of all colors radiated from his body. These "transfiguration scenes" are frequently repeated in Buddhistic legend.

In the Occident, the early centuries of the Roman empire were the ages of the most flourishing belief in miracles and soothsaying.

---

[1] R. S. Hardy, *Mannual of Buddhism*, 190.

[2] Bournouf. *Introduction a l'histoire du buddhism*, p. 151 ff.

The old legends of Hercules, Orpheus, Æneas, Romulus, Esculapi and Pythagoras were told by poets and by historians as stor handed down and therefore trustworthy, and were amplified please the taste of the reader. The historian, Diodorus Siculus,[1] ports, concerning Hercules, that all his life long, as is commo narrated, he endured great hardships and dangers, in order to quire immortality by his benefits to humanity and he recounts detail the marvelous deeds of this hero till he is finally borne aw from the funeral pile to Olympus.

Pausanias[2] tells us that Esculapius, being exposed to dea when an infant, by his grandfather, was found by a shepherd w recognized by the glory radiating from the child that he was divi The rumor spread immediately that this divine child could h the sick and revive the dead. At the time of a pestilence Esculapi is supposed to have come to Rome in the form of a serpent, and have continued his miraculous healing there for centuries. He reputed to have awakened ten persons from death. But because awakened Glaukos, son of Minos, Jupiter killed the wonderful ph sician with a thunderbolt and placed him among the immortals. the god of healing he continued his works at his shrines, amo which those at Epidaurus and at Rome were especially celebrat as resorts for pilgrimages. During the early centuries of the emp he was considered the most "benevolent" god, from whom help w sought in all troubles of body and mind, and his temples were fu of votive offerings and the inscriptions of those that believed the had received help from him. He is said to have appeared in perso to some that were sick like the Egyptian god of healing, Serapi

Even among the philosophers of the Platonic and the Stoic, th neo-Pythagorean and the neo-Platonic schools, the popular belief i miracles and revelations found zealous defenders, who found lines o connection between it and their doctrines of divine providence an of mediatory beings (dæmons) and used its authority as a suppo for their own doctrines. In these circles especially the old legen

[1] *Hist.* I., 2; IV., 8-39.

[2] *Periegesis* II, 26.

of Pythagoras, the founder of the religio-political covenant, were transmitted with fondness and transmuted into an ideal figure of a god-man, a prophet and a miracle-worker. According to the biography of Iamblichus he was not merely the son of Apollo, but his actual bodily incarnation. Aside from his miraculous prophetic knowledge (a knowledge of his previous existences is also ascribed to him, which suggests Buddha), a quantity of the most astounding miracles are told of him, he cured the sick, suppressed a pestilence by magic, stilled the floods of the ocean and of rivers so that his disciples could pass over them unharmed, while the spirit of the floods addressed him by his name in a clear voice that was heard by all. Furthermore, he had been present among his disciples in two distinct places separated by land and sea (at Metapontus in Italy and Tauromenium in Sicily) on one and the same day—an independence of the limitations of space such as frequently occurs in the legends of Buddha.

The neo-Pythagorean school, however, was not satisfied merely with honoring the ideal of the wise and miracle-working god-man in their old founder, but they claimed that it had reappeared in the Pythagorean Apollonius of Tyana (d. about 96 A. D.), whose biography was written about 220 A. D. at the order of the Empress Julia Domna by the rhetor Philostratus.[1] He has a quantity of miracles to tell of his hero both in knowledge and power. He is said to have foretold various future events such as the revolt of Vindex against Nero, the short reign of Galba, Otho and Vitellius, the death of Titus, the sinking of a ship, etc. Being in Ephesus at the time he saw the murder of Domitian as though he had been present; while in the midst of a conversation with friends he suddenly became silent, looked fixedly before him, and then exclaimed, "Down with him, the tyrant!" Thereupon he explained to his surprised friends that Domitian had just been murdered. Soon afterwards the news arrived that this had in fact taken place in the very same hour.

---

[1] Cp. Baur's Treatise "Apollonius and Christ" in three essays on the history of ancient philosophy, ed. Zeller, 1876.

Apollonius also understood all the tongues of men and of animals and could read even the hidden thoughts of people. He freed the city of Ephesus from the demon of the pest, recognizing him in the guise of a beggar and causing him to be stoned, whereupon a great dog was found beneath the stones. At Corinth he unmasked in the bride of one of his disciples a man-eating empusa, or feminine vampire. At Athens he recognized in a young man, who interrupted his discourse with rude laughter, one possessed of an evil spirit, and commanded the demon to leave him with some perceptible sign. Thereupon the demon announced that he would overturn the statue standing in the hall, and forthwith this statue moved and fell down; but the youth was healed from that moment and restored to his right mind. In Rome he met a funeral train which was conducting to the grave the corpse of a young girl accompanied by her mourning lover. He stepped up and bade the bearers stand still, saying that he would dry the tears of the mourners. They thought that he was intending to deliver a consolatory address, but he laid his hands upon the girl and murmured over her some unintelligible words, whereupon she arose, began to speak and returned to the house of her parents. The father attempted to express his gratitude to the savior of his child by a considerable gift of money, but Apollonius refused to accept it, directing that it be devoted to the trousseau of the bride. The biographer remarks, moreover, that we may leave it an open question whether we have here a case of the arousing of one in a trance or of the restoration to life of one actually dead, the same dilemma that presents itself to us in the New Testament accounts of the raising of Jairus' daughter and of the son of the widow of Nain. (Mark v, 41 f.; and Luke vii, 12 ff.)

All these and other similar miracles of Apollonius had a beneficent and philanthropic purpose, serving for the relief of those suffering from all sorts of ills; but some stories are told in which he himself is the person involved in danger, among them the following: When he had been thrown into prison on the order of Domitian and loaded with fetters, a friend asked him when he would probably be freed. He replied: I will give you here a proof of my liberty by shaking off his chains. But then he voluntarily put them on again and the disciple recognized his miraculous power. This miracle with its transparent symbolism—the superiority of the saint to all the power of a hostile world—recalls the miraculous release of the apostles Peter and Paul out of prison (Acts xii, 7; xvi, 26) and the falling down of the Roman cohorts in Gethsemane at the word of Jesus (John xvii, 6).

The legends of the miracles of the Christian saints are in the same line with those of the Pythagorean. The apocryphal acts of the apostles are full of the most remarkable miracles which the apostles are said to have performed among the heathen for the confirmation of the truth of their gospel. According to the Acts of Peter,[1] for instance, Peter drove out a demon from a young man in Rome, and as the demon in leaving overturned and broke a statue of one of the emperors, Peter restored it by the magic power of the holy water. Again, he restored to life a salted herring, gave sight to several blind widows, had a babe proclaim in the voice of a man the punishment impending over Simon Magus, while a dog with a human voice challenged the Magian to a contest in miracle-working. The Magian offered to bring back to life a dead man, whom he had himself killed by his magic arts, but he succeeded only partially, as the man died again immediately. Peter, on the other hand, before the eyes of the Roman people and of the prefect of the city, raised three dead men in succession to new and complete life and cured many sick besides. But when Simon Magus thought to outshine all these miracles by his own ascension into Heaven in bodily form, the attempt at flight was frustrated by the prayer of the Apostle, the Magian fell from a great height and was killed.

When on the persuasion of his friends Peter was about to evade martyrdom by flight, Christ met him at the city gate and replied to the question where he was going, "To Rome, to be crucified again." Peter immediately turned about, was condemned to death on the cross and asked from humility to be crucified head downwards. When this was done, the crucified apostle comforted his mourning friends in a mystical address on the mysteries of the cross, while

---

[1] Lipsius, *Apokryphe Apostelgeschichten*, II, 1.

angels with wreaths of roses and lilies stood about him. But after his death he appeared frequently to his followers and admonished them to remain faithful. But he appeared to Emperor Nero also in a vision, gave him a fearful beating and commanded him to leave the Christians in peace thenceforth.

This reappearance of the martyrs after death to comfort their mourning church is very common, one might almost say a standing feature of the legends of the saints, which must certainly rest upon actual psychic experiences, such as visions and hallucinations.

From the great abundance of church legends of miracles we call attention to two instances from early and middle-age history. In the last book of his work *De civitate Dei* (XXII, chap. 8) Augustine raises the question why such miracles no longer occurred as in the accounts of the gospel time. And he makes answer, first, that they are no longer so necessary as in those days when they were intended to convert the world to the faith, whereas anyone who still required a miracle to help him believe was himself a miracle, refusing to believe in spite of the belief of the world. Besides, he goes on, miracles do still occur in the name of Christ, either through his sacraments or through the prayers or the memorials of his saints, only that these current miracles no longer attract such worldwide attention as those earlier ones.

And then he tells a series of stories of miraculous occurrences from his own time and partly from his own immediate environment. In Milan the bones of the martyrs, Protusius and Gervasius, had been found by means of a revelation in a dream to Bishop Ambrosius, and on the occasion of the resulting celebration a blind man had been cured before the eyes of all those present. In Carthage he had been an eye-witness of how his host Innocentius had been suddenly cured through the prayers of himself and his friends of a dangerous ulcer on which an operation was about to be performed. At the same place a pious woman who suffered from cancer of the breast was cured by a newly baptized convert who made the sign of Christ (the cross) on the diseased part. A physician who suffered from the gout was cured of his disease by baptism. A bit of holy earth, which had been taken from the grave of Christ at Jerusalem and brought to Carthage, expelled the spirits from a haunted house and cured a youth who was lame. In Hippo a maiden was freed from a demon by being anointed with oil which had been consecrated by the tears of the presbyter who was praying for her. In Hippo, too, a miraculous answer was vouchsafed to the prayer of a poor shoemaker addressed to the twenty martyrs for which the place was celebrated; on the shore he found a great fish and in its belly a gold ring; thus the martyrs fulfilled his request for the means to procure clothes. At the celebration of the anniversary of the glorious martyr Stephen, a blind woman was cured by the flowers that had been blessed by the bishop. At the head of the bed of a prominent heathen were laid, while he slept, flowers from the altar of the martyr, and he was moved overnight to the acceptance of the baptism, which before that he had steadfastly refused. A boy who had been run over by an ox-cart and mortally injured was taken to the sanctuary of the martyr and there restored forthwith to his previous complete health. Finally the same martyr caused several restorations from death in this fashion; a garment, consecrated by the relics of the saint, was laid over the corpse, or the body was anointed with oil consecrated in the same way, or it was carried to the holy spot and there laid down while prayers were said over it. "And accordingly," Augustine concludes, "many miracles are still accomplished by the same God, through whom and by what means he will, who performed those of which we read in the Holy Scriptures. Only the former do not become so widely known."

The official biography of St. Francis of Assisi, the founder of the order of Minorites or Franciscans (d. 1226) was written by the general of the order, Bonaventura, in 1260. In this version of the legends of the saint he reports a great number of miracles which are said to have been reported by the first disciples and friends of the saint, accordingly by alleged eye-witnesses. St. Francis kissed a leper upon his very wounds and straightway the leprosy disappeared. In the desert he and his comrades were fed with bread from Heaven. He maintained an entire ship's crew upon a long voyage with the miraculously increased supplies from his wallet. Like Moses he caused water to flow from a rock, and like Jesus he turned pure water into the best of wine. In an assembly of the brotherhood the saint, who was bodily absent, was suddenly seen hovering in the air and blessing the assembly with outstretched arms. The saint was upon an intimate footing with animals; he preached to the birds and they listened to him attentively with outstretched necks; the swallows with their noisy twitter interfered with his address, but on his commanding it they were instantly still; he admonished a wolf to cease from murdering and the beast gave him his paw upon it and became from that moment a tame domestic animal.

The most famous of all is the miracle of the stigmata: During the latter years of his life the saint is said to have borne on hands and feet and side the marks of the wounds of Christ in the form of scars, which bled from time to time, the oldest accounts differing as to the origin and exact nature of the wounds. Later legend spun out this miracle into a series of forty resemblances between Saint Francis and the life of Jesus. Finally, the number of cures from disease, restorations to life, rescues of the shipwrecked and others, which were accomplished by the departed saint, is unlimited. "His memory was so revered that there was a familiar saying regarding him, 'Exaudit quos non ipse audit Deus.' Thus he is more merciful than God himself. This sounds like blasphemy, but it is only the essence of all the worship of the saints frankly expressed."[1]

Otto Pfleiderer.

Berlin, Germany.

---

[1] Hase, *Kirchengeschichte*, II, 387.

THE COMING SCIENTIFIC MORALITY.

THE object of the following article is to show in a concise form the real origin of morality—the dependence of morality upon fundamental scientific principles and the relation of science to good and evil. It proposes no revolutionary ideas, but illustrates the gradually coming effects of scientific knowledge upon the moral sentiments and conduct of mankind. The subject is treated in a comprehensive manner, because the ordinary treatment of morality introduces numerous contradictions.

a. THE REAL FOUNDATION OF MORALITY.

The subjects of science and morality appear so very unlike that it is commonly believed they have no connection with each other; a chief reason for this is, morality is so very much more complex than mechanics, with which it is usually compared, that we cannot so readily understand it. If we examine books on morals we find that notwithstanding human bodies and brains are material substances constantly influenced by numerous scientific conditions, little or nothing is said in them about any scientific relations of the subject. As this fundamental omission requires notice, I beg leave to say a few words on the question, but owing to its inherent complexity and its numerous seeming contradictions, it is impossible to make it clear to all persons, and, as inherent qualities are permanent, the only remedy for this is a prepared mind and attentive reading.

Notwithstanding the seeming absence of any connection between science and morality, I will endeavor to show that the chief principles of science are the great guides of life, and are not only essentially related to morality, but actually constitute its primary foundation. On the authority of sufficient evidence I venture to affirm that the only permanent basis of morality is immutable truth, and as well-verified science is the most perfect truth we possess, we may reasonably expect to find a fixed basis of morality in it.

By the term "science" I mean knowledge derived from proper and sufficient evidence; by "morality" I mean such human conduct as produces justifiable effects on sentient creatures; by "immorality" the infliction of unjustifiable injury upon living beings, and by truth I mean statements consistent with all known facts. The terms "truth" and "science" are largely synonymous, and as science and dogma are incompatible there is no dogmatic science; dogma is not knowledge. Although our knowledge of science is not yet to any large extent absolute, it is gradually becoming so, and is even now very certain in some of its parts. Thus we know to a second of time the periods of coming eclipses, and he who cannot believe that the sun will rise to-morrow because it is not "absolute knowledge" must "sit still and perish." Knowledge and belief are very different; by means of proper and sufficient evidence we may be gradually led to know all things, whilst without evidence we may believe but cannot know anything; the most moral course is to proportion our faith and belief to the evidence.

As natural agents, such as alcohol and our environments, influence our moral conduct, and pain and pleasure are states of the nervous system, morality is a part of science. According to all related evidence, the permanent basis of morality lies in the great principles of universal motion, universal causation, continuity o cause and effect, action and reaction, etc., all of which have bee abundantly established by original research. With these truthfu principles to guide us, all logical thinking on the subject leads truth.

As all material phenomena, manifestly those of astronomy physics, constitute a perfect and orderly system, a correct ve representation of them must be a perfect system of truth, an universal causation and motion present a similar system I ventu say that they are a safer foundation of morality than any unpro statements can possibly be; they are also more reliable guides of conduct than instinct or feeling alone, because moral conduct is a result of feeling after it has been corrected by intellect and training. In the very complex subject of morality, unless we know what is right, we often cannot do it, and even if we do know we often act wrongly, simply because the stronger powers of feeling and desire compel us. Perfect integrity requires ability.

b. DEPENDENCE OF MORALITY UPON UNIVERSAL MOTION.

Unceasing internal motion exists in all material bodies (including human beings), and in the universal ether which pervades all substances and all space. We know nothing of the first cause of it, but we know that it is practically indestructible, that when it disappears it either becomes stored up or reappears in another form or place, and that it is continually being transferred from one body to another by radiation through the ether. The chief proofs of this are the phenomena of conservation of energy and of universal change. We know that this motion differs in form in every different substance, because each substance produces a different spectrum, and we consider that these differences of form of motion are the cause of the unlike properties of different bodies, because when we confer new movements upon a body it acquires new properties, thus a straight chain acquires rigidity when caused to move rapidly in the direction of its length; the gyroscope and Foucault's pendulum are other examples. We know further that bodies of unlike properties act frequently and spontaneously upon each other by mere contact; chemistry furnishes us with an immense number of such instances. They also act by radiation through the ether, thus their spectra, such as those of the sun and of white-hot coke, produce different effects upon a photographic surface, etc.; a mere look may cause hatred.

All material substances are extremely complex, and we can only faintly realize the great feebleness of our perceptive powers in relation to them and their movements. The extremely minute molecular motions of the simplest substance entirely surpass our powers of perception and comprehension; spectrum analysis has shown that the internal movements of the smallest particle of white-hot iron "are more complex than the visible ones of the entire solar system."

Evidence already existing is abundantly sufficient to prove that all bodies (including ourselves) are not only in a state of constant internal motion, but also of continual change of motion; that the cause of this change is largely the unlike properties of different bodies which enable them to act and react upon, and alter, the properties and motions of each other, as we see so often in cases of chemical union, etc., and that all actions, including those of ourselves, occur in accordance with law. Such great truths as these are of the utmost value to mankind, but are not readily accepted, largely because ordinary minds are not sufficiently scientific to receive them. As an example of this, about 300 years ago the English philosopher, Hobbes, said: "There is only one reality in the world; it is movement, external, without beginning, the cause of each and every change." Partly owing to the limited evidence existing at the time in proof of this hypothesis, his idea was neglected, but the evidence in its support has now become so vast that we are compelled to adopt it as a settled truth.

This universal motion in our organs and environments causes our experiences; our experiences and inferences from them produce our ideas, and our experiences and ideas cause our actions through the medium of our nervous system. When our environments act upon our nervous centers the latter, by unconscious "reflex" or "automatic" action through the nerves, largely cause our bodily movements and the changes in our organs. Nearly every organ in our body acts automatically during sleep, and more or less during the waking state; the heart acts automatically at all times, the lungs breathe automatically, the brain thinks automatically during dreams and partly so during the waking state; we walk automatically until we come to a difficulty, and then the conscious intellect, excited by the stronger impression, operates and prevents an accident. Most of the actions, especially of untrained persons, are automatic. When we cease to automatically move we die. Automatic actions have no moral quality because they do not involve conscious intellect.

In nearly all cases of physical and chemical action there are conversions of energy from one form into another, and in all such cases practically no energy is created or destroyed and the total effect is equal to the total cause; this is well known as the principle of universal equivalence and the conservation of energy. Similar conversions take place in us; thus the latent energy contained in food and air gives rise to vital power. Nearly every such act, whether in living things or in dead ones, is, however, attended by dissipation of energy, usually in the form of heat; thus muscular energy warms our bodies, and thinking makes the head hot, and the dissipation of power in a steam engine and boiler between the furnace and fly-wheel is quite 87 per cent. Through similar dissipations of energy within us our "reflex" actions are often weaker than our direct ones, and we know that intellect is often weaker than the animal feelings out of which it arises. It is apparently by process of conversion of energy that our intellectual acts are produced by prior material ones, thus the energy of oxidizing cerebral tissue is accompanied by mental action. We know that one direction of visible motion in a machine can be converted into another, for instance, reciprocating into circular, etc., and as the laws of motion of small bodies are the same as those of large ones it is reasonable to conclude that one kind of invisible molecular motion can be converted into another in the human body and brain as certainly as visible motion is in an inanimate machine. The usual cause of conversion of energy and of the changes occurring in nature is difference of property and motion of adjacent substances.

All cases of morality as there defined are instances of action and reaction, chiefly between human beings and between men and other animals; also between each man and his environments, and between his brain and his bodily organs; thus the mere sight of valuable property causes the thief to steal, and bodily feelings excite moral and immoral ideas. We are always under the influence of motion, from within and without, from the cradle to the grave, compelled to act or to refrain from acting, and are equally obliged to accept, sooner or later, some of the consequences, whether pleasant or painful, of our conduct. This is not fatalism, because scientific effects are always conditional, whilst fatalistic ones are entirely uncondi-

[illegible]. Similar to all other material bodies, man is inexorably bou:
by law and circumstances, though he often does not like to thi.
so, because it curbs his desires.

The world is not governed essentially by what we with o
narrow ideas consider "justice," but by material necessity, and it
only when acts of natural causation happen to agree with those ide
that we consider them just. We are so ignorant and conceited th
we forget our littleness, and cannot believe that great terrestri
powers, such as earthquakes, lightning, etc., are just toward
Why do the weak yield to the strong in all cases? It is simply
cause all natural actions are essentially of a mechanical nature.
consequence of difference of circumstances and property in eve
different substance, all bodies act and react upon each other, ar
each governs in proportion to its power; the large celestial glob
govern the small ones, and the small ones react upon them;
stronger animal feelings govern the intellect and the latter react
in a less degree govern them. The powers of all bodies are limit
by their mass and their motion, and by the fact that they cann
simultaneously possess contradictory properties; the existence of o
property necessarily limits that of its opposite; thus a body cann
be soft and hard, brittle and tough. According to some writers, ev
a Deity cannot possess incompatible powers, thus: "How can infini
justice exact the utmost penalty for every sin, and yet infinite mer
pardon the sinner?" (Dean Mansel.)

As natural laws are invariable, the actions of all material su
stance are regulated, each celestial body has a definite speed of m
tion, and human progress has a definite rate, we cannot "hurry up
millennium." The rate of human progress depends largely up
fixedness of human habits, and upon the fact that when an idea h
been firmly impressed upon the brain it remains until death a
prevents the reception of new ones. Human progress is a very co
plex phenomenon, and its rate is not measurable by us; but, notwit
standing this, its rate must be as fixed as that of the earth in
orbit, because it depends upon the same ultimate causes and law
is the discovery of new knowledge which enables mankind to a
vance, and the diffusion of it maintains the state attained.

All change requires time, and dissimilar bodies require different periods to alter without injury; human beings have often to make many preparations in order to prevent great loss and suffering caused by change. If any substance is too rapidly strained it is damaged; a stick, too quickly bent, breaks; overstrained metals suffer permanent change, and men do not entirely recover from greatly injured moral character.

In our own individual case our actions *seem* to be regulated by energy of volition, but as volition is not an uncaused phenomenon and cannot of itself create energy, we are really governed by the internal and external influences which cause our volitions. A steam engine seems to be regulated by its "governor," but the real energy exerted through that contrivance is that of the steam. Notwithstanding our seeming volitional power, we are nearly as helpless in the power of universal energy as the dust of a road is in the rush of a hurricane. Man desires, but energy performs, apparently in every case; we are incessantly governed by climate, temperature, tides, state of bodily health, etc. All men are more or less controlled by ignorance, largely in consequence of deficiency of knowledge, disease and accidents kill millions of men prematurely every year. Very few die simply of old age, for in every man

> "There is always somewhere a weakest spot,
> Above or below, within or without,
> And that is the reason, beyond a doubt,
> A man 'breaks down,' but doesn't wear out."
>
> O. W. HOLMES.

All substances more or less govern all substances at all distances by means of radiations, and as we are material bodies, radiant energy largely governs us; thus we are held fast to the earth by rays of gravity, and are kept alive by rays of heat from the sun; we are also affected by rays of light, rays from radium, etc.

Man is a storehouse of energy derived from the food and air he consumes and the heat of the sun potentially contained in it. He is a structure in which energy is always active, with nervous organs for consciously or unconsciously liberating it, and producing either moral or "immoral" effects. Energy continually flows through him, it enters his body in the food and air he consumes and escapes largely as bodily heat and movement. His body is always being consumed and renewed, and appears to be as truly kept in action by the energy of chemical union of the oxygen in the blood with his tissues as a steam engine is by the oxidation of the coal in its boiler furnace.

c. SCIENTIFIC VIEWS OF LIFE AND MIND.

All kinds of errors are obstacles to the spread of morality. Books, etc., are continually being written without definitions of the chief terms used in them. Through neglect of properly defining of terms, and of limiting their meanings, the idea of universal molecular motion has been in some cases misused, thus the well-known self-repair of crystals, and the spontaneous recovery of metals from internal strain have been spoken of as "life in crystals" and "life in metals." That inanimate bodies, minerals, magnets, etc., potentially contain the rudiments of some of the properties of animals, such as action and reaction, is quite true, but we require definite terms to indicate complex abstract idea, such as life, mind, spirit, etc., and it is misleading to call the invisible molecular motion of metals a crystal "life," because, as far as we know, "life" only exists in organic cellular structures.

The abstract idea of universal molecular motion is very similar to that of a Deity, and many persons have unscientifically spoken of God as being "an all-pervading mind." It is true that such motion has the qualities of omnipotence, omnipresence, infinity and invisibility, but it has not that of personality; nor is it really "mind," because the existence of mind in the absence of nervous substance has never been proved.

The idea of the existence of a "mind" or "soul" as a separate entity, whether in the body or out of it, is another error opposing moral progress. It is really only a mental abstraction of our collection of thinking faculties; the independent existence of mind has never been proved, and the idea has for ages deceived millions of ns, and even if such an entity did exist, we have no proof that ites energy with which to perform mental actions; if also, as e infers, such actions are really caused by natural influences physiological conditions, there is no need of a separate entity pirit" to produce them. The mere ethereal or mysterious na- of a substance or action does not warrant our calling it a t," "spiritual" or "supernatural."

The idea of the existence of a "second self" within us is another ved assumption, and appears to be explicable by ordinary logy. Under the influence of suitable stimuli all our organs automatically," the legs walk, the lungs breathe, the heart without supervision by the intellect. Similarly, under the lus of indigestion, cerebral excitement, etc., the brain thinks g dreams, and this kind of thinking has been attributed to a nd" or "subliminal" self within us. Thought, whether con- or unconscious, if uncorrected by intellect and training, is unhealthy, and sometimes dangerous. In the *conscious* state, n and women, all kinds of crime are committed under its in- e; similarly with animals, they have less intellect than men re audaciously guilty of instinctive deceit, theft and murder. e *unconscious* state, as in dreams, even suicide and murder been committed, and many somnambulists have seriously in- themselves. Nevertheless, in highly intelligent and trained ns dreams are occasionally correct, and acts of thinking have re occasions been performed during them which could not have done in the waking state, in consequence of disturbing influ- As dreaming, somnambulism, trance, etc., are reasonably able by ordinary physiological automatism, there is no need e assumption of "a second self" to explain them.

We may approximately limit the term "mind" or "soul" to ollection of faculties or actions termed consciousness, observa- comparison, inference and imagination, and, as far as we , these exist only in living nervous organisms. Further, in the series of living structures, from plants up to man, wherever l appears, there also is nervous substance. Mind is a species of life, and life may be scientifically viewed as a kind of motion, but motion alone, separate from organic structure, is neither life nor mind; metals and crystals have internal motion, but do not live. Wherever mind exists questions of morality begin to arise, because moral action is largely mental, and mental action is produced, as far as we can infer at present, partly by oxidation of living nervous substance. Sooner or later, by the aid of new discoveries, life and mind will probably be much more precisely defined as particular forms of internal movement, occurring only under special conditions in suitable organisms, but as the human intellect is nearly powerless in such profound and complex questions without the aid of proper and sufficient evidence, we must work and wait for more discoveries.

In consequence of insufficient knowledge of scientific principles and of how to use them in explaining mental phenomena, a great mystery has been made of consciousness. Consciousness and attention are largely synonymous; each consists merely of a high degree of activity of the senses, and this increases with the strength of influence of the environments upon them; the stronger and more sudden that influence and the more excitable the senses, the more vivid the attention and consciousness. Consciousness is largely increased by the perception by one sense of the action of another in the same organism, and there are all degrees of it. Perfectly automatic actions, such as those of some of the viscera in a healthy state, are not usually noticed by the senses, whilst those which are violent or are accompanied by great pain or pleasure are strongly perceived, and when several senses are simultaneously and strongly excited each one perceives the excitement of the others, and, by coöperation, heightens the effect; thus if we suspect a great danger close at hand, such as our house on fire in the night, several senses are excited; we see, smell and taste the smoke, we hear the sounds of burning, we feel our heart beating, and feel and see our body trembling, and each sense perceives, more or less, the excitement of the others, and thus increases the total feeling. Consciousness is intimately related to morality; the more conscious we are of our actions the more accountable are we considered to be for them.

4. DEPENDENCE OF MORALITY UPON UNIVERSAL CAUSATION.

Next in importance to the dependence of morality upon universal motion is its relation to universal causation. Abundant evidence exists to prove that moral and immoral actions are as much cases of cause and effect as motion produced by steam, and the great assumption that some natural phenomena are produced without a natural cause has never yet been proved; all men are caused to perform acts of "good" and "evil," friendship and enmity, by the influences within and around them. In some cases many causes produce a single effect, as in the maintenance of a good character, whilst in others a single cause produces many effects, as in the sudden destruction of that character by a criminal act. Given unlimited time, the smallest cause may produce a very great effect, as continually occurs in the washing away of mountains by rain, and in the gradual loss of moral character by habitually telling small untruths. In other cases the number of causes between the earliest one and the effect are many, but this, like the number of links in a chain, makes no difference in the result, provided all the intermediate connections are certain. Lapse of time, also, has no influence; thus we are as certainly descendants of the first human couple and inheritors of some of their moral qualities, as of our immediate parents. Many persons want to know "the first cause of all things," not thinking that this is quite beyond our feeble powers and that every cause must have had an earlier one to produce it. Causation acts as surely in a complex machine as in a simple one, in a man as in a windmill, in morals as in mechanics, provided all the necessary conditions are present. This statement is based upon the great principles of indestructibility of motion and continuity of cause and effect, but the degree of certainty in morals *seems* to be less than in mechanics, because the more numerous conditions confuse us; nearly the whole of our difficulty in understanding complex subjects arises from the smallness of our knowledge and the very limited powers of the human brain. As moral qualities are not often measurable, it is not much wonder that we cannot assess moral values.

Under the influence of universal motion and causation, acting according to invariable laws, all material bodies, ourselves included; "do as they must," and we are so far justified in all our actions, whether moral or immoral. Some persons are alarmed at this great scientific statement, as if it were wrong to submit to greater powers than our own, but whether we consider it right or wrong, we have no choice in the matter; even the great globes in space are compelled to obey, and why should not we? It might be supposed that if this was true it would render unnecessary all praise and reward, punishment and blame, but as causation is not suspended in the mutual presence of any two bodies, we are still compelled by the influence of our environments to encourage "right" and discourage "wrong" by all the ordinary means. We may reasonably conclude that even the greatest criminals "do as they must," and this is the truest charity, because whilst it does not prevent correction of "immoral" conduct, it calms revengeful feelings and prevents undue punishment. As the stomach is more clamorous for food than the brain is for learning, the necessity of getting an income is with nearly all men more urgent than love of truth or virtue; multitudes of persons are compelled by this influence to do all kinds of "immoral" and "criminal" acts, and this is largely proved by the great number and variety of "crimes" they commit. Persons are not to be entirely blamed for the acts they commit under compulsion, and we cannot so heavily punish a man for his "evil" actions if we are fully convinced that he "does as he must" under all the conditions and circumstances.

All bodies whatever, men included, have only limited powers, and this is largely due to the circumstance that a body cannot possess contradictory attributes nor perform incompatible actions simultaneously; thus it cannot be both hot and cold, nor move in opposite directions at the same moment. A man cannot be alive and dead concurrently, and as we cannot perform incompatible acts, nor exert superhuman powers, we must not expect too much of each other, but make allowance for human weakness. It is evident from these and other facts that the great scientific truth, "contradictories cannot coexist," lies at the basis of all human conduct, whether moral or physical.

As the influences within and around us are often stronger than our wishes, obedience to them is a necessary condition of life, our internal stimuli requires us to breathe, and we must either do so or die. In going through life we are as truly compelled by natural influences to move or refrain from moving as the blades of grass in a field are by the force of the wind. Ask any man why he did a particular act and he will probably say either that he does not know, that he was compelled to do it, or that he did it by his own free will. In the first case he may have been moved by an unobserved cause, in the second by an observed one, and in the third by an unnoticed one, which coincided with his volition at the moment. When a man retires from business he is usually compelled by the circulation of the blood in his body and brain to seek some other occupation. We cannot carry out our "will" to "do as we like" in any case unless our volitions happen to agree with the natural powers that govern us, and which, by supplying energy, are the real causes of our acts; we cannot by merely "willing it" fly across the Atlantic Ocean, nor even swim across the Straits of Dover, unless those powers are propitious. "Freedom of will" is like a mirage, the farther we scientifically examine it the more we find the effect to be due to ordinary natural causes. The government of the world by universal energy underlies all our arrangements, obedience to greater powers is indispensable to politics, sociology, morality and religion, it allows no distinction between men, all must submit to it; out of it arise all our systems of law and rules for maintaining life and health, and for performing all our legal, social and moral duties.

Every one of our actions, if properly interpreted, proves that we "do as we must;" thus we all must die in order that our successors may live; each man is compelled to be born, to accept his position in nature, and when he ceases to be useful he is usually forced out of sight. He is compelled to suffer pain, anxiety, poverty, ungratified desire; to be praised and blamed, punished and rewarded; to work and wait, to love and to hate; to discover and invent, to fail and to succeed; to acquire numerous mental and bodily diseases and deformities, and numberless false ideas which he can never erase; to commit crimes, to believe untruths and promulgate them; to deceive and be deceived in nearly all directions, because whilst there is usually only one true explanation of a phenomenon, there are often many false ones, especially in the very complex phenomena of psychical research, morals and spiritualism.

Some persons seem alarmed at the numerous changes wrought by science, and ask, "Where is science leading us?" Tell us, oh, tell us, how far will science go? Farther and farther is nearly all we know. As we cannot predict as surely in morals as in mechanics, we should be reasonably content with the knowledge we possess until we can discover more, and probably when more is found, and more is understood, we then shall better see that "all is good." All things, even our ideas of morality, are changing; matter and change are inseparable, and their union and continuance are so perfect that we are practically compelled to accept them as complete.

"Everything that exists depends upon the past, prepares the future, and is related to the whole." (Oersted.) Continuity unites all natural phenomena in one great flowing scene, the present to the past and future; it is the basis of heredity, and of all history of morals and other subjects; it secures fulfillment of prediction of future events, as in eclipses, and in the discovery of substances which we have never seen, but which are subsequently obtained, as in the case of Helium, etc.

e. SCIENTIFIC VIEWS OF GOOD AND EVIL.

The subject of morality is very largely composed of questions relating to "good" and "evil." Scientifically defined, "good" is that which serves some useful purpose, not merely to mankind, but to the entire universe; any narrower definition than this leads to numerous contradictions which prove its falsity, and what we term "evil" is mostly that which unjustifiably produces pain, anxiety or injury to sentient creatures; a common idea of "evil" is anything which produces pain, but this is a great mistake, because pain is simply a sensation which we fear and dislike. It is manifest that if any so-called "evil" prevents a greater one it must be good, thus the pain of amputation of a limb in order to save a life is not an evil; that which does good is good, and as the welfare of this globe and all upon it is vastly more important than that of men alone, earthquakes and volcanic outbursts are good, because they relieve the crust of the earth and prevent the occurrence of greater ones. Actions are not necessarily "evil" because they are violent or rapid, nor is the universe imperfect because all things in it are constantly changing and causing us pain and anxiety.

The belief that pain is "evil" is one of the greatest of human deceptions, nearly every person entertains it, and there is no false idea so firmly fixed or so easy to acquire; this is due to the fact that we all suffer pain, and the idea that it is "evil" has been bred in us, and taught afresh to each new generation; this false idea is, however, often useful to those who cannot realize the truthful one. That pain is not evil is shown in many ways; insensibility to it is often dangerous, because it warns us of approaching disease; thus the incipient pains of gout bid us properly regulate our diet and exercise. Pain is our great disciplinarian; if it were not for the anticipation of it we should often injure ourselves. "The burnt child shuns the fire." The painful prospect of poverty makes us thrifty; without the pains and anxieties of earning an income we should lapse into idleness, luxury and disease. The desire to escape pain and increase pleasure compels us to train ourselves, acquire knowledge, discover new truths, invent contrivances, seek new remedies, etc. As inanimate bodies undergo violent changes, and all animals suffer pain and death, why should not we? We strongly object to having more pain than we are able to bear, but even in this case we often have to submit to greater powers, as in the case of epidemics, etc. Trials are not "evils," but pain to be borne or work to be done.

"As ignorance, untruth and false beliefs are great sources of human suffering, it might be supposed that they are really 'evil,' but we know that in certain cases untruths are more useful than truths to unlearned persons, simply because they are more easily understood; thus the idea of the existence of an evil Deity has been very useful in its time, and so has that of a heaven and hell. We pay physicians to prescribe poisons to cure our bodies, and why not pay for untruths to console our minds? Various false beliefs have been, and are, great consolations to millions of anxious persons who have never had a chance of learning the great truths of science. Untruthful orators have induced multitudes of persons to think and improve who would never have done so, and the immense 'evil' of ignorance affords a livelihood to great numbers of professional men, tradesmen and others, to supply the lack of knowledge in other persons. Anything which gratifies desire will 'sell.' If it were not for ignorant enthusiasm and exaggeration many good undertakings would not be carried out. Men are not to be blamed because they are compelled to believe untruths; probably every false belief would be found to be useful if it were scientifically investigated; nevertheless, truth is more virtuous than untruth. Not the strictest truth, but 'probability,' is the great guide of life."

If we view the subject in a comprehensive manner we find that each seeming "evil" is usually followed by a greater good; thus every man is compelled to pay rates and taxes in order to secure safety of life and property, and the greater good thus acquired more than justifies the lesser "evil" needed to produce it; each man has to suffer for all in order that he may gain the support and protection of all. Even the premature death of multitudes of human beings by disease, etc., has the good effects of regulating the density of population and the speed of human progress, each of which, if too great, would ultimately cause greater disasters to the species.

As pain and pleasure are states of the nervous system, morality is based upon physiology. The scientific basis of morality is further proved by the fact that the variety and number of pains and pleasures increase with the complexity of the animal structure and are greatest in civilized man, and if the human organism was still more complex it would be liable to a still greater variety of pains and pleasures. Good and evil, pleasure and pain, are largely equivalents of each other; thus the greater the pleasure the more usually we have to work or pay for it. As the ideas of good and evil are extremely complex, they are largely unmeasurable and we are often obliged to guess their magnitudes.

Many persons have asked, "Why does evil exist?" The answer is: For the same reason that all phenomena exist, viz., because it is a necessary consequence of universal energy acting upon material bodies. Good and "evil" are produced by the same natural causes, and often there is no essential difference between them; thus "virtue in excess is vice," and pleasure, when too intense, becomes pain. "Evil" is due to our internal and external environments, and these are almost endless in number and variety; it is also largely due to our limited powers, especially to the smallness of our knowledge, the fewness and narrowness of our senses and the undeveloped state of our brains. There are thousands of actions occurring within and around us every instant which our senses cannot perceive, and nature is full of phenomena which we cannot explain. Each of our powers, except our intellect, is surpassed by that of some other animal; thus our vision is weaker than that of an eagle, we cannot run as fast as a greyhound, fly like a bird, or swim like a fish.

"Why has not man a microscopic eye?
For this plain reason, man is not a fly." (Pope.)

In consequence of his limited powers, each man is frequently making mistakes, neglecting the rules of health and moral conduct, injuring himself and others in many ways, resorting to deception, violence and crime in order to effect his objects, and in some cases, through despair of succeeding in life, committing suicide. The moral fall of man and woman is often caused by inability to resist the influence of environments. Nothing, perhaps, shows more plainly the limited powers of man than the multitudes of crimes he commits and the endless variety of pains, errors and deceptions to which he is subject. Not only man, but all inanimate bodies, have limited powers which frequently give rise to disasters; bodies break by their own weight, internal weakness, etc., and it is, therefore, no punishable defect in man that his abilities are not greater than they are; nevertheless, defective machines must be strengthened and wrongdoers must be corrected in order to pre vent future disasters. The more ignorant the person the more is h carried through life by the stream of events, without predictic or reaction on his part, and the more is he subject to accidents.

The problem of "evil" is extremely complex, and is "the gre puzzle of mankind." Numerous moralists, theologians and met physicians have tried to solve it, but have largely failed, part through deficiency of suitable scientific knowledge. The term "evi is an extremely conventional one and very difficult to make clea because it depends on so many conditions; thus what is "evil" one man at one time, is often "good" to another man or at anoth time, or under slightly different conditions; deaths are good f the undertaker. The problem is rendered more confusing by t circumstance that each man's view differs from that of every oth man, and that "evil" may be viewed in two very different aspec viz., the ordinary narrow and deceptive one, and the broad, scie tific and true one, and these two views often contradict each oth As real contradictions do not exist in nature, these must ari from the fact that the narrow view is an imperfect one. T subject is still further mystified by the fact that the whole nature is in a continual state of change, and that our idea of "e is constantly changing with it.

In addition to all this, the innumerable different views t of "evil" are so contradictory that the problem remains inso to nearly everybody. In such a complex case the best gui truth is a correct theory, because it yields true inferences—to the question to great scientific principles and view it in the comprehensive aspect—but even a true theory, aided by mo found meditation, is not a sufficient guide to truth in the mo cult cases, partly because the human mind is unable to true values to all the numerous circumstances. The only which is perfectly consistent with all the evidence is the one, viz., that the Universe and all it contains is perfect, each individual body is perfect in its own sphere and circu at the time, but this idea seems so opposed to our experi it is quite beyond ordinary imagination. Our view of the must not, however, be contracted to suit narrow human capacities, but be expanded so as to represent the Universe as it really is.

Each extreme view has its uses, and both are necessary, the narrow or so-called "practical" one for deciding what is best for the individual, irrespective of the welfare of others, and the broad one for general human welfare and prediction of consequences. In practical life both views should usually be taken and acted upon. Commonly, however, "self-preservation is the first rule of life," but as our automatic impulses are often stronger than our intellect, the selfish man obeys this so-called "first rule" and neglects the rights of his fellow-man. "The real first rule of life is to do the greatest good."

According to the narrow view, "there's something wrong in everything," man is full of sin and very imperfect, and the earth is "badly governed," but according to the broad one "whatever is, is good," and all things are perfect in their respective spheres and fit for future change. Things are not imperfect because they are changing; all are doing so. As no substance can possess contradictory attributes, all bodies are limited in their properties and powers and therefore cannot act otherwise than they do, and as all "do as they must," their so-called "imperfections" are only limitations. Thus an oyster is as perfect in its sphere as a man. A body is not imperfect because it is simple, nor because it is complex, nor because it has limited powers. Thus a pin is as perfect as a watch, a mouse as a man, each in its own particular station. A sleeping man is not imperfect because he is wholly guided by his automatic action, without the help of intellect. He is only a more limited being. A man must not be unreservedly blamed because he is not other than he is, nor for the crimes arising from his environments and limited faculties. These considerations do not, however, exclude the corrections necessary to progress.

> "Then say not man's imperfect, Heaven's in fault,
> Say rather, man's as perfect as he ought.".—*Pope.*

Each man has no choice but to take the special view of nature which his entire environments compel him; and as the influences acting upon the brains of any two men are never entirely alike; each man's view differs, more or less, from that of every other man. The views taken by different persons vary in comprehensiveness and truthfulness directly as the extent of their knowledge of fundamental principles. The narrow-minded man is usually more convinced of the truth of his false ideas than the broad-minded man is of his true ones, largely because his ideas are fewer, simpler and more fixed. The obstinacy of ignorant persons is proverbial, and often continues until death, because their passions are frequently stronger than their intellects, and they cannot erase their false impressions.

The ideas of different men and the actions of different bodies must be either harmonious or discordant, and if discordant with each other, conflict and conversion of energy occur. It is largely in consequence of contradictory ideas that wars in general arise, and these differences are easily traceable to the influence of unlike environments, fixed ideas and limited knowledge. The rudiments of war and crimes are visible in nearly all animals. The phenomena of conflict exist throughout nature. There are "wars of the elements" as well as of men; even plants contest for a living, and all this is due to differences of property and action of material bodies. Conflicting views in politics, morals and theology are necessary parts of human life. They result in evolution, advance, growth and decay, of men and nations. We are often strengthened by conflict which we are able to bear, and trials, if rightly accepted, usually do us good.

The true and broad view of "evil" is, that whilst pain and suffering are all around us, there is no real evil. First, because its existence would prove the Universe to be imperfect; 2d, if the physical constitution of the Universe is perfect, as scientific evidence declares it to be, the moral arrangement, being inseparable from it, must also be perfect; 3d, whenever a case of seeming evil is fully investigated, it is ultimately proved to be necessary and good; 4th, it has been abundantly proved that pain is necessary to human existence and welfare in many ways; 5th, as great "calamities" serve useful purposes and many so-called "evils" prevent greater ones, they must be good; 6th, "evil" acts are produced by natural agents in the same manner as good ones; 7th, the greatest "evil doers" are compelled to act, the same as all other persons and all inanimate substances; 8th, it would be inconsistent if all other animals suffered pain whilst man alone was exempt; 9th, even the feeling of so-called "evil" is limited to an extremely minute portion of nature, viz., animal brain in the waking state, and in that only occasionally; 10th, no consistent theory of human life has ever been framed upon the idea that real evil exists; 11th, the Universe works so as to secure the greatest good to all things; and 12th, belief in the existence of "evil" is easily accounted for by our frequent experience of pain. Considering all this evidence it is incomparably less likely that the moral perfection of the Universe is defective, than that we with our very feeble minds and fixed belief in the existence of "evil," are deceived in such a vast and complex question.

It may be objected that if such a belief was not a true one, it would not exist in nearly every human mind and be irremovable; but we know that some of the greatest errors have been believed by nearly all men during many centuries, until expelled by science; e. g., that of the rotation of the sun round the earth. The question might also be asked: What is the use of the conclusion that the Universe is perfect if it cannot be at once applied to relieve human suffering? The answer is: It has been and can be so applied by intelligent persons who possess suitable and sufficient scientific knowledge. The advantages of scientific morality are immediately applicable, but whether they can be fully realized at once is a minor question. Great ideas require time to grow, and to obtain oaks we must plant acorns many years in advance.

The coming system of morality is a much more reliable one than any at present existing, because it is entirely founded upon truths which have been proved by means of proper and sufficient evidence. "Truthfulness is the basis of all the virtues." When men have true principles to guide them they agree, because their leading ideas are the same. The reliability of science depends largely upon the fact that the testimony of inanimate substances and impersonal powers is free from bias; we cannot alter a fact; it is a fact forever. Uncertainty means danger and truthful ideas are essential to the highest morality.

To believe from sufficient proofs that the Universe is perfect, that real evil does not exist, and that all men "do as they must," affords relief of mind in many trials and constitutes a sound basis for the much-desired "government by love." It diminishes hatred of our fellow-men and requires us to forgive our enemies, but it does not relieve us of the duties of discovering truth or of improving ourselves and others. The greatest preventive of pain is knowledge; new knowledge is the starting point of human progress and the most powerful cause of national advance is the general diffusion of comprehensive scientific discoveries. Fundamental scientific knowledge is the greatest promoter of peace; it enables us to correct error and detect deceit; it makes life more worth living, and that it prolongs life is shown by the fact that scientific philosophers live longer than the average period. Scientific experience makes us more exact, careful and reliable, and by increasing our knowledge of the future enables us to arrange beforehand so as to secure our safety and correctness of conduct. The great uses of science in preventing, alleviating and removing bodily pain, transmitting intelligence, etc., are well known. But notwithstanding all this and very much more, it is often called cold, dreary, etc., by emotional persons, because it does not encourage irrational beliefs and desires.

The idea of universal goodness is an old one, and was originally a mere conjecture, but it is now abundantly supported by facts, and mankind will be gradually compelled by the pressure of advancing knowledge to accept it. At present it needs competent expounders, and it is merely our lack of suitable scientific knowledge and our frequent experience of pain that hinder our believing it. Like other great truths which mankind have been slowly compelled to accept, it is strongly at variance with our feelings whilst perfectly in harmony with intellect.

If the foregoing system of morality were taught in schools it would produce intelligent, practical and moral human beings, each one acting as a law unto himself, and would ultimately result in evolving a more truthful system of religion than any at present existing.

BIRMINGHAM, ENGLAND. G. GORE.

[Among those scientists of England who take an interest in the relation of science to ethics, George Gore, F. R. S., LL. D., of Birmingham, holds a prominent position, and the present paper contains, in a condensed form, the maturest thought of his long and useful life.

Dr. Gore was born of humble parents in Bristol, England, January 22, 1826. His education was scanty and he had to work hard for a living. He left school at thirteen and found employment four years as an errand boy and then four other years as a cooper. Although he had received no scientific training, attended no scientific lectures, did not enjoy access to any laboratory, had no scientific friends, and was not possessed of inherited property, he showed even in his boyhood a love of, and an aptitude for, experiment, and, being fond of science, he was always an eager reader of scientific books. At an age of 26 years, having acquired, by mere self-training, a stock of scientific knowledge, he formed classes for teaching science. In the year 1855 he discovered "explosive antimony," and was soon afterward appointed lecturer on physics and chemistry at the great Grammar School of King Edward VI. at Birmingham, a position which he filled for many years. He made numerous experimental researches for philosophical purposes, which, on account of their originality, etc., were published by the Royal Society, the Birmingham Philosophical Society, the Philosophical Magazine, etc. We count over 200 scientific essays written by him, and most of his researches were of a laborious character; among them was one made with liquified carbonic acid, and one with the most dangerous anhydrous hydrofluoric acid. He discovered the molecular movements of red-hot iron, electrolytic musical sounds, and the electric rotating ball, now used in many lecture rooms.

Dr. Gore's specialty is electro-metallurgy, and in his capacity of consulting chemist and electro-metallurgist he made various useful inventions which proved helpful to the industries of England. He wrote four books on electro-metallurgy, one of which, *The Art of Electro-Metallurgy*, has passed through five editions; another, *The Electrolytic Refining of Metals*, has been used for many years as a text-book in industrial schools.

Although Dr. Gore is a specialist and even a pathfinder in his chosen field, he takes a great interest in the general significance of science and especially its practical application in the common walks of life. His appreciation of the essential value of scientific research is expressed in two books, entitled *The Art of Scientific Discovery* and *The Scientific Basis of National Progress*. His conception of the fundamental scientific nature of morality found expression in a voluminous work, *The Scientific Basis of Morality*.

There is a very laudable method in England of recognizing the merits of citizens who have well deserved the approbation of their country. It consists of a Civil List pension, and this distinction was conferred upon Dr. George Gore by Queen Victoria.—EDITOR.]

THE PRINCIPLE OF THE CONSERVATION OF ENERGY.

FROM THE POINT OF VIEW OF MACH'S PHENOMENO-LOGICAL CONCEPTION OF NATURE.

THE need of an epistemological investigation of the domain of the exact sciences, which has recently been making itself very vividly felt, like similar aspirations of universal and wide-reaching import, has found expression in many varied forms. Leaving out of account the original fundamental ideas of the great inquirers, which afford at all points *aperçus* of epistemological inquiries, the real era of the development in question began with Faraday, Lord Kelvin and Maxwell—although it was not consciously pursued until the present day, when a number of prominent inquirers began to investigate epistemologically the foundations of the exact sciences, not as a matter of supererogation, but as a definite end, sufficient in itself.

In two branches of knowledge which stand in intimate relation with physics, this work had been attempted at a much earlier date; namely, in philosophy and mathematics. In the first field, Berkeley, Hume and Kant had subjected the theory of knowledge to thorough-going scrutiny and criticism, and in so doing had at least demonstrated the necessity of such investigations. A critical examination of the foundations of mathematics by Abel, and by Weierstrass and his school, had proved amply that successful progress in the domain of mathematics was by no means a conclusive demonstration of the solidity of its foundations. It follows at once from the results of these inquiries that a critical examination of the epistemological structure of physics likewise is an imperative necessity, and has its no sense been rendered redundant by the steady progress made in this science.

MACH'S EPISTEMOLOGICAL WORK.

Ernest Mach was undoubtedly the first inquirer to discern clearly the necessity of a reform of the current conceptions of the fundamental principles of physics and to make the epistemological investigation of these notions an independent object of inquiry. For forty years now, in the prosecution of this task, he has produced an imposing array of works and memoirs. For a long time he remained isolated, and, as he himself tells us, for many years the only reception his ideas met with from his colleagues was a shrug of the shoulders. But gradually the number of those who either partly or wholly agreed with his views increased; nay! he was ultimately successful, even, in discovering kindred ideas among inquirers of an earlier period; principally, B. Stallo, a German-American whose *Concepts and Theories of Modern Physics* appeared in 1881 and who in very many points, at times even in minute details, is in surprising accord with Mach; and the celebrated English mathematician Clifford (died 1879 in Madeira), who took a related, if not an identical, point of view with that of Mach.[1]

Mach found substantial support for his views also in the philosophical school of Avenarius, while more recent thinkers, like H. Cornelius in Munich, exhibit even greater affinities. In England, again, Karl Pearson has expressed his full agreement with Mach's views on the epistemological foundations of physical science in his book *The Grammar of Science*, the first edition of which appeared in 1892, and the second enlarged edition in 1900.

POSTULATES, HYPOTHESES, AXIOMS AND NATURAL LAWS.

The discussions on this subject have of late centered chiefly about the definitions of such conceptions as "axioms," "postulates," "hypotheses" and "natural laws," the endeavor being to formulate

---

[1]Goethe and Julius Robert Mayer had given expression to views of a similar character. So also had Adam Smith.

s which these traditional conceptions of physics
xent they are permissible and serviceable.
nce to understand in the first place that the
is an entirely superfluous one. Grassmann
ection with regard to the formal sciences as
Ausdehnungslehre, a book which is collaterally
of importance. At the head of arithmetic, he
instead of the customary *axioms*, the follow-
ings:

nbers are said to be equal numbers, when, in
one of them can be substituted for the other.
is said to be greater than another quantity when
able as a part of the former.

itions may be deduced logically the principle
an axiom in the same connection), that "like
like quantities give like results."

ms of logic may be expressed in the form of
nciple of identity is correctly expressed by as-
ys a," and furnishes a definition of the concept
nciple of contradiction is, according to the vary-
gne to it, either equivalent with the first prin-
finition of negation.

physics, the highest and most general principles
y contain definitions, but their contents are not
hese definitions; they are not pure definitions,
by the so-called principle of "particular deter-
by L. Lange and accepted by Mach.[1]
before the law of inertia can be made to have
ed of a system of co-ordinates and a scale of
this principle we are in need of several bodies,
s, as a result of the definitions, must hold

seen in the case of time. The concept "uni-
ned. For this purpose may be chosen a body,

moving with respect to a given system of co-ordinates, the displacements of which body are considered as the measures of time. That motion, then, of a second body is called "uniform" of which the positional displacements are proportional to the displacements of the body of reference. Such a body of reference, for example, is the rotating earth, and the motion of a body is said to be "uniform" when the displacements which it undergoes between the same points of it are proportional to the angle of hours reckoned from the vernal equinox. Absolutely, there is no assignable meaning in speaking of a uniform motion *per se*. The law of inertia has, consequently, with reference to any second new body, the significance of a natural law. It makes with respect to that body an assertion which can be demonstrated experimentally.

Recapitulating, then, we may say that the law of inertia, and, analogously also, the other so-called "axioms" or "postulates," have only a *partial* definitional value, in that, first, they define certain conceptions, but in that, secondly, their contents are not entirely exhausted with the formulation of these definitions; nay, that, on the contrary, inasmuch as the law asserts the universal applicability of these concepts, it employs assertions, of which the actuality may be controlled by experiment. Principles of this character have, therefore, a validity which stands in part only the test of experience (that is, they may not always be borne out by experience), which isolated exceptions it may be possible to harmonize with the principles by the subsequent construction of new and other principles of a more special character. The only genuine test of the value of principles of this sort is the possibility or impossibility of deducing from them a system, or, in better phraseology, of erecting a system on the foundations which they furnish.

Consequently, the decision with regard to the value of the highest and most general principles of physics rests primarily with the outcome of repeatedly continued experimental tests which directly confirm or refute the truth of the more specific principles. The general principles are demonstrated to be serviceable implements of science when the special principles confirmed by experience permit of their being arranged, along with the former, into a single system in which the so-called "postulates" possess the most comprehensive and most general significance.

From this state of matters the conclusion follows immediately that the difference between "postulates" and "natural laws" is a graduated one only. For, that the latter likewise possesses axiomatic, or, as we might more correctly say, definitional, significance, is upon the face of it obvious, though the statement may be enhanced in lucidity by the consideration of its special application to Coulomb's law. Writing this law in the form

$$f = \frac{M_1 M_2}{r^2}$$

where f represents the magnitude of the force M_1 M_2 the numbers measuring the masses, and r the number measuring the distance, by which assertion (on the mere assumption that it is possible to produce equal masses) the unit of mass, but not multiples of that unit, are defined, it will be apparent that it is impossible to determine the numbers which are the measures of these masses by the consideration of two masses only, for the reason that a product can be separated into two factors in different ways. Three masses may be combined in three ways, and hence permit of being uniquely determined from the three equations so obtained; in other words, the law is just sufficient for the definition of the masses of three bodies. The experimental verification of the proportionality of force to product of masses is still impossible so long as we have three bodies only; for these bodies the existence of the law is given by the definition of the three masses. Not until four masses are presented does the law afford an assertion that can be experimentally verified; for these four bodies may be combined in six ways, giving six equations, of which four are employed for determining the unknown quantities M_1, M_2, M_3, M_4, and of which the other two may be employed in the verification of the law by experience.

THE PRINCIPLE OF THE CONSERVATION OF ENERGY.

Many and numerous as are the applications which the principle of the conservation of energy has found in all provinces of physics; great as its import for science in general has become, nevertheless the conceptions of physicists regarding the theoretical nature of this principle are so far apart and discordant that, as Mach says, "opinions regarding the foundations of the law of energy still diverge greatly even at this late day." Similarly variant are the views regarding the position which this principle occupies in theoretical physics. One school of physicists regards it as the highest and the exclusive law of physics, ascribing to it an almost axiomatic import, whilst other inquirers—to mention only Mach, Hertz and Boltzman—have believed themselves called upon to take a most decisive stand against exaggerations of the scope of this principle. Indeed, so far has the conceptual investigation of this principle been neglected that to-day even the form of enunciation in which it appears in most text-books can lay little claim to precision, let alone to correctness. Considered rigorously and unprejudicedly, therefore, the principle of the conservation of energy is wrongly formulated; at least, to express it in Mach's words, "there are limits beyond which the principle can be only artificially maintained."

Nevertheless, it is difficult to define these limits with anything like precision. The fact is that the principle is in contradiction with the second fundamental law of the mechanical theory of heat, and this contradiction must be removed if the logical harshness of the formulation of the principle is to be removed. But the source of the contradiction in question can be found nowhere else than in the concept of energy itself, from which all our assertions are predicated. In point of fact the elucidations of the first inquirers in this field, for instance, the works of Clausius, do not contain this contradiction; but, then, the term "energy" does not as yet appear in them.

What now is "energy?" It is certainly not a substance; certainly not a substantial or real property inherent in a body, as is erroneously believed in many quarters. It is a concept formed, like all other physical concepts, on the basis of definite given facts, though not ceasing on this ground to be an arbitrary creation of our intellect. And in point of reality the concept of "energy" has been so formed and selected that it shall supply fully the needs of the principle of "energy."

The facts upon which its formation rests are the following: In the domain of mechanics exists a large number of motions of which the property of reversibility is a characteristic feature, just as in the cycle of Carnot. When, for example, a body falls a certain distance, it can be made to rise again the same distance by simply reversing the direction of its velocity. This peculiarity of the phenomenon of motion was conceived as a *capacity* of the body, and was designated "its living force." Inasmuch as the body has at every point of its path "the power" to evoke another like motion, differing in direction only, inquirers were led to speak of the constancy of living force; always positive because direction was not regarded. Hence resulted the principle of the "conservation of living forces," the applicability of which is strictly limited to reversible processes of the kind described.

In the case of friction, which is a non-reversible process, the principle does not hold—a conclusion which is mathematically expressed by saying that the principle loses its validity as soon as forces appear which are dependent on velocity. But since, in such cases, a body loses living force, it was an obnoxious suggestion to regard the heat which made its appearance as the *equivalent* of that force.

The word "equivalent" must not be misunderstood. Heat is not a real "equivalent," for the reason that it is impossible to reverse the process, and because also the process can take place only in one direction. Nevertheless, it is possible to conceive this heat as a partial summand of the total energy of the body and to add it to energy of some other kind. Again, it must not be forgotten that this heat, or this part of the energy of the body, represents no capacity whatever to perform work, but has simply the significance that it can, and actually does, become the equivalent of work when a transformation of heat into work takes place. This condition can under no circumstance be left out of consideration (as has hitherto been the custom in defining energy), for the reason that there is absolutely no necessity that the said transformation should be possible. Consequently, the principle of the conservation of energy simply informs us, when a transformation of energy takes place, what the ratio is in which that transformation is accomplished.

It may be remarked further, that the truth of the principle of energy assumes that the manner of measuring homologous quantities is the same in the different departments of physics. As a matter of fact, the modes of measuring quantities of heat and electrical work are homologous with the modes of measuring mechanical work. But this would not be the case were not the potential, or the difference of level, of the electrical states of two bodies measured by units of mechanical work—for which state of things there is no real logical necessity. Otherwise the law of energy would not be applicable to electrical phenomenon, and, in place of simple proportionality, which can be transformed into equality by the simple choice of an appropriate unit of measure, would be substituted a more complicated function.

The stability of the law of energy is thus essentially dependent on our arbitrarily selected definitions of the fundamental concepts of physics; the possibility of its existence is dependent on the presence of an equation between the different groups of physical concepts of measurement.

A genuine law of nature, in the sense usually supposed, this principle is not, even though certain actual facts are at the basis of the assumption of its validity.

Ordinarily we think, when we hear the law of the conservation of energy—not so much of energy in the sense above described as of energy in the sense of *capacity to perform work*—which, as we have seen from what has gone before, are two distinctly different things. But if in the place of energy we take as the essence of our principle capacity to do work, then this principle assumes an entirely different form. In this last case nothing more can be generally affirmed than that the capacity to do work has remained constant, when the passage from the first to the second state as well as from the second to the first is *possible*, or, when, as we say, we are concerned with a reversible cycle.

The principle of the constancy of capacity to do work *is thus restricted to cyclic processes,* and is none other than Clausius' principle of the equivalence of transformation, which is one of the forms of the second law of the mechanical theory of heat.

Processes which are not reversible, as, for example, friction, or the passage of heat from higher to lower temperatures, result in the *dissipation* of capacity to do work. Since, in considering the principle of energy, it has been customary to adhere rigidly to this last-mentioned meaning of the word, it will be apparent that the principle of the conservation of energy, as thus formulated, was incorrect, and we now know also what the limits mentioned by Mach are, "beyond which this principle lost its validity."

It will at the same time be apparent that this second principle is a more appropriate expression of a characteristic peculiarity of our nature than is the second—which furnishes us merely with an equation between our own concepts. The reason for this is that the second principle is more intimately associated with the phenomena of nature and is not so much concerned with the properties of bodies as they are assumed to be by us.

The results of the foregoing inquiry are, then, the following:

1. The principle of the conservation of energy is in its present form incorrect.

2. A distinction must be made between "energy" and "capacity to do work."

3. Whether the first or the second concept is embodied in the principle mentioned, are obtained in its place two laws; namely, the first and the second laws of the mechanical theory of heat.

Furthermore, and finally, the special importance of reversible cyclic processes in all the departments of physics is made apparent. Thus, without a consideration of the concept of reversible processes, it would appear to be utterly unfeasible to attempt a formulation of the principle of energy, and on the grounds which have been adduced the introduction of the two first laws of the theory of heat into instruction in physics in secondary schools would appear to present no objections.

HANS KLEINPETER.

GMUNDEN, AUSTRIA.

MADAME BLAVATSKY.

I.

THE grand discovery of the nineteenth century is the absolute unity and immutability of Nature's laws. It would seem that this would be the death blow to superstitions of all kinds, particularly of magic arts, etc. But such is not the case. Astrology, chiromancy, theosophy and the occult sciences "occupy a large place in modern thought, literature and polite society on both sides of the Atlantic.

The tendency to cultivate the esoteric manifests itself in the study of the Cabala, the investigation of the mysteries of Buddhism, Confucianism and other oriental philosophies, in researches into the phenomena of spiritualism, so called, and in the foundation of societies to study psychic force and the tenets of the followers of Madame Blavatsky; crystal-gazing, reading in magic mirrors, slate-writing, planchette, the quasi-scientific study of apparitions, of table-turning, of rappings by unseen powers, of telepathy, of the subliminal self, etc. Look, for example, at the advertising columns of the *New York Herald*, and read the long list of clairvoyants, magic healers, magnetizers, palmists, astrologers, and spirit mediums.

The remarkable revival of occult arts in this age of ours is a source of wonder to scientific men. The reason is not difficult to divine. It is a reaction against the rampant materialism of the times. Extremes meet. The pendulum swings as far forward as backward.

Science declares the age of miracles and magic is passed. In one sense this is true. But says Thomas Carlyle: "This world, after all our science and sciences, is still a miracle; wonderful, inscrutable, *magical* and more, to whosoever will think of it. That great mystery of Time, were there no other; the illimitable, silent, never-resting thing called Time, rolling, rushing on swift, silent, like an all-embracing ocean-tide, on which we and all the universe swim like exhalations, like apparitions which *are*, and then *are not;* this is forever very literally a miracle; a thing to strike us dumb."

The materialism of the age seeks to crush out the strivings of the soul after the divine life, to deny God and immortality. The psychic in man is but an epiphenomenon, the result of the "fortuitous collocation of atoms"—dissipated at death. The Cosmos is directed by a blind, insensate Force.

> "A moment's Halt—a momentary taste
> Of BEING from the Well amid the Waste—
> And Lo!—the phantom caravan has reacht
> The NOTHING it set out from—oh, make haste."

Crushed by such negations, tender souls take refuge either in the dogmatisms of historical religious creeds, in liberal Christianity as exemplified by Unitarianism, or else in the various forms of mysticism in vogue to-day: Spiritism, Christian science, Theosophy, etc., etc. There are also many students of philosophy, not attached to any particular religious faith, or school of occultism, who take a spiritualistic conception of the cosmos and man.

Many noted men have been numbered among this latter body of idealistic thinkers. They argue as follows with great cogency: "It is not conceivable that, if only matter existed, it could, by any effort of its inherent forces, produce Reason, Intelligence, Thought, or even that limited Reason which we call Instinct. Nothing can by exercise or operation of the forces which belong to it create qualities of a higher nature than itself possesses. The effect cannot be of a higher nature than the cause, or derive from it qualities higher than any which it possesses, or radically different from them. Only Intelligence, or something higher than Intelligence, could produce the human intellect or the animal instinct. To that Intelligence must be ascribed everything that displays design in the universe."

The learned scientist, Joseph Le Conte, in his *Evolution and Religious Thought*, has written as follows, on the proof of personality behind Nature: "If the brain of a living, thinking man were exposed to the scrutiny of an outside observer with absolutely perfect senses, all that he would or could possibly see would be molecular motions, physical and chemical. But the subject himself, the thinking, self-conscious spirit, would experience and observe by introspection only consciousness, thought, emotions, etc. On the *outside*, only physical phenomena; on the *inside*, only psychical phenomena. Now, *must not the same be necessarily true of Nature also?* Viewed from the outside of the scientific observer, nothing is seen, nothing can be seen, there is nothing else to be seen, but motions, material phenomena; but behind these, on the other side, on the *inside*, must not there be in this case also psychical phenomena, consciousness, thought, will; in a word, *personality?* In the only place where we do get behind physical phenomena, viz., in the brain, we find psychical phenomena. Are we not justified, then, in concluding that in all cases the psychical lies behind the physical? . . . . Thus then we see that our self-conscious personality behind brain phenomena compels us to accept consciousness, will, thought, personality behind nature."

"The star-lit sky above, the law within—
These are of truth the witnesses sublime,
To which man's heart has hearkened in all time,
As to deep voice heard 'mid the battle's din.
Beneath the stars, in presence of the soul
Far from the whirl, the noise, the strife, the glare
Of the vain world, come visions of the whole,
Which His eternal hands make and upbear;
We read the writing of the mystic scroll,
And know that life means hope, and not despair."

"God geometrizes," says the profound Plato. The heavens are crystalized mathematics. Where there is mathematics there is evidence of design, of mind. Writes the great French astronomer, Camille Flammarion: "The existence of God is incontestable, for without it, it would be impossible to explain the existence of intelligence in the creation of mathematics (which man has not invented but discovered), of intellectual and moral truth. . . . . God, then, is a pure Spirit or rather *the* pure Spirit, self-conscious and conscious of each infinitesimal part of the entire universe, personal but without form, infinite and eternal."

Granting the existence of "an eternal and infinite spirit, the intellectual organizer of the mathematical laws which the physical forces obey," and conceiving ourselves as individualized points of life in that greater life, for "in God we live, move, and have our being," spiritual thinkers declare that we bear within us the undying spark of divinity and immortality.

Says Le Conte: "Without immortality there would be no conceivable meaning in human life, nor, indeed, in the complex structure and elaborate evolution of the Cosmos itself. Every evolution must, by definition, have an end. Every cycle of material changes must finally close. Now suppose the human race, or, indeed, the Cosmos itself, to have run its course, as it inevitably must finally. When all is done and the cycle closed—what then? Evidently without immortality it would be exactly as if it had never been at all. The whole elaborate history of the Cosmos and of the organic kingdom, occupying inconceivable time and culminating in man, would be but an idle dream, an idiot tale, signifying—nothing! Can we by reason accept a conclusion which is a stultification of reason? Now the belief in God and immortality is not only universal—unless destroyed by a shallow scientific philosophy—but was at all times, is now, and ever will be, a necessary condition of human improvement. Without it man would never have emerged out of animality into humanity, or, having thus emerged, would never have risen above the lowest possible stages. It is simply inconceivable that what has ever been the necessary condition of human progress should have no foundation in the laws of nature, should have no objective reality corresponding thereto."

Or take the following statement:

> "The Universe is the body of God;
> Humanity is the soul of God;
> God Himself is the spirit of God."

"From this we recognize the truth of the opinion of the Pantheists, who declared that God was the universe; but we also see their error, when they refuse to acknowledge in him any innate consciousness. For as the consciousness of man is independent of the millions of cells which compose his body, so the consciousness of God is independent of the molecules of the universe and of man which form its body and its soul. We might partly destroy the universe without in any way diminishing the Divine Personality, even as the four limbs can be cut off a man without his losing the consciousness of the integrity of his personality. This is why the conclusions of Schopenhauer and Hartmann are partly erroneous. . . . God is the Absolute, the essence of which is impenetrable, formed of the universe as body, of humanity as soul, and of himself as spirit."[1]

Strong minds may hold a rational belief in Theism and immortality, based upon the conclusions of the sanest thinkers of the idealistic school, tempered and restrained by science, like Martineau, Le Conte and John Fiske, without committing excesses in metaphysics, but weak minds with a mystical trend are prone to fall victims to the psychical epidemics of the age, and to follow blindly such leaders as Mary Baker Eddy, Dowie, Blavatsky, and the like.

Of all the occult movements which have affected modern thought, theosophy is the most interesting to the student. Theosophy is on a higher metaphysical plane than spiritualism, and has drawn upon the Orient for its inspiration. We look to the East for light, but when it comes to mental illumination, we find, alas, much that is *dark!* Yes, from out of the mysterious East have proceeded most of the superstitions that have hypnotized the minds of the Western thinkers. It is the land of wonders and paradoxes. Hand

---

[1]Even Nomotheism, which abandons the idea that God is a being, a person, or an individual of any kind, but characterises him as the superpersonal presence of the Eternal that shapes and creates the world, manifesting himself in natural laws, does not brook materialism, nor denies the spirituality that prevades the Cosmos. Dr. Paul Carus may, in the opinion of supporters of the traditional belief in God, go to the verge of Atheism, but he recognizes the significance of facts spiritual and the indispensableness of the idea of immortality.

in hand with the most grotesque idol worship is a metaphysics of remarkable subtlety. It is the land of contrasts. A renaissance in the East, says a well-known writer, means a new religion; a renaissance in the West signifies the death of a religion and the growth of positive knowledge. 'Tis well said! The Orient is immersed in a dream; the Occident is awake and acting. The East is well symbolized by a gigantic sphinx, half buried in shifting sand, brooding upon the problem of existence and dreaming the eternal dream of spirit. To escape repeated transmigration; to become one with Brahma, ah! that is the supreme desire of the Eastern sage.

The modern theosophical movement is chiefly to be studied in the career of a single individual—Madame Helena Petrovna Blavatsky, a Russian by birth, who was the founder of the Theosophical Society. Dr. Elliot Coues has called her "the she-Cagliostro of the 19th Century." In the past centuries, the greatest charlatans have been men, for example, Alexander of Abonitichos, Apollonius of Tyana, Comte de St. Germain, Mesmer and Cagliostro; but *place aux dames*, the wheel is bound to turn. This nineteenth century being the age of woman's rights, it is only natural that the greatest charlatan should be a woman—and such a woman, big, fat, frowsy, and gross-looking, a tremendous smoker of cigarettes; possessed of a horrible temper and a vocabulary of words not to be found in works on etiquette, but withal a female of extraordinary mental acumen and personal magnetism, who had the honor of introducing a religious cult to the Western world—a cult that now numbers its adherents by the thousands.

Let us turn aside at this juncture to ask, "What is Theosophy?" The word Theosophy (Theo-sophia—divine knowledge) appears to have been used about the third century, A. D., by the Neo-Platonists, or Gnostics of Alexandria, but the great principles of the doctrine, however, were taught hundreds of years prior to the mystical school established at Alexandria. "It is not," says an interesting writer on the subject, "an outgrowth of Buddhism, although many Buddhists see in its doctrines the reflection of Buddha. It professes to give its followers the esoteric, or inner-spiritual meaning of the great religious teachers of the world. It asserts repeated reincarnations, or rebirths of the soul on earth, until it is fully purged of evil, and becomes fit to be absorbed into Deity whence it came, gaining thereby Nirvana, or unconsciousness." Some theosophists claim that Nirvana is not a state of unconsciousness, but just the converse, a state of the most intensified consciousness, during which the soul remembers all of its previous incarnations.

I shall now introduce Madame Blavatsky to the reader, through the medium of Colonel Olcott, whose striking pen picture of her is worthy of record.

II.

In the year 1874 Colonel Henry S. Olcott, a special correspondent of the *New York Graphic,* was sent to investigate the alleged spiritistic phenomena occurring in the Eddy family of Chittenden, Vt. The place where the ghosts were materialized was a large apartment over the dining-room of the antiquated homestead. A dark closet, with a rough blanket hung in front of it, was the cabinet. From this cabinet the shades of the departed came forth to hold converse with the awe-struck sitters, who had come from far and near to witness the phenomena. Olcott not only saw the ghosts, but he met his fate in the shape of a Russian occultist, who came to the place to acquaint herself with the methods of American spiritualists. But let me quote the journalist's own words:

"My eye was first attracted by a scarlet Garibaldian skirt the former wore, as being in vivid contrast with the dull colors around. Her hair was then a thick blond mop, worn shorter than the shoulders, and it stood out from her head, silken, soft, and crinkled to the roots, like the fleece of a Cotswold ewe. This and the red skirt were what struck my attention before I took in the picture of her features. It was a massive Kalmuck face, contrasting in its suggestion of power, culture and imperiousness, as strangely with the commonplace visages about the room as her red garment did with the gray and white tones of the wall and woodwork, and the dull costumes of the rest of the guests."

Colonel Olcott scraped an acquaintance with this eccentric character. She informed him that she was Madame Hélène Petrovna

Hahn-Hahn Blavatsky, a Russian lady of distinction, a believer in spiritism and a student of occultism, who had traveled in Egypt and India, searching for "antiquities at the base of the pyramids, witnessing the mysteries of Hindoo temples, and pushing with an armed escort far into the interior of Africa."

She discoursed learnedly of the "astral plane," of French and English spiritism, and fascinated Olcott with reminiscences of foreign travel. Little did he imagine at the moment that she was to develop into the greatest pythoness of the age, the introducer into the Occident of a new religious cult, the modern priestess of Isis; and that he, the prosaic newspaper reporter, would evolute into her coadjutor and Grand Hierophant of the Mysteries, the greatest and most ardent exponent of her so-called system of occultism and magic.

No sooner had Madame Blavatsky arrived than spirits from Russia, the Caucasus, India and Egypt materialized in the Eddy ghost cabinet. The *mise-en-scène* changed to an Oriental and barbaric background, in honor of the great progenitor of modern theosophy. Among other things that took place was "the writing of Madame Blavatsky's name upon a card, by a spirit hand, *in Russian script.*"

"But," says Colonel Olcott, "I doubt if any circle ever witnessed a more astonishing spiritual feat than that which I am about to relate.

"The evening of October 24 (1874) was as bright as day with the light of the moon, and, while there was a good deal of moisture in the air, the atmospheric conditions would, I suppose, have been regarded as favorable for manifestations. In the dark-circle, as soon as the light was extinguished, 'George Dix' (a spirit control of the Eddy brothers), addressing Madame de Blavatsky, said: 'Madame, I am now about to give you a test of the genuineness of the manifestations in this circle, which I think will satisfy not only you, but a skeptical world besides. I shall place in your hands the buckle of a medal of honor worn in life by your brave father, and buried with his body in Russia. This has been brought to you by your uncle, whom you have seen materialized this evening.' Presently I heard

herself to be the messenger of the mahatmas to the scoffing world.

Theosophy would have amounted to little had it not been for the fact that it was exploited by the Theosophical Society, an organization which saw the light of day in New York, October 30, 1875. Madame Blavatsky is generally credited by her followers with being its founder, but there is considerable doubt on this point. As originally organized the society was not intended as a medium for the propogation of esoteric Buddhism and Brahmanism, but for the prosecution of psychical studies. A lecture given in New York City by a certain George H. Felt, before a select coterie of ghost-seers, primarily led to the founding of the Theosophical Society.

The term "theosophy" was chosen expressly on the basis of the first meaning given to that word in Webster's Dictionary: "Any system of philosophy or mysticism which proposes to attain intercourse with God and superior spirits, and consequent superhuman knowledge, by physical processes, as by the theurgic operations of some ancient Platonists, or by the chemical processes of the German fire-philosophers." Hence the first sentence of the original preamble of the Theosophical Society reads: "The title of the Theosophical Society explains the objects and desires of its founders; they seek to obtain knowledge of the nature and attributes of the Supreme Power and of the higher spirits by the aid of physical processes."

Mr. Arthur Lillie, author of the remarkable work, *Madame Blavatsky and Her "Theosophy,"* writes as follows regarding the foundation of the Theosophical Society. He takes his facts mainly from Colonel Olcott and Mrs. Hardinge Britten, an original member of the Society. The Cairo experiences (of the Madame) being more recent than the Thibetan, the Theosophical Society was at first Egyptian as to its local color.

Its moving spirit was a Mr. Felt, who had visited Egypt and studied its antiquities. He was a student also of the Cabala, and he had a somewhat eccentric theory that the dog-headed and hawk-headed figures painted on the Egyptian monuments were not mere symbols, but accurate portraits of the "Elementals." He professed to be able to evoke and control them. He announced that he had discovered the secret "formularies" of the old Egyptian magicians.

Plainly, the Theosophical Society at starting was an *Egyptian* School of occultism. Indeed, Colonel Olcott, who furnishes these details ("Diary Leaves" in the *Theosophist*, November to December, 1892), lets out that the first title suggested was the "Egyptological Society."

Madame Blavatsky's mind, in short, was adaptive rather than original.

"She took spiritualism from Home, the Brothers of Luxor from Colonel Olcott, the notion of controlling "Elementals" from Mr. Felt. And hearing for the first time about Mahatmas from Dayânanda Sarasvati, she promptly assimilated them likewise."

In this occult society Madame Blavatsky came rapidly to the front and began to exploit the vagaries of Indian mysticism. Strange reports were set afloat concerning the mysterious appearance of a Hindoo adept in his astral body at the Society headquarters on Forty-seventh street. It was said to be that of a certain Mahatma Koot Hoomi, who left behind him as a souvenir of his presence a turban, which was exhibited on all occasions by Colonel Olcott.

After seeing the Society well established in America the modern priestess of Isis went to India, accompanied by Colonel Olcott.

She went first to Bombay, thence to Madras, and afterward to Adyar. A rambling East Indian bungalow was fitted up as the headquarters of the Theosophical Society, and a certain M. and Mme. Coulomb were installed as librarian and assistant corresponding secretary. One of the rooms of the bungalow was fitted up as an occult cabinet, or séance apartment, with a cupboard against the wall, known as the "shrine." In this shrine letters were received from the mahatmas, and from it were sent by a sort of spiritual post located somewhere in the fourth dimension of space. Astral appearances of adepts were seen in the room and about the grounds of the building. The news spread like wild-fire. Anglo-Indian theosophists flocked to the place. The genuineness of the phenomena was not doubted. But now Madame Blavatsky quarreled with the Coulombs. During her absence in Europe with Colonel Olcott, in 1884, the Coulombs were expelled from their positions by the general council of the Society. In revenge they published parts o certain letters purporting to have been written them by the high priestess, in the *Madras Christian College Magazine*. "These letters, if genuine, unquestionably implicated Madame Blavatsky in a conspiracy to produce marvelous phenomena fraudulently."

The London Society for Psychical Research sent Doctor Richard Hodgson to India to investigate the matter and report upon the "occult phenomena" produced at the bungalow. His report, published in the transactions of the society for 1885, is most voluminous and painstaking. After perusing it no sane person can doubt the truth of his statements, viz., that jugglery and trickery were used to accomplish the so-called transportation of ponderable objects, including letters, through solid matter; the "precipitation" of handwriting and drawings on previously blank paper; astral appearances, et cetera.

Doctor Hodgson sums up his case as follows:

"1. She (Madame Blavatsky) has been engaged in a long-continued combination with other persons to produce by ordinary means a series of apparent marvels for the support of the theosophic movement.

"2. That in particular the shrine at Adyar, through which letters purporting to come from mahatmas were received, was elaborately arranged with a view to the secret insertion of letters and other objects through a sliding panel at the back, and regularly used for the purpose by Madame Blavatsky or her agents.

"3. That there is consequently a very strong general presumption that all the marvelous narratives put forward in evidence of the existence of mahatmas are to be explained as due either (a) to deliberate deception carried out by, or at the instigation of, Madame Blavatsky, or (b) to spontaneous illusion or hallucination, or unconscious misrepresentation or invention on the part of witnesses."

Sliding panels, secret doors and disguises constituted the *deus ex machina* of the theosophic mysteries.

Sitting in a London drawing room, usually her own, Madame would frequently exhibit her favorite tricks of the precipitated writing and the Indian mail. Someone would express a desire to have certain questions expounded by a mahatma.

"Behold!" the sibyl would cry, "the masters have come to your aid." Suddenly a mysterious envelope, covered with strange characters, would flutter apparently from the ceiling, or else be found in some out-of-the-way spot. On tearing open this envelope a letter from an eastern adept would be found, answering the queries. A confederate, of course, was employed to "materialize" the missive. Thanks to her really remarkable conversational powers, Madame Blavatsky was able to adroitly lead people into asking questions that would tally with the mahatma message.

A number of books have been written about Madame Blavatsky and her theosophy. Perhaps the most interesting is that of the Russian journalist and litterateur, Vsevolod S. Solovyoff, who was in Paris in 1884, studying occult literature and preparing to write a treatise on psychic research. One day he read in the *Matin* that Madame Blavatsky had arrived in Paris. With a letter of introduction from a friend in St. Petersburg he visited the priestess at her residence in the Rue Notre Dame des Champs—a long mean street on the left bank of the Seine. He says: "I climbed a very, very dark staircase, rang, and a slovenly figure in an Oriental turban admitted me into a tiny dark lobby. To my question whether Madame Blavatsky would receive me the slovenly figure replied with an 'Entrez, monsieur,' and vanished with my card, while I was left to wait in a small, low room, poorly and insufficiently furnished.

"I had not long to wait. The door opened, and she was before me; a rather tall woman, though she produced the impression of being short, on account of her unusual stoutness. Her great head seemed all the greater from her thick and very bright hair, touched with a scarcely perceptible gray, and a trifle frizzed—by nature and not by art, as I subsequently convinced myself.

" . . . . I remarked that she was very strangely dressed, in a sort of black sacque, and that all the fingers of her small, soft and, as it were, boneless hands, with their slender points and long nails, were covered with great jeweled rings."

So much for a striking pen picture of the pythoness. Madame received her fellow countryman most cordially. She begged him to join the Theosophical Society, and produced for him her astra-bell henomenon. She excused herself to see to some domestic duty, nd on her return to the sitting room the phenomenon occurred. Says the journalist: "She made a sort of flourish with her hand, aised it upward, and suddenly I heard distinctly, quite distinctly, omewhere above our heads, near the ceiling, a very melodious sound ike a little silver bell or an Æolian harp.

"'What is the meaning of this?' I asked.

"'This means only that my master is here, although you and I cannot see him. He tells me that I may trust you, and am to do for you whatever I can. Vous êtes sous sa protection, henceforth and forever.'"

Solovyoff was not convinced of the genuineness of the phenomenon, but he said nothing to the madame. He asked himself this question: "Why was the sound of the silver bell not heard at once, but only after she had left the room and come back again?" However, he joined the society, and kept his eyes open.

Madame Blavatsky introduced him to the hierophant Olcott, who showed him the turban that had been left at the New York headquarters by Mahatma Koot Hoomi.

In August, 1885, he visited the madame at Wurzberg, Germany. It was after the Coulomb affair, and she was sick at heart and in body. A little Hindoo servant, Bavaji, was her sole attendant at the Spa.

"Every day," writes Solovyoff, "when I came to see the madame she used to try to do me a favor in the shape of some trifling 'phenomenon,' but she never succeeded. Thus one day her famous 'silver bell' was heard, when suddenly something fell beside her to the ground. I hurried to pick it up and found in my hands a pretty little piece of silver, delicately worked and strangely shaped. Hélena Petrovna changed countenance and snatched the object from me. I coughed significantly, smiled, and turned the conversation to indifferent matters."

At another time he was talking with her about the "Theosophist," and she mentioned the name of Subba Rao, a Hindoo, who had "attained the highest degree of knowledge." She requested the journalist to open a drawer in her writing desk and take from it a photograph of the adept.

"I opened the drawer," says Solovyoff, "found the photograph and handed it to her, together with a packet of Chinese envelopes, such as I well knew; they were the same in which the 'elect' used to receive the letters of the Mahatmas Morya and Koot Hoomi by 'astral post.'

"'Look at that, Hélèna Petrovna! I should advise you to hide this packet of the master's envelopes farther off. You are so terribly absent-minded and careless.'"

Terrible was the rage of the high priestess of Isis at thus being detected. Her face grew as black as midnight. "She tried in vain to speak, but could only writhe helpless in her great armchair."

Solovyoff declares he then adroitly drew a confession from her. She said: "What is one to do when in order to rule men it is necessary to deceive them?" She begged him to go into a copartnership with her to astonish the world. He refused.

Then, after repeated denials of fraud, she broke down utterly and wrote him, according to his statement, a full confession of her many impostures. This confession she subsequently denied and declared a forgery. Forgery or not, the Paris theosophists believed it genuine, and their lodges were disrupted in consequence.

Soon after this event the great occultist went to England and made a convert of Annie Besant, the socialist, authoress and atheist. Finally came the end. The high priestess died in London, May 8, 1891. Her body was cremated and the ashes were divided into three equal portions, one of which was sent to Adyar, India, one to New York, and the third retained in London. The American shrine is a marble niche in the wall of the Theosophical headquarters, 144 Madison avenue. The ashes repose in a bronze urn.

And so ended the famous priestess of Isis. To her followers she was the greatest worker of miracles since the Christ. Once a year they celebrate the anniversary of her death. The day is called White Lotus day; why, I know not. The lotus in the East is the symbol of purity; it also typifies the doctrine of perpetual cycles of existence. The reader can make his or her own application of the emblem.

The question may now be asked: "Did Madame Blavatsky really

possess any occult powers, or was she simply a juggler with a well-rehearsed repertoire of sleight-of-hand tricks?" Such phenomena as the materialization of roses, astral-bell sounds and answers to sealed letters are well-known feats to any medium or conjurer. They are not dependent upon the exercise of psychic powers, but are effected by legerdemain. However, after all is said, I am of the opinion that she possessed one faculty bordering on the marvelous, namely, the power of hypnotizing, but like all hypnotizers she had to have a good subject. There are many people that are not hypnotizable, consequently she, like other alleged psychics, had to resort to trickery on many occasions to accomplish her ends.

I quote the following by Hereward Carrington, published in *Mahatma* not long ago. It may not be strictly scientific, but it is very interesting indeed: "Two of the principal phenomena that occurred, and of which Mr. Sinnett (a writer on Madame Blavatsky) makes the most, are 'the brooch incident' and 'the pillow incident.' Of these we will consider the 'pillow incident' only, as being the more perfect of the two. The following is a brief summary of the pillow incident: A party, including Madame, had gone to lunch, and were on the top of a hill, when Madame suddenly asked in what place Mr. Sinnett would like the article to appear, which he was expecting. It was very clearly stated that this expected article, a brooch, was not mentioned by Mr. Sinnett before and the subject had *not been led up to in any way*. This is the crucial point of the whole test. Mr. Sinnett thought a moment and then said: 'Inside that cushion.' He had no sooner uttered the word than his wife cried out, 'Oh, no, let it be inside mine.' This was agreed on. The cushion was now covered with a rug for about a minute; when it was opened, inside that was a second cushion. In the very center of this latter was found the brooch and a note from Koot Hoomi—the more important and communicative of the two mahatmas. But the brooch and the cushion had been in the Sinnett family for a number of years, so that the 'test' appeared to be absolutely conclusive.

"The principal point in this test is that the expected article was not mentioned before in any way. Apparently, then, the answer to the question was entirely haphazard, and had never crossed Mr. Sinnett's mind before that instant. If that was the case the 'pillow incident' was certainly remarkable, but the writer holds that such was not the case.

"It must be acknowledged by all, that if Madame could have by any means foretold the place that was to be chosen as the recipient of the article, it would have been an easy matter to have placed it in there beforehand and triumphantly produced it at the critical moment. The only thing that would require careful manipulation would be the 'forcing' of that particular place on the victim. But there was *no* forcing in this case, as Mr. Sinnett is particular in reminding the reader, consequently it could not have been done in that subtle way.

"Madame pursued a much bolder plan, and, in the writer's opinion, caused the choices to fall upon the prepared places by means of employing post-hypnotic suggestions.

"Hypnotism is, undoubtedly, a true science, though there are so many humbugs playing under its 'role.' That it was known in India many hundreds of years ago, there cannot be the least doubt; moreover, it is much used by the yogis of the present day.

"What would be more natural, then, than to suppose that Madame should have learned the art in her sojourn in the East, and bringing it into the world—to which it was still somewhat new—in a little different form, she should have employed it, in many instances, to startling effect?

"As it does not necessarily follow that all magicians are acquainted with this subject, it may be said that post-hypnotic suggestion is a suggestion given to the *sensitive* (or person under the hypnotic influence), but which is not carried out until after he is again restored to perfect consciousness. Such suggestions seem to rise spontaneously from the mind of the subject, and *not* as if they had been previously suggested by the 'operator.' It seems to be merely the accidental thought of such a person.

"Now in the greatest of all 'tests,' viz., 'the pillow incident' Madame could easily have placed the brooch in the cushion beforehand, then quietly hypnotized Mr. Sinnett and his wife the eveni before, and *suggested* that they should choose the cushion on being asked where they would like the brooch to reappear. When asked, the choice naturally fell on the prepared cushion.

"If Madame had failed, nothing would have been said about it, but as she succeeded, a grand 'test' was the result."

Madame Blavatsky is known to the world of letters as a writer of two ponderous works of a philosophical or mystical character, explanatory of the esoteric doctrine, viz., *Isis Unveiled*, published in 1877, and the *Secret Doctrine*, published in 1888. In the composition of these works she claimed "that she was assisted by the mahatmas who visited her apartments when she was asleep, and wrote portions of the manuscripts with their astral hands while their natural bodies reposed entranced in Thibetan lamaseries. These fictions were fostered by prominent members of the Theosophical Society, and believed by many credulous persons."

Madame Blavatsky had a very imperfect knowledge of Oriental languages, and this fact may account for the ludicrous mistakes in which the volumes abound, despite the aid of the ghostly mahatmas, who ought to have known better. Mr. William Emmette Coleman of San Francisco has made an exhaustive analysis of the madame's writings, and declares that *Isis* and the *Secret Doctrine* are full of plagiarisms. In *Isis* he discovered some two thousand passages copied from other books without proper credit.

Mr. Lillie, who had lived much in India and is an accomplished Orientalist, further questions the stories of Madame Blavatsky's Thibetan training and the Hindoo education, from internal evidence —her ignorance of Sanskrit as exposed by Max Müller, of the meanings of words commonly understood; the use of words professedly native but really inventions of her own; and the anachronisms displayed in her descriptions.

In *Isis Unveiled*, vol. ii, p. 609, is this statement: "We met a great many nuns traveling from Lha Sa to Kandi. . . . They take refuge in caves or viharas prepared by their co-religionists at calculated distances."

What would be thought of a modern traveler who announced that along the roads of Sussex he had met numbers of the "Valas" or prophetesses of Woden, and that at the stone circles, where they stopped for the night, mead and the flesh of the boar Sæhrimmer were doled out to them? Buddhist viharas and Buddhist nuns have disappeared from Hindustan quite as long as the priests of Woden from England.

Besides, as Mr. Spence Hardy tells us, there are no female recluses in Ceylon. (*Eastern Monachism*, p. 61.)

He also shows the discrepancies between historical facts and Madame Blavatsky's autobiography—the gap in the story of her existence between October, 1848, when she fled from her husband, and May, 1857, a period when she was supposed to be in Thibet, though during the same period she was known to be in Paris and also in New Orleans.

Says the journalist, William T. Stead: "She was a woman who allowed herself to become the sport of circumstance, who organized her life by opportunism and ignored principle. The beautiful truths of Buddhism, which have deservedly exercised great influence on human thought, were but very superficially understood by Madame Blavatsky, who utilized them as she utilized magic or spiritualism when it served her turn, for her own ends."

Says Arthur Lillie: Madame Blavatsky's theosophy had one consistent principle—opportunism. Her "Esoteric Buddhism" was designed to win over the rich Hindoos, and to do this she was obliged to dethrone Brahma, Vishnu and Rama, and to put in their places the Mahatmas, the Dhyan Chohans. These Dhyan Chohans made the Kosmos, as Mr. Sinnett tells us. But as they are still alive in Thibet they confront us with a difficulty. Without a world there could be no Dhyan Chohans, and without Dhyan Chohans there could be no world. Then Madame Blavatsky had to get rid of the Indian ghost worship. Her mind, as I have often stated, lacks originality. But a book by an eccentric Frenchman gave her a hint.

This was the *Haute Magie* of Eliphas Levi. We here see how many million miles away the "Buddhism" of Madame Blavatsky was from that of Buddha. Supposing that there are mahatmas and that the Russian lady's miracles were genuine, does that take far? Madame Blavatsky, a pauper, desired to use her magic ain the lakhs of rupees of Mr. Sassoon and Holkar. Buddha, ng a crown and countless gold pieces, desired to become a pauper. ame Blavatsky had an ambition to astound the vulgar with icated diamond rings and astral postoffices. Buddha contemned nonds and false applause. Madame Blavatsky worked entirely he plane of matter, and sought to demolish Brahma and his le-s. Buddha worked entirely on the plane of spirit, and sought immortal world of Brahma, and the soul growth.

Had Madame Blavatsky contented herself with exploiting Ve-taism and the so-called Esoteric Buddhism, all would have been , and her following would have grown like the proverbial rolling wball; but, alas, the madame was not content to pose as a phil-pher of the occult and a missionary of Oriental doctrines, but yed to bolster up her cause with pretended miracles and absurd ies of mahatmas. She was bound, like many mystical thinkers, produce her Apocalypse for the edification and the stultifica-of her disciples. Her miracles were not above the average of inary conjuring and hypnotic feats, and the mahatma stories e as wildly improbable as those invented by the mythical Baron nchausen.

We are living in an age of science where the searchlight of ical investigation is focused upon everything purporting to deal h the Unknown. The age of miracles is passed. The reign of is upon us. Madame Blavatsky failed to take cognizance of this portant factor when she propagated her Theosophical cult. Her hatma revelations—especially those of Koot Hoomi and Morya—re too absurd to be believed. The theosophical card-castle, which I had erected with such patience and care, fell to the ground. ndreds of intelligent theosophists left the Society, among them ctor Elliott Canes, the eminent ornithologist. It is only fair to as regards the societies existing to-day that no more miracles worked to convince the skeptics. The order is largely given to the earnest study of Vedantaism, Buddhism and Neo-Platon-, and much honest and earnest work is being accomplished; es-lally so is this in the city of Washington, where the prime movers of Theosophy are composed of ladies and gentlemen of intelligence. The charlataine side of Madame Blavatsky's character has been forgotton or covered with the mantle of charity. Her name is now revered as that of the founder of the Theosophical movement and the author of many curious works on the occult.

After the death of Madame Blavatsky there arose two claimants for the mantle of the great High Priestess, viz., William Q. Judge of America and Annie Besant of England. A bitter warfare was waged, whereupon the American branch of the general society seceded, and organized itself into the American Theosophical Society. Judge was made life president, holding the post until his death, in New York City, March 21, 1896. Mrs. Besant had to content herself with the English and Indian branches of the Society. She died a few years ago. The present head of the American theosophists is Katherine Alice Tingley, who claims to have been a bosom friend of Hélèna Petrovna Blavatsky, 1,200 years B. C., when both were incarnated in Egypt.

Henry Ridgely Evans.

Washington, D. C.

PSYCHOLOGY ON THE "NEW THOUGHT" MOVEMENT.

IN the Gifford Lectures, delivered at Edinburgh during the year 1901-1902, by Prof. William James of Harvard University, and afterward published in book form,[1] there are many comments upon the movement known as "New Thought." These come from a doctor of medicine, a professor of philosophy and a prominent psychologist, and when brought together show how the New Thought philosophy appears, considered objectively from a psychological and scientific standpoint. Moreover, the book furnishes a kind of background against which the movement can be measured; and it is here attempted to outline that background for the reader by adding some of the lecturer's general summaries and conclusions.

The religious experiences that formed the subject of the lectures were, in Dr. James's words, "the feelings, acts and experiences of individual men in their solitude, so far as they apprehend themselves to stand in relation to whatever they may consider the divine"; and the term "divine" was not taken in any narrow sense, for systems of thought in which the existence of a God is not positively assumed were considered as religious. The lecturer's method of treating this subject was by analysis and comparison; he took up and considered concrete cases of personal religious experience, and deduced their fundamental principles by distinguishing the essential characteristics common to all from such superficial differences as were incidentally due to creed, race, temperament, intellectual force or historical setting. This is analogous to the case method of studying law, which his colleague, Prof. Langdell, estab-

[1] *Varieties of Religious Experience*, by William James LL. D., etc. London and New York: 1903.

lished at Harvard, and which has spread and transformed the study of Common Law. That method has produced a literature of such books as Langdell's *Cases on Contracts,* Ames's *Cases on Torts,* Gray's *Cases on Property,* etc., and this book might not inaptly be called, James's *Cases on The Subliminal Consciousness.*

It is in an early chapter entitled "The Religion of Healthy-Mindedness" that most of the comment on New Thought is found. There is a natural optimism which enables its possessor to enjoy life uninterruptedly. Dr. James gave some cases of this happy temperament, and pointed out that the resulting attitude of grateful admiration for the gift of existence was in itself a kind of religious feeling. Such unreflecting optimism he distinguished as involuntary healthy-mindedness, and then went on to say that a healthy-minded attitude, as such, could be deliberately adopted and systematically practiced as a religion. On that point he makes these psychological criticisms:

"The systematic cultivation of healthy-mindedness as a religious attitude is consonant with important currents in human nature, and is anything but absurd. . . . Every abstract way of conceiving things selects some one aspect of them as their essence for the time being, and disregards their other aspects. Systematic healthy-mindedness, conceiving good as the essential and universal aspect of being, deliberately excludes evil from its field of vision; and although, when thus nakedly stated, this might seem a difficult feat to perform for one who is intellectually sincere with himself and honest about facts, a little reflection shows that the situation is too complex to lie open to so simple a criticism."

Dr. James says that every emotional state is, and must be, blind to opposing facts. If melancholy rules, the thought of good cannot acquire the feeling of reality; while by "the man actively happy, from whatever cause, evil simply cannot then and there be believed in. He must ignore it; and to the bystander he may then seem perversely to shut his eyes to it and hush it up."

There are several modern tendencies that have promoted the growth of healthy-mindedness as a religious attitude. The advance of "liberalism" in the Christian Church during the past fifty years

one; the popular spread of the scientific theory of evolution, with te doctrine of universal progress, is another; New Thought is still nother; and in Dr. James's opinion it is the most weighty of them l. He says:

"To my mind a current far more important and interesting eligiously than that which sets in from natural science towards ealthy-mindedness is that which has recently poured over America nd seems to be gathering force every day, and to which, for the ake of having a brief designation, I will give the title of the 'Mind-cure movement.' There are various sects of this 'New Thought,' to use another of the names by which it calls itself; but their agreements are so profound that their differences may be neglected for my present purpose. . . . It is a deliberately optimistic scheme of life, with both a speculative and a practical side. In its gradual development during the last quarter of a century, it has taken up into itself a number of contributory elements, and it must now be reckoned with as a genuine religious power. . . . One of the doctrinal sources of Mind-cure is the four Gospels; another is Emersonianism or New England transcendentalism; another is Berkeleyan idealism; another is spiritism; another the optimistic popular science evolutionism of which I have recently spoken; and, finally, Hindooism has contributed a strain."

Dr. James says that the practical character of New Thought especially characterizes it. "The plain fact remains that the spread of the movement has been due to practical fruits, and the extremely practical turn of character of the American people has never been better shown than by the fact that this, their only decidedly original contribution to the systematic philosophy of life, should be so intimately knit up with concrete therapeutics. To the importance of mind-cure the medical and clerical professions in the United States are beginning, though with much recalcitrancy and protesting, to open their eyes. It is evidently bound to develop still farther, both speculatively and practically.

"The leaders in this faith have had an intuitive belief in the all-saving power of healthy-minded attitudes as such; in the conquering efficacy of courage; and a correlative contempt for fear and all nervously precautionary states of mind. Their belief has in a general way been corroborated by the practical experience of their disciples; and this experience forms to-day a mass imposing in amount.

"This system is wholly and exclusively compacted of optimism. 'Thoughts are things,' as one of the most vigorous mind-cure writers prints in bold type at the bottom of each of his pages; and if your thoughts are of health and vigor, before you know it these things will also be your outward portion. No one can fail of the regenerative influence of optimistic thinking, pertinaciously pursued.

"The mind-cure principles are beginning so to pervade the air that one catches their spirit at second hand. . . . More and more people are recognizing it to be bad form to speak of disagreeable sensations, or to make much of the ailments of life. These general tonic effects would be good even if the more striking results were non-existent. But the latter abound.

"The blind have been made to see, the halt to walk; lifelong invalids have had their health restored. The moral fruits have been no less remarkable. Regeneration of character has gone on on an extensive scale."

Discussing New Thought belief on its speculative side, Dr. James says:

"The fundamental pillar on which it rests is nothing more than the general basis of all religious experience, the fact that man has a dual nature, and is connected with two spheres of thought, a shallower and a profounder sphere, in either of which he may learn to live more habitually."

The shallower sphere is, of course, the physical; but, whereas Christian theology has always considered frowardness to be the essential fault of this part of human nature, the mind-curers say that the mark of the beast in it is—*Fear;* and this, in his opinion, gives "an entirely new religious turn to their persuasion."

An extract from another part of the lectures, where the immediate subject of discussion was the heroic aspect of asceticism, may be inserted here by way of commentary on this "entirely new religious turn." He there said:

"In these remarks I am leaning only on mankind's common instinct for reality, which in point of fact has always held the world to be essentially a theater for heroism. In heroism, we feel life's supreme mystery is hidden. We tolerate no one who has no capacity for it whatever in any direction. On the other hand, no matter what a man's frailties otherwise may be, if he is willing to risk death, and still more if he suffer it heroically, in the service he has chosen, the fact consecrates him forever. Inferior to ourselves in this or that way, if yet we cling to life, and he is able to 'fling it away like a flower,' as caring nothing for it, we account him our born superior. Each of us in his own person feels that a high-hearted indifference to life would expatiate all his shortcomings."

The profounder sphere of thought with which our dual nature is connected is, of course, the spiritual; the mind-curers' theory of the higher part of human nature also differs strikingly from the theological theory. "The spiritual in man appears in the mind-cure philosophy as partly conscious, but chiefly *subconscious;* and through the subconscious we are already one with the Divine without any miracle of grace, or abrupt creation of a new inner man. As this view is variously expressed by different writers, we find in it traces of Christian mysticism, of transcendental idealism, of Vedantism, and of the modern psychology of the subliminal self."

Of the Subliminal Self, or Subliminal Consciousness, Dr. James says:

"I cannot but think that the most important step forward that has been made in psychology since I have been a student of that science is the discovery, first made in 1886, that, in certain subjects at least, there is not only the consciousness of the ordinary field, with its usual center and margin, but an addition thereto in the shape of a set of memories, thoughts and feelings, which are extra-marginal and outside of the primary consciousness altogether, but yet must be classed as *conscious* facts of some sort, able to reveal their presence by unmistakable signs. I call this the most important step forward because, unlike the other advances which psychology has made, this discovery has revealed to us an entirely unsuspected peculiarity in the constitution of human nature."

Going on to show the importance of this discovery, he explained that the expression "field of consciousness" was a recent term in psychology; that until lately psychologists had considered the unit of mental life to be the single "idea," a well-defined thing; but that now they tended to consider such unit to be the entire wave of consciousness, or field of objects, present to the thought at any one time. He further explained that modern psychology, while admitting that it seemed impossible to outline this "field of consciousness" definitely, had, nevertheless, taken it for granted that "what is absolutely extra-marginal is absolutely nonexistent, and cannot be a fact of consciousness at all."

The discovery of an extra-marginal consciousness changes this, and Dr. James says:

"In particular this discovery of a *consciousness* existing beyond the field, or subliminally, casts light on many phenomena of religious biography."

The suggestiveness of this discovery is emphasized in a final lecture, where Dr. James sums up his conclusions on the whole subject of religious experience. He concludes that under all discrepancies all creeds agree in their testimony on two points: That there is *something wrong about us* as we naturally stand; and that *we are saved from the wrongness* by establishing the right relation with higher powers. He concludes that there are the same progressive stages in every religious experience. The individual who suffers from this sense of wrongness, and begins to criticise it, is to that extent conscious of something higher, if anything higher exists. Along with the wrong part of him there is thus a higher part of him, though this may be but a helpless germ, and though it may not be obvious with which part of him he had better identify his real being. When, however, the crisis is reached, the individual "identifies his real being with the germinal part of himself" in the following way: "He becomes conscious that this higher part is coterminous and continuous with a MORE of the same quality, which is operative in the universe outside of him, and which he can keep in working touch with, and in a fashion get on board of, and save himself when all his lower being has gone to pieces in the wreck."

How much objective truth is there in such psychological feelings? Does that MORE, of the same quality, really exist and really act? If so, in what shape does it exist, and in what manner does it act? Dr. James says all theological creeds agree that it does exist; their differences are in regard to the way in which it acts. Just how "union" between the individual and this MORE is made, is the point over which "pantheism, theism, nature and second birth, works and grace and karma, immortality and reincarnation, rationalism and mysticism, carry on inveterate disputes." But he believes that we can sift out of their differences a body of doctrine common to all, and formulate it in terms to which physical science need not object. He says: "The *subconscious self* is nowadays a well-accredited psychological entity; and I believe that in it we have the term required. . . . Let me propose, as an hypothesis, that whatever it may be on its *farther* side, the MORE with which in religious experiences we find ourselves connected is on its *hither* side the subconscious continuation of our conscious life."

Difficulties commence the moment we ask how far our transmarginal consciousness carries us if we follow it on its remoter side. Here different religions come with their different creeds, which he terms "over-beliefs," and does not pass upon; but he says: "Disregarding the 'over-beliefs' and confining ourselves to what is common and generic, we have in the fact that the conscious person is continuous with a wider self through which saving experiences come, a positive content of religious experience which, it seems to me, is literally and objectively true as far as it goes."

According to New Thought belief, the individual becomes united with the MORE by passive relaxation; or, to be more accurate, each of us is already united with the source of infinite and eternal energy, and the one thing needful is to recognize that fact.

Dr. James is struck by the "psychological similarity between the mind-cure movement and the Lutheran and Wesleyan movements. To the anxious query, 'What shall we do to be saved?' Luther and Wesley replied, 'You are saved now, if you would but believe it.' To the anxious query, 'What shall we do to be whole?' the mind-curers reply, 'You are whole already, if you *did* but know it.' Both doctrines teach that the way is in passivity, not activity; relaxation, not intentness; that the seeker must give up the feeling of responsibility; let go his hold; trust the care of his destiny to higher powers; and he will find that he gains not only a perfect inward reward, but often, also, the particular thing he thought he was renouncing."

He says:

"Whatever its ultimate significance may prove to be, this is certainly one fundamental form of human experience. With those who undergo it in its fulness, no criticism avails to cast doubt on its reality. They *know;* for they have actually felt the higher powers in giving up the tension of the personal will. . . . The mind-curers have given the widest scope to this sort of experience. They have demonstrated that a form of regeneration by relaxing, by letting go, physiologically indistinguishable from the Lutheran justification by faith and the Wesleyan acceptance of free grace, is within the reach of persons who have no conviction of 'sin' and care nothing for the Lutheran theology. It is but giving your little private convulsive self a rest and finding that a greater Self is there. The results, slow or sudden, great or small, of the combined optimism and expectancy, the regenerative phenomena which ensue on the abandonment of effort, remain firm facts of human nature, no matter whether we adopt a theistic, a pantheistic-idealistic or a medical-materialistic view of their ultimate causal explanation."

The psychology of relaxation is explained in a chapter on "Conversion." A great many cases of conversion are reviewed, some voluntary and gradual, others so sudden as to have been called miraculous; and analysis of them shows that there is always a point in the process at which the personal will is either surrendered, or ceases from sheer exhaustion, or is overwhelmed by an inrush or uprush from some source uncomprehended by the individual who receives it. The psychology of our moods and their alternations; of character and the differences of character between different men, and of changes of character in a single individual, is first discussed. These processes are analogous. They result orm a change in the balance between impulses and inhibitions, many which are partly or wholly sub-conscious, a *shift* of the center the field of consciousness, and the substitution of a new group "associated ideas" for the former group. How the process conversion is helped at the critical moment by a temporary etting-go is shown by a familiar illustration. When we try to recall a forgotten name our efforts, *at first*, start up processes in the subliminal consciousness, where all "forgotten" experiences are recorded. But, as we go on struggling to recall the lost name, the efforts of the conscious mind *jam* the operations of the subconscious, just at the "threshold of consciousness." All know the mental discomfort then felt. If now we will turn away our conscious attention from the subject, "in half an hour (to use Emerson's words) the lost name comes sauntering into your mind as carelessly as if it had never been invited."

In a religious conversion the situation is analogous. The candidate has two ideas in his mind—the "sin" from which he would escape and the "salvation" to which he would attain. His idea of "sin" is distinct; his idea of "salvation" is vague; so much so that the ideal actually attained is generally different from that which was sought. The conscious effort toward "salvation" is "a process of struggling away from sin rather than of striving toward righteousness." The new ideal is being formed chiefly in the deeper, sub-conscious mind, and like the lost name it gets *jammed*. Then follow acute distress, desperate self-surrender and consequent release of the pent-up ideal with something like a revelation.

Religion and psychology agree in this. There is a force beyond consciousness which brings help to the individual. Religion attributes this force to Deity; psychology does not affirm that it transcends the individual's sub-conscious self.

The personal will works in the ordinary or primary field of consciousness. To let the will go, to relax the finite personal self, as a means of establishing communication between the primary consciousness and the subliminal consciousness, and through the subliminal consciousness with any MORE beyond, is psychologically reasonable. New Thought philosophy advocates doing this systematically, though the practice did not originate with New Thought. Dr. James says: "Mind-cure has made what in our Protestant countries is an unprecedentedly great use of the sub-conscious life. To their reasoned advice and dogmatic assertion its founders have added systematic exercise in passive relaxation, concentration and meditation."

A like practice has always been a part of Hinduism, Buddhism and Mohammedanism; and in the Christian Church there have always been mystics and a codified system the basis of which is orison. In relaxation, concentration and meditation the mystic's object is to become conscious of the continuity of his finite self with the Infinite. In Dr. James's words, "This overcoming of all the usual barriers between the individual and the Absolute is the great mystic achievement. In mystic states we both become one with the Absolute and we become aware of our oneness. This is the everlasting and triumphant mystical tradition, hardly altered by difference of clime or creed. In Hinduism, in Neoplatonism, in Sufism, in Christian mysticism, in Whitmanism, we find the same recurring note, so that there is about mystical utterances an eternal unanimity which ought to make a critic stop and think."

The psychological condition known as the "mystical state of consciousness" is one both of feeling and of knowing, and always possesses the four characteristics of ineffability, a transcendent insight, transient duration, and a sense of passivity. It is not sustained for long at any time, but it is recurrent; and when it sets in, the mystic feels as if his own will were in abeyance and he were being carried along by a superior power. This is not, however, like the passivity that marks the phenomena of alternative personality, or trance, or any automatism; for in mysticism there always remains a perfect memory of the experience, as well as a deep sense of the importance of its meaning. No state of feeling can be satisfactorily described to those who have not themselves felt it; being in love is an example of this. But the feeling that marks the mystical state of consciousness seems to baffle verbal expression so utterly that it is no wonder we find the term "mysticism" generally used as a term of condemnation to throw at opinions that seem vast and vague and without foundation in fact or reason. As a state of knowing, mystical consciousness is characterized by a sense of perceiving truths that transcend the range of the discursive intellect. This peculiar "noetic" quality marks even the most elementary stages of this psychological condition, while in the more developed mystic states problems of being, so profound that their very investigation had not been dreamed of, seem to be made plain as if by a flash of light; and these illuminations and revelations, articulate though they remain, "as a rule carry with them a curious sense of authority for after time." Sometimes they relate to a familiar phenomena of the objective world, but more often to the attractions of metaphysics or cosmology, so that another name for the mystical state is the "state of cosmic consciousness."

Dr. James said that he could treat the subject of mysticism at second-hand only, for his own constitution shut him out almost entirely from the kind of experiences that were given in his collection of cases on this topic; but there are experiences, not unfamiliar, that must be regarded psychologically as rudimentary states of mystical consciousness and his review of these gives any critic some idea of the nature of the state. The simplest case is the sudden sense of realizing the full meaning of some saying which has been a proverb from the nursery, but the truth of which has never been felt before. This sudden sense of deeper significance is not confined to entire sentences; a single word, an effect of light, an odor or a musical sound may cause it. Poetry and music owe their power to this. "We are dead or alive to the eternal inner message of art according to whether we have kept or lost this mystical susceptibility." A more pronounced case is that peculiar sense that not rarely possesses us of having *"been here before,"* in just this place, with just these people, saying just these things. A little more and we come to a "realm that public opinion and ethical philosophy have long since branded as pathological, though private practice and certain lyric strains of poetry seem still to bear witness to its ideality—the consciousness produced by intoxicants and anæsthetics, especially by alcohol. . . . The sway of alcohol over mankind is unquestionably due to its power to stimulate the mystical faculties of human nature. . . . Drunkenness unites and expands . . . Not through mere perversity do men run after (alcohol). . . . It is part of the deeper mystery of life that whiffs and gleams of something that we immeditely recognize as excellent should be vouchsafed to so many of us only in the earlier phases of what in its totality is so degrading a poisoning."[1]

An example of the mystical state of consciousness, not rudimentary but highly developed, is the peace of mind that immediately follows a religious conversion, filling the very hour of change. It is a state of *assurance* rather than of faith; its characteristics can be specified, but Dr. James says it is probably hard for any one who has not been in the state to appreciate its intensity of feeling. There is in it a sense of being under a higher control. There is a sense of entire *willingness to be,* even though conditions should remain the same. The idea of personal "salvation" that usually accompanies the change in Christians is not essential to this state. It is something apart from the satisfaction of personal salvation. "A passion of willingness, of acquiescence, of admiration, is the glowing center of this state of mind. . . . The second feature in a sense of perceiving truths not known before. . . . A third peculiarity is the objective change which the world often appears to undergo. An appearance of *newness* beautifies every object. . . . The most characteristic of all the elements of the conversion crisis is the ectacy of happiness produced. . . . The transition from tenseness, self-responsibility and worry to equanimity, receptivity and peace is the most wonderful of all those shiftings of

---

[1]*Conf.* "The one thing which we seek with insatiable desire is to forget ourselves, to be surprised out of our propriety, to lose our sempiternal memory, and to do something without knowing how or why; in short, to draw a new circle. . . . 'A man,' said Oliver Cromwell, 'never rises so high as when he knows not whither he is going.' Dreams and drunkenness, the use of opium and alcohol, are the semblance and counterfeit of this oracular genius, and hence their dangerous attraction for men."—Emerson: "Circles."

inner equilibrium, those changes of the personal center of energy, which I have analyzed so often, and the chief wonder of it is that it so often comes about, not by doing, but by simply relaxing and throwing the burden down. This abandonment of self-responsibility seems to be the fundamental act in specifically religious, as distinguished from moral practice. It antedates theologies and is independent of philosophies. Mind-cure, theosophy, stoicism, ordinary neurological hygiene, insist on it as emphatically as Christianity does, and it is capable of entering into closest marriage with every speculative creed."

In another place he writes: "There is a state of mind known to religious men, but to no others, in which the will to assert ourselves and hold our own is displaced by a willingness to close our mouths and be as nothing in the floods and waterspouts of God. The time for tension in our soul is over, and that of happy relaxation, of calm deep breathing, of an *eternal present*, with no discordant future to be anxious about, has arrived. Fear is not held in abeyance as it is by mere morality; it is positively expunged and washed away. . . . This sort of happiness in the absolute and everlasting is what we find nowhere but in religion. . . . In its most characteristic embodiments, religious happiness is no mere feeling of escape. . . . It cares no longer to escape."

Dr. James says that the mere fact that a thing originates in the subliminal part of the mind, or arrives by way of it, is no proof of its divine character, and does not make it authoritative as divine. But he points out that the question of origin is quite distinct from the question of worth. He explains that we follow two orders of inquiry concerning anything: "First, what is the nature of it? How did it come about? What is its constitution, origin and history? Second, what is its importance, meaning or significance, now that it is once here?" The answers are, respectively, what the books on logic term an *existential proposition* and a *proposition of value*; and the second cannot be deduced from the first. To determine the value of these mystical experiences we should criticise them as any other objective fact is criticised, basing our judgment on their "*immediate luminousness, philosophical reasonableness, and moral helpfulness.*" Of course, a "revelation" possesses immediate luminousness for the mystic who receives it. Dr. James says: "Mystical states, when well developed, usually are, and have the right to be, absolutely authoritative over the individuals to whom they come;" the mystic's position is invulnerable to argument; he has *felt;* and that, after all, is all that we have done with our ordinary senses. In his opinion, "no authority emanates from mystical states which should make it a duty for those who stand outside them to accept their revelations uncritically." But as to the reasonableness of these revelations, he notes that they do not *contradict* the facts of ordinary consciousness, but only add new meaning to them; they do not deny that reason has truth, but do not admit that reason has all the truth there is. "They break down the authority of the rationalistic consciousness, based upon the understanding and the senses alone. They show it to be only one kind of consciousness. They open out the possibility of other orders of truth." Finally, the results of mysticism seem to be morally helpful. Dr. James concludes that its practical effect on character is strengthening, not weakening. Although in subjects of feeble disposition and narrow intellect these results have sometimes been stupefaction and an unfitting for practical life, upon natively strong dispositions and intellects the results are quite opposite. "The great Spanish mystics, who carried the habit of ecstasy as far as it has often been carried, appear for the most part to have shown indomitable spirit and energy;" Loyola, the founder of the Jesuits, was "one of the most powerfully practical engines that ever lived."

The mystical state of consciousness is transient, but, as noted above, after it has been felt once, whenever it recurs its peculiar quality is instantly recognized. Dr. James says that between recurrences it "is susceptible of continuous development in what is felt as inner richness," and that in mysticism "personal religious experiences have their root and center." The habitual mental attitude of "saintliness" seems to be always bordering upon cosmic consciousness, and frequently rising to it. Dr. James warned his hearers that "saintliness" must not be mistaken to mean sanctimoniousnes the condition that follows a conversion which effects a pe transformation of the individual's nature. He gives these features of "a composite photograph of universal saintline same in all religions: "1. A feeling of being in a wider li that of this world's selfish little interests, and a conviction, not intellectual, but, as it were, sensible, of the existence of a power." This may or may not be personified. "2. A sense friendly continuity of the ideal power with our own life, and ing self-surrender to its control. 3. An immense elation ar dom, as the outlines of the confining self-hood melt down shifting of the emotional center toward loving and harmoni fections." In a final summary, he says that the cases all sh the following beliefs are characteristic of the "religious life That the visible world is part of a more spiritual univers which it draws its chief significance. 2. That union or harm relation with that higher universe is our true end. 3. That or inner communion with the spirit thereof is a process wherei is really done, and spiritual energy flows in and produces psychological or material, within the phenomenal world." A attributes of saintliness flow "from the sense of the divine, a their psychological center." Whoever possesses this sense s significance of the smallest details in their relation to the divin and the contemplation of this divine order yields him a steadi of spirit with which no other can compare.

Religion is the faith-state combined with a creed. The c a secondary thing, an intellectual growth; religion is essen matter of feeling and conduct, and the characteristic feelings same in all religions, however the intellectual content may var James says these feelings belong to the "sthenic" order; tl expansive, tonic, freshening to vital power. The faith-stat biological as well as a psychological condition, and Tolstoi i lutely accurate in classing faith among the forces by whic live." Considering religions as purely subjective, without re the truth of creeds, he concludes that "we are obliged, on a of their extraordinary influence upon action and endurance, to class them among the most important biological functions of mankind."

To conclude, I briefly recapitulate the foregoing facts and comments, and thus group them:

I. A deliberate mental attitude of optimism is psychologically reasonable. In New Thought practice the experiment of deliberate optimism has been tried on a large scale, and the results, material as well as mental, now form an imposing mass of objective fact.

II. Hero worship is instinctive with mankind. New Thought belief holds that the specific defect of the inferior side of man's dual nature is not positive, but negative; not frowardness, but lack of courage; as a religious creed this is new.

III. The discovery that there exists a fact of consciousness beyond the threshold of our primary or ordinary consciousness, marks a very important advance in the science of psychology. New Thought belief holds that the superior part of man's dual nature trends into the subliminal consciousness, and that through the subliminal mind every individual is united with a Universal Mind.

IV. All religions hold that there is something not ourselves from which we can obtain help; psychology agrees that there is something beyond our ordinary consciousness from which help comes, but cannot say that that something transcends the individual's sub-conscious self. New Thought practice systematically seeks help by way of the subliminal mind.

V. Psychology has suggested that conscious intentness probably raises the threshold of consciousness, and hinders the advent of ideas originating in the subliminal mind. It is a fact of experience that regenerative phenomena ensue upon the abandonment of intentional effort by the ordinary consciousness. New Thought advocates systematic mental relaxation and meditation. As a religious practice this is not new. It is found in the oldest religious systems known, the alleged effect being that the individual thereby becomes sensibly conscious that he is one with the Absolute. New Thought belief further holds that the individual thereby draws upon an infinite energy, and therewith produces physical effects in the objective world. The remarkable growth of the New Thought movement must be attributed to practical "fruits."

VI. The characteristics of the transient state known as mystic consciousness resemble the characteristics of the habitual religious attitude of saintliness. The religious attitude, considered even as a subjective mental condition, must be deemed one of the most important biological functions of mankind.

VII. An alleged result of relaxation, concentration and meditation is the revelation of truths that transcend the knowledge obtained by the senses and reason alone. It has been noted that such quired knowledge, but have only claimed to add meaning to them.

These facts and opinions constitute Dr. James' testimony on "New Thought," so far as he deals with that subject in this particular book. This testimony is incidental. The main purpose of the book is not to criticise the "New Thought" movement, but to study individual religious experiences, as such, and to show under what conditions these have their origin, through what stages they pass, how they terminate, by what results they are followed, and what such "fruits" are worth. Yet this testimony, incidental though it is, is valuable, for, as an ordinary witness to fact, Dr. James is exceptionally well informed, and, as an expert, he is qualified to give opinion evidence. As a rule both the advocates and the opponents of "New Thought" agree in this—they are rather intemperate critics. The former usually make large assertions unsupported by any reasoned argument, and the latter usually dismiss these claims as pure bewilderment and moonshine, undeserving rational refutation. Dr. James' method is refreshingly different from either of these extremes, for it is marked by open-mindedness, reasonableness and moderation of statement.

As stated at the beginning of this paper, its sole object has been to pick out this incidental but valuable testimony and to put it concisely before the reader, leaving him to criticise for himself its relevancy and force, and to reach his own verdict by the exercise of his own judgment. For this reason I have had to refrain from giving any opinion of my own as to these facts, or from going into any critical examination of Professor James' opinion as to these facts. For the same reason I am restrained from making any digressions into those portions of Professor James' book which do not bear directly upon these facts.

JOHN H. NOBLE.

BOSTON, MASS.

THE ÉLITE OF DEMOCRACY.[1]

SINCE the history of the nineteenth century is dominated by the social phenomenon of the universal tendency to promote the education of the masses, it is probable that the history of our new epoch will in turn be dominated by the action of these masses. They are already palpitating with hope. They are expressing their wishes through the agency of the individuals of their choice. By this choice they make known their tastes and their tendencies. These individuals, when chosen, are the units of the new contemporary élite, a "representative" and "variable" aristocracy.

In all civilized countries the problems of sociology are every day more imperatively demanding attention. It seems, indeed, that most of us have agreed, on principle, to work for a better social state. There is a sort of harmony between the vague but enthusiastic thoughts of a workingman summoning the new era, and the persistence of a social philosopher striving to reduce the sum of human suffering. We no longer discuss the value of the expression, "social solidarity;" some of us even pronounce these words with almost religious reverence. "Corporations" and "associations" of every kind abound. "Sociology" is bringing thinkers and people together. And the other sciences no longer disdain popularization. Their devotees are leaving the solitary heights where they formerly enjoyed a selfish pleasure. A great leveling process is going on. The era of democracy is at hand.

The social problems now pressing for solution are essentially modern. The political economists of the last century emphasized

---

[1]Translated by Prof. W. H. Carruth, University of Kansas.

the importance of the economic conditions regulating our style of living and our social relations. Under the powerful leadership of Karl Marx the fine rhetoric of the Utopians of '89 became a system supported by exact documents. Reread *Capital;* from the spherical contact of things common conditions and laws result; the social evolution can be accomplished only as these conditions and free social intercourse are regulated. The *"laisser faire"* of Adam Smith cannot withstand the severe attacks of Lasalle upon wages and their significance. Henceforth the political ideologist must drop anchor; he may no longer sail at random toward the horizon where the mirage is rising. Let him devote his attention to the price of grain, the market quotations. On the other hand, old-time governments, whether empires or kingdoms, seem to our contemporaries antiquated forms of government, obnoxious to minds enamored of justice and anxious to balance reasons, even overlooking all the details for the sake of securing this balance and harmony. At school, on the street, in the universities, in the daily papers, the maxims that the French revolution hurled into the hearts of men are no longer subject to discussion. The words Liberty, Equality, Fraternity are no longer mere symbols of philosophic conceptions; they represent facts. At least, modern democracy has so decreed.

rights but also powers, and excited and carried away by oratorical leaders, their spiritual representatives, form organizations, and in their turn excite and carry away their leaders.

This democracy appears to be the most advanced social form, the ultimate stage. And the problem that occupies us is this:

In this organization which seems to give such exceeding importance to groups of the élite, what are the characteristics of the élite; what are their manifestations; what are their means of action; what are the motives that prompt them to action; how is the membership of the group increased; and are they, belonging to the élite, really élite, or select, individuals?

In order to exhaust this field of study we propose to analyze in a series of articles the whole of contemporary social psychology. We shall find the bulk of our illustrations in France, but we shall not limit our observations to this country; we intend to speak of all the democracies that exist in the world—for example, of the United States and of Switzerland.

Forthwith, at the very threshold of this article, of this bird'seye view which is to serve us as an orientation, we must indicate the spirit in which these essays are to be conceived. We wish to look at existing society as a mildly philosophical enquirer. We shall nowhere attempt to display erudition. We hope to express our indignations and our dislikes with more fire than is permitted by a solemn tone all inflated with learning. And here is the first source of our wroth:

Democracies, or at least the French democracy, neglect systematically to-day the select individual. The heroes whom they admire, whom they patronize, whom they elevate to rule over them, must first of all renounce their own individuality, must be nothing but the echo of the desires and the tastes of social groups. The masses admire themselves in their representatives and they admire nothing but their representatives.

And this is deplorable.

In the first attempts at human society—if we may believe the specialists who have devoted themselves to reconstructing the physiognomy of that society—the victory belonged solely to the possessor of muscular power. The *élite* individual was the *strong* individual. Among savages of the present day, whom, according to Feuerbach, we must consider as belonging to a backward society yet one quite as old as our own, psychical qualities have come into play, and cunning—not to speak of intelligence—is employed in the service of brute force. The élite savage controls his subjects by knowing how to apply his force. He must not forget that these tribes have their traditions, their past, which compels their chiefs to follow certain paths, and which introduces new complications. But even here force retains its aureole. It is always victorious. It has been modified somewhat. Aided by cunning, by intuitive and elementary cunning, this force, which is triumphant from the social point of view, approaches perceptibly that which is manifested by every human organism in the struggle for existence. The élite individual exists as such among savages. It is hard to imagine that groups of élite could grow up among them.

Ancient societies, which became organized under the influence of divers motives—emotional, religious, economic—gave legal sanctions to these individuals. The victors united to impose their will upon the vanquished. They established castes. The superior castes determined the duties, the obligations and even the sensations of the inferior castes. India is the classic example of this sort of social formation. Here the élite are no longer determined in accordance with a criterium of brute force. Barriers are erected in society. Ruling families constitute the élite, and it is only in this privileged sphere that individuals can in their turn distinguish themselves and become élite individuals.

Later a new element enters into play. Among the Greeks we do not find castes, but social classes, and the élite are no longer exclusively the ruling class. Superior individuals may spring from any family. Generals, artists, philosophers, priests and oracles, orators and courtesans labor together to create the genius of the race. Over against Aristides, Leonidas, Themistocles—in whom, despite their readiness to sacrifice themselves for the common good, we shall perhaps recognize after all representatives of the conquerors by cunning force—over against these superior individuals, who direct and govern, these military chiefs, arise Socrates, Plato, Aristotle, philosophers, orators, poets, tragedians, select individuals, themselves holding a very definite place in the history of their city, and this thanks to intellectual works, which present no immediate interest for the government of the city. In another study we shall return to this prodigious period. Never was the individual freer to manifest his powers. But there were so many slaves in this fair Hellos that to be born Greek was after all to belong to a superior caste.

Among the Romans this intellectual and artistic aristocracy, while not attaining quite the same prestige, exists alongside the ruling aristocracy. However, the Hellenic conception was modified; in Rome caste resumed its full power; patricians and plebeians were required by law to maintain the relation of superior and inferior.

From this point it seems as though we were returning upon our steps. The barbarian invasions restored the entire power of brute force and of cunning force. In the train of a chief galloped unorganized troops, and power of muscle alone establishes a hierarchy in the mob that follows Attila. Yet, in truth, the intellectual aristocracy was not dead; it was wretched and persecuted. In Byzantium it appears, emotional and confused. On the banks of the Bosphorus Greek metaphysics mingled with naissant Christianity and with Oriental superstitions. While the emperor, the victorious soldier, owes his throne to his force, he trembles before the religious factions which were led by individuals in a state of exaltation and intoxicated with ideas.

In the Occident when the barbarbians plan to profit by their victory we see an intellectual aristocracy arise; the papacy is organized. The church, and the monasteries especially, with their monks constantly bending over manuscripts brought from the Levant and filled with the knowledge of Greek philosophy, of Aristotle and Plato, cultivate and direct the thoughts of men. And thus we have a new development—two ruling classes organizing side by side: a military and an intellectual aristocracy.

But the second of these is no longer a national élite. It has a tendency to become a cosmopolitan aristocracy. Its power increases daily. Consider the Crusades. Here a few dreamers carry the military élite off their feet and for a time dominate force and use it for their own ends.

Next, alongside these two bodies of ruling élite—the already international church and the military nobility—there appear once more dissenting and independent élite. As in Greece, poets, philosophers, artists contribute to human development. The renaissance spreads over Italy and France. But this third élite seems to be in vassalage to the other two. The church, if it does not absorb it, is flatly hostile to it. Luther and Calvin, the reformers, are individuals who enter into conflict with the reigning intellectual élite, just as the latter in its day had combatted the military élite. The Reformation conquers a part of Europe. As happens in all such cases, its leaders labor to secure organization. The ruling intellectual élite is divided. The Catholic Church remains international. The reformed church is factional, is national, and these two powers alike oppress the individual. The Spanish inquisition scarcely surpasses the pastors of Geneva in intolerance. Michael Servetus, the revolutionary pantheist, is burned at the stake.

Nevertheless the labors of independent individuals go on. A fourth élite is created, or rather the élite consisting of artists and philosophers before the Reformation continues its task, aided and often encouraged by the monarchs.[1] It was individuals independent of all organizations who prepared the way for the French Revolution. Before this is launched we note indeed a certain number of secret societies with more or less power, which afford to these isolated individuals the opportunity to exchange views, but we think that the importance of these fraternities should not be exaggerated. The achievement of a Voltaire, of a Rousseau, was in our opinion more important than the, to be sure, interesting ac-

[1] We shall examine later the part played by monarchs in relation to élite individuals. A Louis XIV., a Frederick the Great constituted, through their desire to be surrounded by men of genius, admirable unorganized élites, and thus did more for progress than the members of contemporary democracies have perhaps done hitherto.

rity of Free Masonry. In fact, the latter will pretty nearly represent the efforts of these free individuals to transfer their conceptions from the field of abstract ideas to the domain of facts. Once again, as in the time of the Crusades and of the Reformation, the labor of individuals animates an organized, intellectual élite, which in its turn, utilizes brute or cunning force, or, in short, the military élite. After the downfall of Napoleon I, despite the power of the "congregation," the élite which really called forth the events of '89 did not disappear. It was merely resolved into its elements. Thus it again became potent. Never were ideologists so plentiful. Economists begin to propound social problems. The coming of democracy is at hand. It is ever the same phenomenon repeated—the isolated individual of an unorganized intellectual élite prepares the way for a social revolution, and the formation of new, organized, intellectual élites; that is to say, of élites which apply themselves directly to transforming the thought of the masses in order to make use of the force of the masses.

To-day this social revolution has been accomplished in France in some measure. Before proceeding to the study of contemporary governments let us make note of the fact that we have observed constantly in this rapid survey that human evolution is guided by individuals. No sooner is an association formed to impose a new conception upon the populace than other superior individuals go to work, and it is their labor that prepares the way for the future. All the great scientific discoveries, all the great religious, metaphysical and social ideas are the work of individuals.

But there are those who claim that these individuals are, on the contrary, merely the echo of organized groups, the representatives of the universal knowledge of their day. To which it may be replied: If Lamarck and Newton, for instance, profited by this knowledge it was surely in themselves and because of their mysterious genius—mysterious, I repeat, for what do we know of the origin of genius?—that the synthesis was accomplished of all the elements which were furnished to them (this we freely admit) by organized élites.

Now they derived from this synthesis new conclusions, which

were not always accepted by those very persons to whom th constructive heroes owed the elementary materials of their str tures. So that, if the élite individuals are the echoes of the lear multitude, we would say that they give back to this multitude t voice so transformed that they themselves do not recognize it. this transformation, which is the peculiar work of isolated indi uals, is the very kernel of progress.

It is therefore necessary, first of all and even solely, to se to each individual his particular and especial development.

II.

The French Revolution, or at least those who prepared way for it, seem to have recognized the value of this thought. T proclaimed the equal right of each to develop unhampered; bu the same moment in which they summoned all the masses to t share in life they found themselves face to face with a new q tion, the question of the relations of these equal individuals, wished not only to live, but to individualize themselves still m to dominate, to conquer. In order to satisfy these energies these ambitions they attempted in theory equitably to distri honors as well as offices; they distributed the spoils of victory the greatest possible number, and since they were forced to re the social categories it was demanded that they be open bro to all citizens. Better still, they demanded that, from top to bott of the social scale, in whatsoever category, each unit should rep sent other units, for to *represent* was to conquer and to contro portion of the power which governed the state. The unanim desire to give to all the elements of the populace the impres of victory explains the creation of these representative éli which took the place of the older organized élites, whether intel tual or military, which we shall call *fixed* élites, in contrast w the newer élites, which are essentially *variable*.

In the constitution of the variable élites of the Revolution account was made of heredity, nor of the environment in which individual had grown up. The principle had been propounded th the free exertions of the units of the nation would tend naturally to realize the common ideal. The intent of every citizen should be, and they did not doubt that it would be, to improve the condition of his fellows. The fact of representing a group of men animated by this specific virtue became a new force, a new value, as Nietzsche would say. In order, therefore, to appreciate an individual, two criteria were used: He was *himself*, and he *represented others*—he had a qualitative value and a quantitative value.

But very soon the quantitative element outweighed the qualitative in the judgment of the masses, as a result of this naïve axiom; all citizens are animated by an equal love for the common ideal. Accordingly, the common ideal is the only thing that counts. Thus the qualitative element is no longer estimated excepting by its relation to the quantitative element; the moral qualities of a man, his physical or his intellectual force, are recognized only in so far as they are imposed upon other men, win their suffrages and hold the favor of the masses for a greater or less period of time.

In order to win the favor of these masses, to obtain this quantitative value, the tribunes of the Revolution tried all the ancient means of conquest. Brute force, cunning, audacity and prudence, which are only the art of employing force, were used in succession. But these ancient devices were now supported by others. A delegate had no existence unless he was sustained by an initial group, and therefore it was necessary for him to remain in contact with this group. He was obliged to please those to whom he owed his power, and he pleased them so long as he could hear their voice speaking within him, so long as he was their faithful echo. . . . Frightened by the fear of falling from favor this delegate found his field of action restricted, and he dared not overstep the limits of the "middle ground" in which centered the aspirations of his electors. And this "middle ground" was of necessity narrow, unless perchance the delegate appealed to the feelings most deeply rooted in the hearts of all men, to those primitive instincts which civilization had tried to suppress.

The victors of the variable élite of 1789 unloosed hatred, fury and envy, not from preference, perhaps, but in order to broaden the field of action in which they wished to manifest themselves.

To be skillful in discovering the passions which stir the greatest number, to be adept in appealing to these passions, in shaping them to any use whatever, to be able to become the echo of a tumult while controlling it, in fine, to be able to assimilate oneself to the multitude, and at the same time remain oneself. Such were the qualities indispensable in these tribunes.

For a century now they have been endeavoring to instruct the multitude, to give them a common ideal which should be at the same time more complex and more noble, and the results obtained deserve to be examined with care. We shall return to this point. For the present we shall insist only upon this:

There are those who declare that the intellectual level of the masses is rising constantly through the action of its élite representatives. We believe this to be false. We believe that all the actual progress accomplished in the century past was such, owing, not to élite representatives, who were constrained, on penalty of suddenly losing their power, to avoid offending the deep feelings and the master instincts of the groups which they represented—not to élites whose intellectual level was established by the intellectual level of the multitude—but rather owing to the labor of superior individuals, who were united by no organization and whose qualitative value was not devoted to being transformed into a quantitative value.

Now, whatever be the instruction given to the multitude, only he can become a member of the governing élite, even now, whose power humiliates itself to the point of accepting as its criterium the number of expressions of admiration which it arouses.

III.

What actually becomes in modern society of these superior and solitary individuals? Formerly the victor by force among the first human families had only to struggle against other more or less robust individuals—not, however, united among themselves. The power of this victor vanished as soon as the vanquished united when collective power was born. And the individual who has conquered hitherto by his intelligence will succumb also when he is obliged to oppose the combined intelligences of the nation. And they will surely combine against him, against his initiative, for, we repeat, the multitude can unite only for the purpose of compelling the acceptance of average ideas, of ideas already accepted by the majority of citizens.

The kingdom or the empire, despite all the criticisms directed at these institutions, were certainly more favorable to the development of these individual heroes. Whether they were already members of a caste that was elevated by law or by birth, or whether they were victorious by virtue of their nature or their intelligence, they did not have to concern themselves about an omnipotent public opinion. It is true they had to combat the prejudices of the already existing social groups. But these groups had to reckon with their own comparative isolation, and thus presented a less imposing surface of resistance than the universal coalition of average minds. Recall here, moreover, what was said at the beginning of this article—the feeling of social solidarity has penetrated even the hearts of men who have reached the highest eminences. In the name of this sentiment they judge the value of their own work according as it is, or is not, directly serviceable to humanity, and humanity responds to them by the voice of its elect, whom they call deputies, senators, ministers, members of universities and academies, and they concede the validity of this response.

The multitude has become the sovereign judge of all activities, and few there be that protest against its decisions. Through this omnipotence, which it uses for the purpose of leveling, democracy is more oppressive toward the true intellectual élite than any monarch or any religious caste that ever existed.

And if we turn now to those other élite individuals, military or political leaders, we see that the same reasoning retains all its force. Only within the brain of a single individual is the synthesis accomplished whence may spring a new deduction. Most, if not all, laws and reforms were conceived by individuals acting independently;

that is to say, acting without any concern for public opinion, without asking the multitude for its immediate approbation. And this is why, however inauspicious be the accession of a tyrant to the throne, it seems to us to be compensated and more than compensated by the accession of a genius. We confess ourselves to be the opponents of a single power, of that power which, resting upon the consent of average minds, seems to us to be committed either to inaction or to the rôle of panderer to the lowest of human passions.

The man of genius, when called to govern the people by the will of all, is obliged to restrain his initiative lest he lose the favor of all. The man of genius, who governs by right of birth, or who depends upon the good pleasure of a king, or again, who governs by right of conquest, enjoys a freedom extraordinarily wider. If hereditary sovereign of a country, he derives his fortune from the traditions and the memories of the past. These memories impose a certain general direction upon his acts, but do not at all prevent him from developing himself in this direction.

If he is minister of a king he has but to satisfy this monarch. And who will claim that it is less easy to mould the mind of an individual than the mind of a mob?

Finally, if he rules by right of conquest, he enjoys absolute liberty. His power depends upon memories which connect directly with previous manifestations of his power. He will increase it by developing his own powers logically; the limits within which he can move are precisely those which are adapted to him. Consider the enormous work accomplished by all founders of dynasties. They begin by destroying; they end by constructing. All human progress, if we admit that there is such a thing as progress, is but the succession of these two functions. Democracies are opposed to them both alike. As soon as they are in the saddle they no longer permit destruction, and they fear new constructions, or at least every construction that would rise above the common level where they stagnate. The majority of the legislators of France regard the constitution which controls their country as detestable. And yet they dare not lay hands upon it, and we doubt whether a deputy, even had he genius, and the greatest genius, could succeed in getting his colleagues to vote for a constitution which would not, all in all, satisfy the present passions of the multitude. Now, these passions would destroy the ideal harmony of democrats. A perfect democracy seems almost committed to immobility.

Thus would the élite individual, who might by chance belong to a representative group, find his activity restricted. And yet, our contemporaries, in a certain measure, recognize that heroes are indispensable to them. They commend, as though it were a new religion, the worship of great men; we permit them to control us—when the marble of their statues makes them incapable of action.

IV.

And, nevertheless, these frantic agents of social leveling, these representatives of the masses, the members of the variable élites, are subject still to the influence of the fixed élites, constituted of old in accordance with the ancient criteria of force and heredity.

In our contemporary democracies the possessors of inherited power, be it the power of gold or that which gives the prestige of memories to one who bears a famous name—these, uniting, drawn together by a common regard for a certain elegance, constitute groups within which the pride of being able to accomplish more than someone else, thanks to capital, and the pride of being able to claim the past, compel the individual not to consider himself merely a social "unit." The sons of wealthy men, the descendants of ancient noble castes, even the sons of representatives of the people, are conscious of possessing an ancient power, accumulated in them and differentiating them from other men. This consciousness is increased by the relations which they maintain with the cosmopolitan élite, consisting of individuals who certainly do not lack vigor, since they bear transplanting without perishing—removal from their social environment, traveling aristocrats, who, becoming the guests of a democratic people, import the mode of thought of races in which other tendencies predominate. In the midst of such extremely complex environments we meet with another variety of conqueror; no longer the sons of the rich, but the "new men," men who have grown rich by their boldness or their energy

This aggregation of such diverse materials constitutes a superior class in the nation, a class which the representative élites admire and detest, assail and imitate. And how can it be otherwise? The elect of a group, aside from his social existence, is subject to human passions. Even if he remains merely the representative of his electors, when he exercises his governing functions, yet he is not always governing. The psychology of his private life has been written many times. We shall attempt to reconstruct it in another essay. It is crammed full of ambitions. Ambition urged him to solicit suffrages. It spurs him to raise himself into a region where power is less ephemeral, less uncertain. He wishes to demonstrate to himself that he possesses a qualitative value and not only merely the quantitative value given by his certificate of election.

Dazzling luxury and the brutal power of financiers hypnotize him. He worships a Lesseps before crushing him; he marvels at the genius of a Morgan or a Rockefeller before creating a law against trusts. He perceives that there is another glory than that which social units have bestowed on him. The rights of the great number are constantly isolated in his mind by the vigor of a single man; he must admit that the majority of the great industrial achievements are conceived in our day by individuals. And he is dazzled not only by the conquerors of wealth, but also, and perhaps even more, by those traditional castes which he has brought low and the remains of which persist in despising him. He would like to admire these castes, as a dilettante, just as he admires, though a rationalist, the manifestations of Christian art with which the museums are filled. But lo! he finds himself copying the morals, the exterior attitudes of these "fossils," of those whom he regards as fossils. If he is a politician, a member of the university or the academy, he will be caught by the fine sound of the famous name which adds to the prestige of this or that deputy or scholar, or artist, the son of some well-known personage. The strangers also whom he meets in the embassies or the cosmopolitan salons, force upon him a certain respect for titles, for decorations, for all the symbols which distinguish men in the name of the past and in the name of heredity.

These fixed élites and these other élites which are at the same time fixed and variable, constituted by the rich, may then teach him to see in a man something else than a fragment of the mass. . . . It would be thus, perhaps, if he hoped to maintain himself in this privileged class without the support of his electors, but he knows too well that his position in the world depends upon them. The lesson that he learns by his transient sojourn among the survivors of ancient régimes is that outward organization is necessary, such as that maintained among the ancient régimes, to oppose them successfully. He joins the Free Masons; he is Grand Master of the Temple; he aspires to the red ribbon of the Legion of Honor. The pomp of Catholicism and the mysteries of the church arouse in him the thought of establishing similar ceremonies in which to shine and similar mysteries from which to derive an aureole for himself. He speaks of the religion of democracy and of its dogmas. He dreams of priests for this religion, and perhaps he fancies also that the dogmas would be better served by the scions of the distinguished representatives of the people.

And still better, since financiers have frightened and seduced him, he demands that private fortunes be subject to the control of the representative élite; he wishes ministers and members of parliamentary committees—in a word, the state—to be sole judge of the future of industrial affairs, to be free to permit or prevent development. He aspires to become à priest, a noble, a great financier. When he is not making laws this chosen one is planning to prove that his quantitative value is the guaranty of his qualitative value. He hopes that the fact of representing a great number of individuals will before long be equal to a brevet of omniscience. And he anticipates the future. He realizes his hopes by means of his decrees and his laws.

Decrees and laws ordain that he shall be a member of the élite.

V.

In truth, our fondness for sociology, this science which sees in men only fragments of a mass, interferes too much with our considering the man himself, the springs of his action, the feelings which cause him to love life for life's sake, and to love science in general, not *your* science.

A century has passed since the Revolution broke the ancient molds in order to permit all citizens to develop freely, and never was the individual who wished to develop freely more trammeled than in our day in his struggles for independence. Never was he more swallowed up in the mass. He constitutes a part of an "amorphous whole"—Society. He possesses rights only in so far as his rights do not embarrass society. He possesses no other power but that devolved upon each social unit—of naming the representative élite. As soon as he has exercised this power he becomes a subordinate wheel in a formidable machine. And even his representative, his delegate, is only a unit of another multitude, which, while commissioned to rule everything, to regulate everything in the name of society, merely devotes itself to trying to establish social *harmony*. To this harmony these beings sacrifice the originality of themselves and of others. They decree that the best morality is that which secures the good operation of the institutions which they govern. They direct us to act in such a manner that our actions will not disturb the order which they have declared necessary to the welfare of the state. They expect to prepare for the future by regulating the emotions of our children by giving them such philosophic instruction as they themselves have chosen. They teach them the code, they mould their doubts, they select their regrets and direct their enthusiasms. And all this, once more, they accomplish by laboring solely to facilitate the mutual *relations* of men.

These relations alone absorb attention. They put oil upon the wheels and do not perceive that these wheels operate because a higher power impels them. They have never turned their eyes toward this power. They do not feel it in themselves. In the motors of to-day the oilers are automatic. They too are parts of the mechanism. It is the same with the chosen representatives of our modern élites. They consider themselves as wheels, as units of the mass.

And they cannot consider themselves otherwise. Their abnegation is natural. Are they not the results of human groups. And are not these groups brought together by the self-denial of each one for the sake of the common interests? The elector has sacrificed his individuality, of his own free will, thanks to the education which society has given him, he has regarded it as soft wax, capable of melting and mingling in a larger mass. Thus he sets an example for his representative; the only power that devolves upon him is used, not independently, but in submission to the discipline of a party, a school, a system, a scientific or political church. He has not chosen the delegate who will best express his personal and individual aspirations, but the delegate who could be chosen also by those units of the mass whom he himself most resembles. He voluntarily obliterates himself in a joint-stock multitude. We shall meet this multitude again in all the social categories, in all classes. It is constantly inferior to the individuals who compose it. Whether we are dealing with a parliament or an academy, it is always dominated by the one of its members who represents the most "values." In order to represent values in a multitude one must be able to bend to its demands at the very time when one would like to impose a new conception upon it, must be able to sacrifice to it a portion of oneself, and since the members of the representative élite make this sacrifice—in fact, the most important of all—in order to mass social units behind their own ambition, why wonder when they endeavor to impose upon their contemporaries and on future generations a uniform mode of thought? They wish to govern beings who will get together easily, and this is why they teach the people uniform morals, official science, and persuade them little by little that the sole duty of an individual consists in solidarity with the rest of mankind, in making the mutual relations of men more easy and agreeable.

They are logical with themselves, these people, who, in the

governing assembly, are forced to shape themselves after the image of their party, when they try to compel the nation also to model itself upon a single type, and they are logical, furthermore, when they declare that the nearer an individual approaches this type, the more worthy he is to take his seat among them and share in their glory.

But this typical individual, being the creation of a majority which is of necessity forbidden to neglect a single one of its members, can be in his turn only an average individual as compared with the members of this majority. However, the entire present social organization is laboring to produce this mediocre being. The university and the government are alike working to this end.

VI.

As soon as he has left his family the pupil learns to submit to the exigencies of programs. He is subjected to masters who themselves are amenable to the decrees of the minister of education, and the minister remains in power only on condition that he show a common purpose with parliament. The social edifice rests with its entire weight upon the originality of the child's mind.

Programs of study guide him to the secondary examinations. The pupil must obtain the "satisfecit" of the managing élite if he wishes to profit by the learning he has already acquired. And now we come to the competitive examinations. We are attempting to discover the best in this gathering of candidates. The best? Those whose originality will jar least the majority of the judges. And thus selection works from one competition to another. Having reached the end of his official instruction, the young man, if, indeed, he is still young, has so devoted himself to avoiding offense to any of his masters by his own initiative that he cannot even recall his early enthusiasms. He is cowed and muzzled. Have no further fear lest he rebel against official learning.

Consider that in order to become doctor or surgeon in the hospitals of Paris the candidate is undergoing competitive examinations from the age of twenty to that of thirty-five. He must satisfy the jury of day treatment and the jury of house treatment, and if he aims to become a surgeon he must be satisfactory to the jury or adjuvants, then to the jury on prosectors, then to the three professors, who will nominate him for assistant chief of some clinique, later chief of this clinique, and finally he will become physician or surgeon at the central office before he can be chosen incumbent of a regular practice.

We know very well that nepotism intervenes and falsifies the results of this series of tests. Certain savants make the task easy to their pupils, and thus succeed in creating a class of superior individuals. But nepotism is regarded as a plague by democracies, and very justly, for while it is profitable in the case we have just cited, it manifests itself frequently in another form: The governing élite, properly so called, the political representatives of the people, bring pressure to bear upon the verdict of the judges, and thus again we meet the confusion between qualitative and quantitative values. Is it not the administration of Public Assistance which appoints as regular incumbent of a practice the physician from the central office?

We have taken as an example medical studies in Paris, but the same criticism applies to all the academies.

While the university is charged with watching over the classification of minds, the government is charged with regulating the relations of social units with one another and with the state.

The average commonplace individual rules in the government—what an absurdity! What a crushing series of wheels! If an official proposes a reform it simply cannot receive consideration until it has been indorsed as necessary by sub-chiefs and chiefs of bureaus, by sub-prefects and prefects, by chiefs of division, by commissions, by the minister's cabinet and the minister himself, and by Parliament.

Every new and original idea, whether belonging to the intellectual realm or touching the organization of the state, must therefore overcome innumerable obstacles before it can be put into execution. Scholars, professors and officials are not ignorant of this fact. They devote themselves solely to the search for what will please the greatest number. To be unlike other people reduces the chances of success. They develop in themselves not merely the spirit of discipline, but that mediocrity which they must attain in order to succeed.

VII.

In the hands of these slaves of democracy, whose brains are like those of Chinese mandarins, and, we believe, of an equally sterile beauty, the masses themselves are constantly oppressed. In the name of their own welfare they are subjected to an intolerable hygiene. Hygiene? The word is very fitting. For have we not invented social pathology?

Yes, society would seem to be like a human organism. In the railways we have the arteries of this unique body; the farmers and workingmen are the cells of the muscles; the government is the brain, or perhaps the heart; the succession of representative élites seems to correspond to a nervous system with its ganglious and brain centers.

Take note that this organism must aim at one single object—to keep in good order. If it is ill it must be cured. If it is not ill we are in fear lest it become so. Close the window in the evening when the air is pleasant to breathe. The dream which you are following along the vault of heaven, and which grows as the light diminishes, will perhaps make you happy—but look out for that awful bronchitis.

Have you ever known the unfortunate man who, being all plastered over with neurasthenia, surrenders himself to twenty doctors, nurses at one and the same time his stomach, his kidneys, his bladder and his lungs, takes his reactions and weighs out the rations of his diet? He is fearful of emotions which may accelerate his heart action. He remains motionless save when he is promenading methodically, watch in hand, in order to obey the rules of hygiene. He is devoting himself with desperation to the equilibrium between the functions of his organs. Their individual gratification is a matter of indifference to him. He even forbids them any pleasure which would excite them individually. Does he ever imbibe alcohol? Does he ever indulge in highly seasoned food? No mistress claims his devotion. And if by chance his brain becomes excited, quick! a bromide will calm the imprudent organ. The brain must care only for the fulfillment of its daily duty, and this duty is to remain in good health. This man exists only to keep from dying. His mental life consists only of a precise picture of the mutual relations of his organs.

And such will be the mental life of a society which regards itself as being like a human organism and concentrates its attention upon hygiene. Melancholy ideal!

But let us turn from this comparison. There is no evidence that it is correct, and if it should become so we should be horrified at the result. For the present at least the individual is something more than the cell of an organism, and the farther removed he is from this degradation the more he suffers from the oppression which society imposes upon him.

In order that his voice may be heard he must ally himself with others like him. But what if he do not find his like? The mob begins to cross-question him and is offended. He is hindering the movements of the passers-by, those regular and precise movements which are the glory of social harmony. All the territory in the streets, the city, the fields and even on the hills has been surveyed. The earth is peopled with automatons who follow with empty gaze their daily tasks. And the independent individual stands still and turns his eyes inward and proposes to develop within his own self in accordance with his beliefs. But they elbow him and drive him away. He is dreaming, the vagabond; well, then, let him write down his dreams. Society is now calling for the analytical drama; to-morrow it will be the drama of chivalry. He is crowded toward the theater, toward the libraries. He must choose. And if he wishes to study here are laboratories, but he must first prove that he has a useful knowledge. Alas! he knows nothing. He is dreaming for his own amusement. He is dreaming to be happy. Is he crazy? Here we dream only to fulfill a social duty, to appease or excite or instruct the masses. He flees. He seeks the neighboring mountain. He climbs into ancient solitudes. They are closely watched. No one is permitted to penetrate them without public

ıd him away. Crazy in fact. They take him there he will live, among real fools, intoxicat- not to die too soon, with the memory of the old lays. And now when he dies, trembling with n to his cry of protest against the ideology against all these systems, all these reasonings, doctors of the people have cured them of their plicity. In the name of grandiose conceptions, ver understood and scarcely the material value in their simple philosophy. Yet it was all they m in tilling their gardens and breathing there rnity. He dies. Around him the automatons, joy, pursue the play of their cadenced move- ıe will come when the initial force will be ex- matons will stop, will coagulate, will die them- ast into a motionless humanity.

VIII.

ll! But what other can be suggested, and shall s to suggest another? We must have that bold- belie our convictions. Yes, we believe that we ety.

s are being absorbed in furthering the triumphal we are forgetting that social life is perpetuated We ourselves exist by virtue of these conflicts. er: It is conflicts that bring us the most agree- ociety, and not respect for law. Social life fur- ments for our disguise, and we are expected to node of seeing and feeling, despite the grand rce, the ego, the imaginary or real individuality ıch one!

to give first place to the question of the relation ety! Let political economy and sociology keep by no means the foremost among the sciences n. The material well-being which they are so h concerned with distributing to us equally is not sufficient. It is oil which lubricates the wheels of the machine, but not the fuel makes the wheels go round. And this fuel, this mysterious en-, is furnished neither by economists nor by sociologists, nor by mediocre representative élites of our present-day democracies. not the present age be reproached for the one that preceded the ach revolution! That was the time when everybody wanted dom of individual development, and freedom is a fair Utopia, ch means precisely the independence of the "ego." The organi-on that is held up to us as a new religion restricts the liberty of 1 in behalf of the liberty of all. It is the very negation of this o," of this grand source of life, of this sole atrium, whence the ividual may constantly derive new vigor.

And if it is impossible to-day to suppress these representative es, these agencies of leveling, these factors of individual weakness, us at least labor to make them better by diminishing their power, tolerating alongside of them élite individuals, by trying in all sible ways to increase the number of these élite individuals, these oes whose activity is not regulated by the needs of the state nor the concerns of the passing hour.

In the society which our economists and sociologists are busy ating the demi-gods will probably be regarded as faulty wheels, too noisy wheels, disturbers of political harmony. Those who named Galileo, or Newton, Lavoisier or Kepler, Spinoza or kespeare, Descartes, Montaigne, Racine, Pascal, Goethe, Schop-hauer or Nietzsche do not produce works for the man who re-icts his rôle in life to being one unit in the multitude, nor for one whose aims and emotions are created solely by the desire to ilve in this multitude without offending anyone else. They pro-ce works that give to life the savor of a divine fruit. They in-ase our consciousness; they rouse those who have fallen into the p of indifference; our dead arise at the sound of their voices. ey stir our ashes and transfuse them with life; they fill our poor stence with suggestions of a thousand other possible existences, for ich our hearts throb. They are the deep and shifting mirror the centuries past. They create resting places of the soul in

poraries has been opposed to morality, and every day we l by the follies that are done in his name. But what of it? s his heart for food. What does it impart against the oethe that Werther led several hundreds of young people

And yet our democracies will be logical if they com- ietzsche and Goethe. And how quickly they will send to n this King Ludwig II of Bavaria, who lived amid the lia of a perpetual ecstasy; this madman, who watched irth of Wagner's tetralogy and who forces us to think ine, and Villiers de l'Isle-Adam, and Poe, the dipso- or the fact is that all these fellows, these diseased beings, lerably the brain of the masses and might impart to some desire to grow.

ow will the society that we would pave the way for deal men? Would not Hugo in his age burst the narrow a phalanstery?

ell! we must create men who burst the bounds of phalan- to bring this about we must struggle with ourselves; we t to ourselves constantly that we must never lower our- e mob, that body whose sole function should be to nourish by consuming itself—that the multitude has not the through the medium of its representative élite, to judge luals; that we need to exalt ourselves for ourselves; that even the average individual must find in himself the force of living, the fuel of his own energy; that he will find this sustenance in himself alone and not in that rhythmic organization where all the data are lacking. We must cry aloud that the élite individual must rise without concerning himself about the opinion of his contemporaries.

Whoever rises, though solitary, toward an ideal labors better for mankind than the tribune who concerns himself about all mankind.

Yes, we hate tight-rope dancers. We are disciples of Nietzsche, presumptuous and beside ourselves. But more mad than Nietzsche himself, for if we were creating a Zarathustra he would not descend to the mob to address it. He would write his book slowly, in his solitude, and forgetting it upon the peak where he was dreaming, he would be unconcerned, for he would know that no force is ever lost that has once manifested itself powerfully, and he would have confidence. Some passer-by would find his book when the time for it was fulfilled.

But behold! We have combined to write these studies. Oh, the melancholy symbol! Who was it that said that it would soon be impossible for a single brain to accomplish the synthesis of the universe? We make no claim of doing it, and yet we have combined. In this association may at least no particle of our two personalities be lost! We do not unite them to bring them toward a commonplace ideal. One shall be added to the other, and if some confusion results, better this confusion, these conflicts, than any most perfect regulation, which should make our discussion mediocre and commonplace!

N. Vaschide.
G. Binet-Valmer.

Paris, France.

CRITICISMS AND DISCUSSIONS.

A REVIEW OF DR. CARUS' "FUNDAMENTAL PROBLEMS" AND "THE SURD OF METAPHYSICS."[1]

These two volumes may be presumed to give a fairly satisfactory account of Dr. Carus' philosophy. His writings are voluminous, but it is fair to assume that his other books are either an explication or an application of the philosophical principles here set forth. And this assumption is justified in that the former of these two volumes purports to be and actually is a careful treatise upon the great themes of philosophy, while the latter, although directed to a specific point in metaphysical inquiry, serves to present more fully and clearly the author's views upon the fundamental questions involved; so that we have here, in a nutshell, the Philosophy of *The Open Court.* This is notwithstanding what is told us in the Preface to the *Fundamental Problems,* namely, that nearly the whole of its contents first appeared as editorial articles in *The Open Court.* A glance at the Table of Contents reveals not only a general connection between the essays, but also a substantial identity of theme, and even a logical consecutiveness and harmony in the treatment of it.

The author is a man of no merely amateur accomplishments in the areas of dialectical thought and discussion. He has convictions of his own and he is not wanting in courage or ability to enforce them. He disclaims originality or, more accurately, he affirms his endeavor to avoid it. In this, whatever his own modesty may lead him to declare, it will hardly be unjust to charge him with some measure of failure.

It may be more surprising to the savants of the opening century that a new and somewhat original philosophy should come out of the utilitarian and Mammon-worshiping city of Chicago than it was to them of old time that any good thing should come out of Nazareth; but in both instances the thing which surprises is the thing that comes to pass. Dr. Paul Carus is the brilliant author and persistent proponent of this new philosophy. It is neither possible nor desirable to set forth in full its postulates and principles

[1] *The Princeton Theological Review.* MacCalla & Company, Philadelphia.

in this review, and yet, as all theology banks up against philosophy, and as this system—in so far true to the philosophical instinct and necessity—explicitly invades the realm of religious thought and ethical motive, we may examine the elements of this American positivism for the sake of its placement in the general scheme of modern philosophical encyclopedia, and of learning what are not only its alleged but also its logical and implicit bearings upon the intellectual elements of the Christian religion.

Dr. Carus conceives the problem of philosophy to be "the arrangement of all knowledge into one harmonious system which will be a unitary conception of the world and can serve as a basis for ethics" (i, 7)[1] He admits that his Monism differs from other philosophies in this, that it "is not a finished system but a plan for a system" (i, 24). The unitary conception is the goal of philosophy. This conception presupposes the idea of the continuity of nature which, however, he significantly says, "has not yet been proved in all its details" (i, 7). This unity of Reality must be unqualifiedly accepted. It is true in thought because it is true in fact. This conception is grounded on positive facts, and therefore the system is called "Positivism"—a term which, although he adopts it, he cannot accept with the connotation of M. Auguste Comte, who introduced it. Facts are ultimates; they are equally real or equally unreal. "Monism" also designates this philosophy of the unitary conception. But this Monism is not a "one substance theory;" Spinoza's doctrine was a pseudo-Monism, a "Henism." The author is Hegelian enough to tell us that Monism is a "recognition of dualities and their reconciliation in higher unities" (ii, 76, 77). Idealism affirms spirit only and Realism affirms matter only, whereas in truth both spirit and matter are mere abstracts and neither exists. True Monism recognizes the oneness of All-Existence. There are no differences of kind in this One; no Creator and created, no supernatural and natural, no divine and human. God and the universe are One. All nature is alive. Haeckel says that all nature has intelligence; this is "panpsychism." Carus says all nature is alive or has the capacity to live; this is "panbiotism" (ii, 170). Life is an immanent property of matter. There is organic life and inorganic life; the former no doubt originated in the latter. But the barrier between them has been broken down by modern thought, and life is now recognized as a fundamental property of matter; indeed, "it must be eternal" (i, 111). Reality is indivisible; the most important abstracts are matter, force and form—these three, but the greatest of these is form.

Epistemologically stated, all knowledge has its root in sensation and sensation is primarily feeling and not choice, as Professor Romanes believed. Feeling is fundamental and the *rationale* of feeling is purely biological. In

[1] For convenience in reference, I indicate the first volume named at the beginning as volume i and the second as volume as ii.

the development of knowledge from feeling the conditioning factor is memory, and this memory is nothing more than the psychological aspect of certain preserved physiological forms in sentient substance (i, 12). Constant special irritation has created special senses; the unity of consciousness is the product of the whole organism and the soul is not an entity; it is not a separate or separable independent something; it is only "the psychical aspect of all the organic forms of our body" (i, 14). The old ego-centric psychology is abandoned and the new is accepted, which regards "the center of consciousness as the strongest feeling at a given time which as such naturally predominates over and eclipses the other feelings of the organism" (ii, 195).

Metaphysically stated, the ultimate category of thought is to be found in the laws of form. These are eternal, irrefragable and everywhere the same. They are always "*correct, i. e.*, the truths of formal thought, but they are not always *real, i. e.*, the truths of a well-ascertained experience" (i, 69). The real is not a necessary existence; but if it do exist, then it must exist in accordance with these laws of form. The ultimate of thought is not any thing-in-itself, but forms-in-themselves.

Kant nodded in overlooking the essential difference between the subjective and the ideal, and the consequent confusion weakens the very foundations of his system. The ideal belongs to the realm of ideas and is therefore metaphysically eternal; the subjective belongs only to the realm of the thinking or feeling agent, and is therefore psychologically variable. Kant distinguishes between the *a priori* and the *a posteriori* correctly enough, but he attributes the former only to subjectivity; and, whereas he erroneously makes the subjective equivalent to the ideal, the truth is that the infinitely important part of the subjective of Kant, namely, the ideal as correctly conceived, is preëminently, if not exclusively, entitled to the honors of the *a priori*. For, indeed, from the evolutionistic and Monistic point of view the subjective is really not *a priori* in any correct sense at all, seeing that it pertains simply to the perceiving or the conceiving subject; and to us men this subject, this soul or mind or ego or what-not, is only a fragment or moment of the Great All-One. Man, like charcoal, is simply "transformed solar heat;" and "mind is not something different from the world, but must be considered as its product and highest efflorescence" (ii, 22). Hence Kant was wrong in regarding the mind as able actively to import forms into phenomena; these mind-forms or categories of thought are only a reflection of the forms of objective existence, preserved in the plastic but ceaselessly crystallizing sentient substance. The subjective *a priori* is liable to all the mutations and fluctuations of a psychological experience; the ideal *a priori*, which is Dr. Carus' *a priori*, resides in these eternal, imperial, immanent and even "supernatural" (ii, 87) laws of form.

So much may serve imperfectly to give to one unfamiliar with this philosophy a rough but true conception of its teachings and tendencies. Its author argues for its truth very earnestly and sometimes with much force. In the course of his arguments he says many things which are both excellent and true, but we are now dealing, not with detached thoughts in his system, but with the system itself.

Dr. Carus frankly acknowledges his indebtedness to Kant. He regards his own position as the natural outcome of the critical philosophy, but not without very important differences. He calls it Kantism developed, broadened, matured and adapted to our time. "It is a protest against the halfness of agnosticism and a rejection of the perverted ethics of hedonism" (i, vi). Both intellectual and ethical excellences are claimed in its behalf. It "means perspicuous simplicity. It is the systematic and clear conception of an intelligible reality." It is the "classical philosophy" (i, 251). Materialism invariably leads to hedonism or utilitarianism; spiritualism or idealism leads to asceticism; but this classical philosophy "finds the purpose of existence in the constant aspiration of realizing a higher and better, a nobler and more beautiful state of existence" (i, 189). In short, it is a new gospel not only for the philosopher in his search for truth, but also for the people in their chase for happiness and fulness of life.

All this is promising, but what is to be expected in the performance? Is this new occidental philosophy pagan or Christian? Does it square well or ill with the things most surely believed throughout the Church of God? Does it ring true or false to what Christendom reveres as the Word of God, and does it acknowledge or regard the fundamental elements of Christianity?

In finding its theological and religious valuation, we have two methods within our reach. We may take the plain utterances of the author himself as bearing upon our inquiry, or we may take his system and decide upon it for ourselves.

For himself, the author, while claiming everything for his philosophy, frankly affirms his radical break with evangelical Christianity. He tells us that he does *not* persist in calling himself a Christian, although to a great extent he gladly accepts Christ's ethics. He regards Christ and Christianity as radically different. He seeks the direct revelation of God in the facts of life and solemnly warns us that "the surrender of science is the way to perdition." If theism is identical with supernaturalism—and it certainly is—then he tells us that he must beg to be classed among the atheists. There is no disputing the correctness of this classification; and, as a confession of faith, we have here enough to place Dr. Carus among the Philistines.

But, passing by the teacher, let us look into his teaching to see whither it tends, theologically. The bottom postulate of a philosophy correlates with the theistic conception in theology. Dr. Carus' final postulate is the "Laws of

Form." Metaphysically, this foundation hangs in midair. Every impulse of the modern philosophical spirit, crying out for the ultimate personality, is ignored and repulsed. We fail to see wherein the positing of these eternal laws has a single advantage in the search for a metaphysical *terra firma;* and certainly the considerations which have brought the sanest and strongest of the accredited philosophers in Christendom, especially in recent times, to acknowledge personality as the highest note and final category of our thinking are, metaphysically regarded, incomparably to be preferred. But with Dr. Carus these laws are God. "By God we understand the order of the world that makes harmony, evolution, aspiration and morality possible" (i, 152). He conceives God to be not less than a person, but more; and yet, building perhaps more consistently than he intended, he calls God "it" and not "Him." The conception of God as a person is poetry, not science. These eternal laws "possess all those qualities which a pious reflection has attributed to God" (see i, p. 54). The Cosmos, which is the One, which is God, is the foundation of morality. "We may compare it to a father and with Christ call it 'Our Father,' just as well as we like to speak of Mother Nature" (i, 323). But it must be remembered that this is only a simile which, if carried out, would lead to serious misapprehension.

This is not exactly the theism of the decalogue. Monism is monotheism, but wait to hear what kind of monotheism it is: "God is not one in number, but one in kind. He is unique. To believe in one God, as opposed to several Gods, is a pagan view which is more advanced than polytheism, but remains upon the same level" (ii, 155, 156). Monism revises the second word of the law and tells us that even as we shall not bow down ourselves to graven images nor serve them, so also we shall not bow down before the true God which is the All-in-All to worship it. "We do not call the All God in order to bow down into the dust and to adore it. We regard adoration as a pagan custom which, it is a pity, survived in Christianity" (i, 261). This is a consistent corollary, it is true; but it is the consistency of a deliberate and downright twentieth century paganism, which not only would smash the shrines of all creeds and cults, but also would throttle the very instinct of religion in man, which leads him upward toward his God. Religion is only man's aspiration to be in harmony with the All; it matters not how well he succeeds; it matters not that, whatever he is or becomes or does, he is still, in spite of himself, a part of the All; only let him *aspire,* and that is the Alpha and Omega of religion.

Nor is this new Positivism less advanced in its doctrine of Man. *Talis Deus, qualis homo.* Man is the flower of nature—not even its fruit. Mr. Edison says that, in its own little way, the atom is everything that man is. Dr. Carus agrees, and yet the atom itself is but a convenient scientific fiction. The ego is no entity. Memory produces selfhood, not *vice versa.* Personlity is the symbolical thread on which are strung the beads of our existence. The ideas which live in us constitute the self. Abstract thought helped to make man man; but, pray, how could it help to "make" him man, seeing that he must needs be man before he could be helped by it? Truth is relation; if it has any meaning, it is correct cognition. Man is the child of the cosmic dust; but the Cosmos is the All-God; therefore, man is the son of God. As a rational being "man's begetter is not his brute progenitor, but the eternal order of the universe" (ii, 224, 225). This is fatalism stripped of every shred of the idea of providence or plan or personality. Such an anthropology is quickly self-interpreting. Man is but a coördinating factor in the living All. Atoms are centers of living spontaneity. There is no push or pull of gravity from without; all nature lives. This all-pervading spontaneity comes to the front in God-like beauty in the moral character of man. But he is dust and only dust; into dust he need not return, for only dust he ever is. "Christ's words are literally true when he says, 'God is able of these stones to raise up children unto Abraham'" (ii, 54). Any doctrine of man which makes his soul to consist only of a series of successive states, whether taught by Emmons or Spencer or Dr. Carus, takes away the franchise for any intelligent notion of immortality which involves a continual personal existence and consciousness after death, and so does violence not only to the Christian religion, but also to the highest extra-Christian faiths of mankind.

But it is needless to compass all sides of this pretentious philosophy. The touchstone of any system of thought is to be found in its attitude toward theism. Its teachings must have either a direct or an indirect theological reference. Not that the philosopher must wait with a "By your leave" for the theologian; but the theologian must find room for himself within the pale of a philosophy or he forthwith declines to abide there.

The principles of this Positivism are a direct negation of many of the most elementary truths of Christianity. Its unitary conception is not the unity of truth, but the essential kinship, the identity of the All; the oneness of the whole enclosing circumference of reality, together with all that it encloses. It is Pantheism robbed of its mystical adorations and its confessedly somewhat redeeming features. It is Cosmism, scorning the more and more generous conceptions to Christianity of the lamented author of *The Outlines of the Cosmic Philosophy*. It is not so far from Comte's Positivism as it imagines; for it regards with patient and patronizing complacency the crude anthropomorphisms and excrescences of mankind's present religious state, remembering that mythology is ever an indispensable ladder to be climbed in making the difficult ascent to truth.

Dr. Carus is at no pains to make his peace with evangelical theology. He has chosen his own way, but he will never win the thought or the heart of humanity. His philosophy will be accurately classed as atheistic, and atheism is false philosophy. To make God One with the Cosmos is, to an ardent scientist who makes the way of science the way of life and the surrender of science the way of death, not acosmism, as Spinoza, the God-intoxicated man, would hold it, but atheism, as the world-intoxicated scientist is bound to hold it in the end. For the human mind is not ingenious enough to be able to hold consistently the same thing as God and the world. Its faith becomes either atheistic pancosmism or pantheistic acosmism. However successful Spinoza was in holding consistently to the latter, this new philosophy, with its commendable but overstated loyalty to empirical science, is essentially the former, pure and simple.

The merit of this philosophy is that it wears no disguise. It spurns the idea of the unknowable and truly argues that all that exists is capable of being known. Like all other implicitly atheistic systems, it is inconsistent enough to substitute eternal law for God and the Cosmos for the basis of the indispensable authority in religion and in ethics. It withholds Mr. Spencer's patronizing but inconsistent sop to the superstitions of the religious and coldly bids men, since there is nothing adorable to adore, to cease from the pagan-folly of adoration. This forbids all worship of God; and why not? for there is no God such as men could worship. The Great Teacher said to the woman of Samaria: "God is a Spirit, and they that worship Him must worship Him in spirit and in truth." The voice of the new Positivism, speaking forth from the shores of Lake Michigan, says: "Spirit is not a substance; spirit is the significance of words;" and, again, "Adoration is a pagan custom which, it is a pity, survived in Christianity."

TRENTON. HENRY COLLIN MINTON.

THE GOD OF SCIENCE.

IN REPLY TO REV. HENRY COLLIN MINTON.

AMONG recent reviews of my works, a criticism of *Fundamental Problems* and *The Surd of Metaphysics* by Rev. Henry Collin Minton of Trenton, which appeared in *The Princeton Theological Review*, is distinguished by fairness and gives upon the whole a correct statement of my views; yet it contains at the same time a vigorous denunciation of my philosophy as atheistic and hostile to Christianity, if not to religion in general, I wish to submit the case to all who are inclined to agree with Mr. Minton for reconsideration, and, in order to let readers of *The Monist* judge for themselves, I take pleasure in reprinting his review in its entirety, and will limit my answer only to the most important point at issue—the objection of atheism.

Mr. Minton overlooks the distinction made by me, between Determinism and Fatalism; he claims that I say "Man is dust and only dust; unto dust he need not return, for only dust he ever was." Obviously, Mr. Minton mixes me up (strange though it may seem) with Yahveh, the God of the ancient Hebrews, who utters a verdict to that purpose in Genesis iii, 19. Yahveh says: "Dust thou art and unto dust thou shalt return." Yahveh does not use the word "only," but he means it, and Ecclesiastes agrees with Yahveh's materialistic philosophy, which he states in shocking crudity (iii, 18-22), saying that "man hath no pre-eminence above a beast." I object to this one-sided view. I say that man, the human of man, is his soul, and man's soul is not of the earth earthy; while the body will turn to dust, the soul is not subject to decay.[1] I have much to say on this subject, but I will drop all points of minor importance and limit my answer to our difference concerning the idea of God.

Mr. Minton says: "The touchstone of any system of thought is to be "found in its attitude toward theism. Its teachings must have either a direct "or an indirect theological reference. Not that the philosopher must wait "with a 'By your leave' for the theologian; but the theologian must find room "for himself within the pale of a philosophy, or he forthwith declines to "abide there."

I agree with Mr. Minton that the God question is the touchstone of any system of thought. I further agree with him that the philosopher need not ask for a "By your leave" from the theologian, and I even agree that the theologian has the right to decline to "abide" within the pale of a philosophy which leaves no room for his God. He calls my philosophy "pretentious," and I will not quarrel with him on points of etiquette, for theologians have the advantage. They can afford to be modest and yet be positive, because they proclaim, not their own private views, but the truth of God. Mr. Minton should consider that I can turn the tables on him. The case can be viewed from the opposite standpoint. The philosopher investigates theologies, and he tries whether he can find room in any one of them for his philosophy. When I compare notes with a theologian I am above all interested in his God-conception, and, if his God-conception gives to science what is of science, I shall be glad to abide with him.

Judging from Mr. Minton's comments, I fear that his God belongs to the old-fashioned circle of deities whose dwelling-place is in darkness and who cannot stand the light of science. If he worship the God who needs nescience in order to have at all a right to existence, I am not specially pained if he prefers to part company. But we may, after all, find some common ground, if his God be (as I am convinced he is) the God of Protestantism, a God that lives in light, a God of truth, not only of the truth of sentiment, but also of the truth of science; further, of righteousness, of good will and lovingkindness, not only in questions of charity, in taking care of the sick, and preaching the doctrine of love, but also in our actual

[1] See my article, "The Ascent of Man," in the March number of *The Open Court*.

intercourse with the people who differ from us in opinion, even if they are infidel philosophers.

The fact is that more than thirty years ago I was in exactly the same place in which Mr. Minton is now. I can understand him, but he does not understand me. I know his God-conception in all details, for it was my own belief when I was either at his age or at least at his stage of mental development. I have given up that God-conception not by any perversity of heart or any objection to Christianity. Nor did I surrender my faith rashly. On the contrary, I gave it up reluctantly and against my will. When I gave up my belief in God, in that individual divine monarch who performed miracles and listened to the prayers of his humble worshipers, all my hopes and moral convictions were so intimately intertwined with my lost belief that my entire religious world broke to pieces and I felt all the horrors of perdition on account of the unbelief to which I had fallen a prey. It was only after years of groping after the truth that I regained my mental equilibrium and that I found again truth in the faith of my childhood if I were only permitted to interpret the dogmas in a symbolical sense. I have ever since tried to see how religious convictions might be adapted to scientific truth, not by compromise, but by a frank surrender of error, and the result was that I formulated a God-conception that is unequivocally tenable on scientific grounds. If Mr. Minton, for the sake of his religion, extends no welcome to my philosophy (or, more correctly stated, to the philosophy of science, for personalities have nothing to do with the case) it is certainly not the latter (the philosophy of science), but only the former (his religion) which in the long run will have to suffer; for (to repeat a sentence of mine, which Mr. Minton disapprovingly quotes), "The religion which opposes science is doomed."

I have lost the God of my childhood and I have become, in the opinion of those who still believe as I did then, an atheist, but the more I think about the God-problem, the surer grows my conviction that the God of science is the true God, and the God of mediæval theologians is a mere makeshift, a substitution for the true God, a temporary surrogate of God, a surrogate which at the time, was good enough for immature minds, but too often only led people astray. The God of heresy trials and witch persecutions is not the true God, and the theology of the inquisition is a sad aberration, whatever its pretensions and claims of Catholicity may be.

Gods will be tried as much as mortals, and they should be judged according to their deeds. Compare the God of miracle and special revelation with the superpersonal God of science whose cause is identical with truth, with righteousness and justice, and then make your choice.

Mr. Minton claims that in my philosophy "every impulse of the modern philosophical spirit crying out for the ultimate personality is ignored and repulsed." The term "ultimate personality" is not fortunate, but I will not haggle about words, whenever I have good reasons to know the meaning; and so I answer that his statement is not true, in so far as I have myself decidedly advocated the justice of speaking of God as a person, only I insist that God's personality is not human, but divine.

God's thoughts are not transient successive representations, but eternal verities, some of which are formulated by naturalists as laws of nature. God's thoughts are everlasting and omnipresent, being all-efficient in every instant. When we consider that actual events in the world shape themselves according to their regulations, we must grant that they prove omnipotent. In so far as they are perfect in every respect, they may be called all-wise, although the term implies a gross anthropomorphism. They are not wise in a human sense; they are all-wise, being the standard of all wisdom. Since nothing escapes the omnipresence of God, they may be characterized as omniscient. Yet here, again, they are not omniscient in a human sense, but in a higher sense, penetrating into the most secret recesses of existence. Finally, in so far as they justify truth, goodness and right, if not at once, yet in the long run, we may call them all-good, omni-benevolent, omni-beneficent, and, at any rate, they are the ultimate standard of morality. Such has been the nature of God, since in the evolution of religion God was identified with justice and righteousness. I am far from denying or ignoring the desire to think of God under the allegory of a person. I only remain conscious of the fact that it is a simile. Further, it is important to stand in a personal relation to God, to bear in mind that He is the God of the whole world and also of me individually; but I am at the same time aware of the child-like confusion which frequently prevails in the God-conceptions of pious souls. If their piety keeps in proper limits and does not ascend the tribunal of the inquisition, their erroneous views are not only harmless, but may be regarded as a surrogate of the genuine piety which has grasped the true nature of a truly divine God.

It is not fair to say that I propose to "smash the shrines of all creeds" or "to throttle the very instinct of religion in man;" for, on the contrary, I see in religion the deepest and most important impulse of man's humanity. My criticism of the errors of religion in its lower phases does not blind me to the enormous significance of all religious aspiration, and I am glad to recognize the goodness of the religious instinct even where it is still obscured by superstitions and idolatrous practices. In my opinion, it is the duty of the philosopher to judge every religion according to the best interpretation that its best representatives have given it. Aberrations should not be concealed, but the motive of the aberration should be explained without personal disparagement.

Mr. Minton characterizes my God-conception as "pantheism robbed of its mystical adornments and its confessedly somewhat redeeming features."

Pantheism identifies God and the world to such an extent that God is the sum-total of all being. I object to pantheism because God is not the sum-total of all things in the world; God is the cosmic order, the entirety of the factors that shape the world. Accordingly, God is not the All, the totality of nature, but a definite feature of the world. God as the cosmic order, it is true, is everywhere in the world, but he is not the material world itself. God is not the whole, but a part of the world, and here the old paradox becomes true, that the part is more than the whole. The determinate factors of the world, the eternal norm of being, the divine in the real, is so much more real, so much better, so much more powerful, than any and all single realities, that it exists independently of nature and would remain, even if the whole world did not exist—a truth which justifies the term "supernatural." God is the super-real in the real, the hyperphysical in the physical, and the supernatural in the natural. Yet the supernatural is not anti-natural, nor is it extra-natural; it is present in the natural; it lies latent in the lower spheres of the inorganic world and becomes apparent in the soul of man.

The fundamental difference between Mr. Minton and myself is this: He believes in a personal and I in a superpersonal God, and to him the superpersonal God is impersonal. Mr. Minton does not call me an atheist, but other theologians have done so, and I will freely grant that in so far (but in so far only) as a truly superpersonal God makes the personal God redundant, my philosophy will naturally appear to many as atheism, because it antagonizes or renders antiquated the old-fashioned theology of a personal (i. e., an individual) God. But the man of science will understand that the idea of a superpersonal God is tenable before the tribunal of the severest critique, and so my God conception will finally be considered as a higher theism, truer, more scientific, and more genuine than the old belief, if only we agree to be serious in the purification of the God idea, if only we mean to think of God as a truly divine being, if only we are serious in looking upon him as truly eternal, omnipresent, omniscient, omnipotent, etc. The theologians of the past have never been serious in thinking out these qualities of God to their very last conclusion. They have illustrated them with a childlike naïveté and made of God, instead of a divine person, an enormously huge human person, a deified individual, an Ego entity, with all its weaknesses, retaining the most human features of the simile and rejecting its truly religious meaning.

Now, I will confess to Mr. Minton and to all theologians who may care to know, that in my theological development I actually passed through an era of unequivocal and avowed atheism. I turned atheist, when I understood that law is supreme and must be supreme, that the highest authority in matters of truth and morality are not verdicts of an individual being, be be ever so huge and powerful, but that they are eternal and unalterable norms. Nothing can be more eternal than eternal law.

Principle is above any deity, truth is higher than any God, and if there is anything divine at all, truth constitutes the very essence of divinity. Says Esdras (1 Esdras, iv, 35):

"Great is the truth and stronger than all things."

The book is apocryphal, but the glorification of the truth which it contains is worthy of being quoted in full. Esdras says (1 Esdras, iv, 38-40):

"As for the truth, it endureth, and is always strong; it liveth and conquereth for-evermore.

"With her there is no acceptance of persons or rewards; but she doeth the things that are just, and refraineth from all unjust and wicked things; and all men do well like of her works.

"Neither in her judgment is any unrighteousness; and she is the strength, kingdom, power and majesty of all ages. Blessed be the God of truth."

The question is not whether or not my God is a personal being, but whether or not my God is the God of Truth.

I will boil down the God problem to the simplest possible statement, and if Mr. Minton will be kind enough to criticise my atheism and correct me where I am wrong, I will be glad to revert to the old theological anthropomorphism.

Uniformities of our experience which naturalists formulate as natural laws are ultimately reduced to principles of the formal sciences, logic, arithmetic, mathematics, etc. We will select the simplest of all, arithmetic, and take as an instance the simplest statement, $2 \times 2 = 4$. This statement is typical of all other purely formal statements in all the purely formal sciences. We might as well take any complicated equation, for instance, the formula of the Newtonian law of attraction or the result of calculations by which we predict with great precision the movements of the celestial bodies, or events in physics, or the result of any natural process. All formulas of scientific certainty, if correctly stated, are finally just as intrinsically necessary as the equation $2 \times 2 = 4$. Now this statement is intrinsically true, and so are all the conclusions of all the purely formal sciences, and since the purely formal features are the determining factors in the laws of nature, the laws of nature themselves are of the same intrinsic necessity. Such as they are, they are immutable; they must be so, and cannot be otherwise, and we can understand that if certain features of reality are given, the consequences are definitely determined, and cannot be otherwise. Scientific comprehension really consists in formulating experiences as uniformities and pointing out their necessity.

Now the question is—Has this equation, $2 \times 2 = 4$, been made such as it is by a God or is it intrinsically necessary? If it (and with it the entire cosmic order) has been made by a God, then God is superior to the formula.

If, however, God, the Creator, when about to create the world, considered the intrinsic necessity of formal laws and like a master-inventor adapted His plans of construction to eternal and immutable norms, He is no longer supreme, but is subject to some higher power, the eternal necessity of law.

Plato's God is not God in our sense. Plato speaks of necessity as above God. Plato's God is the Demiurgos, the master-builder of the world. Further, Brahma, the God of the Brahmans, is the world-soul; and the world-soul, too, is subject to eternal law. The world-soul (as conceived by the Brahmans) is a great and noble creature. It is as much bigger and higher, and, perhaps, also, as much better, than man as perhaps man is superior to an ant, or even to a microbe, or to a white blood corpuscle that courses in his veins; but, after all, the world-soul is not truly God, but an individual being, a creature of the true God; and the principles of truth and goodness and justice are his norms as much, and not a whit less, than they are the norms of man. I for one cannot conceive that God made $2 \times 2 = 4$, or any other purely formal statement. The harmony of mathematics is not extraneous, but intrinsic, and there is no room for an individual lawgiver who made the laws, such as they are, eternal and necessary.

Having been told from my childhood that all other God-conceptions save the traditional interpretation of Biblical theology are atheistic, I jumped to the conclusion that theism is wrong and that atheism is right and, preferring truth even to the faith of my childhood, which was very dear to me, I discarded religion and turned infidel.

I thought at the time that I was irreligious, but I know now, from experience, that all infidelity is only a phase in our religious development.

Ingersoll was the son of a clergyman, and there was more of his father in him than he knew himself. He was a born clergyman, and all his scoffing, his blasphemy, and flippant jokes about things sacred are evidences of his deep interest in theological questions. The disappointment of our expectations naturally turns our love into hatred, our infatuation into spite, our disappointed hopes into bitter denunciations. The historians of a later age will give Ingersoll a place in the development of theology, and will give him more credit and more honor as a theologian than the leaders of our orthodox churches of the present day are inclined to allow.

I remained an atheist so long as I felt merely the need for a negation of errors; but very soon I began to yearn for a positive statement of my convictions, and I tried to construct a new world conception out of the débris of the shipwreck which my religion had suffered. When I inquired into the scientific explanations of the universe, and when I investigated the nature of the moral problem, I found that what I had attributed formerly to an individual being, a great cosmic monarch, or a purpose-endowed world-soul, was actually accomplished in a much grander and a more unfailing way by natural law; and natural law is not the mere formula of the naturalist, but a living factor, an omnipresent power that although unmaterial, rules supreme everywhere in exactly the same manner which must be attributed to God if the conception of God's nature be freed from gross anthropomorphism. Moreover, all the natural laws form one great system of an intrinsic and organic unity—a kind of spiritual organism, and we may in this sense call it a person, only we must understand that this person is not an individual, not a person in the human sense, but the omnipresence of efficient law. It is the norm of being, which, when it illumines the consciousness of sentient beings, through the development of reason, constitutes their personality. There is a standard of right and wrong, of good and evil, of truth and falsehood; there is an objective condition in the constitution of the world that makes man possible as a rational and a moral being. Whatever it may be, that is God.

Thus I had found God again, yet God is to me no longer a particular and concrete reality, but the super-reality of universal and eternal efficiency. Here is an undeniable factor possessed of all the qualities formerly attributed to God, doing all the functions of God and serving at the same time in the broadest way as the ultimate authority in the field of conduct. Here is the prototype of man's personality; for human reason is nothing but the reflex of the cosmic order—the rationality of the universe. Here alone is the standard of truth and untruth, of right and wrong, of goodness and badness; and when I became confronted with the claims of wrong liberalism rejecting all authority in science as well as ethics; when I considered the claims of Mr. Spencer's agnosticism, that the ultimate mystery of the world is absolutely inscrutable, that accordingly in ethics hedonism rules supreme; that there is no good and evil in the moral sense of the word, but that good is merely that which yields most pleasure, I found that in these essential points—in points relating to conduct—agnosticism is wrong and that the traditional religion is right. We have only to mind that the traditional view is expressed in poetical terms.

Mr. Minton calls me a pagan, but whether or not he is right depends upon the meaning of the name. The word, according to its etymology, means "villagers," "country folks," or "people that live in the heath." Hence, the Saxon term, "heathen." The pagan is contrasted to the inhabitant of the city, the "urban." The latter is supposed to be urbane and progressive, but the former is considered a boor, a hayseed, a reactionary conservative. While the urban population had adopted the new faith (Christianity) the pagan still clung to his belief in the ancient gods, and thus pagan came to mean a worshiper of any one of the pre-Christian religions.

To-day the word "pagan" is used in different senses. Some Christians (especially those that are inclined to be dogmatic) call pagans all non-

Christians, fetich-worshipers as well as philosophers. This makes not only the cannibals pagans, but also the ancient Greeks and Romans, the large masses of the Chinese, the Japanese, the Siamese, and the Hindus, including all non-Christian sages, Socrates and Plato, and Buddha.

It seems unfair to use the word "pagan" promiscuously for Plato as well as the idolator, and I propose to use the word "pagan" for all those who are so backward in their religious development that they still believe in the letter of their religious myth instead of accepting the spirit of it. If Plato speaks of Zeus, he does not mean merely the personification of the sky, but God, almost in a Christian sense. However, the idolator who kneels before a Zeus statue and believes that it is the residing place of a spirit called Zeus, is a pagan, and it becomes apparent that if the word "pagan" is used in this sense, that while Socrates and Plato cannot be called pagans, there is much paganism still left in Christianity, not only in Italy and other Catholic countries, where saint-worship bears a strong resemblance to the ancient polytheism, but sometimes even in Protestant countries, where the God-conception in many minds is by no means free from crude anthropomorphic conceptions. It is pagan to think of God as a great benevolent man seated on a throne in the heavens; it is pagan when the dogmas of the symbolical books are believed literally, and not in a symbolical sense: it is pagan to kneel before an icon and expect help through a worship of it.

The dogmatic Christian looks with contempt upon pagan mythology, without being aware that there is also a Christian mythology, and, as a rule, those Christians who call dissenters infidels and pagans are pagans themselves; the Christian pagan, however, is more ingenuous than the pagans of Greek and Roman antiquity, for the latter were mostly conscious of the mythological nature of their gods, while the dogmatic Christian of to-day is still a believer in the letter of his mythology.

When I became aware of the truth that the essential part of a religion, a philosophy, a world-conception, is that feature which determines its ethics, which finds practical application in conduct, I found myself necessitated to revise my atheism, and now I discovered that the very arguments which had upset my belief in an anthropomorphic deity, furnish the most solid foundation for a truer and nobler and better God-conception.

Having regained a positive ground, I learned to judge the situation objectively, and I came to the conclusion that my views are the legitimate outcome of a consistent further development of the faith of my childhood, and I have no doubt that Mr. Minton himself, or his sons and his disciples, will by and by reach the position in which I stand to-day. I am fully aware of my kinship to former stages of my religious development, and since then whenever I feel an Ingersollian irony come over me, I am conscious of its being the criticism of my own prior self.

Far from being averse to religion, I love it, and am deeply interested in it. Other religions that are kin to Christianity, especially the old original Buddhism, and the pure teachings of Lao-Tze, are naturally sympathetic to me, but Evangelical theology takes the place of a direct spiritual ancestry. It seems as if Mr. Minton had noticed the special regard I pay to it, but he views my consideration of it not without distrust, for he says of my philosophy that:

"It regards with patient and patronizing complacency the crude anthropomorphisms and excrescences of mankind's present religious state, remembering that mythology is ever an indispensable ladder to be climbed in making the difficult ascent to truth."

Replace the words "patient and patronizing complacency" by "sympathy" and I will make no objection to Mr. Minton's statement.

There is a peculiar charm in the God-conception. These three letters, G-O-D, are a treasure of uncommon riches. They embody all that is great, and noble, and good, and right, and true. It is one of my greatest efforts in life to preserve this grand idea from the shipwreck which Christian paganism (the dogmatic belief in the letter) is bound to incur. To those who call me an atheist, I answer that I am not a common atheist; I am an atheist who loves God. But, after a careful inquiry into the problems of the nature of God and the history of the God-conception, I have come to the conclusion that my philosophy is not atheistic.

A German scholar writes in a German encyclopedia:

"The conceptions concerning God are very different, and there are many who denounce as atheism every view which differs from their own."

How true is this statement! It may be applied to both my opponents and myself. Mr. Minton calls me "a twentieth century pagan" because I do not believe as he does, and I call him "a Christian pagan" because he believes in the letter of a dogma which was originally not meant to be taken literally, for it was proclaimed as "a symbol," being contained in the collection of Christian credos, officially called "symbolical books."

The more I ponder on the God-problem, the surer grows my conviction

Mr. Minton takes me to task that my God does not stand in need of adoration, and that I condemn adoration as a pagan custom. All depends upon the meaning of the word.

"Adoration" is derived from the Latin "*os*" = "mouth," and means throwing a hand-kiss to a person or deity to whom one is devoted. The usual attitude of pre-Christian pagans before their gods, as represented on the monuments, is with the fingers of the right hand on their lips. I have no objection to lip service of any kind, nor to any form of dignified adoration, but we should not encourage self-humiliating ceremonies. Religion should elevate man, not degrade him, and so I have no room for any God who enjoys the spectacle of prostrate and kneeling worshipers. Remember that even earthly monarchs, if they become civilized, are disgusted with the kowtowing of their subjects.

My view of worship is, briefly stated, this: If worship is taken in the usual sense as an act of submissive flattery, I do not propose to worship God. However, if worship is to signify, what it does according to its etymology (Anglo-Saxon *weordhscipe*), "considering and bearing in mind the worth of something or somebody," I do propose to *worthship* God. All of us should fully appreciate the import of God, for our lives and for those who shall live after us. Such a worship is one "in spirit and in truth," as is commended by Christ. It will keep us in harmony with humanity as well as with the cosmical order of the universe. It will not disparage but elevate man as the first-born son of nature and the legitimate child of God.

The same holds good of prayer. Supplication, with kneeling down in abject self-humiliation, should be discontinued. But if prayer is a severe self-criticism, a moral atonement for trespasses committed, and also a vow to do better in the future, a strengthening of our moral sense for avoiding errors, if prayer thus keeps us in unity with God, the eternal standard of morality, prayer is recommendable.

There is no sense in praying for rain, or for the abatement of a storm, or for a change in the course of nature. If we do so, our prayer may prove an alleviation to our troubled mind, but it will have no effect upon nature, for the laws of nature are immutable. Nor is there any sense in trying to alter God's will; but there is sense in praying for a change in our own will, a change of our attitude in life, of our own mental and moral disposition, and this is not only recommendable, but highly desirable even from the standpoint of science. Man can only gain by the establishment of a personal relation to the divine will, meaning by it the moral demands made of man by the cosmic order. Our hearts are sanctified by a devotional attitude toward that all-presence which we have defined as true divinity. If this personal relation finds expression in words it will assume the form of vows, of self-exhortation, of praying for the power of resistance in temptation, for strength and energy when great tasks confront us, for fortitude in misfortune, for patience and submission to the inevitable ills of life.

There is but one true worship, which consists, as Christ declares, in doing the will of God, and there is but one prayer that is not heathenish, the Lord's Prayer, "Thy will be done," for it is not a beggar's petition but a vow of self-discipline. Finally, there is but one religion; it is the spread of good-will upon earth, yet it cannot be realized without an uncompromising submission to truth. Let us by all means respect the symbols in, with, and under which religious truths are taught; but the significance of a creed is more than its symbols; the meaning is greater than the dogma; the spirit is higher than the letter.

EDITOR.

ON THE DEFINITION OF AN INFINITE NUMBER.

"The whole is greater than any one of its parts," is one of the most useful axioms of elementary geometry. In view of this fact it appears somewhat remarkable that the most useful definition of an infinite multitude should be, "The whole is equal to one of its parts." To understand this definition fully it is necessary to define the terms equal and parts.

One of the most primitive modes of proving the equality of two multitudes is the placing of the units of the multitudes in a (1, 1) correspondence. That is, if it is possible to associate with every unit of each multitude one and only one unit of the other, the two multitudes are said to be equal. The idea of a (1, 1) correspondence is doubtless one of the earliest mathematical concepts, and it is generally supposed to have given rise not only to the number concept, but also to number words.

When the child employs his fingers or other objects in counting, he gives evidence of the early development of the power "to relate things to things, or to represent a thing by a thing, an ability without which no thinking is possible."[1] Hence, there is no simpler or more definite way of proving that a part of a multitude may be equal to the whole than by establishing a (1, 1) correspondence between the units of a part and the units of the whole. The totality of positive real numbers furnishes one of the most interesting examples of such a multitude.

If in the equation

$$y = \frac{1}{x+1},$$

we let x represent any real number whatever y will also represent a real number. For two distinct values of x the corresponding vales of y will be

[1] Dedekind, *Essays on Number* (translated by Beman), page 39.

distinct. Moreover, if x is replaced by any positive real number whatsoever, y will be equal to a positive proper fraction. That is, there are just as many positive real numbers which do not exceed one as there are positive real numbers, including those which do not exceed one.

It should be observed that this is not juggling. Only perfectly valid thought processes are employed. The given equation shows in a clear and definite manner that the positive real numbers which do not exceed unity can be placed in a (1, 1) correspondence with the total number of positive real numbers. That the former constitute a part of the latter is universally accepted. Hence we must say that a part of the positive real numbers is equal to the totality of these numbers.

By employing the equation

$$2y = \frac{1}{x+1},$$

we can show, in exactly the same manner, that the positive real numbers which do not exceed one-half are equal to the totality of real numbers. More generally, by employing the equation

$$ay = \frac{1}{x+1},$$

it appears that the positive real numbers which do not exceed $\frac{1}{a}$ are equal to the totality of these numbers. It deserves to be emphasized that we are not dealing here simply with a mathematical curiosity. The real numbers furnish the foundation of a great part of the work of the student of mathematics, and it appears unpardonable to overlook any of their important properties.

The developments of mathematics have always been greatly influenced by discoveries of facts which are at variance with what was generally accepted. Of such discoveries in comparatively recent times three are especially noteworthy on account of the fundamental principles involved, namely: (1) There are perfectly consistent geometries in which the sum of the angles of a plane triangle is not equal to two right angles. (2) There are algebras in which the commutative law of multiplication does not hold. (3) There are multitudes or aggregates such that a part is equal to the whole.

The first of these discoveries is perhaps better known than either of the other two. In regard to the second, Poincaré recently said:[1] "Hamilton's quaternions give us an example of an operation which presents an almost perfect analogy with multiplication, which may be called multiplication, and yet it is not commutative, *i. e.*, the product is changed when the

[1] Poincaré; *Bulletin des Sciences Mathématiques.* Vol. 26, 1902, page 250.

order of the factors is changed. This presents a revolution in arithmetic which is entirely similar to the one which Lobatchevski effected in geometry."

The third one of the given discoveries has perhaps made the least impression on popular thought, and yet it is certainly not less fundamental than either of the other two nor is it more foreign to the usual trend of human thought and interests. When thought is not artificially restrained it naturally enters upon the infinite, and, as in other domains of science, so in the science of the infinite, nothing capable of proof ought to be passed by without proof. Moreover, it is most important that the facts which do not agree with what has been generally accepted should be popularized, on account of their corrective influence on the human intellect.

In the above proof that a part of the real positive numbers is equal to the totality of the numbers, the term part was employed in its universally accepted sense. In general, we shall say that a given aggregate is a part of a second aggregate, provided all the units of the first aggregate are contained in the second and the second contains at least one unit which is not in the first. For instance, we shall say that the even positive numbers are a *part* of all the natural numbers. Since it is clearly possible to associate with each natural number its double, the natural numbers constitute an infinite aggregate. In fact, we may establish a (1, 1) correspondence between the natural numbers and a part of these numbers in an unlimited number of different ways. For instance, it is possible to associate any multiple or any power of the number with each of the natural numbers.

By the same method it may be proved that time, according to the common conception, is infinite; for there is a (1, 1) correspondence between the total number of hours and the total number of half hours. If the half hours from any period would be denoted by the natural numbers, the hours would correspond to the even numbers. Similarly, it may be observed that space (defined analytically by coördinates) is infinite, according to the given definition.

If it is possible to establish a (1, 1) correspondence between two infinite totalities, they are said to be of the same power. The totality (M_0) formed by the natural numbers is especially important. Any totality which has the same power as M_0 is said to be countable. It is an extremely interesting fact that all algebraic numbers are countable. In particular, it is possible to establish a (1, 1) correspondence between all rational numbers and the natural numbers. The developments along this line belong to the important subject known as the theory of aggregates (ensemble, Mengenlehre), where the full significance of the use of the infinite in mathematics is exhibited.

The simplicity of the given definition may perhaps become more evident if the matter is stated as follows: If a totality (M) of units is given, only two cases are possible. Either M contains a part which contains as many units as M or no such part exists in M. In the former case, M is said to be infinite; in the latter it is finite. It is not difficult to show that the definition does not violate the ordinary conception that the infinite is unlimited, while the finite is limited.

Dedekind was the first (1880) to use this definition of an infinite aggregate or totality as the foundation to establish the science of numbers. Bolzano and others pointed out at an earlier date that infinite aggregates have the property which is here used as a definition. It is now very generally employed, and the mind that can dwell upon it long enough to grasp even the most direct bearings cannot fail to derive from it an unusual amount of pleasure and profit, such as only great thoughts can give.

G. A. Miller.

Stanford University.

NOTE ON "A BUDDHIST GENESIS."

Since my translation of the Buddhist Genesis document appeared in the January *Monist*, I have found that Rockhill rendered it from the Tibetan in 1884. (*Life of the Buddha and Early History of His Order.* Translated from the Tibetan. By W. Woodville Rockhill. London (Trübner's Oriental Series, 1884). I had known this book for years, but it escaped me when making the Genesis translation and also in my *Buddhist Bibliography* (London, 1903). In Rockhill's volume the Genesis document comes at the very beginning. Like the Sanskritised Prâkrit version used by me, it belongs to the Vinaya Pitaka. The Tibetan Canon is that of the sect of Realists (*Sarvastivada*), whose account of the compilation of the Scriptures was translated by Suzuki, also in the January *Monist.* There are two versions of the Genesis document in the Tibetan Vinaya Pitaka: A short one in the Vinaya-vastu (corresponding in part to the Pâli Mahâvaggo), and a long one (translated by Rockhill) in the Vinaya-Vibhâga (Pâli Bhikkhu-Vibhanga). The Theravâda sect, who have handed down the Pâli Tripitaka, do not place this document in the Vinaya, but in the Sûtra Pitaka. Thus do we prove the truth of the Island Chronicle of Ceylon, which says that the Realists, the Great Council, and many other sects, made recensions of the Canon to suit themselves. We must never forget that the Pâli, though the oldest version of the Canon known, is by no means the only one. The Mahâsamghika (Great Council) school also claims to be the oldest, and their Book of Discipline has come down to us in a fifth-century Chinese translation. Suzuki also gave us extracts from this, and we saw therefrom that they had no Abhidharma. This looks as if their Canon belonged to an earlier period than the Pâli, for the Abhidharma was in the nature of commentary, and was compiled after the Buddhists had split up into sects. W know that one ancient sect, the Sautrântikas (*i. e.*, Sûtra-men) refused to admit the canonicity of the Abhidharma and were content with the Sûtra-Pitaka. Moreover, the Great Council sect not only tabooed the Abhidharma, but they also had a very short recension of the Fifth Nikâya. This collection, known as the Khuddaka (Short) in Pâli, was called the Miscellaneous Pitaka by other sects, and consisted largely of commentaries. The Great Council refused to canonize these commentaries, but admitted into it only the Udâna, the Itivuttka and the Nidâna.

It is high time that Japanese scholars translated the books of this early rival sect, which may yet be proved to be older than the Pâli.

Albert J. Edmunds.

Philadelphia, Pa.

PRESENT-DAY SCIENCE AND RELIGION.

At a time when so much scientific literature is being issued to the public the questions naturally arise in one's mind, In what direction does this scientific influence tend? Does it make for religion, or does it favor atheism? Probably there never has been a time when an answer in the negative could be so definitely given to the latter question. Indeed, such is the attitude of religion to science that so advanced and broadminded a preacher as the Rev. R. J. Campbell has said: "I believe the next great rehabilitation of the fundamentals of religion will come, not from the side of theology, but from the side of science." This, no doubt, to many, will seem a daring pronouncement to make. Yet, is it not significant of present-day thought?

Such happy relations, however, have not always existed between religion and science. Science has had to battle hard for a recognition of its services to thought and progress, and, like religion, it, too, has had its martyrs. One has only to mention the names of Galileo, Bruno and Antonio do Dominis. Galileo, it is well known, was cruelly treated and imprisoned for promulgating the doctrine of Copernicus that the earth revolved round the sun; Bruno for teaching the plurality of worlds was sacrificed at the stake, and the body and books of Antonio Dominis were taken and burned after his death, because he attributed the colors of the rainbow to natural causes. If ever the fear existed that a knowledge of science was opposed to religion, that fear certainly was rife in the sixteenth and seventeenth centuries.

But what immense strides progress has made! Compare the situation just described with the condition of thought that now prevails, which makes acceptable such an utterance as that of the Rev. R. J. Campbell, quoted at the beginning of this article. He, apparently, has no fear of science being the foe of religion, but rather looks to it as an aid to strengthen men's beliefs in an All-wise Creator. One might say his attitude is that of the welcoming hand of religion to science, and, what is more, it is an appeal made not in vain. Science, also, has extended her hand. Lord Kelvin, speaking quite recently, definitely stated: "I cannot admit that with regard to the origin of life, science neither affirms nor denies Creative Power. Science positively affirms Creative Power."

The question of the attitude and relationship of science to religion is one of long standing. It seems to have disturbed the thoughts of that great natural philosopher, Lord Bacon, whose judgment is very apropos to-day. In his "Sacræ Meditationes" he says: "This I dare to affirm, in knowledge of Nature, that a little natural philosophy, and the first entrance into it, doth dispose the opinion to atheism; but, on the other side, much natural philosophy, and wading deep into it, will bring about men's minds to religion." This, indeed, seems true. Many readers will remember that when their minds first opened to the elementary truths of natural science, there was a tendency to doubt any agent other than "natural laws." But after "wading deep" into science, gaining further knowledge of the mysterious relations between living and non-living matter, the wonderful possibilities inherent in the elements, and the magnitude of the starry realms, the mind was compelled to bow in reverence before Him who has created so much that is incomprehensible.

The specific influence science has had upon thought, especially religious thought, is admirably stated by the late Professor Drummond, in his *Natural Law in the Spiritual World*. He writes: "Now that science has made the world around articulate, it speaks to religion with a twofold purpose. In the first place, it offers to corroborate Theology; in the second, to purify it." *To corroborate and purify.* That is the special influence science has had upon religion. Again, what does Lord Avebury—better known as Sir John Lubbock—say? "Science has always purified religion. . . . It is in those countries where science is most backward that religion is less well understood, and in those countries which science is most advanced that religion is purest." According to these two great authorities, then, science certainly does not oppose religion, but purifies it of superstition and makes the "world around articulate." Did not Longfellow hear that articulation in Nature when

"He wandered away and away
With Nature, the dear old nurse,
Who sung to him night and day
The rhymes of the Universe."

That science does not "dispose the opinion to atheism" is surely sufficiently shown by the fact that such world-wide scientists as Copernicus, Galileo, Bruno, Newton, Darwin and Drummond have been believers in a Supreme Creator. Indeed, that greatest of living scientists, Lord Kelvin, has said: "We are absolutely forced by science to believe with perfect confidence in a Directive Power." Likewise is the opinion of Sir Oliver Lodge. Scientific literature and scientific inquiry, evidently, do not incline to disbelief, but, as Bacon said, three hundred years ago, "will bring about men's minds to religion."

W. E. Ashwell.

Battersea Park, S. W., London.

BOOK REVIEWS.

Dr. Otto Weininger ueber die letzten Dinge. Mit einem biographischen Vorwort von *Moriz Rappaport.* Wien und Leipzig: Wilhelm Braumüller, 1904.

Dr. Otto Weininger's first and main work, *Sex and Character,* was reviewed in the January number of *The Monist* for 1904 (XIV, 2, p. 316), and we could even then discover in its author a certain nervous condition that indicated a neurotic and unbalanced state of mind. In the meantime his last work entitled *Concerning the Last Things* was edited by one of his friends, Moriz Rappaport, and here we learn more about this strange and abnormal man, who, possessed of high ideals, was nevertheless mainly interesting on account of the pathology of his mental development. Dr. Weininger, as we learn from the preface, handed his unfinished manuscript to his friend with the remark that in case he were incapable of finishing the book, he would entrust him with the work. Soon after Weininger ended his life by suicide.

Weininger was a dualist and his favorite philosopher was Plato. Next to Plato he loved Plotinus, Augustine, Pascal, Schopenhauer and Nietzsche. The latter two, however, he criticised severely, blaming them for regarding pleasure and pain as ultimate realities, and he called theirs, as well as Fechner's philosophy, "the world-conception of neurasthenics."

The favorite composer of Weininger was Wagner. Light was to him the symbol of everything good, the darkness of the deep sea the symbol of crime and evil. His work, *Sex and Character,* gives expression to the idea that woman is principally a sexual being, and he deemed it of importance to show the connection between sexuality and crime. Weininger used to say, "Ethics is never made as a present to anyone," and also that "Good people always have a shallow ethics," meaning thereby that good people, who never feel any temptation or the impulse to do wrong, have no proper idea of the ethical problem and its solution. Guilt was to him the center of all his thoughts. All suffering is due to guilt or inherited guilt. He distinguished between people such as have inherited a guilt and suffer thereby, and he called them "sufferers," and such who transferred their guilt upon others, and he called them "criminals."

Weininger accepted the belief in a soul and conceived the idea of a itual death, which is possible while the material body remains alive. The , in his opinion, is individual. Everywhere man has his own original sin this sin is identical with his guilt. "His aversion against Jews, against nen, and against Schiller," says Moriz Rappaport, "is solely due to their in exhibiting any dualism. Weininger rejected empirical optimism, but elieved in a transcendental one, which he identified with Paradise."

We recapitulate briefly what Herr Rappaport says about the author in preface, page XIX.

"When he had finished his first work, *Sex and Character*, he said to me: re are only three possibilities for me; the gallows, suicide, or a future lorious that I would not dare to think it to its end.' Since then his mental ndition grew worse. He studied the whole summer in Italy and sojourned some time in Syracuse, where he wrote the greatest part of the present k, *The Last Things*. He called Syracuse (a city facing the east) 'The place where one could stand sunset.' Then he visited Calabria, the island schia, Rome, Florence, and returned in the latter days of September to nna. Here he was frequently visited by suicidal intentions. He worked nights on his 'Last Aphorisms,' and found suddenly the solution of the blem which had formerly tortured him, 'Not the souls, not the individuals ultimate realities, even they are an expression of vanity, in that they ch importance to personality. The highest reality is alone the Good which udes all single contents.'

"Weininger proposed to leave Vienna and to travel again, but his condi- grew worse and the catastrophe approached. A dismal pessimism, which also conceived as guilt, came over him. Thus he said: 'All that I have tten is doomed because it has been written with bad intention . . . aps everything is cursed with which I have ever come in contact.' Next he rented a room in which Beethoven had died. There he stayed one t and early in the morning, October 4, 1903, he ended his life abruptly by hot into his breast."

The fate of this man is perhaps more interesting than his books, and ng his books his last and posthumous deserves most of all our attention. thoughts are instructive mainly as documents of a pathological life, a life which we feel sympathy because it was fated to end tragically, yet it ains much that is great and noble.

The contents of the book are as follows: (1) Peer Gynt and Ibsen, con- ing some comments on erotics, on hatred and love, on crime, etc.; (2) horisms, containing comments on the psychology of Sadism and Masoch- (pp. 65 ff.), the psychology of murder, ethics, original sin, etc.; (3) Notes Characterology, the neophytes and the priest, on Friedrich Schiller, frag- nts on Wagner and his "Parsifal"; (4) The One-Dimensionality of Time and Its Ethical Significance, together with speculations on time, space, and will, and the problem of time; (5) Metaphysics, containing the suggestions of a universal symbolism, psychology of animal types, the psychology of criminals, the animal psychology of the dog, the horse, and other general comments; (6) Culture and Its Relation to Faith; Fear and Knowledge. The last chapter concludes with Aphorisms.

PANIDEAL. Psychologie der sozialen Gefühle, von *Rudolf Holzapfel*, mit einem Vorwort von *E. Mach.* Leipzig: Johann Ambrosius Barth. 1901.

A special interest attaches to this book on account of the preface, written by Prof. Ernst Mach, who has considerably influenced the author in the formation of his world-conception, which is practically a reconstruction of man's religious aspirations, with new aims and a new authority in the domain of conduct, the latter, which is called "*Panideal,*" furnishes an appropriate title to the book.

In the preface, dated at Vienna, July, 1901, Professor Mach says:

"During the last winter the author of the present books, who introduced himself as a former student of R. Avenarius, visited me and handed me the MS. for perusal. I had never busied myself with an analysis of sentiments, this part of psychology lying without my sphere of interest, and the abstract mode of presenting the subject was at the start to me very little sympathetic. Thus I began my reading, to say the least, without any preconceived favorable opinion, as a kind of duty, but my interest rose with the progress of my study and I became highly interested in many of its parts. It threw certain light upon certain phases of my inner life, to which I, being a naturalist devoted to the investigation of objective phenomena, had so far paid little attention. Indeed, one may gain here a deeper insight into the psychology of the inquirer, the inventor, the artist, the founder of a religion and to the builder of civilization. One learns to understand how even our own ego in its evolution may become alienated to himself, to the very same ego in another phase of its development.

"One can very well see in this book that the author has lived much; but, of course, the individual psychical experiences upon which his abstract exposition is built and which give to his ideas their concrete contents, appeal to him more in their full reality than they would to the reader who may perhaps never have had analogous experiences of the same intensity and who can only fall back upon shadowy notions of his own experience. Further elucidations of his exposition, through concrete instances, by relating typical events, if not his own personal recollections, would be highly desirable. The efficacy of his labors I confidently believe could thereby only gain. However, even in its present shape, the book will be helpful and may prove that, in spite of all the valuable methods of modern psychology, with its experiments and measurements, the possibilities of simple introspective self-observation are by no means as yet exhausted."

The book itself consists of aphorisms which are arranged in nine chapters under the titles "Solitude," "Longing," "Hope," "Prayer," "Struggle," "Conscience," "Art," "Worlds" and "Ideal." The aphoristic utterances of the author are consecutively numbered and amount to 1,075, with an epilogue which reads as follows:

"No ideal for which I could live,
Even with the highest no [helpful] hint.
Myself I must seek, perhaps find."

The thousand and odd sentences are, as may be expected, of very unequal value. Some of them express fine sentiments, others seem trivial, and a few are obscure. Unquestionably they are all full of significance to the author, being expressions of his inmost convictions. They are of a man who has no faith in the established religions, yet feels an impulse stirring in himself that would be able to reconstruct a new religion, which would be better adapted to his particular needs. There is scarcely a mention of God in the book, yet the chapter containing his thoughts on prayer prove him a man of deep insight and religious feeling. He says:

"Prayer is mostly addressed to mere concepts or fictions, because our conversation with concepts is easier than a communication with realities."[1]

"Therefore prayer mostly assumes the soul and character of a monologic dialogue in which the praying person either speaks himself, while the person prayed to is conceived as listening, viz., assumed to be tacitly present, or the praying person and the adored one are thought to intercommunicate, while both remain to all appearances silent." (337.)

"Each prayer involves more or less a great hope of being answered, a help, or an edification." (344.)

"Prayers can be made, not only in words and music, but also in color, sculpture and architecture; nay! these arts are indispensable for the intensification of the disposition, as well as the effect of prayer." (352.)

Prayer according to Holzapfel depends very much upon the idea of the power or the person prayed to, but even if an individual be deprived of the illusion of its or his God's existence, he may continue to love anthropomorphism, and to address prayers to his ideals, but they will lose much of their former power and significance. A disappearance of illusion may finally lead to an atrophy of the need of prayer, yet prayer is a power in mankind. Holzapfel says:

"Almost all modern empiricists and atheists look upon prayer and the

[1] The text reads. "Wahrnehmungs verkehr," meaning "the actual objects of sense perception," i. e. "realities." A literal translation is here, as in many other passages, impossible.

need of prayer as slavish, barbaric and useless. But the builders of our civilization knew better." (388.)

"Sufficiently oriented poets may be induced to create new prayer poems." (386.)

"Among the most potent means of promoting human and humane developments are prayers addressed to the evolution-ideal and especially the prayer to the Panideal. The Panideal is defined (in 1052) as the pure ideal of a hygio-psychical, maximal, positive, valuation, which in its fullness (as explained in 1056) is unattainable and can only be longed for and aspired for." (381.)

The reviewer believes to know German, but he can only guess at the exact meaning of some new expressions and word combinations, such as *"ethikalische Kopierungen," "menschkheitsentwickelungsrevolutionaere Moralbilligung"* and *"unterschiedsgraduell hygiopsychisches Panideal."*

The Panideal is a kind of new religion which will prove interesting to men of science such as Mach, but it is very doubtful whether this special instance will appeal to large masses, and it is, as Professor Mach hinted at in the preface, too abstract to exercise any effect upon others; and so it may be regarded as a symptom, not merely of the present state of unrest, but also of the tendency toward the formation of a new faith that is budding in the heart of modern man.

Studies in Psychology. Edited by *George T. W. Patrick*, Professor of Philosophy. Volume III. University of Iowa. Iowa City, Ia. 1902. Price, $1.00.

The third volume of these studies contains two essays by C. E. Seashore, entitled "A Method of Measuring Mental Work: the Psychergograph" and "A Voice Tonoscope;" one article by the same, assisted by Miss Mabel Clare Williams, on "An Illusion of Length." A fourth article is devoted to "Normal Illusions in Representative Geometrical Forms," by Miss Williams. and the concluding essay by George T. W. Patrick describes "The New Psychological Laboratory of the University of Iowa."

Studies in the Psychology of Sex. Analysis of the Sexual Impulse. Love and Pain. The Sexual Impulse in Women. By *Havelock Ellis*. Philadelphia: F. A. Davis Company. 1903.

Mr. Havelock Ellis, one of the best authorities in the studies of sex and its various problems, here publishes the first section of a volume which is to treat on the psychology of sex. It analyzes and tries to explain the sexual impulse, and the entire volume will be completed with two other monographs on subjects in the same line to be published by the same publishers.

A French edition of Prof. Mach's *History of Mechanics* has been published.

Geometric Exercises in Paper-Foldi

By T. SUNDARA ROW. Edited and revised by W. W. Bema and D. E. Smith. Pp., x, 148. Price, cloth, $1.00 net (4s. 6d. net)

"Simply a revelation in the possibilities of paper-folding."—*Teachers' Insti tute*, N. Y.

"The editors have performed a genuine service in bringing this work befor our public, and in such neat and attractive form. The twenty-six exquisit half-tone illustrations with which they have replaced the line drawings of th original, are a decided enrichment of the volume."—*Science.*

"For teachers of elementary geometry the book is really of considerable valu and it shows in a forcible and tangible way how properties vaguely known to u by experience are logical and necessary consequences of a few definitions. set of colored squares of paper is provided with the book."—*Journal of Physi cal Chemistry.*

"A most welcome contribution to concrete geometry, well worthy the attentio of teachers."—*Charles DeCarmo*, Cornell University.

"A helpful and stimulating book for teachers."—*E. M. Langley*, Bedford, Eng

THE OPEN COURT PUBLISHING CO., 324 Dearborn CHICAGO

LONDON: Kegan Paul, Trench, Trübner & Co.

ESSAYS ON NUMBE

I. CONTINUITY AND IRRATIONAL NUMBERS.
II. THE NATURE AND MEANING OF NUMBERS.

By *Richard Dedekind*, Professor in Brunswick, Germany. Auth ised Translation by *Wooster Woodruff Beman*. Pages, 115. Pri Red Cloth, 75 cents.

"The Open Court Publishing Company deserves praise for continuing to p lish translations of foreign scientific classics into English."—*Bulletin of the Am can Mathematical Society.*

"The work of Dedekind is very fundamental, and I am glad to have it in carefully-wrought English version. I think the book should be of much servic American mathematicians and teachers."—*Prof. E. H. Moore*, Univ. of Chicag

"It is to be hoped that the translation will make the essays better know English mathematicians; they are of the very first importance, and rank with work of Weierstrass, Kronecker, and Cantor in the same field."—*Nature.*

THE OPEN COURT PUBLISHING CO., CHICA

LONDON: Kegan Paul, Trench, Trübner & Co., Ltd.

THE MONIST

A QUARTERLY MAGAZINE

Devoted to the Philosophy of Science

Editor: DR. PAUL CARUS. *Associates:* { E. C. HEGELER / MARY CARUS.

CONTENTS:

CHICAGO:

HE OPEN COURT PUBLISHING CO

Price, 50 cts.; Yearly, $2.00.

LONDON: KEGAN PAUL, TRENCH, TRÜBNER & COMPANY, LIMITED.

In England and U. P. U., half a crown; Yearly, 9s 6d.

PUBLISHERS' NOTE

The Publishers of THE MONIST propose henceforth to begin each new volume with the New Year, which change will be accomplished by adding a fifth number to the present volume.

OL. XIV, No. 4. JULY, 1904.

THE MONIST

A QUARTERLY MAGAZINE

Devoted to the Philosophy of Science

Editor: Dr. Paul Carus. Associates: E. C. Hegeler, Mary Carus.

CONTENTS:

CHICAGO:

THE OPEN COURT PUBLISHING COMPANY.

1904

. XIV. JULY, 1904. No. 4.

THE MONIST

:HE BIOLOGICAL EVOLUTION OF LANGUAGE.

[Mr. O. F. Cook had the rare opportunity of watching a people primitive gh not to be conscious of the grammar of their own language, and the nt article contains an observation on the subject. One of the most rtant points, which comes out very clearly in his statements, is a condemna- of the theory that a conscious notion of the abstract should exist in man's l when he begins to use abstract ideas, and this is I would say a corollary e theory propounded by Ludwig Noiré who tersely said that "man thinks ise he speaks, not *vice versa*, he does not speak because he thinks." é's theory of the origin of language may be considered as a new epoch e history of philology, and the gist of his theory has been published in ish form in extracts from his works under the title *On the Origin of uage* (Open Court Publishing Co.). Noiré's ideas have not become iently known in this country, and judging from the authorities which Cook quotes, the opposite view which would insist that man speaks ise he thinks, that he forms ideas because he has become conscious ie power of abstraction, is still regarded in many quarters as the dox view. It almost seems as if Mr. Cook were not familiar with é's theory of language, but if that be so, it only corroborates the ctness of the natural and spontaneous growth of language in s mind. He proves from the facts that he had the rare oppor- y of observing that languages are not (to use an Aristotelian term) ; i. e., by construction, but φύσει i. e., by natural growth. They lop not otherwise than, and according to the same laws as, plants ', flowers bloom, and fruits ripen. The regularity of grammatical rules the constructions of the syntax are as much a result of the natural laws iture as are the forms of crystals, of plants, and of animal bodies.—ED.]

OME years ago a party of Americans engaged in a scientific exploration of Liberia made an attempt at learning the uage of the Golah people, one of the numerous small tribes of ralley of St. Paul's River. By those who have become acquainted that part of Africa the Golahs are not considered remarkable ir for stupidity or for brightness of intellect; their language is thought to be easier of acquisition than, for example, that of the Kroo people of the coast, but somewhat more difficult than that of the Vey tribe, with which the Golah tongue is, perhaps, most nearly related. The task of learning either to talk or to "hear" Golah proved, however, to be beset with many obstacles, and although our opportunities of observation and instruction were excellent, they proved to be altogether too brief and intermittent for more than a mere introduction to the musical conversation of our sable friends. The effort resulted, however, in many suggestive incidents, and it was possible to establish one fact which seems to have a general bearing upon so trite a subject as the development of speech.

The point in current theories which our Golah experience affects can probably be illustrated best by reference to two recent papers by eminent anthropologists and philologists. In his "Philology; or the Science of Activities Designed for Expression,"[1] Major Powell, as indicated by the title, places the greatest possible emphasis on the factor of intention and design, and interprets not only oral and formal language as deliberately contrived, but the same theory is extended to explain the origin and application of acts classified as "emotional language," laughing, smiling, sobbing, screaming, frowning, etc.

"Natural expression must be distinguished from artificial expression or language, for natural expression is not designed to convey concepts, while expressions which are designed to convey concepts constitute language. Hence language may be defined as artificial expression of concepts in judgments by words in propositions. . . . *Sobbing as an expression of despair.* Sobbing is caused by sudden or spasmodic inspiration and is accomplished by the facial signs of grief through the action of the muscles of grief. Habit has made it instinctive, but its true nature as an artificial sign is plainly exhibited when sobbing is simulated."

In a more recent address[2] Prof. Boaz draws equally definite inferences regarding the intellectual powers required in the construction of language.

"A developed language with grammatical categories presup-

[1] *American Anthropologist*, N. S., 603-637, 1900.

[2] *Science*, February 22, 1901, XIII., 283.

poses the ability of expressing abstract relations, and since every known language has grammatical structure, we must assume that the faculty of forming abstract ideas is a common property of man.... We must not forget that the abstract idea of a number must be present among these people because, without it, no method of counting is possible."

"We also find that nouns are classified in a great many ways in different languages......It is at once clear that every classification of this kind involves the formation of an abstract idea."

The above opinions may represent somewhat extreme views, and yet they are but expressions of the theory which underlies the philologist's respect for the logical powers of the peoples who are supposed to have constructed the languages in which syntactic relations of words are highly developed and intricately adjusted.

If we had had predecessors in the study of Golah, and had thus been enabled to approach the language through the medium of a formulated grammar, the point of our original investigation might easily have been missed, though the same fact has been encountered undoubtedly by hundreds of pioneer students of unwritten tongues. Contrary, however, to the impressions commonly reported by missionaries and philologists, our respect for Golah linguistic ingenuity, instead of continuing to increase, was soon rudely shattered by the discovery that, with the exception of a few nouns and verbs, the wisest men of the tribe had no suspicion of the meaning of the words of their own language, much less a comprehension, however slight, of its grammar or syntax. Of such a sentence as, Where is the ax? ("*Cul bu-leah,*" "Where ax-at?"), we could ascertain without delay that *bu* means *ax*, but when we attempted to learn which sounds conveyed particular parts of the remainder of the idea it soon became apparent that the Golahs were more ignorant than ourselves, for by comparing a few sentences we were soon able to inform them, much to their surprise and satisfaction. They were unable to understand the grammatical structure of their language, much less to contrive and elaborate it, and they were in total ignorance, not only of the nature and existence of such a structure, but of any separate existence and definite meaning for a large proportion of their linguistic elements or word-symbols.

To infer deliberate design from the existence of complex adjustments is not a new method of argument, nor one in especial favor at the present time. It is indeed wonderful that utterly illiterate savages should possess intricately complicated linguistic systems which require years of expert philological study before they can be adequately comprehended and described. The philologist knows that an even greater period would be needed to invent, elaborate and popularise a new language, and bows in spirit before the nameless, primitive originators of Sanskrit, Greek, or Arabic; but the biologist has less confidence in this theory of prehistoric inventors, because of his acquaintance with other systems of intricate organic adjustments which have developed by gradual processes and through natural, continuously active causes.

The degeneration of languages is another venerable theory, related, evidently, to that of the fall of man, though we are now learning that languages, like men, "fell up." It begins to be appreciated that grammatical regularity is not necessarily a sign of age and gradually attained perfection, but may indicate just the contrary. Arabic, for example, one of the most regular and grammatically logical systems of human speech, is now thought to have been reduced to writing within a comparatively short period after its formation. Languages, like organisms, can develop and degenerate; indeed, the same language may be undergoing both processes at the same time.

The language of the Golahs is in essential respects like those of their numerous neighbors, though differing from Vey probably as much as English from German, and completely different from some of the linguistic types of the eight or ten tribes which could be reached in a day's journey. When one knows the people it seems obvious that these languages are to be interpreted as the result of the evolutionary subdivision and integration of others like themselves and not as products of conscious effort on the part of individuals, ancient or modern.

Among the plants and animals cross-breeding and the resulting combination of characters can take place only between related and similar organisms, but in building languages the most heterogeneous constitutents may be united.[1] When the child of three years produces from his own subconsciousness such words as "knewed," "broked," and "oak-corn," he is but furnishing an example of the constructive tendency which in primitive society would incorporate and bring to the grammatical regularity of one language, word-symbols of diverse origin, and this is done without any abstract ideas or intentions of forming or arranging words in accordance with the categories and classifications to be recognized by the philologist's subsequent study of the resulting compound type of speech. That Homer should have used a word only in the plural, while the singular became current later, has seemed very remarkable to those who have thought of language as deliberately constructed from roots[2] and inflectional particles, but to borrow a word in the plural and afterward make a singualr for it is quite as possible in practice as the opposite course.[3]

[1] The natives of West Africa did not divide time into weeks, and when, for example, the Kroo tribe of the coast of Liberia adopted the system from the slave-traders, they secured also their word *weekay*, while among the Golahs of the interior missionary influence may be perceived in the fact that the word for week is *Sunday*. By using English words with the grammatical constructions and vocal inflections of his own language the native makes a literal translation or "jargon." Having had no equivalent for our "to be" he refuses to adopt it, and uses "live" instead. The result is such expressions as, "No rice live here," "Man live for come" (is coming), or "Man live for die" (is dead). Such gibberish, with intonations which render even the most familiar words quite unintelligible to the newly arrived traveller, is the chief medium of communication in West Africa, and if that quarter of the world were left to itself would soon crystallise into a distinct language. Similarly, the Japanese language is said to have exactly the grammatical structure of the Corean, but with an entirely distinct vocabulary, indicating that Coreans who colonised Japan talked at first a jargon to the natives and then adopted it among themselves. In numerous other instances, such as the Polynesians, Malays, and Egyptians, conquest and colonisation resulted in keeping two more or less distinct languages in use together, one for the royal family, nobility, upper class, medicine-men, or priests, and another for the common people. Among the predaceous Caribs of the West Indies the language of the women is said to have remained distinct from that of the men, and the same is also true to a notable extent in Japan.

[2] The non-existence of roots as origins of words has been ably argued by r. A. L. Kroeber, *American Anthropologist*, N. S., III., 334, 1901.

[3] Dictionaries recognise English plurals for memorandum and index, but not, as yet, admit that date is an English singular for data. The natives Guam mistook the Spanish plural *santos* for a singular, and proceeded to

As the existence of numerals is held to imply the possession of the abstract idea of number, so Professor Boaz might reason with even greater logical propriety that euphonic changes imply an abstract idea of euphony, in accordance with which the Golahs have introduced certain modifications of what the philologist would take to be the normal or original structure of their language. And yet after acquaintance with the mental habits of the Golabs the theory that they or any of them were ever separately conscious of the nature, purpose, or methods of speech, or of any design or intention of modifying or improving their language, seems about as probable as that the brooks of their country run down bill by deliberation. Euphony is, indeed, a phonetic gravitation,[1] and when the Golah man says *cum* or *culum* instead of *cul mu* (whither you) it is because his tongue falls more easily to it. The apparent design is simply the result of motion on the line of least resistance, an evolution rather than an involution, a physical quite as much as a mental process. It is true that not all the elements and principles of linguistic structure and change are as obviously related to the physical and automatic faculties, but if we keep close to the facts of the primitive mind it becomes evident that among the Golahs, as elsewhere, there are many indications that language is a product of the subconscious rather than of the rational phase of the human intellect, and that the designs of its structure and the abstractions of its categories exist only *in posse* until they are discovered and formulated by the philologist. Indeed, it is little less than obvious that language is as much an instinct as an art, and that with the race as with the individual it was a preliminary, rather than result, of the development of abstract ideas.

The linguistic opportunities of primitive man of the Golah and neighboring varieties exceed those of their civilized brethren in that their waking hours are spent in an almost incessant exercise of the "activities of expression." The Golah man talks mostly from habit rather than from purpose or intention, and is limited by no formal

---

form a plural *mañantos* in conformity to their own "laws" of etymology and euphony, which Mr. W. E. Safford has recently formulated and published for the first time. *American Anthropologist*, N. S., V., 303, 1903.

[1] The Samoans have an expression for euphony, the literal translation of which is "lifting it easily." See Turner's *Samoa*, p. 223.

standards of grammar or requirements of reason, as we understand it. He finds no difficulty in metrical improvisation by the hour, and is ready on the shortest notice to deliver an impassioned oration with rhetorical balance and rhythmical periods impressive from the sound alone, all the more when one understands nothing of the childish subject-matter. Natural orators, masters of language, shall we say? Rather does the language master the savage and deceive his undeveloped judgment.

On form, as the concomitant or the counterfeit of emotion, depends much of the charm and efficiency of language, and most languages have never been used as vehicles of deliberately clarified perceptions and logically elaborated ideas; they have never really attained to the status of activities *designed* for expression. As well might we hold that primitive man would not have eaten had he not entertained an abstract idea of nutrition as that he contrived language by the assistance of abstractions. Beyond the symbolic languages of mathematics and other sciences, Volapük and its imitations are probably the only tongues thus elaborated.

"Inspiration" and "divine afflatus" are commonly invoked to explain the beauties of religious and poetical literature of Mediterranean and European peoples; outside of these it is also recognised that the form rather than the substance has been the chief element of permanence and influence for the masterpieces of many languages, as, for example, the Arabic and the Chinese. The language itself becomes, as it were, a fetish, and the perfection realised in the form becomes also an unquestioned quality of the ideas expressed. The mind is charmed and convinced by the formal perfections of language largely because it is utterly unconscious of having contrived them, much as the school-child is sure that he has the right answer when the example "comes out even." Much of the poetry and oratory of former times is now dismissed as useless word-making, or "empty verbiage," but even in our advanced civilisation the most important truths and finest sentiments secure appreciation only as they are expressed in words able to command our instinctive respect for excellence of speech.

There is a sense, indeed, in which language might be called a function of the human intellect, but in a far more important respect it appears that the intellect is itself a product of man's power of expression. The possession of simple languages by many of the lower animals is an indication that man did not need to invent speech, and there has undoubtedly been mutual increase in scope and perfection of organs and faculties, which is so obviously true also of the human hand. Neither is there any indication that man ever had an intention or a motive for the diversification of languages, which even in primitive times was recognized as a misfortune and explained as the curse of a jealous deity. Philology affords the amplest proofs that languages have become what they are by a process of universal evolution with but little direct influence of artificial selection, and with endless divergences and intergraftings which hopelessly obscure their origins and relationship. Between languages, as such, natural selection also effects relatively small and slow changes, the selection is racial, national, or social, and important linguistic movements have been incidental to the history of great political, commercial, intellectual, or religious empires.

Custom, not reason, has ever been the lawgiver of language. Intellectual progress, including even the advancement of science itself, is obviously conditioned on the tardy improvement of the arts of expression, and these are still controlled by usage, tradition and the æsthetic sense through which they have always been elaborated. The ascendency of intellect is in some respects inimical to the evolution of language; civilised man has contrived to write and print his words that they may not be forgotten or changed,[1] but live words continue to vary in form and sense even after lexicographers have at-

[1] The careful memorising and frequent recital of genealogies and poems, as among the Polynesians and the ancient Greeks, may be even more effective than printed literature in preventing modification of language. In spite of the immense distances and the multiplicity of small islands, one language is still spoken throughout the Polynesian islands, from Hawaii to Easter Island and New Zealand. Indeed, these three apices of the triangle, according to Mr. W. E. Safford, have the language in greater purity and similarity than Samoa, Tonga, and other equatorial archipelagoes. The eastward movement of dark-skinned, curl-haired Melanesians seems to have extended to Tahiti and even to the Marquesas group, subsequent to the colonisation of the Pacific islands by the original Polynesian stock.

tempted to embalm them. The extent of man's designed interference in language is well illustrated by the continued failure of his spelling reformers during a period which has added to the English language and brought into general use hundreds of new words and expressions in spite of the most strenuous objections of the purists.

Linguistic forms are still dictated, as they were originally elaborated, not by a deliberate or conscious exercise of judgment or inventive ability, but by the æsthetic or proportional sense which is the common base of man's progress in all constructive and artistic activities, the same sentiment or feeling which was long since personified as the "genius of language," in apparent recognition of its subliminal and involuntary nature. Expression has an infinite variety of purposes, but these are momentary and incidental; they affect details of words and phrases, but they do not furnish either the power or the pattern for weaving the fabric of language. It is only at an advanced stage of intellectual progress that tasks of expression transcend the capabilities of existing language, and result in designed additions to the vocabulary. But even such novelties consist mostly of individual words, and do not affect the structure of language. Many new ideas are, however, conveyed by old words, both idea and word having been gradually adapted in use. Such adaptation is a concomitant of evolution, but not of design, and we may invoke again the analogy of organic evolution where some of the higher animals have, as it were, interfered in details of their own evolution, although the general process is quite without their ken and was only recently approached by human comprehension.

Direct evidence of the subliminal character of the linguistic powers of the mind had long been available in the numerous instances where languages long since forgotten or never consciously acquired are brought to the surface and used with fluency in abnormal mental states. To this class of phenomena may be added the even more pertinent fact occasionally afforded to students of foreign languages by dreams in which they are able to carry through without hesitation or error, extended and difficult conversations quite impossible to the waking intellect. Moreover, the studies of Flournoy would seem to carry the matter a step farther by indicating that the

ıbconscious mind may have not only an apparently unlimited sensi-
ǝness in acquiring and retaining languages, but that in an abnormal ate the talent natural to the child and to the savage may become ypertrophied, and may elaborate on an extensive scale new symbols speech.

This view of the origin and nature of language affords, in ad-
tion, an obvious and adequate explanation of the practical ineffi-
ency of all methods of instruction which attempt to impart languages rough the medium of the rational powers. In a much truer sense ıan Goethe's oft-quoted denial of the existence of the species in ıture which "knows only the individual," might it be said that, a ith the Golahs, language knows only the sentence. Etymology an ntax represent but the analyses and generalisations of the con ious intellect from phenomena to which it stands in no causal rel on, and to expect that a knowledge of the generalisation can affect even facilitate the transfer and use of linguistic symbols and form to bid defiance to all pertinent psychology. Fluency in the use language has always been, and is likely to remain, a matter of bitrary memory and individual skill, just as correctness of gram-
atical construction and literary style are questions of taste and prac-
ce. The learning of language is one department of education where ere is no danger or disadvantage in the use of the arbitrary memory, oviding the effort be expended on the speech itself, instead of upon neralisations regarding its formal structure. Language was ither invented nor developed by the methods of comparative philol-
y, and these are a demonstrated failure as means of imparting it.

Since the establishment of the doctrine of organic descent many her series of gradual changes have been termed "evolutions," ough often having but slight analogy with biological evolution. o call something an "evolution" in this literary or philosophical nse may mean merely that there has been a continuous sequence of ents, instead of disconnected periods and independent causes. anguage, however, is one of the characters acquired by the human ıimal in virtue of the same properties and influences to which his ore tangible bodily perfections and diversities are due. And as ental progress has been more rapid and extensive than bodily change, the greatest diversity among men lies in language and in the consequent intellectual and social arts, habits, and instincts. With language, too, it is even more apparent than with physical characters that divergence is not caused by environment, but appears whenever isolation permits separate manifestations of the ever-present tendency to change.[1] It is also more obvious with language, but no more true, that the rapidity of evolutionary progress does not depend upon segregation, but is greatly accelerated by the contact and combination of characters. The Norman invasion changed the English language and people much more than centuries of isolation would have done. And when languages and other characters are thus brought into synthesis it is apparent that their differences are not always useful, but much more often useless, and that the perpetuation of a new character or variation does not depend so much upon its fitness with reference to an external environment as upon its fitting into the existing structure, organic or linguistic.

The development of language has, accordingly, an interest wider than that of the science of comparative philology, since it is not an artificial contrivance of the mind but represents the natural, spontaneous and unconscious growth of a human talent. The evolution of language is not a figure of speech or a subject apart, but a genuine, familiar and instructive instance of biological evolution. The power of expression made possible the attainment of general and abstract ideas, but the philologist's classification of linguistic symbols and forms affords no evidence that primitive man designed language, or that abstractions have influenced its evolution.

The ancient theory that languages were created along with the peoples who speak them had the merit of logical consistency, a virtue not apparent in the modern opinion that the diverse characteristics of the peoples are due to evolution, while their languages are looked upon as the artificial result of deliberate constructive effort.

WASHINGTON, D. C. O. F. COOK.

[1] "Kinetic Evolution in Man," *Science*, N. S., XV., 927. June 13, 1902.

ON SOME CONCEPTUAL ERRORS RELATING TO FORCE AND MATTER.

PROFESSOR W. STANLEY JEVONS, an orthodox authority in science, of high standing, merely repeats the statement of all capable scientific writers in saying, "Science does nothing to reduce the number of strange things that we may believe. When fairly pursued it makes absurd drafts upon our powers of comprehension and belief."

This is true in every field of the natural sciences; no superstitions of what are called the pre-scientific or dark ages ever exceeded in absurdity many of the statements which science, fairly pursued, and ready to present its problems openly and boldly, makes and asks us to accept as the necessary corollaries of what are deemed infallible scientific facts and principles. The same writer says, "Is it not rather true that we have but to open a scientific book and read a page or two, and we shall come to some recorded phenomenon of which no explanation can yet be given? In every such fact there is a possible opening for new discoveries."

But they who speak in the name of Science are not always honest in presenting these unexplained facts; they are apt, sometimes, to jump the question, and ignore differences which no scientific knowledge can reconcile with natural principles or established facts, as we know them. The same writer says,—"I am inclined to find fault with mathematical writers because they so often exult in what they can accomplish, and omit to point out that what they do is but an infinitely small part of what might be done. They exhibit a general inclination, with few exceptions, not to do so much as mention the existence of problems of an impracticable character."

Science, as taught, in other words, is often likely to present its case as would a skilled lawyer addressing a jury, for the one side or for the other, and not as an impartial judge, fairly weighing the evidence presented by both sides; perhaps indeed the evidence for the opposite side has been refused any consideration, or even a hearing. And yet the vast importance of these unexplained facts, to realise what, and how imperfect even, science really is, and to open the way for such new discoveries as have often unwillingly enough shifted the whole kaleidoscope of sciences, Sir John Herschel has emphasised in his great work on Astronomy by saying, "Almost all the great discoveries in astronomy have resulted from the consideration of Residual Phenomena, that is to say, such as remain outstanding and unaccounted for after subducting and allowing for all that would result from the strict application of known principles."

Dogmatism is no part of genuine science, and a moment's consideration will demonstrate the fact; for if science to-day may dogmatise, then it might have dogmatised in the past, and so back to the days when there was little or none of what is now called science; and hence science could never have had so much as a true beginning, and all we now know of science, would be classed, by so-called men of science, merely as gross and ignorant superstition. For there is no fixed centre in science; all is changing with the changing observations of new facts, and its dogmatism is mere bigotry, comparable with which religious bigotry becomes respectable, for it at least claims some fixed centre around which to revolve, while science can only claim to imperfectly record a few observed phenomena, and deduce a few inferences, which never can be stronger than the value and relative scope of the observation, nor more certain than the proportion existing between the few observed facts, in any case, and the vast aggregate of unobserved and possibly discordant facts in the same case.

The Holy of Holies in Science is merely a dark chamber set up by a few teachers who require, for their own purposes, a straight road for teaching, in which extraneous matters are merely stumbling blocks and interferences, of which the least said the better; of which, in fact, nothing at all is said, they are simply ignored.

Says Jevons, speaking of such writers as Comte and John Stuart

Mill, with whom are to be classed Huxley, Tyndall, and Herbert Spencer,—"At least these and many other writers fail to impress upon their readers a truth which cannot be too constantly borne in mind, namely, that the utmost successes which our scientific method can accomplish will not enable us to comprehend more than an infinitesimal fraction of what there is to comprehend."

Recollect that he says "our scientific method," for he does not deny that we can comprehend to an indefinite, almost to an infinite extent, possibly, and can constantly learn to comprehend more and more, and to reach certainty, if need be; but that we cannot do this to any considerable extent at all by "our scientific method," which excludes, of necessity, those Residual Phenomena, lying outside, of which Sir John Herschel speaks, and which are merely disturbing factors lying beyond the bounds of known science at the time, and yet by means of which nearly all, perhaps all, the great scientific discoveries and advances have been made. Says Jevons, of these cases,—"The supply of new and unexplained facts is divergent in extent, so that the more we have explained, the more there is to explain. The further we advance in any generalisation, the more numerous and intricate are the exceptional cases still demanding further treatment. Can any scientific man venture to state that there is less opening now for new discoveries than there was three centuries ago?"

It is well to guard ourselves against the contemplation of so-called Science as a rotund and complete thing, a perfect whole, to be bowed down before and worshipped; it is, on the contrary, a vast battle-ground on which the combatants, in the pursuit of truth, are not arrayed in opposing armies, but are fighting each other man to man, individually, all over the field, and from every point of vantage, and with the ally of this instant the antagonist of the next. And this is the only proper conception of Science as a living thing, and out of it, thus contemplated, vast good must come, and has already come: all the good of science, in fact, has come; and its scope will include, nay, it even now includes, those researches and determinations which find brute or crude materialism to have failed utterly when pushed even measurably toward the ultimate, and those other researches and determinations which bring the psychism of a universe, or of deity, into the problem as a demonstrable factor.

All science asks, or can ask, is that scientific means shall be employed in examining and deducing, and that the field be broad and not narrow, and that the facts be many and not few, that they be well authenticated, and proven and reproven, and that the investigators be true and capable, and not false and incapable.

And it is no derogation from the scientific value of these investigations and determinations that they may, perchance, find their controlling principles, in whole or part, previously deduced or discovered by methods coming down to us from an age which we denominate the pre-scientific, or unscientific; because, until we have pushed our investigations to a logical and tactical conclusion, far, far beyond present possibilities, we do not know whether we may not ourselves land in a region in which means of acquiring knowledge may be discovered higher, or broader, and more secure even, than those we work with in our own limited field of to-day, and it is merely begging the question to discredit such scientific results because they may chance to resemble "pre-scientific" knowledge. As well might the ledge-miner for gold, who excavates and blasts and crushes and decomposes his metal-bearing rock, discredit the value of the great open placers where barbaric and untaught men of old gathered the finest gold from the open sands of the desert, or the beds of prehistoric streams, to deck their persons with magnificent breastplates and necklaces, or braid their banners, and line the walls of their homes and palaces. The mint, the test of all, makes no discrimination, for the law of the miner is the law of Science — "the gold is where you find it."

With these prefatory remarks, I wish to speak of some erroneous popular views of what have been called Force and Matter, which views are not held really by men of science themselves, but which, as an easy way of settling the question, have become widely

hensive explanations of what has not been personally investigated or pursued by them themselves, but accepted like a faith, as a convenient rule of belief: It is, in fact, on the same plane as some of the dogmas of certain sects of religions, whether Christian, Buddhist or Pagan, and it may be described as the tenaciously held dogma or superstition of the priesthood of irreligion.

It is absurd, of course, to conceive of a thing which is inconceivable, and still worse to believe and swear by a thing which is inconceivable. New force which is not acting on something is totally inconceivable; it is movement without motion, strain without anything to strain against, or impulse without anything to act against; it is, in fact, not only inconceivable, but is a contradiction in terms. It is only when something is moved that we have motion, or when some impulse is operative on something that we can have any conception of it. If there were no matter, in a merely physical universe, there could be no force in that universe; that is to say, no self-caused cosmical force. With the force of will I will deal hereafter; but in this case there can be no will without an existent and intelligent willer.

As of force, the same is true of matter. If matter were deprived of all its properties, solidity, color, taste, smell, hardness, coldness, heat, electricity, and the like, it would cease to be matter, for it would not have the properties of matter; matter is only known, and can only be conceived of, as having properties. Yet these properties are all manifestations of force or forces, acting to produce the perception or conception of matter. Hence *force* and *matter*, as separate entities or existences, are simply inconceivable mental vagaries, having no actuality—are in fact mere transcendental abstractions, purely metaphysical, and by holding to which, those who adhere to them in the guise of materialists, merely show that they may be capital metaphysicians, dealing with the baseless and hypothetical, but can have no standing as men of science, and above all no standing as materialists, which is what they claim, nevertheless, to be.

All we know is *energy*, that is, matter undergoing change of form or place. This is conceivable and actual.

The alternative result, in dealing with force and matter, was early shown by the sequence of the philosophies of Locke, Berke-y and Hume, in which Locke set up his theory on the working out matter in the development of mental phenomena (although he imself did not really claim to do this, but left an accepted *terra in-ognita* of divine mentality behind); then Berkeley, taking advan-age of a statement of Locke, that at different periods of our lives the ame object appears to us quite different, built up his theory that natter as matter was non-existent, and that we only conceived of it y a sort of mental jugglery. Then came Hume, who took hold of erkeley's thesis, and showed that, since mental changes were as arious and obvious as material or physical changes, and hence as nreliable, all existence could be reduced to nihilism, leaving only a niverse filled with floating and haphazard ideas or streams of un-aused and useless consciousness, dreams within dreams, and with-ut the individuality of even a dreamer.

So far as we know, whatever is the basis of matter is the basis f force, whatever is the manifestation of matter is the manifestation f force; and they are only known when co-acting as energy. We ave a material universe, and we have, in this universe, mentality; hether it be confined to the human race, animals, and perhaps veg-ables, or whether it extend elsewhere, we know that there is mind, or without mind there would be nothing cognisable, nothing con-eivable, nothing to cognise or conceive, nothing existent, unless as wild and senseless chaos, if at all.

What Lamarck called the "Order of Nature" is what we ontemplate around us and in us. It existed before we were born, d we know that it will continue to exist after we are dead.

Science deals with this order of nature, and with it alone.

Has it always existed, or has it had a beginning? This, of urse, is the great question.

Materialists, who deny any mind in the universe, except that hich is or may be a by-product of the order of nature, are logically mpelled to assume that this order of nature has been eternal in past. It is not because this particular order now exists that it st be assumed by materialists to have always existed, for it may be the outcome, they might say, of another order, and so of another, and so on eternally.

But this position is untenable for three reasons. First,—since materialism claims its basis in natural science, it can find no stability unless natural science is stable, and natural science owes all its stability to the stability of the present order of nature. To assume another order at another time, when we have nothing but a bare assumption behind it, is like the feat once attributed to the rope-walker Blondin, who proposed to wheel a wheel-barrow along a rope stretched across the whirlpool of Niagara, and coil up the rope in the wheel-barrow as he passed across the chasm. Or like the feat of Jack and the Bean-stalk, who found himself on the moon, and let himself down to the earth by weaving a rope of chaff forty-five miles long, attaching it to one of the horns of the moon, and climbing down to the end of it, unfastening the upper end, and tying that to the lower, and so on alternately till he reached *terra firma*.

Another reason for denying, as a scientific assumption, any other order of nature, lies in the fact that it does not simplify the problem, but merely sets the solution back one step, for, as has been well said, "an infinite series of causes is not a cause."

Of course materialists may fall back on the fact that in such a series there may be found somewhere an initiative cause, but this also begs the question, for, if so, there may just as likely have been an initiative cause in the present order of nature, which concession, of course, abandons the whole argument.

I shall show, later on, that such successive orders of mere physical nature are not possible, if the present order of nature is itself possible; and that it is possible we all know, because it exists, for we see it all around us.

As a part of the present order of nature we have the attraction of gravitation. As stated by Newton, and accepted by all natural science, every particle of matter in the universe attracts every other particle of matter in the universe, and is attracted thereby, with a force varying directly as the masses and inversely as the squares of the distances between them, and they tend, in consequence, if not held apart by a stronger energy, to approach each other in accordance with the terms of this law, gradually but rapidly accelerating their rate of approach as they advance toward each other, inversely as the squares of the distances diminish. This law of gravitation, and the presence of gravitation, appear to be co-extensive throughout the universe, as they ought to be, and must be. The most distant binary stars, far, far beyond the reach of the most delicate parallax to determine their distances, are found to rigidly obey this law, as their components rotate around each other.

Hence all the particles and masses of matter, all the suns and planets, comets, meteoric bodies, nebulæ, and "all the host of heaven," are and must be constantly drawing nearer and nearer to each other, as dissipation of energy continues its wasteful course among the working factors of the universe, for dissipation of energy is the only possible means for the transformation of energy.

Astronomers picture what will be the fate of our own system when all the planets have been drawn by retardations into the sun, (for every little shooting-star or meteor which enters our atmosphere or falls to the earth retards the earth's motion, and space is filled with such material, massive or diffuse), and when the sun itself has cooled down, by the dissipation of its energy, to a black, dead and relatively inert mass. And so of all the universe; the same attraction will be drawing together other solar systems, and other galaxies, and our own with them, and all will end in one mass of eternal stillness, darkness and death. During these processes there will be collisions in space, and these cataclysms will spasmodically and temporarily expend themselves in space, for dissipation of energy will continue, and in a little while quiescence will be resumed, and the great orbs will be ready for new collisions, till all have collided, and the process has become complete.

No student of natural science will deny this inevitable ending, for all nature is dissipating energy throughout space, and the tendency is down-grade as a whole, from a starting-point of high and unbalanced potential to a culmination, by equilibrium of energies, in silence and darkness. I do not believe that such events will necessarily occur, because I do not believe in a merely physical universe of this sort, but in one prepared and carried on by creative power; but, assuming a merely physical universe, science is right, and such an ending is inevitable.

Now, if the present order of nature has been eternal in the past, and dissipation of energy and the attraction of gravitation have been, as they must have been, efficient throughout the eternal past, it is obvious that all these possible changes must have taken place already in the unnumbered æons of the past, and that the present order of nature could not now be in operation at all. But it is in operation, for we see it; hence, the present order of nature has not been eternal in the past, but must have had a beginning in finite time; and no sequence of successive orders of nature could possibly have prevented this, but at most could have only retarded the result, which must still have been completed long before

> "The foundations thereof were fastened,
> Or the corner-stone laid thereof,
> When the morning stars sang together,
> And all the sons of God shouted for joy."

Unless, as I have said, there was somewhere a power of initiative (and, as I shall show, any reversal of the order of nature demands an initiative), this result could not have been avoided; and if initiative ever existed, it might just as well have originated the present order of nature, as to have originated or reversed another order of nature for which, in the absence of initiative, there is not the slightest warrant or possibility in science, observation, or good sense.

What has been said above of gravitation is not confined to gravitation. Every process of nature demands and employs the same principle of degradation; the whole universe is running down-grade from an accumulated high potential at the time it began its down-grade course. During this down-grade progress, work has been done; enormous work is still being done. Measured in foot-tons, the expenditure of energy is incalculable.

Now to raise the universe to the potential of its starting-point would, to-day, require the expenditure of as many foot-tons of outside energy as have been expended throughout the universe to reach its present low level. What possible source of such energy can be conceived of?

I will, at this time, therefore, indicate the third reason why a new order of nature, to reverse the present order of nature, is not only inconceivable, but impossible, if the present order of nature itself exists.

Take a cannon-ball and elevate it a hundred feet above the earth's surface, and let it drop. On its contact with the earth it will manifest a definite amount of distributed energy, a part as heat, a part as displacement, and a part as light, electricity, etc., and it will then rest on the earth's surface with the same weight as it had before it was raised. Now everybody knows that it required just as much of an expenditure of energy to raise that cannon-ball to the height of a hundred feet as it manifested in its fall. That is a self-evident proposition, and, if applied to the universe, will clearly demonstrate that no new order of nature, an "order of elevation" instead of one of degradation, could possibly exist, whether as a sequence, an alternation, or an antecedent. It is a contradiction in terms, for the following reasons:

The universe, in running down, becomes quiescent by dissipating or satisfying its opposing energies, so as to reach a position of stable equilibrium from one of unstable equilibrium, which is that from which the present order of nature started. We find the energies of repulsion existing everywhere, just like the energies of attraction, but with this difference. All the energies of repulsion are themselves necessarily secondary, and are the results of the same processes of degradation which are operative throughout nature, and which, in fact, constitute the manifest order of nature. Electrical repulsion is merely the manifestation of unsatisfied electrical polarities which have been sheared off the balanced electricities of the universal ether. A dynamo will so shear these electricities apart, but it requires as many foot-pounds of energy, not considering the waste or dissipation, to place these opposing electricities in such separation as either to attract or repel each other, as the same electricities will develop in again flowing back and uniting in a state of equilibrium. Gases repel each other, but this is simply because their molecular heat has not yet been dissipated into space. When gases reach a temperature not so low even as the temperature of interstellar space, they will have first become liquid, then solid bodies, and repulsion will have ceased, just as in a mass of rock. Repulsion is kinetic and, so to speak, artificial, while gravitation depends on aggregation and when the whole material substance of the universe shall have become compacted into one vast whole, then its attractive force will have increased by contiguity to an almost inconceivable extent, in first forming and then maintaining the mass.

An analogy for a new order of nature has been imagined in a counting-machine, constructed to count up, one by one, to a vast total, and then, as the machine continues to run, by a pre-calculated change of a tooth in a gear, to count backwards, one at a time, and so reverse the process. But the process is not reversed; the counting is not the significant factor at all, but the running of the machine is, and that will require not only the same amount of energy, but the same energy, to count backwards as to count forwards. And the count, too, will be all the same, one more is added at every beat of the lever, whatever you may call the result. A dog does not acquire five legs by calling his tail a leg. Now let us suppose that the present order of nature has run its downward course to its culmination, and that a new order of nature is to begin, reversing the old order, and in which every process is reversed, and potential is piled up instead of dissipated or satisfied, as at present.

First the attraction of gravitation, or at all events the cohesion or gravitation of the mass, must be dispensed with, or neutralised. To neutralise this, which will certainly not neutralise itself if it is a dynamic phenomenon, will require, *ab initio*, as much expenditure of energy as would be required to accomplish the same work by an ideally perfect set of rock-breakers and crushers, run by steam-power.

If attraction must be neutralised it must be mechanically overcome, and where, in the present order of nature, is this new mechanical energy to be derived, because we have assumed that our entire present universe has run down to its culmination, in the dissipation and balancing of potential and kinetic energy throughout?

Surely this energy cannot be derived from the energy of one part of the universe lending itself to another, because this would only prolong the apparent time, but would not alter the process or result. Nor can we overcome the difficulty by assuming that the new order of nature may begin before the old one has completely run out, for this partial reversal is quite as difficult as an entire reversal; nay, more so, as the kinetic agencies would have to be violently taken hold of and mechanically turned about and made to work backward and upside down, henceforth, against their own energy. So this new energy to reverse the old energy cannot come from the material universe as a whole, nor from any part of the material universe. Hence it must come, if at all, from outside the material universe, and what is outside? If the present order of nature is co-extensive with the universe, then there is nothing outside; if it is not co-extensive with the universe, then the same process of degradation must go on, however often supplemented from outside sources, only the rate being changed, the process and result remaining the same; and in a past eternity, or a future eternity, the rate does not affect the problem in the slightest degree, and the end would long ago have been reached just the same.

Of course an infinite creator could halt all processes of nature, or reverse, or start them up again at will, for an infinite creator, by the very nature of the conception, possesses an infinite initiative. But a merely physical, self-contained, self-propelled and self-destroying or dissipating order of nature certainly has no power of arrest, and no power of reversal, as Lamarck, whom I shall quote later on, clearly shows, and we can never have a new order of nature substituted therefor without mechanically accounting for all the residue of the present order, and building up against it an artificial power sufficient to coerce and reverse it, for which there is no material anywhere, and for which there never can be any, whatever superstition may project or fancy predicate.

But if there is no power to institute a reversed order of nature, much less could there be any power in the machine to subsequently erect itself into higher and higher potentials, in the absence of a constant external reserve, which has been excluded, or of a creative agency with unlimited power of initiative, which is the point at issue, and which materialism denies.

It is an axiom of philosophy, as well as of ethics and physical science, that "you cannot grind with the water that is past."

A universe in which attractions are changed to repulsions would never build up a potential, for it is of the very essence of repulsions that they dissipate themselves; they operate radially outward to split themselves up into space, and, unless arrested in spots by an extraneous obstacle, this radiant escape must continue forever, along right lines; whereas, in building up a potential, it is absolutely necessary, whatever sort of universe be predicated, that there shall be condensations, gatherings together, concentrations of energy above the environment, to which dissipation is fatal, and with which it is eternally irreconcilable.

In such a new order of nature there could be no light, heat or electricity, and nothing which could serve as substitutes for them, because there could be no vibration or oscillation; for vibrations themselves by their very terms are compelled to dissipate themselves away from all their sources, more and more widely apart through space.

Nor could gravitation in the mass, when overcome by a stronger energy (which is impossible, as I have shown, since there is and can be no possible physical source of such energy), so as to cause water to habitually run up-hill, and stones, first, and afterwards molehills, and then mountains and continents, to fly forth and scatter into outer space, accomplish any such results by its reversal. The power required to accomplish this, as I have shown, is precisely the mechanical power required to accomplish it to-day, and it does not exist. And, if atoms and molecules did take flight by some power of repulsion, it could only be by such inter-atomic activities as now keep the particles of gases apart; and potential for these new movements would have to be accounted for, and the heat provided to accomplish these results. But having nothing analogous to heat in the new order of nature, and nothing capable of acting as its substitute, such events as the dissipation of atoms universally through space could not occur in any conceivable alteration of the present order of nature. Nor, if they could occur, would it be possible to have potential piled up thereby, but more and more dissipated, which is the prolific source of the present progressive ruin.

It is for these reasons that I have said that nothing of the kind could occur either as a sequence, an antecedent, or an alternative, provided the present order of nature has any existence at all. Of course, if this is all a sham, then we can have any number of similar shams, either forward or backward, right-side up, or upside down, and without waiting for the end of anything, merely using those senseless and discoördinated streams or streaks or clouds of consciousness without connection or sequence, those dreams within dreams, and without a dreamer, to which Hume, in his splendid *reductio ad absurdum* of Locke and Berkeley, reduced all the phenomena of the physical in the flash-light of one universal and eternal nihilism.

There can be no rational doubt, therefore, that the present order of nature has had a beginning, and that, at the period of this beginning there was stored up, by some adequate agency, a potential energy, ready to be unloosed, that is to say, in unstable equilibrium, sufficient in amount and persistence to carry along all the transformations which we know to have passed, and all those now passing, or which will pass.

Or else, when this beginning appeared, there was some adequate agency which could build up all the potential required for the beginning, and supply all that required for its running, as events transpired, and transformations progressed.

In either of these cases something at that beginning must have had the power of initiative, the power of creation. Herbert Spencer supposed that the law of persistence of force might account for all down-grade transformations which have occurred in the order of nature, not seeking, however, to account at all for the primordial store of unstable energy, which omission destroyed his argument at the start. But as that brilliant pupil of, and co-worker with, Charles Darwin, the lamented George J. Romanes, says, in almost his last work,—"It may be true that causation depends upon the 'persistence of force'; it does not follow that all manifestations of force should on this account have been directed to occur as they do occur. For, if we follow back any sequence of physical causation, we soon find that it spreads out on all sides into a net-work of physical relations which are literally infinite both in space (conditions) and in time (antecedent causes) * * * Physical causation cannot be made to supply its own explanation, and the mere persistence of force, even if it were conceded to account for particular cases of physical sequence, can give no account of the ubiquitous and eternal direction of force in the construction and maintenance of universal order." Long before Romanes, Sir John Herschel, in his magnificent paper "On the Origin of Force," concludes as follows: "Will without Motive, Power without Design, Thought opposed to Reason, would be admirable in explaining a chaos, but would render little aid to account for anything else."

But it has been asked, if the present order of nature arose in finite time from the intelligent activity of an infinite creator, what was the condition of things before that period? Was there matter or force in the form of energy there? If not, how did this creator make something out of nothing, create the universe from nothing, create the energy to carry it on from nothing, create the sequences and transformations, and all the past, present, and future, out of nothing? What was he doing before that date? Well, nothing so violent need be asked or predicated; we simply do not know what other universes may have preceded, or what will follow this one. We know that if there were initiative intelligence and power enough to start and maintain the present order of nature, that intelligence and power were greater than the present order of nature, while we are but a very subordinate portion of merely the present order. We need not know, for we are no part of it, and there is no call to speculate, if we have once found a rational and scientific origin for the present order, one sufficient in scope, adequate in power, and comprehensive in plan; for if that intelligent creator ever lived he still lives; if he ever was sufficient, he still is sufficient; if the harmonious order of nature is of his devising and executing, he is a lover of order and harmony; and if creation has culminated in living forms, and these have advanced from lower to higher, from narrower to broader, from less intelligent to more intelligent, from more gross to more spiritual, from worse to better, from enmity to fellowship, from cruelty to kindness, from servitude to freedom, from ignorance to knowledge, and from the carnal and earthly to the psychical and the spiritual, then we know that we are aspiring and ascending, somewhat at least, towards him, so that we can understand him and grow more and more like him, in a weak and feeble way it is true, but as rapidly and as perfectly, we may be sure, as our present physical limitations will permit.

What is this great governing psychism of the universe? Lamarck defined it, a hundred years ago, as "An order of things composed of objects independent of matter, which are determined by the observation of bodies, and the whole amount of which constitutes a power, unalterable in its essence, governed in all its acts, and constantly acting upon all parts of the physical universe. . . . The power which has created Nature has, without doubt, no limits, cannot be restricted in its will or made subject to others, and is independent of all law. It alone can change Nature and her laws, and even annihilate them. . . . If Nature were an intelligence, it could exercise volition, and change its laws, or rather there could be no law. Finally, if Nature were God, its will would be independent, its acts unconstrained; but this is not the case; it is, on the contrary, continually subject to constant laws, over which it has no power; it hence follows, that although its means are infinitely diversified and inexhaustible, it acts always in the same manner in the same circumstances, without the power of acting otherwise."

Says Sir John Herschel, "Whenever, in the natural world, what we call a phenomenon or an event takes place, we either find it resolvable ultimately into some change of place or of movement in material substance, or we endeavor to trace it up to some such change; and only when successful in such endeavor do we consider that we have arrived at its theory. In every such change we recognise the action of FORCE. And in the only case in which we are admitted into any personal knowledge of the origin of force, we find it connected with volition, and by inevitable consequence, with *motive*, with *intellect*, and with all those attributes of mind in which—and not in the possession of arms, legs, brains, and viscera—personality consists. Constituted as the human mind is, if nature be *not* interpretable through these conceptions, it is not interpretable at all."

Says Romanes, "Throughout this universe of infinite objectivity—so far, at least, as human observation can extend—there is unquestionable evidence of some one integrating principle, whereby all its many and complex parts are correlated with one another in such wise that the result is universal order. And if we take any part of the whole system—such as that of organic nature on this planet—to examine in more detail, we find that it appears to be instinct with contrivance. So to speak, wherever we tap organic nature, it seems to flow with purpose; and as we shall presently see, upon the monistic theory the evidence of purpose is here in no way attenuated by a full acceptance of any of the mechanical explanations furnished by science. Now these large and important facts of observation unquestionably point, as just observed, to some one great integrating principle as pervading the Cosmos; and, if so, we can scarcely be wrong in supposing that among all our conceptions it must hold nearest kinship to that which is our highest conception of an integrating cause—viz., the conception of psychism. Assuredly no human mind could either have devised or maintained the working of even a fragment of Nature; and therefore it seems but reasonable to conclude that the integrating principle of the whole—the spirit, as it were, of the universe—must be something which, while as I have just said holding nearest kinship with our highest conception of disposing power, must yet be immeasurably superior to the psychism of man."

In the orderly progress of the universe, organised by illimitable power and intelligence, there must have been purpose, and that purpose a high one. Looking over the whole realm of nature, we concededly find nothing so high as living form, and of these nothing so high as the human, and of mankind we have a vast range of relative capacities and qualities, the upper members of which are nearly Godlike, or, as a sacred writer has expressed it, "only a little lower than the angels."

These are the men and women who lead the way and point to still further triumphs beyond. They find their kindred in that divine galaxy of the great and good who have gone on before, enriched th the priceless lessons of education, self-control, and experience, d filled with that inscrutable psychism which could only have come om the eternal and omnipresent psychism of such a creative agency, hether it be pictured as an individuality, a pervasion, an influx, an mosphere, a surrounding nimbus, or as you may, but always as that in whom we live, and move, and have our being."

In the lines of Wordsworth:

"Our birth is but a sleep and a forgetting:
The soul that rises with us, our life's star,
Hath had elsewhere its setting,
And cometh from afar:
Not in entire forgetfulness,
And not in utter nakedness,
But trailing clouds of glory do we come
From God, who is our home."

PHILADELPHIA, PA. I. W. HEYSINGER.

THE STELE OF TEIMA IN ARABIA

A WELCOME OF THE GODS

SOUTHERN Arabia, the country of the Sabæans and Minæans, and of the fabulous Queen of Sheba, has yielded hundreds of inscriptions written in an alphabet, which, although at first appearance it does not very closely resemble Phœnician script, was nevertheless derived from it, and cannot therefore be much older than about 1000 B. C. These inscriptions furnish us a considerable amount of information concerning the history, the religion, and the life of the ancient South-Arabians. But Northern Arabia seemed for a long time shrouded in a cloud of darkness, before a sudden light was thrown upon it, by the advent of Islam, that shone up brightly like a flash of lightning.

A country situated between the two great centers of civilisation, Egypt on one side and Babylonia on the other, could not have remained without influence from either side; but until the last quarter of the past century very little was known about pagan Northern Arabia, except what was gleaned from a few passages in the Old Testament and in Greek authors.

Within a decade, i. e., between 1875 and 1885, the country was visited by three dauntless explorers, Charles Doughty, an Englishman, Charles Huber, an Alsacian in French service, and Prof. Julius Euting, at present Director of the Imperial Library at Strassburg. A large number of inscriptions in Aramaic, Nabatæan, and so-called Proto-Arabic characters were brought to light by these men, and the deciphering of these documents has greatly increased our knowledge of these regions in ancient times. Among these in-

THE STELE OF TEIMA.

scriptions the one on the stele of Teima belongs to the oldest monuments of Northern Arabia and is rightly regarded as the most important.

The city of Teima, located in Northern Arabia, about half way between Mecca and Damascus, has been known since the times of Isaiah for its abundant water supply and its palm groves, bearing the finest dates. As it was situated on the ancient commercial road from Southern Arabia to Egypt and to Syria, it was but natural that here a wealthy emporium grew up.[1] Even at the present time the place is famous for its enormous spring which keeps sixty water-wheels constantly busy, and for its luxurious date crops. Soil is appraised to-day according to the number of palm-trees in exactly the same way as in olden times, described in the inscription of our stele—another proof of the stability of the East. A striking parallel to this custom is found, e. g., in other oases, viz., in the Sahara, where a man's wealth is judged by the number of palm-trees which he owns, and the amount of water to which he is entitled.

All of the above-named three travellers visited Teima. M. Huber went there twice, once alone in 1880, and a second time in the company of Professor Euting in 1884. During his first visit he saw the inscription which afterward was to become so famous, and copied a few lines of it.

No sooner had Professor Euting seen the stone himself than he recognised that this was a monument of extraordinary importance. Copies and squeezes were taken and sent to Germany, and the stone itself was purchased.

The inscription was published by Professor Noeldeke in the Proceedings of the Berlin Academy in 1884, and after the unfortunate death of M. Huber at the hands of his treacherous Arab guides, the stone was secured for the Louvre by Dr. Lostalot, at that time French Consul in Djeddah, Arabia.

The stele is a slab of lime-stone, 110 centimetres high, 43 centimetres wide, and 12 centimetres thick, or, in Assyrian measures,

[1] Isaiah xxi. 14. Job vi. 19.

2 cubits high, 4 hands wide, and 1 hand thick. The front bears the inscription in raised characters. On the left end we find bas-reliefs and two copies of one very short inscription.

The bas-reliefs may be described as follows:

Beginning at the top we see first a winged disk, a very common symbol of the sun-god in Egyptian art. This symbol was borrowed by the Assyrians, and from them it seems to have passed to the inhabitants of Teima, for here it is executed according to the Assyrian fashion.

Directly under the disk there is the figure of a god, who is represented as a bearded man clothed in Assyrian fashion and wearing a mitre like that of the Assyrian kings. In his left hand he has a staff or a spear, while with his right hand he seems to indicate that he grants protection to, and accepts the offerings of, a priest whose picture is carved underneath his own and is represented on a smaller scale, as is customary where divine and mortal persons are pictured side by side. He is likewise clothed in an Assyrian toga, his head is uncovered, and with his hands he performs the offering on the altar before him. On the top of the altar, and underneath, the name of the priest is given: "Salmshezeb, the priest."[1]

The inscription itself is much mutilated at the beginning, but thanks to the sagacious comments of a number of French and German scholars the sense of the whole is now well understood, and even the missing parts can be restored to some extend with reasonable certainty.

The document may be entitled "A Welcome of the Gods," for in it we read that the gods of Teima agree to receive in their midst a newcomer, the god Salm of Hagam, who was brought to Teima by Salmshezeb, son of Petosiri, furthermore to sanction this man and his descendants as the new god's priests, and finally to endow the new temple with an annual income.

The name Petosiri, "devoted to Osiris," shows us that the donor of the temple was of Egyptian origin; his son Salmshezeb,

---

[1] צלמשזב כמרא.

in Aramaic "Salm has preserved," had probably adopted a name, perhaps chosen because he wanted to express his grati- to the god Salm of Hagam for having preserved him from e danger. Then Salmshezeb may, possibly in fulfilment of a , have built a temple for Salm of Hagam in Teima, for which gods and the king of Teima gave the assurance: first to recog- him and his descendants as the priests in the newly built ple, and secondly, to grant the temple a certain income from sacred (or public) palm grove (field) and from the king's estate.

The editors of the *Corpus Inscriptionum Semiticarum*[1] have cor- ly divided the inscription into three parts.

1. Lines 1–8: must have contained the reasons why the gods the king of Teima recognised Salmshezeb as priest and en- ed the temple of Salm of Hagam.

2. Lines 8–15: speak of the erection of the monument and en- erate the rights of the priest; further, those who should des- it are cursed.

3. Lines 15–20: specify the endowment.[1]

4. Lines 20–23: contain Salmshezeb's invocation for his own ection and for that of his descendants.

The following are the text and an English translation of this iption:

1 [בירח ...] בשת 22 [למלכא ...]
2 [צדקו בתימ]א צלם [זי מחרם ושנגלא]
3 [ואשירא אלהי תימא לצלם זי
4 [הגם להן] שמה ביומא ז[נה בתי]מא
5 [צלמשזב בר פטסרי] ..... זי
6 ....
7 ....
8 .....א להן והא סותא ז[א
9 זי [הקי]ם צלמשזב בר פטסרי
10 [בבית צ[ל]ם זי הגם להן אלהי
11 תימא צ[דק]ו לצלמשזב בר פטסרי
12 ולזרעה בבית צלם זי הגם וגבר
13 זי יחבל סותא זא אלהי תימא
14 ינסחוהי וזרעה ושמה מן אנפי

[1] Part II, No. 113. The present article is mostly based on this edition.

15 תימא והא זא צדקתא זי י[הבו]
16 צלם זי מחרם ושנגלא ואשירא
17 אלהי תימא לצלם זי הגם א[נו]
18 מן חקלא דקלן 16 ומן שימתא
19 זי מלכא דקלן 5 כל דקלן
20 21 [הא] שנה בשנה ואלהן ואנש
21 לא יהנ[פקו] צלמשזב בר פטסרי
22 מן ביתא זנה ו[ז]רעה ושמה
23 כמ[ר]יא בביתא זנה [לעלם]

1 [In the month...] of the 22d year [of the king....]
2 [in Teim]a, Salm [of Mahram and Shangala]
3 [and Ash]îra, the gods of Teima, [sanctioned] Salm of
4 [Hagam]. Therefore he was introduced on this day [in Tei[ma
5 [by Salmshezeb, son of Petosiri]............ who
6 ....
7 ....
8 ......This is therefore [the stele]
9 which Salmhezeb, son of Petosiri, [set] up
10 [in the temple of S]alm of Hagam. For the
11 gods of Teima [sanction]ed Salmshezeb, son of Petosiri,
12 and his seed in the temple of Salm of Hagam. And any man
13 who shall destroy this stele, may the gods of Teima
14 pluck out him, and his seed, and his posterity from before
15 Teima! And this is the grant which
16 Salm of Mahram and Shangala and Ashira,
17 the gods of Teima, have [given] to Salm of Hagam, na[mely]:
18 from the field 16 palms, and from the treasure
19 of the king 5 palms, in all
20 21 palms year by year. And neither gods nor men
21 shall bring [out] Salmshezeb, son of Petosiri,
22 from this temple, neither his [see]d nor his posterity, [who are]
23 prie[sts in] this temple [forever]!

Scarcely anything is known concerning the gods mentioned in this inscription. It has been suggested that Shangala is the same as the Babylonian goddess Shagal or the moon-god Sin-gala, and that Ashîra is contained in the Palmyrene name Rabasira,[1] or that Ashîra is identical with the goddess Ashêra, known from the Old Testament. In Salm of Mahram and Salm of Hagam we must see

1 רבאסירא *'Ραβασιρα.*

local gods whose cult spread beyond their original place of worship; parallels from the Semitic as well as the Greek and Roman religions are known, for instance: Ilat of Salkhad (in the Hauran) אלמקה ד הרן in Southern Arabia, Jupiter Olympius, Venus Paphia, etc. A place called al-Hagm is found in Southern Arabia, and Mahrama in Northern Arabia. Moreover, Mahram has been compared with the Abyssinian war-god Mahrem, who is mentioned in the ancient inscriptions of Axum and corresponds to the Greek Ares.

The date of this inscription may approximately be fixed by a comparison of its script and of its language with those of other Aramaic inscriptions. We are led to conclude that it is not older than the sixth nor younger than the fifth century B. C.

The importance of this document lies in the fact that we learn from it:

1. A well established civilisation with temples, hereditary priesthood, and other public institutions existed in Northern Arabia as early as about 500 B. C.

2. This civilisation was influenced from Egypt, Syria, and Assyria: Egypt is represented by the priest himself, Syria by the Aramaic script and language, Assyria by the sculptures on the left side of the stele.

3. A fact established on other evidence is here corroborated. We see how closely all the countries and communities of the ancient East were interconnected in their history.

Modern scholarship is fully justified when it recognises the conclusion as true, that the Hebrew nation, too, cannot have developed in isolation, and that Israel's political history must have been strongly influenced by the civilisation of the surrounding countries, particularly of the great empires of the ancient East, Babylonia, Assyria, and Egypt.

ENNO LITTMANN.

PRINCETON, N. J.

THE FRONT DOOR OF PALESTINE.

SOUTHWARD from Damascus runs a great caravan route to Arabia Felix, making Damascus the metropolis—or rather the "cross-roads"—in past days, for Semitic commerce. Along this rude highway have also crept the moving clans who sought in other lands an easier environment. Running nearly parallel with the Jordan, some 30 miles east of it, it traverses the border of the irreclaimable desert. But to the west of the road lie the broad meadows and rolling plains of Moab and Bashan, and the breezy heights of Gilead; not universally tillable, but affording excellent pasturage in the southern region, and becoming marvellously fertile as the road nears Damascus. The posession of this route gives two great advantages to the Oriental nomad. On the one side lies luxuriant pasturage and an excellent water supply, on the other the fastnesses of the desert afford a refuge from superior forces, while the passing caravan affords unlimited opportunities for "blackmail"—an institution as fixed in the East as the East itself. Travellers following in the wake of the Arab trader find they must pay roundly for their passage through savage tribes. "Go not empty into the presence of princes" is an Oriental dictum now hoary with age. Throughout Africa the traveller must fight his way through or pay toll for the privilege of passing. The Arab trader has established the habit, and the white man must conform to established precedents. So in the East the incessant cry of the submerged tenth is "Backsheesh, howwajji! backsheesh!" while the itching palms of officials create a permanent market for "ointment of Mexico"—to use a Spanish phrase. With these fundamental features of primitive clan life still persistent, we may comprehend the course of development of an ancient Semitic empire. The petty city-state imposes toll for ıe right of passage upon the trader—our word "tariff" being de- ;ved from this very practice at the port of Tarifa. Raids for plunder egin also to assume larger proportions; the demanding and securing n annual tribute from wealthy neighbors results. That was the /hole of international politics in the earliest stages of the Orient. 'urely intellectual culture and improved social organization do not ppear to have occupied the energies of early Semitic life. They re- ıult from the contact with other people. The Semite's progress in hese departments somewhat suggests the progress of a cow tied at he tail of a wagon.

With the wants of a primitive Semitic in mind, it is clear ıat the broad tract between the Arabian caravan road and the ›rdan is an ideal situation for him. Fertile lands well tilled, lay yond the river; the fruits were to be had for the raiding; while the ealth of the Indies, of Yemen, of Oman and Hadramant, are ought to his door by the traders of the time. Now add the "back- oor" road of Palestine, the route through the coast plain and Es- aelon, connecting with the front door route east of the Sea of Gali- e, and we have possible the political problem of the ancient world; e ceaseless struggle for the control of the commerce of these two ads.

Now the Hebrew records place this possibility before us as a ality. The Aramaic nomads seize this region; the method of ap- rtionment being "might makes right." When strife arises, the lot ns gain the tract (the Lōtān of some ancient records: the Rutennu the Egyptian inscriptions). The other clan, of which Abram is ikh, secures the less fertile uplands, toward Hebron, and allies itself h three Hittite chieftains; while later Moab and Ammon absorb rly half the eastern plateau. Later, upon a further division of the n, a strong tribe seizes the red lands and the rocky ridges south of Dead Sea, finding strong natural fortresses in the ravines and fts of the rock, and hewing out remarkable cities there in the solid one. Later there is another division, and two pastoral clans seize he great plains northeast of the Dead Sea, as far as northern Bashan.

Now the importance of this road becomes the more marked,

when we find these kindred clans struggling persistently with each other for the control of this road. We find David endeavoring to establish his authority in this region, and destroying the commanding Ammonite fortress; finding also that he must contest its possession with the original Aramaic clans centered at Damascus, the Mesopotamian and Egyptian empires being disastrously weak and anarchic at the time. The Hittite federation being a thing of the past, and the northern Aramean power not being fully developed, David has temporary success; but the control is speedily lost by his successors. Rather than fight Aram, Solomon tries to establish a new route across the desert south of Damascus; a scheme which is revived with much better success in Græco-Roman times, as the ruins of Baalbek testify. We may also remember Solomon's effort to divert traffic at the southern end of the road by seizing the Gulf of Akaba; a direct result of his policy being a diplomatic visit from a Saharan princess. We find Amaziah later striving to regain control of the road by reconquering Edom, which Solomon had lost; while Samaria and Aram are for years at war over the tract, the strategic fortress of Ramoth-Gilead being the centre of the struggle. Aram's position is desperate in this period; for Assyria has cut off her control of the eastern overland route to India—travelling along which Aramean traders had carried the alphabet into the Punjab. Samaria by reason of her natural position controls the sea-coast road to Egypt; Babylon is mistress of the route through the Persian Gulf; Tyre controls the Mediterranean. If Aram cannot control the direct southern route from Damascus, her control of the overland route to the sea-coast of Asia Minor will be largely deprived of value. Samaria's position is similar; her control of the Egyptian road could be of value only so long as she had a free outlet to the eastward; while Mesha of Moab has no interest in their differences, so long as he can collect toll from caravans of any people, bound north or south, a thing which Israelite traders would prevent; and Mesha, so soon as he is independent, manifests no desire to conquer western Israel, or to extend his dominion beyond the fortified cities that control this road.

This barely suggests the field of action, and the political significance of tribal struggles. Looking now at Western Palestine, it is clear that an immense difference from the beginning could be predicted of the development of the tribes. Northern Israel could not possibly escape contact with the world and collision with the world-powers of the time. She would be involved in their movements in spite of herself. All that is meant by culture, learning, art, commerce, would in some measure flow through her territory. She was as certainly predestined to be cosmopolitan, liberal and humane, if she could maintain herself, as Jerusalem was destined to be conservative, provincial, narrow and even bigoted. The latter could not readily get in contact with the cultured world. Could or would the world come to her? Not while Samaria stood. Jerusalem was a mountain town, out of the track of the world's commerce. No Assyrian would meddle with her, if she did not go out of her way to meddle with him. No Necho cared to give her a passing thought, if she would let the Esdraelon commercial road alone. The world's armies could march to and fro through the coast plain, but none would climb her barren hills, if she kept the peace.

The Dead Sea protected her eastern border. Moab and Ammon and Edom held the fortresses beyond. Samaria on the north protected her from interference from that quarter, but absorbed the culture to be derived in that position. Even Philistia in her effort to dominate Israel fought for Dothan, Megiddo, Gilboa, little concerned about the passes from the Shephelah into Southern Judah. No wonder that Judah came to feel a peculiar sense of protection in the hills of Zion. It was the "accident" of her geographical position. So Isaiah in his disputes with Ahaz and Hezekiah, that Judah had only to let the world-powers alone, and they would let her alone. If she would raid the coast plains, or meddle with the politics of the region, entanglement with Assyria was certain. Beyond the coast plain lay a sea whose harborless eastern shore afforded little opportunity either to go out or to come in; a steady northward current was ever bringing Nile mud to make new banks and shoals, so that the "isles of the sea" were not disposed to exploit this coast nor to explore its *hinterland*. Such was the situation of Judah with regard to the " hindersea."

But at her front door, "Oedemah," the situation was different. Save for the precipitous edges of the Ghor, the land was defenseless. The fords of the Jordan were too numerous for that stream to be considered a serious barrier. Raids from the great table-land beyond the Jordan might be looked for at any time; as well as immigration of those disposed to adopt a more settled life. We catch glimpses here and there of such events. But this influx was naturally of a people in a more primitive social and religious state. The tendency of such influences was to retard progress. It is but natural that Judah then should remain for centuries more heathenish than Israel ever was, as Ezekiel declares.

We have already seen that from this difference in the geographical situation of the northern and southern kingdoms some very important consequences follow. Northern Israel was from the beginning to the end compelled to be more warlike, and to take a ceaseless interest in world-politics. She could take the initiative, or stand steadfastly upon the defensive, waiting till she was attacked. But fight she must, against the leading empires of the time. If, on the other hand, she strove to secure herself by diplomacy, she was placed the more surely under the influence of peoples more cultured and experienced than herself. The warlike spirit is shown in the early attitude of Mt. Ephraim toward her neighbors, and her real hegemony. The ceaseless struggle makes militarism prominent; the northern prophets are inevitably affected, suggesting and advising in the matter of campaigns. The "pretorian guard" becomes dominant; revolution after revolution originates in the army, with the "captain of the host"; in its latest and proudest days, Amos invades the domain of the mighty Jeroboam II., to sneer at the "war hunger" of the great nobles, to denounce the oppressiveness of this militarism, and to announce vengeance for the revolutionary tactics of Jehu. The influence of cultured peoples is suggested by the earlier and more rapid development of literature and religion in the northern kingdom; and the influence of that development is in part suggested by the Josianic reform, which made it possible for a pious northerner to consent to worship with his southern brethren. Such centralisation of worship was impossible while the two divisions were far apart in their religious doctrines and purposes. The northern elements in Deuteronomy we cannot discuss here.

In the south, *per contra,* the assailants of Judah could be expected at the "front door." They were of her own kith and kin; Kenites and Edomites were constituent parts of the early clan of Judah. Relations with Moab were familiar. All these were not greatly different from the primitive people of Judah, these raiders, or home-seekers, they were not organized empires. Pastoral and nomadic, they had no world-politics nor world-ambition. They could exert no influence for progress; make no contribution to culture. Such influence as they could exert would be for the retention of primitive modes of life and the earlier crude religious ideas. Judah could not gain from her contact with them any experience in organized warfare. The sudden foray, the tactics of the desert; beyond these there is no hint of development in these semi-nomadic peoples. Judah's one general learned much, no doubt, from his alliance with the methodical Philistine. We may expect, in consequence, that the ideal of Judah would be more peaceful; but in like manner it is certain that the idea of a mission to the world would be much harder to produce in this uncultured people of the hills. The active interest in world-politics soon produces prophets in the north who consider themselves charged with missions to Sarepta, to Cherith, to make kings in Syria, to go to Nineveh and cry against it; to set up and pull down kings. The " stormy petrels " of their time, they are ever to the front in time of war or trouble. But nothing could be more unlike the southern prophet. He wishes to be let alone; he wishes Judah to be let alone. If the king has military aspirations, the prophet declares he prefers a prince of peace. The world empires can take care of themselves. The great chasm between the Pharisee and Sanhedrim on one side, and the Galilean Carpenter and Fisherman on the other is becoming discernible. If the Galilean zealot was too full of the old militarism of the days of Elisha, he at least was full of the idea of a world-mission. While he mis-estimated in a measure the purport and scope of his mission, he had not the narrow exclusiveness toward the Gentile that characterised the pedantic ritualist of the south. Nor did he care for the forms of the latter, nor for his consequent sneer at the Galilean: "This people that knoweth not the law is accursed." While the southern priest would not touch a world's burdens with one of his little fingers, the Galilean would move some of them, if he knew how.

Such is a bare suggestion of what it would take many pages to elaborate. How the two different ideals of destiny and method were utilised in the production of the environment through which the Nazarene and his co-laborers were to come, and what was His attitude toward each element of the Jewish atmosphere, may be left largely to the reflection of the reader. Certainly He was more northern than southern.

It may be added that the habit of centuries clung to the Judean to the last. To the east he looked for light: the children of the east were the wise in his eyes. From Babylonian schools came the legislation and priestcraft of Ezra: in the same schools the earlier Targums grew. There is no more suggestive reversal of Jewish prejudices than in the tale of the wise men who turned their faces westward, seeking for light. Yet so it was to be. From the west came the Jew's intellectual enlightenment, Hellenism, even though he knew it not. And in the Hellenised Jews the Galilean Carpenter found the great nucleus of His church, the great opponents of Jewish narrowness, and an early martyr to a broader faith. The southern Jew could not set his face in this direction. Accustomed to the yearly influx of ancient conservatism from the east, speaking of the east as the "front," he resolutely sets his back to all that the west implied, the Arabian caravan road—that meant Aram, Mesopotamia, Hanan, Armenia, Babylonia, Arabia, Persia, even India, to him: all his ancient world and ancient order of ideas. Nothing new, no element of progress, could come to him thence. Over this same road later came the great Arabian in whom Khadijah believed when no one else would: and immediately there came into being a new synonym for fanatical conservatism. From the northern kingdom, by the great highways there, have come those great elements in the Hebrew religion that make for the progress and liberty of the world.

A. H. Godbey.

Chicago, Ill.

CERBERUS, THE DOG OF HADES.

HERMES, the guide of the dead, brings to Pluto's kingdom their psyches, "that gibber like bats, as they fare down the dark ways, past the streams of Okeanos, past the gates of the sun and the land of dreams, to the meadow of asphodel in the dark realm of Hades, where dwell the souls, the phantoms of men outworn." So begins the twenty-fourth book of the *Odyssey*. Later poets have Charon, a grim boatman, receive the dead at the River of Woe; he ferries them across, provided the passage money has been placed in their mouths, and their bodies have been duly buried in the world above. Otherwise they are left to gibber on the hither bank. Pluto's house, wide-gated, thronged with guests, has a janitor Kerberos, sometimes friendly, sometimes snarling when new guests arrive, but always hostile to those who would depart. Honey cakes are provided for them that are about to go to Hades, the sop to Cerberus. This dog, nameless and undescribed, Homer mentions simply as the dog of Hades, whom Herakles, as the last and chief test of his strength, snatched from the horrible house of Hades.[1] First Hesiod and next Stesichorus discover his name to be Kerberos. The latter seems to have composed a poem on the dog. Hesiod[2] mentions not only the name but also the genealogy of Kerberos. Of Typhaon and Echidna he was born, the irresistible and ineffable flesh-devourer, the voracious, brazen-voiced, fifty-headed dog of hell.

Plato in the *Republic* refers to the composite nature of Kerberos.[3] Not until Apollodorus (2. 5. 12. 1 ff.), in the second cen-

[1] *Iliad* viii. 368; *Odyssey* xi. 623.
[2] *Theogony*, 311 ff.; cf. also 769 ff.
[3] *Republic*, 588 C.

tury B. C., comes the familiar description: Kerberos now has three dog heads, a dragon tail, and his back is covered with the heads of serpents. But his plural heads must have been familiarly assumed by the Greeks: this will appear from the evidence of their sculptures and vase-paintings. Classic art has taken up Cerberus very generously; his treatment, however, is far from being as definite as that of the Greek and Roman poets. Statues, sarcophagi, and vase paintings whose theme is Hades, or scenes laid in Hades, represent him as a ferocious Greek collie, often encircled with serpents, and with a serpent for a tail, but there is no certainty as to the number of his heads. Often he is three-headed in art as in literature, as may be seen conveniently in the reproductions in Baumeister's *Denkmäler des klassischen Altertums.* Very familiar is the statue in the villa Borghese of Pluto enthroned, three-headed Cerberus by his side.[1] A Greek scarabacus shows a pair of lovers, or a married couple, who have died at the same time, crossing in Charon's ferry. As they are approaching the other bank of the Styx, where a three-headed Cerberus is awaiting them, the girl seems afright and is upheld by her male companion.[2] On the other hand, a bronze in Naples shows the smiling boy Herakles engaged in strangling two serpents, one with each hand. The figure rests upon a cylindrical base upon which are depicted eight of the wonderful deeds which Herakles performs later on. By a rope he leads a *two-headed* Cerberus from Hades.[3]

This last of the wonderful deeds of Herakles is a favorite theme of vase pictures. Herakles is regularly accompanied by Hermes and Athena; the dog, whose marvelous shape Homer fails to reveal, is generally two-headed. Such a vase may be seen in Gerhard, *Auserlesene Vasenbilder,* ii. 131.[4] Or still more conveniently Professor Norton has reproduced[5] an amphora in the Louvre with a picture of the dicephalous Kerberos. Upon the forehead of each of the

[1] Baumeister, volume I., page 620 (figure 690).

[2] Baumeister, volume I., p. 379 (figure 415).

[3] Baumeister, volume I., page 653 (figure 721).

[4] Baumeister, volume I., page 663 (figure 730).

[5] *American Journal of Archæology,* volume XI., page 14 (figure 12, page 15).

o heads rises a serpent. Herakles in tunic and lion's skin, armed th bow, quiver, and sword, stoops towards the dog. He holds a ain in his left hand, while he stretches out his right with a petting sture. Between the two is a tree, against which leans the club of erakles. Behind him stands Athena.

Neither Greek literature, nor Greek art, however, really seems to : either the shape or nature of Kerberos: it was left to the Roman ets to say the last word about him. They finally settle the number his heads, or the number of his bodies fused in one. He is *triceps* hree-headed," *triplex* or *tergeminus* "threefold," *triformis* "of three dies," or simply Tricerberus. Tibullus says explicitly that he has th three heads and three tongues: *cui tres sint linguæ tergeminumæ caput.* Virgil, in the *Æneid*, vi. 417, has huge Cerberus barking th triple jaws; his neck bristles with serpents. Ovid in his *Metarphoses*, x. 21, makes Orpheus, looking for dear Eurydice in rtarus, declare that he did not go down in order that he might in the three necks, shaggy with serpents, of the monster begotten Medusa. His business also is settled for all time: he is the terle, fearless, and watchful janitor, or guardian (*janitor* or *custos*) Orcus, the Styk, Leke, or the black Kingdom.[1] And so he nains for modern poets, as when Dante, reproducing Virgil, cribes him:[2]

Or Shakespeare, *Love's Labor Lost,* v. ii: "Great Hercules is sented by this imp whose club killed Cerberus, the three-headed *is.*"

Such classical explanations of Cerberus' shape as I have seen : feeble and foolishly reasonable. Heraclitus, *Περὶ ἀπίστων* 331, tes that Kerberos had two pups. They always attended their her, and therefore he appeared to be three-headed. The mythrapher Palacphatos (39) states that Kerberos was considered three-

[1] *Custos opaci pervigil regni canis.* Seneca.

[2] *Inferno,* Canto vi., 13 ff.

> "When Cerberus, that great worm, had seen us
> His mouth he opened and his fangs were shown,
> And then my leader with his folded palms
> Took of the earth, and filling full his hand,
> Into those hungry gullets flung it down."

headed from his name *Τρικάρηνος* which he obtained from the city Trikarenos in Phliasia. And a late Roman rationalistic mythographer by the name of Fulgentius[1] cites Petronius defining Cerberus as the lawyer of Hades, apparently because of his three jaws, or the cumulative glibness of three tongues. Fulgentius himself has a *fabula* in which he says that Cerberus means *Creaboros*, that is, "flesh-eating," and that the three heads of Cerberus are respectively, infancy, youth, and old age, through which death has entered the circle of the earth — *per quas introivit mors in orbem terrarum.*[2]

"*Lasciate ogni speranze che voi entrate*": Can we bid this "*schwankende Gestalt,*" this monstrous vision, floating about upon the filmy photographs of murky Hades, stand still, emerge into light, and assume clear and reasonable outlines?

"Hence loathed melancholy of Cerberus and blackest Midnight-born."

An American humorist, John Kendrick Bangs, who likes to place his skits in Hades, steps in "where angels fear to tread," and launches with a light heart the discussion as to whether Cerberus is one or more dogs. The city of Cimmeria in Hades, having tried asphalt pavement, which was found too sloppy for that climate, and Nicholson wood pavement, which kept taking fire, decides on Belgian blocks. In order to meet the new expense a dog-tax is imposed. Since Cerberus belongs to Hades as a whole the state must pay his tax, and is willing enough to do so — on Cerberus as one dog. The city, however, endeavors to collect on three dogs — one license for each head. Two infernal coppers, sent to impound Cerberus, fare not well, one of them being badly chewed up by Cerberus, the other nabbed bodily and thrown into the Styx. In consequence of this they obtain damages from the city. The city then decides to bring suit against the state. The bench consists of Apollyon himself and Judge Blackstone; Coke appears for the city, Catiline for the state. The first dog-catcher, called to testify, and asked whether he is

---

[1] See p. 99 of the Teubner edition of his writings.

[2] Fulgentius, Liber I., Fabula VI., de Tricerbero, p. 20 of the Teubner edition.

familiar with dogs, replies in the affirmative, adding that he had never got quite so intimate with one as he got with him.

"With whom?" asks Coke.

"Cerberus," replies the witness.

"Do you consider him to be one dog, two dogs, or three dogs?"

Catiline objects to this question as a leading one, but Coke manages to get it in under another form: "How many dogs did you see when you saw Cerberus "

"Three, anyhow," replies the witness with feeling, "though afterwards I thought there was a whole bench-show atop of me."

On cross-examination Catiline asks him blandly: "My poor friend, if you considered Ceberus to be three dogs anyhow, why did you in your examination a moment since refer to the avalanche of caninity, of which you so affectingly speak, as him?"

"He is a him," says the witness. After this Coke, discomfited, decides to call his second witness: "What is your business?" asks Coke, after the usual preliminaries.

"I'm out of business. Livin' on my damages."

"What damages?"

"Them I got from the city for injuries did me by that there — I should say them there — dorgs, Cerberus."

And so on. Catiline gains the day for the state by his superior logic: the city of Cimmeria must content itself with taxes on a single dog. But the logic of the facts, it will appear, are with the dog-catchers, Judge Coke, and the city of Cimmeria as against the state of Hades; Cerberus is more than one dog.

India is the home of the Cerberus myth in its clearest and fullest development. In order to appreciate its nature we must bear in mind that the early Hindu conceptions of a future life are auspicious, and quite the reverse of sombre. The statements in the Veda about life after death exclude all notions of hell. The early visions are simple, poetic and cheerful. The bodies of the dead are burned and their ashes are consigned to earth. But this is viewed merely as a symbolic act of preparation — cooking it is called forthright — for another life of joy. The righteous forefathers of old who died before, they have found another good place. Especially Yama, the first mortal, has gone to the great rivers on high; he has searched out, like a pioneer, the way for all his descendants: "He went before and found a dwelling which no power can debar us from. Our fathers of old have traveled the path; it leads every earth-born mortal thither. There in the midst of the highest heaven beams unfading light and eternal waters flow; there every wish is fulfilled on the rich meadows of Yama." Day by day Yama sends forth two dogs, his messengers, to search out among men those who are to join the fathers that are having an excellent time in Yama's company.

The tenth book of the *Rig-Veda* contains in hymns 14-18 a collection of funeral stanzas quite unrivaled in mythological and ethnological interest in the literature of ancient peoples. In hymn 14 there are three stanzas (10-12) that deal with the two dogs of Yama. This is the classical passage, all depends upon its interpretation. They contain detached statements which take up the idea from different points of view, that are not easily harmonised as long as the dogs are merely ordinary canines; they resolve themselves fitly and neatly into a pair of natural objects, if we follow closely all the ideas which the Hindus associated with them.

In the first place, it is clear that we are dealing with the conception of Cerberus. In stanza 10 the two dogs are conceived as ill-disposed creatures, standing guard to keep the departed souls out of bliss. The soul on its way to heaven is addressed as follows:

"Run past straightway the two four-eyed dogs, the spotted and (the dark), the brood of Saramâ; enter in among the propitious fathers who hold high feast with Yama."

A somewhat later text, the book of house-rite of Açvalâgana, has the notion of the sop to Cerberus: "To the two dogs born in the house of (Yama) Vivasvant's son, to the dark and the spotted, I have given a cake; guard me ever on my road."

The twelfth stanza of the *Rig-Veda* hymn strikes a somewhat different note which suggests both good and evil in the character of the two dogs: "The two brown, broad-nosed messengers of Yama, life-robbing, wander among men. May they restore to us to-day the auspicious breath of life, that we may behold the sun." Evidently the part of the Cerberi here is not in harmony with their function in anza 10: instead of debarring men from the abodes of bliss they ick out the dead that are ultimately destined to boon companionship ith Yama. The same idea is expressed simply and clearly in prayers r long life in the *Atharva-Veda*: "The two dogs of Yama, the ark and the spotted, that guard the road (to heaven), that have een dispatched, shall not (go after) thee! Come hither, do not ng to be away! Do not tarry here with thy mind turned to a disance!" (viii.1-9.) And again: "Remain here, O man, with thy oul entire! Do not follow the two messengers of Yama; come o the abodes of the living." (v. 30, 6.)

These prayers contain the natural, yet under the circumstances ather paradoxical, desire to live yet a little longer upon the earth in he light of the sun. Fitfully the mortal Hindu regales himself with ccharine promises of paradise; in his every-day mood he clings to fe and shrinks with the uneasy sense that his paradise may not aterialize, even if the hope is expressed glibly and fluently. The al craving is expressed in numberless passages: "May we live a undred autumns, surrounded by lusty sons." Homer's Hades has iped out this inconsistency, only to substitute another. Odysseus, on turning from his visit to Hades, exclaims boldy: "Better a swineerd on the surface of the earth in the light of the sun than king of e shades in Hades." It is almost adding insult to injury to have e road to such a Hades barred by Cerberus. This latter paradox ust be removed in order that the myth shall become intelligible.

The eleventh of the *Rig-Veda* stanzas presents the two dogs as uides of the soul ψυχοπόμποι to heaven: "To thy two foured, road-guarding, man-beholding watch-dogs entrust him, O ing Yama, and bestow on him prosperity and health."

With the change of the abode of the dead from inferno to heaven e two Cerberi are *so ipso* also evicted. That follows of itself even we had not explicit testimony. A legend of the Brāhmana-texts, e Hindu equivalent of the Talmud, tells repeatedly that there are wo dogs *in heaven*, and that these two dogs are Yama's dogs. I hall present two versions of the story, a kind of Γιγαντομαχία in rder to establish the equation between the terms "two dogs of Yama," and "two heavenly dogs."

There were Asuras (demons) named Kālakānjas. They piled up a fire altar in order to obtain the world of heaven. Man by man they placed a brick upon it. The god Indra, passing himself off for a Bràhmin, put on a brick for himself. They climbed up to heaven. Indra pulled out his brick; they tumbled down. And they who tumbled down became spiders; two flew up, and became the two heavenly dogs." (Brāhmana of the *Tāittirīyas* I. 1. 2.)

"The Asuras (demons) called Kālakānjas piled bricks for an altar, saying: 'We will ascend to heaven.' Indra, passing himself off for a Brahmin, came to them; he put on a brick. They at first came near getting to heaven; then Indra tore out his brick. The Asuras becoming quite feeble fell down; the two that were uppermost became the dogs of Yama, those which were lower bcame spiders." (*Brāhmana of the Māitra* 1. 6. 9.)

This theme is so well fixed in the minds of the time that it is elaborated in a charm to preserve from some kind of injury, addressed to the mythic figures of the legend:

"Through the air he flies looking down upon all beings: with the majesty of the heavenly dog, with that oblation would we pay homage to thee.

"The three Kālakānjas, that are fixed upon the sky like gods, all these I have called to help, to render this person free from harm.

"In the waters is thy origin, upon the heavens thy home, in the middle of the sea, and upon the earth, thy greatness; with the majesty of the heavenly dog, with that oblation would we pay homage to thee." (*Atharva-Veda* vi., 80.)

The single heavenly dog that is described here is of no mean interest. The passage proves the individual character of each of the two dogs of Yama; they cannot be a vague pair of heavenly dogs, but must be based each upon some definite phenomenon in the heavens.

Yet another text, Hiranyakeçin's book of house-rites, locates the dogs of Yama, describing them in unmistakable language, in heaven: "The brood of Saramā, dark beneath and brown, run, looking down upon the sea." (ii. 7. 2.)

There are not many things in heaven that can be represented

a pair coursing across the sky, looking down upon the sea, and ıving other related properties. My readers will make a shrewd ıess, but I prefer to let the texts themselves unfold the transparent ystery. The Veda of the Katha school (xxxvii. 14) says: "These wo dogs of Yama, verily, are day and night," and the Brâhmana f the *Kâushitakins* (ii. 9) argues in Talmudic strain: "At eve, hen the sun has gone down, before darkness has set in, one should acrifice the *agnihotra*-sacrifice; in the morning before sunrise, when arkness is dispelled, at that time, one should sacrifice the *agnihotra*-acrifice; at that time the gods arrive. Therefore (the two dogs of 'ama) Çyâma and Çabala (the dark and the spotted) tear to pieces he *agnihotra* of him that sacrifices otherwise. Çabala is the day; yâma is the night. He who sacrifices in the night, his *agnihotra* yâma tears asunder; he who sacrifices in broad daylight, his *agni-otra*, Çabala tears asunder." Even more drily the two dogs of ama are correlated with the time-markers of heaven in a passage of he Tâittirîya-Veda (v. 7. 19); here sundry parts of the sacrificial orse are assigned to four cosmic phenomena in the following order: . Sun and moon. 2. Çyâna and Çabala (the two dogs of Yama). . Dawn. 4. Evening twilight. So that the dogs of Yama are andwiched in between sun and moon on the one side, dawn and vening twilight on the other. Obviously they are here, either as special designation of day and night, or their physical equivalents, un and moon. And now the Çatapatha. Brâhmana says explicitly: The moon verily is the divine dog; he looks down upon the cattle f the sacrificer." And again a passage in the Kashmir version of the 'tharva-Veda says: "The four-eyed dog surveys by night the phere of the night."

Even the theosophic Upanishads are compelled to make their ay through this tolerably crude mythology when they come to eal with the passage of the soul to release from existence and bsorption in the universal Brahma. The human mind does not asily escape some kind of eschatological topography. The Brahma self may be devoid of all properties, universal, pervasive, situated below as well as above, the one true thing everywhere; still even the panishads finally fix upon a world of Brahma, and that is above, not below, nor elsewhere; hence the soul must pass the great cosmic potencies that seem to lie on the road from the sublunary regions to Brahma. The *Kânushîtaki Upanishad* (i. 2, 3) arranges that all who leave this world first go to the moon, the moon being the door of the world of light. The moon asks certain theosophic questions; he alone who can answer them is considered sufficiently emancipated to advance to the world of Braham. He who cannot—alas!—is born again as worm or as fly; as fish or as fowl; as lion or as boar; as bull or tiger or man; or as something else—any old thing, as we should say—in this place or in that place according to the quality of his works and the degree of his knowledge; that is, in accordance with the doctrine of *Karma*. Similarly the *Maitri Upanishad* (vi. 38) sketches salvation as follows: When a mortal no longer approves of wrath and ponders the true wish he penetrates the veil that encloses the Brahma, breaks through the concentric circles of sun, moon, fire, etc., that occupy the ether. Only then does he behold the supreme thing that is founded upon its own greatness only. And now the *Chândogya Upanishad* (viii. 13) has the same idea, mentioning both moon and sun by their ancient names and in their capacity as dogs of Yama. The soul of the aspirant for fusion with Brahma resorts purgatorio-fashion alternately to Çyâma (the moon-dog) and Çabala (the sun-dog): "From Çyâma (the moon) do I resort to Çabala (the sun); from Çabala to Çyâma. Shaking off sin, as a steed shakes off (the loose hair of) its mane, as the moon frees itself from the maw of Râhu, the demon of eclipse, casting aside my body, my real self delivered, do I enter into the uncreated world of Brahma."[1]

Hindu mythology is famous for what I should like to hear called arrested personification, or arrested anthropomorphism. More than elsewhere mythic figures seem here to cling to the dear memories of their birth and youth. This is due in part to the unequaled impressiveness of nature in India; in part to the dogged schematism of the Hindu mind, which dislikes to let go of any part of a

[1] Both Çankara, the great Hindu theologian and commentator of the Upanishads, as well as all modern interpreters of the Upanishads have failed to see the sense of this passage.

ing from the beginning to end. On the one hand, their constant, almost too rhythmic resort to nature in their poetry, and on the other. their Vedânta philosophy, or for that matter their *Ars amatoria* (*Kâmaçastra*), the latter worked out with the painstaking and undignified detail, illustrate the two points. Hence we find here a situation which is familiar enough in the Veda, but scarcely and rarely exhibited in other mythological fields. Dogs, the two dogs of Yama, are, but yet, too, sun and moon. It is quite surprising how well the attributes of things so different keep on filling them both well enough. The color and brightness of the sun jumps with the fixed epithet "spotted," of the sun-dog Çabala; the moon-dog is black (Çyâma or Çyâva). Sun and moon, as they move across the sky, are the natural messengers of Yama, seated on high in the abode of the blessed, but Yama is after all death, and death hounds us all. Epithets like "man-beholding," or "guarding the way," suit neutrally both conceptions. Above all, the earliest statements about Yama's dogs are relieved of their inconsistencies. On the one hand the exhortation to the dead to run past the two dogs in order to get to heaven, suits the idea of the heavenly dogs who are coursing across the sky. On the other hand, by an easy, though quite contrary, change of mental position, the same two heavenly dogs are the guides who guard the way and look upon men favorably; hence they are ordered by Yama to take charge of the dead and to furnish them such health and prosperity as the shades happen to have use for. Again, by an equally simple shift of position, sun and moon move among men as the messengers of death; by night and by day men perish, while these heavenly bodies alternate in their presence among men."[1] Hence a text of the Veda can say in a similar mood: "May Day and Night procure for us long life" (House-book of *Çvalâyana* ii. 4. 14). Conversely it is a commonplace of the Veda to say that day and night destroy the lives of men. One text says that, "day and night are the encircling arms of death" (Brâhmana of the *Kânshîtakin*, ii. 9). Another, more explicitly, "the year is death; by means of day and night does it destroy the life of mortals

[1] Cf. the notion of the sun as the "highest death" in Tâittirîya Brâhmana i. 8. 4.

(*Çatapatha Brâhmana* x. 4. 3. 1.). He who wishes to be released from the grim grip of day and night sacrifices (symbolically) white and black rice, and pronounces the words: "Hail to Day; hail to Night; hail to Release" (Brâhmana of the *Tâittirîya*, iii. 1. 6. 2). Who does not remember in this connection the parable widely current in the Orient, in which two rats, one white, the other black, gnaw alternately, but without let-up, the plant or tree of life?

Norse mythology also contains certain animal pairs which seem to reflect the two dualities, sun and moon, and day and night. There is here no certainty as to detail; the Norse myth is advanced and congealed, if not spurious, as Professor Bugge and his school would have us believe. At the feet of Odin lie his two wolves, Geri and Freki, "Greedy" and "Voracious." They hurl themselves across the lands when peace is broken. Who shall say that they are to be entirely dissociated from Yama's two dogs of death. The virgin Menglödh sleeps in her wonderful castle on the mountain called Hyfja, guarded by the two dogs Geri and Gifr, "Greedy" and "Violent," who take turns in watching; only alternately may they sleep as they watch the Hyfja mountain. "One sleeps by night, the other by day, and thus no one may enter" (*Fiölsvinnsmál* 16). It is not necessary to suppose any direct connection between this fable and the Vedic myth, but the root of the thought, no matter from how great a distance it may have come, and how completely it may have been worked over by the Norse skald, is, after all, alternating sun and moon and their partners, day and night.

No reasonable student of mythology will demand of a myth so clearly destined for fructification an everlasting virginal inviolateness. From the start almost the two dogs of Yama are the brood of Saramâ. Why? Saramâ is the female messenger of the gods, at the root identical with Hermes—Hermeias; she is therefore the predestined mother of those other messengers, the two four-eyed dogs of Yama. And as the latter are her litter the myth becomes retroactive: she herself is fancied later on as a four-eyed bitch (*Atharva-Veda*, iv. 20. 7). Similarly the epithet "broad-nosed" stands not in need of mythic interpretation, as soon as it has become a question of life-hunting dogs. Elusive and vague, I confess, is the persistent and important attribute "four-eyed." This touch is both old and widespread. The *Avesta*, the bible of the ancient Iranians, has reduced the Cerberus myth to stunted rudiments. In *Vendidad*, xiii. 8, 9, the killing of dogs is forbidden, because the soul of the slayer "when passing to the other world, shall fly amid louder bowling and fiercer pursuit than the sheep does when the wolf rushes upon it in the lofty forest. No soul will come and meet his departing soul and help it through the howls and pursuit in the other world; nor will the dogs that keep the Cinvad bridge (the bridge to paradise) help his departing soul through the bowls and pursuit in the other world." The *Avesta* also conceives this dog to be four-eyed. When a man dies, as soon as the soul has parted from the body, the evil one, the corpse-devil (Druj Nasu), from the regions of hell, falls upon the dead. Whoever henceforth touches the corpse becomes unclean, and makes unclean whomsoever he touches. The devil is expelled from the dead by means of the "look of the dog": a "four-eyed dog" is brought near the body and is made to look at the dead; as soon as he has done so the devil flees back to hell (*Vendidad*, vii. 7; viii. 41). It is not easy to fetch from a mythological hell mythological monsters for casual purposes, especially as men are always engaged in dying upon the earth. Herakles is the only one who, one single time performed this notable "stunt." So the Parsis, being at a loss to find four-eyed dogs, interpret the name as meaning a dog with two spots over the eyes. Curiously enough the Hindu scholiasts also regularly interpret the term "four-eyed" in exactly the same way, "with spots over the eyes." And once more the Vedic ritual has occasion to realize the mythological four-eyed dog in practice. The horse, at the horse-sacrifice, must take a bath for consecration to the holy end to which it is put. It must also be guarded against hostile influences. A low-caste man brings a four-eyed dog—obviously the symbol of the hostile powers—kills him with a club, and afterwards places him under the feet of the horse. It is scarcely necessary to state that this is a dog with spots over his eyes, and that he is a symbol of Cerberus.[1]

[1] Similar notions in Russia and Russian Asia are reported by Wsevolod Miller, Atti del iv., *Congresso Internazionale degli Orientalisti*, vol. II. p. 43;

The epithet "four-eyed" may possibly contain a tentative coagulation of the two dogs in one. The capacity of the two dogs to see both by day (the sun) and by night (the moon) may have given the myth a slight start into the direction of the two-headed Greek Cerberus. But there is the alternate possibility that four-eyed is but a figure of speech for "sharp-sighted," especially as I have shown elsewhere that the parallel expression "to run with four feet" is a Vedic figure of speech for "swift of foot."[1] Certainly the god Agni, "Fire," is once in the *Rig-Veda* (i. 31. 13) called "four-eyed," which can only mean "sharp-sighted."

The two dogs of Yama derive their proper names from their color epithets. The passages above make it clear that Çyāma (rarely Çyāva), "the black," is the moon dog, and that Çabala, "the spotted, or brindled," is the sun dog. In one early passage (*Rig-Veda* x. 14, 10) both dogs are named in the dual as Çabalāu. But for a certain Vedic usage one might think that "the two spotted ones" was their earliest designation. The usage referred to is the eliptic dual: a close or natural pair each member of which suggests the other, may be expressed through the dual of one of them, as when either *mātarāu* or *pitarāu*, literally, "the two mothers," and "the two fathers," each mean "the two parents." From this we may conclude that Çabalāu means really Çabala and Çyāma, and not the two Çabalas, that is, "the two spotted ones." More than a hundred years ago the Anglo-Indian Wilford, in the *Asiatic Researches*, iii., page 409, wrote: "Yama, the regent of hell, has two dogs, according to the Purānas; one of them named Cerbura, or varied; the other Syama, or black." He then compares Cerbura with Kerberos, of course. The form Cerbura he obtained from his consulting Pandit, who explained the name Çabala by the Sanskrit word *karbura* "variegated," a regular gloss of the Hindu scholiasts.

About fifty years later a number of distinguished scholars of the past generation, Max Müller, Albrecht Weber, and Theodor

---

and by Casartelli, *Babylonian and Oriental Record*, iv. 266ff. They are most likely derived from Iranian sources.

[1] See *American Journal of Philology*, Vol. XI., p. 355.

Benfey, compared the word Çabala with Greek Κέρβερος (rarely Κέρβελος), but, since then, this identification has been assailed in numerous quarters with some degree of heat, because it suffers from a slight phonetic difficulty. One need but remember the swift changes which the name of Apollo passes through in the mouths of the Greeks —Ἀπόλλων, Ἀπέλλων, Ἀππέλλων, Ἀπείλων, Ἄπλουν[1]—to realize that it is useless to demand strict phonetic conservation of mythic proper names. The nominative Çabalas, translated sound for sound into Greek, yields Κέβερος, or Κέβελος; *vice versa*, Κέρβερος translated sound for sound into Vedic Sanskrit yield Çalbalas, or, perhaps, dialectically, Çabbalas. It is a sober view that holds it is rather surprising that the two languages have not manipulated their respective versions of the word so as to increase still further the phonetic distance between them. Certainly the burden is now to prove that the identification is to be rejected, and, I think, that the soundest linguistic science will refuse ultimately to consider the phonetic discrepancy between the two words as a matter of serious import.

But whether the names Çabalas and Kerberos are identical or not, the myth itself is the thing. The explanation which we have coaxed step by step from the texts of the Veda imparts to the myth a definite character: it is no longer a dark and uncertain touch in the troubled visions of hell, but an uncommonly lucid treatment of an important cosmic phenomenon. Sun and moon course across the sky: beyond is the abode of light and the blessed. The coursers are at one moment regarded as barring the way to heaven; at another as outposts who may guide the soul to heaven. In yet another mood, as they constantly, day by day, look down upon the race of men, dying day by day, they are regarded as picking daily candidates for the final journey. In due time Yama and his heaven are degraded to a mere Pluto and hell; then the terrible character of the two dogs is all that can be left to them. And the two dogs blend into a unit variously, either a four-eyed Parsi dog, or a two-headed—finally a plural-headed—Kerberos.

---

[1] See Usener, Götternamen, p. 303 ff.

The peace of mind of one or the other reader is likely to be disturbed by the appearance of a hell-dog here and there among peoples outside of the Indo-European (Aryan) family. So, e. g., I. G. Müller, in his *Geschichte der Americanischen Urreligionen*, second edition, p. 88, mentions a dog who threatens to swallow the souls in their passage of the river of hell. There was a custom among the Mordwines to put a club into the coffin with the corpse, to enable him to drive away the watch-dogs at the gate of the nether world.[1] The Mordwines, however, have borrowed much of their mythology from the Iranians. The Hurons and Iroquois told the early missionaries that after death the soul must cross a deep and swift river on a bridge formed by a single slender tree, where it had to defend itself against the attacks of a dog.[2] No sane ethnologist or philologer will insist that all these conceptions are related *genetically*, that there is nothing accidental in the repetition of the idea. The dog is prominent in animal mythology; one of his functions is to watch. It is quite possible, nay likely, that a dog, pure and simple, has strayed occasionally into this sphere of conceptions without any further organic meaning—simply as a baying, hostile, watch-dog. But we cannot prove anything by an ignorant *non possumus;* the conception *may*, even if we cannot say *must*, after all in each case, have been derived from essentially the same source; the dead journeying upward to heaven interfered with by a coursing heavenly body, the sun or the moon, or both. Anyhow, the organic quality of the Indo-European, or at least the Hindu myth makes it guide and philosopher. From dual sun and moon coursing across the sky to the two hell-hounds, each step of development is no less clear than from Zeus pater, "Father Sky," to breezy Jove, the gentleman about town with his escapades and amours. To reverse the process, to imagine that the Hindus started with two visionary dogs and finally identified them with sun and moon—that is as easy and natural as it is for a river to flow up the hill back to its source.

The rudiment of the present essay in Comparative Mythology

[1] Max Müller, *Contributions to the Science of Mythology*, p. 240.

[2] Brinton. *The Myths of the New World*. Second Edition, p. 265.

was published by the writer some years ago in a learned journal, under the title, "The two dogs of Yama in a new role."[1] My late lamented friend, Max Müller, the gifted writer who knew best of all men how to rivet the attention of the cultivated public upon questions of this sort, did me the honor to notice my proposition in an article in the *London Academy* of August 13, 1892 (number 1058, page 134-5), entitled "Professor Bloomfield's Contributions to the Interpretation of the Veda." In this article he seems to try to establish a certain similarity between his conception of the Kerberos myth and my own. This similarity seems to me to be entirely illusory. Professor Müller's own last words on the subject in the Preface of his *Contributions to the Science of Mythology* (p. xvi.), will make clear the difference between our views. He identifies, as he always has identified, Kerberos with the Vedic stem *Çarvara,* from which is derived *Çarvarī,* "night." To quote his own words: "The germ of the idea . . . must be discovered in that nocturnal darkness, that *çārvaram tamas,* which native mythologists in India had not yet quite forgotten in post-Vedic times." With such a view my own has not the least point of contact. Çabala, the name of one of the dogs, means "spotted, bright"; it is the name of the sun-dog; it is quite the opposite of the *çārvaram tamas.* The name of the moon-dog, and, by transfer, the dog of the night, is Çyāma or Çyāva "black," not Çabala, nor Çarvara. The association of the two dogs with day and night is the association of sun and moon with their respective diurnal divisions, and nothing more. Of Cimmerian gloom there can be nothing in the myth primarily, because it deals at the beginning with heaven, and not with hell; with an auspicious, and not a gloomy, vision of life after death.

In conclusion I would draw the attention of those scholars, writers, and publicists that have declared bankruptcy against the methods and results of Comparative Mythology to the present attempt to establish an Indo-European naturalistic myth. I would ask them to consider, in the light of the Veda, that it is probable that the early notions of future life turn to the visible heaven with

[1] Presented to the American Oriental Society at its meeting May 5, 1891; and printed in its Journal, Vol. XV., pp. 163 ff.

its sun and moon, rather than to the topographically unstable and elusive caves and gullies that lead to a wide-gated Hades. In heaven, therefore, and not in hell, is the likely breeding spot of the Cerberus myth. On the way to heaven there is but one pair that can have taken shape reasonably in the minds of primitive observers into a pair of Cerberi. Sun and moon, the Veda declares, are the Cerberi. In due time, and by gradual stages, the heaven myth became a hell myth. The Vedic seers had no Pluto, no Hades, no Styx, and no Charon; yet they had the pair of dogs. Now when Yama and his heaven become Pluto and hell, then, and only then, Yama's dogs are on a plane with the three-headed, or two-headed, Greek Kerberos. It is not likely that the chthonic hell visions of the Greeks were also preceded by heavenly visions, and that Kerberos originally sprang from heaven. Consider, too, the breadth and the persistence of these ideas, their simple background, and their natural transition from one feature to another in the myth of Cerberus, and the notions of sun and moon (day and night) in their relation to the precarious life of man upon the earth, his death, and his future life. For my part, I do not believe that the honest critics of the methods and results of Comparative Mythology, though they have been made justly suspicious by the many failures in this field, will ever successfully "run past, straightway, the two four-eyed dogs, the spotted and the dark, the Çabalāu, the brood of Saramā."

MAURICE BLOOMFIELD.

JUSTICE.

> ". . . . Judges and officers shalt thou make thee in thy gates . . . . and they shall judge the people with just judgment. Execute ye judgment and righteousness, and deliver the spoiled out of the hand of the oppressor: and do no wrong, do no violence to the stranger, the fatherless nor the widow . . . ."

A PROCLAMATION, the firing of a few guns in salute, the hauling down of one flag, the raising of another, a few ragraphs, or at most a few columns in the newspapers very inade- ately signalised to the world the most extraordinary event history s ever had to record; yet—busy people that we are—as notable and :ent as is that event and notwithstanding we were the principal :ors in it, you have to be reminded that I allude to the cession of ıba to its people by our government!

That the probabilities are that it will not be long before that ıntry applies for admission to the Union, and that a powerful com- :rcial-political element here seems to be striving to hasten that ısummation, should not lessen in the slightest degree the glory that aches to the giving of such a precedent to the world. It *was* ex- ıordinary magnanimity, inspired by the highest motives on the part the administration and in accordance with the real desires of our ople. The unworthy ulterior motives of the clique just referred simply facilitated the performance of that act by estopping opposi- ın to the President's carrying-out of the people's well-known wish. bove all else, however, it was a splendid example of national justice.

Note also that, too, in our treatment of the Chinese indemnity matter and the Venezuelan affair we are striving to have other nations join us in rendering a higher quality of international justice than most of them are used to.

What surprises most people in all this is that as fond of advertising, as immodest as we are generally believed to be we are making so little noise about this new brand of Justice we are so mildly yet firmly endeavoring to have established as standard.

Strange how little understood that term, Justice, has always been, how misapplied, illogically conceived and wrongly administered it has remained through ages, even in the most advanced civilisation. That we seem to grasp some of the significance of the word and are willing, at times at least, to live up to its proper application justifies us in indulging in some self-gratulation, if nothing more. We will attend to that, however, in the privacy of our several closets. It is not my purpose to suggest or inaugurate any flapping of our national wings just now, but, if you will bear with me awhile I will endeavor to briefly review how Justice has been regarded, interpreted and administered before our day.

Such a glancing back need not be time wasted; it may assist us to a clearer appreciation of our manifold duties in the complicated administration of our growing interests and of our wonderfully diversified transactions with other peoples.

History and the splendid writings of antiquity reinforced by the sound logic of such moderns as Crazowski, Bishop, Schenider and particularly de Coulanges have made the task of compilation an easy one. If it be as interesting and instructive as it is earnest then am well repaid, indeed, for the labor it involved.

Men have ever been prone to attempt to soar in the very heights of political organisation, even to rise to the clouds and misty reveries of waters humanitarian rather than to settle right down to the prosaic details of practical life; to create systems of government, to organise states, is so much more worthy of our genius than is it to bother with the trivialities of mere administration. Still, if we pause to really seriously think it over we must realise that there are some things even more precious than our political rights, for there are involved in this question of Justice, our well-being, our civil rights and liberty our property, our conscience, our very lives, all that constitutes our material and moral existence.

Of old Greece, Athens was the best governed city, the most prosperous and most intelligently organised. Whatever her faults we must admit that of all ancient republics her's was the least undemocratic. There were rich and poor but there was no privileged class or caste. No chiefs or judges were appointed; the entire city, all the people, established the laws, united in declaring war, in arranging treaties, in governing themselves. Every citizen was indeed a judge, a representative in Congress. The laws were administered by the people in jury assembled. Every year six thousand jurors were drawn and *all* sat in judgment all that year. There was no class of jurists or specially trained administrators. To be upon that jury one had to be over thirty years old and free from criminal indictment or judgment. The entire body sometimes sat upon the one case, but oftener they were divided into sections of two to five hundred, each section presided over by a member, a temporarily elected archon, and sitting in different parts of the city.

The people governed themselves and judged themselves. There could be no tyranny; the rights of all were guaranteed by all; each victim of a crime had the entire city behind him to punish the criminal; justice was absolutely gratuitous and was oftener invoked by the poor than by the rich.

Then, again, there is the reverse side to consider. None of these judges could well be deeply versed in law, nor could he have a very clear insight into human weaknesses or an intuitive appreciation of true and false testimony. Those things come only with years of training and study.

Such large bodies were easily carried away by specious, eloquent pleading, whatever the real merits of the case; intrigue was more easily practised in such a crowd than with a judge directly and solely responsible for his verdicts. A crowd becomes as a single individual when properly handled by a spell-binder; it is swayed by his every emotion; he can carry it to a certain point then even his control ends, the crowd becomes a frenzied, unreasoning mob. So it often was with the Athenians. Would any judge or an intelligent jury have condemned Socrates?

Such a court is as wrong an organisation of Justice as is an absolute monarchy. The judge was the state; what chance had an individual whose rights clashed with those of the state, or who might be suspected of treason? Witness Demosthenes' second trial for instance.

We notice that all the Athenian pleadings laid great stress upon the poverty of the pleader. Punishment was generally meted out in fines, confiscations, rarely in a death sentence. The state throve upon fines, it was dangerous to be wealthy, for just think how necessary it was to insure funds sufficient to pay the six thousand judges.

That justice was pretty in theory, it had a fine flavor of democracy, but in application, exercised by the people, it necessarily was subordinate to the interests, the passions of the people. We find no sufficient guaranty in it to safeguard individual liberty, the rights of property, man's conscience, or even his life.

Roman justice has been the basis of that of most modern nations. It varied with the constitution of the state, but was never disassociated from politics. Its constant and fundamental principle was that it emanated from state authority and necessarily was part of and one with the latter. A judge, a magistrate, was always also an administrator, the *magister* was invariably the representative of the central authority, the chief, the arbiter and judge as well as the commander of the troops of his district. Call him prætor, consul, dictator or what you will, but in him was vested *all* authority. True there were prætors to whom was assigned the duty of judging, but they also commanded the troops, they constituted the *provincia urbana* but really were sub-consuls acting under the consuls who could at any time hold court themselves and set aside the verdicts of their subalterns. According to the Romans, law was by reason of authority alone; equity, reason and conscience counted for but little in the question.

There were also special officers called *judex* wrongly supposed by many to be judges. They were but "district-attorneys," they prepared state cases, took testimony, heard pleadings and reported to the administrator who then passed judgment. Justice was necessarily subservient to public interest and reasons of state, hence the maxim, *salus populi suprema lex esto,* and from that old source are derived all the iniquitous laws of *lèse majesté* with which the old world has since been burdened. These laws were equally handy of application under the Republic and under the Empire. In either case it meant an absolute power, an arbitrary and often cruel one before which all personal rights were effaced. Now, all offences against those laws were tried before a consul, prætor or other officer of the state. Could there be a case in which the judge was not interested to the extent at least of upholding his own dignity, or, as chief of that particular community, the dignity of the state?

The ancients never seemed to recognise that republican despotism was as crushing as that of any other ruler. Under the latter it became tyranny; under the former people voluntarily submitted and called it liberty.

True there was an appeal from the consul's decision direct to the people, but those assemblies were presided over by that consul, and brave indeed was the individual who walked not on the line laid down by that officer. The right of appeal was really a dead letter. They tried to revive it at least seven times during a period of three centuries but only in the last two hundred years of the Republic was it really effective.

At times the people sat in judgment in a case direct, not an appeal, but such a court was convened by and presided over by the consul. It partook of the nature of a political gathering rather than a court of justice; witness the trials of Coriolanus, Claudius Pulcher and of Scipio Africanus; passion, hatred and party ruled.

In the latter years of the Republic there grew up an institution much resembling our jury system—in sound, at least. Tribunals of some thirty or more were chosen by ballot, they were presided over only by a questor or prætor, who merely read the sentence agreed to by the jurors. These sat for a year and were called *quæstiones perpetuæ.* Several such bodies sat at a time, one attended to crimes against the person, another to civil cases and so on, though it does not appear that any of the jurors had previously received any training in the laws relating to the particular branch assigned him.

I said this system *sounded* well, it had the ring of true democracy, but in application it was the mightiest bulwark of the aristocracy. Rome, you remember, even as a republic never was frankly democratic. Athens was. In Rome when the patrician caste was weeded out, destroyed, there immediately sprang up an aristocracy of wealth. Apparently all men were equal politically and at law, but in fact classes divided off according to the ciphers of respective wealth. Men were elected to the senate from such a class only, to other offices from such and such classes. One had to be rich indeed to reach the higher offices—the suffrage of the people was expensive; the services were gratuitous but the pickings were tempting. A man could not vote unless he had a certain income. Representation was so juggled that the property-owners had thirty-one seats, in the Assembly the proletariat but four. All the offices were purchased. As a matter of fact the Senate became a close corporation, an hereditary office, controlled by the rich families, and to these fell all the honors, sacerdotal, martial and civil. It was from this senate that the lists of these juries we have noted were made up. They robbed the people and the magistrature of their authority and subserved the interests of this new oligarchy, becoming its strongest shield as well as most potent weapon of offence. Politics again ruled Justice.

The Republic really succumbed in consequence of the bitter strife between the classes as to who should compose these juries; the middle class demanded recognition upon them, not to give a better quality of justice but, mark you, on account of the pickings; the oligarchy haughtily refused to yield any of its rights; the former then aimed higher, even aspired to the senatorial toga, and civil war upset the whole order of things.

But justice remained as strongly bound to and controlled by politics as ever. The emperor was supreme judge, in fact the only judge. He delegated *legati* and *procuratores* to administer the laws but it was in his name, according to his instructions and solely for his interests they were administered.

There were lawyers to assist, to defend the accused but the judge paid as little attention to them as he did to their clients. He had other functions to attend to, military, social, etc., and wasted little time trying cases. The most important matters were expedited about as our police courts mete out justice and with about the same results; the accused was almost invariably fined. That made a quite important asset in the finances of the empire and added somewhat to the emoluments of the judges. There was an appeal, of course, but what did it amount to? From judge to the governor, then to the vice-prefect, to the prefect of prætorians and so on up. A costly proceeding and of little advantage. All their instructions were from the same source and the laws themselves were given by the emperors, mere whims often, in the form of *edictum rescriptum* or *responsum*, depending whether he "simply spoke, or wrote, or answered special questions." There was no law but the will of the ruler.

Naturally, under such a régime terrible abuses grew up. "Preventive detainer" was inaugurated, a man was imprisoned for fear he *might* commit crime. Such a procedure was absolutely unknown to the ancients. Bail under heavy bonds secured the "suspect's" release. Torture and "forceful inquiry" became potent factors in the administration of justice. Old Rome had permitted the torture of slaves; under the Empire it was applied freely to all classes, flagellation, "refined barbarities," confiscation of property, hard labor in the mines, slavery, were some of the *lesser* punishments inflicted upon the subjects of the mighty emperors. Confiscation was particularly in vogue, it added so to the imperial coffers. The number of slaves increased and they were not all taken from conquered peoples, neither property nor other rights were respected, agriculture languished, the trades were abandoned, public as well as private works ceased, and the Empire went the way of all despotisms.

Tacitus, some of the traditions of the Sagas, and a few old Germanic codes show us the condition of Justice and its administration, locally, nationally and internationally among the Germanic, Celtic and Frankish peoples of Europe, laws and customs that, naturally, left a powerful influence upon the successors to these peoples in feudal times and hence a strong impress upon us, their more or less direct descendants. At first these laws were in the hands of a sacerdotal theocracy, then followed tribal rule. The evolution was slow, these people were phlegmatic, more stable than, albeit not so wise as, the Greeks and Romans. The latter period was necessarily one of interdependence. There were three classes, the nobles, the freedmen and the bondsmen or serfs. The nobles depended somewhat upon the king, the freedmen very much upon the nobles, and the serfs absolutely upon the others.

Mundium was the word: a lot of followers and serfs were attached to a noble, they formed a group, a family, and hence the present confusion and paucity of our names.

Some would have us believe these old peoples had no idea of property and its rights. They had a very well-defined one. The chief or lord, or head of the composite or real family, held all of the principality or section—later, counties—that is, all that was granted him by the king or that he could get by "conquest" from his neighbors. It was parcelled out to his followers on leases, some extending unto the fifth generation and some even in perpetuity, but mostly for short terms; indeed the farming lands changed hands nearly every year.

These families or groups grew in importance, they yielded scant fealty to the king, and increased their authority in their own domain. We see there the germ and soon the full flower of feudal institutions. There was "public justice," and also "private justice." Treason or cowardice on the part of the chief were about the only crime tried under the former in a court composed of all the chiefs about, merely presided over by the king who exercised the same authority over the court as does our vice-president over the senate. The sentence of the court was rendered by a priest and always executed by him—a relic of the ancient form of "justice in the name of the gods." "Private justice" covered or punished all other offences. The chief of the tribe was sole judge of and had the power of life and death over all his retainers and serfs. Inter-tribal disputes were never taken before the king, they were settled by arbitration or by blood and a family or tribe that could not manage its own affairs was soon absorbed by the stronger ones. This arbitration court, or *mall* as it was called, was composed of a hundred sub-chiefs. They were as often called together by the offender as by the offended, they could not summon witnesses but merely tried to patch up the difficulty, or as a not always last resort, suggested a duel or even a battle. They frequently counselled an indemnity to be paid to the offended; particularly in the case of a murder they set a price that the murderer should pay the son of his victim or to the latter's chief, and when once that *Wehrgeld* was paid the matter was settled and the murderer could hold up his head as high as any one.

The Frankish kings attempted a sort of composite justice made up from the traditions of the old Roman Empire and the customs of their Germanic kinsmen. It read well, but its application, judged by the records and legislative documents of the time, was not a startling success. Charlemagne vainly endeavored to bring order out of chaos, his repeated exhortations to his nobles and officers to administer justice "justly" are really pathetic; they give us a clue to the brand of justice customarily meted out. For centuries no sort of law really obtained and justice was but a hazy memory. The individual had absolutely no rights but those he could defend by the sword. Society protected no one. Force became the law and the sword its sole administrator. Warfare was not the exclusive privilege of kings and the nobles; ecclesiastics, peasants, all classes of men warred among themselves and banded together against a common enemy; it was continual strife, pillage, murder and rapine and even the more sensible among men, yes the mighty (Saint) Louis of France himself, hardly dared express an adverse criticism of the habit, or attempt to stem the tide of bloodshed; it had become a fixed custom; a man entered into a bloody individual quarrel, or plunged a whole province into war, with as little or less hesitancy than one to-day instructs his lawyer to collect a bill "by any reasonable means."

For three hundred years force was the only law recognised by the individual as well as the nation. Individually we have fairly outgrown that idea, but as nations I do not see that the conditions have changed very much; we have an occasional "peace conference" and all that sort of thing, but force remains a pretty potent factor in the settlement of international difficulties.

From the very beginning of the eleventh century men realised something was wrong. Life was not worth living, everybody and everything suffered, individuals and nations were going to rack and ruin, fields remained untilled, no manufacturing could safely go on, and famine was common. People rebelled *against* war, they clamored not for Justice, they had forgotten the word, but they did yearn for peace. The great revolutions of the twelfth century had but that one purpose! Nations were not establishing laws to govern their people; there was *no* public authority to rebel against; it was the individual begging and fighting for a law to be governed by. Societies with that end in view were organised, seemingly spontaneously, all over the civilised (?) world. They grew in importance and, little by little at least, private warfare fell out of fashion. It was forbidden the peasantry, then the middle classes and, by easy steps, the nobles. At first they were restricted only as to times when they could not fight, so many days a week had to be observed as "peace days," and it went hard with the princeling who infracted the rule; *all* the others were glad of the opportunity of joining in his punishment. Then a law was established that compelled the nobles to wait forty days between the dispute and actual hostilities. That gave them time to think it over and much trouble was thus averted.

Civil order grew apace, charters were respected, codes of law were established, the king became more potent, a central administration was possible and municipalities and courts were organised and magistrates took the place of the sword—among individuals: nations still glared at one another, the stronger brandishing their swords and shaking their plumes in the hope of intimidating the lesser ones, and these hatching up combinations that would enable them to glare back.

In affairs of any importance the magistrate or tribal chief, and in inter-communal matters the suzerain himself, sat as the president of the court, and the accused had the right to be judged by his "peers," four, six, ten or more men of exactly his own rank, and punctilious indeed was he in his "peremptory and privileged" challenges. The presiding judge but rendered the verdict agreed upon by the peers. Strange it seems, too, that if that verdict was not to his liking the accused or the disgruntled litigant transferred his enmity from his opponent to the "peers" who did him the "injustice." Spite of the peaceful tendencies above noted, many bloody quarrels, real wars, were waged twixt litigant and jury as results of these trials.

Trouble between men of different ranks was tried before the peers of the *lesser* one. Vassals and serfs were still judged by their chiefs, but even they were often given the benefit of a jury of their fellows, and in any event they were not the abused class in that period we sometimes imagine them to have been; their condition was certainly superior to that of the peasantry of the seventeenth and eighteenth centuries. They were protected by certain laws, unwritten ones, but "customs that obtained among gentlemen in the treatment of their people" that were religiously observed and jealously guarded. The chief held court (without power of inflicting death) always at the same spot, under some particular tree or arbor in the great court of the castle, hence the term "court." It was a place of sanctuary, accused and witnesses had the right to say *anything* there without its prejudicing against them later, and once a man claimed it as asylum no enemy, or even the master, could do him harm until after he had been judged.

In the cities the mayor and aldermen (the old men and principal ones of the place) held court and tried minor cases. While the aldermen debated after the evidence was all in, the mayor retired so as not to "intimidate their decision." The chiefs levied fines that reverted to themselves, and imprisoned evil-doers in their "dungeons"; the cities turned their fines into the municipal treasury and maintained (usually well filled) great city prisons. Village justice was administered either by a mayor and his council or by a provost or deputy, subject to the lord of that particular feudality. Still these courts were not altogether dependent upon the will of the lord, the jury of peers obtained there, too, and the old records show us some strange findings that indicate indeed that the lord often came out of the small end when such courts adjudicated disputes between him and his tenants.

The quality of this justice was simple, rugged, yet eminently more logical and just than could often be obtained under the involved laws of later date that were framed, one would think, for the express purpose of allowing lawyers to quibble. The people were well balanced, simple if you wish, but society, nevertheless, was fairly well constituted. Every one was tired of the warfare and the never-ending quarrels of his predecessors. Under other conditions such a system of justice would have miscarried and been the handmaiden to conflict and disorder. The thirteenth century was notable for the calm that reigned all about. It was ominous.

For with the fourteenth century there came troublous times; strife in the state, in the church, in the community, between sects, between countries, aye and between members of the one family. Kings grew over-ambitious and classes first mistrusted each other, then mistrust turned to implacable hatred. The "plain people" lost their hold upon the administration of justice; village courts were abolished; the jurisdiction of municipal courts was cut down; kings and princes grew more and more despotic and the people more and more rebellious.

I trust this leafing over of the musty old tomes of the past has not been too wearisome to you: I lay particular stress upon it, for the older I grow the more impressed am I with the influence that that past exercises over us in absolutely everything we do. Our government, our politics, our faith, our mode of life, are based upon *how* we have *read* that past. Differences of opinion even about matters of to-day, and trivial ones, may be traced to the prejudice, inspired by that past, with which we observe things and forecast their results. Does such a man believe in the Divine rights of kings? Depend upon it he has not only an hereditary bent that way, but his reading of history and natural admiration for the grandeur and valor of this or that mighty ruler of the past, have much to do with his opinion whatever may be his environment. Is such another rabidly democratic? That too is an hereditary trait handed down through generations from the time some poor wretch was cruelly wronged by a "noble" feudal baron; but mark you, he has read of and been impressed, stirred-up by the cruelty of kings and has absorbed advanced notions anent the rights of the down-trodden people and all that sort of thing in his early youth and reading. And that prejudice seizes hold of us in our very childhood, our first books are responsible for it and the efforts of a lifetime are not sufficient to eradicate it. True, the old régime does not govern us, but the idea we have of it dominates and governs each one of us.

The trouble is that our knowledge of that past is so very imperfect, and, indeed, generally derived from romantic fiction. Each one fashions to himself an imaginary past. Do you ever find two men with the same notion of any detail of history? There are so many different ways of mistaking history, and each one of us models his political credo about the errors to which he has given his preference or to which he is chained by his early education. We have about as many political parties and subdivisions in the world to-day as there were different school histories in our youth. A famous German scholar tells me he would gladly give up ten years of his life could he but forget, or at least get away from, the influence of what he read before he was fourteen!

Scientific, exact and as unprejudiced a study as we can give history is of the greatest value to society. Would that we had time to look into this question of justice, as it was dealt with in the past with leisure and thoroughness. We are striving to establish universal peace, equity among nations and men, let us first try and weed out our prejudices and errors regarding the past. It is time well spent. History wrongly interpreted keeps us divided; it is by a more intimate knowledge of it, a clearer appreciation of its details and keener insight into and comparison of the old time systems of justice that we may hope to begin the work of conciliation, of unifying our views, of ennobling our common purposes, and of finally establishing that peace that at present does certainly seem to be far beyond our understanding.

But let us back to the middle ages, they are of particular interest to us, for, with a change of name, some slight variation and an injection of new as well as of very old ideas, their laws, their notions of justice are still doing duty for us.

We noted the advance of monarchical supremacy in the fifteenth century. Kings were ambitious, yes, but the people contributed to the overthrow of their "cherished" rights, they abdicated them. Liberty is always a burden; to govern one's self is tiresome and only the most energetic of peoples make a success of it; to be one's own judge is positively unbearably irksome. It was not only the men of *those* days who shirked jury duty; the excuses we read of, given to evade that task, have a strangely familiar sound to us. It meant time lost to business or pleasure, annoyance, responsibility and often —in those days, not now—a fight. So difficult was it to get a jury that frequently but four men sat and upon most important cases, indeed we have record of only one man being selected to try a case involving life.

A suzerain was supposed to call all his vassals to sit at certain assizes. They were pretty independent of him, however, and those who did not ignore the summons "begged off" very formally, being certain they would be excused, or paid their fine for non-attendance as nonchalantly as does the automobilist for fast riding, so that the king could but depend upon his lesser vassals, the weaker ones, those absolutely under his thumb and anxious to do his beck. One of the most famous trials in feudal England was tried before but three peers, two of whom fell in mortal combat waged with the unsuccessful plaintiff, who, later was crippled for life by the third. Jury duty had its dangers as well as discomforts in those days. It was so much easier (and safer) to have those things attended to by others, and the kings were not slow in availing themselves of the opportunity to attend to *all* the dispensing of justice. Still it is a mistake to say that trial by one's peers was *wrested* from the people by violence or ruse.

Naturally the kings and suzerain chiefs could not, or would not attend to all the petty disputes and legal quibbles. We have but scant notion of the mass of litigation and prosecution carried on; there were crimes innumerable besides those we punish to-day, sorcery, "blasphemy of relics," and what not, and in civil matters barons and common folk alike seemed to walk about with the proverbial chip on the shoulder. They were far more litigious than we are and, Heaven knows, that is bad enough. Those kingly duties were

:putised, men studied the laws, precedents and procedures, they :came adepts at questioning, extracting evidence by the rack and her effective means. Légistes, procurators, assizors, deputy idges they were called. Their's became a science, a profession, the pplication of the old Roman code a fine art.

The clergy, with ample time for study, and a boundless ambition satisfy, were particularly adept, for, forsooth, the law could be trned to good advantage, and they became great jurists. Archishop This and Prior That, princes of the church and common tonks sat upon the benches and bent every energy toward getting all thers off, but among their number there were barons and titled adges, so that even the upper classes still deluded themselves with ae idea they were being tried by their peers. To all intents, for a me at least, all courts of justice of Europe were ecclesiastical, hough the kings and Rome itself sought to curb this holy zeal.

Whatever their formation the transition of these courts from the ld trial by peers was an easy one, not particularly slow but without aock. How unconscious we are of absolute changes, complete evolutions, when they do not come as sudden surprises! Contemoraneous writers chronicle these changes but without comment; aey apprehended not the effects of what was going on. It upset the atire social structure, the conditions, the politics, the religion of the Iiddle Ages and of all succeeding times.

Monarchical rights were wonderfully enlarged through the un- onscious intermediary of these courts, and feudality received its eath blow through their unintended instrumentality. Under the ld régime a man either obeyed the verdict of his peers in judgment ssembled, or fought those peers and defied all hands to enforce the entence; under the new dispensation appeal was the order. No ne thought of fighting a book-worm, a priest, a grave and ancient adge, as most of the judges were, so he went from petty court up the seignorial tribunal, from it to king's court, and from the latter o the ruler himself. The dukes and barons maintained great rmies; the kings had few troops, but they governed by force withal, *hrough* the courts; they reigned by virtue of the law which they manipulated and enforced by playing one feudal lord and his troops, his wealth and his ambition, against the other, and wound up by the destroying or absorbing the power of both.

This magistrature, incipient, subordinate, the plaything of kings at first, grew in independence apace with its importance. Early in the thirteenth century terms of office were insecure and short at best, depending solely upon the good will of the crown; then they became life offices. Kings, always more or less pressed for funds, sold the appointments and collected rentals during their continuation. These offices actually became hereditary (again history repeated itself) transmitted from father to son, and were "as hot coals unto the fingers of royalty" to such an extent that the latter voluntarily gave up the appointive power and made them elective by the privy councils and "parliaments" (of which these judges formed part). Men spent fortunes in influencing, buying these elections and justice became a veritable monopoly. It is passing strange, too, that the justice administered under such conditions was of pretty fair quality. Men sought the office for the power and the glory; there were no salaries attached to these high offices, but the emoluments were considerable, the fees levied upon litigants were many and all reverted to the courts. The judges had large retinues, bailiffs, clerks, readers, expounders, mace-bearers, criers, and so on, and all had their pickings from off the litigiously inclined—who seemed to thrive under and enjoy the operation. Have things changed since then so very much?

Venality crept in little by little, however, dishonest judges were not the exception, in fact those who were above suspicion were looked upon as heroes. Henry IV. of France declared that all his courts were corrupt. He said he *knew* for he had purchased verdicts in *every* one of them. Hand in hand with venality came ignorance. Judges as well as "pleaders" (lawyers) still passed through the farce of an examination before taking their places, but their ignorance of the first principles of equity as well as of law was sometimes monumental. The world has not yet gotten over the tangles and evil precedents bequeathed it by that judiciary. And these conditions obtained for full three hundred years. Worst of all, the magistrates not only administered the laws but very largely enacted them, originated them. As constituted in the thirteenth century the magistrature was the origin, the grandparent of the senates of to-day. Kings devised laws, but they were inoperative until passed upon by those courts or "parliaments"; they really exercised the right of veto. James I. swore his courts were "a sort of republic in an alleged monarchy whose ruler danced to its tune."

Still the courts were loyal, they were never adversaries to the crown, they simply opposed it when its wearer overstepped certain bounds, they jealously insisted upon its attending to its own business, which no longer was the administration of justice. At the same time this judiciary became the "defender of the people's rights," however royalist its tendencies.

As if by very reason of its conception, in very disgust, it purged itself thereof—those things do happen you know—and as it became purer so grew its power. To the judiciary of that time belongs the honor of inspiring, devising a constitutional monarchy from which sprang the idea of its being a co-ordinate branch of government in monarchical as well as republican forms. It kept kings straight, people satisfied, and despite the sins of its youth that judiciary of the fifteenth century, corrupt, venal, purchasable and purchased as it was, has given us the firmest bulwark society has to-day.

For centuries did kings seek to minimise that authority that thwarted their schemes and anchored them in quiet waters, but without success. Yet each was dependent upon the other. Once—in France—did the judiciary attempt a revolution, a rebellion against the king. It lacked material force, so had to ally itself with the nobles or with the "masses"; in either company was it most ill at ease, and it was but a little while before it went back into the royal fold and redoubled its devotion to that cause. It could neither brook an absolute monarchism or stand without a king.

The old judiciary waged a constant warfare upon the excesses of that absolutism, the men who sat upon its benches were living synonyms for "liberal conservatism"; but then, excesses are as common to other forms of government, even republican; moderation and discretion are no more inherent in the one than in the other. There have been times, even in our day, when the conservative influence of a judiciary was all that saved a nation from ruin. The interests of a day, the caprice of a man, influence legislation that unless counteracted by the conservative rulings of a wise court of review—based upon a written constitution that has withstood the shock and storms of years—might work incalculable and irremediable injury upon the entire nation.

Of all the nations of to-day our's stands the most in need of preserving intact the integrity, the freedom from party and other influence of not only its supreme court, but also of its state and petty courts.

The greatest danger that threatens the judiciary, and through it the nation, is our tendency toward—aristocracy. A strange word to use in connection with a democratic form of government, is it not? But republic and democracy are not necessarily two correlative terms. That they are is what has been preached for years, though history shows us the fallacy of the claim. There is no nobler form of government than a republic, yet it is the most propitious formation for the founding of an aristocracy that ever existed. It is so essentially aristocratic in its ultimate tendency that wherever a democracy has established a republic, that government has invariably, sooner or later, either resolved itself into a severely exclusive oligarchy or else it has been overthrown by the people who replaced it with—of all things!—a monarchy.

We saw that tendency in the South before the Rebellion, there was an unmistakably aristocratic flavor about its politics, its society; the simpler habits, the sturdier stock and puritanical training of the men of the North counteracted that element and a democratic Republic was preserved. But for how long?

Remember, rather should we watch and pray and keep our loins ready girded for the fray than to sit idly by, indulging the while in ostentatious vauntings. We may feel that we are founded upon a rock and laugh at the precedents, the falls of other nations that have gone on before. but, I tell you, a thinking man shudders when he notes some of the tendencies of the times. We are strong, yes, but is our brief span of scant a century and a quarter of national existence a criterion, a sufficient guarantee, that we shall go on thus in contravention of what seems to have been the invariable, the immutable order of things, as we know them to have been for at least thirty times the duration of that period?

There are essentials to our continued and true democracy: equal suffrage and representation; absolute separation of government, law and religion; regular times when the people (I mean the people, not so-called conventions) have an opportunity to completely change the personnel of their representatives in government; and a most jealous guardianship of the Constitution, particularly wherein it limits official powers.

Our judiciary generally is composed of high-minded, noble men, still we observe with regret, if not with positive fear, the infusion therein of a party spirit. Even our Supreme Court is expected to divide upon strictly party lines upon all great questions submitted to it. That is a relic of olden times we might well lay aside. The judiciary should be a class by itself, unhampered by obligations to appointive powers, forgetful of previous affiliations and unprejudiced by party desires or necessities, then would there be perfect justice and equity.

If we can but preserve our judiciary as it is, however, we ought to be well pleased, our every effort at reform is needed far more in other directions. Our municipalities need, nearly every one of them, a moral as well as physical cleansing. If our federal and state governments were administered as are most of our little as well as great cities the nation would go to the dogs in a generation's time. (It is a peculiar coincidence at least, that in our only really well-governed city, Washington, there is never an election, all offices are appointive and the people have no voice in any branch of its administration, yet they are happier, freer, better protected, and have more privileges and rights than the citizens of any other municipality.)

The trouble is, like in the Middle Ages in the matter of judgment by peers (preserved, by the way, intact by the peers of England) we do not care to bother with details; the men of those times were willing that judges should relieve them of irksome duties; we are willing that those who make a business and traffic of politics should do our voting and necessarily our governing, and that the riffraff of society should sit upon our juries. Then we wonder at the verdicts rendered and at the calibre of the men who sit in solemn council squandering our money and granting suicidal franchises. What opposition do we offer to the ambitions of such men, and do not many of them, creep up or boldly walk into still higher places, in state and federal offices?

There *are* dangers lurking about, there *is* a possibility of history repeating itself. We are too lazy or too busy to give more than a passing thought or moment to our government, let alone justice and our laws. We are perfectly satisfied to let things go and we dread anything like reform, or change or experiment. Experiment! Ah, that is the word most of us balk at. All reforms are branded "experiments" and our good people hold up their hands in horror. For instance, some of us are advocating the Bérenger method of treating first offences being adopted in this country (Senator Bérenger, of France, has been laughed at for years because he succeeded ten years ago in passing a law that every first offence, not involving over two years' imprisonment, should have that penalty suspended and ultimately remitted, provided the offender commits no misdemeanor during the subsequent five years). We are laughed at, called dreamers, assured that we are suggesting dangerous experiments and what not, yet there are the records to show that the percentage of second offences in France has been reduced—by that law—from 46 to 5.4! But we should not speak of it for it's only an — — — — experiment.

We can afford to experiment along these lines. Mercy is an accompaniment to Justice. We should clear our minds of the fog that shrouds the justice, the methods of the past, that we may correctly appreciate the effects of those methods and be guided thereby in our experiments of the future. The past may indicate to us what cannot, should not be done. The great questions of the future that confront us are social questions. The alleged statesmen of Europe are afraid of seeing them settled; some of their antics in the endeavor to keep them unsettled are positively grotesquely amusing if they were not so pitifully effective. They keep the people, the parliaments, the cabinets discussing such petty themes. Here, on the contrary, all is so vast! And the eyes of the world are upon us.

Our natural tendencies are toward a true democracy, the air we reathe is that of Freedom. Justice must accompany Freedom, and rith Justice, Equity.

We must recognise that there is an equity superior to social ower, that there are rights of individuals that cannot be judged by ie State and that conscience never can.

Let us cultivate that spirit of regard for conscience, let us follow s dictates; they will not lead us astray. We may centre all our fforts upon our individual selves, they will not be wasted, nor will re be deemed selfish. Let each man be just unto his neighbor and eaceful, and you will observe how very quickly the municipality. he State, the Nation, the World is infected with that holy contagion.

> . . . "The fruit of righteousness is
> sown in peace of those who make peace . . ."

WASHINGTON, D. C. F. W. FITZPATRICK.

AN INTERNATIONAL AUXILIARY LANGUAGE.

AN active campaign is being carried on in France with a view to securing the adoption of an international auxiliary language. There would be no occasion to speak of it if the commission established for this object cherished the chimera of giving to an artificial language the value and use of a living language. The present is an undertaking that is being conducted in a practical way and which deserves examination. I do not mean to intimate by this that I regard its success as easy or even probable. For indeed a first observation forces itself upon every one who faces this question of a common linguistic medium with an open mind. Even if this instrument were found and adopted by academies and prescribed by governments, what would be its office and scope?

Among the languages spoken to-day—leaving aside the yellow races, that is to say, the third part of the population of the globe approximately—we can recognize three principal groups: the Anglo-Germanic, the Neo-Latin and the Slavic. In the first group the advantage of number belongs at present to the English; in the second group to the Spanish including the Portuguese; and then to the French; the Russian ranks after the English and before the German. Now if we weigh carefully the conditions of the success of a language, the extent of its actual possession (I mean the number of those who speak it), its political influence, its simplicity, etc., it will appear convincingly that the English language has the greatest chance. German presents difficulties which embarrass the efforts made to propagate it. French world policy by its weakness compromises the success of the French language, despite very definite advantages on its part. In brief, and without pushing this discussion too far, it seems that the struggle must come in the future between two or three of our living languages, so that the adoption of an auxiliary language would not yield a permanent result. But leaving aside these conjectures regarding a possible evolution, let us consider the question of immediate utility.

We may well doubt whether an artificial language if written will translate easily the movements of thought and can be applied to other subjects than the most ordinary themes of life; it is one thing to give such a language the benefit of the qualities of a text that one may be translating, and quite a different thing to use it as a direct instrument. And as a spoken language (if indeed it can actually be spoken) it would be no more likely to give real expression to thought, since language is *par excellence* a personal matter, adequate to each individual. The use of it, therefore, would necessarily be limited from every point of view. Furthermore we are supposing that it would be easier to learn and understand an artificial language than a living one, which seems to me far from being demonstrated.

One last observation is forced upon me straightway. If I learn a living language, English for instance—if I learn it practically and not scholastically, I have the immediate advantage of being able to converse with 150 million men; and so with the other languages, in proportion to the number of people who speak them. Hence one may say that any individual who possesses two foreign languages in addition to his mother tongue, or even one such, receives at once a benefit which no artificial language could possibly yield him.

Commercial interests are already satisfied in large measure by the partial unification of the universal business vocabulary. As for the advantage which a few scholars might have from nearly understanding one another in a Congress, I confess that I do not estimate it very highly. I do not think it will be very much worth while to set academies and governments to work and resort to scholastic constraints for a result which seems to me so slight.

How can we give life to that which is by its very definition dead? This is one great objection among many others. I hasten to add that MM. Couturat and Leau who are the most active members of the "commission," have foreseen and occasionally refuted some of these objections, either in pamphlets published by them, or in the book which they are now offering us and which I make it my duty to call the attention of your readers.[1]

The authors have had the patience to analyze all the systems that have been proposed, to classify them and criticise them. Their very curious work is a genuine monument. Their preference, we can infer, is for "Esperanto," but they give us all the details of the case and leave the reader to judge for himself. I have just expressed with all freedom some general and not altogether favorable thoughts. I beg MM. Couturat and Leau not to charge them to invincible ill will. I do not claim to have exhausted the discussion, and I would have hesitated to oppose an interesting attempt.

PARIS. L. ARRÉAT.

---

[1] *Histoire de la langue universelle.* Paris, Hachette, 1903.

PASIGRAPHY—A SUGGESTION.

SEVERAL attempts have been made to create a world-language, a Volapük, a pasiglossy, but all of them have sooner or later proved abortive. Without saying that the scheme is impossible, we recognise that it is confronted with serious difficulties, among which the sundry national and even dialectic idiosyncrasies of pronunciation seem so light and are so grave.[1] Volapük, relatively the greatest success among the world-languages was so differently pronounced in England, France, and Germany that its adherents when visiting their sympathisers abroad had considerable trouble to understand each other.[2] Critics contend with a great semblance of plausibility that even if a pasiglossy could be generally agreed upon, it would only add one more language to the Babylonian confusion of tongues. This much is sure, that so far, all world-languages have been purely artificial conceits; they were spoken by heir inventors and a few of their friends only, and the several failres of this great ideal might almost be taken for an indication that ie scheme is either unfeasible or premature.

The case is different with pasigraphy, that is, a writing that ould be read by people of different nationalities. Pasigraphy, at is, an "all-script," would consist of symbols denoting the *eaning* of language, not its sounds, nor even its words: and such n attempt, so far as the writer knows, has not as yet been made or any practical purpose, for the pasigraphy of logicians (such as

---

[1] The very word "Volapük" is unpronounceable to the average Englishman who will say either "Volapyook" or "Volapeek."

[2] This statement has been challenged by M. Leau, with whom I had some correspondence on the subject.

proposed by Ernst Schröder of Karlsruhe[1]) consists of logical symbols invented to describe logical relations, and had better be called in Schröder's own nomenclature the "algebra of logic." It serves theoretical purposes only.

The idea of a pasigraphy was suggested to the writer by his study of Chinese. The Chinese script is, among all written languages, the only one that in its way may be called a pasigraphy. The Chinese script may be read by every one in his own language: the Japanese read it in Japanese and the several provinces of the Chinese Empire are inhabited by nationalities which are more varied than the nationalities of Europe; and yet all of them use the same script, and every educated person of the Chinese Empire reads the Chinese script in his own way. This is possible because the Chinese symbols are ideograms; they represent ideas, the meaning of words and not the sounds of speech.[2]

It may seem that the Chinese script being actually in existence might be introduced as a pasigraphy for the whole world, but there are some serious objections. The Chinese script, though in its elements ideogrammatic, is after all conditioned by the Chinese spoken language, for it reproduces its many idiomatic and grammatical expressions and cannot be understood without a close study of the significance of compound words, phrases, clauses, etc., which contain innumerable allusions to Chinese modes of thought that have become established by tradition. Moreover, the Chinese script is extremely difficult to write, and a good caligraphy is a rare accomplishment in the Celestial Empire. A practical pasigraphy ought to be simple in every respect; its symbols ought to be easily written, easily remembered, and easily understood.

We may mention that all kinds of writing were originally pasigraphic. The invention of the alphabet is a comparatively late

---

[1] See Ernst Schröder's article "On Pasigraphy" in *The Monist*, Vol. IX, No. 1. Compare Charles S. Peirce's ingenious article "The Logic of Relatives" *ibid.*, Vol. VII, No. 2, pp. 161–217.

[2] The sound sometimes determines the shape of a Chinese character, but even then it remains an ideogram. The transcription of Sanscrit and other foreign words into Chinese is a peculiar case and an exception, which need not detain us here.

step on the line of human progress. The North American Indians at the time of the arrival of the white man were still in the habit of employing an ideographic script; and the hieroglyphic inscriptions of Egypt still show traces of it. There we find words spelled out according to their sounds, but at the same time accompanied with ideograms,—a practice which offered considerable help in the decipherment of these venerable monuments. It seems to be but natural that mankind should return to a pasigraphy, the utility of which is obvious, and it would only abolish itself when in the course of historical progress all the languages are swallowed up in one common human speech,—a result which may very well be accomplished in the long run through the establishment of a common and universal civilisation, according to the law of the survival of the fittest.

An ideal pasigraphy would be a symbolical writing of meanings, which with little or scarcely any trouble or study should be readily understood by people of any speech. The fewest possible rules should cover the greatest possible ground, and the symbols should be so obvious in their meaning as to be easily remembered, or even easily guessed.

The grandest beginning that has so far been made in the direction of a truly perfect pasigraphy is the Arabic numeral system which in the simplest possible way by mere position of ten cyphers denotes sums of any description, fractions and proportions with unsurpassable precision. It is fully equaled by the symbols of musical notes and to some extent also by the method of chemical denotation, which, however, is confronted with the difficulty of requiring familiarity with the facts upon which the science is based.

It is the purpose of the present article to offer a suggestion how a pasigraphy which would meet all reasonable demands could be established; and we have devoted special care to the grammatical relations, including prepositions as well as other particles of speech, and the logical interrelation of the ideas that constitute sentences. They being established, the meaning of a sentence could easily be determined even if the principal words,—the subject of the sentence, the predicate, or the object, perhaps all three,—were to be expressed in the writing of the writer's own language. The difficulty of understanding a foreign tongue rises less from a lack of our knowledge of the vocabulary than our inability of determining the grammar. If the construction of a sentence is unequivocal we can easily and quickly make up for our lack of knowledge with the use of a dictionary. Moreover, in a correspondence between the inhabitants of different countries, which deals with definite commercial transactions, the subject nouns of a communication are nearly always determined by well-known conditions, they being either the goods to be bartered, or their quality, or their value.

We will now submit a brief synopsis of the methods and symbols proposed for pasigraphy.

* * *

The writing of the symbols is arranged on a staff in the same order as our script from the left to the right. The staff is divided into three horizontal partitions, the Middle or Main, the Upper, and the Lower. The Main is utilised for root signs, while the Upper shall contain symbols for further specification. The Lower remains reserved for the writer's own language and is superrogatory, but may sometimes serve as a help and will let the recipient of a letter know the writer's meaning as he would express it in his own vernacular.

The Upper

The Main or the Middle

The Lower

DIAGRAM OF THE STAFF.[1]

RADICALS.[2]

The ultimate elements from which symbols are constructed are called "Radicals," and it goes without saying that they ought

[1] Beginners might use paper in which the three lines of the staff are marked, but they should be very lightly printed, or merely dotted, or printed in a light color. They are as redundant as the lines in the caligraphical copy books of children.

[2] The symbols have been devised, first of all, to make them handy for writing by hand, and the first draft of them was made by the author with this special purpose in view. As they here appear in the text they have been adapted to the printed

to be simple and easy to remember. It will be advisable to utilise mathematical and other signs to which a great part of mankind has become accustomed, and having accepted a radical we must utilise it to the utmost and modify its sense by slight changes or such simple additions as are quickly understood.

We propose a few radicals as working material for our examples:

ARTICLES AND SOME OTHER GENERAL CONCEPTS.

❙	One item, symbol of noun.
↑	Male gender, definite masculine article.[1]
Y	Female gender, definite feminine article.[2]
I	Definite neuter article.
T	Person, personality.[3]
S	Plural, plurality.[4]
∪	Any.[5]
∩	Some (i. e., a definite determination).[6]
ω	Possible, (i. e., one in any).
m	Choice, (i. e., one in some).
⋈	Probable, (i. e., some in any).
⋈⋈	All, universality.[7]
_	The symbol of a verb.
=	Equality.
‖	Parallelity, agreement.
∽	Similarity.
:	Relation.
+	Addition.
∞	Infinitude.
?	Query, to ask a question.
▬	Equality.
<	Sign of the past.
V	Sign of the present.
>	Sign of the future.
⊍	Any of two, either.
⊍	One of two chances, or.

style and according to a standard measure. The drawing has been executed with great accuracy by the skillful hand of Mr. Teitaro Suzuki.

[1] The lance (in ancient Babylonia the emblem of Marduk, in Greece and Rome of Mars) is commonly used as a symbol of masculinity.

[2] The feminine symbol is chosen to be clearly different from the male symbol. While the latter is angular downwards, the former is rounded upwards.

[3] In jurisprudence, the essential part of the person is the head. Thus "one" with a head means personality.

[4] The fact that *s* is the plural ending in almost all Indo-Germanic languages, is a sufficient justification to adopt for the same purpose a symbol resembling the letter *s*.

[5] Resembles a bowl from which any may be selected.

[6] The symbol "any" turned upside down resembles a chicken-coop which covers a definite number, viz., "some."

[7] The symbols "one" and "some" and "any" combined.

Yes or yea.[1]

No, not or nay.[1]

Symbol of time.[2]

Symbol of space.[3]

The present one, this one.

That one.

This person.

That person.

Present time, now.

Present space, here.

Much.

Little.

Great.[4]

More.

Less.

Most.

A couple, a pair.

A few.

Many.

Who? interrogative.

What.

Who, relative pronoun.[5]

PERSONAL PRONOUNS.

I, the person present.[6]

Thou, the person addressed.[7]

The third or absent person.

He, the third person, masculine.

She, the third person, feminine.

It, the third person, neuter.

We.

You.

They.

They, masculine.

They, feminine.

They, neuter.

FURTHER SYMBOLS.

Event [8]

Cause.

Effect.

Open

Door.[9]

Closed.

---

[1] Yea, representing parallel lines on an outlined subject, means agreemen Nay, in contrast to it, may be regarded as cancellation.

[2] The symbol represents an hour-glass.

[3] The symbol represents the four quarters of space.

[4] This symbol agrees pretty closely with the Chinese symbol 大 (ta) great

[5] The meaning of this combination will be explained further down. It co sists of the symbol "person" on the oblique line over the verbal-symbol (—). dicating that a dependent sentence is to follow.

[6] The symbol is intended as a combination of "the one" and an abbreviat of the symbol "present."

[7] The second person "thou" means "the one in front," while the third per means "the one behind."

[8] The symbol depicts by an involved line an involved process

[9] The opening that can be barred.

want.[1]

interfere.

ıoney determined.)

y.[5]

[6]

seous state.[7]

or fluid.[7]

r.[7]

merchandise.[8]

.[10]

Fish.

Bird.

Animal.

Sun.

Light.

Moon.

Star.[11]

Day (sun above the horizon).

Night (sun below the horizon).

Year (circuit of the sun).

Month (circuit of the moon).

Hour (hour-glass as marked "run off").

Temperature.[12]

Cold.

Heat.

High.

Low.

Close by, near.

---

ing with the symbol of nothing in it.

ıbol represents the right angle, the plumb line on the horizontal.

like the sky or heaven.

ersion of the symbol "good."

indedness.

ng a closed front, or a shield.

ıbol of matter is space filled. Matter tending down is solid. Matter the gaseous state. Between the two is matter as a fluid, and the matter before it was solidified, is ether. A locality is a place mapped

ıbol of merchandise represents a bale.

ıe Egyptian hieroglyph denoting "town." It represents an enclosed ts.

isions represent the districts of a country.

yptians represent the star with five rays.

ature is represented by a thermometer. The thermometer, if marked cold," and if marked high, means "heat."

Distant, far.

This side.

The other side, yonder.

Long.

Short.

Quick.

Slow.

Eat.

Drink.

Lips.

Mouth.

Tongue.

Speak.[1]

Teeth.

Eye.

Weep.

See.

Watch.

Ear.

Hear.

Listen.

Within, inside.

Without, outside.

Above.

Below.

Before.

Behind, after.

For (purpose.)

From.

Into.

Out of.

Between.

Through.

Mountain.[2]

House.

Church.

Temple.

Heart.

Apple.

Use.[3]

Abuse.

Gain.[4]

Waste.

Salary.[5]

Interest, rent.[6]

Bribe.[5]

Loss of money.

Standard, norm.[7]

Join.

Separate.[8]

Book.

Write.

Read.

Machine.[9]

---

[1] The verbal sign underneath means "action of tongue."

[2] This is the Chinese symbol for mountain.

[3] The line of transaction turned upward.

[4] The symbol "gain" is turned "toward." The symbols "abuse" and "wa are the opposites of "use" and "gain."

[5] "Salary" is "gain" with money; "bribe" is "abuse" with money, etc

[6] Compound root, consisting of the symbols "merchandise" and "house"

[7] Picture of a flag.

[8] "Separate" is "space between two lines."

[9] The symbol represents a wheel and a crank.

ng.

ity.

d.

e.

rant.

ought, thinking for-

, thinking backward.

ion, thinking down-

Assumption, thinking upward.

Planning, devising.[1]

Bearing in mind.[2]

Hope, anticipating good.

Fear, anticipating evil.

Expect, anticipate.

Recollect.

Fiction.

Generalise.[3]

Subject, subjectivity, feeling.

Object, objectivity,[4] concrete bodily reality.

Wish, feeling going out.

Resistance.

Will, intention (feeling directed).

Opposition (purposive resistance).

Exertion, labor.

Success (resistance overcome).

Satisfaction (the object wished, obtained).

Pain (feeling cut).

Energy, force, resistance of object overcome.

Experience, friz., compre-

---

is "to give," "buy" is "to take"; the former has added "money latter "money left."

elsewhere, the discriminating marks are mere dots, to denote "any-

bol denotes "thinking upward to universals."

symbols, "subject" and "object," represent the former, the boun- ject or the bosom of a sentient being, the other the boundary of the urface of concrete things opposed to the subject.

hension, knowledge, the obobject grasped by the subject.

Ӕ Skill.

★ Orderly arrangement.

† Life.

Youth, ascending life.

Old age.

Store.[1]

Beautiful.

Ugly.

Pleasant.

Unpleasant.

The root-symbol of a word is called a ROOT, and roots are placed in the Main.

The space in the Main at the beginning of a word is called the Initial, at the end, the Terminal. In order to separate the words clearly from each other, the Initial is left free and the Terminal is marked by a dot.

THE INDICATOR AND DETERMINANT.

The space above the Initial is used to indicate what part of speech a word belongs to and thus we call it the Indicator.

The Indicator of a noun may be the definite or any other article (the, a, any, some,) or, if none of them is needed, a vertical line (❙).

The Indicator of a verb is any personal pronoun, or, if none of them be needed, a horizontal line (—).

The Indicator of an adjective, which for convenience sake we will call an "ad-noun," is a dot before a vertical line (.❙).

The Indicator of an adverb is a dot with a horizontal line (.—).

The Indicator of an interjection is a vertical line over a dot (!).

With the help of indicators, we can easily make of the same root a verb or a noun, or an adjective, or an adverb, or an interjection, and thus the use of our symbols is greatly increased by a very simple method with the use of a few signs, all of which are easily remembered.

The place above the Terminal is reserved for the Determinant.

The Determinant of a word determines its nature and corresponds to what in classical languages (Latin and Greek) finds ex-

---

[1] A compound root, meaning "merchandise house."

ession in endings. In verbs it determines the tense and in nouns e character of a noun.

DETERMINANTS OF NOUNS AND ADJECTIVES.

Property (for adjectives it means "holding," or "filled with").

Essence or quality (for adjectives it means "like," corresponding to the endings -ly, -some, etc.).

Action, or activity.

State, or condition.

: Habit, function.

Psychological state, feeling, sentiment.

Concrete things, objects.

Knowledge, science.

Skill, faculty.

Personality.

Animal.

Any abstract thought.

Imaginary things, fiction.

Locality.

EXAMPLES OF NOUNS.

Life, viz., the act of living.

Life as a biological function.

Vivacity.

Biology, the science of life.

EXAMPLES OF ADJECTIVES.

Alive.

Living, participle present.

Lively, possessing the essence characteristic of life.

Vivacious.

THE MODIFIER.

The number of roots can be multiplied by inserting above the ›ot some symbol that should modify its sense, which is called the Modifier." The sign "general" placed over a definite root gen'alises its sense. For instance, if it is placed above the symbol apple," it will change the sense to "fruit." The symbol "figurive" or "similar" ~ indicates that the root over which it stands should be interpreted in a figurative sense. Thus it will change the meaning of the symbol "heart" into ♡ "love."

Indicator	Modifier	Determinant
	Root	•

THE POSITION OF SYMBOLS IN THE STAFF.

THE VERB.

It is of special importance to recognise the verb, which serves as the predicate of sentences; hence verbs are indicated by lines which are placed either below or above the roots. A line below the root indicates the active, and a line above, the passive voice. The former, the active line runs along the boundary of the Main and Lower; the latter, the passive line, lies between the Main and the Upper, and both lines serve as the reflexive mood, corresponding to the Greek "medium."

The pronouns of a verb, whenever needed, are placed above the Initial, and the determinations of tense, which are expressed by any of the three symbols "Past," "Present," and "Future," above the Terminal.

	Pronoun		Tense
Passive line			
	Initial (Free space)	Root	Terminal (A dot)
Active line			

STAFF OF THE VERB.

EXAMPLES.

Imperative forms are determined by an exclamation sign which takes the place of the tense symbol.

I advance.

It is lifted up.

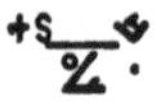

They (these things) have been sold.

VERBAL ROOTS.

To have, to hold, to contain, to possess.

To be contained in, to be subsumed under, to be.

To start, to try.

To be started, to begin.

To complete, to finish.

To be completed, to attain full growth, to develop into.

To act, to do, to be active.

To be passive, designating any state or condition.

To move, motion.

To be moved, movement.

To do again, to repeat.

To be in the habit of doing, function.

Semitic scholars know, how by a clever modification of the t a series of new verbal forms are evolved in Hebrew, Arabic, kindred languages, the Piel, Pual, Nipbal, Hiphil, etc. The an languages possess similar formations in a limited degree. as the verb "*fall*" acquires a causative meaning by a weakening he *a* to *e*, in the verb *fell*, "to cause to fall." In the same way causative of "*to sit*" is "*to set*," which means "to cause to " The verbal symbols quoted above enable us to imitate, or n surpass, the Semitic languages in their elegant formation of ds. They will in the simplest way perform the function of iliary verbs.

The following examples will explain:

AUXILIARY VERBS.

To have a choice, the auxiliary "may."

To be determined, the auxiliary "must." Also analogous to "is to."

To deem right.

To be deemed right, ought.

To feel like, to like.

To have the wish.

To have the intention.

To be sorry.

To compel, to force.

To exert one's self.

To cause, to make.

To be skilled in.

A few special symbols are needed for the coördinate conjunctions such as "and," "also," "but," "however," etc. The simplest ones need no Indicator. Their symbols are "&" for "and," and "+" for "in addition". Other simple coördinate conjunctions are "either... or," "on this side... on the other side," "on the one hand... on the other hand." If for any special reason more complicated word-forms should be used as coördinate conjunctions, they must be marked as such in the Upper by a cross as their indicator.

COMPOUNDS.

Two or several roots may be combined into compounds, as is customary in all languages. Thus the root part of the words "steam engine," "steamship," "gas meter," etc. would show a simple succession of the two radicals.

Other methods of compounding words would be by joining the two roots either with the symbol of the Saxon genitive, or by symbols that mean "made of" or "serving the purpose of" etc., e.g., "road-made of-iron," imitating the French "*chemin de fer*."

THE POSSESSIVE CASE.

The Chinese have a peculiar sign 之 pronounced *che*, which somewhat looks like a capital Z and may sometimes be translated by the Saxon genitive, for instance, 天之道, "Heaven's Reason," and 人之道, "man's reason." We propose to utilise this sign in a simplified form in the same sense, analogous to the Saxon genitive, and produce with its assistance all the possessive pronouns, thus:

My, mine; gen. of "me."	Ours.
Thy, thine.	Yours.
His.	Theirs, masculine.
Hers.	Theirs, feminine.
Its.	Theirs, neuter.

THE OBLIQUE.

The Oblique is a symbol consisting of a slanting line which will be found useful not only to denote what Latin grammarians call the "oblique cases" (*casus obliqui*) of a noun, but all oblique relations including dependent sentences which are introduced by conjunctions and relative pronouns.

The objective case, commonly called "accusative," is marked y a simple Oblique with a noun sign.

The other oblique cases, genitive and dative, are formed after ie same pattern by adding either the genitive symbol or the dative rmbol (the latter being the mathematical sign of relation used in roportions). On these principles we decline the nouns.

DECLENSION.

 The ship (nominative.)

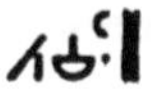 The ship (accusative.)

 Of the ship.

 To the ship.

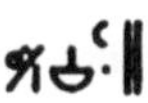 By the ship (ablative case, i. e., through the instrumentality of a ship).

 In a ship.

The Oblique which introduces a sentence shows underneath on s right side the indicator of a verb, while the Oblique which introuces a noun shows the indicator of a noun. The former represents onjunctions of dependent sentences, the latter prepositions. Reltive pronouns introduce sentences, accordingly they exhibit above he Oblique the pronoun symbol, and underneath the verbal indiator.

Here are a few simple sentences which will explain the use of oth obliques, prepositions, and conjunctions:

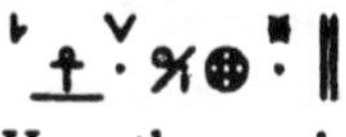 I live in the town.

Here the symbol "within" ⊙ over the oblique is accompanied nderneath by the symbol of the definite neuter article.

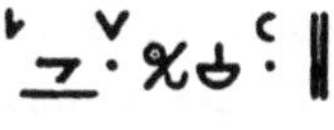 I move in a ship.

Here the preposition "in" ⊙ is accompanied by the indefinite rticle "a" ᴗ.

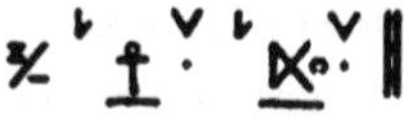 While I live, I hope.

The verbal line under the oblique indicates that the symbol "time" demands a verb, and so it introduces a dependent sentence. Accordingly, the symbol means "time as a conjunction," to be translated "so long as," or "while."

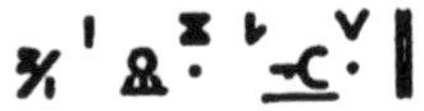 During the day time I work.

Here the same symbol "time" is accompanied by the noun-symbol, which proves it to be a preposition and calls for its translation by "during" or "at the time of."

The relative pronoun may be declined in the normal way by prefixing the noun oblique (/ı) to the verbal oblique (/–); but here an abbreviation may recommend itself, which can easily be introduced by attaching to the left upper corner of the relative-symbol the requisite case symbols, viz., the simple slant (/) for the accusative; the genitive-symbol (Z) for the possessive, and the colon (:) for the dative.

The comparative is formed by attaching as a Determinant to an adjective the symbol "more," the superlative by prefixing the symbol "most."

EXAMPLES.

 More painful.

 Most energetically.

THE PARTICIPLE.

The participle has not been discussed as a form of the verb because it is an adjective. The participle is derived from a verb but has ceased to be a truly verbal form, it only partakes of the tense and the voice of verbs, and pasigraphy can represent every shade of meaning of any participle without resorting to the invention of new symbols. We must use the adnoun initial and treat it in every respect as an adjective, but add in the Terminal its tense and voice value

For present active participles thus Y, e. g., loving, *amans*.

Past passive participles thus Z, e. g., loved, *amatus*.

Future active participles thus ≥, e. g., about to love, *amaturus*.

Future passive participles thus ≽, e. g., to be loved, *amandus*.

Participles as adverbs simply change their adnoun indicator › the adverb indicator.

DATES.

The date is expressed by writing first the day in Arabic figures, ıen the month in Roman numerals, and finally the year again in rabic figures.

INTERJECTIONS.

Interjections are marked by two exclamation signs, one serving ı Indicator and the other as Determinant.

PUNCTUATION.

Since the point has been utilised too much for other purposes, ıe period cannot be a simple dot but must be replaced by another gn. We propose a double vertical line running from the top to ıe bottom of the entire staff. Questions will be indicated by the ıery mark between the two period strokes. In the same way, we troduce the colon and exclamation sign. A simple line will take ıe place of our comma, and if there be any need of inventing a ıbstitute for the semicolon, we let the simple line be followed by ıother short vertical stroke.

LIST OF PUNCTUATION MARKS.

|?|	|:|	|!|	|	|ı	| |
nery Mark	Colon	Exclamation Sign	Comma	Semicolon	Period

CONCLUSION.

In these few pages we have disposed of the grammar of pasig-aphy, symbolising the relations to be described in signs which are oth simple to make and easy to remember.

The author does not intend to present in this article a perfect ystem of pasigraphy. He only offers a suggestion how the scheme ıight be acomplished. He has presented only enough symbols to xplain the methods which he deems advisable to adopt and has urposely abstained from an attempt at making their number complete. He believes that the selection of symbols ought to be the result of a coöperation of many minds, and therefore he would prefer to leave all details of a pasigraghy to a commission of men interested in the subject,—men, who in their own sphere of life stand in need of a pasigraphy and would, for practical reasons, welcome the invention. They will be best fitted for the purpose and more than others prove qualified to devise and choose the most appropriate signs.

EDITOR.

LITERARY CORRESPONDENCE.

FRANCE.

'N *Études de psychologie physiologique et pathologique,* M. E. · Gley gives his report and a résumé of his experimental rearches, made largely upon himself, into the physiological contions of mental activity; the state of the carotid pulse, the rculation of the blood, central temperature, thermic and physical ata, and nutritive fluctuations. It is beyond question that the facts f consciousness and cerebral alterations "have a mutual relation," as loffory says: or better, that there is a parallelism between conscious nd cerebral activity, and that these facts are "interrelated," as M. ley himself says. But at present we cannot go further; reason does t succeed in giving an adequate reason for thought.

The author's investigations in the realm of unconscious muscular vements as connected with mental images or representations and se on the muscular sense are not less interesting than the preced- :- Especial interest attaches also to his study of the aberrations l perversions of the sexual instinct which closes the volume. In Gley we have a serious mind, a scholar of high repute, and ler his guidance we are walking upon solid ground.

M. Ch. Féré brings us in his turn new experimental studies in cho-mechanics under the title of *Travail et Plaisir.* The consion of these painstaking studies is, that in all conditions which are companied by pleasure, labor becomes easier and more productive. is demonstrated besides that labor without artificial stimuli is also ore productive because it exhausts the organism less rapidly and ss completely.

M. G. Saint-Paul, in *Le Langage intérieur et les paraphasies* (*La fonction endophasique*) takes up and pursues still further the analysis of the subjective phases of language (*langage intérieur*) as related to the anatomical and physiological data involved, to the motor centers, to visual memory, to psychic processes and ideation. He proposes a new classification of types based upon the relative complexity of the component elements. His study is supported by an investigation which has been pursued at great length; some of the evidence thus supplied is indeed curious and may be profitably consulted. However, I must criticise the work for lack of precision and of résumés summing up the results.

* * *

Many readers will wish to get their knowledge of Mr. J. Maxwell's *Psychic Phenomena* at first hand. The tone of the book, with its preface by M. Charles Richet, and the very position of the author, who is a judge and a doctor of medicine, are a sufficient guarantee of perfect sincerity. Laying aside all prejudices Mr. Maxwell undertook personal investigations of the facts presented by mediums. He understood that the prime problem is to make sure of the reality of the facts, and despite all his care these facts remain questionable; doubt is inspired by the very abundance of operations employed to obtain results in the séances. Moreover he rejects unhesitatingly the hypothesis of the presence of "spirits" or othr supermundane personalities. In his opinion we must seek in the nervous system the cause of these mediumistic phenomena which seem so extraordinary and even absurd, and of which he believes that a large part are to be attributed to fraud and error. Disposed as I am to make this proportion still greater, it does not seem to me impossible that our nervous system may possess powers not known to us, or that there even exist forms of energy which our science, still in its beginnings, scarcely suspects. But it is proper to walk cautiously upon this slippery ground, and Mr. Maxwell has perhaps not always kept within the bounds which he had wisely set for himself.

* * *

I have now to consider two works which are very unlike in contents and yet closely related in tendency. In our life an excess of social integration is succeeded by a work of dissolution which threatens to be no less excessive. The evidences of this may be derived from many books in literature and philosophy. It is a sort of tide in which we may discern the influence of Tolstoi, of Nietzsche and of still others.

In *L'idéal esthétique* M. Fr. Roussel-Despierres aspires to suggest a new ideal which shall be superior to every other ideal, religious, moral, utilitarian or scientific. The apprehension of this ideal will bring in its own rule of life; or rather, it will impose upon every individual a harmony with the world and with himself which will permit the liberty, the autonomy of the person and dispense with all strict rules imposed from without. The esthetic life will not preclude the moral life; it will contain it and dominate it.

The author seems to forget that our arts, our systems of morality, our religions are natural products of life, corresponding to various sorts of needs, desires and actions which must not be confused. He does not keep sufficiently in mind that the esthetic life is an achievement, a result, but that it cannot be a means and bring about by its own power the very social conditions which alone rendered it possible. Esthetics will never entirely absorb morality nor religion nor science; it does not cover the same territory. M. Roussel-Desquierres sets up an ideal man, in whom all the powers of intellect and of feeling shall be blended in perfect harmony. But individuals are incomplete beings, different beings, in whom the primacy cannot always and absolutely be reserved for the sense of beauty, or the sense of goodness, or the sense of truth.

In his book, *The Man versus the State*, Spencer treated a clear and well-defined question. In *Le combat pour l'individu* M. Palante has attempted to extend the scope of the discussion so as to include all forms of social organization, and thus has made it vague and inexact. In fact the various social groups differ in character and scope. Moral restraints which arise from custom are one thing; legal restraints which are supported by the force of the law are quite another. On the other hand, while certain organizations are oppressive toward the individual, or are liable to become so, there are some that serve to protect him and are natural requisites for personal defence. Let us suppose the emancipation of the individual, as some are pleased to call it, carried to its ultimate consequences; there would reappear such intolerable wickedness and disorder that men would set themselves to build up anew what they had destroyed, and the work of reformation would commence in a literal sense.

I do not mean to say that there is nothing tenable in the criticisms of M. Palante and of other sociological philosophers of his school. I even congratulate him on having recognised the excess of oppression to which a democracy may lead when it becomes merely a government of cliques. I should only wish him not to forget that the individual lives in a society or in some sort of group quite as inevitably as a fish lives in water. I should wish also that he had perceived how much dilettantism enters into individualism. Furthermore, a controlling psychological fact in this problem is that some men are born to obey and others to command. We may be able to change the forms within which obedience is expressed and command exercised, but the law remains the same. From a purely abstract point of view I should say that the Individual and the State are the two extremes of a series; neither one of these terms can exist in and for itself. Their opposition is only a figure of antinomy and like a logical frame for a relation which alone represents the living reality.

* * *

In his *Nouveau programme de sociologie esquisse d'une introduction générale à l'étude des sciences du monde surorganiques*, M. de Roberty once more presents his views (1) on the place of the social fact in the universe, (2) on the essential modes of the social thought, (3) on the new moral order which is dawning. These are the divisions of the book itself.

According to M. de Roberty, sociology should be classified between biology, which precedes it, and psychology, which follows. Its domain is the "superorganic," a product of "social psychism," this latter term being a synonym of sociality, of mental interaction, of collective experience, comprising also the moral sense, the basis of all sociology. The psychologic school, says M. de Roberty, seems to be ignorant of the reality of this new mode of universal existence; it sees in sociology only a chapter of psychology, whereas we ought, on the contrary, to regard psychology as "elementary concrete sociology," the progress of which depends on the discovery of the abstract laws of mental interaction.

"Mental interaction," "social group," "social individual," such then would be the first terms of a great "evolution" continuing in the varying phenomena which constitute civilisation. Science, philosophy, art, action, such would be the four groups in which we should arrange these phenomena, bound together by a law of close correlation which explains the philosophical status by the scientific status, the state of the fine arts by that of beliefs and general convictions, and finally explains human conduct by the preceding conditions which all end in this. The law of evolution, which controls this long series of events is, according to M. de Roberty, the most general law that sociology can establish; it seems to him to solve the fundamental problem of history, making it possible for us to explain why and how one social state produces the state which succeeds and replaces it.

I come now to a most curious work: M. Armand Sabatier, who is a savant and one of the best intellects of French Protestantism, continues in his *Philosophie de l'effort essais philosophiques d'un naturaliste* the series of his studies on the two fundamental features of Christian faith: God and the soul. His position is original; he bases the defence of his beliefs upon the very doctrine of evolution which to so many other philosophers seems to undermine them. Of the twelve essays contained in the volume all are interesting from one or another point of view. I can give here only the general idea of them.

Evolution, as M. Sabatier understands it, can show forth only the development of germs, of tendencies, enclosed in matter; the involution in the germ, the evolution in time. And thence he affirms the Spencerian thesis and the mathematical thesis of Descartes and Spinoza. As would appear at first sight this would be, then, the static, mechanical, and at bottom materialistic, conception of the universe. But M. Sabatier imagines that he is avoiding materialism by treating this matter, this potential, as emanating from God, from the divine essence and developing "by effort" to return thither. Thus his materialism becomes a dynamism controlled by finalism. The end of all beings is God, that is to say, the realisation of the divine attributes; they become God by will power and by suffering. Being free and moral by the very fact of their participation in the nature of the Creator, they have a tendency to take cognisance of their destiny and to complete it. While in the genetic conception liberty and morality appear to be wholly new things and independent creations, according to this conception they merely reappear or manifest themselves, but are not created.

The author is pledged by his thesis to posit liberty as inherent in matter; he says there is room for zones of indeterminism, room for contingency in the mineral kingdom, in the animal kingdom, in the world of mind. Furthermore, we ought to think of matter as "energy become sensible" to organized beings, endowed with sensorial apparatus. This granted, the possibility remains open for material beings to become pure spirit by a simple change of condition. Psychic energy is found distributed throughout the universe in a diffused state, and constitutes the true substance of it. Still more, there is no fact which invalidates the assumption that man has power or permission to draw, by means of prayer from the first source of all energy. (I call especial aatention to this study on prayer.)

In fine, M. Sabatier professes the doctrine of universal psychism and at the same time that of evolution, and yet remains "true to the belief in a personal God and Creator, superior to the world, yet controlling the evolutionary progress of the universe and consequently mingling in its life to exercise a salutary attraction destined to elevate and bring it nearer to himself." Not only does evolution seem to him not to exclude God, but on the contrary God seems to him to be less necessary in the conception of a stable universe. Such a world can dispense with all divine intervention much more easily than a world which is evolving in a thousand different ways in a definite line of perfection and melioration. In the latter there is needed an "incessant influence" which "excludes quite logically the rôle of chance."

This diffused psychic energy with which all things are suffused is recognised further by M. Sabatier in instinct, just as he discovered contingency in the inorganic world. One of the problems that he meets upon his way is that of a present infinity. He believes, however, that he has avoided the paradox of an infinity really present, without violating the principle that nothing is created or destroyed. Since in his view creation is not the appearance of a new quantity of energy, but "the setting apart of a quantity of energy which was merely detached from the divine source," it suffices to assume that the Creator gave to this portion set apart "a special form which permits it to evolve," the "form of matter." And if such were the beginning of the universe, cannot one rationally consider the end of the same universe as being properly accomplished by the return of this material energy into the state of psychic energy? In fact, we may well ask whether matter has never had another form than that which we know. The consideration of ether, of dark rays, of X-rays, of bodies with spontaneous radio-activity, suggest many reflections on special modes of energy unknown to earlier physics.

* * *

Under the head of history I have to mention M. Elie Halévy's *Le radicalisme philosophique*,[1] the third volume of a learned and instructive work, reaching from the death of Bentham to the rise of the Manchester School; also an extensive and very interesting study by Mr. P. F. Thomas, devoted to Pierre Leroux, *His Life, his Work, his Teaching, his Contribution to the History of Ideas in the Nineteenth Century;* from M. Victor de Swarte a curious volume with portraits, drawings and autographs, the title being *Descartes, directeur spirituel, correspondante avec la Princesse palatine et la Reine Christiane de Suede;* by M. Ch. Adam *Études sur les principaux philosophes.*

In the philosophy of science I note J. Perrin's *Traité de chimie physique, les principes*,[2] a work of 300 pages, which I have not myself examined, but which seems to me to be of great importance from the review of it that has just been given in the *Revue philosophique* over the signature of M. Abel Rey.

Under the head of psychology I will mention: A. Binet, *L'étude experimentale de l'intelligence;*[3] J. S. von Biervliet, *Esquisse d'une éducation de la mémorie;* Bunge, *Principes de psycho-*

---

[1] Paris, Hachette; the other volumes are from the *Libraire F. Alcan.*

[2] Gautier-Villars, pub.

[3] Schleicher, pub.

logie individuelle et sociale; Dugas, L'imagination[1] and *L'absolu,* regarded as a "normal and pathological form of the feelings."

There only remains to note the appearance of two new reviews. One, which is published by Alcan, is entitled *Journal de psychologie normale et pathologique,* and is edited by MM. Pierre Janet and G. Dumas; it appears bi-monthly and the two numbers already issued give promise of a most valuable collection which will constitute in a way a complementary appendix to the *Revue philosophique,* a place where one may find collected analyses of all the interesting papers in the domain of more special studies, and the importance of which will constantly increase. "The other journal is entitled *La revue des idées,* and will appear monthly; its programme is very general. M. Ed. Dujardin is the manager and M. R. de Gourmont the editor in chief. This publication, though of very different character from the preceding, deserves high praise.

---

[1] O. Doin, pub.

CRITICISMS AND DISCUSSIONS.

DR. OSTWALD'S PAMPHLET ON UNIVERSAL LANGUAGE.

WE are in receipt of a pamphlet written by Dr. W. Ostwald, entitled *Die Weltsprache*, published by the committee for the introduction of an international auxiliary language.

Dr. Ostwald is an enthusiastic adherent of the idea and the following passage in which he discusses and rejects the advisability of making English the world-language is an extract from his pamphlet:

"Having granted the desirability of a world-language, the question arises as to its possibility. The answer is: 'It is possible, for in America, everyone, whatever his vernacular may be, speaks English, for English is the language of business and all other intercourse of that immense country.'

"Some one to whom I mentioned my argument answered, 'Very well, let us use English as an international auxiliary language,' and indeed this proposition pops up again and again, and has been frequently considered. A prominent German professor has upon a solemn occasion made this suggestion to me and has recommended it, but I am convinced of it that it is impracticable.

"Suppose that in Germany a majority of thoughtful people would be—let us directly say so—unselfish enough to choose English as the international language, we would find much opposition among the nations with a more decided national sentiment who would not be willing to make so great a sacrifice. Accordingly, there is no prospect of establishing a world-language by choosing one of the living tongues, and an attempt to endorse one of them would therefore from the start be destined to become a failure.

"First, there are national objections which have to be considered, but in addition great practical interests are at stake. The nation whose language would be raised to the prominence of a world-

[illegible]

[illegible] factors.

[illegible] language Professor Ostwald sets [illegible] of the living languages, instanced in [illegible] German [illegible]. He shows how it contains many endings and determinatives which are redundant. First, the [illegible] redundant; [illegible], the declension of adjectives is quite ecessary, and thirdly, the repeated indication of the plural form ne and the same sentence is not needed, etc. The German sen- e *"Die steinernen Häuser brennen nicht,"* consists of nine sylla- and contains all these redundant determinations. Professor Ost- d declares that if the redundant determinations were omitted sense would be just as clear, and shaved of them the sentence ht read as follows: *"De steinern Häuser brenn nicht."* This is ving of two syllables and would render the language consider- easier. Professor Ostwald forgets that the development of lish consists exactly in the omission of these redundant forms. his attempts of letting the German approach the ideal of niversal language, he saves only two syllables. Why does he ct to the English which expresses the same sense in five sylla- "Stone-houses don't burn"?

The objections which Professor Ostwald offers against English irrelevant, and, judging from his own characterisation of what iversal language ought to be, it seems rather inconsistent that s not an advocate of English as the best medium of international munication, especially as English is a language based upon his German vernacular. English is but Saxon universalised.

There are objections that can be made to English as an inter- onal language, but they lie in another field than sentimental con- rations of jealousy. The most important ones are the English ing and certain awkward methods of English pronunciation. instance, the English do not pronounce the initial "p" before "s". thus no German or Frenchman would recognise the words lms" or "psychology" when they are pronounced in the English , unless they are specially prepared for it. The same is true of "k" and "g" before "n" as in "knight," "gnome," etc.

But the English spelling is worse than the pronunciation and fact is so generally conceded that we need not enter into de- . It is an old *crux* from which English grammarians and teach- suffer greatly, and reforms are being attempted constantly but ly in vain. We will not decide the question here, but will only hat if English is to become the world-language, it will have to e several important concessions and undergo some changes in ethods of spelling and pronunciation.

If any living language is to become the international world- ch, (and I grant that if there is any one that has a chance to fill office, it will be the English,) the decision will not be made by te of delegates of international committees but by the force of s. If English should continue to increase as it does now, it will be found to be the most practical means of international communication. Business will more and more be transacted in English and news will find quickest circulation if divulged in English.

In the beginning of the history of every nation we find several dialects spoken, but, by and by, one of the dialects becomes the common speech of all literary and educated people. This is not done by a vote taken by the representatives of the nation, but is simply due to a survival of the fittest. In Greece, Athens was the most active city among the Greek states. Its Ionic dialect was modified by contact with other Greek tribes, and thus the speech of Attica became the classical language of ancient Hellas. It is quite probable that the international language of the future will develop in the same way. That language will be spoken most which best fulfills the main conditions that are needed for this special purpose, and so far as we can see, of all the languages English is the fittest.

The teeming millions of India speak a number of languages, and a man from the South would not understand a man from the Northern country, such as Burma or Nepal. The result is, they have to use a language that is easily acquired and easily understood everywhere. English is spoken in India only by a few hundred thousand foreign, (and let us grant it, even hated,) invaders, and yet the English language fulfills the conditions, and we need not doubt that within a hundred years the language of the country will be English

Suppose we have in a foreign, not an English, country, families of several nationalities dwelling together,—say for instance in Jerusalem or in Peking. There the children of French, of German, of English, of Spanish, of Portugese, of Italian, and also of Russian families who happen to live there for some reason or other, play together. What will be the language of the children? There will be scarcely any doubt that anywhere in the world, be it China or Asiatic Turkey, that English will be the common speech of such international gatherings. In fact, wherever we inquire, English does become the language that is understood by everyone, not because English is the most beloved of all nationalities, but because it is the easiest language, and even if it is not well spoken, it is easily understood.

English is least hampered by redundant determinatives, its grammar is very simple, and so the language is acquired almost without effort. It is true that the use of correct literary English in which all scholarly linguistical and elocutionary requirements are observed is almost as difficult as the acquisition of other languages, but that is another question which has nothing to do with the fact that English lends itself best to the purpose of international communication.

We do not venture to decide here the question whether or not English will actually become the international language. We only point out that Professor Ostwald's arguments that militate against it, induce us to think that English among all the living languages has the best chance, yet we would grant that in case English should become the international language, there is no doubt that it would have to make certain concessions, especially in spelling and pronunciation, and these modifications would to some extent change the English language into a new language which we might call world-English.

* * *

Professor Ostwald objects to the introduction of English as a world-language because together with the language, we would come into possession of the entire world-conception, including the views of art and science that have been deposited in English speech. We would say, that far from being a disadvantage, this is a preference for the English, and, closely considered, the English literature and the English sciences are not national but international. How much of the German and French literature, science, and arts has been incorporated and is still being incorporated into the English language! In fact English, especially since the rise of the United States, has become the receptacle of human, of international thought, and there is nowhere in the world a proposition of importance uttered in any language but it is at once translated into English and becomes accessible to the English-speaking world.

English is not the speech of Great Britain alone, but of North America, Africa, Australia, India, the European colonies of China, and so it has actually ceased to be the exclusive speech of the English people and has become an international medium. It is the only language that is being spoken by many nations of decidedly different nationalities.

In the course of its evolution English accepted so many foreign elements, especially here in America, that it is frequently denied to have a character of its own. The legend is well known that God made all the other languages but that Satan made English and he made it by mixing up all the God-created languages and calling the result "English." The legend has been told by Heine who is well known from his antagonism to English, but though it is sarcastic it expresses very well the international character of English speech.

If English itself has an international character, English literature and English science are even more international, and rather than construct an empty receptacle for thought, it would be by far preferable to inherit with the acceptance of a world-speech the wealth of intellectual life of several great nations, whose fate is strongly identified with humanitarian and international ideals. An artificial language would be not less difficult to learn but would be empty and, being an utter blank, would oblige us to start the world of thought all over again.

We must not forget that language is φύσει, not θέσει. It is of natural growth and does not originate by social contract. It seems to us that if the development of the national languages has been such in the past, why should not the development of an international language be the same means?

The intellectual institutions of mankind are not less products of nature than is the physiological development of animals and plants. To some extent we can direct the natural course of life, but in its main outlines the spiritual development of the world, of political, of legal, of educational, and of all other institutions, is as much a result of natural growth as the structure of the human body or the shape of trees or the formation of crystals. If the word could be understood in the scientific sense as we define it, we would say briefly that finally not man will shape the international language, but God.

At the present juncture, it seems of little consequence whether or not, in the distant future, English or a modified world-English, or an artificial auxiliary language, shall become the universal means of communication. We have to deal with conditions such as they are now, but I would insist that *the aspiration of constructing a world-language is in itself a factor that should not be underrated as a symptom of the growing spirit of international good will and friendship*. International exhibitions have been held in London, Paris, Chicago, etc., and foreign delegates have been welcomed in these centres of different nationality. We have the Hague tribunal which, though it will not prevent wars, will gradually tend to establish an international conscience, and the development of an international conscience will be an important factor in making for peace. Among the symptoms of international good will the aspiration of creating an international language is one that we deem of highest importance even if its actual aim may be destined to be a failure.

WHERE PHILOSOPHY FAILS.

The conclusions of a layman who has spent more or less time very greeably in the suburbs of the city of Philosophy can be of no value from technical standpoint, but I venture to think that they may well enough xpress certain current lay criticisms upon philosophy as she is commonly romulgated which the technicians might afford to consider more seriously han they do.

My rambles in the aforesaid environs were inspired by the hope that I night find there the solution of some very vital practical problems involving hose much disputed matters — right, justice, etc. And my difficulty is that ow, finally, I have arrived at the commonplace conclusion that all serious hilosophers are trying to formulate, each in his own way, the same root lea. Also I conclude that they more or less unconsciously desire controersy and do not desire agreement. If these conclusions are warranted it ollows — in view of the natural ineffectiveness of lay arguments upon such oints — that only those should speculate who can afford to do so for the ndeniably great charm of the game. Nevertheless, before taking my own dvice and going about my lay business, I give way to a perverse desire to ay what I think must be in the minds of many laymen, however variously hey might express themselves. And I shall say what I have to say more irectly by being boldly personal.

The one somewhat variant aspect of my experience in these philosophical egions is that I have been led to form my judgments as to other men's conictions from their *actions* rather than from their *words*, where the choice s possible. Of course, we all do this largely, in point of fact, but we are pt to forget that we do it. I do not by any means impute conscious disonesty to the professed pessimist, for example, who continues to live. I nerely think that he allows his feeling to obscure his vision unduly. Just so, s long as I see men *act* as if the universe were One and somehow purposeful, I cannot take their materialistic or pluralistic professions very seriously. This attitude has no theoretical novelty, of course, but very few hilosophers seem to adopt it practically. What sticks in my mind is that its doption dissipates philosophical problems, and not to adopt it is neither tional nor common-sense-ical. The view is too simple and obvious to be opular; indeed, there seems to be in us humans an instinctive aversion to o much simplification. To urge this view is perhaps to give offence resultsly: yet silence here is far from golden to the honest skeptic.

Every man's *actions*, then, reveal his conviction that the universe someow hangs together in a way which he cannot grasp and yet dares not ignore. lso, and at the same time, his *actions* reveal his acceptance of himself, for all practical working purposes, (not in the ultimate absolu genuine individual.

If men's actions do *not* reveal this acknowledgment of (two flatly contradictory standpoints one would welcome ex failure. But if examples are not to be found then men's acti ment of themselves as parts of a complete (i. e., a statical) wl Our behavior in this respect is not logical, of course; only tl logically formulate the absolute. I do not know *how* or *wl* is thus out of all reason: I do not expect to know.] to the undeniable fact that men accept their fate of finitude they were absolutely self-determining, knowing all the wh ideal ultimate sense they are not so. I urge, moreover, tha this (thoroughly irrational thing or die—and when did a refusal to accept his contradictory fate?

Mr. Haldane, in his *Pathway to Reality*, says: "It is n the purposes of these lectures 'to determine' whether the ful exhibited in a system such as Hegel attempted. The remarl one of a sort that seems generally to suggest the gratuitous it is not necessary to determine for *any* purpose, whether th be exhibited by any finite system. But what we know, and wh forget, is that by our acknowledgment of our finitude we there, and by that sign, acknowledged that the full (i. e., the can *never* be determined by finite men. It is this hoping, certainty, that absolute truth may some day be attained by the layman dabbling in philosophy, seems to be the root of n evil. Our *actions*, then, acknowledge the absolute, alias the *ought to be*, just as surely as they acknowledge the re *it is* of finitude.

Surely there is nothing obscure in the distinction be *toward* what *seems* to be a goal, and *arriving at* what *is* a that the ideal is unattainable is not to weaken the unaccounta able authority of our ideal sense as giving us the directio finite judgments should look.

And so in regard to "justice," etc., I see no difficulty have always *two* possible connotations, the one absolute, ideal, tive, practical. Real justice we attribute to the statical i Absolute which our every action presupposes: the tentativ tice is reflected in man-made laws. I am not forgetting ou more or less fleeting, private judgments as to what would mo our ideal sense of justice in this, that, or the other, finite c that these judgments of the moment are what most men mind when they talk about "justice." But justice in this sense is obviously an unstable subjective affair, and the mere thought of a final criterion of such misnamed justice morally or legally obligatory upon others is repugnant even to common sense when it stops to reflect.

I am not doubting that these judgments are to be formed and *urged upon* others. Such judgments are the necessary raw material for the operation of a selective process the results of which, men being as they are, can be obligatory upon all only when they are duly erected into that *working* criterion which we call the law. All of these old trite truths remain. I merely emphasise the well-known but lightly-forgotten fact that the distinction between the absolute and the relative connotations of such words as justice, right, freedom, etc., is perfectly clear. No one ever knew this better than did Spencer, yet he said, in substance; Because the real absolute justice is not for us we might as well use the convenient term "absolute justice" to signify the *nearest approximation* to the genuine article that is conceivably compatible with finitude. So he planted his standard of "absolute ethics" and "absolute justice" *not* in the actually infinite (i. e., The Unknowable) where it belonged, but at an assumed limit of finitude. But after a few pages the mantle of real absoluteness had fallen upon his relative absolute. He nodded and presently awoke to find himself seated in the "tea-table elysium" together with ideally perfect *finite* men. I think that the chapter on "Absolute and Relative Ethics" (vol. I. *Prin. of Ethics*) warrants this characterisation. He there explicitly disavows reference to The Absolute when he uses the term "absolute"; not because The Absolute is not, for him, confessedly *there*, but because the conception of The Absolute is, *for us*, contradictory, and hence absurd. But, throughout, his perfect, ultimate finite man—that reconciliation of the statical and the dynamic—is as contradictory and inconceivable as is The Absolute. It is Spencer's inevitable and willing acknowledgment of The Absolute, with all of its contradictoriness *from our standpoint*, which finds utterance in his expression "absolute ethics."

I think there can be no doubt that Spencer had the right idea but was so much under the influence of his time, after all, that he could not keep clear of the hopeless attempt to formulate a completely logical finite system: and so he did not *say* what we may feel sure he *meant* to say.

Spencer's faith in an ultimate extension among all men of the filial and parental attitude is peculiarly un-Spencerian; yet that faith has influenced many excellent men to believe that the dream of a state of attainable automatic social harmony is a sound scientific postulate. Why, in view of such a precedent, should not men like Mr. Mitchell and Mr. Roosevelt, taking them merely as conspicuous examples of widespread types of mind, hope for the finite realisation of a criterion of justice above the law but less than the infinite, and teach uncritical men to hunt for this snark? When Mr. Mitchell says that he looks forward "to the time when right and justice shall be secured for those who toil," or when Mr. Roosevelt sends a message to the people declaring that it shall be the purpose of the executive to see that justice is done between man and man, it may, indeed, be said that what they *mean* is all right enough. And of this I, for one, have small doubt. But, after all, the practical question is: Are such statements taken literally by the generality of men — or not? And, speaking for one again, the evidence that they are usually taken literally is overwhelming — and thereupon rests the main burden of my complaint. Moreover, does their good intention usually keep the distinction clear for those who use the term justice in this determinate fashion? Decidedly not, I should say.

Take the two cases cited above. Each speaker, I suppose, meant only to voice the common desire of men that our social life be more nearly ideal. Neither, it is safe to say, had conscious reference to a perfect social state. Neither used the word justice in the absolute sense. We may assume with equal safety that neither would think of imposing his personal judgment upon others as their criterion of justice. What, then, could they mean by justice? Obviously nothing remains but the relative working sense of the term which civilised men try to embody, as best they can, in the law. And did Mr. Mitchell merely mean that he looked forward to the time when the law should be enforced for the protection of those who toil? Was he advocating the "open shop," and have we all slipped a cog? And did the President get much excited about that state of lawlessness in the anthracite coal fields of which his Commission says: "The practices, which we are condemning, would be outside the pale of civilised war"; and did he throw the immense weight of his influence in the direction of suppressing that — or did he try chiefly to settle other men's troubles?

I choose these instances merely for illustration. They are in no wise peculiar. What the President did millions of other excellent men would have done in his place. And I have not here a thought for the merits of that case. I am only trying to suggest, by concrete example, how easily we shift from the absolute to the relative pole, and back and forth, in our thought and speech about justice; and to suggest, also, that the very inadvertency of our slip is what makes it so dangerous and so difficult to combat.

It is not strange that men busy with the world's more concrete work should have fallen into this inadvertency; but should trained philosophers — and Spencer was not one — do as ill or worse?

I suppose there is no answer. The thing is done; it has been done and it doubtless will be done. If men all kept the plain distinction of absolute and relative always before them life would be an affair of judging and acting in a well-recognised direction, and there would be no room for philosophising. I don't say that would be much fun. I don't see how not to say it.

S. D. MERTON.

ST. LOUIS, MISSOURI.

EDITORIAL COMMENT.

We publish Mr. S. D. Merton's letter because philosophers by profession may be interested to know what a layman who tried to post himself in philosophy thinks of the usefulness of their speciality. Mr. Merton expresses the impartial view of a bystander who witnesses the quarrels among the adherents of different philosophical schools, and he gains the impression that philosophers more or less unconsciously avoid agreement and desire controversy. The truth is that many philosophers who are supposed to be antipodes agree much better than they seem to be aware of themselves. It is well known for instance how Kant misinterpreted Berkeley, and it is no exaggeration to say that more than half of the philosophical discussions are due to a lack in the precision of terms. Further, Mr. Merton is right when he proposes to judge philosophers, not from their words, but from their actions, and he finds that pessimists continue to life; pluralists act as if the universe were One; materialists as if it were purposeful, and as if they themselves were persons, etc. We grant that most philosophers hanker after brilliancy while their aim should be clearness and precision. Most of their problems are self-made puzzles and the solutions offered mere verbiage.

The term "justice" is perhaps the most misused word in our language. Every one has his own ideas of justice, and as a rule he understands by justice a full consideration of his own rights to the disregard of others. We cannot discuss the subject here, but we suggest that there is as little sense in speaking of absolute justice as there is in speaking of absolute truth. Reality consists of relations and thus the relative alone is real. The absolute, in the rigid sense of the word, is a fiction.

The same is true of the infinite. Infinitude is not a real thing, not a concrete object, not an actualised existence. To treat infinitude as if it were a thing leads to absurdities. Infinitude is a possibility; it is an unlimited procedure, a state of things fraught with unbounded potentialities. Nothing is infinite, but everything contains infinitude. Man is not infinite, at a given moment he is finite; but he holds infinitude in his soul.

The phrase that the finite cannot comprehend the infinite, or that only an infinite being can understand infinitude, is not (as is generally assumed) a truism but a falsehood. Infinitude (I mean the idea of infinitude) is perfectly clear and is even simpler than finitude. Infinitude is only unthinkable if the attempt is made to substantialise it into a concrete thing. In our boldest flight of imagination we cannot represent a thing that is actually infinite, because it is an impossible and self-contradictory assumption. But for that reason the idea of infinitude is not a vain fiction; it serves useful purposes and there are conditions in the actual world (especially in the domains of space and time) to which it finds an appropriate application.

Mr. Merton's choice of Mr. Spencer for showing the looseness of philosophical argument is perhaps unfortunate, as Mr. Spencer ought to be considered, not as a philosopher, but as a brilliant dilettante. This statement may be startling to many whose knowledge of philosophy is limited to Spencerianism, but it will not be unexpected to professional philosophers. Yet I grant that Mr. Merton might have made as strong a case if he had chosen Hegel, or Kant, or Aristotle, or Plato, for even the great philosophers are sometimes guilty of most flagrant inconsistencies; *interdum bonus dormitat Homerus.* In the mean time philosophers will be wise to mind the complaints of laymen such as are voiced by our correspondent. Philosophy is not and should not be a mere intellectual legerdemain. Philosophy should provide people with the daily bread of their spiritual needs. All the sciences ultimately exist for the purpose of satisfying some practical need and the practical needs unto which philosophy ministers are the most universal and most urgent of all. Let us philosophers mind the children's cry for bread, and let us cease to offer them stones. P. C.

REJOINDER OF MR. SETH D. MERTON.

I return herewith your sheets of "editorial comment." I am afraid that you find in my article more complaint against philosophy than I intend. My feeling toward philosophy is warm. I think that philosophy has the answer to our problems, and my only complaint is that she hesitates to proclaim it. Agreeing that the "full" truth (i. e., the absolute truth)[1] is not attainable by men she holds out the hope that maybe, after all, we may some day attain to it. The whole world, it sometimes seems to me, refuses to stand firmly for its acknowledgment of our imperfection, when its very wabbling on this point creates most of our "problems." I do not expect common sense to stop wabbling so long as philosophers wabble.

It is not that I blame the philosophers especially. It is not a case for blaming at all. I criticise the philosophers because, as things stand in the world, it seems to be up to them to rectify matters—if ever they are to be rectified in this respect. And I criticise them for our common fault only in the forlorn hope that they may yet see their opportunity.

---

[1] There is a difference between the statement that "absolute truth is not attainable" and that ' absolute truth does not exist." In my conception of philosophy truth is always a relation between subject and object. Accordingly it is always relative, and the idea of absolute truth is self-contradictory. The same is true of "absolute justice." Justice is always a relation and depends upon special circumstances in which the demands of both parties are of great importance.—EDITOR.

While I say there should be no room in life for philosophising I do *not* say there is no room for philosophers. I mean that there is but *one* philosophy that our *actions* warrant. I mean that this one philosophy will always need to be taught, and the reasons why there can be no other must be constantly explained to new generations as they arrive. I cannot imagine a higher calling in life than to be such a philosopher.

If my article reads like a general condemnation of philosophy I would not on any account wish it printed.

Kindly start with me at the concrete end of this "justice" business. Unionists declare that certain conditions which they desire would be "fair." Economists approve. Papers like *The Outlook* endorse. Well-meaning people, by the million, chime in. Then, of course, the commercial press "hops on." A moral quality is presently found to have been imported, from nowhere, into the question. We are ready to turn the world upside-down in order to get things "right" and "just." We forget that it cannot ever be done. Call the attempt nonsense and Spencer is thrown at you. I agree that Spencer was a dilettante, but especially I agree that he was a brilliant one, and he shed a lot of light. But he looked forward to a time when finite life should have become automatically perfect, i. e., statical, knowing well that life, so long as it is life, is dynamical. He wabbled just as the philosopher wabbles who clings to the hope of ultimate attainment of the "full" truth after he has, in a cooler mood, definitely set that hope aside. Fortunately our instinct is better than our philosophy. They haven't *thought* out anything, perhaps, in Colorado, but at last men have been driven to the only alternative, and they are *fighting* things out, as we must eventually fight them out here and elsewhere unless we can somehow be made to remember that our only conceivable working rule of fairness (i. e., of justice) is the law, and that while the world may in time voluntarily adopt our point of view as to the justice of this or of that, there is positively no way of *enforcing* our view even though Theodore Roosevelt, Mr. Mitchell, Dr. Lyman Abbott, and all the rest combine as one man for the effort.

Let a layman rail and men will say that he is off his beat—he speaks of matters philosophical. So be it, if only the philosophers would attend to the job. But the philosopher wants to dig out the *full* truth before he will commit himself dogmatically to those acknowledgments which his *actions* exhibit.

I have had too much consideration and advantage from philosophers to be willing to risk giving offence without being understood.

I leave the matter thus in your hands. S. D. MERTON.

ST. LOUIS, MISSOURI.

BOOK REVIEWS.

Histoire de la Langue Universelle. Par *L. Couturat*, docteur ès lettres, et *L. Leau*, docteur ès sciences; respectively Treasurer and General Secretary of the "Délégation pour l'adoption d'une langue auxiliaire internationale." Paris: Librairie Hachette et Cie. 1903.

Those who wish to study the history of man's aspiration to create a universal language can have no better source of information than this stately volume of 576 pages which rehearses the development of the idea, beginning with Mersenne and bringing it up to date by announcements of the very latest attempts at creating a panglossy in one form or another. The authors are the most enthusiastic leaders of the movement, and they act, M. Couturat as treasurer, M. Leau as general secretary, of a society which at the Paris Exposition in 1900 held a congress devoted to the purpose of making a propaganda for an international language.

The idea of MM. Couturat and Leau is not that an international language should replace the existing national languages but that it should serve as an auxiliary international means of communication between representatives of different nationality. The need of such an auxiliary international language is not denied by any one, and its utility is also generally recognised; there is only a difference of opinion as to the acceptability of the several propositions that have so far been made. Volapük enjoyed an ephemeral triumph, but its failure could be predicted by those who were familiar with its vocabulary and grammar. Other propositions have been made in recent times, and judging from the comments of the book in the form of a postscript on page 569, made while the book went to press, they are still being made, three new propositions being mentioned as having appeared in 1903.

The first one to mention a universal language is Descartes, the great philosopher who by general consent is placed at the beginning of modern philosophy. He expresses his opinion on the problem in a letter of November 20, 1629, to P. Mersenne, a friend and correspondent of his who had sent him a Latin prospectus written by an unknown author containing six propositions in favor of creating a universal language. Descartes discusses point after point and treats the idea as quite feasible, but it is characteristic of the philosopher that he loses sight of the practical feature and speaks of "a philosophical language" of which he expects the elucidation of philosophical ideas without considering the practical result of benefitting the exchange of thought of the common a-lack-a-day life.

A very interesting pamphlet on Universal Language appeared in 1661, written by George Dalgarno, a Scotchman, born at Aberdeen about 1626, for some time director of a private school at Guernesey, later on at Oxford; he died 1687. Dalgarno published a book on a method of instruction for deaf mutes under the title of *Didascalocophus* in 1680. His book on Universal Language, after the fashion of those days written in Latin, bore the title, *Ars Signorum, vulgo Character universalis et Lingua Philosophica* (London, 1661), and it propounds a philosophical language of a universal character. In the sub-title which is significant, he declares that through it, people of different languages will in the space of two weeks be able to communicate all that they have in their mind concerning common things, not less intelligently either in writing or in speech, than in their own vernacular. He adds further that thereby our young men will more quickly and easily imbibe the principles of philosophy and the practice of true logic than from the current philosophical writings.

Dalgarno was followed by another Scotchman, Sir Thomas Urquhart (or Urchard) of Cromarty (1611-1660), known through his translation of *Rabelais* which has become classical in English. He published a treatise under the title *Logopandecteision, or an Introduction to the Universal Language* (London, 1653), but Sir Thomas did not enter into details and presents merely the theory of a Universal Language without suggesting either a vocabulary or a grammar.

These two Scotchmen most probably drew their inspiration from John Wilkins, Bishop of Chester (1640-1672) and one of the most eminent scientists of England, the founder of the Royal Society of London and its first secretary. Twenty years before the appearance of Dalgarno's book he published an essay on cryptography, or a method of secret communication. Afterwards Wilkins undertook to improve Mr. Dalgarno's philosophical language, but upon the whole his classification of ideas and other methods are the same.

The comments of Leibnitz on the subject are very important but they are scattered over his numerous works. This great thinker, the founder of the Royal Academy of the Sciences, of Berlin, did not devote to the problem a special essay, but M. Couturat, who is perhaps the best Leibnitz scholar now living, has collected Leibnitz's utterances even from books that are as yet unedited and quotes them in his edition of Leibnitz's works.[1]

---

[1] *Opuscules et fragments inédits de Leidnitz*, éd. Couturat, pp. 27-28: Paris: Alcan. 1903.

A new practical attempt was made by Delormel, a Frenchman, who during the French Revolution offered his proposition of a universal language to the National Convention and published a pamphlet on the subject in the year 3 of the Republic (1795) at Paris.[1]

There are several propositions to be mentioned; Sudre's Solresol, a music-language, and an obvious failure; Grosselén's Symbol Language, a kind of spoken pasigraphy; Vidal and Letellier's Letter Script; Soto's Ochando, Renouvier's Linguistic Society; Reimann's Etymological Language; Maldant's Natural Language; the Spokit of Dr. Nikolas, Hilbe's Number Language, and Dietrich's Neutral Art Language, all of them artificial constructions *a priori*, some of them absolute failures, and none of them easy enough to be acquired without difficulties and much study.

The first universal language that seemed promising and became a temporary success was "Volapük," invented by Rev. Schleyer, a Catholic clergyman of Litzelstetten near Constance in the German Duchy of Baden. He succeeded in creating a great enthusiasm for his world speech, but in spite of his numerous disciples his attempt was soon neglected and may now be considered as having become an event of the history of the past.

The latest and most significant attempt to replace Volapük was made by a Russian physician, Dr. Louis-Lazarre Zamenhof, born at Bielostok, Russia in 1859. He called his universal language "Esperanto" and it seems that MM. Couturat and Leau are looking with great favor upon this most prominent proposition of recent times.

The American Philosophical Society took up the question in 1887 without coming to a definite conclusion. They adopted, however, several principles which should be mentioned. They declared that in the construction of a universal language there was no objection to a mixture. All international languages, "pidgin-English" and even English itself are the results of mixtures. As to spelling they declared that orthography should be absolutely phonetic. Every letter should always have the same sound and it was recommendable to let it be in agreement with the most common usage among the Aryan nations. There should be no diphthongs nor double consonants (such as "ch," "sh," "th"). The sense should never depend on intonation, accent, quantity of vowels or inflection of voice. There should be only five vowels, *a*, *e*, *i*, *o*, *u*, pronounced as in Italian. Gutturals, aspirants, nasals, sibilants should be avoided. The characters should be the so-called Latin letters, adjusted in a fashion so as to combine all letters without lifting the hand in writing a complete word. All words should be easily pronounced

[1] *Projet d'une langue universelle, présenté à la Convention nationale, par* le Citoyen Delormel. Paris, *Chez l'auteur, au ci-devant Collège de la Marche*. An 3.

and pleasing to the ear. The heaping of consonants should be avoided and brevity aimed at. The vocabulary should be derived from the six principal languages and the grammar should be a simplification of the Aryan grammars.

Other recent attempts to be mentioned are Henderson's *Lingua*, Bernhard's *Lingua Franca Nuova*, Lauda's *Kosmos*, Hoinix's *Anglo-Franca*, Stempfl's *Myrana*, recently simplified (1894) in his *Communia*, Dr. Rosa's *Nov Latin*, Julius Lott's *Mundolingue*, Dr. Liptay's *Langue Catholique*, Heintzeler's *Universala*, Beermann's *Novilatiin*, Puchner's *Nuove-Roman*, Kürschner's *Lingua Komun*, Rosenberger's *Idiom Neutral* of the International Academy, etc., etc.

We cannot say that there is any hope for any one of these schemes that has any chance of permanent success, but the idea itself is noteworthy and no one can be blind to the fact that the interest which the movement has gained in recent years is constantly increasing.

THE SIX SYSTEMS OF INDIAN PHILOSOPHY. By the *Right Hon. Prof. Max Müller, K. M.*, late Foreign Member of the French Institute. New Edition. London, New York, and Bombay; Longmans, Green & Co. 1903.

The Six Systems of Indian Philosophy was the last work of Prof. Max Müller published only two months before the beginning of his fatal illness, and the widow, Mrs. Georgiana Max Müller, had so many letters from friends in India as well as in England expressing a desire for a more accessible edition of it than the one in the Professor's collected works that she had it republished by Longmans, Green & Co., in a cheaper form and as a separate volume in order to bring the book within easy reach of his many admirers in both countries. While Mrs. Müller hesitated to do so because she thinks the book shows already some signs of her late husband's illness, and that the materials are here perhaps less clearly gathered up and set before the reader than in his other works, we think that on the contrary the work shows Prof. Max Müller at his best; his thoughts are fully matured and the book contains passages which are as brilliant as anything he ever wrote. There are books on the same subject among which the one by Prof. Richard Garbe[1] of Tubingen deserves special mention for setting forth the meaning of the six darsanas, the orthodox systems of India, most succinctly and in clearest terms, but Max Müller excels the scholarly Garbe by the literary finish and the presentation of interesting detail. Thus the present book clothes with life the dry bones of the old Brahman thinkers

[1] *Philosophy of Ancient India.* Chicago: The Open Court Pub. Co.

and we see them risen to life again, for it is Prof. Max Müller's forte to tell the story of a budding thought in the most attractive way, finding out those points which interest us most deeply.

In the present volume he characterises Hindu philosophy in general, describes the Vedas, Vedic gods, originated under philosophical influences, and then points out the significance of the Upanishads which he dates at about 700 B. C. Prof. Max Müller describes the period in which they were composed as follows:

"For gaining an insight into the early growth of Indian philosophic thought, this period is in fact the most valuable; though of systematised philosophy, in our sense of the word, it contains, as yet, little or nothing. As we can feel that there is electricity in the air, and that there will be a storm, we feel, on reading the Upanishads, that there is philosophy in the Indian mind, and that there will be thunder and lightning to follow soon. Nay, I should even go a step further. In order to be able to account for what seem to us mere sparks of thought, mere guesses at truth, we are driven to admit a long familiarity with philosophic problems before the time that gave birth to the Upanishads which we possess.

"The Upanishads contain too many technical terms, such as Brahman, Atman, Dharma, Vrata, Yoga, Mimamsa, and many more, to allow us to suppose that they were the products of one day or of one generation. Even if the later systems of philosophy did not so often appeal themselves to the Upanishads as their authorities, we could easily see for ourselves that, though flowing in very different directions, like the Ganges and Indus, these systems of philosophy can all be traced back to the same distant heights from which they took their rise. And as India was fertilised, not only by the Ganges and Indus, but by ever so many rivers and rivulets, all pointing to the Snowy Mountains in the North, we can see the Indian mind also being nourished through ever so many channels, all starting from a vast accumulation of religious and philosophic thought of which we seem to see the last remnants only in our Upanishads, while the original springs are lost to us forever."

Chapter IV. is devoted mainly to the Vedanta philosophy, the aim of which is to understand the meaning of the Veda. Chapter V. sets forth the Mimamsa, Chapter VI. the Samkhya, Chapter VII. the Yoga, Chapter VIII the Nyaya, and Chapter IX. the Vaiseshika philosophy. Professor Garbe in his treatise above referred to, covers the same ground in 88 pages to which Max Müller devotes 459 pages, and what an abundance of interesting details turn up during the discussion.

The ancient Hindu has a philosophical turn of mind. At the time when the Veda originated, philosophy and religion were hardly as yet differentiated. The tendency to monism in philosophy and monotheism in religion is plainly rceptible, especially in the conception of the Visve Devas, which are the gods their totality.[1]

Monotheism is formed in several ways, but all the attempts to produce philosophical theology tend in the same direction and even then, when the a of the deity as a totality has been conceived, the Brahman feels dis-isfied, for God must still be higher, and he finds God in the "Braham," the "atman" (i. e., the self), or the "Tad Ekam" which means in eral translation "That One." The one highest god receives several names, ong which Prajapati (i. e., the lord of creatures), is one of the most nmon, and we find in an ancient hymn the following passage:

"O Prajapati, no other but thou has held together all these things; atever we desire in sacrificing to thee, may that be ours, may we be lords of wealth."

Prof. Max Müller adds the following exposition on the rise of notheism:

"With this conception of Prajapati as the lord of all created things and the supreme deity, the monotheistic yearning was satisfied even though existence of other gods was not denied. And what is curious is that we t the same attempt repeated again and again. Like Visvakarman and Pra-pati we find such names as Purusha, man; Hiranyagarbha, golden germ; ana, breath, spirit; Skambha, support (X. 81, 7): Dhatri, maker; Vid-tri, arranger; Namadha, name-giver of the gods; and others, all names the Eka Deva, the one god, though not, like Prajapati, developed into ll-grown divine personalities. These names have had different fates in later mes. Some meet us again during the Brahmana period and in the Athar-ana hymns, or rise to the surface in the more modern pantheon of India: thers have disappeared altogether after a short existence, or have resumed heir purely predicative character. But the deep groove which they made in he Indian mind has remained, and to the present day the religious wants of he great mass of the people of India seem satisfied through the idea of the ne supreme god, exalted above all other gods, whatever names may have een given to him. Even the gods of modern times, such as Siva and Vishnu, ay goddesses even, such as Kali, Parvati, Durga, are but new names for what was originally embodied in the lord of created things (Prajapati) and the maker of all things (Visvakarman). In spite of their mythological disguises, these modern gods have always retained, in the eyes of the more enlightened of their worshippers, traces of the character of omnipotence that was assigned even in Vedic times to the one supreme god, the god above all gods."

---

[1] *Visva*, i. e., "together" is different from *sarva*, "all." The Visve Devas are not "all gods" but the *Gesammtgotter*, the gods taken together, the totality

A beautiful hymn of a philosophical belief in God is the Nasadiya hymn which reads as follows:

"There was then neither what is nor what is not, there was no sky, nor the heaven which is beyond. What covered? Where was it, and in whose shelter? Was the water the deep abyss (in which it lay)?

"Darkness there was, in the beginning all this was a sea without light; the germ that lay covered by the husk, that One was born by the power of heat (Tapas).

"Love overcame it in the beginning, which was the seed springing from mind; poets having searched in their heart found by wisdom the bond of what is in what is not.

"Their ray which was stretched across, was it below or was it above? There were seed-bearers, there were powers, self-power below, and will above.

"Who then knows, who has declared it here, from whence was born this creation? The gods came later than this creation, who then knows whence it arose?

"He from whom this creation arose, whether he made it or did not make it, the Highest Seer in the highest heaven, he forsooth knows; or does even he not know?"

Another hymn expressing the desire to worship that god alone who is worthy of adoration (reiterating the refrain "Who is the god to whom we should offer the sacrifice?") is not less interesting. It reads as follows:

"In the beginning there arose the germ of golden light, Hiranyagarbha; he was the one born lord of all that is. He stablished the earth and this sky.

"Who is the god to whom we should offer our sacrifice?

"He who gives life, he who gives strength; whose command all the bright gods revere; whose shadow is immortality and mortality (gods and men).

"Who is the god to whom we should offer our sacrifice?

"He who through his power became the sole king of this breathing and slumbering world—he who governs all, man and beast.

"Who is the god to whom we should offer our sacrifice?

"He through whose greatness these snowy mountains are, and the sea, they say, with the Rasa, the distant river, he whose two arms these regions are.

"Who is the god to whom we should offer our sacrifice?

"He through whom the sky is strong, and the earth firm, he through whom the heaven was established, nay the highest heaven, he who measured the light in the air.

"Who is the god to whom we should offer our sacrifice?

"He to whom heaven and earth (or, the two armies) standing firm by his help, look up, trembling in their minds, he over whom the rising sun shines forth.

"Who is the god to whom we should offer our sacrifice?

"When the great waters went everywhere, holding the germ and generating fire, thence he arose who is the sole life of the bright gods.

"Who is the god to whom we should offer our sacrifice?

"He who by his might looked even over the waters, which gave strength and produced the sacrifice, he who alone is god above all gods.

"Who is the god to whom we should offer our sacrifice?

"May he not destroy us, he, the creator of the earth, or he, the righteous, who created the heaven, he who also created the bright and mighty waters.

"Who is the god to whom we should offer our sacrifice?"

Orthodox in the traditions of ancient India does not mean either theistic or atheistic, but simply implies a recognition of the Veda as divine revelation. All tendencies that would raise objections to the Vedas were regarded as heterodox, and it is strange that Brihaspati, the teacher of the gods, is supposed to have been the inaugurator of heterodoxy. The Brahman argument is that Brihaspati, for the sake of the preservation of the gods and for the destruction of the Asuras, the demons, decided to teach error so that the demons should be misguided to their own perdition; yet gods and Brahmans should know that it will be injurious to study that false knowledge, and so it is branded as heretical. It is commonly called after Barhaspatya, a follower of Brihaspati. Prof. Max Müller explains the situation of philosophical speculation in India as follows:

"It must have been observed how these six, or, if we include the Barhaspatya, these seven systems of philosophy, though they differ from each other and criticise each other, share nevertheless so many things in common that we can only understand them as products of one and the same soil, though cultivated by different hands. They all promise to teach the nature of the soul, and its relation to the god-head or to a Supreme Being. They all undertake to supply the means of knowing the nature of that Supreme Being, and through that knowledge to pave the way to supreme happiness. They all share the conviction that there is suffering in the world which is something irregular, has no right to exist, and should therefore be removed. Though there is a strong religious vein running through the six so-called orthodox systems, they belong to a phase of thought in which not only has the belief in the many Vedic gods long been superseded by a belief in a Supreme Deity, such as Prajapati, but this phase also has been left behind to make room for a faith in a Supreme Power, or in the Godhead which has no name but Brahman or Sat, 'I am what I am.' The Hindus themselves make indeed a distinction between the six orthodox systems. They have no word for orthodox; nay, we saw that some of these systems, though atheistic, were nevertheless treated as permissible doctrines, because they acknowledged the authority of the Veda. Orthodox might therefore be replaced by Vedic; and if atheism seems to us incompatible with Vedism or Vedic orthodoxy, we must remember that atheism with Indian philosophers means something very different from what it means with us. It means a denial of an active, busy, personal or humanised god only, who is called Isvara, the Lord. But behind him and above him Hindu philosophers recognised a Higher Power, whether they called it Brahman, or Paramatman, or Purusha. It was the denial of that reality which constituted a Nastika, a real heretic, one who could say of this invisible, yet omnipresent Being, Na asti, 'He is not.'. Buddha therefore, as well as Brihaspati, the Charvaka, was a Nastika, while both the Yoga and the Samkhya, the former Sesvara, with an Isvara, the other Anisvara, without an Isvara, the one theistic, the other atheistic, could be recognised as orthodox or Vedic."

The most prominent representative of heretics is Buddha and, although Prof. Max Müller is decidedly an adherent of Brahman Philosophy in contrast to Buddhism, which denies the existence of the atman, the favorite idea of Brahmanism, he speaks very highly of Buddha, saying:

"Out of the midst of this whirlpool of philosophical opinions there rises the form of Buddha, calling for a hearing, at first, not as the herald of any brand-new philosophy, which he has to teach, but rather as preaching a new gospel to the poor. I cannot help thinking that it was Buddha's marked personality, far more than his doctrine, that gave him the great influence on his contemporaries and on so many generations after his death

"Whether he existed or not, such as he is described to us in the Suttas, there must have been some one, not a mere name, but a real power in the history of India, a man who made a new epoch in the growth of Indian philosophy, and still more of Indian religion and ethics."

There is no need of recommending the book to the reader. The passages quoted speak for themselves. Even where we cannot follow Prof. Max Müller in his arguments or take issue with his propositions, we admire the penetration of his thoughts and the brilliancy of his style.

P. C.

Henri Poincaré, Wissenschaft und Hypothese. Autorisierte deutsche Ausgabe mit erläuternden Anmerkungen. Von *F.* und *L. Lindemann*. Leipsic: B. G. Teubner. 1904.

Professor Ferdinand Lindemann, one of the leading mathematicians of Germany, has undertaken the laudable task of translating a series of essays written by his French colleague, Prof. Henri Poincaré, and Mrs. Lindemann the translator's wife, has done so much of the literary labor of the work that her name also appears on the title-page.

Poincaré's position in the philosophy of mathematics is in its main outlines well known to mathematicians and perhaps also to those of our readers who have studied the essays which he contributed to *The Monist*, but we offer here a résumé in quotations, methodically compiled by Professor Lindemann, which covers almost the entire field and affords a bird's-eye view of Professor Poincaré's position as regards the foundation of geometry and arithmetic and the definition of mechanics. Professor Lindemann selects the following passages from Poincaré as specially characteristic:[1]

"Our understanding has a direct conception of the power of mind (which implies the conviction that an infinite repetition of the same procedure can be imagined), and experience can be only an opportunity to make use of it and to become conscious of it." (Page 13.)

This is good Kantian doctrine according to which experience is not the main source of our knowledge. But let us proceed in our quotations:

"The geometrical axioms are neither synthetic judgments *a priori* nor experimental facts. They are determinations based upon general consent, which is to say, they are concealed definitions. Geometry is not a science of experience, though experience guides us in the proposition of axioms. Experience does not decide which geometry is the right one but which is the most convenient one. It is just as irrational to investigate whether the fundamental principles of geometry are true or false as it would be to ask whether the metric systems be wrong or false." (Pages 51, 73, and 138.)

Next in order are three quotations on physics and mechanics:

"The law of gravitation which in some special cases has been proved by experience can be boldly universalised, because we know that in all cases experience can neither prove nor disprove it." (Page 99.)

"The principle of action and reaction being equal cannot be regarded as an experimental law but only as a definition." (Page 102.)

"Experience can serve as a basis for the principles of mechanics but it can never contradict them." (Page 107.)

"The principles of mechanics are based on consent and are concealed definitions. They are derived from experimental laws. These laws are, as it were, presented as principles, for our understanding attributes to them absolute validity." (Page 140.)

Without taking exception to Poincaré's statements as to the validity of a universalisation of gravitation, we wonder at the argument which he adduces in its favor. That experience can neither prove nor disprove a generalisation, is no sufficient reason to make us bold. Further, that experience can never

[1] The pages in parentheses refer to Professor Lindemann's translation.

contradict the principles of mechanics is exactly the crux of the main problem. Finally, we must express our doubt as to the propriety of two terms, viz., "consent" and "definition." Both are employed by Poincaré and occur in the last quoted passage. It is not a mere "consent" if the physicist claims an absolute validity for his principles of mechanics, and mathematical axioms are more than "definitions"; they are definitions, the formulation of which is inevitably forced upon the mathematician. Their inevitableness is their most significant feature.

After this digression we revert to Poincaré:

"If one wants to regard the principle of the conservation of energy in its sweeping universality and apply it to the universe, one sees it as it were volatilised and nothing remains except the sentence: 'There is a something that remains constant.'" (Page 134.)

"Experiment is the sole source of truth." (Page 142.)

This statement must be understood so as not to contradict previous propositions savoring of Kantian apriorism. It means simply that experiment is the sole method of extending our knowledge of facts, for Poincaré adds that experiment must be improved. Something has to be added. He says:

"Mathematical physics has the duty to guide generalisation so as to increase the efficiency of science." (Page 144.)

"Each generalisation presupposes to a certain extent the faith in the unity and simplicity of nature." "But" adds he, "it is not sure that nature is simple." (Page 152.)

We conclude this summary of Poincaré's views with three more passages:

"The purpose of mathematical science is not to explain the true nature of things. Her sole aim is to interconnect physical laws with which experience makes us acquainted, but which cannot be expressed without the assistance of mathematics." (Page 212.)

"We care little whether ether really exists. It is essential, however, that everything happens as if it existed and that this hypothesis is convenient for an explanation of phenomena." (Page 212.)

"The goal which it is possible for science to attain is a cognition of things in their interrelations. Outside of these relations there is no cognisable reality." (Page xiii.)

Professor Lindemann adds in characterisation of Poincaré's standpoint:

"The reader will notice that we have thus returned to Kant's proposition according to which the understanding does not derive laws from nature but prescribes them to nature and that the highest legislator of nature lies in ourselves, i. e., in our understanding or, as Goethe expresses it: 'Everything transient is but a simile,'—a simile which refers to the same thought if one is conscious of the relativity of all knowledge. All such universal propositions are possessed of a high subjective significance, for they satisfy in a certain sense our need of a completion of inquiry and cognition. For the empirical inquirer, however, there is no such completion. Every general proposition needs according to him a continued investigation under the guidance of experience, and to him it is valid only so long as he finds himself in agreement with experience, whether we have to deal with a universal necessity of our mind or with a special doctrine of the exact sciences." * * * "Even those who do share the purely empirical standpoint" adds Professor Lindemann, "will feel the need of pursuing the leading principles throughout all the intricate paths of the exact sciences, and they will gladly accept the guidance of the author (Poincaré) in order to temporarily remove the exuberant vines of detail and to gain an outlook upon the interstices between the firm tree trunks of experience for the sake of orientation. The apparent ease with which our author attains his aim is the main cause that will prove attractive; it did so at least with me.

"We must not lay main stress upon the results gained in the present work but upon the method of treatment, and the method which has been pursued by M. Poincaré is the one which during the last decades has led to satisfactory results in the field of the foundations of geometry and arithmetic. It consists in replacing an hypothesis, admissible according to our experience, when its relation to other theories is to be investigated, by an assumption which would satisfy our logical thought without agreeing with experience. In this way we are enabled to make the mutual dependence of the different hypotheses or axioms conceptually evident."

Professor Lindemann has not only selected essays which allow us to understand Poincaré's thought as a systematic whole, but has also added to them explanations and notes and in addition furnished literary references for a further study of the several questions.

Considering the difficulties of the translation in which Mrs. Lindemann has been a faithful helpmeet to her husband, we must acknowledge that the work could scarcely be surpassed. The work reads as if it had originally been written in German. The subject-matter of the work is discussed in four parts: I., number and magnitude; II., space; III., "Kraft" (i. e., force or energy); IV., nature.

The first part contains articles on the nature of mathematical and syllogistic deduction, verification and proof, the elements of arithmetic, algebraic methods, recurrence, induction, mathematical construction, mathematical magnitude and experience, the incommensurable, the physical, and the mathematical continuum, measurable magnitude, the physical and the mathematical continuum of many dimensions.

The second part discusses such subjects as the several non-Euclidean geometries, those of Lobatchevski and of Riemann, that of curved space and the fourth geometry, so called, and Lie's proposition. Further, geometrical space and space conception, the space of vision, the space of touch, and of motion, change of place, solid objects and geometry, the laws of homogeneity, the non-Euclidean world, the four-dimensional world, geometry and astronomy, law and relativity, the applicability of experiment, and a ventilation of the question, "What is a point?"

Among the articles treated in the third part are the following: the principle of inertia, the law of acceleration, anthropomorphic mechanics, the school of the thread (referring to Andrade's method which implies the use of a thread), relative and absolute motion, the methods of Newton, energy and thermo-dynamics.

The fourth part opens with a discussion of the significance of experiment and generalisation, the unity of nature, the use of hypothesis, the origin of mathematical physics, the theories of modern physics, physics and mechanicalism, the present state of science, the calculus of probabilities, *rouge et noir*, the probability of causes, the theory of mistakes, etc., optics and electricity, Fresnel's and Maxwell's theories, the mechanical explanation of physical phenomena, electro-dynamics, Ampère's and Helmholtz's theories and their difficulties, Maxwell's theories, Rowland's experiments, and Lorentz's theory.

The annotations by Professor Lindemann are a valuable addition comprising ninety pages, almost one-third of the whole volume.

The work is important for the student of mathematics and especially the philosophy of mathematics, for it summarises the life work of a prominent thinker along these lines.

GRUNDRISS DER RELIGIONSPHILOSOPHIE. Von *D. Dr. A. Dorner*. Leipsic: Dürr'schen Buchhandlung. 1903. Pp. xviii, 448.

One of the leading and most prominent theologians of Germany expounds in the present volume of over 400 pages the theological convictions that may be regarded typical of orthodox protestant theology modernised by philosophy and science. Our author recognises philosophy as an independent science, but assures himself of the ground which is taken by religious philosophy, and he comes to the conclusion that the object of faith presupposes something real and objective; it cannot be the product of mere subjective fancy, but all the data of our experiences point to it that we have to deal not with hallucinations but with experiences based on actual facts. The province of metaphysics according to Dorner is "to comprehend the being which constitutes the basis of existence of the world" and this being cannot be a simple substance, nor can it be a manifold, a combination of many realities of spiritual monads, but "it must be one substance conceived in such a way as to show that it is the source of the many, the source of all life, the source of manifoldness and of all intelligence in the world" (pp. 25-26). Professor Dorner passes in review the several attempts made to satisfy this ideal of metaphysics and then contemplates the metaphysics of absolute being of the world of spirit and the relation of metaphysics to ethics and religious philosophy.

Religion to Professor Dorner is the relation that obtains between God and man. He devotes much space to the phenomenology of the religious process in mankind and discusses first the ideals of the several religions, and then the absolute ideal of religion, finding the aim of the human mind centred in the ideal of a unity of intelligence with will. This ideal becomes manifest in the God-man which is characterised by an immanence of the divine spirit in the human spirit. Dorner rightly states (p. 117) that the Christ idea, the principle of the God-man, involves two sides, egoity and love, and he invents a new name for it, *Gottmenschkheit*, i. e., "God-man-hood."

In the chapters devoted to the problems of monotheism Dorner recapitulates the old and well-known proofs for the existence of God which he deems necessary in spite of the criticisms that there can be no absolute proof of the existence of God, for though the pious may be satisfied with the God-feeling, the demand of the intellect cannot be refused a satisfactory solution of the problem. He further enters into a psychological appreciation of faith and its psychological conditions.

A large part of the book, pages 287 to 406, is devoted to church institutions and the external forms in which faith finds its actualisation, viz., sacrifices, sacraments, revelations, miracles, prayer, contemplation, holy objects considered as symbols, symbolic actions, religious conviction expressed in words, language and writing, holy places, sacred times and the communion of the church. He further proves that there is no conflict between religion and morality, nor between religion and science, and least of all between religion and art. In reviewing the laws of religious life (pages 406 to 437), he views religion as a normative science, the laws of which are not necessary, as are laws of physics, but find expression in demands. Thus religion is closely connected with the teleology of natural laws, which is not incompatible with causation but forms a contrast to it. A reconciliation of the two kinds of causality forms the conclusion of Dorner's voluminous work. He grants that his views of natural law may be onesided because they require the assumption of divine action, but he is satisfied that divine action manifests itself in all stages of the spiritual development of the world.

We cannot help thinking that the theological modes of inquiry are antiquated and will have to be dropped even by the religious philosopher, but we take an interest in Dorner's book and views on account of the thoughtful and earnest personality that is revealed in the arguments and conclusions of his work.

Friedrich Nietzsche, Darstellung und Kritik. Von *Jakob J. Hollitscher, Ph.D.* Vienna and Leipsic: Wilhelm Braumüller. 1904. Pp. xiv, 270.

Among the Nietzsche literature this new work by Prof. Jakob J. Hollitscher is one of the most thoughtful and critical productions. No one denies that Nietzsche is full of contradictions, yet after all his propositions are derived from the character of this philosopher of anarchism, and Professor Hollitscher attempts to show the consistency of Nietzsche in spite of the contradictions that appear in his arguments, his logic, and his ideals. Nietzsche is an individualist and as such he advocates an atomistic social life. Society has no rights, the individual is everything. History does not exist for him. There is only a general struggle between individuals, and the general idea is that the overman, who is the individual which with all man's cunning has a dislike of the rights of others, will assert himself, but if the social atomism be correct, the ideal theory of the overman as the aim of all human development will necessarily collapse, for according to Nietzsche there is no evolution of society, and the individual is supreme.

The most original part of Professor Hollitscher's paper may probably be found in his conclusion that Nietzsche's conservatism, although it seems to contradict his radicalism, is simply the consistent result of his anarchistic principle. Proudhon said that every anarchist is at once the most radical and the most conservative man, and this appears plain in Nietzsche whose contempt for the herd is practically a justification of the most barbarous methods of tyrants in asserting their sovereignty. Nietzsche despises the ideals of democracy and recognises the privilege of the powerful to ignore and suppress the rights of the masses who are too weak to defend themselves. Professor Hollitscher says: "The philosopher Nietzsche is actually anarchistic, but he is anarchistic only for himself. He recognises above himself nothing that may guide, rule him or regulate his conduct except himself. His own conscience is the king whom he serves and to whom he looks with reverence, before whom he bows, and he justifies it in respect to his position which establishes in regard to others a complete absolutism, consisting in this that he is a philosopher." *Quod licet Jovi, non licet bovi.* This Latin proverb, "What is right for Jove is not right for the ox," is the basis of his anarchism. Translated in Nietzsche's interpretation, "What is allowed to Jove, because it is consistent with his nature and therefore necessary and just, should not be allowed to the ox as being contrary to his nature and therefore unjust," or simply in principle that this social form is quite compatible with conservatism is obvious, especially as it is based upon the same practice.

The spirit in which Hollitscher conceives his subject is characterised by the motto which he inscribes over his preface which is a quotation from

Eckermann *Colloquies with Goethe*. Goethe said: "I will reveal to you something and you will find it frequently verified in your life. All epochs which are regressive and decadent are subjective, but all the epochs that possess an objective tendency are progressive." Measured by Goethe's proposition Nietzsche is decidedly one of the strongest symptoms of a decadent epoch.

THE EDUCATIONAL THEORY OF IMMANUEL KANT. Translated and Edited by *Edward Franklin Buchner, Ph.D.* (Yale). Professor of Philosophy and Education in the University of Alabama. Philadelphia and London: J. B. Lippincott Company. 1904. Pp. xvi, 309.

Dr. Edward Franklin Buchner publishes in this fourth volume of Lippincott's Educational Series, a comprehensive and thorough exposition of Kant's educational theory, incorporating all the necessary data which a student of the subject would be in need of knowing: The chronology of Kant's life and writings; a history of Kant's "Lecture-Notes on Pedagogy"; the sources of Kant's educational theory, its philosophical basis; Kant's psychology; Kant's evolutionary and educational theories; Kant's conception of education; the division of educational activities; and finally a criticism of Kant's educational theory.

There are added also four pages of literature, English translations of Kant's writings.

The main body of the book contains a translation of Kant's "Lecture-Notes on Pedagogy" and selections on education from Kant's other writings. It goes without saying that whatever Kant says is of importance and of interest even where his ideas may be regarded as antiquated. Professor Buchner declares: "Kant was a pedagogue in the fullest and best sense of the term, and is another brilliant instance of the double truth that the true teacher must be philosophical, and that the true philosopher finds a perennial theme in the problems of education."

As an instance of Kant's views on education we quote from paragraphs 106-107 his advice in matters of religion, and we see at once the important rôle which his *Critique of Practical Reason* plays in practical affairs. Kant says (pp. 215-216):

"The reproaches of conscience will be without effect if it be not considered as the representative of God, who has His lofty seat above us, but who has also established a tribunal in us. On the other hand, if religion is not joined with a moral conscientiousness, it is without effect. Religion without moral conscientiousness is a superstitious worship. People imagine that they serve God when, for example, they praise Him and extol His power and His wisdom, without thinking how they can fulfil the divine laws; yes, without even knowing and searching out His power and His wisdom, etc. These praises are an opiate for the conscience of such people and a pillow on which they hope to sleep tranquilly.

"Children cannot comprehend all *religious concepts*, but a few, notwithstanding, must be imparted to them; only these should be more negative than positive. To make children repeat formulas is of no use, and produces only a false concept of piety. True reverence consists in acting according to God's will, and it is this that children must be taught. Care must be taken with children, as with one's self, that the name of God be not so often misused. Merely to use it in congratulation, even with pious intentions, is a profanation. The thought of God should fill a man with reverence every time he speaks His name, and he should therefore seldom use it, and never frivolously. The child must learn to feel respect for God as the master of his life and of the whole world; further, as the protector of man; and, finally, as his judge. It is said that Newton always stopped and meditated a moment whenever he spoke the name of God."

Noveau Programme de Sociologie. Esquisse d'une Introduction Générale à l'Étude des Sciences du Monde Surorganique, par *Eugène de Roberty*, Professeur a l'Université de Bruxelles, Vice-Président de l'Institut International de Sociologie. Paris: Félix Alcan, Éditeur. 1904. Pp. 268. Price, 5 fr.

Eugene Roberty, a native Russian who has found a more congenial home in Western Europe and is now Professor at the new University of Brussels, publishes in the present volume "a new programme of sociology," which he calls an attempt of a general introduction of the study of the sciences of the super-organic world. By "super-organic" he understands those important relations which are not represented in the organism of the individual, but constitute the factors of social relations. He traces the process of socialisation, and in this sense he contrasts collective psychology with individual psychology. His work consists of three divisions: The first part is a résumé of the fundamentals of the author's sociology, who, after a discussion of different hypotheses of the nature of the social phenomenon, offers his own solution, which he discovers in the most general law that governs the evolution of society, and which explains why and how a social state necessarily produces another which follows and replaces it. The second part is devoted to an inquisition of the main factors of civilization and progress. He regards inter-sexual love as a great æsthetic manifestation, as the prototype of the beautiful arts, and he finds in the ideal of liberty the determinant of the sociological development. Professor Roberty rejects the freedom of the will and speaks of it as the illusion of the *libre arbitre*. He deems that a new definition of the concept of liberty is needed which would set liberty in contrast to oppression. The third part is devoted to the new moral order which is to be established upon the basis of the sociological laws with the decay of the present relations and metaphysics that has become inevitable. A new formation must be expected and Professor Roberty prognosticates the rise of a new morality which will reanimate our hopes and our courage.

Transitional Eras in Thought with Special Reference to the Present Age. By *A. C. Armstrong, Ph.D.*, Professor of Philosophy in Wesleyan University. New York: The Macmillan Company. London: Macmillan & Co., Ltd. 1904. Pp. 347. Price, $2.00.

Prof. A. C. Armstrong discusses the conflict between science and religion, and confidently offers his solution of the problem as sound and rational. The present age, which like all eras of transition is decidedly marked by negativism, is a phase in the growth of mankind. He believes that though our religious views may be modified, they will be reformed in the struggle for truth. Theism is not endangered. "The grounds of theistic belief are numerous and varied; the complete argument for theism is cumulative, composed of many convergent lines of proof. To different minds the several elements which compose it appeal in different ways and with varying degrees of force. Not least important, however, and far from least in its coercive influence over the modern mind, is the conviction of the supreme significance of the theistic postulate. * * * The instinctive disposition of the human spirit to crown its feelings and its action, as it completes its thinking, by belief in a Supreme Spiritual Being, may be a delusive impulse rather than a mental tendency which is worthy of all trust. But these convictions and the ideal appreciation of their object, these strivings toward the assurance that God exists and reigns, themselves constitute a principal obstacle to the successful defence of the sceptical position. * * * Or to employ the more accurate, because more simple and spontaneous, words of St. Augustine, 'God has made us for Himself, and our heart is restless till it finds rest in Him.'"

Our author comes to the following conclusion:

"In order to complete the advance from a negative to a positive age, developmental synthesis must conform to two different yet related standards: it must satisfy the demand for conclusions in accord with the results of advancing knowledge; it must meet the need for principles fitted to serve as the foundation and the vehicles of a vigorous life. These constitute the criteria by which the value of constructive movements is to be tested. * * * Thought must become conviction, reason find an ally in will, belief pass over into joyous faith, for so only can they accomplish their appointed work."

Die Willensfreiheit. Eine Kritisch-Systematische Untersuchung von *Oskar Pfister, Dr. Phil.,* Pfarrer in Zürich. Berlin: Georg Reimer. 1904. Pp. xii, 405.

The present volume is a defense of the freedom of the will which is done, if not always with acumen, yet with great circumspection and with the introduction of much detail argument, mainly based upon lines of thought after the style of the Kantian school, as interpreted among liberal theologians. Obviously the author is first of all a pastor and educator, and incidentally a philosopher, and so naturally the last chapter discusses the consequences of the question in the domain of religion, which is perhaps the most important part of the whole book. Dr. Pfister is orthodox enough to be a conservative representative of Christianity, but he assimilates some of the Christian dogmas to his philosophical conceptions. He finds, e. g., the key to the Christological conception in the loving sacrifice of Jesus, which is the greatest possible actualisation of human duty. For that very reason he attempts to conciliate the ideals of justice and mercy in God the Father which the popular conception finds better united in the person of Christ. God is rather feared than loved, which Mr. Pfister characterizes in the story of the child who on his death-bed is asked whether he would not gladly go to Heaven: "Yes I would like to go to Heaven" replied the dying child, "if I but knew that God were not at home." This serves as an explanation why the average man shows more confidence to the more human figure of Christ than to God himself who is made a bugbear of the moralist, and Dr. Pfister claims (we think, rightly) is mostly prayed with a thought of Christ than with a thought of God. The book closes with the significant words which to our author practically settle the whole problem, "and the secret is this: where the spirit of the Lord is, there is freedom."

A Short History of Monks and Monasteries. By *Alfred Wesley Wishart.* Sometime Fellow in Church History in the University of Chicago. Albert Brandt: Trenton, New Jersey. 1902. Pp. 452. Price, $1.50.

This book, now in its second edition, is not so much a history, not even a short one, of institution of monasticism, as a series of contemplations on the institution itself as instanced in several orders that have been successively founded. The author claims that "the monastic institution was never entirely good or entirely bad. In periods of general degradation there were beautiful exceptions in monasteries ruled by pure and powerful abbots. From the beginning various monasteries soon departed from their discipline by sheltering iniquity and laziness, while other establishments faithfully observed the rules. But during the eighth, ninth, and tenth centuries there was a widespread decline in the spirit of devotion and a shameful relaxation of monastic discipline." Our author claims in the preface: that the power of monasticism "was practically broken in the sixteenth century and no new orders of importance or new types have arisen since that time." However, he should bear in mind that the Jesuits are a reaction against the reformation and thus one of the most powerful orders is a product of the Roman Church since the reformed churches broke away from its fold. Moreover in modern times the Paulist brothers, founded by Hecker in America, exhibit a decidedly new type of their own which, though faithful to the Catholic Church, shows monasticism modernized and reformed. The book is interesting, but we need not say that the author would have accomplished his task more successfully if he had not limited his investigations to second-hand sources and in addition, if he had considered the institution of pre-Christian monks, especially those of Egypt and India. It would have thrown more light upon the origin of monasticism and probably also on its psychology.

PHILOSOPHY AND ITS CORRELATIONS. *Alexander T. Ormond.* Reprinted from the *Philosophical Review,* Vol. XII, No. 2, March, 1903.

In a lecture delivered before the second meeting of the American Philosophical Association, Alexander T. Ormond, Professor of Philosophy at Princeton, undertakes to justify philosophy against modern attacks, and he formulates his question thus: "How shall philosophy vindicate itself against the scepticism with which its claims are liable in our time to be met?"

Professor Ormond answers:

"I. By defining some point of view that is clearly philosophical, so that the complete occupation of this point of view will have the effect of translating an inquiry into one that is distinctly philosophical.

"II. By determining some concept of method that will stamp as distinctly philosophical any inquiry that conforms to its requirements."

As to the first part Professor Ormond says: "A construction of things, in order to be truly entitled to the name philosophical, must take its departure from mind itself and must follow the processes in which mind reduces its world to terms of its own experience."

The second point is disposed of as follows: "That philosophy has its problems for the solution of which it supplies the only or the most favorable point of view need scarcely be argued. We need only mention the problems of the unification of the elements of our culture, the development of a rational conception of the world, the question of the ultimate meaning of life, the problems of man's freedom and destiny, the ultimate problems of ethics and religion, the great perennial issues of God and Immortality."

Professor Ormond concludes: "Philosophy has positive insights and may be of some value in grounding and rationalizing our theories of life and conduct; it may yet have an important part to play in determining our conceptions of reality and our theory of religion. We will still entertain the hope that philosophy may help us in completing our ideals of being and of truth and duty, and in making up our minds about freedom, God, and immortality. And, so long as we entertain this larger hope, we will not be willing that philosophy should be shorn of its theoretic criteria and aims, even though the alternative offered us be a pragmatism with whose larger spirit we may find ourselves much in sympathy."

L'Individualisme Anarchiste Max Stirner. Par *Victor Basch,* Professeur à la Faculté des Lettres de l'Université de Rennes. Paris: Félix Alcan, Éditeur. 1904. Pp. vi, 294. Price, 6 fr.

Max Stirner is a modern thinker who is closely allied to Nietzsche, yet he is more systematic than the inventor of the overman. He bases all his views upon the valuation of the individual and thus stands for the uniqueness of each personality. His system of thought may be briefly characterised, as is done by Professor Basch, as anarchistic individualism, but it is understood that Stirner is not an anarchist of violent temper. He does not see in anarchism a mere destruction of the present form of society but a new organization in which the individual feels its uniqueness, by being freed of all religious chains, of all gods, of morality, of all conventions in which it can manifest all its energies and level all its powers, be his own creator and own proprietor, look with contempt upon every outside influence and to be unhampered by any scruple or regard. Professor Basch characterises Stirner "the unique one." He describes the background from which his theories proceed and investigates the peculiarity of this apostle of anarchistic individualism with appreciation of his ingenious work.

Handbuch der Gemaldekunde. Von *Dr. Theodor v. Frimmel.* Zweite umgearbeitete und stark vermehrte Auflage. Mit 38 in den Text gedruckten Abbildungen. Leipsic: T. T. Weber. 1904. Pp. 286.

Dr. Theodor von Frimmel, director of the *Schönborn-Wiesentheidsche* Gallery of Vienna, who has made a reputation as an art critic, especially by his thoughtful investigations of the history and philosophy of art, offers in this little volume a summary of his views of art, particularly the art of painting. The book will be valuable not only for connoisseurs, but also for those of the general public who are interested in painting. Students will be exceedingly grateful for the explanations of the technique of painting which is discussed in the first chapter, as to the background and materials the different woods, metals, canvas, stones, etc., tempera and oil, r's marks, varnish, etc., etc. There are also hints given as to the ring of old pictures when they have suffered by rents, by cracks or injuries.

he second chapter is devoted to the judgment of the artistic values, tic considerations and the difficult question of good and bad in art. author waives a definition of the beautiful, but he finds many points ich he deems it possible to offer objective norms by which the artistic of a painting may be judged.

he third chapter is devoted to the history of art, historical criticism, ethods of utilizing published sources, the different ways of exegesis, ption of the several styles, methods of comparison, questions of eness of copies made from the originals, frauds, and intentional as s unintentional misleading features of nomenclature.

he fourth chapter is devoted to a not unimportant question for lovers t—the price. The last chapter will be especially welcome for those appy ones who are able to have a gallery of their own. It contains advice for making collections and here as well as in all other chapters author falls back upon historical references. In his field he is an rity of the first rank, and we will incidentally mention that he is ed to Ruskin's as well as Tolstoy's æsthetical views. The book is well rated and we ought to add that Dr. Frimmel is engaged in writing a work which will treat of the problems of the philosophy of art.

L BUDDHISMO ANTICO. By *Giuseppe de Lorenzo.* Bari: Gius, Laterza & Figli. 1904. Pp. 299.

The author devotes this book of nearly three hundred pages to a study cient Buddhism in India. He begins with a comparison of India and nt Greece, and Brahman wisdom with Hellenic philosophy. Some of arallels which he draws between the Indian and the Greek conception e immortality of the soul, Braham and Buddhistic rites on the one hand Orphic and Pythagorean notions on the other, are very striking. ama Buddha he compares to Plato. The second chapter is devoted to founder of Buddhism, the archæological and epigraphical testimonials s existence, his family and home, priestly and worldly life, and the em of death or extinction. The third chapter is devoted to the dis-les of Gautama Buddha, and he is compared not only to Plato but to espeare. Special sections are devoted to parables and allegories, the on with God and divinity, the negation of wisdom and the immortality e soul, his philosophy compared to Kantism, the problem of caste, e, the piety of the apathetic attitude of the Buddhists compared to the charity conception of Christianity, the four noble truths and the gospel concatenations.

The fourth chapter discusses Buddhism in India after Gautama's death, its spread and degeneration, and finally the Buddism of Europe. Lorenzo concludes with a quotation of the *poeta poetarum:*

> "If all were minded so, the times should cease,
> And threescore years would make the world away."

MAINE DE BIRAN'S PHILOSOPHY OF WILL. By *Nathan E. Truman, A.M., Ph. D.,* formerly Fellow in the Sage School of Philosophy. Cornell Studies in Philosophy. No. 5. New York: The Macmillan Company. London: Macmillan & Co., Ltd. 1904. Pp. 93.

Maine de Biran, sometimes called the French Kant, is a philosopher whose importance lies not to such a degree in the strength of his own thoughts as in the mental and moral influence which he exercises over his countrymen, and it is strange that no special translation of his philosophy has as yet appeared in English. Dr. Nathan E. Truman has taken the task upon himself to present us in a monograph of ninety-three pages a résumé of Biran's philosophy and to outline his religion to both his predecessors and successors. Mr. Truman objects to Neville's views of Biran's development. He shows the influence which earlier thinkers, Locke, Condillac, Kant, and Reed, exercised upon him, the psychological basis of his arguments, his views of the categories, and his divisions of psychology. He compares Biran's psychology with Condillac's *Treatise of Sensations,* discusses his ethics, æsthetics, and religion, and shows how much his views have influenced Cousin, Comte, Renouvier, and Fouillée. Dr. Truman has apparently overlooked one interesting and important reference, viz., Maine de Biran's influence upon Schopenhauer, who learned from Biran the significance and the superiority of the will. The book contains a fine frontispiece of Maine de Biran which is taken from Lévy-Bruhl's *History of Modern Philosophy in France.* Any one who wishes to be familiar with Maine de Biran, and has not the time to study his several works in the original, will find Dr. Truman's compendium a very useful and handy memoir.

DAS PROBLEM DER WILLENSFREIHEIT. Ein neuer Versuch seiner Lösung von *Karl Fahrion.* Heidelberg: Carl Winter. 1904. Pp. 63.

Karl Fahrion believes he has discovered the solution of the problem of free will in the feeling of freedom which accompanies our actions. He believes that every deed can be judged from a double point of view. Man does not possess absolute liberty in the sense of arbitrariness but a relative y, which, if it did not exist, would annihilate all responsibility and guilt. annot see that Herr Fahrion is happy in his presentation of his case, ve think that he neither sees the salient point of the problem, nor that olution will prove satisfactory.

ONCTION DE LA MÉMOIRE ET LE SOUVENIR AFFECTIF. Par *Fr. Paulhan.* Paris: Félix Alcan, Éditeur. 1904. Pp. 178. Price, 2 fr., 50c.

'his treatise on the function of memory by a prominent French savant, f the best known contributors to the *Revue Philosophique,* attempts to stand the problem of recollection by analysing the process of effective ry and then applying it to intellectual memory and generalizing it. book contains many valuable suggestions, but is upon the whole disnting as it does not really give a definite solution or offer a clear nation of the nature of memory.

ONCTIONNISME UNIVERSEL. Essai de Synthèse Philosophique. Monde Sensible. Par *Henry Lagrésille.* Paris: Librairie Fischbacher. 1902. Pp. 580.

This stately volume offers under the title "Universal Functionism," a ed attempt at a philosophical synthesis, the first part of which forms eral introduction, and the second part treats the physical orders which xplained by sixty instructive illustrations in the text. M. Lagrésille with the proposition that metaphysics must form the summit of science nust lead to the establishment of the identity of the constitutive elements ason and actual cognition or sense-experience. Metaphysics should not parated from its base but should remain in connection with the objective s. This leads to a theory of functionism which serves as a metaphysics e object, and of the subjects, and of the moral world. The second er is devoted to a methodical conception of functionism, the third to lative science, the fourth to the science of principles, the fifth to the of phenological principles, the sixth to hypotheses as the method of opment, the seventh to concepts as the principle of definition for the ces.

The second part, which treats of the physical orders of the external l, discusses a series of sceintific problems, such as the constitution of r: (1) matter and atoms; (2) a representation of the imponderable l and the atomistic principle of ether; (3) molecular genesis, which is a sentation of the chemical world and chemical atoms; (4) the motions ght; (5) the motions of electricity; (6) chemical motions and the harsation of the different motions. The third book discusses the problems e organized world and shows how we must comprehend its develop-; its different phases as peaceable and active evolution of nature, its spirit and its directive forces as follows: (1) the government of nature is like a personal and intelligent power; (2) the physiological conception of nerves and the cell; (3) pleuri-cellular systems; (4) biological considerations; (5) treatises on paleontology; (6) speculations of anthropology. The fourth and last book treats of the cosmic world; (1) the evolution of the sun as a star; (2) of the planets and the earth; (3) the formation of the earth in its different phases; Plutonic, Neptonic, and changes of the atmosphere at different epochs, taking into consideration also the life of planets in general and the natural end of the earth; (4) nebulas and higher worlds; (5) the intelligible nature which directs the thought on evolution; (6) general recapitulation and final reflections. This last book contains a classification of the phenomenal world and draws a parallel between the natural and the artificial systems of the sciences. It explains the evolution of the sciences and gives us a bird's-eye view of the entire sensible world.

Combat pour l'Individu. Par *Georges Palante.* Paris: Félix Alcan, Éditeur. 1904. Pp. 232. Price, 3 fr., 75c.

Since Nietzsche gained prominence in the philosophical world, the problem of individualism has come to the front, or possibly the reverse is the case. Individualism is asserting itself, and so the philosophy of individualism gains recognition. The present book by Georges Palante is an independent essay which sets forth the struggle for and of the individual against the factors which from all sides appear to hem it in. The author looks upon society as the environment of the individual and thus society appears as his enemy. Therefore the individual has to assert itself against its tyranny which appears in several forms as *l'esprit de corps*, as the administrative spirit, as the spirit of the family, of the class, of the social conditions of his home, of politics, etc. Authors of education appear as infringements upon the individual, even the social dilettante and the philosophy of the overman, the social dogmas, and the democracy of the present age threaten the liberty of the individual. The book is practically an argument of the individual against society. The author is a strong individual, and to some extent his booklet reminds one of Mr. Spencer's *The Man versus the State*.

If our author and more of his ilk had ever analysed the nature of society they would find that society after all is the product of many individuals, and that the individual in its turn is nothing but the product of social factors. Our very language is a product of social institutions, the exchange of thought among members of a social group. Thus the whole idea of isolating the individual and setting society, to which it owes its origin, up as its worst enemy, is a miscomprehension of the situation.

Unser Verhältnis zu den bildenden Künsten. Sechs Vorträge über Kunst und Erziehung. Gehalten von *Dr. August Schmarsow.* Leipsic; B. G. Teubner. 1903. Pp. 160.

Dr. August Schmarsow is Professor of the History of Art at the University of Leipsic, and the present pamphlet is a series of enthusiastic lectures on his specialty. He points out the importance of the arts and shows that in the study of art the entire man, head and heart, is engaged. The origin of all artistic creation is expression, and thus art is first of all realized in pantomime. Mimicry develops the plastic, and the language of expression is a preparation for true language. The height of beauty is reached in the representation of organic beauty, finding its highest realization in the human body. The human body is and must remain the center of all the arts. Our author shows us the contrast and the connection of architecture with sculpture as being a utilization of space. The architectural building finds its limit in the wall and the wall is enlivened by fresco and painting. Dr. Schmarsow appreciates also music and poetry, but we can read between the lines his preference for the quiet unassuming plastic arts. He characterises differences of text by a contrast of the monument of Canova's tomb at Venice with the Monument of the Dead by Bartholomé on the Père Lachaise at Paris. While appreciating the former, our author appears to give the palm to the latter. Without depreciating the Teutonic spirit and its tendency to defame the significance of artistic productions, he decries the narrowness of a doctrinary taste which glories in the narrow Teutonism and yet restricts German art to an inferior place; above all he condemns the apron strings by which the German artists have so far been tied.

Le Problème du Déterminisme Social. Déterminisme biologique et Déterminisme social par *D. Draghicesco,* Membre de la Société de Sociologie. Paris: Éditions de la Grande France. 1903. Pp. 99. Price, 2 fr., 50c.

The author of this book discusses the problem of necessity in the domain of social development, in consideration of the fact that it is subject to natural laws. In this sense he speaks of social determinism and contrasts it to biological determinism. Social determinism is different from the determinism of nature, and so he proposes the question:

"Are there at all moral and social laws, and are these laws independent of biological and natural laws in such a way as to form a distinct determinism which may be contrasted to biological determinism?

"Which are the aspects under which these two determinisms present themselves in the social individual, and which are their relations?

"Which is the scientific formula of the social determinism with reference to the biological determinism, and which is its specific feature?"

Our author undertakes to demonstrate that the ethico-social determinism is real but cannot be comprehended under other natural and biological laws. The scientific formula of the social determinism is a social heredity which is an actual element in the existent conscience which may be compared to a bundle of social relations frequently materializing in an actual life. Its principal laws are justice and solidarity.

Our author insists on the difference between the spiritual nature of man and the physical. Man is conditioned by the factors of social life, by social relations and social sanctions which shape him anew and graft upon his biological nature a novel life and being, spiritual, rational, and *sui generis* which is superadded to his bodily life. It is a new and artificial personality built upon the natural personality. Thus the social is the spiritual and the ideal, but it is a realistic ideal and an experimental spiritual idea, for what is more experimental than education and tradition. "Spirit," as says Mr. Ward, "comes as a new power into the world and our whole civilization is a product of art which stands in opposition to nature." Yet the ethico-social reality is different from biological and physical facts. It appears to us as a duty and is therefore called the "ought" and not the "is." Biological nature exists as an accomplished fact in spite of us and without our existence, but the social reality can be accomplished only through our efforts and volition. Never can the realization of ethico-social laws be accomplished without our active intervention, such as finds expression in the formulation of duties. This difference results in the impossibility to foresee or foredetermine the final outcome of the social evolution, with the same precision as can be done in natural events.

Bulletin de la Société Francaise de Philosophie. Paris: Librairie Armand Colin. 1904.

The congresses which in 1900 were held at Paris during the time of the Exposition have given a powerful stimulus to the interest taken in intellectual pursuits and among the societies founded at that time the French Society of Philosophy[1] survives and prospers to this day. Its officers are M. Xavier Léon, Administrator, M. André Lalande, General Secretary, and M. Élie Halévy, Treasurer. So far it seemed as if Félix Alcan and Company possessed the monopoly of the publications of French philosophical literature, but this society has taken a start of its own and publishes its bulletins through the Librairie Armand Colin, 5 rue de Mézières, Paris. They are now in their third year and contain a series of important discussions which

[1] *Société Française de Philosophie.*

are characterised by a breaking away from the narrow limits of the materialistic and agnostic tendencies of the scientific school of France, and venture into broader fields.

Most of the bulletins contain a thesis for a discussion in which the most prominent members take part and thus almost every one of them is actually a symposium, viewing the subject from different standpoints.

Here is a summary of the three volumes: Vol. I, No. 1, M. Le Roy discusses the objective value of physical laws; No. 2, M. Bergson criticises the old views of the psycho-physical parallelism and insists that psychological metaphysics is possible on the basis of positive facts; No. 3, M. André Lalande attempts to elucidate and specify a number of important philosophical terms such as morality, ethics, ethology—the normative (a term coined by Wundt), individuality and personality, virtue, merit, moral value, life, nature; No. 4, M. H. Michel discusses the political doctrines of democracy, in which he defines democracy as that political system which allows each citizen to attain the maximum of his human value.

The second volume contains: No. 1, a discussion of the idea of being, by M. Weber; No. 2, M. Rauh discusses details of the admission to philosophical chairs involving examinations and diplomas; No. 3, M. A. Darlu analyses the contemporary conscience as to the Christian elements it contains; No. 4, M. Couturat explains the relation of logic to metaphysics according to Leibnitz; No. 5, M. Sorel expounds historical materialism, speaking mainly of its social exposition in the works of Marx and Engels; No. 6, M. Belot proposes a thesis on luxury, its effects, its value, and its drawbacks; No. 7 and 8 contain the scheme of a philosophical vocabulary (continued in Vol. III, No. 6 and 7) by MM. Belot, Couturat, Delbos, and Lalande.

The third volume, No. 1, contains M. Émile Boutroux, on Comte's philosophy and metaphysics; No. 2, M. Belot on the place which philosophy should hold in school; No. 3, M. André Lalande on the objective appearance of visual perceptions; No. 4, M. Brunschvicg on the idea of moral liberty; No. 5, M. P. Tannery on the value of Kantian classification of judgments in analysis and synthesis; No. 8, M. G. Tarde on the social philosophy of Cournot.

ELEMENTE DER VEKTOR-ANALYSE. Von *Dr. A. H Bucherer.* Leipsic: Teubner. 1903. Pp. 91.

Since the invention of geometry and algebra, no single advance in mathematics can, perhaps, compare in importance with that introduced by Descartes in 1637, by which geometrical methods are reduced to mere numerical computations.

Disappointment has been felt, in some quarters, that the generalization of Descartes's work which was devised by Hamilton—the Calculus of Quaternions—has not proved itself a more practical and influential mathematical weapon. But it is to be remembered that "natural selection" is a secular process. Accordingly, just at present, something a little less general than the method of Grassmann and a little less unwieldy than the method of Hamilton appears to be "fittest" and is, therefore, "surviving" easily. It is this modern treatment of vectors, embodying the essential features of the systems of Heaviside, Gibbs, and Grassmann when limited to three dimensions, that Dr. Bucherer gives in the present volume. What then is this Vector Analysis that has grown up between Cartesians and Quaternions? This question is one which can be made easily clear provided the inquirer has already firmly grasped the idea of the complex variable—the "double algebra" of De Morgan—the idea that each equation between complex quantities is equivalent to two equations between real quantities. Just as the complex variable $a+ib$ is a special case of a quaternion, so is the vector $ia+jb+kc$ a special case of Grassmann's n-dimensional vector. The difference between these two algebras lies essentially in the different meanings which are given to products of the operators i, j, and k.

As Tait remarks, the equation $ijk=-1$, together with the equations $i^2=j^2=k^2=-1$, "contains essentially the whole of quaternions." While in vector analysis the corresponding defining equations are $ijk=-1$ and $i^2=j^2=k^2=+1$. Each of the products here mentioned are *scalar* quantities. If we consider *vector* products, we find that the two systems have the following feature in common, namely $ij=k$, $jk=i$, $ki=j$.

To those who are familiar with the elements of physics the difference between scalar and vector multiplication is, perhaps, most easily understood by thinking of the difference between *work* and *torque*, each of which is a product of a force by a distance. In the former case the force and the distance are each in the same direction, while the product, *work*, has no direction and is hence only a scalar. In the latter case, the force and the distance are mutually perpendicular, while the product, *torque*, has a direction (axis) at right angles to both. It is, therefore, a vector.

Returning now to the i, j, k of vector analysis, we have for scalar products, $ij=0$, $jk=0$, $ki=0$.

Vector products $ij=k$, $jk=i$, $ki=j$.

This usage, it will be observed, is quite different from that of the electric engineers who, like Hamilton, employ i as a quadrantal vector

The volume under review is made up of essentially four parts: (1) general discussion of vector addition, multiplication and differentiation; (2) applications to some of the simpler problems of dynamics; (3) a brief discussion of the potential theory with electrical applications; and (4) a discussion of the motion of a sphere in a perfect fluid together with the derivation of the general equations.

Students of mathematical physics will be especially interested in the elegant forms here given to Kepler's First Law, the theorems of Gauss and Stokes the two fundamental electro-magnetic equations of Maxwell Green's theorem, the solenoidal condition, the lomellar condition, and numerous other formulæ. The determinantel expressions for curl for vector product, and for certain scalar products are very attractive.

The size of the volume, as it stands, is excellently adapted to the needs of graduate students in physics. When, however, it comes to a second edition the author might find it wise to add a little more "connective tissue." For in discussions of this type it is very easy for every trace of physical meaning to drop out and leave nothing but bare equations — unless interpretation is insisted upon either by author or teacher.

If it were not considered "going over to the enemy," a chapter on the symbolic method employed in the treatment of alternating currents would prove useful and attractive.

The style of the book is clear and altogether admirable. It is to be hoped that it may soon receive an English translation. On page 72, the printer has inserted a gratuitous *r*, thus transforming a distinguished Irish name (Fitzgerald) into perfect German vernacular.

HENRY CREW.

IMMANUEL KANT, EIN BILD SEINES LEBENS UND DENKENS. Von *Dr. Max Apel.* Mit einem Bildnis. Ein Gedenkblatt zum hundertjährigen Todestage des Weltphilosophen. Berlin: Conrad Skopnik. 1904. Pp. viii, 102.

Kant said in his younger years when teaching his students: "Philosophy cannot be learned, for there is no absolute, sure, and universally recognised philosophy. What we can learn, however, is philosophising, viz., we can render clear with a critical spirit the problems in their whole significance and importance." Our author, Dr. Max Apel, adds: "The old master's voice went out from the narrow lecture room into the world and still sounds forth through centuries. Kant has become the philosophical teacher of mankind, but he is not only an incomparable educator in philosophical thinking, he not only makes clear heads and hearts, he is not only the bold revolutionary, but also a powerful creator of new conditions, the thoughtful center of the sciences of human knowledge and action. His philosophy is not *the* philosophy, not the truth but it teaches the way to truth. For this reason, one studies Kant's writings more seriously than ever, and must let them pass in spite of all their unavoidable implications and unsolved difficulties."

In the evening of his life, Kant uttered the proud melancholy words: "I have come with my writings a century too soon. Only after a hundred years will I be properly understood, and then my books will be studied and allowed to stand."

"This prophecy," says Dr. Apel, "is partly true, partly wrong. There are many who now believe they understand Kant properly, but every one has his Kant and every one's Kant is a reflection of his own self."

In the present pamphlet Dr. Apel first reviews briefly the life of Kant—parentage, school and university life, his years as tutor and magister, and finally as professor, his success, his troubles with the censors and his death (1-18).

The second chapter introduces us to Kant's personality, his appearance, his character, the circle of his acquaintances, his relation to State and Church (18-33).

The second part of the book is devoted to Kant's philosophy, his pre-critical writings (37-52), his conversion to criticism (53-59), then his *Critique of Pure Reason* (60-83) of which he gives his usual careful analysis (84-97). The last chapter, which is perhaps too short, discusses Kant's moral philosophy.

Kant's *Critique of Judgment* has been passed over with the mere reference that it exercised a great influence upon Goethe.

The pamphlet contains as a frontispiece, a reproduction of a painting by an unknown artist discovered in 1897 at Dresden, representing Kant in his fifties, the time when he wrote the *Critique of Pure Reason*.

DOVE SI VA? Appunti Di Psichologia Politica. Del *N. Fornelli.* Napoli: Luigi Pierro Tip, Editori. 1903. Pp. 235. Price, 3 Lire.

The question, Whither? (*Dove Si Va?*), when applied to society, is, of course, a most difficult one to answer. Social prophecy has not yet been reduced to a science. The opinion expressed in this book, however, is that we are headed towards a revolution unless the ruling classes curb quickly and effectually the social malcontents whose hostility to the state is expressed in contempt for the political powers that be, and in daring to proclaim a social order based on human brotherhood.

The author attempts to account for the failing powers of modern liberal and parliamentary governments. They are due, he thinks, to the confession and ambiguity of the ideas entertained by those in authority, and to the inadequate means employed with respect to desired ends, namely, the preservation and perpetuation of existing forms of government. At present, the State is entirely too lenient toward enemies of the social order these "new Jacobites," who are for the most part selfish fomenters of trouble, or deluded idealists.

Socialism is the main object of attack in the book. It has been thought worth while to devote considerable space to refuting the prophecies of Karl Marx with reference to the concentration of capital and the expropriation of the small landholder.

The viewpoint of the book is distinctly that of the conservative. The ruling class is represented as standing to the disinherited *in loco parentis*. Liberty is regarded as a good thing, but the people must be prepared for and adapted to liberal institutions before these are to be granted.

I. W. H.

Saggio di Uno Studio Sui Sentimenti Morali. Del *Dott. Guglielmo Salvadori*. Firenze. Francesco Lumachi, Editore. 1903. Pp. v, 139. Price, 3 Lire.

The author of this book disclaims the purpose of constructing a new theory of the moral sentiments. His aim is critical, but constructively so. His doctrine, to use his own language, is a kind of rational eudemonism, founded upon experience, in which he attempts to reconcile, by applying the theory of evolution, the empirical realism of the utilitarian school and the abstract idealism of the metaphysical school. The book professes to sum up in large part the conclusions arrived at in a larger work, by the same author, entitled *L'Etica Evoluzionista*.

I. W. H.

Osservazioni Sullo Svolgimento Della Dottrina Delle Idee In Platone. Parte I. Del *G. Lombardo-Radice*. Firenze: Tipografia Galileiana. 1903. Pp. 91. Price, 2 Lire.

Students of the dialogues of Plato may find in this book a scholarly presentation of the Aristotelian criticism of the Athenian philosopher in which the researches of others are given due prominence but which is by no means a compilation, or a sifting of old material thrown up by former excavators in this fruitful field. The author deals directly with Platonic ideas, and assumes a familiarity with the dialogues, especially the moral and Socratic. The first division of the work, after the introduction, deals with the value of stylistic researches. This is followed by some observations on the fantastic elements of the Platonic dialogues. The work is concluded by a chapter on the premises of Plato's philosophy.

I. W. H.

Die Erlösung vom Dasein. Leipsic: Verlag von C. G. Naumann. Pp. xvii, 286.

The anonymous author of this strange work *Salvation from Existence* was born in Basel, Switzerland, and judging from the preface which also is anonymous, he must have been one of the most unfortunate of mortals. He died December 4, 1901, sixty-seven years old, and he quitted life without remorse, without regret and without attachment of any kind. The sum-total of his life, of his views, of his ideals, of his philosophy, of his poetry, of his convictions and religion, if we may so call his negative views, are contained in this book which he leaves as a memorial for the inhabitants of Basel, the pious Christian city, to serve them as an atheistic breviary of a salvation from existence.

We learn from the preface written by the anonymous executor of his literary remains that he was born in 1834 at the time when Basel was implicated in wars, in which his father took an active part as a voluntary combatant. The worry of these years never left him and impressed him with a timidity that became for all time a characteristic feature of his. His mother died early, and in his eighth year he attended the gymnasium, but by an unfortunate accident he fell into a caldron of hot water which caused him great suffering. The case became aggravated by a tuberculosis of the bone which confined him for months upon a sick bed; and the greatest pleasure of our little patient consisted in this, that he, the timid little boy, was now removed from the wild games and plays of his comrades. He now indulged exclusively in the fairy world of *A Thousand and One Nights*. We need not touch upon all the incidents of his suffering and the cure to which he was submitted in an orthopedic institution. In 1850 the father married again, so did his only sister, and the companion of his younger years also plighted her troth to a rich suitor. His father now took him out of school and made him a clerk in some commercial business. He went to Lyons, France, whence he was called home by the death of his father. Being not on good terms with his stepmother, he was now cast upon himself, and he went to Paris where he accepted a modest position; but he found leisure enough to attend lectures in the Collége de France and the Sorbonne. On his temporary return to his home he dared to take hold of earthly happiness, but his dream was soon dispelled. His experiences are here only indicated and we must assume that he was engaged or married for a short time, but that the object of his affections died. This transient hope of earthly bliss matured his mind, yet he remained isolated, friendless, broken in his health, and suffering from an incurable heart disease which set the possibility of death constantly before his eyes. At this period of his life he became an author and he says of himself: "As I look back upon my life, it is nothing but a series of accidents, privations, disappointments, sufferings, and pain. I had not one joyful hour, not one moment in which I could say 'Stay, thou art so beautiful!' and now with every hour hope more and more disappears that the evening of my life might throw a last silver lining upon the dark clouds of my fate. I merely enjoy with every hour that is past to approach the goal of my journey. The entire fate of my life is the resultant of one fundamental quality of my character, or rather of one fundamental want, viz., weakness and incapacity to live. It was weakness which made all my accidents affect me unfavorably; it was weakness that I suffered so many mishaps; weakness that I could not secure any permanent position and a name, weakness that I was timid in the presence of people who had only contempt for me and used me, weakness that I could not found a family, weakness that I was generally speaking one of the most unfortunate of men." The silver lining for which he had hoped came, however, in the idea that he might advance the knowledge of human soul life by his own writing. He intended to confer with Nietzsche, who happened to live at that time in Basel, but he could not make up his mind to do so, and so it remained undone. Yet he continued to live in his own ideas and grew milder, more friendly, and more serene with advancing years. Courageously and without remorse he met death on the 4th of December, 1901.

The biography of this solitary sufferer is perhaps the most important part of the work, and it seems to the reviewer that the redactor of the MSS. should have taken more pains to have entered into details. These mysterious quotations from the manuscript writings of the anonymous author together with the brief allusions to his fate are not sufficient to form an insight into his real character.

The literary remains of our anonymous author are very irregular in importance and value. Unquestionably his poetical effusions range higher than his essays and discussions. These latter, however, have the precedence in the book and fill the greater part of it. We learn that he was an atheist, or at least an agnostic, who begins his first essay with the exclamation "God! There is no word which means so little as this one." He calls the God of the Old Testament a duodecimo God, and he says of the doctrine of the unit of God: "Why should there be one God only? Why not a plurality of divinity? We do not think of an Areopagus of gods as the vision of Greek mythology but rather of an *in* and *super* existence of divine being in such a way as the earth is the deity of man, the planetary system the deity of planets, our world system, the God of the starry heavens within the domain of the Milky Way and the cosmos, the god of all these islands of worlds. Perhaps there are many grades of divinity. What do we know of it? Will there not be other solutions of the God problem possible?"

His essays on sin and morality, on the dogma of the vicarious atonement of Christ, on the human side of the life of Jesus, on humanity and eternity, show a thoughtful layman, but may scarcely be considered as either up-to-date or exhaustive in philosophical breadth. Nevertheless they contain much that is interesting and instructive, for both the psychologist and the philosopher. Christianity is decidedly not his ideal. He rejects it with a decisiveness which betrays his disappointment. Apparently he was hungry for a religion that might have given him comfort in his peculiar situation in life, and Christianity seems to have attracted him at a certain phase of his development, but left his heart unsatisfied. Among his poems we find a few stanzas inscribed "My Last Will" in which he prays to be buried without a priest, quietly at night while the stars shine, without words or speech, but in mute contemplation. He wants a stone unhewn and rough, without inscription, without even bearing his name. His desire is to live on in the choir of noble spirits, to rest in the soft soil of the earth and in the memory of his friends, nameless, and such indeed has been his lot. Such is the character of this book and as such he will go down to posterity, "The Nameless Sufferer."

The last piece of his poetical sketches is entitled "The Three Balls, a Thanatopsis." Here he describes his own world-conception in the form of an allegory. A messenger comes to him dressed in a flowing white garment who leads him first to the temple of the great Cosmos, then to the temple of Eidos and finally to the abode of rest.

The first place is the deification of actual life as it exists in the world. Cosmos is blessed as the infinite universe which is all that is. It is worshipped and millions of lives are sacrificed in its service. The naked picture of Cosmos is a horrible display of reality in its terrible details, struggles and suffering.

The worship of Eidos is the realm of platonic ideals. Its main characteristics are, beauty, harmony, and immutability. There is no contrast of youth and old age, of birth and death, only the enjoyment of pure Heavenly light. It is a sphere which elevates and beautifies, and the poet almost feels as if he would here find his highest satisfaction.

But his guide leads him further to the vale of contemplation where everyone enters a cell with a view upon the horizon at an infinite distance. The symbol of the world of Cosmos is a red ball, of the world of Eidos is a blue ball, and of the world of peace is a black ball. The hymn which is intoned in this realm of eternal rest speaks of strife as the father of things through which all contrasts originate from nothing. Each Yea is contrasted by its Nay; to every pleasure corresponds a pain, and light finds its counterpart in darkness, good in evil. Tired from being a constant play ball between two contrasts, as the plaything of blind accident, life will find here its final refuge and from the purely phenomenal will sink down into the naught. The poet chooses the latter and stands in the country that is symbolised by the black ball. He now awaits the hour of darkness and rest when he will be cognisant of the all and the naught.

The British Journal of Psychology is a new periodical that comes from the University Press of Cambridge. It is edited by James Ward, the famous English psychologist, and W. H. R. Rivers, with the collaboration of W. Mc-

Dougall, C. S. Myers, A. F. Shand, C. S. Sherrington, and W. G. Smith. Thus it represents the best sources of English psychologists. The first number which lies before us contains an article "On the Definition of Psychology" by James Ward, and further investigations "On Binocular Flicker and the Correlation of Activity of 'Corresponding' Retinal Points" by C. S. Sherrington, a memoir of "Bernardino Telesio, a Sixteenth Century Psychologist," whose interesting work *De Rerum Natura* has almost been forgotten, by J. Lewis McIntyre, and an article "The Sensations excited by a Single Momentary Stimulation of the Eye, a Study in Experimental Psychology," by W. McDougall of the University College in London. The price of the journal is five shillings.

A new translation into German of Aristotle's Metaphysics by Dr. theol. Eugene Rolfes is now appearing in the *Philosophische Bibliothek, Vol. II.*, published by Dürr, Leipsic. The book contains fascicles 1 to 7. A short introduction of 18 pages surveys Aristotle's system and contains in laudable brevity the necessary references as to the text, commentaries, and translations. Dr. Rolfes's translation is literal, almost too literal, but his method can only be commended. It is a faithful imitation of the original without being unreadable or even awkward, so much so as to enable the reader to reconstruct the original Greek.

The *Annual Literary Index* for 1903, edited by W. I. Fletcher and R. R. Bowker has now been published by the New York office of the *Publishers' Weekly*. It is indispensable for litterateurs and authors in general who wish to keep abreast with the times. The contents show a list: first, of the Periodicals; second, an Index to General Literature; third, of Modern Authors; fourth, Bibliography; fifth, Necrology, and sixth, dates of Principal Events.

The University of Chicago is publishing now, under the editorship of its President, Dr. William R. Harper, a series of constructive Bible studies, the latest volume of which, belonging to the elementary series, is written by Georgia Louis Chamberlin and bears the title *An Introduction to the Bible for Teachers of Children*. It is intended for use in Sunday Schools or in the home, and supplies us with suggestions how Bible lessons should be directed and how the spirit of instruction can be modernised and brought up to date. The forty lessons of the book are reverent in spirit and at the same time dictated by a respect for scientific inquiry as well as the assured results of the higher criticism. Never is there a term used which would cause a conflict in a truth-loving teacher with his conscience, for the attitude of the instructor is entirely changed. The child learns to look upon the several Biblical passages presented in the Sunday school as compositions of a given time, by a man of definite character who pursues a special purpose. which is mostly the edification and instruction of the reader. From this standpoint the child will learn to love and respect the Bible without fostering the spirit of credulity, and thus the Bible study will prove helpful as a means of character-building.

The third number of the quarterly, *Buddhism* opens with an editorial on "The Law of Righteousness" and contains a series of contributions from prominent Buddhist scholars. Professor Rhys Davids writes on "Seeing Things as They Really Are," pointing out the position of Buddha's doctrine in which he anticipates modern science. "Gotama," he says, "showed the genius of a great pioneer of thought in thus feeling out after what is termed a dynamical conception of things." The term Bhutama characterises the thought of becoming, and thus he anticipates even in important details the theory of evolution, and here Rhys Davids agrees with the exposition of the editorial by Ananda Maitriya, who takes as a motto the following lines of *The Light of Asia:*

> "Before beginning, and without an end,
> As space eternal and as surety sure,
> Is fixed a Power divine which moves to good,
> Only its laws endure."

J. Newman treats "Hypnotism" from the standpoint of modern psychology. Several articles are of local interest, such as "The Origin of the Burmese Race" and "Education in Burma." Dr. R. Ernest discusses the temperance question after the fashion of temperance preachers in saying that "alcohol is a poison both to the body and the mind, and its poisonous influence on the mind is obvious even in small doses." Mr. Maung Tsain writes an article on the Fifth Buddhist Council which took place in Burma under King Mindon Min, reports of which in stone inscription are still extant.

The fifth edition of Haeckel's *Anthropogony, or the History of the Development of Man* has just appeared at Leipsic, published by Wilhelm Engelmann. The book has been greatly increased both in illustrations and text, but the main idea, a representation of the natural history of mankind, has remained the same as in former editions. The book is richly illustrated and is one of Haeckel's best books, being written in the fascinating style of this enthusiastic scientist.

L'Année Psychologique, of which the tenth volume will soon appear has changed publishers and will now be brought out by the Librairie Masson, 120 Boulevard St. Germain, Paris. The editorship will remain as before in the able hands of Dr. Alfred Binet of the Sorbonne.

·XIV. No. 3. APRIL, 1904.

THE MONIST

A QUARTERLY MAGAZINE

Devoted to the Philosophy of Science

: Dr. Paul Carus. Associates: { E. C. Hegeler, Mary Carus.

CONTENTS:

CHICAGO:

…E OPEN COURT PUBLISHING CO

Price, 50 cts.; Yearly, $2.00.

LONDON: Kegan Paul, Trench, Trübner & Company, Limited.

In England and U. P. U., half a crown; Yearly, 9s 6d.

10 Cents Per Copy **$1.00 Per**

The Open Court

An Illustrated Monthly Magazine

Devoted to the Science of Religion, The Religion of Science and the Extension of the Religious Parliament Idea.

Science is slowly but surely transforming the world.

Science is knowledge verified; it is Truth proved; and Truth will a conquer in the end.

The power of Science is irresistible.

Science is the still small voice; it is not profane, it is sacred; it is not hu it is superhuman; Science is a divine revelation.

Convinced of the religious significance of Science, *The Open Court* bel that there is a holiness in scientific truth which is not as yet recognised in it significance either by scientists or religious leaders. The scientific spirit but be a genuine devotion to Truth, contains a remedy for many ills; it lead way of conservative progress and comes not to destroy but to fulfil.

The Open Court on the one hand is devoted to the *Science of Religio* investigates the religious problems in the domain of philosophy, psychology, history; and on the other hand advocates the *Religion of Science*. It bel that Science can work out a reform within the Churches that will preser religion all that is true, and good, and wholesome.

Illustrated Catalogue and sample copies free.

SUBSCRIPTION FORM

To THE OPEN COURT PUBLISHING CO.

324 Dearborn Street, Chicago, Ill.

Gentlemen,—

Please send THE OPEN COURT for.................. yea

beginning with.................190...to the address given below.

I enclose.............for $..........

Signature.................................

Address..................................

Date....................................

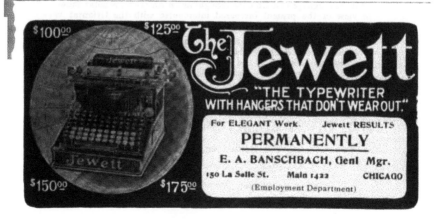

The Surd of Metaphysics. An Inquiry Into the Question, Are There Things-in-Themselves? By *Dr. Paul Carus.* Pp., vii, 233. Price, cloth, $1.25 net (5s. net).

The subject discussed in this book (the idea of things-in-themselves) is one of the most important of the problems of philosophy, and is of a paramount practical nature in its application to real life, especially in the domains of ethics and religion.

A Brief History of Mathematics. By the late *Dr. Karl Fink*, Tübingen, Germany. Translated by *Wooster Woodruff Beman*, and *David Eugene Smith.* With biographical notes and full index. Pp., 345. Cloth, $1.50 net (5s. 6d. net). Second edition.

"Dr. Fink's work is the most systematic attempt yet made to present a compendious history of mathematics."—*The Outlook.*

"This book is the best that has appeared in English. It should find a place in the library of every teacher of mathematics."—*The Inland Educator.*

Fundamental Problems. The Method of Philosophy as a Systematic Arrangement of Knowledge. Third edition, enlarged and revised. By *Dr. Paul Carus* Pp., xii, 373. Cloth, $1.50 (7s. 6d.).

The Gathas of Zarathushtra (Zoroaster) in Metre and Rhythm. Being a second edition of the metrical versions in the author's edition of 1892–1894, to which is added a second edition (now in English) of the author's Latin version also of 1892–1894, in the five Zarathushtrian Gathas, which was subventioned by His Lordship, the Secretary of State for India in Council, and also by the Trustees of the Sir J. Jejeebhoy Translation Fund of Bombay, and is now practically disposed of. (See also the literary translation in the Sacred Books of the East, XXX., pp. 1–393 [1887], itself founded by especial request upon the limited edition of 1883.) By *Lawrence H. Mills, D. D.*, Hon. M. A. Professor of Zend Philology in the University of Oxford. Large octavo. Pp., 196. Price, cloth, $2.00.

The Temples of the Orient and Their Message; in the light of Holy Scripture Dante's Vision, and Bunyan's Allegory. By the Author of "Clear Round!" "Things Touching the King," etc. With Map showing the Ancient Sanctuaries of the Old World and their relation to Abraham's Pilgrimage. Pages, x, 442. Price, cloth, $4.00.

A work dedicated to the intending missionary, with a view to broadening his conception and appreciation of the great religions of the East

The Age of Christ. A Brief Review of the Conditions Under which Christianity Originated. By *Dr. Paul Carus.* Pp., 34. Price, paper, 15 cents net.

The Canon of Reason and Virtue (Lao-Tze's Tao Teh King). Translated into English from the Chinese by *Dr. Paul Carus.* Separate reprint from the translator's larger work. Pp., 47. Paper, 25 cents.

Karma, A Story of Buddhist Ethics. By *Paul Carus.* Illustrated by Kwason Suzuki. American edition. Pp., 47. Price, 15 cents.

Devoted to the Philosophy of Science

Editor: DR. PAUL CARUS *Associates:* { E. C. HEGELER. MARY CARUS.

CONTENTS:

CHICAGO

HE OPEN COURT PUBLISHING CO

Price, 50 cents; Yearly, $2.00.

LONDON: KEGAN PAUL, TRENCH, TRÜBNER & COMPANY, LIMITED.

In England and U. P. U., half a crown; Yearly, 9s 6d.

VOL. XIV. No. 5. OCTOBER, 1904

THE MONIST

A QUARTERLY MAGAZINE

Devoted to the Philosophy of Science

Editor: Dr. Paul Carus. *Associates:* E. C. Hegeler, Mary Carus.

CONTENTS:

CHICAGO:

The Open Court Publishing Company.

1904.

L. XIV. OCTOBER, 1904. No. 5.

THE MONIST

THE ORIGIN OF SPECIES BY MUTATION.

HISTORICAL REVIEW.

THE CONCEPTION OF THE SPECIES AND PRE-DARWINIAN EVOLUTION

RIOR to the publication of the work of Darwin, and contemporaneous with him, there obtained several widely differing opins concerning the origin of species. There was the philosophical ool, in which the most prominent figures were Lamarck and offrey St. Hilaire, defending the common origin of all species. ere were those who regarded the genera as created and the spes and subspecies as derived from these. There were the adherents the Linnæan species who insisted that these were created. Finally re were others who regarded the elementary forms which proved stant under cultivation as created.

The theories of the times were dependent upon the extent of loitation of the systematic opportunity. Before Linnæus the era were commonly accepted as the systematic units, and the spes regarded as their minor modifications. Numerous genera had mon names, while the species were usually not so distinguished. e view that the genera were created and that the species had ginated from them by transmutation had many advocates. Many ngs show that the present conception of a species was hardly own before the time of Linnæus. In the older works on natural story, a very short diagnostic description was written after the neric name, and as often as the plant was mentioned this diagsis was, of necessity, repeated. So long as the number of plants recognized was small, this occasioned no great inconvenience, but with more detailed and extensive investigations the originally brief diagnosis could not but become elaborate and detailed. The simplification of this complex and unwieldy mechanism was the work of Linnæus, who proposed the binary system of nomenclature, in which the plant or animal is described and assigned a specific name to replace the brief description previously appended to the generic name. To give the essential authority to his system, he made the species the units; and his predecessors and he himself in earlier years had regarded the genera as created and the species derived from them, he now maintained that the species had been created and that the minor forms had arisen from them in a natural manner.

But the Linnæan species are collective species. He himself seems to have recognized this fact more clearly than his followers, although he rarely distinguished varieties among his species and forbade his students their study, as has been said by some to assure so far as possible the dignity of his new systematic units. The history of the period following the establishment of this new system is similar in many respects to the earlier times when the genera were regarded as the units. While the unstudied material was copious and easily accessible, there was no reason to ignore the master's injunction against the study of minor forms or to doubt that they were descended in a natural manner from the created species. As the material, especially in the European flora, was more thoroughly studied and the opportunity for descriptive work became less, the necessity of considering minor forms became increasingly greater, until it was clearly recognized that the Linnæan species are built up of a number of forms showing small but clearly defined differences. Probably the finest illustration is *Draba verna*, a species described by Linnæus himself, which has been split up into over two hundred minor species. *Viola tricolor* has suffered a very similar fate. Not only were these minor species found to be distinguished by small but sharply limited morphological characteristics, showing well defined differences, not of one but often of all the parts, so that a comprehensive characterization is of necessity very extensive, but they also proved themselves quite true to seed under cultivation. Many of them, grown for many generations, proved quite as true to their minute differences as did the larger groups currently dignified by the term species. Individual variability was everywhere seen by the students of these minor forms, but the transition from one form to another, never, and it was but natural that they should regard species as immutable. They opposed the transmutationists and adherents of the Linnæan school, basing their contention upon the Biblical records and the constancy of the minor species through a series of generations, and dismissing as artificial and arbitrary the grouping of such real forms into larger "species."

The contest before Darwin led to two important results, the experimental demonstration of the existence of numerous constant, independent types of the Linnæan species, and the very general conviction that such constant types had arisen by transmutation, as the process was generally designated at that time, from the larger units. There were four more or less clearly distinct conceptions of the origin of species. The adherents of these schools were prepared in very different degrees for the revolutionary writings of Darwin. Those least prepared for the new doctrine were the adherents of the minor species. Variation they knew very well, but this never led to the transgression of specific bounds, and mutation they never saw. And yet it is strange that this escaped these keen observers, for it is to be oserved both in cultivation, where it produces the so-called single variations, and in nature as well.

b. THE THEORIES OF DARWIN AND WALLACE AND THE HYPOTHESIS OF MUTATION.

To have generally established the theory of descent, the scientific explanation of systematic relationship, is the immortal honor of Darwin. In doing this he revolutionized biological science and influenced most profoundly all other fields of intellectual activity. At and before the time of the publication of the *Origin of Species* the origin of varieties from the species was generally admitted. He insisted that "varieties are incipient species" and that "species have descended, like varieties, from other species." For the establishment of these fundamental hypotheses he collected data still of great value in present work in the same field. The task of Darwin was the establishment of the theory of descent, and his work was so effectively done that this is now generally accepted. The theory of descent finds its support in the data of comparative morphology, embryology, and paleontology. This is very different from that upon which the physiological side of the theory of evolution must be based, and upon just this side of the question the great master was never quite clear, or at least never expressed himself finally. In his earlier works it was the spontaneous variations to which he attached the greatest importance as material for natural selection, while in his later works, and under the influence of his critics, he attributed more significance to individual variability, though between the two he never sharply distinguished. Such was not necessary to his main task and would have introduced many difficult problems whose solution, had data for their elucidation been available, was not necessary for the establishment of the great theory and would only have detracted from the main object. Quotations might be cited to show Darwin's attitude toward the two kinds of variability, which he surely recognized, but between which he never very closely distinguished; but so long as it is borne in mind that he did recognize and distinguish *individual differences* and *single variations,* and that he did ascribe to the latter a very significant rôle in the origin of species, it is hardly necessary to discuss in detail the different ways in which he has expressed his valuation of the two types of variability as material for natural selection.

In his attitude toward this question—fundamental for future evolutionary work though not for the establishment upon comparative grounds of the broad lines of his theory—he showed all his characteristic caution, even exhibiting some of the weak points of his theory to those who were glad enough to avail themselves of any assistance in the criticisms they were so eager to hurl against it. It was another who restated the theory of Darwin, and in a simpler, more attractive form. Wallace presented to the public a work on Darwinism in which he attempted to show that species are the product of the selection of the differences of individual variability. His great purpose was to show that animals and plants do perpetually vary in the manner and to the amount requisite for the formation of new specific forms." The single variations of Darwin he regarded as quite without significance in descent. Not only did he assume as the basis of his theory a rapid increase in numbers with the consequent early death of numberless individuals, variability, and the survival of the fittest in the struggle for existence, but he went even further and assumed as an additional principle the inheritance of variations and the bettering of the race through the selection of the breeder. But the meaning of the term "race" must be very carefully defined. The various cultivated plants whose specific identity with wild forms is hardly to be recognized, are by no means necessarily the result of selection of individual variations. Many of the cultivated races are as old or older than their cultures; they are minor species, and their origin from a given wild form is as much a matter of conjecture as that of the common ancestry of the species of a genus. It must be said that it is upon very questionable grounds that Wallace concluded that: "It is therefore proved that if any particular kind of variation is preserved and bred from, the variation itself goes on increasing in amount to an enormous extent; and the bearing of this on the question of the origin of species is most important." This can only be assumed as a working hypothesis, not accepted as an established basis for further constructive work. That selection may carry individual variation to "an enormous extent," practically may be freely admitted, but this is very different from an enormous biological difference, and that it may extend to the "amount requisite" for the origin of specific form is a quite unestablished assumption. He shows the admirable explanation of the systematic and biological facts which the simplified theory of selection offers, but how the elementary or sub-species of which he furnished so many examples, originated, he does not satisfactorily prove. He does not show that the races produced by selection are constant when this selection is discontinued, or that specific characters may actually be the product of the action of selection upon the material of individual variability.

It must not be thought by those not well acquainted with the literature of evolution that the only critics of Darwin's theory have been those who opposed it on dogmatic grounds. The sufficiency of common variability with natural selection has often been called in question, and a paper upon the theory which has reached its present culmination in the two volumes of Professor DeVries would be incomplete without a brief mention of the attitude of some of those who have not joined in the general acceptance of natural selection.

Among the earliest of these was Cope, who granted that natural selection accounts for the survival of the fittest, but could not admit that common variability accounts for the origin of the fit, and for this he assumed special causes which he summarised as *Bathmism*. Semper discarded the explanations of selection and ascribed to the environment an important rôle, returning to the so-called *monde ambiant* of the French school. Upon the basis of a large series of data Louis Dollo declared that evolution is discontinuous, irreversible, and limited, thus opposing directly the logical conclusions to be drawn from the grounds assumed by Wallace.

A most important criticism of the current theory of descent is Bateson's well known *Materials for the Study of Variation, Treated with Special Regard to Discontinuity in the Origin of Species*. He maintains that the theory of descent must explain not only the relationship of organisms but their discontinuity as well. Species as they exist to-day are sharply separated from each other, and this great objection to the theory of gradual or continuous individual variation is not removed or surmounted by a reference to the numerous transitional forms which are to be found. These have been shown in many cases to be themselves sharply defined and constant units which, except for the amount of their differences, are just as deserving of specific designation as are the larger groups of forms, and do not indicate a continuous origin. Another important argument brought forth by Bateson against the selection theory is that it does not account for the useless differences which often appear as specific characters. Bateson concludes that: "The evidence of variation suggests in brief that the discontinuity of species results from the discontinuity of variation."

The geologist Scott opposed many statements of Bateson's work, referring to the continuous paleontological series in which progress, so far as we may judge from the historical fragments, seems to have been by almost imperceptible gradations. But it must be seriously questioned whether the continuity of paleontological remains is not that of a series of numbers and the differences in this series such as Bateson would designate as steps, rather than the difference of continuous variability. The term mutation has been used in geology more than in any other field of study, and many important considerations are taken up by Scott.

Korschinsky termed the mutation or spontaneous changes of earlier authors "heterogenesis," and brought together a large number of examples of garden forms, often distinguished so sharply from the parent type that, were their origin not known, they would be designated by the systematist as distinct species, which originated suddenly and without transition, and he concluded from the examination of his data that in horticulture all new forms, or more properly all new characteristics, originate by heterogenesis. According to him new varieties are not secured by selection or accumulation of individual variations does not occur. Selection is a conserving element, fixing varying characteristics of previous origin and preventing further variation, but is not able to produce new forms. In his writings, then, the cardinal principles of the selection theory and the mutation theory are stated and contrasted.

Other expressions of dissatisfaction with the current selection theory have been many and from men who could speak with authority, but they cannot be detailed here.

THE SEVERAL KINDS OF VARIATIONS.

The mutation theory is very little concerned with the origin of the larger groups or with the broad outlines of the theory of descent. These rest upon comparative and historical data, and, so far as the scientific world is concerned, have long been firmly established. But with the physiological aspects of the evolution theory it is quite different, and to it, especially to its experimental side, the author of the mutation theory directs our attention.

In a work dealing primarily with variation and its inheritance, the first thing to be done is to examine the different meanings of the term and discern exactly what it comprehends in the several phenomena which it has been made to cover. An analysis shows that under the term variability four essentially different phenomena have been included. There is the systematic polymorphism and the polymorphism produced by hybridization, there are the differences of organs and individuals obeying the law of Quetelet, and finally there are the so-called spontaneous modifications or single variations. For a clear understanding of the position occupied by the mutation theory these groups must be examined in some detail.

As to systematic polymorphism, the Linnæan species are collective species, artificial groups composed of a greater or lesser number of forms as sharply and completely distinguished from each other as the best species, but usually designated by the names of varieties and subspecies; varieties when they differ in but a single characteristic, but generally subspecies when they differ in the totality of their characteristics, in their habit, as it may be called.

In practice all possible differences of opinion upon this point have been defended by systematists. Some have insisted that these are elementary species and have given them binary names, breaking up the Linnæan species into minor forms. This is being done very extensively at the present time. The botanist who sees the mass of current literature can hardly look through the accumulation of a fortnight without finding papers devoted to the segregation of some of the older species. In Europe *Rubus*, the raspberry and blackberry, and in America *Crataegus*, the hawthorn, furnish striking examples.

A few years ago not a score of hawthorns were described for North America, while at the present time the number is ten times as great and being constantly increased. The most recently published flora of the Southern States contains 6300 species as compared with 3400 of the preceding flora of the same region, which was, however, published some years before. Such work is criticized unsparingly by many who see in it only confusion and useless labor, and insist that the characteristics of these new species are only individual variations, perhaps dependent upon special life conditions, pointing with unfeigned satisfaction to the cases where separate "species" have been described from the same plant when grown under different conditions. But evidence of special interest and importance is that furnished by *Draba verna,* a species of Linnæas which, as mentioned above, has since been divided into over 200 minor forms. Jordan had the most of these under cultivation in his garden and was so thoroughly convinced of their constancy as to regard the minor forms as created and species as immutable, while others have satisfied themselves in the same way of the constancy of many of the minor forms,

Some emphasize the minuteness of the differences which separate these minor forms from each other, and regard their use as specific characters as unjustifiable. Those of the opposite opinion point to the fact that these forms differ from each other not in a single or a few characteristics but in all, so that a complete description must be very elaborate, and to their constancy in culture, the lack of transition between the individual types or between these types and the ideal species from which they are supposed to have sprung. The treatment of these forms by the descriptive botanist must be largely a matter of judgment on the part of the one concerned with the elaboration of the group in hand. So long as consistency is maintained, it matters little whether they are designated as varieties or all given binary names. Possibly the most convenient and simple solution of the problem would be the establishment of a ternary nomenclature in which, with all the minuteness of subdivision characteristic of modern systematic work, the old familiar generic and specific names under which the complexes have long been known might be retained. The specialist would then refer to a plant by its generic, specific, and minor species name, while the amateur or the morphologist or physiologist would simply refer to the larger group, the genus or the genus and Linnæan species. But with all the talk of species, subspecies, varieties, and nomenclature it must not be forgotten that the essential question is whether forms are actually differentiable and constant in their characteristics.

Before and since the time of Darwin it has been assumed that varities are of common ancestry, but only in the rarest cases is there a historical record. Even in the garden varieties this holds true; the record of their origin is generally wanting or untrustworthy. This part of the field of variability must be largely comparative; its data are morphological, and only very rarely is it to be approached from the historical or experimental side.

The polymorphism produced by hybridization is due to the changed combinations of the heritable characteristics of the parents. For scientific investigations the simplest possible combinations should be selected. The investigator selects the least "variable" species. The plant breeder, on the other hand, prefers parents of which at least one is very "variable," so that the range of variation of the hybrid may be increased and the possibility of securing a new form thus heightened. To a discussion of these problems a second paper is to be devoted, and so we shall not consider it further here.

Variability in its restricted sense, or individual variability, comprehends the differences of individuals and organs which are amenable to the law of Quetelet, which was formulated since the time of Darwin, and which, with the labors of Galton, Weldon, Bateson, Davenport, Duncker, and others of recent years has given rise to an entirely new phase of biological investigation, the statistical study of variation and heredity, and the application of the results of these studies to the problems of organic evolution. The results of these investigations show that common, individual, or fluctuating, variations group themselves around a mean value, the frequency of occurrence of individuals or organs varying on either side of the mean, decreasing as the degree of their deviation from the mode increases. In fact, when a large series of observations are taken and the curve plotted, it is found to coincide with the curve of the probability of error.

We may take an illustration from Professor DeVries's own work, though others equally good may be found in the literature in almost unlimited number. Seeds of the common red-spotted garden bean were found to vary in length from eight to sixteen millimetres. In the lot of 448 beans, the numbers with the different lengths were found to be as follows:

Length, millimetres, . .	8	9	10	11	12	13	14	15	16
Number	1	2	23	108	167	106	33	7	1

It will be seen that by erecting upon a base line in which the different seed lengths serve as abscissas, ordinates corresponding in length to the number of beans in that class, and connecting these ordinates, a very symmetrical curve closely corresponding to that secured by the expansion of a binomial will be secured.

Numerous illustrations of this kind might be given. The fruit length of *Oenothera*, the number of the ray flowers of the Compositæ, the height, and weight, and strength of pull, and keenness of vision of man, as well as his social traits, all follow the same law. The validity of this law for various characteristics of a very large series of organisms, both animal and vegetable, has been established by direct observation and measurement. This type of variability has been variously designated as fluctuating, gradual, continuous, reversible, limited, statistical, and universal. Of these terms, individual has been used most frequently in zoological and anthropological studies, while the best general term is fluctuating or flowing. In botany there is a distinction to be made between individual and partial variability, the former designating the difference between individuals, the latter the equally numerous differences between the organs of the same individual. Darwin repeatedly insisted that this form of variation "perpetually occurs," and Wallace laid even greater emphasis on this point. It might then be termed perpetual or uninterrupted.

Now the generally accepted theory of natural selection is that environmental conditions continually select only a certain class or classes of individuals, or, to state it more precisely, eliminate all not having the peculiar characteristics adapting them to their life conditions. So in the course of a longer or shorter period of time one or more good species would be developed, showing as the fundamental distinguishing mark the perfection and fixation of the fortunate variation which determined its superiority over all the other individuals in the competition for existence. Of course such new species would be expected to vary somewhat.

Let us use again the illustration of the bean and consider for the sake of argument that the small seeds have in some way a great advantage over the larger ones under the conditions in which the plants grow. In the course of a few or many generations all but small-seeded individuals would disappear. These would vary in length from four to twelve millimeters, but the most of the individuals would have a mean value. The curve would be similar to the original one but with a mean representing an entirely different species. Had the larger seeds been selected, the same thing would have occurred, but the mode of the new species would have been large instead of small.

Supposing that both large and small seeds were especially adapted to certain life conditions, then two divergent species would have been developed. There would be a form with large and another with small seeds, each showing a considerable range of variation. Perhaps this variation might be so great as to cause the limits of the species to overlap, so that a continuous series of lengths from the shortest of the short seeds to the longest of the long seeds would result, and from the measurement of any individual seed it would be impossible to say to which species it belonged. Such transgressive variability, as it is called, very frequently occurs.

This illustration may make clearer the distinction between common or fluctuating variability, and mutation, to which we must presently turn, and at the same time depict a purely hypothetical case of evolution by selection according to the theories of Darwin, or more especially Wallace, for it must be borne in mind that Darwin attached much importance to the single variations.

The illustration is not an altogether satisfactory one, since species are not based upon a single characteristic. But it is a very convenient one for illustrating the supposed action of selection, and for our present purposes it is unnecessary to assume a more complicated situation. One of the strongest supports for the Darwinian theory has always been the evidence of garden selection with its consequent improvement. Many cases are known in which artificial selection has produced just such results as those we have assumed for the seed lengths in the bean. But for the origin of specific characters it is not necessary merely that a modification may be effected by selection. It must become fixed, become independent of selection.

"The true danger reef of the Darwinian theory is the transition from artificial breeding selection to natural selection," says Paul Janet. Garden selection has not yet secured the fixation of the modifications of selection. Common variability may also be termed linear variation, occurring as it does toward plus or minus. It is also characterized by reversion to the type. It does not lose its plasticity: the long- and short-seeded races of beans, to use again our illustration, might be developed with great ease, but so soon as selection ceased, the variations would again group themselves around the old mode in the course of but a few generations. In evolutionary speculation the different processes which have been included under the general term of horticultural improvement have not been carefully enough distinguished, and this looseness of expression has led to error and confusion. To this we shall refer later.

As has already been suggested, the fourth type of variation is that in which the changes are not gradual and flowing, but sudden and unmediated. Saltatory variations they have sometimes been called, but it seems better to speak of the individual transitions as steps and of variation by steps. To this class belong those known as bud variations, in which certain buds of an individual give rise to a branch of essentially different character from the rest of the plant. Another group includes the so-called single variations of Darwin. These are solitary individuals of characteristics markedly different from those of their parents or neighbors, which are at rare intervals to be found in a garden bed and which sometimes become the ancestors of a new and constant race. Many examples of such might be given, but these may be reserved for later paragraphs. Each type has advantages and disadvantages as material for study. The bud variations demonstrate beyond question the genetic connection with another form and show most perfectly their unmediated origin.

They must always be investigated with caution, since they are likely to be produced from hybrids or from plants belonging to varieties with mixed and only partially fixed characters. The single variations have the disadvantage of leaving some uncertainty as to the possible origin of the plant. The new form appears suddenly and unmediatedly. Nothing is known of it until it is there, and then it is usually too late to be absolutely sure of the source or purity of the seed and many other considerations of importance.

The impression that these steps are longer than the range of common or fluctuating variations, and perhaps differ from this type of variation chiefly in their magnitude, is very common, and not a surprising one. One sometimes hears the remark that the mutation theory merely disregards the smaller and considers only the larger variations.

But the difference is not merely quantitative, it is qualitative as well. The difference between these steps is often smaller than the range of common variability. The numerous minor species into which *Draba verna* has been divided differ from each other very slightly, and less than the range of the fluctuating variability of some species, or even less than the different parts of a single individual of some others, and yet years of cultivation have shown them to be sharply differentiated and constant systematic units. Other examples might be given to establish this point, but the space will be better employed in giving a very apt illustration used by Galton, showing the differences between mutation and variation. A polyhedron rolling upon a smooth surface has a centre of gravity for every side. On any side it may oscillate back and forth without passing away from the center of gravity of the side upon which it rests. This may represent common or fluctuating variability. But a greater force may change the centre of gravity of the polyhedron, and then it will come to rest upon another side where it may oscillate indefinitely in response to some small force until some force as great as that which caused the original change, again changes the centre and moves it backward or forward. A change in the centre of gravity and the consequent shifting of the whole polyhedron represents a step or mutation. The number of the sides of the polyhedron determines the magnitude of the steps; increase this number, and the difference in character between the successive positions becomes less and less. And to carry the figures a little farther and let the path of the rolling polyhedron represent the history of the species, we see that each change of position has represented a step —a mutation.

THE COMPARATIVE DATA OF THE MUTATION THEORY.

The supporters of the theory of natural selection must show not only that common variability may be carried to the extent of specific differences by the requirements of natural forces, and the modification thus secured then become fixed, so as to be independent of these forces in heredity, but it must also account for discontinuity—the absence of transitional stages of the nature of those attributable to fluctuating variability. The mutation theory, if it is to be considered on a basis of equality with the old theory, must show that while explaining their discontinuity, the assumption of a variability by steps, a special species-forming variability, can account for the high degree of differentiation exhibited in the vegetable kingdom.

One of the most essential things is to examine as searchingly as possible the nature of the species, to have clearly in mind just what is to be understood by the term "species" as used in the terminology of experimental and comparative evolution. Once it was assumed that the Linnæan species were created, just as earlier it had been thought that genera had that distinction. Since this is no longer held to be true, the conception of the species has been linked with the binary nomenclature—that which was given a generic and a specific name was a species. Earlier in this essay some emphasis was laid upon the statement that species are collective groups. Linnæus himself recognized this fact, and it was pointed out by others of the old masters of systematic botany. Collective species are imperative necessities in all fields of biological work. The grouping of plants into species has the same value as their arrangement in genera and higher systematic divisions but must be regarded as equally artificial.

Let us take an illustration. A systematist may examine material which falls clearly into three or four distinct species, composed each of a number of minor forms, separated by wide differences over which no fluctuating variability can furnish transitions. Later collections or those from widely distant localities may fill the gaps, and the problem becomes an exceedingly difficult one. The whole series is composed of a large number of slightly differing units, each well characterized, but in the opinion of the student of that particular group of too small denomination to merit separate specific designation. So long as certain groups of the slightly differing forms were lacking the others stood well isolated and could be given specific rank, but when the series becomes complete there appears no point at which it can be divided. This group might represent a wider range of variation than all the other species of the genus combined, but, so long as all the differences are of lesser rank than those selected as specific, consistency demands that it be retained a simple species or that the whole genus be resolved into its most elementary forms.

Had some of the elementary types been exterminated or never collected, the several species originally described would have stood as valid, valid from the standpoint of the descriptive systematist, but not from that of the experimental evolutionist who must recognize as the unit only the smallest constant type, the so-called elements of the species, if such exist,—and to show this is the primary object of the mutation theory—and not artificial conveniences.

The demand has always been made that the origin of a species be the subject of direct observation, and, while the broad theory of evolution is so firmly established on comparative and historical grounds that the observation of the origin of a species is no longer needed to convince the learned world of the validity of the theory, the requirement is a perfectly legitimate one.

The emphasis which has frequently been laid upon the slowness with which selection may modify and transform species has doubtless had its influence in deterring investigators from approaching the subject of the influence of selection from an experimental point f view, but a more serious hindrance has been the vagueness of eas concernig species, subspecies, and varieties.

It is obviously unreasonable to demand that the origin of a innæan or collective species be observed. The origin of such an tificial group is a historical phenomenon, consisting in the elimi- ation by natural selection of certain of the elementary types in e chain and the consequent dividing of the one continuous series to smaller ones separated by gaps of greater or less extent. The rigin of these species is a subject for historical and comparative it not for experimental investigations.

But when it is admitted that it is unfair to ask for the observed rigin or still more for the experimental production of artificial roups of forms, there still remains another and very serious diffi- ilty. So soon as evidence for the origin of a new type from an- ther is brought forward, it is immediately opposed by the assertion iat it is only a *variety* of the species from which it sprung. It is iscouraging to the investigator to have the results of laborious re- :arches set aside by a mere juggling of ill defined terms in that l forms whose origin is more or less definitely known are desig- ated as varieties, and it becomes necessary to examine the nature f the most minute systematic units as carefully as the larger arti- cial groups.

Few things are more variable than the terms variability and iriety. The comprehension of all forms—except hybrids—whose rigin is more or less definitely known, under the term variety in- udes the improved or acclimatized races and the widely different ngle or sudden variations. In nature, on the other hand, varieties e regarded by the best systematists as those forms which are fferentiated by a single characteristic. A very good example is iat of the common and the purple Jamestown weed, described as vo species by Linnæus but now made species and variety, since e only difference is the presence of coloring matter in the stem, aves, and flower of the purple one. Such varieties are usually just s independent and just as constant in culture as the best species. 'ariety in this case then means only a special kind of species. Varieties are only small species," says Darwin.

Varieties differ greatly from the numerous elementary species of Jordan. The latter differ in almost all their characters. If it is true that species in nature consist of a number of individual and constant types, then it is to be supposed that those selected by man for cultivation will also be composed of a number of types.

Pliny recognized numerous varieties of many cultivated plants, 43 of pears, 29 of apples, 10 of plums, 8 of cherries, etc., while the *Théatre d'agriculture*, published in 1600, listed a few more. It is quite possible that some of these forms originated in cultivation or even under the influence of cultivation, but whence they came is entirely unknown, and it is quite possible that all the different types were present when agriculture began and were brought as such under cultivation from the same or different habitats. There is no reason to assume that wild plants were brought into cultivation but a single time, and with repeated gatherings of the seed of wild plants from different localities the probability of securing a number of different types would be greatly increased.

In the beginning of the nineteenth century the wheat fields of Le Couteur on the Isle of Jersey were found to be not a homogeneous culture but exhibiting numerous well defined types of which Professor La Grasco recognized at least twenty-three. Seed from these was selected, and when grown separately they showed themselves pure and constant, and the better kinds were cultivated and profitably placed in the trade, where some are still to be found.

In Scotland much the same method was followed with various cereals by Patrick Shirreff and with closely corresponding results. Several types hitherto unrecognized were found, the seed increased for two or more generations, and placed at once on the market. These experiments show that wheat, oats, and barley were at that time a mixture of constant subspecies, just as has been seen for wild plants. Of the origin of these subspecies as little is known in one case as in the other.

Perhaps of even greater interest to the general reader than the origin of the different varieties of cultivated cereals is that of the history of the hundreds of varieties in our orchards and vineyards. The common origin of our varieties of apples and pears need not be questioned, but except in the case of a few of the more recent introductions, for which there is a trustworthy record, this must be regarded as a deduction from the accepted fact of descent rather than historically recorded data. Some of the most interesting observations available are those of a Belgian plant breeder, Van Mons, of the first half of the nineteenth century, who introduced many of the best-known sorts of the present time. He disclaims the credit of the production of any new forms, "*La nature seule crée.*" All the forms he introduced he found growing wild, mostly in the Ardennes.

With cultivation in the garden the wild scrubs lose their thorns, and the coarse, small fruits become larger, fleshier, and juicier. But form, flavor. color, and other distinguishing characteristics do not originate in or through cultivation. They are already present, and the only effect of cultivation is to bring them to their fullest perfection. Van Mons was so fully cnvinced of the independence and constancy of his forms that he called them subspecies instead of varieties. To introduce a new sort, then, one must not select seeds of the best cultivated types but rather, according to Van Mons, seek for the seed of a small, poor fruit, but of a type as yet unknown.

Flax, red clover, and the poppy show such sup-species, or minor species. The principal types of *Chrysanthemum indicum* were brought as such into Europe, and more recent varieties have been derived from these by crossing. Numerous so-called varieties, even many monstrosities, are almost as old as the cultivation of the species itself and are figured or listed in the old herbals, while of the most important cultivated plants, such as hyacinths, tulips, and Ranunculus hundreds of varieties were known.

Only one more illustration may be given. The cactus dahlias of the present time are so universally known and admired that the history of their origin might be read with interest. A Holland grower received from a correspondent in Mexico a chest of bulbs, roots, rhizomes, and tubers, which had spoiled in transit so that only a single tuber produced a plant. This was the dahlia, and when in flower was found to be of the hitherto unknown cactus type. From it the numerous cactus varieties have been produced by crossing with forms already cultivated. All effort to find the plant in the region where the chest was filled has been fruitless—all that is known is that it was there. How it originated is not known. New forms are wont to be found only in the largest cultures. Wier found his cut-leaved maple among about a million seedlings, and the first double dahlias were found in a culture of about 10,000 plants.

The agreement of wild and cultivated species in their polymorphic composition has been considered. The importance of the composite nature of cultivated forms has so impressed itself upon breeders and some of the earlier botanists as to lead to the saying: "The first essential for the production of something new is to possess it already." In these paragraphs the fact has been emphasized particularly that not nearly all the cultivated forms are to be considered as originating in or especially through cultivation. The establishment of this thesis is a strong argument against the theory of natural selection, for which the triumphs of cultural selection have been the strongest pillars of support. But it must not be inferred that new forms never do originate in cultivation. It is to a few trustworthy records of this occurrence that we shall now turn. The data available for this examination strongly emphasize the assumption of a fundamental difference between the improved races and subspecies. So convinced of this was Von Rümker, for instance, that he divided his well known work on the breeding of wheat into two sections, the one treating of selection for improvement, the other of production of new forms. The first of these has, according to him, the object of fixing, more sharply differentiating, and increasing the superiority of characters already present, while the second consists rather in the search for new forms which occasionally appear. One of the best known records is that of *Chelidonium laciniatum*. This form, characterized by its deeply cut leaves and petals, was first observed in a bed of *Chelidonium majus* in the garden of a Heidelberg apothecary in the year 1590. Neither he nor any other botanist to whom he sent specimens of his novelty had ever seen or found described a similar form, nor has it been found wild up to the present time. Since the time of its appearance it has been and is still constant with no reversion to the characteristics of the typical *C. majus*.

In a garden Cyclamen, in which the impossibility of crossing prevents the assumption of hybrid origin, a number of forms seem to have originated in this same way. A strawberry without runners, the Gaillou strawberry was found as a single example among a lot of the ordinary type and has been found to be quite constant. Cauliflower and kohlrabi of the kitchen garden, and other varieties as well, originated as monstrosities of the common cabbage, and the same might be shown of other well-fixed garden forms.

Sometimes these new types have originated independently in widely separated localities or at different times. Several good examples might be given of the discovery of similar and constant novelties in different régions. A double Syringa was recently found in a garden and was introduced as an entirely new form, and was so considered until it was found recorded in an old work bearing the date of 1671.

Other examples of constant and heritable subspecies and varieties might be given, but enough have been mentioned to illustrate the comparative data of the mutation theory. This has led to the conclusion that the gradual development of the elementary species has not yet been demonstrated among cultivated plants, but that numerous cases of the sudden origin of new "species" may be considered valid or at least highly probable. Considering the fewness of the cases in which the new forms are isolated and kept from the swamping incident to free cross-fertilization, they show themselves very generally heritable and as constant as the older so-called good species.

THE EXPERIMENTAL DATA OF THE MUTATION THEORY.

a. THE INSUFFICIENCY OF VARIABILITY WITH SELECTION.

It is of great interest to establish on comparative grounds the theory that the discontinuity of systematic units as they exist at the present time is due to discontinuity of variation. But, however strong this comparative evidence may be, however complete the series of forms showing no transition stages, it cannot carry with it the conviction which experimental proof may offer, and it is the production of this experimental proof which lends such weight to the mutation theory.

In the preceding pages variation has been divided into four classes, systematic polymorphism, the polymorphism of hybrids, common or fluctuating varibility, and mutation. Systematic polymorphism is largely a problem of descriptive botany and concerns only indirectly the experimental evolutionist. The different combinations of elementary characteristics found in hybrids offers a most promising field for experimental work, and to it the second volume of *Die Mutationstheorie* is a contribution. Our present purpose is to examine carefully the nature of the third and fourth classes of variability, fluctuating or flowing variability, and mutation. and fourth classes of variability, fluctuating or flowing variability, and mutation.

Comparative evidence may stand for much, but it is upon experimental grounds that the greatest weight must be laid. The evidence in favor of the selection theory is drawn in great part from the data of artificial selection. This has necessarily constituted the mass of the experimental data of the selection theory. Beyond this it has depended upon comparative investigations, and this evidence has been very satisfactory for the establishment of the theory of morphological and historical descent.

Experimental work may be undertaken along three different lines. The ability of selection to develop new and constant forms may be investigated as searchingly as possible, the hypothesis of a special species-forming variability may be given the greatest weight by actual observation of the origin of distinct and constant forms, and finally the conduct of the elementary characters of plants may be studied in hybrids. All of these methods have been employed in the development of the mutation theory, but it is with only the first two that we are concerned in the present paper.

In approaching the question as to the ability of natural selection to develop new species it is first necessary to examine the validity of the data upon which much of the theoretical discussion has been based. It may be safely asserted that in the past too much theoretical significance has been attached to the practical achievements of horticulturists. By many every new garden form has been attributed to artificial selection. To this we shall recur later.

It must be borne in mind that practical plant breeding is carried on not for the purpose of collecting scientific data, but for financial profit, and while the breeder may be quite willing or anxious to gain an insight into the scientific laws underlying his profession, it is usually more profitable to experiment at haphazard and upon a larger scale, saving the promising individuals and burning the rest, than to undertake the detailed and laborious researches necessary to the formation of detailed laws of conduct. For this reason accurate accounts of experiments are usually dispensed with. When a particularly desirable form is secured, the process by which it was obtained is generally unknown. It came from a series of broad and varied experiments, but which particular condition or combination was the fortunate one is unknown or alleged only from a chance memory, which may or may not be trusted. An accurate and painstaking record of all experiments would usually cost more than it is worth to the man of practical aims. The biologist must necessarily work with the fewest and simplest factors possible to avoid the hopeless confusion incident to an admission of all factors. The originator of new forms, on the other hand, seeeks to increase rather than to decrease the multiplicity of factors in his experiment. Systematic polymorphism, crossing, enrichment of the soil, mutation and the gradual improvement by selection may all be thrown together indiscriminately in the hope that something good may be secured. That many thousands of failures are made, matters little so long as there is occasionally something good which pays for the whole experiment.

To attribute the whole success of horticultural improvements to selection is far from the truth. There are several quite distinct processes to be borne in mind. There is the improvement by hybridization with newly discovered and in some respects more desirable forms. Genera which are very rich in species or those in which there have been occasional discoveries of new types in little known regions have been crossed in so many different ways that they present an insoluble tangle of garden forms which owe their origin almost exclusively to varied combination of the elements of the various wild forms. Examples of this are Fuchsia, Dahlia, Chrysanthemum, Begonia, Gladiolus, Caladium, and Amaryllus. Hybridization is a so much surer and easier method of securing forms that it is rarely to the interest of the breeder to exclude the possibility of crossing. Only when a new race is to be fixed or where the process of pure selection has been decided upon is this done. And only when this factor is excluded have the results of the breeder any significance for the selection theory. In selecting examples to illustrate the effect of horticultural selection, too great care cannot be exercised in making sure that there is no possibility of a previous cross-fertilization by the wind or insects.

Horticultural and agricultural "improvement" may be here compared. The varieties introduced every year in greater or less numbers by trade gardeners may be new elementary species or varieties, originating suddenly and unexpectedly in the garden, they may be newly introduced elementary species or varieties hitherto uncultivated, or they may be hybrids representing new combinations. These forms are then freed from the effect of previous crossing, a process which requires a period of time of from two to five years, which time is also necessary for obtaining sufficient seed to make it profitable to offer the variety to the trade. The entire profit of such a new form is in the first year of its introduction, since, once introduced, seed may be supplied by any firm or by the kitchen garden as well as by the one first offering the novelty. For this reason a newly originated or discovered from is often offered to the public simultaneously by a combination of several houses so that the first year's profits may be the greater.

With the true improved races the case is quite different. These depend upon the careful and constant selection of the best individuals, and the one who secures the best forms may be sure of his yearly profits from the sale of seeds until some rival introduces a more desirable article, since constant selection is required to maintain the betterment secured and seed cannot be saved from th crops grown for commercial purposes, but must frequently be secured anew from the original source or from some other where selection is just as keen as in the original.

To account for the origin of species by natural selection it must be assumed that this selection may carry the differences offered by common variability to the extent of specific characteristics, and that the degree of differentiation from the original type shall then become independent of the selective influences. The first of these assumptions is quite possible, since common variability in some forms shows a wider range than that offered by the specific limits of others; but that selection may so fix these that they become independent of it, can be admitted only with a much greater weight of evidence than that at present available.

Before speaking at greater length of this let us examine a few cases in point. To secure the horticultural betterment which has so often served as proof for the theory of natural selection does not require the great length of time many suppose, nor is the improvement unlimited in extent. The universally known fact that certain plants have been in cultivation for centuries and are widely different from the wild forms from which we assume they have sprung does not necessarily indicate that these forms have been constantly and uniformly improved by selection during this period, or indeed that they owe their fixed characteristics to selection at all. In our orchards we have a vast number of varieties of apples, but the apple is in its wild state a very polymorphic genus. This and hybridization, and the origin of new forms by mutation in culture, are to be taken into consideration.

Historical evidence is almost, if not quite, wanting. Almost the only method of obtaining an insight into the action of selection is the study of such records of exact experimentation as are available, and the accumulation of such other data as opportunity will permit. That available is very limited in amount.

In making this examination of the sufficiency of natural selection it seems that two points are of especial importance. The one is the rapidity with which an individual characteristic may be brought to the maximum of its possible improvement, and the other is the certainty of regression when the selective influence is removed. The most of the betterment of a form may be secured in from two to five generations, depending largely upon the number of characteristics to be modified. Lévêque improved the wild carrot so much in from three to five generations that the roots were as fleshy and suitable for culinary purposes as the common cultivated form. Carrière had the same success with the wild radish, and Buckmann found that the wild parsnip could be rapidly improved by cultivation. An unusually interesting case is furnished by certain alpine primulas which have developed two seasonal forms, one of which blossoms before and the other after the cutting of the principal harvest of hay. Of course, in this case it cannot be determined whether it is a case of slow selective or of sudden and unmediated chance adaptation to the peculiar conditions. One of the finest series of data for the study of selection is furnished by the history of the sugar beet, the lines of improvement being not too complex, and the record of a nature suitable for statistical comparison.

Of the origin of the sugar beet we can say little. At the beginning of the nineteenth century numerous varieties were known, but of their origin we know as little as of most cultivated plants. It is simply with the selective improvement of the beet that we wish to deal. From 1830 to 1840 Vilmorin selected the sugar beet with reference to external characteristics, but not until 1851 did he test the sugar content of the individual roots, when he found that they contained an amount of sugar varying from 7 to 14 per cent. The seeds of those richest in sugar were selected for the next planting, and in the second generation he secured beets with 21 per cent. of sugar. The methods available were not highly accurate or convenient, permitting an examination of but a limited number of specimens, but it is probable that he found too little rather than too much sugar. In 1874, when the vastly improved method of the determination of the sugar content by means of the polariscope and selection according to its indications was begun, the sugar content was 10-14 per cent., in poor years showing a mean of 10 per cent., in good years 12-14 per cent., while variations from 9.5 to 17.5 per cent. were not rare. The new method spread gradually in Germany from 1878 to 1881. At present an immense number of beets are polarized each year in a large manufactory. The sugar percentages are found to form a very symmetrical curve which is in close agreement with Quetelet's law. Some individual figures from the establishment of a Holland firm may be of interest. In 1892 roots containing less than 14 per cent. were not utilized for seed, those with 14 to 16 per cent. furnished plants the seed of which was sold, while those with 16 to 18 per cent. furnished seed plants for their own race, the so-called élite, from whose seed the beets to be polarized in the next generation were to be grown. In this year only four out of 180,000 specimens examined showed more than 18 per cent. of sugar. Since 1892 the number of roots polarized has been increased to 300,000 with the result that the upper limit of 21 per cent. of sugar was reached. The plants commercially grown from the seed offered to the trade showed a mean of 13 to 14 per cent. of sugar.

The commercial profit to be derived from increasing the percentage of sugar from 7-8 to 14-16 or over is evidently enormous, but when it is noted that the highest limit reached in the hundreds of thousands of specimens tested by the Holland firm coincides with the highest percentage observed by Vilmorin, 21 per cent., it will be seen that twenty-five generations of selection seem to have produced very little biological difference. Other races grown under different conditions may yield an upper limit of 26 per cent., but it must be borne in mind that the present scope of the beet sugar industry offers the possibility of higher maxima.

Selection is not carried on with regard to the sugar content alone but for all other characters which have been found of importance, only about one tenth of the harvest being selected in the field for the final chemical examination. The development of the sugar content of the beet has been slow and more or less uniform, but this is attributable in a large measure to the gradual improvement of methods. Never has the betterment become independent of selection. With the exceedingly sharp selection described above the quantity of seed procurable is far too small for commercial purposes, and an intermediate generation must be grown to increase this quantity. Even in this one generation the reversion is very great, and should more than two generations be grown it would be so great that the gain of the laborious selection for the so-called élite culture would be lost. A half a century of labor and experience has produced results of the highest commercial importance, but so far as can be seen, has accomplished nothing toward the establishment of a constant systematic form.

Here we may not take the space necessary for a discussion of the cereals in their relation to the problem before us. It must suffice to say that the evidence they offer confirms that furnished by the sugar beet—that selection does not lead to the formation of constant characters but only to a betterment which is dependent upon constant selection for its maintenance.

We may not discuss further comparative data. In our necessarily much condensed review this seems the most suitable place to mention one of the most interesting chapters in the first volume of Professor DeVries's work—a chapter in which he has, as everywhere else in his researches, sought to introduce the experimental methods. The simplification of the study of variation by the recognition of the two fundamentally different types of variability is not sufficient. Each of these must be subjected to the most searching experimental study.

One method is the placing in opposition of the two apparently different influences. Selection and nutrition forms one of the most suggestive chapters of evolutionary literature. The detailed treatment of this interesting section is quite out of question in the present place, since the description of the experiments and explanation of the statistical methods used in the exact comparisons would lead too far. We must simply state in the most general way that the common or fluctuating variability of certain plants was accurately measured by the statistical methods which have shown such a development of recent years, and then the influence of selection and mutation upon the variability measured as they acted separately and combined or antagonistically. The effect of the best possible conditions of nutrition in its broadest sense, and of the sharpest selection were compared and then opposed to each other by giving the plants the best possible conditions for growth while selection was made of the poorest individuals for seed plants or vice versa. Experiments were made with the fruit lengths of *Oenothera Lamarckiana,* the number of branches in the inflorescence of the Umbelliferæ and the number of rays of the composite flowers. The results of these studies show that when selection and nutrition are opposed to each other sometimes the one and sometimes the other has the controlling influence, while again it remains undecided. The investigations indicate that selection and nutrition influence the plant in the same way, and that it is a matter of circumstance which predominates in its influence. In other words, to express this more significantly, fluctuating variability is a manifestation of the physiology of nutrition. The external causes of mutation are as yet quite unknown.

Of such vital importance to the mutation theory is the establishment of the hypothesis that selection does not lead to the origin of specific characters, that we shall give here, in the form of a summary, the supporting evidence for this hypothesis, after which we must pass directly to the second class of evidence for the mutation theory, the direct observation of the origin of species or specific characters.

1. Statistical investigations have replaced the old vague idea of an all-sided variability with that of linear variation in a plus or minus direction. Existing characters may be increased in magnitude, but something new does not come into existence, and since the differentiation of organisms depends in the main upon the development of new characteristics, the necessary material is not to be found in linear variations.

2. The view that linear variation is unlimited and may be carried farther by the selection of centuries than by that of a few years is entirely unsupported. In the betterment of individual characteristics, two or three generations under favorable conditions, and three to five generations under ordinary conditions, are sufficient to bring the improvement to its maximum. Further selection in the absence of special conditions serves only to maintain what has already been secured.

3. The limits of selection are no more sharply marked than those of fluctuating variability. By vastly increasing the number of individuals the range of variability may be slightly increased, and the same is true of selection. This has been illustrated in the development of the sugar beet. The idea that with selection variability in a certain direction increases is quite contrary to the better known cases in which progress soon becomes less rapid and gradually ceases. Darwin's idea that in the first years of their introduction into cultivation plants showed themselves increasingly more variable, probably depended in part upon the discovery of elementary species, latent or overlooked until that time.

4. Upon every selection there follows a regression the greater the sharper the selection, and independent of its duration. Apparently more than one half of the betterment is lost in each generation. In improvement a doubling, or, when selection is in the opposite direction, a halving of the value of the original characteristic is all that may generally be obtained in the best cases, and usually much less is attainable; the striking examples furnished by fleshy roots and fruits furnishing only an apparent exception.

5. The principal difference between improved races and species—and even the most minute elementary species—is the inconstancy of the former and the constancy of the latter. The improved races are just as dependent upon selection for their permanence as for their development; when selection ceases to act, the race characteristics revert to the original type in about the same time as that required for their development.

6. Constant improvement of the methods of selection may secure constant betterment of the race. Every improvement of method signifies a sharper selection, but if the method remain the same the limit attainable is constant.

7. Scientific investigation should, so far as possible, be confined to individual characteristics. The laws of correlation will rarely allow this. In practical work, since general betterment is desired the time necessary is greater, just twice the number of generations being required with two characteristics with cultures of the same extent.

8. Every improved race is adapted to a special environment, soil, climate, and manuring. Only when their special requirements are met is the promised yield assured. In this they agree with the local races of the wild flora.

9. The importance of natural selection as influencing artificial selection in the fields has often been taken too little into account in theoretical biology. Cold, frost, moisture, crowding, lateness in maturing "select" in the field with the same surety as the best breeder. In rare cases, as in acclimatization where the object is mainly elimination of those not adapted to the conditions, natural and artificial selection coöperate, but in most cases they strongly oppose each other, natural selection tending to favor the stronger, but according to the special taste of the breeder, less desirable individuals. The problem of the breeder becomes then first the maintenance of his race.

The discussion here given to the first of the three paths open to the experimental evolutionist in considering the problem of the origin of species is meager and with many gaps, but it must suffice for the present while we pass by the second to indicate some of the results which have been obtained in the third, the path which Professor DeVries has broken for the scientific world and the one in which it is to be hoped that other investigators will eagerly follow.

J. Arthur Harris, Ph. D.

St. Louis, Mo.

[TO BE CONCLUDED.]

THE CHRIST OF PRIMITIVE CHRISTIAN FAITH IN THE LIGHT OF RELIGIO-HISTORICAL CRITICISM.[1]

IV.

CHRIST AS CONQUEROR OF DEATH AND BRINGER OF LIFE.

TO the faithful believer, Christ is the Saviour because he conquered Death and Hell (Hades), deprived death of its power, and brought life and incorruption to light. (1 Cor. xv. 55 ff., 2 Tim. i. 10.)

In order to understand this belief in its original and actual significance, we must take into consideration that for the ancients death was not a natural occurence, but the result of supernatural causes. Either an angry god decreed death as a punishment, (as befell the whole human race after the fall of Adam, Rom. v. 12 ff.) or else demoniac powers tainted men with the destructive poison of sickness and sin, thus bringing them into the power of Death, who as a ruler of the underworld keeps souls imprisoned in his dungeon.

Consequently deliverance from death is accomplished in three ways: the son of God reconciles sinful mankind with God by the atonement of his vicarious death, thus redeeming them from the curse of the law which condemns them, and restoring them to the favor of God (Rom. iii. 24 f., 2 Cor. v. 19 ff., Gal. i. 4, iii. 13); or he cleanses them from the demon's taint of sin and death by the purifying power of his sacred blood (Heb. ix. 11 ff., x. 14, xxii. 29);

---

[1] Translated from the original manuscript by Prof. W. H. Carruth, University of Kansas

or again, by his own death and resurrection he wrested from the dictator of death, the devil, and from the evil spirits, their power over mankind (Heb. ii. 14, Coloss. ii. 15, i. 13 f., 1 John iii. 8).

According to the first and second views, the resurrection of Christ is the divine recognition of the atoning and purifying effect of his death (Rom. iv. 25); according to the third the resurrection and ascension[1] of Christ is the proof of the victory gained by him over Hades and death, whereby he became the "Prince of Life," possessor, pledge, and mediator of life for us (Acts iii. 15, Rev. i. 18, John xi. 25, iii. 13 ff., 1 Peter iii. 18 ff.).

The means by which Christ, being raised up, imparts his life to his followers, are (1) belief in his name, which includes confessing and calling upon it (Rom. x. 9 ff., John iii. 15 ff., xx. 31, xvi. 23 f.); (2) baptism in his name (Acts ii. 38), the washing of regeneration (Tit. iii. 5, John iii. 5), mystical purification (1 Cor. vi. 11, Eph. v. 26), the participation in Christ's death and resurrection (Rom. vi. 1 ff.); (3) the eating and drinking of the Lord's Supper (1 Cor. x. 16 ff., xi. 23 ff., John vi. 51 ff., Rev. iii. 20, xix. 9).

For all these features of the picture of Christ as Saviour of the world, as we find it in the New Testament, there are many parallels in the history of religion. The belief that the unmerited suffering of the pious is a vicarious atonement for the salvation of sinners, is found for the first time in the prophet of the exile, the Deutero-Isaiah, Chapter liii, and from the time of the Maccabees became dominant in the theology of the Pharisees.

The Hellenistic-Judaic writing known as the fourth book of the Maccabees, represents the dying heroes of the Maccabean period as praying (vi. 29):

"Make my blood a sacrifice of purification and accept my soul as a ransom for theirs (the people's)!"

And in xvii. 22 we read:

---

[1] The ascension, as the opposite of the "descent into hell," originally the same as the resurrection, both of them expressing the "lifting up" of Christ from the realm of death into Heaven. (Eph. iv. 8 ff.).

"By the blood of those holy men and by the atonement of their death divine Providence has saved Israel."

This conception of a vicarious atonement dominated popular opinion concerning the sacrifice of animals in the religious service among the Jews as well as among heathen nations. On the one hand these were regarded as substitutes in a visible representation of an execution, and in that capacity served as vicarious satisfaction of divine justice, to re-establish the connection that had been broken between the congregation and the deity. On the other hand they served as an effective means of purification, the sacred powers present especially in the flesh and blood of the sacrifice washing away the impurity that prevented communication with the deity.[1]

Among the Greeks, too, the services of atonement for reconciling angry gods and spirits, and those of purification for removing infection produced by demons, were frequently identical. Vicarious sacrifices of animals served in both instances, and for special occasions even of human beings, whose death was regarded as sacrificial atonement for the city.[2]

In Athens, at the spring festival of the Thargelia (in honor of Apollo and Diana) two condemned criminals were led in a solemn procession through the city, and were afterwards stoned or burned to death as expiatory sacrifices. The same ceremony occurred annually at Abdera and at Massilia in times of public calamities. In the Ionic cities of Asia Minor an animal sacrifice was commonly substituted for the human sacrifice, or the slaying of the victim was performed symbolically, being represented by blows with sacred twigs. The substitution of the animal sacrifice for the human is easily recognized in the stories of the offering up of Isaac by Abraham and Iphigenia by Agamemnon. But this substitution was not practiced by all the heathen Semites. Even at the time of the Kings of Israel, the Canaanites, as is well known, sacrificed their first-born as burnt-offerings to Moloch, and down to the time of Jeremiah the prophets had to contend constantly with the ineradi-

---

[1] W. Robertson Smith, *The Religion of the Semites.*

[2] Rohde, *Psyche*, p. 247 f., 366 f.; Frazer, *The Golden Bough*, III, 125 f. II, 39 ff.

cable tendency on the part of the Israelites toward similar heathen aominations. This proves how deeply the notion of the necessity for human sacrificial atonement was rooted in Semitic religion. Moreover, the sacrifice was regarded as the more effective, the more the life offered up was of high rank and value.

Philo of Byblus[1] tells us that it was an old custom for the ruler of a city or of a people, in times of great danger, to give up his beloved son as a vicarious sacrifice to the evil spirits for the whole people, and the children thus sacrificed were put to death with mystical rites.

An instance of such a sacrifice of a king's son is recorded concerning the king of Moab in 2 Kings iii. 27. We are told of the Carthaginians that they attributed their defeat and the siege of their city by Agathocles (308 B. C.) to the wrath of Baal, because for some time the sacrifice of the children of noble families had been replaced by that of the children of slaves. Consequently they decided to reconcile their god by throwing a hundred children of the noblest families into the fiery throat of his brazen image, and this number was increased by three hundred voluntary sacrifices in addition.[2] This horrible practice was still secretly kept up among the Carthaginians even at the time of Tertullian,[3] in spite of all the endeavors of the Roman authorities to suppress it.

This opinion that the sacrifice of royal children is especially efficacious, is connected with time-honored belief of the Orient in the incarnation of the deity in kings. In such cases, therefore, it is a divine or semi-divine life that is offered up to the deity, and this leads us to the fundamental idea of the dying and resurrected god, which was the basis of the mysteries. In its original form it is one of the earliest factors in religious legends and customs, and is due to the annual dying off of the vegetation in the fall, and its renewed life in the spring. Childish imagination everywhere looked upon these natural processes as the fate of the spirits and deities that work in nature, and gave expression to this view in correspond-

---

[1] According to Eusebius, *Praepar. evang.*, IV. 16. (156 d).

[2] Diodorus, XX, 14.

[3] Apologeticus, 6.

ing acts of worship, indicative of sorrow or of joy. These acts of worship, however, were not merely symbols, but were intended to be at the same time magic means for averting the threatened annual destruction of the divine life in nature, and for assisting in its victorious resurrection.

Survivals of this primitive belief are to be found almost everywhere in the form of popular customs, such as the driving out of winter and death in the spring-festivals of the May-queen, or in the harvest-festivals of the "corn-mother" or the "maiden," the personification of the corn-demon, and other similar celebrations. From these universally diffused primitive conceptions and customs there were developed among the nations of Asia Minor, Egypt, and Greece more distinctive myths of the death and return of a god whose former life was represented by the rites of every recurring yearly celebration. With increasing culture, anxiety for the preservation of the life of nature was overshadowed by the need of a guarantee for the preservation of individual life after death. Then these myths and rites, dealing originally only with the annual death and revival of vegetation, or of the indwelling spirits and deities, became the symbols and mystic means of the mysteries guaranteeing to the initiates future life.

The Egyptian Isis-mysteries were based upon the myth of Osiris, originally a god of vegetation. Osiris was killed by his brother Set, the demon of the parching summer-heat, and afterward ruled the underworld as king and judge of the dead, but lived again on earth in his son Horus, who avenged his death upon Set, his enemy. This myth was commemorated by a religious drama at the autumnal celebration the seventeenth to the twentieth of Athyr (November), first by a service of mourning on the seventeenth, the day of Osiris's death, then by a festival of joy upon the nineteenth, the third day after his death, when the body of Osiris was found again by Isis, his sister and wife.[2] In a similar manner

[1] A profusion of further particulars is to be found in Frazer's *The Golden Bough*, II, Chapter 3, §§ 2 ff. The same source is authority for the following statements concerning the mysteries.

[2] Plutarch, *Isis and Osiris*, ed. Parthey, chap. 13, 39, and p. 235.

the death of Adonis was commemorated in Byblus at the spring festival by the mourning of women, and on the next day his resurrection and ascension to heaven was celebrated with rejoicing.[1]

According to another legend, Adonis is said, like Persephone, to spend half the year in the underworld, and the other half on this upper world with his beloved Aphrodite (Astarte).

The part played by Adonis in Syria, was taken in Phrygia by Attis, the beloved of the "great mother," Cybele. The festival of the vernal equinox, lasting four days, was celebrated in his honor. In this, first the death of the god, the result of his voluntary emasculation, was mourned with dirges and symbolically represented by the priest's making an incision in his own arm, and offering up the flowing blood as a sacrifice, while others by voluntary emasculation entered the ranks of the god's followers.[2] Then on the fourth day came the "festival of joy," in celebration of the resurrection of the god, when the priest anointed the lips of the mourners with oil, uttering the formula:

"Be glad, ye pious, since the god is saved
We too shall rescue find from our distress!"[3]

The mysteries of Demeter and Persephone have for their basis substantially the same myth, but in this case the goddess mourns the death of her daughter instead of that of husband or lover. The daughter (who like her mother, Demeter, is the personification of vegetation) was snatched away from the flowers of the meadow by Pluto, the lord of the lower world, was carried down to his realm of shadows and sought by her mother everywhere on land and sea. Then, because the grief of the goddess checked the fruitfulness of all vegetation on earth, theatening to produce a universal famine, the daughter was restored to her mother by the behest of Jove with the stipulation that she should remain half the year with her husband in the lower world and the other half with her mother

[1] Lucian, *De dea Syra*, 6.

[2] Prudentius, *Peristephanon*, X, 1061-1075.

[3] Firmicus Maternus, *De errore prof. rel.*, chap. 3, 22.

in the upper world. The dramatic representation of this story of the two goddesses, especially of Demeter's search and lamentation, were the subject matter of the Eleusinian mysteries. Doubtless the original purpose of these mysteries was merely the preservation and fostering of the fertility of nature by means of the magic symbolism of the ceremonials; but later, under the influence of guaranteeing to the initiates a happy future existence.[1]

Dionysos, like Osiris, with whom the Greeks frankly identify him,[2] is among the nature-gods, whose violent death, dismemberment and subsequent resurrection were recounted in legends of varying forms, and represented in corresponding mystic rites. Among these rites was that of the dismemberment of the god, in which the worshippers tore the flesh of a steer with their teeth and consumed the bloody flesh in order to become thereby participants in the imperishable life of the god, who was incarnate in the steer. In this mystic communion the death and life of the god were constantly renewed and assimilated.[3]

Closely connected with these legends of the violent death of a deity are those of the voluntary descent of a god or a hero into the lower world and of his safe return. The oldest of these is the Babylonian myth of Istar's descent into hell.[4] In order to find the water of life, which is to bring back to life her lover Tammuz, the goddess descends into the "land without return." Arriving at the gate of the lower world she peremptorily demands admission of the gate-keeper, theatening, in case of refusal, to force the gates open and to lead back to the upper world all the spirits imprisoned within. Reluctantly the mistress of the underworld permits her entrance, "according to the ancient laws," that is, at each of the seven gates a portion of her clothing is taken from her so that she

---

[1] Firmicus Maternus, *De errore profan. religionum*, chap. 7. Hyginus *Fabulae*, 146. Ovid, *Metamorph.*, V., 509-571.

[2] Plutarch, *Isis and Osiris*, chap. 35. Firmicus Maternus, *De errore prof. relig.*, chap. 6.

[3] Clemens Alex., *Protrept.* I, 12, 17 f. Compare Rohde, *Psyche*, 301 f. Frazer, *The Golden Bough*, II, 165.

[4] Schrader, *Höllenfahrt der Istar*, also *Keilinschriften und das Alte Testament*, second edition, 561 ff.

finally enters the underworld quite naked, is there immediately put behind lock and key and is attacked by sixty diseases.

But since the removal of the goddess of fertility threatened to put an end to all propagation of men and beasts on earth and to bring on universal death (Compare the same thought in the Demeter legend, *ante* p. 677), the supreme god, Ea, created the hero Assusunamir and sent him to the underworld to liberate Istar. At the command of the messenger of the gods the mistress of the underworld releases the captive goddess, has her sprinkled with the water of life and at each of the seven gates through which she has to pass on her return one of her garments is given back to her. The poem seems to close then with the account of how the lover of Istar, Tammuz, is washed with the water of life, anointed with oil and thus recalled to life, whereupon the lamentation passes over into the playing of flutes accompanied by the shouts and games of those taking part in the ceremonies, evidently a description of the same rites of a spring festival as were performed in honor of Osiris, Adonis, Attis, Demeter, and Persephone.

The nearest relationship to this Babylonian myth of a descent into hell is one found among the Mandæans, a Judæo-Babylonian sect. Here the divine hero, Hibil-Ziwa, is called into existence to

exit. Therefore, the hymn proceeds, the celestial saviour-spirit Christ prayed to his father: "Send me! In possession of the seals I will go down, will wander through all æons, disclose all secrets, make known the figures of the gods, and impart the hidden features of the sacred way, called 'Gnosis.'" According to the Gnostic conception, then, salvation consists in the descent of the heavenly Christ-spirit into all the realm of earth, liberating the souls held captive by the (earthly and infernal) powers that are hostile to God, by means of the mysterious knowledge of these powers and the control over them thus acquired. Thus, too, according to the wisdom of the Egyptians, the souls in the netherworld are obliged to protect themselves against the assaults of demoniac powers by the possession and use of mysterious names and formulæ.

From the circles of syncretic Gnosticism the myth of the descent into hell went over into ecclesiastical Christianity. It is found frequently in the apocryphal gospels and acts of the apostles which were widely read in the first Christian centuries. Thus, for instance, in the Gospel of Peter, the resurrected Christ is asked by a heavenly voice: "Hast thou preached obedience to those who sleep in death?" and his answer is "Yes." This indicates that in the interval between his death and his resurrection Christ descended into hell and presented himself before the world of shades as its ruler and master. How important this thought was to primitive Christians, and how earnestly they boasted of this particular superiority of the Christian faith over the kindred mysteries of paganism is shown by the eloquent disquisition of the old apologete and polemic Firmicus Maternus: While in the case of the pagan divinities only their death is known but their resurrection is neither prophesied nor attested by eye-witnesses, on the other hand the Son of God accomplished what he promised in advance, "he closed the gates of the infernal regions and broke the spell of the harsh law of death; in three days[1] he assembled together the host of the just that

[1] This "triduum" does not harmonize exactly with the Gospel account, since there are between Good Friday afternoon and Easter Sunday morning not three times twenty-four, but only about forty hours. The expression "triduum" is well chosen with reference to the festival of Attis-Cybele.

wicked death should no longer have dominion over them. In order that their merits might no longer lie in endless hopelessness he broke open the eternal prison-house, and its iron doors fell down at the command of Christ. Then the earth trembled to its very foundations in the presence of the divinity of Christ, the sun sank into night before completing his daily course, and darkness covered the face of the earth. All the elements were agitated when Christ fought the fight against the tyranny of death. Three days this struggle lasted until the evil powers of death were conquered and broken. Then behold, after three days the dawn breaks more brightly than ever; the sun with dazzling rays pays homage to the almighty God, Christ; the beneficent divinity conquers and the host of the just and holy accompany his triumphal chariot. Then in exalted joy humanity exclaims: O death where is thy sting? The divine Saviour marching in front commands the opening of the gates of heaven: Open, open! Break the eternal seals! The God, Christ, has trodden death under foot and calls back to heaven the men whom death had taken captive! Forthwith the guardian of heaven recognize the Son of God; they see the spoils of the defeated enemy and recall the primal order, and they and all those rising to heaven cry together: Lift up the gates, ye gatekeepers, that the King of Glory may come in! The Father gives back to his returning son the scepter of the kingdom and concedes to him a throne of equal authority, in order that he may reign and rule in the eternal majesty of his divinity."

Græco-Roman legends also are familiar with many descents into hell and ascents into heaven. The descent into hell of Odysseus in Homer, and its development along the line of gradually growing vividness in the conceptions of the future life, was early followed in epic poetry by stories of similar journeys of other heroes,[1]

---

where the joyful feast of the resurrection of the god followed the mournful ceremony for his death on the fourth day, that is, after three days. On the other hand, the Gospel reckoning corresponds to that of the festival of Osiris and Isis, where the mourning on the seventeenth of the month Athyr was followed by a jubilee on the nineteenth. Finally it should be observed that the New Testament Easter tradition itself hesitates between "on the third day" and "after three days,"—a very noticeable parallel!

as of Theseus, Peirithous, Orpheus, Heracles, Æneas, and Pythagoras. Primitive legend, poetic imagination and religious speculation had about equal share in the development of these legends. Most familiar of all is the descent into Hades of the mythical singer Orpheus, whom legend represented as a prophet, thaumaturgist and lustratory priest, and upon whose revelations the Orphic sect founded their occult doctrines and mysterious rites, which were intended by means of the recognition of its divine origin and by mystic rites and ascetic practices to release the soul shut up in its bodily prison, and to elevate it to immortal life.

In the writings attributed to Orpheus there are detailed desciptions of the other world, its punishments and rewards, as the hero is said to have seen them on his journey to Hades. Indeed in these Greek legends of the descent into Hades the chief concern was to obtain a knowledge of the affairs in the other world, which might serve incidentally to preserve the life of the initiated in that world, and not to enable him to overcome the powers of death directly. However, there may be found a beginning in this direction in the legend of Heracles who is said to have subdued Cerberus, the dog of Hades.

The ascents into heaven are found in various forms, partly as a final translation of a divine, or divinely favored, hero to the regions of perfect bliss, partly as a temporary elevation of a soul in a state of ecstasy, in which it gets an opportunity to see the stages and dangers of the way to heaven—a visionary prototype, followed further by the eschatological conception of the ascent into heaven of pious souls in general. Hebrew legend tells of but two "translations," that of Enoch, who was "lifted up from the earth and translated unto God," or "passed away," and that of Elijah who went up to heaven in a fiery chariot.[2]

But in the Greek legends translations occur very frequently and in many different forms, to the Elysian fields, to the islands of the blest, to a cave, a mountain, the depths of the sea, or, finally,

[1] Rohde, *Psyche*, p. 278 ff.

[2] Gen. v. 24; Sirach xliv. 16, xlix. 14; Josephus, *Antiq.* I, 3, 4; 2 Kings ii. 11.

to the ideal hights of Olympus, the heaven of the gods.[1] Here the notion originally was that the entire man, body and soul, was transported directly into future bliss without having to pass through the gates of death. But later the sceptical came to consider the bodily ascension, as ancient legend had represented it in the case of Heracles and Romulus, no longer credible and accordingly restricted the transition to the incorporeal soul.

The legend of Heracles[2] is, moreover, of special and typical interest in several respects: He is the son of Zeus and a human mother, Alcmene; he has to contend all his life with the hostile destiny which the jealous Hera inflicted upon him; he demonstrates his divine power in great tasks and combats which consist for the most part in the conquest of hostile powers in both this world and the next (for instance that of the dog of Hades); in particular, he liberates Prometheus, the representative of curse-laden humanity, from the punishment inflicted upon him by the gods, his fetters, and the vulture that daily tore his flesh; finally he mounts the funeral pile of his own free will and is transported thence directly to the side of Zeus upon Olympus and becomes a sharer in the immortality of the gods through the draught of ambrosia. Nothing less than this seemed to the authors of the legend a worthy close to the life of such a divinely begotten hero who had expended it in struggles for the welfare of humanity.

But the mythical heroes of prehistoric times are not the only ones of whom has been told the legend of an ascension to heaven. It was transferred also to the great men of history, as was the legend of divine descent. "After divine honors had been paid to the kings and queens of the Macedonian Empire of the East, following the example of Alexander the Great himself, the fable ventured into the light that the divine monarch did not die at the close of his earthly existence, but had only been 'snatched away by the divinity,' and continued to live."[3] Suetonius tells us of Cæsar

[1] Details on this subject are collected by Rohde, *Psyche*, 64 ff., 658 ff.

[2] Hyginus, *Fabulae*, 29 ff. Diodorus Sic., *Hist.*, IV, 8-30.

[3] Rohde, *Psyche*, p. 663.

(*Julius*, 88) that he was placed among the number of gods after his death not merely by imperial decree, but in accordance with the conviction of the people, for during the games decreed in his honor by Augustus a comet appeared in the heavens for seven days, and this was regarded as the soul of Cæsar which had ascended into heaven. And likewise of the Emperor Augustus it was believed that he soared up to heaven from the pile that consumed his earthly remains. A prætor is even said to have testified under oath that he saw the image (the soul) of the Emperor flying up to heaven. (Sueton, *Octavius*, 100.)

Later at the funerals of the emperors an eagle was made to fly up from the funeral pile, which was supposed to bear the soul to heaven. That this was not simply fawning flattery, but that it corresponded to the superstition of the time is evident from the fact that similar things were told and believed regarding other remarkable men. When Peregrinus Proteus cast himself into the flames at Olympia, in order to follow his model, Heracles, even in this close of his life, a venerable old man asserted directly after that he had seen a vulture fly up to heaven out of the flames, and that he had met Peregrinus himself, transfigured and wearing a white garment, with the wreath of victory on his head. Soon after this he was worshipped as a god in his native city, and in his sanctuary it was believed that oracles were received and miraculous cures experienced.[1]

So also concerning the end of the remarkable man, Apollonius of Tyana, various legends were circulated of his mysterious disappearance in the temple of Athena at Lindus, or in that of the Cictynna in Crete, and his biographer Philostratus (8, 31) finds a confirmation of his apotheosis in the fact that the grave of Apollonius is nowhere to be found on earth.

The notions of the ascension of a soul to heaven in a state of ecstasy, and of such ascension by souls of the departed in general, such as are found in Jewish and Orphic apocalypses, in Gnostic,

---

[1] According to the account of Lucian, which is also confirmed by Anaxagoras's *Defence of the Christians*, chap. 23.

Mandæan and Mithaic[1] liturgies, must be passed over here, being too remote from my theme. This would be a proper subject for a comparative treatment of the doctrines of the end of things (eschatology), which would be a very profitable task. On the other hand, essential features of the primitive Christian belief in Christ as lord and giver of life are found in the notion that his life was imparted to his followers through the belief in his name, in that of baptism in his name, and also in that of partaking of his flesh and blood in the Lord's Supper. Many parallels are found to these three points in the religious history of both Orient and Occident.

In the very instructive book by W. Heitmüller, *In the Name of Jesus* (an investigation into the New Testament on the lines of historical philology and religion, especially on primitive Christian baptism), there is to be found a vast collection of material on the theory and practice of the "belief in the name" in both Biblical and extra-Biblical religions. I must restrict myself here to giving a few specimens from this collection. In early religions the name is never a mere word or image, but has a very real value, standing in the closest mystical relation to the nature and destiny of the one who hears it, indeed, it is in some sort presented as an independent representative of his essence and effective power. A change of name signifies a regeneration of the person, his release from the destiny that clings to the old name. A curse that is pronounced upon the name of a person brings mischief to the person himself. One who knows and utters the name of any divinity or demon obtains a certain power over the being himself, which he can then use for good or evil purposes, for attack and defence, whence the use of the sacred or mysterious names in all sorts of sorcery.

On the other hand, the appeal to the name of a divinity brings the divinity himself near to the one who prays and establishes a mystic union between them, whereby the man who prays is charmed against maleficent powers. One who is "blessed in the name of Yahveh" gains the protecting power of this god and is

---

[1] Cp. Bousset, "Die Himmelsreise der Seele," in the *Archiv für Religionswissenschaft*, IV, Nos. 2 and 3. Dietrich, *Eine Mithras-Liturgie*, p. 179 ff.

under his especial guardianship. By "the name of the great gods" the messenger of the gods, Assusunamir, conjures the mistress of the underworld and compels her to release Istar. By means of the seal ring with the inscription of the cryptonym of darkness Hibil-Ziwa forces the passage through the gates of the underworld. By knowing and uttering the names of the spirit powers which control the gates of the celestial world the soul compels her admission on the journey to heaven.[1] By the name of his father and his mother the prince in the hymn of the soul in the Acts of Thomas[2] charmed the serpent and lulled it to sleep, and thus got possession of the pearl which it was guarding, which made possible his return from foreign parts (the world) to his heavenly home. By the acquisition of mysterious names the initiates in the Eleusinian and Orphic mysteries attained the pledge of bliss in the world to come. In the Phrygian mysteries the priests bore the name of the god Attis in order to identify themselves with him. Thus we read in the Leiden charm-papyrus II[3]. "Thou art I and I am thou: whatever I say must come to pass, for I bear thy name as amulet in my heart; not all Styx, when roused, shall overcome me, nothing will oppose me, no spirit nor demon nor other mischief of Hades, for the sake of thy name which I have in my heart and which I call upon. Therefore hear me in everything, O gracious one; give me unassailable (i. e., proof against witchcraft) health, welfare, success, honor, victory, strength, amiability, hold in bound (invalidate) the (spellbinding) glances of all my adversaries, give me favor for all my undertakings!" Although this prayer comes from a charm-papyrus, nevertheless it may be regarded as a typical expression of the belief in the power exerted by names that was common to antiquity, with its mysticism and its magic. According to this belief, to "believe in a sacred (divine) name," is the same thing as bearing it in one's heart and thus being filled with the

[1] Cp. Origen's account of Orphian Gnosticism, *c. Cels.* VI, 30 ff., and the report of Hippolytus on the Gnosticism of the Naassenes (*Philosophumena*, V, 11 at top, and p. 67).

[2] Lipsius, *Apokryphe Apostelgeschichten*, I, 293.

[3] Dietrich, *Abraxas*, 196. Heitmüller, *loc. cit.* 214.

supernatural powers which are represented by the being appealed to; to "call upon his name" is not an empty form of words, but the establishment of a real connection with this supernatural power whereby it is manifested and experienced in marvellous effects.

If we apply this thought to the Christian sphere, believing in the name of Jesus Christ and calling upon it signifies a mystical union with the nature of the son of God, the vanquisher of Satan and death, the miraculous saviour and lord of the world, and thereby an appropriation or absorption of all the vital forces peculiar to this being and proceeding from him. The mysticism and sorcery of the ancient belief in the power of a name is by no means eliminated here, but it does become the vessel for a higher content of spiritual experiences of truly ethico-religious value; it is, in brief ethically exalted.

The same is true of baptism in the name of Jesus Christ, save that here there is added to the magic power of the name pronounced, as a supplementary means, the sacramental purifying and animating power of the water, which, by calling upon his name, is filled with its magic powers, like a storage battery charged with elecric force. The view which is at the base of this is connected with the most elementary conceptions and usages of faith and worship among all nations. The myth of the descent of Istar into hell brings us near to the source of it: she went down in order to fetch the "water of life" to revive Tammuz. Being attacked in the underworld by sixty diseases, she is then, at the command of the queen of hell, sprinkled by the infernal water-nymphs with the water of life and is enabled to return again safe and sound to the world of the living; then Tammuz is recalled to life by being washed with the animating water. This was dramatically represented at the summer fesival in the month of Tammuz (June or July), he lamenting women pouring water over the statue of Tammuz.

Just so at the feast of Adonis the image of the god, sometimes in human form, sometimes in the form of plants (Adonis), was thrown into the water in order to accomplish the revival of the god of fertility by this symbolic-magic performance. In the processions of the Osiris festivals the water vessel was always carried ahead in honor of the god,[1] water being regarded in Egypt as an exhalation of Osiris, and accordingly a divine substance.

Upon this assumption are based all the widely recurring ceremonies of purification: the divine power inherent in the water serves to expel demons and their baneful poison. Among the Persians, for instance, the person who has become impure by touching a dead body is sprinkled with water to drive the devil out of him, the evil spirit gradually retiring from all the limbs of the body as they are touched by the water, escaping finally through the toes of the left foot.[2] Among the Greeks and Romans, too, all those who took part in a funeral were wont to purify themselves from the defilement by the use of consecrated water. But since sin and guilt, as well as disease and death, appeared from the primitive standpoint of animistic conceptions as a demoniac taint, the sprinkling with pure water taken from running springs was also regarded as a means of washing off sin and guilt.[3] In the familiar verse,

> "Ah, nimium faciles, qui tristia crimina cædis
> Fluminea tolli posse putetis aqua!" (*Fasti*, II, 45),

Ovid ridicules this convenient manner of religious purification and expiation of guilt (which, however, does not come, as he thinks, from Greece alone, but was distributed equally over all countries).

As late as the third and fourth centuries we find in books of sorcery directions for purification which recommend as an effective spell against every evil of body or soul the waters from three or seven springs (in case of murder from fourteen springs).

But the same divine power of water which expels demons and counteracts their harmful influence, serves elsewhere to impart beneficent spiritual powers and to transport man into a condition of divine inspiration, of enthusiasm. Thus the Pythia, the priestess of the Delphic Apollo, was filled with the spirit of the god (ἔνθεος)

---

[1] Plutarch, *Isis and Osiris*, chap. 36. Further examples from popular customs are collected in Frazer's *The Golden Bough*, II, 120-126.

[2] Chantepie de Saussaye, *Religionsgeschichte*, 2d ed., II, 191.

[3] Rohde, *Psyche*, p. 361 ff.

by a draught form the Castalian fountain, and thus inspired to prophesy. In the initiations of the various mystery cults sacred ablutions were not merely the means of purification, but also of a rebirth, of securing a participation in the imperishable life of the god, of resurrection. According to Tertullian,[1] in the Eleusinian mysteries and in those of Isis and of Mithras the initiate was dipped into water as a means for the expiation of his sins and as a symbol of resurrection. This is confirmed for the mysteries of Isis by the description in the Metamorphoses of Apuleius (11, 21, 23): the act of consecration consisted in a symbolical pilgrimage to the land of the dead and a return to the light, a "rebirth for the course of a new salvation," whence the day of the consecration was called the "sacred birthday." The initiates of the mysteries of Mithras were said to be "born again forever." In the recently edited Mithras liturgy[2] the initiate prays: "If it has pleased you (gods) to surrender me to the birth unto immortality, in order that, after the present distress which so sorely besets me, I may behold the immortal primal cause with the immortal spirit and the immortal water, so that I may be regenerated through spirit and the holy spirit may move within me when I am purified and exempt from guilt by sacred ceremonies. . . . After this man, born from a a mortal mother, has been begotten of thee anew to-day, being called into immortality from among so many thousands according to the counsel of the exceedingly good god, he strives and longs to worship thee to the best of human ability. Greetings to thee, O lord of the water, founder of the earth, master of the soul! Being born again, I perish by being exalted, and when I am exalted I die; born by the birth which brings forth life, I am ransomed through death and go the way which thou hast marked out according as thou hast established the law and founded the sacrament." As the editor of this litury remarks, this is the clearest and most thoroughgoing application of the figure of death and regeneration that we

---

[1] *De baptismo*, 5, and *de praescript. haer.* 40: in the mysteries of Mithras an *imago resurrectionis* is represented.

[2] Dieterich, *Eine Mithrasliturgie*, pp. 5, 13, 15, 166.

have in any liturgical text of antiquity. It finds its closest analogy in the Pauline characterization of baptism as a symbolical participation in the death and resurrection of Christ (Rom. vi).

It is no wonder that this resemblance seemed to Tertullian and other early apologists so striking that they thought it could be explained only on the assumption of diabolical imitation of Christian usages. But in fact it is to be explained from the fundamental views common to animistic nature religions, and Tertullian himself reveals this most clearly in the manner in which he refers the virtue of baptism to the miraculous power inherent in water from the time of the creation, when the spirit of God brooded upon it, a power which could be restored and increased by calling upon the name of Christ: "With the increase of the mercy of God more virtue attached to water: that which had formerly cured bodily ills now restored the spirit, that which had accomplished temporal welfare now renewed unto eternal life."[1] That is to say, baptism is the fulfilment of the ancient rites of lustration infused with an ethical sense. . . How strong and how long the magical element persisted in the ceremonies of primitive Christian baptism is clearly shown by the custom of the church at Corinth, mentioned without condemnation by Paul, of receiving baptism for the benefit of deceased relatives, (1 Cor. xv. 29), to which a perfect parallel is offered in the Orphic intercession for the souls of sinful ancestors, and the "ransom and purification of living and dead" promised by Orphic priests through the rites of Dionysius.[2]

The same relation as between Christian baptism and the ancient rites of lustration exists between the Christian supper, or, according to Paul, Lord's Supper, and the ancient sacrificial meals, the ground thought of which is that partaking of sacred food brings the partaker into mystic communion with the life of the divinity.[3]

---

[1] Tert., *De baptismo*, 5. Cp. the same thoughts in the homilies of Clementin, 11, 22 ff., and among the Elkesaitic Gnostics, Epiphan., *Haer.* 53.

[2] Plato, *Rep.*, 2, 364; Rohde, *Psyche*, 420, f.

[3] Cp. Robertson Smith. *The Religion of the Semites*, translated into German by Stübe, p. 239 (of the translation).

This too can be traced back to primitive Babylonian myths.[1] Ea's son Adapa had been endowed by his father with extraordinary wisdom, indeed, but not with eternal life. He might have obtained this also and thus have attained to entire equality with the gods if he had accepted the "food of life" and the "water of life" which were offered to him by Anu, the god of the sky. But because he refused to partake in this divine food, on the advice of the (suspicious or jealous?) Ea, he cast away forever his chance of immortal life (just as our first parents in the Bible did, because, on the advice of the serpent they laid hands upon the fruit of the tree of knowledge and were expelled from Paradise for so doing). According to this conception, then, the possession of immortal life depends upon partaking of the celestial bread of life which is peculiar to the divinity and under certain circumstances is shared with his favorites. By partaking of the food of the gods, nectar and ambrosia, Heracles was accepted into the company of the immortal gods of Olympus, while, on the other hand, Persephone, by partaking of the fruit of the underworld, is bound to remain there.

From the earliest times the religious rites of all peoples have embraced the eating of consecrated food, which not only represents the life of the divinity, but also contains it in some mysterious fashion. Upon this is based the sacramental significance of sacrificial meals: they establish a holy communion with the life of the divinity, which is contained in the flesh and blood of the sacrificial animal—itself an incarnation of the nature god—and which is accordingly appropriated by the one who partakes of it.

Thus in the worship of Dionysius a bull, who was regarded as the incarnation of the god of fertility, was torn to pieces by the teeth of the devotees, and the flesh eaten raw,[2] in order to transfer the divine life of the god to those who took part in the ceremony by this symbolical repetition of the sacrifice of the god himself. But instead of the real flesh the sacramental meal consisted only

---

[1] Schrader-Zimmern, *Die Keilinschriften und das Alte Testament*, p. 520 ff.

[2] Cp. the quotations already cited, p. 678, note 3.

of a substitute in the form of bread baked in the shape of the sacrificial animal.[1] Similar substitutes for the earlier sacrificial flesh seem to have been customary under manyfold forms in the later mysteries. Thus, for instance, in the mysteries of Attis the initiate before being admitted into the innermost sanctuary, declared by eating from the drum and drinking from the cymbal that he had become a devotee of Attis. We do not know the nature of the food and drink which were partaken of from the ritual vessels of the priest of Cybele, but that it was a sacramental eating and drinking, which was to give to the initiate a means for attaining eternal life, is clearly to be inferred from the polemic remarks added by Firmicus Maternus, who reports it to us:[2] "Unhappy man! Thou hast swallowed poison and drunken the draught of death! It is a very different food that gives life and salvation, refreshes the languishing, recalls the wandering, raises up the fallen, and gives to the dying the symbols of eternal immortality: seek the bread and the cup of Christ to fill the human substance with immortal essence!"

This contrast is notable from two different points of view: it shows, on the one hand, that the fundamental conception is the same in both cases, that the sacramental eating and drinking is "a remedy for death and recipe for immortality" (as Ignatius, *Ad Eph.*, 20, 2, formulated the church view of the Lord's Supper, which also finds pronounced expression in John vi. 51-59). On the other hand, it shows that the Christian sacrament also works as an ethical remedy for the erring and the fallen; the background of magic remains the same but is transformed ethically in the Christian spirit. This is acomplished in the Gospel of John by the addition of verse 63 to the theory of the sacrament which preceded.

Among the mysteries of Mithras also there was celebrated, along with the sacred lustration and the marking of the forehead

---

[1] Many details of this sort from ancient and modern times (popular customs) are collected in Frazer, *The Golden Bough*, II, 260-300.

[2] *De errore prof. relig.*, chap. 18.

with the symbol of the covenant,[1] a holy meal of which only the initiates of the higher degrees were permitted to partake. It was regarded as an imitation of the meal in which, according to the legend, Mithras himself had once sealed his compact with the sun-god Helios. Upon a relief of sculpture which is still preserved[2] we may see the two gods sitting together in the middle on cushions, each holding a cup in his right hand, before them a table with four small loaves of bread, each marked with a cross. On either side stand the initiates, their faces covered with masks that represent the nature of Mithras under various attributes—that is, they have "put on" the god in order to bring themselves into mystical communion with him. (Cp. Gal. iii. 27, "put on Christ.")

Concerning the meal of Mithras, Justin (*Apol.* I, 66) tells us that "bread and a cup of water are served and certain blessings spoken," and Tertullian[3] speaks of an offering of bread and of an image of the resurrection, while both apologists considered this a diabolical imitation of the Christian sacrament, partly overlooking the unquestioned priority of the pagan mysteries as compared with the Christian, partly explaining it as due to prophetic anticipation on the part of the demons. It is a remarkable coincidence, that, with regard to the contents of the cup of Mithras, whether is was only water or perhaps wine, the same uncertainty prevails as concerning the original cup in the Christian sacrament, which certainly did not always contain wine, since wine is nowhere mentioned in conection with the earliest Christian love-feasts in the Acts of the Apostles.[4] But in the church at Corinth, according to 1 Cor.xi. 21, the celebration with wine had become customary. This gave to the

---

[1] Whether a brand or an anointing with oil, is uncertain. Cp. Revelation xiii. 16 f., xiv. 9, "the mark of the beast on brow or hand"; is this perhaps a reference to the symbol of Mithras? And in xiv. 10 also, might not the "cup of the wine of the wrath of God, poured out without mixture" contain an allusion to the cup of Mithras?

[2] Cumont, *Textes et monuments relat. aux mystères de Mithra,* I, 157 f.

[3] *De praes. haer.,* 40: "Mithras signat in frontibus milites suos, celebrat et panis oblationem et imaginem resurrectionis inducit."

[4] Cp. on this question: Harnack, "Brot und Wasser, die eucharistischen Elemente by Justin," in *Texten und Unters.,* VII, 1892.

apostle Paul (who moreover never speaks of "wine" but always of the "cup") the welcome occasion for a mystical interpretation of the Lord's Supper as a communion, not only with the body, but also with the blood of Christ. (1 Cor. x. 16.)

It is true, no parallel for this symbolism of blood is found in the meal of Mithras, but it is found in the baptism of blood of the bull and ram sacrifices connected with the mysteries of Cybele, and perhaps also with those of Mithras. This sacrifice of a ram or a bull, adopted into the worship of Mithras, received in that religion probably the significance of a sacramental imitation of the sacrifice of the bull, once performed by Mithras himself for the salvation of the world, and represented in all the pictures of the ceremonies. Here the bull was very likely thought of as the incarnation of the god himself, as was certainly the case in the worship of Dionysius. The one who was to be initiated allowed the blood of the slaughtered bull or ram to drip upon him,[1] and this blood baptism served him as a sacramental means for obtaining participation in the life and death of the god. The thought of purification and regeneration through the sacramental symbol of death, which according to the above quoted liturgy, was a fundamental thought of the religion of Mithras, received very drastic expression in this baptism of blood. We may recall in this connection the Christian doctrine of purification and cleansing "in the blood of the lamb."[2] (Rev. vii. 14.)

CHRIST AS KING OF KINGS AND LORD OF LORDS.

This apocalyptic name of Christ (Rev. xix. 16) indicates the dignity and power which belong to him in the belief of the early Christian communion. It comprises: (1) Lordship over the communion of the faithful, whose "head" Christ is as the saviour who

---

[1] Prudentius, *Peristephanon*, X, v. 1008-1050.

[2] In the expression peculiar to the Apocalypse of John: *το ἀρνίον το ἐσφαγμένον*, there is a probable connection with the Phrygian sacrifice of the ram

established and insured their salvation, as the lawgiver whose will is the guide of their lives, and as the judge who will one day reward each one according to his works; (2) Lordship over the world as the mediator and agent of its creation, government and completion.

With this may be compared the following parallels from the various religious systems. The belief of the Buddhist communion in the supremacy of their founder is expressed in the most extravagant attributes[1]: He is called the joy of the whole world, the help of the helpless, a mine of mercy, god of gods, Brahma of Brahmas, the only saviour, the truly compassionate, the royal preacher who dispenses the ambrosia of justice, the father, helper, friend, treassure, jewel of the world; stronger than the strongest, more merciful than the most merciful, fairer than the fairest, more meritorious than the most meritorious, mightier than the mightiest; who grants salvation to every being that merely utters his name or gives even a handful of rice as alms in his name; eye cannot see, ear cannot hear, mind cannot conceive anything more glorious and more adorable than Buddha.

To this may be added a few hymns from Chapter 23 of the Laudations of the Lalitavistara: "In the world of beings which had long been tormented by the ills of natural depravity, didst thou appear, king of physicians, who dost save us from all evils. Upon thy arrival, O leader, anxiety disappears, and men and gods are filled with satisfaction. Thou art the protector, the firm foundation, the head, the guide of the world with thy gentle, benevolent spirit; thou art the best of physicians, who dost bring the perfect panacea and heal suffering for a certainty. Eminent for thy compassion and sympathy, thou dost order the affairs of the world; eminent for thy severe morality and thy good works, acting independently, perfectly pure, thou hast attained perfection, and being saved thyself, thou wilt, as the annunciator of the four truths, save other creatures also. The power of the evil being has been overcome by wisdom, courage and gentleness; thou hast attained supreme and undying honor; we greet thee as the conqueror of the legions of the liar

---

[1] Collected in Hardy's *Manual of Buddhism*, p. 360.

(Cp. John viii. 44). Thou, whose word is infallible and who, free from error and passion, hast trodden the path of eternal life, dost deserve in heaven and upon earth honor and homage beyond compare. Thou quickenest gods and men by thy exceeding clear words, by the rays of light which proceed from thee art thou the conqueror of this universe, lord of gods and men. Thou didst appear, light of the law, destroyer of unhappiness and ignorance, completely filled with humility and majesty; sun, moon, and fire are without light in contrast with thee and the imperishable splendor of thy perfection. Thou who dost teach us to know what is true and what is false, spiritual guide with sweetest voice, thou whose soul is calm, whose senses are subdued, whose heart is perfectly at rest, who dost teach what should be taught, who dost instruct the assembly of gods and men: I greet thee, Sakyamuni, as the greatest of men, as the wonder of the thousand worlds, to whom are due honor and homage in heaven and on earth, from gods and from men!"

Finally I add the prawer of a pious believer in Buddha[1] who was obliged to flee from his home in the eleventh century A. D. on account of his faith: "Whether I dwell in heaven or in hell, in the city of spirits or of men, let my soul be planted firmly upon thee, for there is no other happiness for me. Thou art my father and my mother, my brother and my sister, thou art my faithful friend in dangers. O my beloved, thou art my lord, my teacher, who dost give me wisdom that is sweet as nectar. Thou art my wealth, my joy, my delight, my greatness, my boast, my knowledge and my life, thou art my all, O all-knowing Buddha!"

When the pious believer lifts his soul in such ardent prayer to the object of his faith—it matters not under what name—reason hesitates to come forward with the dry question, whether Buddha, who has entered into Nirvana, still exists, and whether he is omnipresent and omniscient to hear the prayers of the faithful. The

---

[1] According to the *Proceedings of the Royal Asiatic society of Bengal*, Feb. 1890, p. 127. I am indebted for this quotation to Professor Carpenter of Oxford.

historical founder of their faith is for the Buddhist indeed only the temporal and transient manifestation of the eternal spirit of wisdom and goodness, who has come not merely once, but will forever continue to come in visible human form to carry on the work of salvation for mankind who will forever be in need of it. It is this eternal spirit of salvation then, which is the real object of the Buddhist belief in salvation, while the historical founder of the faith, as the most prominent of the manifestations of that spirit until now, is the immediate and tangible image in which the invisible spirit becomes concrete for the worshipping eye of faith in his followers.

And since Buddhism finds the desirable end of the individual life in general, and accordingly of its founder also, in "Nirvana," meaning either complete dissolution or at least completely inactive calm and blessedness, therefore the historical founder cannot be conceived with the same dogmatic positiveness as in the case of Christianity to be the enthroned lord who is eternally ruling his followers in the exercise of divine authority. Nevertheless, in Buddhism too he is practically, in the worship of the faithful, the ever and everywhere present object of their confiding love. Whence it becomes clearly evident that here as everywhere it is simply the psychological demand of faith for a human manifestation of the eternal which led naturally to some sort of apotheosis of the historical saviour. To faith it is just as natural to combine the finite human person with the eternal principle of the spirit as it is inevitable to the thinking mind to distinguish the two from each other clearly and sharply. From the crossing of these two tendencies results the diagonal of the parallelogram of forces, the dogmatic figure of a miraculous god-man.

From the mythology of polytheistic religions, too, many parallels to the kingship of Christ may be cited. Marduk, the city god of Babylon, first-born son of Ea, was called the "lord of lords and king of kings," because he accomplished the conquest of chaos and the creation of the world, and because he controls the destinies of earthly kings. This last function is also ascribed to Nabu, the bearer and writer of the celestial tablets of fate, who is also called "king and lord of the gods of heaven and earth";[1] he was perhaps originally identical with Marduk, and was distinguished from him later as the celestial scribe, patron of wisdom and oracles, the Babylonian Hermes and Thot.

In Egypt after the foundation of the new Theban kingdom the city god of Thebes, Ammon-Ra, was worshipped as the hidden creator, "the lord of the thrones of earth and king of the gods," uniting in himself all the qualities and powers of the other gods. But the judge in the realm of the dead is Osiris, beside whom is stationed as divine scribe, Thot, who, as god of the wonder-working word, shared also in the creation of the world and became the patron of wisdom, of oracles, and of magic, in some measure a personification of the divine word of revelation, or Logos.

In the Persian religion[2] Ahura-Mazda, the wise lord, is the creator, sustainer, and guardian of the world; with him are associated as personifications of his two chief attributes, wisdom and justice, the spirits Vohu mano, "the good thought" (Logos), the first-created of good spirits, mediator of creation and of the revelation of the law, and gatekeeper of heaven, and Asha vahista, the spirit of justice, guardian of the cosmic order and mediator of the cosmic government, executor of the court of rewards and punishments in the next world. Along with these are also Sraosha the pure and victorious hero, conqueror of the demons, guide of souls, and judge in the world to come, who also plays a decisive part in the last crucial combat at the end of the world; and last of all Mithras, the friendly god of light and truth, the foe of the demons and champion of the faithful, the judge of souls in the underworld, of whom it is said in an ancient hymn that Ahura-Mazda created him just as great and adorable as himself, that is, that he occupies a place in the rites of worship equal to that of the supreme god.

---

[1] Schrader-Zimmern, *Die Keilinschriften und das Alte Testament*, pp. 374 and 402.

[2] Chantepie de la Saussaye, *Religionsgeschichte*, II. 173 ff. Cumont, *Textes et monuments relatives aux mystères de Mithra*, I, 240 ff. Böcklen, *Verwandtschaft der jüdisch-christlichen mit der parsischen Eschatologie*, p. 48 ff.

As this very "mediator," who stands nearer to men, Mithras was halfway identified in the Perso-Babylonian-Phrygian hybrid religion with the sun-god and worshipped in the rites of the mysteries as the special saviour of the initiated. Legend represents him as performing a mediatorial part even in the creation of the world, producing the germs of all life in plant and animal by the sacrifice of the cosmogonic bull. But then again he is the perpetual mediator of all salvation for his devotees in this world and the next, exemplar and helper in their conflict against all the powers opposed to the divine will, guide and guardian of the souls of the pious on their perilous journey to the upper realms of heaven. But at the end of things he will bring about the renewal of the world by a repetition of the sacrifice of the cosmogonic bull, will raise all the dead and prepare for the just the lifegiving drink of immortality.

In the worship of the believers in Mithras Sunday was observed as the sacred day of the sun-god, and the annual chief festival was the celebration of the victoriously rising sun at the winter-solstice; the 25th of December was the birthday of the *sol invictus* of the Mithras religion long before it became the birthday of the Christian saviour. How fervently the relation to the god of their salvation was conceived and felt we may see in the liturgy already cited above, from which these additional hymns may be quoted:[1]

"Greetings to thee, O lord, most mighty, most powerful king, greatest of the gods, Helios, lord of heaven and earth, god of gods; mighty is thy breath, mighty is thy power; lord, if it pleases thee, present me to the supreme god who begot and fashioned thee!" And then the person who is himself lifted up into the presence of Mithras, speaks: "Lord of my life, remain with me in my soul; leave me not! I greet thee, lord, ruler of the water, founder of the earth, master of the soul! Lord, being lifted up I depart as one born again, etc." (Cp. *ante*, p. 689.)

While the saviour divinities of the mysteries, such as Mithras and Serapis, were credited by their worshippers with unlimited dominion over the world of nature and spirit—since otherwise they

[1] Dietrich, *Eine Mithraliturgie*, pp. 11 and 15.

would not be able to protect their devotees—yet the manifestation of this power was looked for only in the guidance of the destinies of the individual worshippers in this world and the next. On the other hand, we miss here the social-ethical ideal of the regeneration and conquest of earthly humanity by the victorious power of the heavenly lord. This ideal was peculiar to the Jewish Messiah belief, at first, indeed, with the limitation to a period of earthly salvation for the Jewish people, but with a tendency, becoming ever stronger in the later apocalyptic writers, to extend these national limits to a universal kingdom of God embracing the entire human race.

In this broadened form, for which Hellenism had paved the way, the social ideal of a kingdom of God to be realized on a regenerated earth, was assimiliated by the early Christian faith, assuring to it from the beginning its unqualified superiority over the belief of the various mystery-cults in their saving divinities. The belief of the Church in the kingship of Christ united in itself the two ideals of religious hope and longing: the guarantee of the perfection and blessedness of the individual life, such as was promised to the faithful by Buddhism and the Oriental-Greek mysteries, and the social-ethical regeneration and transformation of mundane humanity into an ideal state of God, such as was the hope of Jewish-Hellenistic faith.

It is self-evident that the heavenly lord, who guaranteed to his worshippers the fulfilment of this double ideal, was from the beginning destined and qualified for the conquest of all other lords and for the sole dominion over the world. His most serious rival was not, however, Mithras, but the Roman emperor, the occupant of the *imperium* in the earthly world. For the personal needs of the pious soul individual pagans might find a certain satisfaction in the rites of their mysteries; but here the no less mighty longing of the nations for a new social order, in which justice, peace, and goodness should prevail, found no satisfaction and clung with so much the more persistent, though ever disappointed, hope to the earthly gods on the throne of the Cæsars. In an inscription recently discovered at Priene, coming probably from the year 9 B. C., occurs this hymn to Emperor Augustus[1]: "This day (the birthday of Augustus) has given the whole world a new aspect; it would have gone to ruin had not a common happiness dawned for all men in him who was born this day. Well does he judge who sees for himself in this birthday the beginning of life and of all life's powers; at least the time is past when one must needs regret being born. For the blesing of all men, the providence which rules over everything in life has endowed this man with such gifts that he is sent to us and coming generations as a saviour; he will put an end to all warfare and will gloriously develop all things. In his coming the hopes of them of old are fulfilled; he has not only excelled all the former benefactors of mankind, but it is impossible that a greater should ever come. The birthday of the god has brought with it the good tidings ("Gospels") naturally connected with it. A new era must begin with his birth."

A similar inscription comes from Halicarnassus:[2] "That our life may be joyful the divinity has brought to mankind Cæsar Augustus who is the father of his fatherland, divine Rome, but also the paternal Zeus and saviour of the human race, whose foresight has fulfilled and surpassed the prayers of all. For land and sea are blessed with peace, the cities flourish in harmony and wealth, and every good thing is to be had in abundance."

Finally, a certain connection of the Mithras faith with the belief in the emperor is to be detected in the address of the Armenian king Tiridates, who had come to Rome in company with magi, to Emperor Nero:[3] "I am thy servant, my lord; I have come to thee, my God, to worship thee even as I do Mithras."

We see from these evidences that the belief in a human in-

---

[1] Edited by Mommsen and Wilamowitz in the German Archæological Institute, XXIII, No. 3, translated and discussed by Harnack in the *Christliche Welt*, 1899, No. 51.

[2] In the British Museum, No. 994, according to Harnack's report in the *Christliche Welt*, *ibid.*

[3] *Dio Cassius*, ed. Becker, II, p. 253. Suetonius, *Nero*, 13 and 30 . According to the attractive conjecture of Dietrich (*Ueitschrift für neutestamentliche Wissenschaft*, III, 1 ff.) this historical fact is the basis of the Gospel legend of the homage of the Wise Men before the newborn king of the Jews (Matt. ii).

carnation of the divinity in the Roman emperor and in a divinity worshipped in the mysteries, who brought salvation for the next world, not only existed side by side in Asia Minor, but that they tended to some sort of union. But this tendency, which is so easily understood from a psychological point of view, could never be fulfilled on pagan soil because of the basic difference in the respective objects of worship.

The conception of a saviour-god who was to guarantee not only the salvation of the individual soul in the next world but also an earthly kingdom of prosperity and peace, was already present in the dreams and longings of the nations at the beginning of our era; the only question was whence the certainty of his realization should come. The church received the answer to this question in the belief in Christ, which combined the Messiah-king of the earthly kingdom of God with the mystical conqueror of death and mediator of life into a single personality in the ideal figure of the eternal son of God who within the bounds of time became a man, died, descended into hell, subdued death and the devil, arose triumphant and ascended into heaven where he sits as a ruler of the world at the right band of God, and will come again, upon the clouds of heaven, to judge the quick and the dead. All of these dogmas are found, indeed, here and there in the religious worship of dying antiquity, in Orient and Occident, in the manifold forms of the Jewish apocalyptic writings, of Oriental mysticism and gnosticism, of Greek speculation and Roman emperor-worship: the one thing lacking was a single subject to constitute the synthesis of these qualities, the center of crystallization about which this chaotic and fermenting mass of religious ideas might take shape in a new world of faith and hope which should comprehend both the next world and this. This central point was given in the person of Jesus, the Galilean tribal saviour and king of the Jews, who by way of the cross became the saviour of the world and king of the all-embracing kingdom of God.

CONCLUSION.

One who surveys this mass of parallels between the belief in Christ held by the primitive Christians and the religious ideas of the surrounding world, can scarcely avoid the impression that Christianity cannot have fallen from the skies as something absolutely new and unique, but that it developed out of the historically prepared soil of the contemporary world as the fruit of the evolution of thousands of years.

Now it is conceivable from the psychological standpoint that this new and evolutionary view has upon many, both conservatives and radicals, such a startling effect that they forthyith draw from it the most extreme conclusions, thinking that Christianity is thereby deprived of all peculiar character and permanent value, because it seems to them to be merely a collection of ideas which had been known long before and which have become altogether antiquated for us. But this would be a very hasty conclusion, involving many errors, exaggerations and onesided judgments which careful investigation in religious history might regard as its office to reveal and refute. I would only wish to indulge in a few hints in this direction at the present moment.

Before all else we should guard against the frequent and widespread confusion between the inner kinship of religious conceptions and their outward historical relationship. It is entirely unpermissible to infer the latter from the mere existence of the former; such a procedure overlooks the fact that kinship of conceptions is not necessarily to be explained by borrowing and transference from one sphere to another; but on the contrary, from similar psychological reasons and similar social conditions, like conceptions may arise in different places quite independently of one another, and have certainly thus arisen in vast numbers of cases. Accordingly, when similar conceptions are proven to exist, we should first inquire carefully whether their similarity maw be explained as the result of similar conditions, or whether perchance some close or remote historical connection is with any probability to be assumed as existing between them. And in the answering of this question, in view of the present status of archæology and ethnology, the greatest caution is everywhere to be urgently recommended.

An historical connection, whether direct or indirect, is to be assumed with considerable probability only in those cases where the resemblance consists not merely in a general conception or an accidental similarity of sound, but where it involves very definite details. In the preceding pages many instances of this kind may be found; I recall the similarities between the Buddhist and the Lucanian stories of the infancy of the hero: supernatural birth, the song of praise of the heavenly hosts, apparitions of light, the prophecy of a pious seer, the adoration of the wise men, and the parallel to the story of the twelve-year old Jesus in the temple (*Monist*, XIV, 3, pp. 336-38) and also the parallel between the Indian Krishna legend and the account in Matthew of the persecution of the infant Jesus by Herod and the slaughter of the children in Bethlehem, (*ibid.* p. 344), and again, the parallels of the Christian stories of the temptation of Jesus (*ibid.* p. 340-41), or again, the dating of the resurrection "on the third day" in the Egyptian worship of Osiris, or "after three days" in the rites of the Phrygian Attis (*ante* p. 681), the parallel of the apocalyptic purification by the blood of the lamb and the Phrygian purification by the sacrificial blood of the ram (*ante*, pp. 693-694), the Mithras sacrament of bread and wine, the sign upon the brow, the celebration of Sunday and of the 25th of December as the birthday of the god (*ante*, pp. 692 ff., 699). With such individual details at least the possibility of historical influence is to be conceded and to some extent its probability presumed.

On the other hand it would certainly not be warranted to derive the general notion of the divine sonship of Christ historically from a certain pre-Christian legend. In some sense or other this thought was common property among religious men in ancient times, and accordingly must find its ultimate ground in the depths of the universal religious consciousness, in the feeling natural to men, that "we are of divine origin," a feeling which was aroused everywhere by the sight of extraordinary gifts and achievements on the part of individual men, and which accordingly attached itself to these elect heroes of human knowledge and power as the representatives and guarantors of our universal kinship with God. And the double form in which the conception of divine sonship is found, without as well as within Christianity, that of the apotheosis of man and that of the incarnation of the godhead, can easily be explained on a psychological basis from the two equally true points of view: On the one hand the divine sonship, meaning the resemblance to God, appears as the desirable ideal and goal of human destiny; on the other hand the attainableness of this ideal presumes supernatural reality existent from the beginning, a divine capacity and essential tendency which can be comprehended only as the result of an inborn divine spirit.

Furthermore, the thought of the god-man who dies and is resurrected and ascends to heaven found its parallels in pagan religions, with roots reaching back into the most primitive conceptions of animistic nature religion, the annual death and resurrection of the divine vitality in nature. But the Christian myth is not to be derived from these nature myths, because it had its immediate origin in the historical facts of the death of Jesus and of the following Easter visions of his disciples. Nevertheless, these parallels may be regarded as important in so far as they remind us that the religious interpretation of those historical facts in the mind of the primitive Christian community did not rest upon whim or chance but was the expression of the same eternal cosmic law the truth of which has impressed itself upon mankind from the beginning: that the seed must die in order to bring forth fruit, and that the son of man must suffer in order to enter into his glory (John xii. 24 ff., Luke xxiv. 25). The dominant motive of the Christian drama of salvation, "Through death to life," has some sort of archetype in the myths and rites of many religions, and by this very fact

noring the differences, or of so underestimating them that the higher of the two seems almost brought down to the level of the lower.[1] This affords a perfect historical companion-piece to the abuse by natural scientists of the theory of evolution, placing man upon a plane with the ape as a not essentially different variety of this species. Such aberrations contribute much to discredit the just claims of the notion of evolution. But the theory is not to blame for these perversions of it, but only its onesided and superficial application by many empiricists who seem to be entirely ignorant of the fact that every new stage of development rests upon a "creative synthesis," which does not simply combine the old elements in a mechanical fashion, but completely reshapes them, subjecting them to a new and dominant law, so that the new outcome is in fact something entirely different from the sum of its former elements. This general observation finds its most brilliant confirmation precisely here, in the relation of Christianity to earlier religions, from which it developed as their higher unity and purer truth.

Primitive Christianity transformed the Jesus of history into the Jesus of faith by giving the objective form of an independent Christ spirit to the impression it received from his life and death, after the manner of ancient "animism." It fused into one this incorporate spirit with the celestial son of man found in the apocalypses and the son of God and Logos of gnosticism, and then represented this supermundane celestial spirit as descending upon earth, becoming man, dying, returning to heaven and ruling there as co-equal regent with God until his return for the last judgment. In this human-divine drama of salvation the Christian faith had taken on a form of expression that was the better fitted to subdue paganism the closer its formal relation with the myths of paganism. But in this process who could fail to see that the old forms had been made a vessel for an essentially new content, and had thus received a much deeper religious meaning and a much purer ethical significance than they had ever had before? All of the phantas-

[1] I would cite the familiar Babel and Bible Lectures of Delitzsch, which have received their most adequate criticism in Gunkel's pamphlet, *Babylon and the Religion of Israel*, 1903.

tic spirits, gods and heroes of the nature religions, as well as the earthly gods on the throne of the Cæsars, sank into nothingness in comparison with the one lord, Christ, who thenceforth was regarded as the Spirit pre-eminently (1 Cor. iii. 17), because in his nature faith saw combined all that which had been called into life in the soul of the believer by the influence of the personality of Jesus, and all the new life which the believer recognized as actual and efficient in himself and as coming from God.

Even though this belief in the god-spirit Christ clothed itself again in the garment of the old myths and found its sacramental expression in forms of worship similar to their rites, nevertheless, in content and essence this Christian faith was something entirely different, for its dominant principle, to which the old forms were subjected, was no longer the alternation of life and death in nature but the ethical ideal of holy love recognized in the life and death of Jesus, which has compassion on the weary and heavy laden, which seeks its greatness not in ruling but in serving, and sacrifices life for the cause of God and of its brethren. This ideal was not merely devised, like the ethical ideals of the Stoics, the Platonists, and the Pythagoreans, which were devised by sages for sages, and were accordingly always problematical and never efficient among the people; on the contrary, it had appeared as an actuality in the life and death of a divinely inspired prophet and friend of the people. From his words and works, and most of all from his death, it appealed to the reason and heart of all without distinction, to children and philosophers, to low and high, to sinful and righteous. Moreover, its inspiring power was not extinguished with the death of the master, but it never let go of the souls of his followers, continuing to work in them as the indissoluble bond which kept them united to him and to one another, and assured them of his continued life for their benefit in the communion of the saints.

At bottom it was perfectly natural that this ideal, which had been seen as a reality in the historical man, Jesus, was personified by the faith of the early Church in a supermundane celestial being and son of God. It was not only consistent with the animistic thought of antiquity, according to which states of consciousness in general and lively spiritual emotions in particular were given objective form as spiritual beings and explained as the influences of these on and in men, but there is in this procedure a permanent esence of truth, if only we are able to translate the early animistic-mythical language into the psychological and abstract language of to-day. No one will deny that every ideal is a transcendent quantity to which no single historical phenomenon is equivalent. Now love, which overcomes the demon of selfishness, which lifts the individual out of the narrow bounds of his particular interests, and in society transforms the natural struggle for existence into the ethical solidarity of all—should not this love be conceived rightfully as a supernatural power, as a revelation of the all-uniting spirit of God in the souls of men, just as the force of gravitation in the physical world is such a revelation?

Kant, it is remembered, recognized the revelation of God in the laws of the heavenly bodies and in the law of righteousness within the breast of man; now love is the fulfilling of the law, changing the challenging commandment into the heart's free impulse and efficient power. Why then should we not be permitted to recognize in love the "incarnation of the divine Logos," which not only has taken place, but continues to take place wherever love unites the hearts of men and consecrates society into a kingdom of God? And since love in its highest manifestation, the sacrifice of the individual self for the common welfare, is confident that she does not lose her own self but really gains it for the first time (Mark viii. 35), then in fact the divinely-human act of love's sacrifice in the service of her brethren must be the way to eternal life. And so the drama of salvation, with its guiding motive, "Through death to life! Die to live!" is giving representative expression to an eternal truth of the moral order of the universe.

The question might further be raised, why it was not possible to represent this ethical ideal directly as such without the veils of myth, in the teaching and example of Jesus, that is, why the Jesus of history instead of the Christ of faith could not become the subject of the Gospel proclamation. Two answers may be given. First, in the pagan world the Gospel proclamation had to adapt itself to the prevalent mode of thought—which was the mythical—in order to be understood by it; it could conquer the myths and rites of nature religion only by dressing the new ethical ideal substance in those forms already given and thus transforming them from within. And secondly, we must not forget that the historical Jesus, even though he was the first to be mightily inspired by the new spirit of love and divine sonship, and gave the chief initiative to the awakening and control of this spirit in mankind, was after all not simply identical with this ideal principle. That is inherently impossible, because a principle or ideal can never be identical with an individual phenomenon in time and space but is always far broader than all such.

And this is confirmed by a thoughtful glance at the reports of the Gospels, which show us Jesus as a child of his time and of his people, submissive to the law of Moses, sharing the Messianic hopes of his race, and especially, in accord with the apocalyptic mood of his contemporaries, expecting the early end of the present world and the marvellous coming of a new one. It was this apocalyptic mood which stamped upon his ethical demands their deep earnestness and also their ascetic-eschatological spurning of the "world." Now it is simply self-evident that neither that side of Jesus's thought which is attached to his national laws, nor that which connects with apocalyptic asceticism could become an object of religious faith and ethical observance for all peoples and all times. Accordingly it was an inevitable necessity that the universally valid and eternal ideal content, the real saving principle, should be separated from these individual and transient limitations of his personality and fixed in a supermundane form. Now what other form could this have been than the symbolical language of myth, of religious poetry, in which at all times the imagination has clothed the world of the divine and the eternal, under the sensual but yet supersensual figures and actions of miracle and legend?

The liberation of the Christian idea from the stubborn fetters of Judaism was possible only at the cost of arraying it in the mutable forms of myth and cult. While to be sure these were often closely connected with the ancient forms of nature religions, on the other hand they had the great advantage of being independent of that historical restriction which is inseparable from the Jewish religion or from any other religion of laws and codes. It is true, the myths removed the divine activities into the past, but it was an indefinite and fluctuant past, which, in the rites that interpreted the myth, was completely transformed into a timeless present, the symbolical repetition of the mythical story representing it as an ever renewed activity. Even such was the significance which the sacraments had for the early Chuch: they served to obliterate the temporary form of the myth of salvation by giving under symbolical forms an ever-present realization of the eternal spiritual truth hidden within it, the perpetual incarnation of God in the hearts of the faithful believers and the perpetual thank offering of the believing congregation brought to God in obedience and love.[1]

Hence myths and rites were the most suitable expression for primitive Christian faith. But they still have many lessons for us also. They show us how we should allow history to guide us out beyond and above history to the eternal and everpresent God, who is a God of the living and not of the dead; they admonish us to free ourselves from the baneful spell of the historical letter, which looks for the revelation of God only in the documents of a dead past and, absorbed in this, forgets to see him in the living present. "Why seek ye the living among the dead? He is not here; he is arisen! But go to your brethren; there ye shall see him." We shall see the living spirit of Christ, this divine principle planted forever in mankind, wherever the spirits of men are open to the recognition of all truth, wherever hearts glow for all goodness, wherever love brings the daily sacrifice of its own self for the common welfare, wherever men struggle and suffer for right and justice in society, wherever they believe in the perpetual coming of the kingdom of God among us, and where in this sign the world is vanquished.

BERLIN, GERMANY. OTTO PFLEIDERER.

---

[1] Augustine, *De civitate Dei*, X. 6, 20: Hoc est sacrificium Christianorum: multi unum corpus in Christo. Hoc etiam sacramento altaris frequentat ecclesia, quod in ea re, quam offert, ipsa offeretur....quæ, cum ipsius capitis corpus sit, se ipsam per ipsum offerre discit. Huic summo veroque sacrificio cuncta sacrificia falsa cesserunt.

PAUL RÉE.

AN OBITUARY TRIBUTE TO A MAN WHO THOUGH NOT A PROFESSIONAL PHILOSOPHER WAS A DEVOUT SEARCHER FOR THE TRUTH AND AN INDEPENDENT THINKER.

SCHOPENHAUER says that when a German hears the word "Idea" unctiously pronounced, his head commences to swim, and he feels as though he was going up in a balloon. This is a very tame description of the sensation one feels, and the mental torture endured by the inquirer, who attempts to hew his way through the jungle of barbarous concepts, out of which is constructed the metaphysical "system" of a Fichte or Hegel; and then alas! to find out that this "system" is a phantasm of the brain, which only explains the sort of head which invented it, but throws no light upon the world we live in.

On the other hand, Schopenhauer proved to the students and lovers of philosophy, in his incomparable, lucid style and wealth of concrete illustration, that the problems of metaphysics could be made as clear and comprehensible as any other branch of human knowledge, and that absence of obscurity was the *bona fides* of a philosopher.

The reader who takes up the philosophy of Paul Rée[1] will be pleased to learn that in this modest brochure there is no attempt in a metaphysical jargon to reduce "All unto One" and then out of "One" to hatch the universe; which, if you could understand it, could only serve as a kind of intellectual chewing-cud, without an atom of digestible matter. Nor will he be confronted with the usual thick volume of German metaphysics, containing chapter after

---

[1] Dr. Paul Rée, *Philosophie*. C. Duncker, Berlin, 1903, Price, M. 6.

chapter, and page after page of technical terminologies, building up some labyrinthine structure, any insight into which is exceedingly difficult, and as it is not based upon any intuitions of real life, becomes "stale, flat, and unprofitable" in theory as well as practice.

Paul Rée has no philosophical "system" to evolve; he neither attempts to explain the incredible, nor to solve the insolvable. He treats this inquiry into the powers, cogitations, and faculties of the human mind as a scientist, as an accomplished physiologist; and his paragraphs are short, clear, and logical, and the style is as terse and epigrammatic as the maxims of La Rochefoucault, whom he evidently admired.

The following description of Paul Rée's philosophy is intended as an introduction to his scientific and philosophical method of treatment, with a few excerpts freely translated of his paragraphs, illustrative of his style, matter and pithy mode of expression, rather than a comparison with other philosophical works, or a criticism of his conclusions. He treats philosophy as a science and not as an art or a teleological supplement. Without expressing it in words, he may have thought with Lord Bacon, that any inquiry into final causes is fruitless, and whether it was like a "virgin dedicated to God" or not—it nevertheless produces nothing. His style is as clear, direct, and precise as that of a chemist describing the elements of which bodies are composed; and he neither visits the "cloud-cuckoo-town" of abstraction, nor appeals to his imagination to supply data for a fictitious harmony of life.

The book is divided into parts entitled: *Origin of Conscience in Childhood and Humanity; Matter; Theory of Knowledge* (cognition); *Philosophical Thoughts upon the Systems of Kant and Schopenhauer; Vanity,* etc., etc. And each subject is dealt with in certain labelled paragraphs, which facilitate the task of the reader, and make it easier of comprehension.

THE ORIGIN OF CONSCIENCE IN THE CHILD.

As this was the subject of one of his first published books it may be considered as embodying his earliest and later revised investigations. Here our author claims to have made the most important distinction, and one entirely overlooked in previous works on moral philosophy. Hitherto neither the German, Scotch, nor English philosophers have asked or answered the question,—how does the child of a cultured or civilized age arrive at the judgment opinion or feeling, that certain acts like cruelty, robbery, and murder are blameworthy and wrong, and, on the other hand, that acts of benevolence and love of one's neighbor, are praiseworthy and right?

Does the child of the aborigines or uncivilized races think and feel that cruelty, robbery, and murder are blamable: and that benevolent acts towards members of other races are worthy of praise? Certainly not.

Take the case first of the child of the cultured age. The three great moulders and fashioners of its opinions, feelings, and judgment are religion, authority, (parental and magisterial), and its social companions. The child as taught by its parents, kneels and prays in the church, this most impressive edifice with the spire reaching towards heaven; and there it hears the command, as though it were the voice of God, "Love thy neighbor as thyself," "Thou shalt not kill, nor steal, nor lie, nor practice cruelty." Hell gapes for those who disobey, and blessedness in heaven awaits those who obey. The mind of the child is like a phonograph, what is spoken into it, comes out word for word. Then comes the lesson which the State teaches it. The judgment that certain acts are blamable, is constantly taught it. It sees, hears, or reads that the murderer has been arrested, imprisoned, and finally executed. It is a moral lesson.

So with its social companions. They also have been similarly instructed; and the child finds, in every-day speech, in all the books it reads, the plays it witnesses, and the talk of its companions, that certain acts of cruelty, stealing, or murder, are condemned, and that acts of benevolence and love of others are praised. The child does not criticize, but judges precisely as it has been taught.

But how about the child of the uncivilized epoch? Does it blame acts of robbery or murder? No, it praises them. The boy hears his parents boasting of successful robbery or murder. He is taught that such deeds are rewarded by the gods; and he hears his mother pride herself in having a son who has killed his victim. The boy goes to his companions, and he hears the same thing. They may reproach him and say: "We will not play with you, you have not yet shed the blood of even an animal."

Poesy and religion teach him that robbery and murder are praiseworthy. The father who is also a priest, initiates the boy in the religious poesy of a murder.

"As Odin hurled his spear among the people, murder came into the world."—*Edda.*

In some piratical voyage he learns that cruelty receives the highest praise. He who can tear the infant from its mother's breast and carry it off on the point of his spear, is brave, stout-hearted; but the soft-hearted who cannot endure the sight of such cruelty is scrorned and earns the epithet of child-man.

To return to the child of the cultured age. How does there arise in the child, and in the history of mankind, the judgment, that love of one's neighbor is praisable? What is the love of one's neighbor? It is an offshoot of mother love. Its most important manifestation is pity and sympathetic joy. The mother love feels pain when the child suffers, and joy over his joy. Here we have the fact that one being can love another being: an *ego* loving a *non-ego*. And this mother love, which not only covers her own children but includes the children of another, is love of one's neighbor in the widest sense. Take the simplest case. A mother sees a strange child in pain; its cries, by the association of ideas, awake in her mind the pity she feels for the sufferings of her own child, and for the sufferings of every other human being. Consequently, this love is a natural product existing in mankind.

But the opinion or judgment that praises this love is a product of culture, created by legislatures, founders of religion, which afterwards appear in the cultured pupil as an established customary opinion. And the author sets forth the different judgments held of it, in the successive stages of culture. How it was first condemned as a weakness by the uncivilized, but when once the people became cultivated the blame was changed into praise.

Benevolent emotions were not foreign to the Fiji Islanders, but it was considered a weakness to give in to them. A chief at the funeral of his favorite son praised as his most distinguished virtue "that he would have killed and eaten his own wife if she had insulted him."

In fact, the useless shedding of human blood was considered praiseworthy. In all parts of the world, according to the reports of missionaries, travellers, and explorers, most of those acts which are punished as crimes by all civilized peoples, are either treated as virtues by the uncivilized or passed over as trifles. And this is in accordance with their religion, usage, and mode of life It is also true of the heroic age of Greece. The Thracians sold their children into slavery, and considered robbery as the only honorable occupation for men. It was only in cultivated Greece in the time of Plato and Aristotle that these barbarous feelings were changed and the precepts of morality inculcated. If the reader insist that whenever he hears the word "murder," instantly his judgment condemns it, as it were by instinct, he forgets that from infancy the notion has been planted within him, and so repeatedly brought to his ears, eyes, and understanding, that it has become a constant usage. The seed was sown before he learned to reflect.

Words fall into two classes: those which convey an approval or disapproval; those which simply describe the process. For instance: Words like "murder," "treachery," "cruelty," are words expressing a judgment. You can separate them into two halves: the objective half, which means that some one out of revenge, avarice, or jealousy has killed a fellow being. In the other half the word conceals a judgment upon the act, viz., condemning it. In our childhood we learn to conceive in one word, the event and the judgment upon it. This is how the latter apears to us as self-evident.

Legislatures, moralists, and founders of religions have stamped with blame certain actions and feelings which are injurious to others, such as revenge, malice; and also impregnated with praise those feelings and actions which are useful to others (mercy, love of our neighbor)—merely on account of their utility. But the child is taught categorically, absolutely, "Thou shalt not be revengeful! Mercy is praiseworthy." Thus being educated as a child, the man finds in himself a conscience, which absolutely commands "Thou shalt" or "Thou shalt not," and accepts them as self-evident and as inborn.

Schopenhauer correctly perceived that the categorical imperative of Kant, "Thou shalt," had its origin in his early religious instruction; but strangely enough, he did not perceive that his own "pity," instead of being innate, born within us, was also a reminiscence of the catechism learned when a boy.

Schopenhauer asserts that "pity" is an incontestable fact of the human conscience and is not based upon suppositions, concepts, dogmas, myths, education, or training; but is original and innate in human nature itself, and reveals itself in all lands and ages. To this Paul Rée replies: "I agree with you in all that you say about pity. But the opinion, the judgment, of praise or blame which is passed upon pity is not innate. This opinion, this judgment, is no part of human conscience, nor is it essentially proper to it; but is in fact based upon suppositions, concepts, dogmas, myths, religions, education, and training; and does not lie in human nature itself, nor reveal itself in all lands and ages."

Morality is a complicated system; it teaches that you must love your neighbor, but in war you must kill him.

Is a man naturally good? The answer depends upon whether he belongs to the lower or higher stage of civilization. In the lower stage you ask, is the natural man revengful, cruel, and hard-hearted? Yes. But with these good (praisable) qualities, bad ones are mixed; he is naturally placable, soft-hearted, compassionate. Thus he is tolerably good, but not entirely so.

In a higher stage of civilisation: Is the natural man placable, soft-hearted, compassionate? Yes. But mixed with these praisable (good) qualities are bad ones; the man by nature is revengeful, hard-hearted, and cruel. And these bad qualities outweigh the good ones: thus by nature he is not good but bad.

What actions are universally blamed, permits of no answer. By the ancient Norwegians a pirate, sea-robbber, was not blamed, but considered a hero. It was only for utilitarian reasons, viz., that the soil of the country should be cultivated, that piracy fell into disrepute, and was ultimately punished with mutilation and death.

As for the law of nature, that exists only in the heads of the professors of jurisprudence. Paul Rée analyses with clearness and insight the origin of the concepts, natural right, duty, justice, obligation, ownership, etc., which would take up too much space to quote here. In relation to the so-called moral sense, he has this to say: The moral sense is the relation or connection between certain acts and the praise or blame which we attach to them. A special moral sense does not exist.

Hume's ethics which he considered his best work, if devoid of error, has still a gap in it. He teaches that those qualities which are useful to us are stamped as virtues; but he forgets to explain why morality, if dependent upon utility, nevertheless appears to be independent. This appearance is thus accounted for: To the child or pupil only the moral precept is delivered; but not its cause, utility. Utility is the spool around which moral precepts are spun; the moralist who understands how to unwind them sees the spool, but the others see only the precepts.

"He who makes the distinction, or discriminates between the child and the adult mankind, has eaten of the tree of knowledge: he alone knows what is good and evil."

After the laws of morality have been established for the good of humanity, they are impressed upon the minds of each succeeding generation. And the children of each succeeding generation must learn the rules and precepts of morality and its exceptions for themselves. And as they grow up, these rules and precepts appear as self-evident and born within them.

THE ORIGIN OF CONSCIENCE IN MANKIND.

The history of the evolution of man traces this development from an animal. Mankind were first herders of cattle; naked hunters and fishermen, leading insecure lives in dirt and misery. Although the intervening stages cannot be traced, one of the succeeding steps of evolution was the appearance of family life. Single families scattered over large areas of territory, lived in isolated huts, the head of which became king and priest. The family morals forbade a member to rob or murder one of the same family; but if it happened that he killed or robbed one belonging to another family, the act was not considered blamable by his own family. Each family lived in a sea of blood. Stern necessity alone prescribed certain rules of conduct.

In due course of time, as the family multiplied in numbers to a people or a nation, the family morals became the morals of a nation. At the time when mankind were scattered and living in isolated families it was not blamable to rob or murder members of other families. The act was not punished by the chief or head of the family, nor condemned by the community. But the relatives of the murdered man would take revenge as a matter of course; and the more fearful the revenge, the more glorious the deed. As the families increased and became a people, a change took place, not only in their mode of thought or manner of regarding such acts, but also in the punishment awarded them. The historical origin of punishment teaches us that it was founded upon utilitarian reasons. To stop the shedding of blood in acts of revenge, came compensation to the murdered man's relatives in arms or cattle, peace-money, blood-money, and finally punishment by the laws of the State.

The author traces with great clearness and illustrates with abundant concrete instances the various stages from individual vengeance to the erection of asylums for refugees—the buying off of revenge, by compensation and peace-money, up to the institution of fixed punishments and penalties by the State.

He then undertakes to answer two important questions: How does the idea of god arise? How does the notion or conception arise that actions punishable by men are also punishable by the godhead? He goes back to the stage of the uncivilized. When the savage hears the coming storm growling in the distance and watches in fear its approach nearer and nearer, until it suddenly bursts in tremendous thunder claps above his head, and sees the lightning flashes, not only splitting trees but killing men and cattle; in that moment of horror his heart quakes within him, and in the raging tempest he also hears the voice of some mighty power, and sees an angry threatening countenance with eyes that kill.

Pay attention to this moment, for in it a god is born. Like a child the savage asks: Who thunders? Who storms? Who strikes the earth? He naturally conceives this power in the form of a man; with a man's voice, a man's eyes, but eyes whose flashes kill men.

Thus the gods are men, but being born of human terror, they are human monsters. *Deos facit timor.* Consequently the gods are the personifications of certain terrifying events in nature. That fear created them is not so important for this subject, as that they are created in the image of man: anthropomorphism is the fundamental insight by which it is explained, but not without it. The gods of the uncivilized men are in the likeness of the uncivilized; and the gods of the civilized, cultured, are in the likeness of the cultured peoples.

After the Homeric period, agriculture, trade, the arts, and sciences were cultivated. And these foster children of peace required that actions like robbery and murder should be condemned and threatened with punishment. The requirement was fulfilled by the legislature and the spirit of the age. And the gods? They were behind the times. They did not yet blame those actions that were condemned on earth. And the gods had to be transformed and fitted to the improved mode of thought; but for a long time they maintained their old character and morality. The more cultured men became, the more striking became the contrast between the grossness of the gods and the refinement of the people. Lucian remarks that a Grecian youth, who has been instructed in Homer and Hesiod and finally goes out into the world, finds to his amazement that the very same deeds which Homer and Hesiod attributed to the gods in heaven are threatened with punishment on earth. The incongruity between the morals of the gods and men became a scandal of the age; and the morals of the former had to be modified to suit the spirit of the times. Accordingly the Homeric heart is torn out of the body of poor old Jupiter and a new one put in its place; and then the new Jupiter threatens with punishment those very actions hitherto committed with impunity.

Heaven and earth might then be compared to two clocks that at first kept time together; but gradually the former lost ,and when they were too far apart it had to be put forward again.

To recapitulate: So long as cheating, robbery, and murder did not appear blamable to the people it was not blamed by the people's god. When the people arrived, however, at such a stage of culture that such actions were forbidden and punished, they were also forbidden and threatened with punishment by the people's god. In other words, the law did not come down but *came back* from heaven.

World, or universal, morality differs from a people's or nation's morality in two points. A nation's morals is only concerned with certain actions; universal morality includes also the feelings, sentiments, and dispositions. The Old Testament teaches the morals of one nation or people, the New Testament teaches the morals of humanity: one commands certain actions, the other feelings, sentiment. The former commands "Thou shalt not kill," the latter "Thou shalt not even harbor anger against thy neighbor."

It was for the good of humanity that Jesus of Nazareth broadened the morality of actions to also include the morality of feelings. Out of pity for the poor, the lame, the cripple, the blind, and out of love for humanity at large, Jesus preached love of others.

Would the doctrines of Jesus have lasted and spread over a great portion of the earth, if he had simply *preached* love of one's neighbor? Probably not. But Jesus was not only a moral leader, but a founder of religion. And here is verified how anthropomorphism is the universal explainer. Jesus was personified love of others, consequently "God is love."

In the historical development of humanity this has often happened. All peoples at their highest point of culture attain to this conception of universal morality. Thus the stages in the history of the moral-religious evolution of humanity are:

Family morals—family divinity.
People's morals—people's divinity.
World morals—world divinity.

Morality is like a tree which at first only shelters a family, then a whole people rests in its shadow, and finally humanity.

MATTER.

In this chapter, one of the most important in the book, Paul Rée sets forth in a most uncompromising manner his subjective idealism, and specifically analyses with great particularity the various sensations of pain, hearing, sight, touch, and taste, and traces in each concrete instance the physiological process with elementary clearness. As he had received the degree of Doctor of Medicine at Berlin and Munich, his scientific presentation of these sensations are of value to the reader. One or two of these illustrations are here given in substance but not in detail.

Take the sensation of pain. One who suffers from toothache will assert that the pain is in the toooth. Between the troublesome tooth and the brain there runs a thread called a nerve; if the tooth end of the nerve is irritated, say by pressure, a nerve-current is stimulated which, on reaching the brain, produces the sensation called pain. This is a case of false localization.

Take another case. A foot, on account of some disease, is amputated above the ankle; nevertheless, after the amputation, certain sensations of pain, or itching, are localized by the patient in the foot which is no longer attached to his body. The proof that the pain is in the brain and not in the foot is thus given. He puts the case of a sound foot which has not been amputated. If the nerve is cut, say in the leg, which ultimately reaches the brain, and afterwards a hot iron is applied to the sound foot, not the slightest sensation of pain is felt by the patient. The message was not delivered.

So with sound and the sense of hearing. If you clap your hands, there arise (silent) air-waves which reach your tympanum, and the latter communicates these silent vibrations to the three small bones, the membrane, the mucous, and finally the auditory nerve; here the nerve-current is stimulated, which ultimately stimulates the brain-cell and produces the sensation of sound, tones. If the brain-cell, where the nerve of the tooth enters, is stimulated by a nerve-current, "pain" is felt, but if the brain-cell, where the auditory nerve enters, is stimulated as above, sound is produced. Whence this difference? No one can answer it. Let us discriminate between the sound and its cause. The clapping produces *silent* air-waves; these silent air-waves, vibrations, cause through the various connecting links a silent nerve-current, which stimulates the brain-cell and produces "sound." Thus a transformation takes place, silence becomes sound. The expression "sound" or "sonorous waves," strictly taken, is false; these air-waves are silent.

Take the roar of a great city. The motor screams, a trumpet blows its fan-fare, thousands of wheels go rattling over the stones, men are shouting, talking, you add your own speech to the tumult; but if you think that all this noise comes from the locomotive, the trumpet, the mouths of men, and the wheels on the stone pavement, you are mistaken. Those motions only produce *silent* air-waves; the noise is in your brain. Outside the stillness of death prevails. It is another case of false localization.

So with light. According to the hypothesis of the physicists an almost infinitely attenuated and elastic medium fills space, which they call ether, which they call non-luminous, and which like air can be made to vibrate in waves.

Physiologically expressed, a non-luminous object, a lighted candle, generates non-luminous ether-waves, which reach the eye as air-waves reach the ear, and stimulate the optic nerve; of course the intervening links of the process being taken into consideration, the nerve-current stimulates the brain-cell, and the result is light. The light which appears to be in the candle is, in fact, in the brain.

Strictly speaking, the expression light-waves is misleading. It will be noticed that here the effect is totally different from the cause: non-luminous ether-waves producing light.

Idealism can be thus popularly presented. It is evident that the bodies do not possess all the qualities which are arbitrarily attributed to them. For example: does what we call "sweet" lie in the sugar? Impossible, for "sweetness" is a taste, a sensation; that is in me and not in the sugar. Now, if "sweetness" is not present in the sugar, and yet it calls forth in me the sensation, taste of "sweetness," then my taste of "sweetness" is caused by something "non-sweet" in the sugar. But this discrimination is by no means made involuntarily. If sugar melts on my tongue, I do not separate the sensation "sweet" in me from the something "non-sweet" in the sugar. But the process is precisely opposite: I misplace my sensation of sweetness in the sugar and impute to it one of my sensaions, taste, as one of the qualities of the sugar.

The same process takes place with my sensation of color; I also impute to the sugar my sensation of "white" as one of its qualities, also my feeling of hardness, and still other sensations. What is it that excites in me the sensations of "sweetness," "whiteness," "hardness," complex-perceptions, complex-ideas? An unknown something, ether-waves, $X\,Y\,Z$. If sweet, smooth, hard, sharp, and the other perceptions of qualities of bodies are without any independent existence, then "bodies," complex-sensations, complex-ideas, are also without any independent reality. My own body is a mere complex of ideas. "I am a conglomerate of perceptions! It is inconceivable, but true."

What is matter? The sum total of my perceptions, ideas, feelings, which are falsely localized outside of me. To the bodies which I perceive belong also the bodies of my fellow men. But where they appear to me to be, is the unknown exciter, stimulator of my perceptions, viz., hypothetical ether-waves $= XYZ$.

The proportion *cogito ergo sum* is false: It should be: *Sum cogitans*. Plainer and clearer it cannot be made.

The following epitomized dialogue describes Kant's relation to Bishop Berkeley, or "poor Berkeley" as Kant calls him.

Berkeley. "Kant, I have just come from reading your philosophy, and am delighted with it. I said to myself, Kant evidently understands me. He has taken up my ideas and confirmed them from different points of view. I laid the egg, and Kant has hatched it!"

Kant. "Don't make me angry. My doctrine differs from

yours heaven high. I have a *Ding an sich* (*the-thing-as-it-is-in-itself*), but you have not."

Berkeley. "You amaze me. Is your refutation of idealism put forth seriously? I took it for a joke. Besides it is inconceivable that you should claim that I have no *Ding an sich* (*thing-as-it-is-in-itself*). We both assert that everything perceptible, viz., form, color, and material, is merely an idea, perception. You teach that the idea of 'house' is produced in me by your *Ding an sich* of the 'house.' Now I teach that the idea 'house' is produced in me by God. Let me ask you, what do you know of your *Ding an sich?* Nothing, absolutely nothing; except that by some unknown cause it produces in you the idea 'house.' What do I know of God? Nothing. except that he causes the idea 'house' to arise in my mind."

Kant. "You cannot reason away my doctrine in that manner. There is a second thing which you have overlooked. According to my doctrine, things are phenomena of the noumena (*Ding an sich*), while with you they are merely phenomena, appearances."

Berkeley closes the argument by telling Kant that he is not dealing fairly with the question, and quoting his own words:

> "External objects belong just as much to the thinking subjects as all other thoughts; only they possess the deception that they, as it were, detach themselves from the soul, and appear to hover outside of us; for the space in which we perceive them is nothing but an idea. Bravo Kant! More idealistic than that I could not express myself. If all objects exist only in our thoughts, then my body exists nowhere but in my thoughts; my body is my idea, my perception. 'I' am only a conglomerate of ideas."

Dr. Rée asks, if bodies are merely ideas, why do they not appear to us merely as ideas, perceptions, and not as bodies outside of us? That we do not know. Whoever presents a problem clearly and unmistakably as inexplicable, deserves credit for this statement. Pseudo explanations are the corruption of philosophy.

CAUSALITY.

In his analysis and exposition of causality he arrives at the conclusion that Hume and Mill are right; and that the claims of Kant and Schopenhauer that the causal law is known to us *a priori*, is not proved.

What is the meaning of the word "cause"? It may be thus defined: "the course of nature is regular, invariable." For instance, motion invariably follows a blow, thrust, or push of any kind; that is to say, not sometimes only, but regularly. Cause is an event in so far as it regularly succeeds another event or change. But it must be noted that causality means to us something more than regular, constant succession. And this is due to the fact that from childhood we have always seen motion to follow from a blow or push, and have becom econvinced that through all time and eternity a similar result will follow; we think involuntarily that there is a necessary connection or band between the two. Between cause and effect in general there is only an external connection but no inner band of necessity. He then outlines the origin of the causal conscience. For instance, a child has repeatedly learned through experience that the point of a needle pricks; and if it unexpectedly feels the pain of being pricked, it involuntarily thinks of, and looks around for, the needle. So with the fire: experience has taught it that fire burns, and if it approaches unawares the fire and feels the pain of being "burnt," it naturally thinks of a fire and looks for it. And having repeatedly seen a ball roll when struck, if it happens to see one rolling along, without having noticed the blow, it naturally looks around for the striker. Now, after witnessing for a hundred thousand times one event always succeeding another event, it forms the conception that every event is always preceded by another event.

Thus the concept of causality is a concept drawn from experience. If it be objected that the two events are bound together by necessity, this word, necessity, distinguishes the causal concept as a concept *a priori*, which is a spurious necessity.

The child in the first place never sees a ball moving of itself, that is without a blow preceding it; and therefore the conception of a ball moving of its own accord is difficult to conceive, almost an impossibility. And giving expression to this thought-difficulty, one says a blow must precede the movement of a ball. "One can't think otherwise." This "must," this "cannot think otherwise," is simply a habit, usage of the mind.

Ask an unsophisticated person: Can a ball of itself, without cause, commence to roll? No. It is an impossible thought. Can it stop of itself, without cause? Certainly, the ball generally stops of itself.

Thus the opposite of the causal law is not inconceivable, but simply difficult to conceive. He repeats: The necessity of the causal law is not genuine, but spurious; its necessity is merely imaginary. But can we imagine an effect without cause? Certainly not. One must distinguish between a change and an effect. Change means merely an alteration of a state or condition, but does not mean that the change of condition or state has a cause. An effect also means a change of condition or state, but at the same time expresses the thought that change of state has a cause. You can no more think of an effect without a cause than of a nephew without an uncle. After a long detailed analysis, illustrated with numerous concrete instances, he asserts that there is no inner band or necessary connection between cause and effect. As to Kant's claim for the apriority of the causal law, he attacks it repeatedly as in the following instance:

At twelve o'clock I perceive a ship outside the mouth of a river; and fifteen minutes later I perceive the ship to be some distance inside of it. Am I certain that my perception corresponds in fact to the thing perceived? Only under the presupposition of the law of causality can I know whether, when I saw it outside, it was really there and not inside;—I must conceive the change of position to have been causally effected. This is Kant's claim. Causality is not subtracted from the constant succession of events, as Hume thought, but on the contrary, the succession of events, in order to be perceptible, presupposes the concept of causality.

One would naturally expect Kant to explain and prove the assertion, but he simply repeats it over and over again, as though it were a self-evident proposition. Kant's treatment of causality, so far as Hume is concerned, is a step backward, and made, too, in seven-leagued boots. He admits that Hume is right in teaching that individual causal relations we learn from experience; that a push or blow causes changes of position in space, and changes of temperature from heat. But the universal law of causality—every change has a cause—we know *a priori*—is born in us.

Yet in all branches of human knowledge the rule is drawn from the cases; but Kant teaches the opposite, viz., the rule is known to us *a priori*, born within us, as it were; and the cases are only known to us *a posteriori*. This is extremely improbable and needs irrefutable proof, which he does not furnish. According to Kant, causality is not, as Hume claims, abstracted from the succession of events, but on the contrary, the succession of events, in order to be perceptible, presupposes the concept, causality.

Hume and Kant remind one of the two advocates in Scott's romance of *Redgauntlet*. After Hume, with wonderful skill and art, had disentagled the various difficulties of the case, Kant with equal art and skill entangled it all up again.

Passing from Kant's theory of causality, here is an amusing instance how Dr. Rée combats Kant's category of space. If Kant's assertion be true, that space has no independent existence or reality outside of us, but is merely a subjective condition of perception, born within us, some of the consequences are quite lamentable. For instance: Where am I? In space? But the only space is in me. The space of Cæsar was different from that of Pompey. Where was the battle of Pharsalus fought? In Cæsar's space or Pompey's space? As there are millions of men, each with the only space in his head, so there must be millions of spaces; but Kant teaches that there is only one space, and that is infinite. With the first man came space into the world; when the last human being dies infinite space also vanishes.

Think of the probable fate of the lovers, Hans and Gretel! They are in love with each other, and yet no meeting-place can be found. Hans possesses infinite space and endless time, and Gretel is also in possession of infinite space and endless time. But how can the infinite space which is in Hans's head arrive at the infinite space which is in Gretel's? It is no good suggesting that each one should go to the boundary of his or her infinite space, and there find a rendezvous; for space, being infinite, has no boundary. And there the lovers stand, with arms outstretched, and no possible space upon which they can meet. What a pretty philosophical romance could be made of this Kantian notion of space!

In discussing idealism and realism in his chapter upon the theory of cognition, he claims that the nature of things forces the scientific, philosophical thinker to be both idealist and materialist. Idealism is at once true and yet inconceivable; but materialism is no more conceivable than its opposite. For instance: a person has a hole in his head through which can be seen not ouly his brain, but also, let us suppose, its molecular action. And this molecular action one must accept as thinking; the grey matter is calculating the course of the stars, or perhaps animated with passion, or arriving at some difficult conclusion, or willing. Now this assumption is just as incomprehensible as its opposite idealism, according to which one is a conglomerate of ideas, feelings; and the grey matter of the brain is one of these ideas.

The materialist says: The simple organisms probably are evolved out of inorganic matter, and out of the simplest organisms, evolution has produced animals, apes, man. The brain is an organ of man, and the brain thinks; consequently, ideas, feelings, perceptions, are a product of the brain, and brain is matter.

The idealist says: the matter of the brain is not the primary—the *matrix*— of the perceiving subject; but the latter is the primary, and matter is one of its ideas. Both are right, and yet how incomprehensible it is, that both intuitions are correct. He who can answer this question has solved the problem of the universe.

Immanent, transcendental speculations have harmonized these opposing tenets, but not by any honest thinker. There is no great philosopher in the sense that Hervey was a great physiologist and Copernicus a great astronomer. They established certain universal truths. Idealism is irrefutable, and yet it is incomprehensible. As Hobbs says "from hence followeth that whatsoever accidents or qualities our senses make us think there may be in the world, they be not there, but are seeming and apparitions only.—We conclude such things to be *without*, that are *within* us."

As can be seen from the above extracts, Dr. Rée subjects Kant's theories to a very drastic criticism; and the *Ding an sich* (thing-as-it-is-in-itself), the doctrines of space and time, the categorical imperative, and *a priori* ideas and judgments, are treated with grim Carlylean humor. He claims that Kant slaughtered in his theoretic philosophy, God, freedom of the will, and immortality; but that they re-appear again as ghosts in his practical philosophy.

A philosopher who had not studied the philosophy of Kant, once said of him, "I hear, Herr Kant, that on one side of your philosophical system, you have destroyed God, freedom, and immortality, and yet they nevertheless peep out of the windows of the other side of your philosophical system. How did you manage that?"

"Oh," replied Kant, "I postulate God, freedom, and immortality," and turned away from his astonished inquirer. Dr. Rée thinks that there are only two grains of wheat in a bushel of chaff in the Kantian philosophy, and what they are we will leave to the reader to find out. Schopenhauer's theories do not fare much better than those of Kant. He concedes to Schopenhauer the merit that his presentations are clear, clever, and ingenious, and interwoven with the finest observations of nature; and that one could compile a volume of quotations from his works, containing nothing but what is true, excellent, and rich in intellectual thought. But he, too, has been the victim of his own theories, and Dr. Rée proceeds to subject the offenders to his usual painstaking, analytical criticism.

The following is a fair specimen: The production of a system like Schopenhauer's demands a rare combination of qualities. One must possess a good judgment, but also know when to use and when to ignore it; be blind to the facts which oppose and believe the most incredible things that favor it.

For example: Schopenhauer asserts that the blood, with a metaphysical freedom of will, flows *without cause* back to the heart! In order to do justice to this crazy thought we will accompany a little drop of blood on its circulating course. It starts from the heart as a common citizen of this causal world, and this common causal character clings to it on its path through the capillary vessels. But while it creeps through these capillary arteries it approaches the greatest event of its career, and this takes place the moment it leaves the last capillary artery and arrives at the first vein. At this instant, O envied drop of blood! the law of causality falls like a chain away; and with elevated head it flows, or runs, *without cause* back to the heart. And yet, no sooner is it in the heart, than this poor little drop of blood is once more a slave to the law of causality. Thus two-thirds of its course it is subject to the causal law; but enjoys at least one third of its journey free from the propelling force of causality. What proof does he offer to sustain this assertion? There being no serious proof at his disposal, he had none to offer.

Schopenhauer perceived clearly enough that man's thinking organ, far from being his real essence, an immortal thing, was only a tool, like other organs of the body which ministered to life, and desired to perpetuate itself. The same was true of all other organisms. But here closes according to Paul Rée the acceptable portion of Schopenhauer's philosophy. When he arrived at this point he made two phantastic leaps, a small one and a colossal one. The small one is the extension of this principle over the thing-as-it-is-in-itself; as even this, in a very indecent maner, desires to live and to propagate. In truth, its first desire is the will to live; and its last the will not to live.

The imagination cannot invent so many contradictions as are gathered together in the head of a philosopher. It rains assertions in the ethics. A compassionate onlooker is transcendentally identical with the one who suffers from an injury. To the impertinent who asks for proof, Schopenhauer full of divine wrath thunders: "You want proofs? Go to the miserable, contemptible sciences! Intuitive genius alone reigns in philosophy. The veil of Maya which covers the eyes of the rest of mankind has a hole in it, and I, Arthur Schopenhauer, have looked through this hole, and I see the nature, the essence of all things, and I perceive that the artistic thing-as-it-is-in-itself *wills* the world; but that the moral thing-as-it-is-in-itself *wills* it to perish!"

"The power of words over thought is densely illustrated by that phrase *thing-as-it-is-in-itself*."

And so on to the end of the chapter. No wonder that Voltaire in his time cried, "O metaphysics, we are about as far advanced as were the Druids in their time;" and we might ask: are we any further advanced to-day?

Dr. Rée was a very ardent admirer of the works of La Rochefoucauld, and as a result he has inserted in his philosophy a chapter upon Vanity, in which he endeavors to show that, as in the days of Solomon and Marcus Aurelius, not only all is vanity, but that it is the great motive power of human action. To quote only one of his maxims: "If vanity were suddenly to vanish, the painter before his easel, the author over his manuscripts, and the warrior on his battle-steed, would all fall asleep. Like the Sleeping Beauty, only the kiss of vanity could awake them!" They must be read to be appreciated.

He closes his work with the following remarks upon the insolvable problems of philosophy: "Has the world for ever existed? Incomprehensible thought. We cannot comprehend eternity. Has the world had a beginning? Also incomprehensible. We cannot comprehend the origin of something out of nothing. Man perceives externally, forms, colors, etc.; and internally, observing himself, he comprehends that he feels, imagines, wills.

"But every attempt of the human race to break through the world of perception, ideas, in order to discover more or less clearly what lies behind, constantly miscarries; and the new discovery always turns out to be merely a new combination of old concepts. Man is not essentially different from the animal, as the latter also perceives, connects, and combines. It is true, it does not philosophize. Man is the animal that philosophizes; and he is precisely just wise enough to understand that he knows nothing."

As Dr. Rée has no "system" to construct he does not deal with abstractions, which, as he says, are the ever prolific source of error. The unbiased reader may and probably will differ from many of his conclusions—it is always a disappointment to be forced at this late day, to agree with Socrates that we know nothing;—but nevertheless, the epoch-making character of this book, and the honesty, fearlessness, and the logical acumen of its gifted author will be denied by no independent and reasonable thinker.

HENRY HOOPER.

CINCINNATI, O.

THE "HOLY EDICT" OF K'ANG-HI.

A CHINESE ANTI-MACHIAVELLI.

SHORTLY before Frederick the Great ascended the throne, he wrote a criticism of Machiavelli's doctrines of statecraft, which . those times were considered the sum-total of political wisdom, a treatise entitled *Anti-Machiavelli*. Machiavelli, an Italian atesman, educated in the school of Italian politics with its in-igues and *coups d'état*, advised princes to maintain their sover-gnty by crooked means, by treachery, and violence, but the young rown Prince of Prussia condemned the book not only as immoral ıt also as very unwise,—in a word, as absolutely wrong; and he ated his own views that a prince could maintain himself best by rving the people with ability and honesty. Government is eded," the young Frederick argued, "and so long as a prince will) his duty, his people will need him and will be grateful for the rvice he gives." In contrast to the notion of Louis XIV. of rance, who said, *"L'état c'est moi,"* Frederick's maxim was that king is, and should consider himself, "the first servant of his ople." The statesmen of Europe smiled at the ingenuity of the ntastic idealist, as which they regarded him, but Frederick proved them by deeds that his maxims were superior to the intricate iles of the old diplomacy.

It is interesting to learn that in China too there lived a sover-gn who came to the conclusion that honesty is the best policy, ıd whose main maxim of government may be summed up in the inciple, to serve the interests of the people. The man of whom we speak is K'ang-Hi, and the famous document which expresses his views on the subject is called the "Holy Edict."

THE HOLY EDICT OF K'ANG-HI.

K'ang-Hi 康熙, the second emperor of the present dynasty called Ch'ing, was distinguished not only in the field as a successful general, but also as a good ruler by the wisdom of his government. He published in the latter part of his glorious reign an advice to government officials in sixteen maxims, known under the name *Shêng Yü* 聖諭, i. e., "Holy Edict." They were written on slips of wood and hung up in all the imperial offices of the country.

Yung-Ching, the son and successor of K'ang-Hi, republished his father's edict with a preface and amplifications of his own. He says in the preface:

"Our sacred father, the benevolent emperor, for a long period taught the method of a perfect reform. His virtue was as wide as the ocean, and his mercy extended to the boundaries of heaven. His benevolence sustained the world, and his righteousness guided the teeming multitudes of his people. For sixty years, in the morning and in the evening, even while eating and dressing, his sole care was to rouse all, both his own subjects and those living outside his domain, to exalt virtue, to rival with each other in liberal-mindedness and in keeping engagements with fidelity. His aim was that all should cherish the spirit of kindness and meekness, and that they should enjoy a reign of eternal peace.

"With this purpose in view, he graciously published an edict consisting of sixteen maxims, wherein he informed the soldiers of the Tartar race (at the capital), and also the soldiers and people of the various provinces, of their whole duty concerning the practice of the essential virtues, the duties of husbandry and the culture of cotton and silk, labor and rest, common things and ideal aspirations, public and private affairs, great things and small, and whatever was proper for the people to do; all this he elucidated thoughtfully. He looked upon his people as his own children. His sacred instructions are like the sayings of the ancient sages, for they point out the right way of assured safety.

"Ten thousand generations should practise his maxims. To improve them is impossible.

"Since we succeeded to the charge of this great empire and are ruling now over the millions of people, we have conformed our mind to the mind of our sacred father and our government to his, morning and evening, and with untiring[1] energy, we endeavor to conform to the ancient traditions and customs....

"With great reverence, we publish the sixteen maxims of the Sacred Edict on the principles of which we have deeply meditated. We have amplified them by an addition of ten thousand characters, explaining them with similes from things far and near, quoting ancient books in order to fully explain their meaning."

The preface is signed "Yung Ching," bearing the date of the second year of his rule, the second day of the second month. His seal consists of two impressions: one shows the characters "Attend to the people," the other "Venerate heaven."

My source of the Chinese text is a manuscript copy, written by an unknown Sinologist as marginal notes in an old translation of the Sacred Edict by the Rev. Willliam Milne, Protestant Missionary at Malacca, printed in 1817 at London for Black, Kingsbury & Allen, Booksellers for the Hon. East India Co. The handwriting of the Chinese characters is awkward but clear, obviously made with a Western pen, not a native's brush. It contains two mistakes, which were corrected by Mr. Teitaro Suzuki, who also assisted me in the translation.

The copy here reproduced has been written by Mr. Kentok Hori of San Francisco, California, well known among his countrymen for his elegant penmanship.

---

[1] The larva of the mosquito is an aimalcule which is constantly wriggling in the water. It has a name of its own in Chinese, being called *Chieh-Chieh,* which serves as a well-known symbol of an indefatigable activity. For the sake of simplicity, we have simply translated it "untiring."

TEXT OF THE SIXTEEN MAXIMS.[1]

聖諭

敦孝弟以重人倫、篤宗族以昭雍睦、和鄉
黨以息爭訟、重農桑以足衣食、尚節儉以惜
財用、隆學校以端士習、黜異端以崇正學、講
法律以儆愚頑、明禮讓以厚風俗、務本業以
定民志、訓子弟以禁非為、息誣告以全善良、
誡匿逃以免株連、完錢糧以省催科、聯保甲
以弭盜賊、解讎忿以重身命、

[1] The text of the Holy Edict has been incorporated in an edition of the *T'ai Shang Kan Ying P'ien*, published by the Association of the Middle Flower,

TRANSLATION OF THE HOLY EDICT.

MAXIM I.

Cultivate filial piety and brotherly love, for thereby will be honored social morality.

MAXIM II.

Render family relations[1] cordial, for thereby appears the bliss of harmony.

MAXIM III.

Let concord prevail among neighbors,[2] for thereby you prevent quarrels and law suits.

MAXIM IV.

Honor husbandry and silk industry, for thereby is supplied raiment and food.

MAXIM V.

Esteem thrift and economy,[3] for thereby is saved money in business.

MAXIM VI.

Promote academic institutions, for thereby are established scholarly habits.

MAXIM VII.

Do away with heretical systems, for thereby is exalted the orthodox doctrine.

MAXIM VIII.

Explain laws and ordinances,[4] for thereby are warned the foolish and obstinate.

---

a Chinese society at Yokohama. The text agrees with the present one with the exception of two cases, viz., Maxim II ,word 7, and Maxim XIII, word 2, which are replaced by homonyms, and in Maxim XII the order of the characters 6 and 7 is inverted. Our translation is as literal as possible.

[1] Literally: "Make cordial ||relatives|| [and] kin."—Here as well as elsewhere, two synonyms are used to express one idea. They had perhaps been better translated by one word.

[2] Literally: "Harmonise ||the village's|| inhabitants."

[3] See note to Maxim II.

[4] See note to Maxim II.

MAXIM IX.

Recommend polite manners, for thereby is refined the social atmosphere.[1]

MAXIM X.

Develop legitimate business, for thereby the people's desire is rendered pacific.

MAXIM XI.

Instruct the youth,[2] for thus you prevent crime.

MAXIM XII.

Suppress false denunciations, for thereby you protect the good and the worthy.[3]

MAXIM XIII.

Warn those who conceal deserters, for thereby they escape being entangled in their fate.[4]

MAXIM XIV.

Enforce the payment[5] of taxes,[6] for thereby you avoid the imposition of fines.

MAXIM XV.

Keep disciplined the police forces,[7] for thereby are prevented thefts and robberies.

MAXIM XVI.

Settle enmities and dissensions, for thereby you protect human lives.[8]

---

[1] Literally: "Wind and habits"; 風 *Feng* = "wind," means also "climate," and "atmosphere." Both characters together are best translated "social atmosphere."

[2] Literally: "Boys and youngsters." See note to Maxim II.

[3] See note to Maxim II.

[4] Literally: "Escape bush entanglement," which means "being entangled in the (same) bush," i. e., "being caught with criminals."

[5] Literally: "Complete," which means "be punctual in collecting."

[6] The term "taxes" means in Chinese "cash payments and food products," because the tax payers have their choice to pay either in coin or in produce.

[7] Literally: "Protecting armies."

[8] Literally: "Persons and their destinies."

Each maxim of the Holy Edict consists of seven characters, and exhibits the same grammatical construction. The first three characters express the advice given; the fourth character is uniformly the same word *i*, which means "thereby," "thus," or "so that": the concluding three characters contain the result to be obtained.

The style of the Holy Edict will naturally appear pedantical to a Western reader, but if we consider its contents and the spirit in which it is written, we must grant that it is a remarkable document which reveals to us the inmost thought of a great Chinese ruler.

YUNG CHING'S AMPLIFICATIONS.

Yung Ching, the son of K'ang-Hi and his successor, adds to the sixteen Maxims of his father his amplifications, as he styles them, which may be characterised as sermons on the bliss of virtue and the curse of evil-doing.

Yung Ching's comments on the first Maxim are typical Chinese expositions of the significance of 孝 *hsiao,* i. e., "filial piety," the cardinal virtue of Confucian ethics. It reads as follows:

"Filial piety is the unalterable statute of heaven, the corresponding operations of earth, and the common obligations of all people. Have those who are void of filial piety never reflected on the natural affection of parents to their children?

"Before leaving the parental bosom, if hungry, you could not feed yourselves; if cold, you could not put on clothes. Parents judge by the voice and anxiously watch the features of their children; their smiles create joy, their weeping, grief. On beginning to walk they leave not their steps; when sick, they do not sleep or eat; thus they nourish and teach them. When they come to years they give them wives, and settle them in business, exhausting their minds by planning and their strength by labor. Parental virtue is truly great and exhaustless as that of heaven.

"The son of man that would recompense one in ten thousand of favors of his parents, should at home exhaust his whole heart, abroad exert his whole strength. Watch over his person, practise economy, diligently labor for, and dutifully nourish them. Let him not gamble, drink, quarrel, or privately hoard up riches for his own sake! Though his external manners may not be perfect, yet there should be abundant sincerity!

"Let us enlarge a little here by quoting what Tsang-Tsze says: 'To move unbecomingly is unfilial; to serve the prince without fidelity is unfilial; to act disrespectful as a mandarin is unfilial; to be insincere to a friend is unfilial; to be cowardly in battle is also unfilial.' These things are comprehended in the duty of an obedient son.

"Again, the father's elder son is styled viceroy of the family; and the younger brothers [after the father's death] give him honorable appellation of family superior.

"Daily, in going out and coming in, whether in small or great affairs, the younger branches of his family must ask his permission. In eating and drinking, they must give him the preference; in conversation, yield to him; in walking, keep a little behind him; in sitting and standing, take the lower place. These are illustrative of the duties of the younger brothers.

"If I meet a stranger, ten years older than myself, I would treat him as an elder brother; if one five years older, I would walk with my shoulder a little behind his; how much more then ought I to act thus towards him who is of the same blood with myself!

"Therefore, undutifulness to parents and unbrotherly conduct are intimately connected. To serve parents and elder brothers are things equally important.

"The dutiful child will also be the affectionate brother; the dutiful child and affectionate brother will, in the country, be a worthy member of the community; in the camp, a faithful and bold soldier. You, soldiers and people, know that children should act filially and brothers fraternally; but we are anxious lest the thing, becoming to you all, should not be borne in mind, and you thus trespass the bounds of the human relations."

In his amplification of the third Maxim, Yung Ching quotes a saying of his father, which reads:

"By concord, litigation may be nipped in the bud."

Yung Ching's further comments on Maxim III are a sermon on concord:

"It is evident that a man should receive all, both relatives and indifferent persons, with mildness; and manage all, whether great or small affairs, with humility. Let him not presume on his riches, and despise the poor; not pride himself of his illustrious birth, and contemn the ignoble; not arrogate wisdom to himself and impose on the simple; not rely on his own courage and shame the weak; but let him, by suitable words, compose differences; kindly excuse people's errors; and, though wrongfully offended, settle the matter according to reason.....

"Let the aged and the young in the village be united as one body, and their joys and sorrows viewed as those of one family. When the husbandman and the merchant mutually lend, and when the mechanic and the shopman mutually yield, then the people will harmonise with the people.....When the the soldiers exert their strength to protect the people, let the people nourish that strength. When the people spend their money to support the soldiers, let the soldiers be sparing of that money; thus both soldiers and people will harmonise together.....

"The whole empire is an aggregate of villages; hence you ought truly to conform yourselves to the sublime instructions of our sacred father and honor the excellent spirit of concord: then, indeed, filial and fraternal duties would be more attended to, kindred more respected, the virtue of villages become more illustrious, approximating habitations prosper, litigations cease, and man enjoy repose through the age of ages! The union of peace will extend to myriads of countries, and superabounding harmony diffuse itself through the universe!"

Concerning the fourth Maxim, Yung Ching writes:

"Of old time the emperors themselves ploughed, and their empresses cultivated the mulberry tree. Though supremely honorable, they disdained not to labor, in order that, by their example, they might excite the millions of the people to lay due stress on the essential principles of political economy."

Learning is perhaps more highly honored in China than in any other country. Yung Ching amplifies the sixth Maxim in a sermon on the duties of a scholar:

"The scholar is the head of the four classes of people. The respect that others show to him should teach him to respect himself, and not degrade his character. When the scholar's practice is correct, the neighborhood will consider him as a model of manners. Let him, therefore, make filial and fraternal duties the beginning and talent the end; place enlarged knowledge first and literary ornaments last. Let the books he reads be all orthodox, and the companions he chooses all men of approved character. Let him adhere rigorously to propriety, and watchfully preserve decency, lest he ruin himself, and disgrace the walls of his college, and lest that, after having become famous, the shadows of conscious guilt and shame should haunt him under the bed cover.

"He who can act according to this maxim is a true scholar.

"But there are some who keenly contend for fame and gain, act contrary to their instructions, learn strange doctrines and crooked sciences, not knowing the exalted doctrine. Giving wild liberty ot their words, they talk bigly, but effect nothing. Ask them for words, and they have them; search for the reality, and they are void of it....

"With respect to you, soldiers and people, it is to be feared that you are not aware of the importance of education, and suppose that it is of no consequence to you. But though not trained up in the schools, your nature is adapted to the common relations. Mung-Tsze said: 'Carefully attend to the instructions of the schools—repeatedly inculcate filial and fraternal duties.' He also said: 'When the common relations are fully understood by superiors, affection and kindness will be displayed among inferiors.' Then it is evident that the schools were not intended for the learned only, but for the instruction of the people also."

As to the seventh Maxim, we find what may be considered as a suppression of religious liberty in China, and such it is in a certain way and with certain limitations.

Professor De Groot has devoted an elaborate essay[1] on the subject which we have reviewed in *The Monist* for January, 1904. The present edict truly expresses the spirit of the Chinese government in matters of religion. The great emperor K'ang-Hi is anxious to establish the orthodox religion of China which is practically Confucianism, but he tolerates Taoism and Buddhism. His son, Emperor Yung Ching, amplifies his father's maxim by saying that it discriminates only against the corruptors of the doctrines of Confucius, Lao-Tze, and Buddha, and also condemns secret fraternities, such as exist all over China and become easily centers of sedition, as we have seen in the Boxer movement which has recently originated.

[1] *Sectarianism and Religious Persecution in China.* Amsterdam: Johannes Müller.

[As a rule religions are tolerated until they come in conflict with the basic principle of Confucianism, which is expressed in that one syllable *hsiao*, i.e., "filial piety." There are millions of Muhammedans in China who are practically unmolested in their faith. The Muhammedan rebellion in 1865 was a purely political affair and had nothing to do with religion. Further the Jews lived in China undisturbed for many centuries; they could build synagogues and worship God in their own way without any interference from the government. The fact is that both Muhammedans and Jews complied with the main request of Confucianism and inculcated reverence for parents and a recognition of the emperor's authority. The Nestorians met with a hearty welcome from the government and flourished for some time

Marco Polo tells us how much Kublai Khan was interested in Christianity, and that he wrote a letter to the Pope which, however, was never delivered, requesting him to send missionaries to China. The great K'ang-Hi, the author of the Holy Edict, favored the Jesuits and not only allowed them to preach Christianity, but did not hesitate to entrust them with high and important government positions. The animosity against Christianity is of recent date and is mainly based upon the notion that native Christians must despise the sages of yore, that they must repudiate their family (which is frequently demanded by missionaries on account of the ritual of ancestor worship), and that they place the authority of Christ (which practically means the church) above the authority of their parents, as indicated in the passage (Luke xiv. 26) where Christ says: "If any man come to me and hate not his father, and mother, and wife, and children, and brethren, and sisters, yea, and his own life also, he cannot be my disciple." The very words "to hate father and mother," whatever the interpretation may be, jars on the ear of the Chinese. This verse in combination with denunciations of missionaries who call Buddha "the night of Asia," Confucius "a blind leader of the blind," etc., has done much harm to Christianity.]

Yung Ching says:

"From of old three sects have been delivered down. Beside the sect of the learned, there are those of Tao and Füh. Chu-Tsze says: 'The sect of Füh regard not heaven, earth, or the four quarters, but attend only to the heart; the sect of Lao exclusively to the preservation of the animal spirits.' This definition of Chu-Tsze is correct and impartial and shows what Füh and Tao originally aimed at.

"Afterwards, however, there arose a class of wanderers, who, void of any source of dependence, stole the names of these sects, but corrupted their principles.

"And what is still worse, lascivious and villainous persons creep in secretly among them; form brotherhoods, bind themselves to each other by oath, meet in the night and disperse at the dawn, violate the laws, corrupt the age, and impose on the people,—and behold! one morning the whole business comes to light. They are seized according to law, their innocent neighbors injured—their own families involved—and the chief of their cabal punished with extreme rigor. What they vainly thought would prove the source of their felicity becomes the cause of their misery...

"By his benevolence, our sacred father, the benevolent Emperor, refined the people; by his rectitude he polished them; by his most exalted talents he set forth in order the common relations and radical virtues. His sublime and luminous instructions form the plan by which to rectify the hearts of the men of the age. A plan the most profound and excellent!....

"The injury of torrents, flames, robbers, and thieves, terminates on the body; but that of false religions extends to the human heart. Man's heart is originally upright and without corruption; and, were there firm resolution, men would not be seduced. A character, square and upright, would appear. All that is corrupt would not be able to overcome that which is pure. In the family there would be concord; and, on meeting with difficulties, they would be converted into felicities.

"He who dutifully serves his father and faithfully performs the commands of his prince, completes the whole duty of man, and collects celestial favor. He who seeks not a happiness beyond his own sphere and rises not up to evil, but attends diligently to the duties proper for him, will receive prosperity from the gods.

"Attend to your agriculture and to your tactics. Be satisfied in the pursuit of the cloth and the grain, which are the common necessaries. Obey this true, equitable, and undeviating doctrine. Then false religions will not wait to be driven away: they will retire of their own accord."

Concerning the knowledge of laws, Yung Ching says:

"Though the law has a thousand chapters and ten thousand sections, yet it may be summed up in this sentence: 'It agrees with common sense, and its norm is reason.' Heavenly reason and man's common sense can be understood by all. When the heart is directed by common sense and by reason, the body will never be subject to punishment."

In the amplification to Maxim XII we find the following exhortation:

"The commandment is exalted and most perspicuous, yet there are some who dare presume to transgress. The lust of gain having corrupted their hearts, and their nature being moulded by deceit, they spurt out the poison lodged within, vainly hoping that the law will excuse them. But they consider not that, if a false statement be once discovered, it can by no means pass with impunity. To move to litigations with the view of entrapping others, is the same as to dig a pit into which they themselves shall fall."

Yung Ching's sermon on the fourteenth Maxim on taxes shows that the Chinese officials had sometimes great trouble in collecting the taxes. He says:

"Since our dynasty established its rule, the proportions of the revenue have been fixed by a universally approved statute; and all the other unjust items have been completely cancelled: a thread or a hair too much is not demanded from the people.

"In the days of our sacred father, the benevolent Emperor, his abounding benevolence and liberal favor fed this people for upwards of sixty years. Thinking daily how to promote the abundance and happiness of the people, he greatly diminished the revenue.....

"Pay in all the terms and wait not to be urged. Then you may take what is over and nourish your parents, complete the marriage ceremonies of your sons and daughters, satisfy your own morning and evening wants, and prepare for the annual feasts and sacrifices. The district officers may then sleep at ease in their public halls. The villages will no more be teased in the night by the calls of the tax-gatherers. Above you or below you none will be evolved. Your wives and children will be easy and at rest. There is no joy greater than this.

"If you be not aware of the importance of the revenue to the government, and that the law cannot dispense with it, perhaps you will positively refuse or deliberately put off the payment. The mandarins, being obliged to balance their accounts, and give in their reports at the stated times, must be rigorously severe.

"The collectors will have to apply the whip, cannot avoid pressing their demands for money on you. Knocking on your doors, like hungry hawks, they will devise numerous methods of getting a supply of their wants. These nameless ways of spending will probably amount to more than the sum which ought to have been paid; and after all, the tax cannot be dispensed with.

"We know not what benefit can accrue from this. Rather than to give presents to satisfy the rapacity of the police officers, how much better would it be to clear off the just demands of the nation! Rather than prove yourselves to be obstinate, refusing the payment of the revenue, would it not be better to keep the law as a peace-abiding people? Every one, even the most stupid, knows this.....

"Try to think that the daily and nightly vexations and labors of the palace are all in the service of the people. When there is an inundation, dykes must be raised to keep it off. When the demon of drought appears, prayer must be offered for rain; when there are locusts, they must be destroyed. If fortunately the calamity be averted, you all enjoy the profits. When unfortunately it comes, your taxes are remitted and alms liberally dealt out to you.

"If it be thus, and the people still can suffer themselves to evade the payment of taxes, and hinder the supply of the wants of the government, ask yourselves how it is possible for you to be at ease? This may be compared to the conduct of an undutiful son: while with his parents he receives his share of the property, and ought afterwards to nourish them, and thus discharge his duty; the parents also manifest the utmost affection, diligence, and anxiety, and leave none of their strength unexerted; yet the son appropriates their money to his own private use; diminishes their savory food; and feeds them with reluctant and obstinate looks. Can such a person be called a child of a human being?

"We use these repeated admonitions, solely wishing you, soldiers and people, to think of the army and the nation above you; and of your persons and families below you. Then abroad you will have the fame of having faithfully exerted your ability, and at home, peacefully enjoy the fruits of it. The mandarins will neither trouble you, nor the clerks vex you—what joy equal to this!"

The sixteenth Maxim is practically a sermon on anger. Yung Ching says:

"Our sacred father, the benevolent Emperor, in consequence of desiring to manifest regard to you, closed the sixteen maxims of the admonitory Edict by teaching to respect life. The heart of heaven and earth delights in animated nature; but fools regard not themselves. The government of a good prince loves to nourish, but multitudes of the ignorant lightly value life. If the misery rise not from former animosities, it proceeds from momentary anger. The violent, depending on the strength of their backbone, kill others, and throw away their own lives.....

"Cherish mildness, disperse passion; then you need not wait for the mediation of others: habits of contention will cease of their own accord. How excellent would such manners be!

"Kung-Tsze said, 'When anger rises, think of the consequences.' Mung-Tsze said, 'He that repeatedly treats one rudely is a fool.' The doctrines delivered down by these sages, from more than a thousand years ago, correspond exactly with those explained in the Edict by our sacred father, the benevolent Emperor.

"Soldiers and people, respectfully obey this: disregard it not. Then the people in their cottages will be protected; the soldiers in the camp enjoy repose; below you will support your family character, and above reward the nation. Comfortable and easy in days of abundance, all will advance to a virtuous old age. Does not this illustrate the advantages of settling animosities?"

EDITOR.

CRITICISMS AND DISCUSSIONS.

"HUMANISM."*

It appears that philosophy once more has an "issue." Since the days of T. H. Green's attack upon the fortifications of English empiricism, neo-Hegelian Idealism has held most of the field in England and America. The legends on its banners are : "Reality consists of an absolute system of immutable ideas." "Truth consists in the reflection, representation, or symbolization, by finite ideas of this absolute system." Though, incidentally, thought may perform a reconstructing function in experience, its chief business as the subject matter of logic is to "represent" or "correspond to" the unchanging and unchangeable system of ideas.

The problem set by these conceptions, since the days of Plato, is that of a criterion for truth thus defined. How is this "correspondence," "representation," etc., to be tested? The difficulty is Janus-faced. On the one side we are confronted by the ancient and honorable problem of "The Finite and Infinite"; on the other, by the no less honorable and ancient one of "Permanence and Change." The latter has been rendered particularly acute by the work of psychologists of the last twenty-five years in showing up the dynamic character of ideas. How can anything so flexible, as psychologists have shown ideas to be, reflect or represent an unchangeable reality?

It would seem that the logical and epistemological treatises based on the conceptions embodied in the above "legends" must needs have kept this crucial problem steadily in view. But strangely enough, at any rate certainly enough, such has not been the case. Volume after volume of logical theory has appeared in which the topic of "Validity" appears as an incidental but always a troublesome matter, yet one which, belonging to the field, must be covered.

* The title of a volume of philosophical essays by F. C. S. Schiller, M. A., Fellow and Tutor of Corpus Christi College.

Hence, too, after several hundred pages have been filled with an account of how this correspondence is effected (though it is indeed difficult to recognize much of it as an account of "correspondence") we find the chapter on "Validity" consisting chiefly of a confession that the account of correspondence has ended in failure. It would seem that the necessity of such confessions must long ago have led to a suspicion of the assumed conceptions upon which such confessed failures are constructed. Instead, it has for the most part only stimulated more subtle and refined analyses within the limits prescribed by these assumptions.

However, these conceptions have meanwhile not gone entirely unchallenged. Over twenty-five years ago, Mr. C. S. Peirce wrote in *The Popular Science Monthly:* "Consider what effects, that might conceivably have practical bearings, we can see the object of our perception to have, then our conception of these effects is the whole conception of our object." A few years later, the challenge again appears in Mr. William James' chapter on "Reasoning." Although that chapter was bound in a large volume labelled "Psychology" in large gilt letters there were statements in it very important for logic and epistemology. These statements were to the effect that thinking takes place at the point where activity encounters difficulty in going on in a non-thinking fashion; and that the chief business of thinking, from the psychologists' stand-point, at any rate, appears to be that of resolving this difficulty. (Of course it is equally in order to regard the "difficulty" as teleological for thought, i. e., it occurs that thought may go on; each is teleological to the other. Teleology is thus inside, not outside, the process.)

No one who remembers his history of philosophy would think of calling this in either its content or its method a "brand new" discovery. Such a claim would and should quickly be met with such names as Augustine, Fichte, Schopenhauer, to say nothing of the "primacy" of Kant's *Practical Reason*. On the other hand, this same historical sense should make it equally impossible, even from a very superficial survey, to regard the movement as a mere masquerade of some earlier type of voluntarism.

Since the appearance of Mr. James' psychology this instrumental character of thinking has been the dominant standpoint for its treatment by psychologists, and in the meantime the conviction has been growing that this must have its significance for the relation of thought to truth and reality; that if it is sound psychology, it must be good logic and epistemology. Within the past few years, this conviction has found explicit expression to such an extent as to constitute what is now a recognized movement and issue in philosophy. To these expressions Mr. James has continued his contributions in his *Will to Believe*, more explicitly still in his *Philosophical Concepts and Practical Results*, in 1896, and in his more recent *Varieties of Religious Experience*. Much also of Prof. J. M. Baldwin's writings, e. g., his article on "Selective Thinking," is essentially of the same import. The most detailed and articulate contribution to this period of literature, however, is Mr. Dewey's article on "The Reflect Arc Concept," (*Psychological Review*, Vol. III, 1896), the logical implications of which, most readers apparently failed to discover at the time it appeared. This failure is doubtless another witness to the intensity of the ancient prejudice between logic and psychology. Scarcely less significant, if not so explicit, have been many contributions from Germany, and especially from France.

While the literature of the movement clearly shows it to be a general one, the most self-concious and detailed manifestations of it have appeared within the past two years in America and England, and interestingly enough, almost simultaneously. In England, Mr. F. C. S. Schiller is by far the most thorough-going and militant representative. Mr. Schiller has recently put his contributions to the movement into a volume which he calls "Humanism." By Humanism Mr. Schiller means "the philosophic attitude which, without wasting thought upon attempts to construct experience *a priori*, is content to take human experience as the clue to the world of human experience; * * * to remember that man is the measure of all things, i. e., of his whole experience-world and that if our standard measure be false all our measurements are vitiated; to remember that man is the maker of the sciences which subserve his human purposes; to remember that a philosophy which analyses us away is thereby merely exhibiting its failure to achieve its purpose; * * * this is the real root of Humanism."

Mr. Schiller feels that "more than the usual amount of apology" is due for the small proportion of new matter in the volume, all but one of the fifteen essays having appeared in more or less complete form elsewhere. However, I think that Mr. Schiller may be sure that his readers will be glad to have these essays in the revised, permanent and attractive form which they now possess.

Mr. Schiller prefers the term "Humanism" to "Pragmatism" on the ground that the latter "is in reality only the application of Humanism to the theory of knowledge." However valid Pragmatism may be as a method of logic, "we must yet concede that the man is greater than any method he has made and that our Humanism must interpret it." (pp. xxi.) This certainly appears well taken. But some, even of those most in sympathy with Mr. Schiller's general view, may feel that however central human experience may be, it may not after all include all experience and they may continue to long, therefore, for a term that shall express the instrumental, reconstructive character of thought in experience as such.

The most explicit exposition of Mr. Schiller's Humanism is to be found in the essays on: "The Ethical Basis of Metaphysics," "Useless Knowledge," the new essay on "Truth." "The Metaphysics of the Time Process,"—an illuminating discussion of that much befogged subject; "Reality and Idealism," "On Preserving Appearances," and Essay XII, on "Activity and Substance."

In the first two essays we get some very general variations of the central *motif* announced in the preface. The theses of "The Ethical Basis of Metaphysics" are: (1) "The purposive character of mental life generally must influence and pervade also our most remotely cognitive activities " (p. 8); (2) Reality is not something which cognition is to merely represent. Hence "is awarded to the ethical conception of good, supreme authority over the logical conception of true, and the metaphysical conception of real. The good becomes a determinate both of the true and the real. For from the pursuit of the latter we may never eliminate the reference to the former." (p. 9)

As an illustration of the competition between old and new habits of thinking, and of the eternal vigilance necessary to a consistent maintenance of the latter, it is interesting to note that even Mr. Schiller's thoroughly sophisticated consciousness of the problem is almost betrayed into an identification of reality with the "objective" as opposed to the "subjective." (Note p. 11.) I say "almost," for the case is perhaps saved by the statement immediately following: "The actual situation is, of course, a case of interaction, a process of cognition, in which the subject and object determine each other and both we and reality are involved, and we might add—*evolved*."

The central theme,—cognition a function in conduct—is further elaborated in the dialogue "Useless Knowledge," which is in Mr. Schiller's most characteristic style and which serves as an excellent introduction to the chapter on "Truth." In the latter, after a negative criticism of the views of truth as: (1) "agreement with reality," (2) "as systematic coherence," Mr. Schiller sets forth his conception of truth as "a form of value" and finds that the logic which expounds this view with truth is hand in glove with psychology. The outcome of Mr. Schiller's analysis is: "As regards the psychical fact of the truth valuation, truth may be called an ultimate function of our intellectual activity." As regards the object valued as true, "truth is that manipulation of them which turns out upon trial to be useful, primarily for any human end, but ultimately for that perfect harmony of our whole life which forms our final aspirations." (p. 61.)

The essay "On Preserving Appearances" is a very telling criticism of "the familiar antithesis between 'appearance' and reality," the vogue of which Mr. Schiller regards as the chief constructive result of the work of Mr. F. H. Bradley. (p. 184.) Again we read (p. 199) "our inferences must approve themselves * * * by the power they give us to *transform* our experiences. * * * The transmutation of appearances, therefore, must not be represented as an inscrutable privilege of the Absolute; it must be made a weapon mortal hands can actually wield."

The last thesis of this chapter, viz., that Ultimate Reality must be absolutely "perfect" and "harmonious" and the contents of the essay following on "Activity and Substance" develop a conception of Mr. Schiller's that is likely to give some of his most sympathetic readers pause, and is certain to be seized upon by the critic looking for "internal inconsistencies." The conception is that of an ultimate "changeless activity," and immutable "beatific consciousness" as the goal of thought-burdened experience. The limits of these remarks forbid even an outline of Mr. Schiller's very incisive argument. But it would not be strange if some should have trouble with the conception of "a changeless activity." Not that activity is to be identified with *mere change* (as most of the critics of "Pragmatism" assume) but that it is to be change*less*, that there is to be no change anywhere in it, is surely a hard saying. Some will be puzzled also on reading (p. 105) "if therefore the ultimate explanation of the world is to be in terms of ends, it would seem as though it must be in terms of individual ends realized in and through the time-process"; and then to find (p. 227) that "self realization must assume the form, not of a hideous, barbarous neurotic restlessness, nor of an infinite, and therefore futile struggle, but of an activity, which, *transcending change and time* [italics mine] preserves itself in an harmonious equipoise." Nor is it inconceivable that some one should profess to find in this conception of an "ultimate," "unchangeable" "completely beatific" experience certain features not altogether unlike Mr. Bradley's and Mr. Royce's Absolute. However, one gathers that the conception has an interrogation mark after it in Mr. Schiller's own mind, and its exposition is made in quite an hypothetical spirit. And one is here reminded that the complaints by critics of "lack of system," of "the ignoring of fundamental points," etc., in "Pragmatic" literature is certainly premature. Nothing so far has been put out that pretends to be anything more than prolegomena.

On the whole it is safe to say that whatever becomes of the "Pragmatic movement," when the history of "the revival of Pragmatism" or "Humanism," or "Teleological Empiricism" is written, Mr. Schiller's contributions are certain to have a prominent and permanent place.

THE UNIVERSITY OF CHICAGO. A. W. MOORE.

THE RELIGIOUS EXPERIENCE.

The least religious experience is so mysterious and so complex, that a moderate degree of reflection upon it tends to a sense of intellectual impotence. "If I speak," says Emerson, "I define and confine, and am less." One would gladly set down religion among the unspeakable things and avoid the imputation of degrading it. It is certain that the enterprise of defining religion is at present in disrepute. It has been undertaken so often and so unsuccessfully that contemporary students for the most part prefer to supply a list of historical definitions of religion, and let their variety demonstrate their futility. Metaphysicians and psychologists agree that in view of the differences of creed, ritual, organization, conduct and temperament that have been true of different religions in different times and places, and may as well abandon the idea that there is a constant element.

But on the other hand we have the testimony afforded by the name religion; and the ordinary judgments of men to the effect that it signifies something to be religious, and to be more or less religious. There is an elementary logical principle to the effect that a group-name implies certain common group-characters. Impatience with abstract or euphemistic definitions should not blind us to the truth. Even the psychologist tends in his description of religious phenomena to single out and emphasize what he calls a *typical* religious experience. And the same applies to the idealist's treatment of the matter. Religion, he reasons, is essentially a development of which the true meaning can be seen only in the higher stages. The primitive religion, is, he argues, only implicit religion. But lower stages cannot be regarded as belonging to a single development with higher stages, if there be not some achial promise of the latter in the earlier, or some element which endures throughout. It is unavoidable, then, to assume that in dealing with religion we are dealing with a specific and definable experience.

The profitableness of such an undertaking as the present one is another matter. It may well be that in so human and practical an affair as religion, definition is peculiarly inappropriate. But is there not a human and practical value in the very defining of religion? Is there not a demand for it in the peculiar relation that exists between religion and the progress of enlightenment? Religion associates itself with the habits of society. The progress of enlightenment means that more or less all the time, and very profoundly at certain critical times, society must change its habits. The consequence is that religion is likely to be abandoned with the old habits. The need of a new religion is therefore a chronic one. The reformer in religion, or the man who wishes to be both enlightened and religious, is chiefly occupied with the problem of disentangling religion pure and undefiled from definite discredited practices and opinions. And the solution of the problem turns upon some apprehension of the essence of religion. There is a large amount of necessary and unnecessary tragedy due to the extrinsic connection between ideas and certain modes of their expression. There can be no more serious and urgent duty than that of expressing as directly, and so as truly as possible, the great permanent human concerns. The men to whom educational reform has been largely due have been the men who have remembered for their fellows what this whole business of education is after all for. Comenius and Pestalozzi served society by stripping educational activity of its historical and institutional accessories and laying bare the genuine human need that these are designed to satisfy. There is a similar virtue in the insistent attempt to distinguish between the essential and the accessory in religion.

Although declining to be discouraged by the conspicuousness of past failures in this connection, one may well profit by them. The amazing complexity of religious phenomena must somehow be seen to be consistent with their common nature. The religious experience must not only be found, but must also be reconciled with "the varieties of religious experience." The inadequacy of the well-known definitions of religion may be attributed to several causes. The commonest fallacy is to define religion in terms of *a* religion. My definition of religion must include my brother's religion, even though he live on the other side of the globe, and my ancestor's religion, in spite of his prehistoric remoteness. Error arises here through the attempt to define religion in terms of what it ought to be. There is a question as to the relation between ideal religion and actual religion; but the field of religion contains by common consent religions that must on their own grounds condemn one another, religions that are bad religions, and yet religions.

A more enlightened, and therefore more dangerous, fallacy, is due to the supposition that religion can be defined exclusively in terms of some department of human nature. From this standpoint religion has been defined in terms exclusively of feeling, of intellect or of conduct. It is always easy to overthrow such a definition by raising the question as to the treatment of definitely describable religious phenomena that belong to a department of human life avowedly excluded by the definition. Religion is not feeling, because there are many phlegmatic God-fearing men whose religion consists in good works. Religion is not conduct, for there are many mystics whose very religion is withdrawal from the field of action. Religion is not intelligence, for no one has ever been able to formulate a creed that is common to all religions. Yet without a doubt we must look for the essence of religion in human nature. The present psychological interest in religion has emphasized this truth. How, then, shall we escape a facultative or departmental account of it? Modern psychology suggests an answer. As Dr. Leuba has pointed out, the most illuminating conception of human nature in connection with this inquiry is that which points out the interdependence of knowledge, feeling and volition.* The perfect case of this unity is belief. The believing experience is cognitive in its intent, but practical and emotional as well in its content. I believe when I take for granted. The object of my belief is not merely known but also felt and acted upon. What I believe expresses itself in my total experience.

There is some hope, then, of an adequate definition of the religious experience if it be regarded as belonging to the psychological type of belief. Belief, however, is evidently a broader category than that of religion. An account of religion in terms of believing, and the particular type of it here in question would, then, constitute the central stem of a psychology of religion. But belief is more than believing. There is an object believed, and the believing experience means to be true. Hence to complete an account of religion one must consider its object, that is, its cognitive implica-

* Leuba: "Introduction to a Psychological Study of Religion." *Monist*, Vol. XI, p. 195.

tions. The program properly contains three topics: first, the religious experience as a believing state; second, the religious type of belief: and third, the religious object of belief.

The present discussion limits itself to the first two of these topics Its sources will be the experiences of religious people as viewed from within out. Critical opinion of a man's religion is not here in question, but only the content and meaning which it has for him. "I would have you," says Fielding, "go and kneel beside the Mohammedan as he prays at the sunset hour and put your heart to his and wait for the echo that will surely come; yes, surely, if you wait as a man who would learn, who can learn. I would have you go to the Hill Man smearing the stone with butter that his god may be pleased; to the woman crying to the forest god for her sick child; to the boy before his monks learning to be good. No matter where you go, no matter what the faith is called, if you have the bearing ear, if your heart is in unison with the heart of the world, you will hear always the same song far down below the noises of the warring creeds, the clash of words and forms, the differences of place, of climes, of civilizations, of ideals, far down below all these lies that which you would hear. I know not what you would call it.*

1. The general identification of religion with belief is made without serious difficulty. The essential factor in belief is, as we have seen, the reaction of the whole personality to a fixed object or *accepted situation*. A similar principle is employed in common judgments about a man's religion. He is accounted most religious whose religion penetrates his life most intimately. In the man whose religion consists in the outer exercise of attendance upon church, we recognize the sham. He *appears* to be religious. He does at any rate one of the things which a religious man would do. But an object of religious faith is not the constant environment of his life. He may or may not feel sure of God from his pew, but God is not among the things that count in his daily life. God does not enter into his calculations or determine his scale of values. Again, discursive thinking is regarded as an interruption of religion. When I am at pains to justify my religion, I am already doubting; and for common opinion doubt is identical with irreligion. In so far as I am religious, my religion stands in no need of justification, even though I regard it as justifiable. In my religious experience I am taking something for granted; in other words I act about it and feel about it in a manner that is going to be deter-

* Fielding: *The Hearts of Men*, p. 322.

mined by special conditions of mood and temperament. The mechanical and prosaic man acknowledges God in his mechanical and prosaic way. He believes in divine retribution as he believes in commercial or social retribution. He is as careful to prepare for the next world as he is to be respectable in this. The poet, on the other hand, believes in God after the manner of his genius. Though he worships God in spirit, he may conduct his life in an irregular manner peculiar to himself. The different moods of the same individual life may be judged by the same measure. When God is most real to him, brought home to him most vividly, or consciously obeyed, in these moments he is most religious. When, on the other hand, God is merely a name to him, and church a routine, or when both are forgotten in the daily occupations, he is least religious. His life on the whole is said to be religious in so far as periods of the second type are subordinated to periods of the first type.

Further well-known elements of belief, corollaries of the above, are evidently present in religion. A certain *imagery remains constant* throughout an individual's experience. He comes back to it as to a physical object in space. And although religion is sporadically an exclusive and isolated affair, it tends strongly to be social. The religious object, or God, is a social object, common to me and to my neighbor, and presupposed in our collective undertakings.

This reduction of religion to the type of the believing state should thus provide us with an answer to that old and fundamental question concerning the relative priority of faith and works. The test of the faith is in the works, and the works are religious in so far as they are the expression of the faith. Religion is neither the doing of anything nor the feeling of anything nor the thinking of anything, but the reacting as a whole, in terms of all possible activities of human life, to some accepted situation.

2. We may now face the interesting but difficult question of the specific character of religious belief. In spite of the fact that in these days the personality of God is often regarded as a transient feature of religion, that type of belief which throws most light upon the religious experience would seem to be the *belief in persons*. Such belief consists in the practical recognition of a more or less persistent attitude and disposition to ourselves. The outward behavior of our fellow-men is construed in terms of the practical bearing of the attitude which it implies. The extraordinary feature of such belief is the disproportion between the vividness of the belief and the evidence upon which it is grounded. Of this we are

most aware in connection with those personalities which we regard as distinctly friendly or hostile to ourselves. We are always more or less clearly in the presence of our friends and enemies. Their well-wishing or their ill-wishing haunts the scene of our living. There is no more important constitutent of what the psychologists calls our "general feeling tone." Indeed there are times when we are entirely possessed by a state that is either exuberance in the presence of those who love us, or awkwardness and stupidity in the presence of those whom we believe to suspect or dislike us. The latter state may easily become chronic. Many men live permanently in the presence of an accusing audience. The inner life which expresses itself in the words "Everybody hates me!" is perhaps the most common form of morbid self-consciousness. On the other hand, buoyancy of spirits springs largely from the constant and obstinate conviction that "everybody likes me." In this case one is filled with a sense of security, and is conscious of a sympathetic reinforcement that adds to the private joys and compensates for the private sorrows. And this sense of attitude is wonderfully discriminating. We can feel the presence of a "great man," a "formidable person," a superior or inferior, one who is interested or indifferent, and all the subtlest degrees of approval and disapproval.

A similar sensibility may quicken us even in situations where no direct individual attitude to ourselves is implied. We regard places and communities as congenial when we are in sympathy with their prevailing purposes or standards of value. We may feel ill at ease or thoroughly at home in cities where we know no single human soul. Indeed in a so misanthropic an individual as Rousseau (and we all have our Rousseau moods), the mere absence of social repression arouses a most intoxicating sense of tunefulness and security. Nature plays the part of an indulgent parent who permits all sorts of personal liberties.

> "The view of a fine country, a succession of agreeable prospects, a fine air, a good appetite, and the health I gain by walking; the freedom of inns, and the distance from everything that can make me recollect the dependence of my situation, conspire to free my soul, and give boldness to my thoughts, throwing me, in a manner, into the immensity of things, where I combine, choose, and appropriate them to my fancy, without restraint or fear. I dispose of all nature as I please."*

In this confidence or distrust, inspired originally by the social environment, and similarly suggested by other surroundings of life,

* Rousseau: *Confessions*, Book IV.

we have the key to the religious consciousness. But it is now time to add that in the case of religion these attitudes are concerned with the universal or supernatural rather than with present and normal human relationships. The religious consciousness is such practical acknowledgment of a *residual environment*, which lies beyond the range of ordinary communication. This profounder realm of tradition and nature may have any degree of unity from chaos to cosmos. For religion the idea of original and far-reaching power is more significant than that of totality. But that which is at first only "beyond," is *practically* the same object as that which comes in the development of thought to be conceived as the "world" or the "universe." We may, therefore, use these latter terms to indicate the object of religion until the treatment of special instances shall define it more precisely. My religion is, then, my *sense of the disposition* of the universe to myself. We shall expect to find, as in the social phenomena with which we have just dwelt, that the manifestation of this sense consists in a general reaction appropriate to the disposition so attributed. In view of it I shall be fundamentally ill at ease, profoundly confident, or habitually cautious. The ultimate nature of the world is here no speculative problem. A dog that could wag his tail at the universe would be more religious than the sublimest dialectician. It is in the vividness of the sense of presence that the acuteness of religion consists. I am religious in so far as the whole tone and temper of my living reflects a belief as to what the universe thinks of such as me.

The examples that follow are selected because of differences in personal flavor that serve to throw into relief their common religious character. Theodore Parker, in describing his own boyhood, writes as follows:

> "I can hardly think without a shudder of the terrible effect the doctrine of eternal damnation had on me. How many, many hours have I wept with terror as I lay on my bed, till between praying and weeping, sleep gave me repose. But before I was nine years old the fear went away, and I saw clearer light in the goodness of God. But for years, say from seven till ten, I said my prayers with much devotion, I think, and then continued to repeat, 'Lord, forgive my sins,' till sleep came on me."*

Compare with this, Stevenson's Christmas letter to his mother, in which he says:

> "The whole necessary morality is kindness; and it should spring, of itself, from the one fundamental doctrine, Faith. If

* Chadwick: *Theodore Parker*, p. 18.

you are sure that God, in the long run, means kindness by you, you should be happy; and if happy, surely you should be kind."*

Here is Destiny frowning and Destiny smiling, but in each case so real, so present, as to be immediately responded to with grateful warm-heartedness and with helpless terror.

The author of the *Imitatio Christi* speaks thus of the daily living of the Christian:

> "The life of a Christian who has dedicated himself to the service of God, should abound with eminent virtues of all kinds that he may be really the same person which he is by outward appearance and profession. Indeed he ought not only to be the same, but much more, in his inward disposition of soul; because he professes to serve a God who sees the inward parts, a searcher of the heart and reins, a God and Father of spirits: and therefore, since we are always in His sight, we should be exceedingly careful to avoid all impurity, all that may give offense to Him whose eyes cannot behold iniquity. We should, in a word, so far as mortal and frail nature can, imitate the blessed angels in all manner of holiness, since we, as well as they, are always in His presence * * * * And good men have always this notion of the thing. For they depend upon God for the success of all they do, even of their best and wisest undertakings."†

Such is to be practical acknowledgment of God in the routine of life. The more direct response to this presence appears abundantly in St. Augustine's conversation and reminiscence with God:

> "How evil have not my deeds been; or if not my deeds my words; or if not my words my will. But Thou, O Lord, art good and merciful, and Thy right hand had respect unto the profoundness of my death, and removed from the bottom of my heart that abyss of corruption. And this was the result, that I willed not to do what I willed, and willed to do what Thou willedst. . . . . How sweet did it suddenly become to me to be without the delights of trifles. And what once I feared to lose, it was now a joy for me to put away. For Thou didst cast them away, and instead of them didst enter in Thyself, sweeter than all pleasure, though not to flesh and blood; brighter than all light, but more veiled than all mysteries; more exalted than all honour, but not to the exalted in their own conceits.

* Stevenson: *Letters*, Vol. I, p. 229.

† *The Imitation of Christ*, p. 40. Translation by Stanhope.

Now was my soul free from the gnawing cares of seeking and getting. . . . . And I babbled unto Thee my brightness. my riches, and my health, the Lord my God."*

In these two passages we meet with religious conduct and with that supreme religious experience, the direct worship of God. In each case the heart of the matter is an individual's indubitable conviction of the world's favorable concern for him. The deeper order of things constitutes the real and the profoundly congenial community in which he lives.

Let us now apply this general account of the religious experience to certain typical religious phenomena: first, *conversion;* second, *piety;* and, finally, religious *instruments,* and *modes of conveyance.*

Although recent study of the phenomenon of *conversion* has brought to light a considerable amount of interesting material, there is some danger of misconceiving its importance. The psychology of conversion is primarily the psychology of crisis or radical alteration rather than the psychology of religion. For the majority of religious men and women conversion is an insignificant event, and in many cases it never occurs at all. Religion is more purely present where it is normal and monotonous. But this phenomenon is nevertheless highly significant in that religion and irreligion are placed in close juxtaposition, and the contribution of religion at its inception thereby emphasized.

In general it is said that conversion takes place during the period of adolescence. But this is the period of the most sudden expansion of the environment of life, a time of introduction into many new presences. This is sometimes expressed by saying that it is a period of acute self-consciousness. Life is consciousness of itself as over against its inheritance; its whole setting sweeps into view. Some sort of solution of the life-problem, some coming to terms with the universe, is the normal issue of it. Religious conversion signifies then, that as part of this fundamental adjustment, the individual defines and accepts for his life a certain attitude on the part of the universe.

The examples cited by the psychologists as well as the generalizations which they derive, bear out this interpretation. According to Professor James:

"General Booth, the founder of the Salvation Army, considers that the first vital step in saving outcasts consists in making

* St. Augustine: "Confessions." In Schaff: *Nicene and Post-Nicene Fathers,* Vol. I, p. 129.

them feel that some decent human being cares enough for them to take an interest in the question whether they rise or sink."*

The new state is one of courage and hope stimulated by a sense of the glow of friendly interest. The convert is no longer "out in the cold." He is told that the world wishes him well, and this is brought home to him through representations of the tenderness of Christ and through the direct ministerings of those who mediate it. But somehow the convert must be persuaded to realize all this. He must *believe* it before it can mean anything to him. Hence he is urged to pray—a proceeding that is at first ridiculous to him since it involves taking for granted what he disbelieves. But therein lies the critical point. It is peculiar to the object in this case that it can exist only for one who already believes in it. The psychologists call this the element of "self-surrender." To be converted a man must somehow suffer his surroundings to put into him a new heart, which may thereupon confirm its object. Such belief is tremendously tenacious because it so largely creates its own evidence. Once believe that "God, in the long run, means kindness by you," and you are likely to stand by it to the end—the more so in this case because the external evidence either way is to the average man so insufficient. Such a belief as this is inspired in the convert, not by reasoning, but by all the powers of suggestion that personality and social contagion can afford.

The psychologists describe *piety* as sense of unity. One feels after reading their accounts that they are too abstract. For there are many kinds of unity, characteristic of widely varying moods and states. Any state of rapt attention is a state of unity, and this occurs in the most secular moments of life. Nor does it help matters to say that in the case of religion this unity must have been preceded by a state of division; for we cannot properly characterize one state of mind in terms of another, unless the latter be retained in the former. And that which is characteristic of the religious sense of unity would seem to be just such an overcoming of difference. There is a recognition of two distinct attitudes, which may be more or less in sympathy with one another but which are both present even in their fullest harmony. And were I to be taken out of myself so completely as to forget myself I should inevitably lose that sense of sympathy from which arises the peculiar exultation of religious faith, a heightened experience of the same type

* James: *op. cit.*, p. 203; cf. Leuba, *loc. cit.*; and *Amer. Journ. of Psychology, Vol.* VII, p. 309; Starbuck, *Psychology of Religion*, Part I.

with the freedom and spontaneity which I experience in the presence of men with whom I have most in common.

The further graces and powers of piety readily submit to a similar description. My sense of positive sympathy expresses itself in an attitude of well-wishing; living in an atmosphere of kindness I instinctively endeavor to propagate it. My buoyancy is distinctly of that quality which, to a lesser degree is due to any sense of social security; my power is that of one who works in an environment that reinforces him. I experience the objective or even cosmical character of my enterprises. They have a momentum which makes me their instrument rather than their perpetrator. A paradoxical relation between religion and morality has always interested observers of custom and history. Religion is apparently as capable of the most fiendish malevolence as of the most saintly gentleness. Fielding writes that:

> "When religion is brought out or into daily life and used as a guide or a weapon in the world it has no effect either for good or evil. Its effect is simply in strengthening the heart, in blinding the eyes, in deafening the ears. It is an intensive force, an intoxicant. It doubles or trebles a man's powers. It is an impulsive force sending him headlong down the path of emotion, whether that path lead to glory or infamy. It is a tremendous stimulant, that is all."*

Religion does not originate life purposes or define their meaning, but stimulates them by the same means that works in all corporate and social activity. And to work with the universe is the most tremendous incentive that can appeal to the individual will. Therefore in highly ethical religions the power for good exceeds that of any other social and spiritual agency. Such religion makes present, actual, and real, that good on the whole which the individual otherwise tends to distinguish from what is good for him. In daily life the morally valid and the practically urgent are commonly arrayed against one another; but the ethical religion makes the valid urgent.

The *instruments* of religion are legion, and it is in order here to mention only certain prominent cases in which their selection would seem to have direct reference to the provocation and perpetuation of such a sense of attitude as we have been describing. This is true in a general way of all symbolism. There is no essential difference between the religious symbol and such symbols as serve to remind us of human relationships. In both cases the per-

* *Op. cit.*, p. 152.

ceptual absence of will is compensated for by the presence of some object associated with that will. The function of this object is due to its power to revive and perpetuate a certain special social atmosphere. But the most important vehicle of religion has always been personality. It is after all to priests, prophets and believers, that religious cults have owed their vitality. The traits that mark the prophet are both curious and sublime. He is most remarkable for the confidence with which he speaks for the universe. Whether it be due to lack of a sense of humor or a profound conviction of truth, is indifferent to our purpose. The power of such men is undoubtedly due to their suggestion of a force greater than they, whose designs they bring directly and socially to the attention of men. The prophet in his prophecy is indeed not altogether distinguished from God; and it is through the mediation of a directly perceptible human attitude that a divine attitude gets itself fixed in the imagination of the believer. What is true of the prophet is equally true of the preacher, whose function it is not to represent God in his own person, but to depict Him with his tongue. It is generally recognized that the preacher is neither a moralizer nor a theologian, but it is less perfectly understood that it is his function to suggest the living presence of God. His proper language is that of the imagination, and the picture which he portrays is one of a reciprocal social relationship between man and the Supreme Master of the situation of life. He will not define God or prove God, but introduce Him and talk about Him. And at the same time the association of prayer and worship with his sermon, and the general atmosphere created by the meeting together of a body of disciples, will act as the confirmation of his suggestion of such a living presence.

The *conveyance* of any single religious cult from generation to generation affords a signal illustration of the importance in religion of the recognition of attitude. Religions manage somehow to survive any amount of transformation of creed and ritual. It is not what is done, or what is thought, that identifies the faith of the first Christians with that of the last, but a certain reckoning with the disposition of God. The successive generations of Christians are introduced into the spiritual world of their fathers, with its furnishing of hopes and fears remaining substantially the same; and their Christianity consists in their continuing to live in it with only a slight and gradual renovation. To any given individual God is more or less completely represented by his elders in the faith in their exhortations and ministerings; and through them he fixes as the center of his system an image of God, his accuser or redeemer.

The complete verification of this interpretation of the religious experience would require the application of it to the different historical cults. Although a general examination of such instances is entirely beyond the scope of this paper, a brief consideration may be given to those which seem to afford reasonable grounds for objection, such as *primitive* religion, *atheistic* religion, and *reflective* or *critical* religion.

First, it may be said that in *primitive* religions, notably in fetichism, tabooism and totemism, there is no recognition of a cosmical unity. It is quite evident that there is no conception of a universe. But it is equally evident that the natural and historical environment in its generality has a very specific practical significance for the primitive believer. It is often said with truth that these earliest forms of religion are more profoundly pantheistic than polytheistic. Man recognizes an all-pervading interest that is capable of being directed to himself. The selection of a deity is not due to any special qualification for deification possessed by the individual object itself, but to the tacit presumption that, as Thales said, "all things are full of gods." The disposition of residual reality manifests to the believer no consistency or unity, but it is nevertheless the most constant object of his will. He lives in the midst of a capriciousness which he must appease if he is to establish himself at all.

Secondly, in the case of *Buddhism*, we are said to meet with a religion that is essentially *atheistic*.

> "Whether Buddhas arise, O priests, or whether Buddhas do not arise, it remains a fact and the fixed and necessary constitution of being, that all its constituents are transitory."

The secret of life lies in the application of this truth.

> "O builder, I've discovered thee!
> This fabric thou shalt ne'er rebuild!
> Thy rafters are all broken now,
> And pointed roof demolished lies!
> This mind has demolition reached,
> And seen the last of all desire!"

The case of Buddha himself and of the exponents of his purely esoteric doctrine belong to the reflective type which will presently be given special consideration. But with the ordinary believer, even where the extraneous but almost inevitable polytheism is least in evidence, the religious experience consists in substantially the same elements that appear in theistic religions. The individual is here living appropriately to the ultimate nature of things, with the ceaseless periods of time in full view. That which is brought home to him is the illusoriness and hollowness of things when taken in the spirit of active endeavor. The only profound and abiding good is nothingness. While nature and society conspire to mock him, Nirvana invites him to its peace. The religious course of his life consists in the use of such means as can win him this end. From the standpoint of the universe he has the sympathy only of that wisdom whose essence is self-destruction. And this truth is mediated by the imagination of divine sympathy, for the Blessed One remains as the perpetual incarnation of His own blessedness.

Finally there remains the consideration of the hearing of this interpretation upon certain more *reflective* and disciplined types of religion. The religion of the critically enlightened man must be less naive and credulous in its imagery. God tends to vanish into an ideal or a universal, or congeal into some object of theoretical definition. But here we are on that borderland where the assignment of individual cases can never be made with any certainty of correctness. We can generalize only by describing the conditions that such cases must fulfil if they are properly to be denominated religious. And there can be no question of the justice of deriving religions. An idealistic philosophy will, then, be a religion just in so far as it is rendered practically vivid by the imagination. Such imagination must *create and sustain a social relationship*. The question of the legitimacy of this imagination is another matter. It raises the general issue concerning the judgment of truth implied in religion, and this must be treated at length in another discussion. But at any rate the religious experience may be realized by virtue of the metaphorical or poetical representation of a situation as one of intercommunication between persons, where reflective definition at the same time denies it. The possibility of such a representation may best be understood from the fact that the important element in the religious experience is not God in and for Himself, but the worshipper as judged by God. And just as a keen awareness of the presence of other men is a kind of self-consciousness, so in religion one may be viewing *one's self* from the divine standpoint. The human worshipper may himself supply all the personality that is necessary. But whatever faculty be the source of supply for this indispensable social quality of religion, he who defines God as the ultimate goodness or the ultimate truth, has certainly not yet worshipped Him. He begins to be religious only when such an ideal determines the atmosphere of his daily living; when he regards the immanence of such an ideal in nature and history as the object of his will; and when he responds to its presence in the spirit of his conduct and his contemplation.

HARVARD UNIVERSITY. RALPH BARTON PERRY.

DEFINITION OF RELIGION.

It is an old experience that emotional people frequently show a contempt for the labors of the intellect. The heart ever and anon rebels against the head, and feelings defy definitions. No wonder that religion and religious devotees casually exhibit a dislike for science, and mankind is only now finding out that this opposition that obtains between the two most salient features of our spiritual life is not an irreconcilable contradiction but a mere contrast.

It is for these reasons that some of the simplest notions have been declared to be undefinable and inexplicable. Human sentiment revolts against the idea that a cold and clear formula should cover all that is stirring in our inmost soul, and so it appears more satisfactory to the average sentimentalist to rest satisfied with the verdict that certain things are undefinable. Among them are mainly the words, "God," "soul," and "religion." But we ought to remember that a definition is a description of the salient features of a thing and not the thing itself. A definition helps us to understand the nature of a thing, and a definition does not contain anything that would describe its relation to our own self or its paramount importance for our life. Thus it happens that the so-called undefinable ideas are some of the simplest concepts, and their very simplicity is objectionable to one who does not understand the nature of scientific precision, and this is now and then true even of a man such as is Emerson whose words Professor Ralph Barton Perry quotes: "If I speak, I define and confine, and am less."

Professor Perry himself opens his article on "Religious Experience" with the words: "The least religious experience so is mysterious and so complex, that a moderate degree of reflection upon it tends to a sense of intellectual impotence." We might say the same of any event that takes place in this world, the simplest of all being the fall of a stone which takes place according to the well known Newtonian formulas of gravitation. Though our definition of the fall of the stone is perfect, the act itself is so complex that a real comprehension of all the details of a single instance would [illegible] to reveal our intellectual impotence. We are capable of [illegible]

tion, i. e., to mark and describe those features which a set of events has in common, and our generalisations, because they point out the salient features, enable us to comprehend the world, but while generalisations are mere words, the real events are aglow with action. The cold formulas of science lack the life of reality and if the falling stone could think and speak, it would feel that its own case of rushing toward the ground on account of the attraction with which its mass is animated under the particular circumstances of the special event is so mysterious, so complex, so absolutely beyond any description in a scientific formula that it would scorn the idea of being subsumed with all other analogous cases under one general law.

In defining events we must not be too over-anxious to satisfy the demands of emotion. Definitions describe the salient feature of a number of events and there is no set of facts which cannot be classified, named and described.

Religion is an ideal and its emotional character is its most characteristic element. Accordingly we need not be astonished that religious minds scorn any scientific definition of religion. Nevertheless religion is as much definable as any other affair or event.

The old traditional definition of religion has been "man's union with, or relation to God." Those who would try to make a concession to polytheism, add the words "or to gods," that is to say, in general to supernatural beings who answer prayers and exercise an influence upon the world. Since we have become acquainted with atheistic religions (such as is Buddhism) or purely ethical systems (such as is Confucianism), our religious philosophers have become puzzled and have not as yet found a definition which would be broad enough to comprehend also such views as must appear irreligious to our traditional dogmatism. They have resorted either to the theory that religions which do not recognise, or ignore, the existence of God, or gods, or a supernatural world, cannot be regarded as religious in the proper sense of the term, but they recognise philosophical interpretations of God, and so they replace the definition of religion as our "union with God" by a broader term such as belief in a supernatural world order, or they define religion (with Schleiermacher) in purely subjective terms as "the feeling of absolute dependence."

The definition of religion as our union with God has proved satisfactory to religious minds only on account of the other emotional term, "God." The word "God" too has been proclaimed as undefinable for the very same reasons as the term "religion." Our notion of God is so replete with sentiment and fills us with so much awe that we hesitate to believe it could be described in a simple formula, and when thinkers began to reject the traditional conception of God as an individual being while at the same time attempting to retain the substance of their emotional reverence for the word, they replaced it by such words as "the Infinite," "the First Cause," "the Eternal," "the Highest Being," etc., but for all that the words God and Religion, whatever their import for our feelings may be, are and will remain very simple ideas.

God, whatever notion of divinity man may have had has been from the beginning and is still an idea of moral significance to everyone who uses the word and believes in the existence of a God. God to the savage as well as to the Christian apologetic of the twentieth century is that power which forces upon man a definite line of conduct and every believer in God considers that, the duty of his life which in his opinion he trusts to be the will of his God.

When Jephtha, the judge of Israel, thought that Yahveh demanded of him the sacrifice of his daughter as a burnt offering, he obeyed with a bleeding heart. From the standpoint of his belief, his act was moral for it was according to his religion and his conception of God.

Ximenes, one of the most uncompromising inquisitors of Spain, had thousands of victims burned at the stake, and yet, it is said, that he was so tender hearted that he could not bear the groans and cries of the suspected heretics whom he ordered to be tortured on the rack. He appears to us as a villain and a hard hearted scoundrel, but the truth is that, from the standpoint of his conscience, his infamous *autos da fé* were truly moral acts which with logical necessity were derived from his conception of God. As was his religion so was his morality. We can not blame him, we must blame his religion. From the higher standpoint of a modern God conception his acts were immoral, if judged by present standards, and their badness only proves how important it is for us to have the right kind of religion.

Judging from all instances of the different deities that exercise their influence upon human hearts I have come to the conclusion that the best definition of God in a religious sense would be to say that God is that something in a power beyond our control which determines our actions, or in other words, "God is the highest authority for moral conduct." Whether or not this authority for moral conduct be conceived as an individual being, natural or supernatural, as a general idea, or as a law of nature, or as a mysterious power is another question which will prove of importance whenever we investigate the God conceptions of the several religions or of different philosophers. The truth remains that the common feature of all God conceptions is that God represents the ultimate authority for our actions.

Religion refers to the entire man; it covers his whole life, intellectual, emotional and practical. The roots of our religion lie deeply buried in our world conception and therewith religion permeates our intellect, our sentiments and our will. It resides in the head, it pulsates in the heart, it guides the hand. It appears as dogma, as the tenor that gives a definite character to our aspirations; as worship, ritual and prayer; as sacrifice, devotion and rule of conduct. Further it is the quintessence of our hopes and our dreams and the guiding star and mariner's compass on our voyage through life.

The triple nature of religion as being at once the dominant of the intellect, of the emotions and of the will, is best expressed in the word "conviction," for by "conviction" we understand an idea that is backed by sentiment and serves as a regulator of conduct. Accordingly, religion is a world-conception that has become our conviction.

Religion is different in different ages, under different conditions, in different temperaments, and in people of different characters. Although it always affects the whole man, it is to the intellectualist mainly a doctrine; to the sentimentalist, mainly a feeling ("Gefühl ist alles," says Faust); to the moralist, mainly a rule of action; to the man of practical life, mainly endeavor; to the traditionalist, mainly a matter of observances; to the pietist, mainly devotion, etc. All these phenomena are characteristic of religion, but none of them exhausts its nature completely.

It becomes obvious that religion is the natural product of human nature. Wherever there are rational beings who can form a systematic view of the world, religion will inevitably develop and religion will be of the most varied character, savage or civilized, vulgar or noble, superstitious or lofty and pure, according to circumstances and the nature of the people.

Purely intellectual ideas are scientific; they may be true or, if not exactly true, we may be convinced of their truth. They are not religious, but they may become religious. An idea becomes religious as soon as it becomes an authoritative truth, a truth to mind which we deem to be a duty. Thus the doctrine of evolution has become a religious tenet to many by implying the duty of being progressive and working for the advance of the human race.

In brief, religion covers man's relation to the entirety of existence. The characteristic feature of religion is conviction, and its contents a world conception which serves for the regulation of conduct.

This definition of religion is as broad as it sweeping; it covers not only the theistic faith, but also the atheistic religions, such as Buddhism and Confucianism, and also all philosophies, for religion is the philosophy of historical movements, while a philosophy is the religion of an individual thinker. Our definition includes all serious convictions, even those which pride themselves on being irreligious. Irreligion, according to our definition would alone that man be who had no rule of conduct, no maxim according to which he could regulate his life, and thus the irreligious man would practically be identical with the thoughtless man, the man without convictions, without principles, who lives only for the present moment, who never thinks of the future or the past and who, animal-like, only satisfies the immediate impulses of his instincts.

By offering this comparatively simple definition of religion we do not mean to describe all the awe and reverence which the religious man cherishes for his God, for the authority of his conduct, for his ideals. That is indescribable, as much so as any reality in its peculiar idiosyncracy defies definition, but our definition, it is to be hoped, will prove sufficient for scientific purposes, as a satisfactory generalisation of all religious phenomena.

P. C.

THE BASLE CONGRESS FOR THE HISTORY OF RELIGION.

The Parliament of Religions which was convened at Chicago in 1893 could not be repeated in Paris because in France the principal of a separation of church and state is interpreted in such a was as to allow the official authorities to do nothing whatever in the line of religion. Accordingly a religious parliament of any character could not have been tolerated on the Exhibition grounds at Paris; but scientific congresses were quite in order, and so there was no opposition to a historical treatment of religion. Accordingly those who advocated a religious parliament proposed to have the next best possible, which was a congress of scholars who represented not churches or congregations but a scientific inquiry into the history of religion. Thus it came about that a congress for the history of religion was held at the Paris Exposition.

The first Congress of the History of Religion was opened by

the venerable theologian, Professor Albert Réville and was conducted mainly by his well known son of equal scholarly repute, Professor Jean Réville of Paris, ably assisted by Professor Leon Marillier, a most congenial man who, I regret to add, together with his whole family two years later met with a tragic death in the waves of the sea off the coast of Bretagne. A report of the plans of the Paris Congress has been published in the May number of *The Open Court*, 1890 (pp. 271-275. Before the conclusion of the meetings the delegates organized themselves into a permanent body which would meet every four years in some convenient city of Europe, and it was then decided that the second meeting should be held at Basle.

This Basle congress was opened by its new president, Professor von Orelli, on Tuesday, August 30th of the current year, and we propose here to publish a condensed report of the lectures of those scholars who addressed the congress in plenary sessions.

Professor Von Orelli insisted that the congress was not a religious gathering. Its object was neither the propaganda of any confession of faith nor an alliance between different religions against irreligion, and least of all the establishment of a new religion of mankind. Its purpose was not even an inquisition into the divine power which governs the fate of man but simply and solely of the response which this power finds in the human heart. Representatives of different opinions would certainly learn to understand one another better and would by personal contact and mutual exchange of thought be prevented from arriving at wrong conclusions; but the congress itself stood on a neutral basis. Any serious scholar could take part in it, even the man who regarded religion as a pathological phenomenon. Yet after all, Professor Orelli concluded, our practical religious life would be benefitted by the congress for while on the one hand only he who himself is imbued with religious sentiment can correctly interpret the parts of religious phenomena, it is on the other hand to be expected that a knowledge of other religions could only serve to intensify our own religious convictions.

Professor Naville of Geneva greeted the members of the Congress in the name of the Swiss government. Dr. Burckhardt-Finsler, rector of the University of Basle, extended a cordial welcome to the Congress in the name of the City of Basle, and the venerable Professor Albert Réville of Paris spoke in the name of the French Ministry of Education. Among the visitors may be mentioned: Professor Holtzmann, of Strassburg; Professor Paul Haupt, of Baltimore; Professor Richard Garbe, of Tübingen, Professor Von Schröder, of Vienna; Dr. Mahler, of Budhapest; Dr. Linaker, of Florence; Dr. Balfour, of Oxford; and M. Bonet-Maury of Paris.

Professor Albert Dietrich of Heidelberg read an essay on the "Religion of Mother Earth," showing how the Romans knew the divinity Levana, a name of Mother Earth, which is explained to signify the goddess who at the birth of the child lifts it up from the ground and hands it over to the powers of life. In connection with this religious belief the speaker mentioned the ritual of burying the bodies of dead children, which is done even among those nations who habitually burned their dead, the idea being that corpses of infants ought to be returned to Mother Earth so as to enable her to form new souls from the material. The same views concerning Mother Earth obtained in Greece and the horror of the people that their bodies might not be properly buried seems to suggest the fear that possibly they could thus be deprived of the chance of returning to life in future reincarnations. Even in our days suicides are refused burial in religious cemeteries. The veneration of Mother Earth seems to have been gradually superseded by the worship of male deities, when after the matriarchial period a change in the significance of the sexes deprived woman of her ancient prerogatives.

Professor Deussen of Kiel spoke of the kinship of Indian religions, Brahmanism and Buddhism with Christianity. All three are centered in the idea of salvation or redemption; Brahmanism preaches redemption from error through the recognition that the world is illusion; Buddhism seeks redemption from suffering by the suppression of desire; and Christianity is a redemption from sin through regeneration and a renewal of the will. Brahmanism attempts to reform thought; Buddhism, sentiment; and Christianity, the will. Considering the fact that man is at once, thinking, feeling, and willing, the three religions are complementary to each other. Professor Deussen specified further some detailed similarities between Buddhism and Christianity.

Professor Jean Réville of Paris discussed the general significance of the history of religion in its relation to the history of the church. The history of religion is not an enemy to the history of the church nor is there any competition between the two. On the contrary they are of mutual assistance and the history of the Bible cannot be understood without a knowledge of those religions which have influenced its formation. The writings of the New Testament cannot be understood without a knowledge of Judaism and Alexandrian philosophy, while the rise of Christian dogma and ecclesiastical hierarchy must remain obscure without sufficient information concerning the influence which pagan religions exercised upon the growing church. Paganism did by no means cease at the moment when

Christianity became victorious. It's influence continued to be felt during the Middle Ages in folklore and in ceremonies as well as in sectarian movements. From this standpoint the change of Oriental Christianity to Islam becomes quite comprehensive. The Renaissance and Reformation show again influences of paganism upon Christianity, nor can we predict that never again other religions will exercise an influence upon Christianity. Thus a familiarity with the general history of religion is indispensable to the theologian and, in connection with a study of religious psychology, it will afford us a better insight into the nature of religion and the religious spirit that animates mankind.

At the conclusion of the first session Rev. Weber of Menziken, in the Aargau, Swithzerland, exhibited a number of religious objects from Thibet and declared that the Lamas of Thibet and the Thibetan monasteries should not be considered as the preservers of Buddhist orthodoxy for, on the contrary, Lamanism is a degeneration of the original Buddhism. Instead of practising a religion in the sense of Buddha the Thibetans externalized his doctrines, using prayer-mills and prayer-flags, and instead of seeking Nirvana, "the extinction of all sin," by means of self-abnegation and a purification of the heart, the majority of the people attempt to reach their aim on the short cut of magical incantations. The speaker further dwelt on some superstitions of the Thibetans which will remind one of Jewish ceremonies, viz., the scape-goat, and the besmearing of the door-posts with blood; and also of Roman Catholic institutions such as masses for the dead, processions, the eternal light, holy water, etc., which as Rev. Weber said might have reached Thibet by the way of Russia, but which (as we may be permitted to add parenthetically) appear to have been introduced by the Nestorians.

A Japanese gentleman, Kaikioku Watanabé, Professor of the Buddhist College, Endiodotin, Tokyo, spoke of religion in Japan. He said that the Japanese were distinguished by great toleration which was eminently sown in their present friendly attitude toward Christianity. Buddhism in Siam, Burma, Corea, and China has become stagnant and does no longer show its missionary spirit. In Japan, however, things are different. Mr. Watanabé compared Christianity to flowing water, the Buddhism of Siam, Burma, Corea, and China, to the rigid stone of the Buddha images, but the Buddhism of Japan to a spreading tree, and he said, that this spreading tree utilised without hesitation the Christian waters that could give nourishment to its roots. Christianity had come to Japan in 1548 through the Jesuits and had been for a time very successful until the Jesuits destroyed their own influence through their interference with politics. Japan enjoys religious liberty in the widest sense of the word. Shintoism, the old national religion, can scarcely be regarded as a religion, for it is simply a ceremonial which is still used for festive occasions. Confucianism is important as an ethical system, Taoism as a kind of nature-philosophy, for fortunately in Japan, the superstitious Taoism of China has not taken roots. There are a number of smaller religious societies such as the Tenri and the Remmon, which entertain belief in superstitious and degenerate doctrines but they exercise no influence upon the country as a whole. All the sects of Buddhism, which are altogether twelve, belong to the Mahayana Church. There are 300,000 Christians in Japan, among which the Roman and Greek Catholics are numerically the strongest. The Protestants are divided into Methodists, Baptists, Lutherans, Presbyterians, etc. Professor Watanabé concluded that formerly Christianity was considered as an enemy by the Buddhists but of late the representatives of both great faiths have begun to meet on friendly terms and there are symptoms of a mutual approach on both sides. Buddhists do not hesitate to accept some Christian ideas while vice versa, Christians become assimilated to the old faith of the country by adopting much that is Buddhistic.

Professor Von Schröder of Vienna spoke of the belief in a highest and good Being among the Aryans which he assumes to be one of the most primitive notions. He sees remnants of it in the belief of Diaus-Pitar, i. e., Jupiter, the heavenly father, and he thinks that it found a noble expression in the Zoroastrian belief in Ahura Mazda.

Professor Furrer of Zurich spoke of the significance of the history of religion for theology, but he insisted that the investigator should do his work with good intentions. He should endeavor to understand the meaning of other religions and should not mark only those features that are offensive. On the contrary he should point out the attractive features of other faiths and should above all beware of drawing consequences which are not positively drawn by the authorised representatives of that faith themselves, for we must bear in mind that some religions are not consistent. "A theologian," Professor Furrer declared, "cannot sustain the claim of the universality of Christianity unless he is familiar with other religions. We must grant that the conceptions of the fatherhood of God and the ordeals of a high and elevating morality are also met with in other religions. The greatness of Christianity," he added, "lies in the personality of Jesus Christ, for it was Jesus Christ only who deepened the meaning of God as Father, who liberated man from the horrors of suffering and death, and ransomed him from sin. Jesus has made life worth living again."

M. Guimet, Director of the Musée Guimet in Paris, spoke of Lao Tze, the old philosopher of China, and defended the theory that Lao Tze should be explained from Indian Brahmanism. The Chinese language, however, lacked the finer structures that reproduce the results of Indian speculation. Nevertheless, Lao Tze's philosophy introduced not only moral reform but prepared the way also for Buddhism, another religious theory that came from India.

Rastamji Edulji Dustoor Peshotan Sanjana, Deputy High Priest of the Parsees, Bombay, read a lecture on Ahura Mazda in the Avesta, pointing out the strictly monotheistic character of Zoroastrianism and rejected the wrong notions of dualism and nature worship. Ahura Mazda is worshipped as the first cause of all things, as the immaterial creator of the material creation and he is characterised by the attributes of immutability, omnipresence, omniscence, and above all, justice. The four elements: air, fire, water, and earth, are not worshipped but are only regarded as glorifying Ahura Mazda's wisdom.

Thursday, the 1st of September, had been reserved to the inspection of a hagiographical exposition, while the evening was devoted to an excursion to Flühen.

On Friday, Dr. Paul Sarasin spoke about the religious notions of the lowest human races, which in his opinion are certain dwarf negritos in the interior of Africa, in both East Indias, in Ceylon and on the Sunda Islands. They are lower than any other people in the world both as to their bodily development and their spiritual capacities. They continue to live in the simplest way, although they are surrounded by people who possess a higher civilisation. Sarasin divided these races into two species: those with wooly hair and those with curly hair. They seem to have existed in Europe and South America.

Dr. Sarasin had studied especially the Weddas in the interior of Ceylon, and the Toallas in the interior of Celebes. The Weddas are the lowest of all. They have no herds and live exclusively of the spoils of hunting, and of roots and fruits gathered in the forest. Every family has its own hunting revier and they remind one very much of animals. Indeed, the Singalese whose civilisation has very little influenced their habits, call them with the Singalese word which means "animals." They have adopted the Singalese language but are unable to count. Their receptivity as well as their productivity is almost *nil*. Their morality is primitive but not vulgar. It is simply an absence of a higher development. They have no avarice. They do not lay up treasures. They are content with whatever they have. Stealing and lying is unknown to them. They are grateful, courageous and patient in suffering. It is interesting to learn that they are strict monogamists and althought the connubial relation which is entered into with perfect freedom by both parties is never concluded under any formality or impressive ceremony, both mates are faithful to one another throughout life. It is perhaps characteristic that jealousy is strongly developed. In answer to the question whether these nations exhibited any typical religious notions Dr. Sarasin replied in the negative. There is no trace of any worship of a higher being. They show no interest in Buddhist doctrines and simply declare that they no nothing of Buddha. They give no thought to the idea of life after death. They are satisfied with their present existence. Isolated vestiges of religious ceremonies take place at the tomb of the dead, consisting of a dance around an arrow stuck in the ground, which suggests their belief in a soul, but it seems to be unconscious and the Weddas themselves are unable to explain anything of their ritual, for they simply say that they learned it from their parents. The Toallas of Celebes are similar but not quite primitive. They are just beginning to cultivate the soil but, like the Weddas, they are strict monogamists and show no interest in religion. They have adopted nothing of the Mahommedans that live in their neighborhood. There are traces of tree worship among them, but the priest who attends to the ceremony can give no explanation why he does so. These tribes, Dr. Sarasin declared, are the most primitive of all mankind but they are not incapable of civilisation.

Rev. Dr. Jeremias of Leipsic discussed the monotheistic tendencies of the ancient Babylonians. He granted that such tendencies existed but these ideas had not become the common property of the nation, for the official polytheistic worship continued in spite of it. Things were different in Israel where a higher conception of God prevailed among the people at large. Moreover Babylonian monotheism rests upon the scientific progress of purely mundane scholarship, while the monotheism of Israel is based on the historical revelation of God himself.

Professor Kessler of Greifswald read a paper on the religion of Mani, commonly called Manicheism. Formerly our historians thought that they had to deal with a Christian sect, but now we know that Manicheism was a great world religion which had not only spread to the Occident (for instance St. Augustine was a Manichian for some time during his youth), where it continued down into the Middle Ages, but prevailed also in the East and even in China, yea—in Manchuria. So far Manicheism was known only through the opposition of its adversaries, but in 1902 Professor Grünwedel discovered in Turkestan several great fragments of an unknown script which by Prof. Müller of the Ethnological Museum in Berlin were deciphered and explained as Manichean writings in the Middle Persian language. These fragments which are not yet published, corroborate the reliability of the information we have from Arabian historians concerning Manicheism.

Dr. Kohlback of Kaposvar spoke of the mutual influences of religion on art, and of art on religion.

Professor Paul Haupt proposed a reconstruction of Ecclesiastes, insisting that the main idea of the book exhibited a sceptical pessimism.

Professor Samuel Ives Curtiss of Chicago could not be present because he was suffering on his return from Syria from a sudden collapse and lay sick in Zürich. His paper on "Primitive Semitic Religion Today" was read by a friend and greatly appreciated by the audience. We regret to state that Professor Curtiss died very soon after the Congress in Zürich, and his death is the more to be lamented as he had collected much interesting material on his journey through the Orient. We have published an article, explaining the resuts of his former work in the July number of *The Open Court* (1904, pp. 121ff.), entitled "The Religion of Proto-Semitism," and we had an almost buoyant letter from him, dated September 19th, in which he expressed his confidence of a speedy recovery. He further mentioned the results of his explorations in the Orient, and his hope of having them published in a strict scientific form by the Carnegie Institute and also in a popular book which would render them accessible to the general public. On September 22, Professor Curtiss suffered from a sudden relapse and died unexpectedly.

We believe that his investigations throw a new light upon the development of religion, especially the religion of the Semites, and it is to be hoped that his papers are in such a condition as to enable the Carnegie Institute to publish them without difficulty.

THE FREETHOUGHT CONGRESS AT ROME.

The Freethinkers of Europe had planned to hold at Rome, the seat of ultra-Montanism and the stronghold of all reactionary movements, a congress under the very eyes of the Pope, so as to show their strength in the face of the most irreconcilable enemies of Freethought, and we have information that their meeting was a great success. Men from all countries attended the meetings and among them were several prominent scientists of international repute, especially Professor Ernest Haeckel of Jena, Germany, Professor Mercelin Berthelot of France, and the poet Björnson of Norway. The center of interest was the aged but ever youthful Haeckel, his hair white and his face radiant, his eyes beaming with enthusiasm, and the irresistible amiability of his character gaining him the hearts of everyone. Newspaper statements declared that there were no less than 5,000 visitors in attendance, and when on the second day a procession started for the Porta Pia, the gate through which Garibaldi had entered Rome, which finally led to the secularisation of the Eternal City, there were no less than 12,000 people to listen to the speeches made on that occasion. It proved the greatest procession since times immemorial. Apparently the days when the Papacy would still be favored by the people to retain possession of Rome are past. The tide of popular opinion tends the other way.

Professor Haeckel delivered his speech in three languages: in German, in French and in Italian, and at the end of his address he moved that the American idea of free church in a free state as independent and separate of one another should be adopted in European countries and it was further moved and carried that the Premier of France, His Excellency Mr. Combes should be addressed in a petition in favor of the adoption of this policy. Another mass meeting was held on Mount Palatine and here the motion was made to elect Professor Ernest Haeckel as a Monistic Pope which was carried under enthusiastic applause. Professor Haeckel accepted the honor and sent out a greeting in his new dignity to the Editor of *The Open Court.*.

It is impossible here to enter into further details, especially as our information is based on haphazard correspondence, but we may state that among the speakers were Giuseppe Sergi of the University of Rome, and Count De Gubernatis, the editor of the monthly review entitled *The Latin Awakening,* and Mr. Mangasarian of Chicago.

Another Freethought Congress has been planned in St. Louis in connection with the World's Fair under the auspices of the Alliance of Freethought Congregations and Freethought Societies of North America, the governing board of which consists of the following names: William Petersen, President; William Roehling,

Vice-President; Fritz Gerecke, Recording Secretary; Fritz Schleicher, Treasurer; Dr. Max Hempel, First Corresponding Secretary; Franz Hillig, Second Corresponding Secretary; Franz Starz, Financial Secretary.

THE CONGRESSES OF ARTS AND SCIENCES AT ST. LOUIS.

In connection with the World's Fair a congress has been held the purpose of which seems to have been to set a monument to civilization in the shape of a series of resumés of the history and present standpoint of the arts and sciences, by competent speakers, and so a number of foreign and American professors as well as other authorities in their respective branches were invited to meet at St. Louis. The responsible managers of the congresses were Simon Newcomb of Washington, Albion W. Small of the University of Chicago, and Hugo Muensterberg of Harvard University.

During the session of the Congress much criticism could be heard, part of which may be regarded as justified, and part of it pointed out conditions which must be attributed to unfavorable circumstances beyond the power of adjustment.

The best resumé of the several sessions that has come to our knowledge appeared in *The Daily Picayune* of New Orleans, and is written by Professor W. B. Smith of Tulane University who attended a great number of the lectures in person and being many-sighted himself is specially capable of delineating a correct and vivid picture, from which we propose to quote some of the most interesting passages.

Professor Smith having first dwelt on the unevenness in achievement as well as in ability, continues:

"A more serious criticism would seem to be that there *was rather overmuch retrospection and circumspection.* Not a few of the addresses sounded very like annual reports to stockholders in some steel trust or tobacco combine. They told of the past history and present condition of their subjects in a more or less perfunctory fashion, but avoided suggesting new methods or new points of view. There was much looking backwards and some looking around, but very little looking forward. Perhaps this also was to be expected in addresses made to order on assigned themes wherein there was small room for freedom and spontaneity. Creative thought is not kept anywhere on tap; it comes unasked, unbidden."

The writer has attended congresses at Chicago, Paris, and St. Louis, not to mention others, and has come to the conclusion that it is very bad policy for the managing committee to dictate to speakers the subject which they should discuss. If they want good lectures they must allow the speaker the choice of his subject, otherwise the result will be as Professor Smith calls it, "cut and dried and made to order." Further allowance ought to be made for free discussion, for free discussion and divergency of opinion give life to scientific as well as other discourses.

After all, the main purpose of international meetings, aside from the publication of the reports in which the speeches are to be entombed as in a great monument, is the personal contact and the exchange of thought among all those many people who live in different parts of the globe and know each other by reputation. They have thus a chance to see each other face to face, and this purpose of the St. Louis congress has no doubt to some extent been fulfilled, though not completely, for there were several among the delegates who sought one another in vain. The mission of the congress would have been better fulfilled had their headquarters been more comfortable so as to form a centre where people could rest and see each other. The audience halls were too much scattered over the grounds and there were a number of men who having come from great distances had hoped to meet their colleagues, yet were unable to find some of those that were present. It is to be hoped that the managing committee of future congresses will provide for ample opportunities for personal contact and mutual acquaintance.

In an attempt at recapitulating the most significant speeches, it will be difficult, if not impossible, to do justice to all; but we will follow Professor Smith's report, who has done his best to seek out those sessions in which popular interest would naturally centre. He says of the meetings of September 21st:

"The principal focus of interest was Hall 2, where in the afternoon the Darwinian hypothesis came up for discussion. The leader was the renowned Hugo De Vries, of Amsterdam. This savant, whose name now spans the largest angle in the field of biologic speculation, has for years fixed the attention of both continents by his *Mutation Theorie*, the most far-reaching contribution to the general subject since *The Origin of Species*. At many points the Dutchman antagonizes the Englishman most sharply. He discredits largely the efficiency of natural selection, claiming that it is a mere seine, catching the big, letting the small go to death, and not a directive force of nature. But did Darwin really think of it as more?

He still further minimized the significance of the struggle for existence. In a word he rejected the Darwinian causes of variation and species origination as quite inadequate to the task imposed upon them.

"But he is very far from questioning for a moment the general doctrine of descent with modification. This counts everywhere, and especially with DeVries, as certain and almost axiomatic. However, those modifications have not been minute, often insensible, variations, gradually accumulated through generations; they have been considerable, sudden and permanent mutations, completely establishing a new variety, and even a new species, in one or two generations. De Vries bases his doctrine on a long series of careful experiments and wide-extended observation, especially on plants, which fall remarkably in line with the now famous researches of Mendel.

"The Amsterdamer was immediately followed by Professor Whitman, of Chicago, who forcibly contested the validity of his explantations, and maintained that there was a wide margin of observational fact uncomprehended by the thought of De Vries and Eimer, no less than by that of Darwin.

"Other speakers took part in the discussion, and the general interest was aroused to the highest pitch.

"It was made vividly and publicly evident what has for some years been an open secret, that the whole question, not of the fact, but of the manner and agency of modification in descent, had entered upon an entirely new and most important stage of its history.

"In the adjoining hall the greatest living philosopher of religion, Professor Otto Pfleiderer, of Berlin, discussed in a lucid and masterly manner the relations of religion and especilly Christianity, to the surrounding forms of human knowledge. Professor Pfleiderer is in every way a most notable man, but especially remarkable for the freshness, fluidity and receptivity of his intellect, maintained in all of its youthful vigor and enthusiasm to his present advanced period of life. How steadily his thought had pressed onward and still presses onward is manifest to the reader of his works for the past generation. His very latest work, *Das Christusbild*, shows him still the same unwearied mountain-climber. His address today was delivered in English. It does not lend itself readily to recapitulation, even with the manuscript before me. Enough that he has no fears for the essential element in Christianity and no hesitation in making the largest concessions to the widespread illumination of science around the whole intellectual horizon. To many these concessions might be disturbing, but not in the least to the Berlin theologian, whose motto seems to be ever tested, ever grounded. Professor Pfleiderer is an altogether amiable and charming personality, so less at home in the salon than on the platform.

There was another theologian of interest whom Professor Smith describes as follows:

"Conspicuous among these, indeed conspicuous among all the speeches of this occasion, was that of Professor Adolf Harnack, of Berlin, on 'The Relations of Ecclesiastical to Universal History.' Professor Harnack is the illustrious author of the *History of Dogma*, and of other works innumerable of historical research. Recently his *Essence of Christianity* has gone through edition after edition, and has agitated the Fatherland like the *Babel und Bibel* of Delitszch in manner and measure scarcely comprehensible to an American. Professor Harnack is an exceedingly stimulating and inspiring teacher, and his indirect influence on theology through his enthusiastic students, some of whom are pushing his methods to consequences that may surprise him, is even greater than his direct. He is a notable personality. Of very moderate proportions, with a student's face, slightly florid, a mustache reddish and inconspicuous, he is remarkable for his iron-gray hair brushed back straight from his brow and bristling like a field of wheat bent under a strong wind. His eyes have a dreamy, almost weary, and far-away look, and he seems paying little heed either to speeches or to conversation. But when he himself begins to speak his face lights up with a pleasant, even jovial, expression, his brow seems to broaden and the veins become distent as with thought. He is distinctly an orator of the American type. At once he lays aside all formality, disowns notes entirely, speaks in an earnest conversational tone, rivals a Frenchman in gesticulation, leans on the desk behind him, crossing his legs inartistically in front, dashes the gathering dew from his brow and spices his discourse with frequent jests, witticisms and anecdotes. We are tempted to minuter description, but let this suffice.

"He began by apologizing for speaking in German, on the ground that he loved the English language too much to hurt it. He proceeded to dispose of the notion so popular in certain circles that church history dealt with a peculiar train of events and in a peculiar way—this he did in a half-critical, half-facetious fashion. There was no diagnostic mark to distinguish the ecclesiastical from the profane. All history was of a piece. He hurried on to elaborate this idea by showing how ecclesiastic history was woven out of the same threads, political, religious, philosophic, scientific, economic, that make up all history in all lands. There was no exoteric and esoteric history. His plea for the unity of history was replete with illustrations drawn from a wide range of critical knowledge."

Professor Smith continues: "This splendid orator was followed by Professor Jean Réville, of Paris, in a lecture on the 'Progress of Ecclesiastic History.' This well known savant read in excellent English piquant with occasional Gallicisms. He discussed the rise and development of the notion and methods of church history, gave critical appreciations of some principal historians, especially of Baur, whose disciple he seems still to be, and closed with a sketch of the demands and ideals of the present day."

Many more men were present whom it was a pleasure to meet and to hear discourse on their various specialties. We mention among them: W. T. Harris, the Commissioner of Education, of Washington; Yves Delage, the famous French physiologist; Professor Hertwig, a leading embryologist and the new rector of the University of Berlin; Ettore Pais, a famous Italian savant; Richard Muther, the art historian; Alfred Guerard of the Sorbonne, Paris; Professor Mary W. Calkins, of Wellesley College; Brander Matthews; Maurice Bloomfield, of Johns Hopkins University; D. A. W. Jackson, the Zendavesta scholar of Columbia University of New York; Charles Lanmann, Professor of Sanscrit and Pali at Harvard, etc.

The chemical section was especially strong, as may be seen from the presence of Sir William Ramsay, J. H. Vant' Hoft, and Professor Liebreich.

P. C.

PAUL REE. OBITUARY.

A PHILOSOPHICAL GENIUS AND A SYMPATHETIC CHARACTER.

Paul Rée, the son of a wealthy owner of feudal estate, was born on November 21, 1850, in Pomerania; and received his early education at the Schwerin Gymnasium. In 1869 he studied jurisprudence at the University of Leipsic.

The natural bend of his mind, however, and his previous acquaintance with the moral philosophy of Schopenhauer, induced him to abandon his legal studies and devote himself to philosophy, for which his contemplative nature and analytical intellect eminently qualified him. He pursued his studies at various universities; and in 1875 published anonymously his first book, entitled, *Psychologische Beobachtungen* with the motto "L'homme est l'animal méchant par excellence."

In the same year his thesis *Ueber die moralischen Empfindungen* obtained for him the degree of Doctor of Philosophy from the University of Halle. During the following years, he travelled extensively, and continued his studies in various branches of knowledge.

At Basel he became intimately acquainted with Friedrich Nietzsche, for whom personally he had the highest regard, but took very little interest in his philosophy. Later in life they became estranged from each other.

He spent the winter of 1881-2 at Sorrento, in company with Richard Wagner and his wife, and also with Malvina von Meysenburg and Lou Andréas Salomé, two well-known authoresses of Germany.

In 1885 he published *Die Entstehung des Gewissens* and also *Die Illusion der Willensfreiheit*. It was while composing the above that he felt the want of a more comprehensive knowledge of the natural sciences, than was offered to the students by the schools of his time, and he devoted five years of unremitting study and close application to the science of medicine in all its branches.

In 1890 he passed his examinations in Berlin and Munich with honors, and received the degree of Doctor of Medicine. From 1890 to 1900 he lived on his brother's estate at Stibbe, West Prussia, practising as a physician, and devoting his time and princely income to the care of the poor and suffering; while he himself lived in Puritanical simplicity. On account of his philanthropy he was revered by his fellow-citizens as a saint.

It was during the last ten years of his life, that he wrote his main work upon philosophy (referred to in the present number of *The Monist*, in the article entitled "Paul Rée," by Mr. Henry Hooper), the publication of which was deferred until after his death . Being naturally inclined to a solitary life, he, in 1900, after the sale of his brother's estate, removed to Celerina in the Engadine, where, as before, he gained the love and veneration of the poor and suffering and all those with whom he came in contact. His medical services were invariably given without remuneration, and serious cases he would frequently send to the clinics at Munich and Vienna at his own expense.

On October 28, 1901, he met his death by falling into the river Inn, and was buried at Celerina. He was never married. He was an industrious and prolific correspondent; and the letters written to his brother-in-law, Dr. G. Sellin, and others, are said to be innumerable; but the letters were seldom dated, and never signed in full.

MRS. ANNIE BESANT AND THE THEOSOPHICAL SOCIETY.

A LETTER FROM INDIA.

In the conclusion of his interesting article on Madame Blávatsky in your April number, Mr. Evans informs us that Mrs. Annie Besant, the present head of the Indian and English branches of the society founded by Madame Blavatsky, died a few years ago.

Permit me to say that this is a mistake. Mrs. Besant is still very much alive. I saw her and heard her lecture at Lucknow in the cold season of 1901-02. And I have since repeatedly heard of her movements in the Indian papers.

Whatever may be the truth about Madame Blavatsky, there is no question, to any who know her, about the genuineness and sincerity, the wide and profound sympathy, the high-souledness, the lofty altruistic aims, and the great intellectual ability of Mrs. Annie Besant. By their fruits ye shall know them. She is now most actively engaged in good work—stirring up the Hindus—trying to rouse them to religious zeal, unworldly ambition, and fidelity to their own race and country. She has founded a Hindu College at Benares, and is now starting Hindu schools all over India, with the object of training up and educating, in the highest sense of the term, Hindus as Hindus, restoring their religion to its original purity and strengthening their adherence to it, teaching them to be proud of it instead of ashamed of it; and thereby remedying the great evil of the purely secular education of the British government, which only seduces them from the wholesome moral restraining influences which with all its faults their old faith still possesses, and leaving them stranded with *nothing* to replace what has been taken from them.

Thanatpin, Pegu, Burma. W. E. Ayton, Wilkinson.

A LETTER FROM AN AMERICAN THEOSOPHIST.

I have been a member of the Theosophical Society since Mrs. Besant's last visit to this country in 1896 and positively affirm that Mrs. Besant is alive and well—is just now back in England. She, and she alone in connection with Colonel Olcott, is the head of the American Theosophical Society.

Mrs. Catharine Tingley has never been accredited a member of the society by either Madame Blavatsky, or Colonel Olcott, or Mrs. Besant.

Mr. Judge did accredit Mrs. Tingley as a member and did nominate her as his successor, and a large number of the American lodges seceded with Madame Tingley. This falling away, however, did not hinder the main society founded by H. P. Blavatsky going on with its original work.

You surely know of the magnificent work Mrs. Besant is doing for the English government in India, and all about the Central Hindu College of which she is president.

I visited the Theosophic Lodges in London, Paris, Florence, and Rome, and can speak first hand of the growth of the societies in these countries, and of the high character of their membership.

Why don't you take the *Theosophical Review*, edited by Mrs. Besant and Mr. Mead, on your exchange? I am sure, either the Chicago or London Office would be delighted to receive *The Monist*. Mr. Mead some months ago reviewed your *Lao-Tze's Tao Teh King*, recognising its deep philosophic import.

You cannot afford to overlook the meaning and work of the Theosophical Society in America and its widespread societies all over the world, for believe me, they are not the followers of an empty or vain cult but are the accredited instruments for evolution and are under the guidance of the "Masters of Wisdom."

The false rumor of Mrs. Besant's death is very immaterial to a Theosophist, compared with the larger foundational fact as to who has administered and is administering the affairs of the Theosophical Society since the removal of H. P. B.

For such a person or persons are to us members, the accredited agents of the super-human Masters to whom our society owes its origin. There are to my knowledge about 2000 Theosophists in America to whom Mrs. Besant and Colonel Olcott stand in this light and to whom Madame Tingley is simply a passing sensational name.

HOLLYWOOD, CALIFORNIA. JOSEPHINE C. LOCKE.

THE GENUINE THEOSOPHICAL SOCIETY.

So many people are now becoming interested in Theosophy and the Theosophical Society that it may be well to correct some public misconception as to the relation of the latter with other bodies using its name but not its spirit. The original and genuine Theosophical Society was founded by Colonel H. S. Olcott and Madame H. P. Blavatsky at New York in 1875, but its headquarters were subsequently removed to Adyar, Madras, India, where the President-Founder still lives and presides. In April, 1895, a secession from the American Section of the Theosophical Society was carried out by the adherents of Mr. William Q. Judge, at that time General Secretary of the American Section. Grave charges of imposture and even forgery had been brought against Mr. Judge, which charges he refused to meet, and he was on the point of being expelled from the Theosophical Society when his friends rallied around him, seceded from the T. S., and formed a new organisation whereof he should be President and where he could not be reached. One year later Mr. Judge died, and the control of his Society passed into the hands of Mrs. Katherine A. Tingley, a former trance-medium. Soon afterwards Mr. Judge's Society adopted a new constitution which made Mrs. Tingley an entire autocrat thereof, but a portion of his Society refused to accede to this, seceded in its turn, and continued its former organisation, Mrs. Tingley being left in absolute control of the remainder. It is understood that Mr. Judge's society has dwindled to a small number of members, something over 500, and that it is engaged in no propaganda work. Mrs. Tingley's Society, calling itself "The Universal Brotherhood," is likewise understood to have withdrawn from the field of Theosophic teaching and propaganda, and it is largely confined to a land enterprise at Point Loma, California.

The purport of the above explanation is this, that neither Mr. Judge's Society, falsely calling itself the "Theosophical Society of America," a title belonging in its constitution to the American Section T. S., nor the organisation headed by Mrs. Tingley, in any way represents the genuine Theosophical Society established in 1875, both of these organisations being wholly apart from the original Society and in more or less opposition thereto. No organisation has the right to pilfer either the name or the property of the body which it has left, and the grievance is in this case the greater because to so many of the proceedings and methods of the two seceded bodies, genuine Theosophists have the utmost repugnance. It is hardly possible in a public journal to specify these; it is sufficient to say that loyal Theosophists hold unflinchingly to the teaching and policy of the original and genuine T. S., and that they are obliged to disclaim any sympathy with organisations which contravene these and which mislead the public by the assumption of a name to which they are not entitled. There is but one genuine Theosophical Society, its headquarters are at Adyar, Madras, India; its President is Colonel Henry S. Olcott, and it is honored by the continued literary work and eminent oratorical ability of Mrs. Annie Besant, the most illustrious of its members.

Some additional facts respecting the above matter may be found in a circular prepared by the Countess Wachtmeister and Mr. Alexander Fullerton, General Secretary of the American Section, which is entitled "The Theosophical Society and the Secession therefrom." It may be had on application to the undersigned, at No. 7 West 8th Street, New York City.

ALEXANDER FULLERTON,
General Secretary American Section T. S.

EDITORIAL COMMENT.

On account of changes that were made in our composing room, the greater part of the articles that appeared in the April and July numbers of *The Monist* had to be set outside, and since the Chicago printing establishments were greatly crowded with orders, the work was delayed, and so it happened that the proofs came in late and all in a bunch, which caused an unusual rush, making it impossible for the editor to give them any closer attention. He had read the article of Mr. Henry Ridgely Evans on Madame Blavatsky in the manuscript, but he had concentrated himself on the state-

closely correspond to the the expectations of the so-called transmutationists of the time."

The other principle of Darwin's selection theory is the doctrine that common individual variation can by constant selection lead to the origin of new species. This idea was quite new at the time and found many adherents, among whom Wallace was the most prominent. In fact, Wallace restated the selection theory with greater precision by eliminating entirely the principle of mutation. Single variations have, according to his opinion, no significance in the theory of descent.

Professor De Vries points out the fact that many naturalists before him, as Cope, and Semper, and Dollo, have expressed their dissatisfaction with

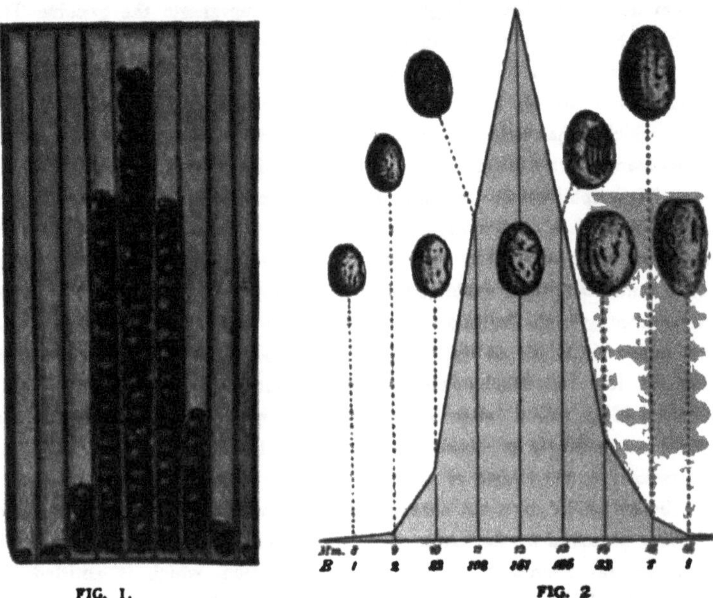

FIG. 1. FIG. 2

the theory of selection as it has been quite commonly accepted since the time of Darwin, and attempts to express the method of the origin of specific characters and of descent in a way which shall be in closer agreement with observed facts.

Variability has of recent years been studied quantitatively by many investigators, Galton, Weldon, Bateson, Ludwig, Duncker, and others, who thus indicate the method of a more exact conception of evolution. These statistical methods are given a prominent place in the volumes before us. As an instance of this we reproduce an illustration from the work of our author showing the variability of the common red-spotted garden bean, *Phaseolus vulgaris*. Figure 1 shows the beans arranged according to size be-

BOOK REVIEWS.

Die Mutationstheorie. Versuche und Beobachtungen über die Entstehung von Arten im Pflanzenreich. Von *Hugo De Vries*, Professor der Botanik in Amsterdam. Leipsic: Veit & Comp. 1901.

Hugo De Vries, Professor of Botany in Amsterdam, especially distinguished for his investigations in the problems of heredity as well as certain other phases of botanical science, insists that the current conception of evolution, which is mainly based on Darwin's famous investigations, stands in need of important corrections. The principle *Natura non facit saltus* does not agree with facts with which all are familiar who have had much experience in horticulture—facts which any one may verify in his own garden. Professor De Vries claims that certain mutations which now and then make their appearance, are of more importance than has yet been conceded; that is to say that the development of species proceeds by "jumps" or "starts," more properly called "steps" or "mutations," and these mutations are frequently immediately productive of new species.

Darwin in his *Origin of Species* relies for explanation on two principles between which he does not always sharply distinguish. The one is mutation, a sudden change by which new species originate abruptly, the assumption of a discontinuous progress in nature by which a new species would originate immediately from a preceding one.

If the new form were distinguished from the original one by only a single characteristic, the process would clearly be a very simple one, and prior to the time of Darwin this was the point about which the controversy turned; especially the French school of the middle of the nineteenth century taking exception to the possibility of such mutations, since it was claimed that they were never observed. At that time they were acquainted with individual variations and often described them, but they saw no relation between them and the origin of new species. Our author says: "I find it impossible to understand how the actual occurence of mutations could have escaped investigators at that time, for they are lacking neither in cultivation, where they are known as single variations, nor in nature, where, as I hope to show, they

author, "are the gaps produced which separate at present all the different species so constantly and definitely from their nearest relatives?"

It is this discontinuity which he seeks to explain. We reproduce from his work two figures of *Chelidonium* The first is *Chelidonium majus*, while the second represents *Chelidonium laciniatum*. But it is known that *C. laciniatum*, distinguished from *C. majus* by its deeply cut leaves and petals, was first discovered about the year 1590 in a lot of *C. majus* growing in the garden of an Heidelberg pharmacist. Since that time the new form—never found wild then or since—has been perfectly true to seed, showing no tendency to revert to the parental *C. majus*.

We also reproduce his figure of *Alnus glutinosa* and *Alnus glutinosa laciniata* which originated from it as a sudden variation. These may serve as striking illustrations of the kind of variations which Professor De Vries would designate as mutations. In common variability the series is continuous, all the forms being connected by transition stages, but in mutation there is no such connection, the mutants being sharply defined, differing from each other in the elements or the combination of the elements of which they are composed.

FIG. 5.

It is these mutations which Professor De Vries deems of importance in the origin of new species. Natural or artificial selection may eliminate all but certain portions of the series of uniformly differing individuals offered by common variability, and so the species may become adapted to local conditions or improved for garden purposes, but selection must be constant if the characteristics desired are to be maintained, since so soon as selection ceases to act, the species reverts to the ancestral form. With mutation this is not the case. By some physiological process not yet understood there appear in certain individuals characters, or groupings of characters, entirely different from those of the parent species, and these characters are from the first strongly hereditable, showing no tendency to revert to the parent form. As individuals of the new forms become numerous, the struggle or competition for existence between the individuals of the new species as such and also between the class of individuals representing the old and the new species, becomes severe. In the competition between the individuals of a species those least fitted to meet their life conditions will succumb in the struggle, so that local races or garden varieties, where the selective influence of man is brought to bear, are developed; but the origin of new specific characters is impossible since the modification obtainable is limited in degree and only maintained by sharp selection. In the competition between the new species and the parent species, or between the several new species which may have originated suddenly from one great species, in the course of a few years the *weaker* species will perish. It is to be assumed that of the vast numbers of species which have originated during past ages only the smallest fraction have been able to persist. In the struggle for existence species have not originated but perished.

In considering the present theory it must be borne in mind that Professor De Vries in speaking of the origin of species by mutation refers to the smallest differentiable systematic unit—small species, minor species, or specific characters and not to the groups of such units which are generally assigned the name of species. Such groups represent isolated portions of an original series of slightly differing minor species, most of which have become extinct, leaving those which remain widely separated.

Evolutionary writings have been so largely speculative that the appearance of a work presenting with the theory the evidence of many years of laborious and successful experimentation must make a profound impression. Such is the contributibn before us. We cannot describe the experiments or state the results beyond saying that Professor De Vries seems to have been able to observe the origin of fixed specific characters in his cultural experiments. He feels confident that investigations in other fields will show facts analogous to those he has discovered in his study of plants ,and that the same law holds good for all forms of life.

It is difficult to form a final judgment of the significance of this voluminous and profound work, but we are impressed with the fact that Professor De Vries is a keen observer and a reliable theoriser. His propositions certainly deserve the attention of all naturalists and their merits will surely not remain hidden.

P. C.

THE HAMMURABI CODE AND THE SINAITIC LEGISLATION. With a Complete Translation of the Great Babylonian Inscription Discovered at Susa. By *Chilperic Edwards.* London: Watts & Co. 1904. Pp. xiii, 168. Price, 2/6 net.

Mr. Chilperic Edwards is a well-informed scholar who in the present volume not only gives us a reliable translation of the text, but also the most indispensable expositions as to the significance of this ancient law book and its relations to the past and the present. The tenor of the book is decidedly scientific and the facts are—making sufficient allowances for personal equations among scholars of different opinions—stated with impartiality and reilability, although it contains a few passages betraying an animosity against traditional orthodoxy, which, if omitted, would have enhanced the dignity of this otherwise well-written book. Thus our author observes in the preface "that the ensuing chapters are not besprinkled with the name of Abraham," adding the reason for such an ommission in Appendix B, which is a condensation of Nöldeke's work[1] on the unhistoricity of Genesis xiv. A few reflections culled from the pages of Mr. Edwards's book will be sufficient for its characterisation .

The Code of Hammurabi is unequivocally the most important ancient law book that has as yet been discovered. It is useful to the historian of civilisation as well as of the evolution of law, for it is the oldest codification that is in existence. The importance of the relation of the Code to Hebrew legislation sinks into insignificance in comparison to its intrinsic worth as an anthropological and historical monument.

It presupposes more ancient laws, and happily some of them have been preserved.

The Semitic Babylonians derived their civilisation from the Sumero-Accadians, whose language died out about 2000 B. C., but fortunately we are in possession of a text book of Accadian which in the Semitic times of Babylonia was regarded as a sacred tongue, and was taught in temple schools and used for special sacred purposes as long as Babylonian religion and civilisation lasted. The great text book of Accadian, which is entitled "Ana Ittishu" constitutes our main source of information and contains specimens of this ancient tongue, and among them laws which prove that the Accadians too were in possession of a highly developed jurisprudence.

We select from the quotations such as refer to family relations, because they give us the best insight into the state of civilisation, and when we compare them to the Code of Hammurabi we learn that civilisation must have been considerably advanced in the days of Hammurabi. Punishments had grown more humane, and the rights of individuals, especially the weaker members of society, slaves and women, are treated with more consideration. We read in the Accadian law:

"If a wife hates her husband and says, 'Thou art not my husband,' into the river they shall throw her.

[1] Nöldeke's contention as to the mythological character of many names in Genesis xiv may be fully granted, and yet, we need not for that reason doubt that it contains genuine historical reminiscences. Of course, Mr. Edwards's position remains true that no definite conclusions can be drawn from it.

"If a husband says to his wife, 'Thou art not my wife,' half a mina of silver he shall weigh out to her."

How much more considerate is the Code of Hammurabi in sections 142-143, which reads as follows:

"If a woman hate her husband and says, 'Thou shalt not possess me,' the reason for her dislike shall be inquired into. If she is careful, and has no fault, but her husband takes himself away and neglects her; then that woman is not to blame. She shall take her dowry and go back to her father's house.

"If she has not been careful, but runs out, wastes her house and neglects her husband; then that woman shall be thrown into the water."

As to the maltreatment of slaves the Accadian law has the following provision:

"If a man hires a slave, and he dies, or is rendered useless, or is caused to run away, or is caused to rebel, or is made ill, then for every day his hand shall measure out a half a *qa* of corn."

Similar provisions are made in the Code of Hammurabi. If freemen are injured the same injury shall be inflicted upon the trespasser, but if the injured person be a slave the punishment is considerably less. We read in sections 196-201 of the Code of Hammurabi the following enactments:

"If a man has destroyed the eye of a free man, his own eye shall be destroyed.

"If he has broken the bone of a free man, his bone shall be broken.

"If he has destroyed the eye of a plebeian, or broken a bone of a plebeian, he shall pay one mina of silver.

"If he has destroyed the eye of a man's slave, or broken a bone of a man's slave, he shall pay half his value.

"If a man has knocked out the teeth of a man of the same rank, his own teeth shall be knocked out.

"If he has knocked out the teeth of a plebeian, he shall pay one third of a mina of silver."

As to the relation of the Code of Hammurabi to Hebrew legislation we must know that our Old Testament contains several law books which represent very different ages and have been preserved side by side. They are as follows:

The Book of the Covenant, Exodus xx-xxiii, to which is related Exodus xxxiv. 11-26.

The Book of Deuteronomy.

The Law of Holiness, Leviticus xvii-xxvi.

The Priests' Code, which claims to be the balance of the Mosaic legislation.

The Priests' Code is for our present purpose the most important constituent of the Pentateuhc. In its present shape it has been compiled by post-exilic priests and cannot be earlier than the time of Ezra, while it received additions at even later dates.

The Law of Holiness belongs to the time of Ezekiel. Deuteronomy is the law which Hilkiah, the high priest of Jerusalem, professes to have found in the Temple in the eighteenth year of Josiah, 621 B. C.

The Ten Commandments, which are inserted in the twentieth chapter of Exodus, are a later addition which cannot be older than the Priests' Code, for it refers to the six days of creation (as well as the institution of the Sabbath) in the sense in which they were understood in the post-exilic days. While the materials for the creation story are drawn from Babylonian stories, the conception of its having been completed in six days is a Jewish interpretation and decidedly un-Babylonian. While the Ten Commandments are of comparatively late origin their source is as yet unknown, and we have nothing that could thow any light on their author, origin, or circumstances of formulation.

The similarity of Hebrew legislation to the Code of Hammurabi is remarkable. The Book of theCovenant for instance begins like the Code of Hammurabi. It is supposed to have been given by Yahveh under impressive circumstances. Both legislations presuppose three estates. The Babylonians know of the freemen, the slaves, and an intermediate class of inhabitants called *Mash-en-kak*, which later corresponds to the Hebrew *Ger*, translated in the English version "stranger," and meaning a sojourner or client who did not enjoy the right of citizenship, yet stood under the protection of the law. In the Book of the Covenant this sojourner or *Ger* shall not be wronged or oppressed. He is simply recommended to mercy. In Deuteronomy he is still a mere object of pity, while the Book of the Covenant directs that the flesh torn by wild animals should be given to the dogs to be eaten. The more humane Deuteronomist allows it to be given to the *Ger*. The time of the Priests' Code, however, is sufficiently advanced to recognise the rights of the *Ger*, and it provides that there shall be one law for both the *Ger* and the freeborn Israelite.

The Psychology of Child Development, with an Introduction by John Dewey. By *Irving King*, sometime Fellow of Philosopy in the University of Chicago. Instructor in Psychology and History of Education in Pratt Institute. Chicago: The University of Chicago Press, 1903. Pages, xxi, 265.

The author is aware of the fact that child study has fallen into disrepute, and he partly seeks the cause of it in the unscientific fashion of "an out-of-date psychology, which dealt with 'powers' rather than the life as a whole." He offers in his book a help to the teacher, and the drift of the book may be characterised in his own words. In summing up the first four chapters he says on page 71:

"The uphsot of the inquiry thus far is this: The newly born infant is at least able to make certain movements. Whether it is conscious or not is purely hypothetical. We know at least that it moves, and that these movements are responses to stimuli of various kinds. Most of its movements are unco-ordinated. There are, however, simple reflexes, and we have chosen to confine the term to those movements which are the result of simple inherited co-ordinations of muscles and neural tracts."

And further down near the end of the book he condenses in the following sentences the immediate pedagogical bearings of his genetic treatment:

"There are two points that have come out in the body of our discussion, about which it will be convenient to center our practical deductions. About these two points the whole psychology of elementary education, in particular, centers. The first point is the undifferentiated character of the child's experience. The second is the imperfect organisation of his experience with reference to the social whole within which he lives. In other words, the first point gives us the organisation of the child; the second, the organisation of his world.

"There is a third point of great importance, but it is one common to the psychology of the adult as well as of the child. It is this: Differentiations in experience occur with reference to the necessities of action. This has been one of our most fundamental propositions, but it is not a deduction from child psychology alone. The modifications of adult experience occur after the same fashion, and it is from this point of view that we have maintained that adult psychology should be studied. But the first two points are the pre-eminent contributions of genetic psychology to elementary school work."

EDUCATIONAL PSYCHOLOGY. By *Edward L. Thorndike*, Adjunct Professor of Genetic Psychology in Teachers College, Columbia University. New York: Lemcke & Buechner, 1903. Pp. vii, 177.

The author, an expert in educational psychology, offers us in this book an insight into the methods and ideals of his science, the importance of which no one will contradict. "What we think and what we do about education is certainly influenced by our opinions about such matters as individual differences in children, inborn traits, heredity, sex differences, the specialisation of mental abilities, their inter-relations, the relation between them and physical endowments, normal mental growth, its periodicities, and the method of action and relative importance of various environmental influences. For instance, schemes for individual instruction and for different rates of promotion are undertaken largely because of certain beliefs concerning the prevalence and amount of differences in mental capacity; the conduct of at least two classes out of every three is determined in great measure by the teacher's faith that mental abilities are so little specialised that improvement in any one of them will help all the rest; manual training is often introduced into schools on the strength of somebody's confidence that skill in movement is intimately connected with efficiency in thinking; the practical action with regard to coeducation has been accompanied, and doubtless influenced by arguments about the identity or the equality of the minds of men and women; the American public school system rests on a total disregard of hereditary mental differences between the classes and the masses." The author discusses the following subjects: The measurement of mental traits.—The distribution of mental traits.—The relationships between mental traits.—Original and acquired traits.—Mental inheritance.—The influence of the invironment.—The influence of special training upon general abilities.—The influence of selection.—The development of mental traits with age.—Sex differences.—Exceptional children; mental and moral defectives.—The relationships of mental and physical traits.—Broader studies of human nature.

The author concludes his book with this consideration:

"The science of education when it develops will like other sciences rest upon direct observations of and experiments on the influence of educational institutions and methods made and reported with quantitative precision. Since groups of variable facts will be the material it studies, statistics will everywhere be its handmaid. The chief duty of serious students of the theory of education to-day is to form the habit of inductive study and learn the logic of statistics.....We conquer the facts of nature when we observe and experiment upon them. When we measure them we have made them our servants. A little statistical insight trains them for invaluable work."

The Federation of Religions. By *Rev. Hiram Vrooman.* Philadelphia and London: The Nunc Licet Press, 1903. 138 pages.

The Rev. Hiram Vrooman, President of "The Co-Workers' Fraternity," and the "Federation of Religions," launches in this booklet a new enterprise which he intends to identify with himself and his life work—viz., a federation of religion, upon the ground that every man with strong religious convictions should join him and the federation should build altars so sacrificial tests can be made to prove whose Lord is God. The primary work of this federation would be investigation rather than instruction, and ought to be carried forward by a permanent parliament of religions whose members are thoroughly representative men. Their common basis should be open-mindedness and loyal-heartedness to truth.

Having explained his purpose and plans, he sets forth in a series of little chapters his views concerning the principles of carrying on such investigation. In chapter 2 he proposes to distinguish phenomena from philosophical conclusions; in chapters 3 and 4 he discusses the inmost and supreme essence of the mind, which he discovers to be spiritual substance; in chapter 5 he arrives at the conclusion that the mind is a microcosm. In chapter 6 he discusses the spiritual sciences and spiritual forms, the subject of the next chapter is spiritual philosophy, and chapter 8 treats the important subject of the method of discriminating between evidences. The conclusion of the book leads up to his initial purpose to establish a federation of religions, for which first of all money is needed, and then the support of lay membership. The address of the treasurer to whom checks should be made out is given as Arthur D. Ropes, 291-293 Congress St., Boston, Mass., or to Rev. H. Vrooman himself, at Roxbury Sta., Boston.

Balance, the Fundamental Verity. By *Orlando J. Smith.* Boston and New York: Houghton, Mifflin & Co. The Riverside Press, Cambridge, Mass. 1904. Pp., ix, 146.

Mr. Orlando J. Smith, the author of *Eternalism*, discusses in the present volume the equilibrium which characterises the universe and forms the basis also of our intellectual and moral life. Noticing that the sea throws up the dunes that form its shores, he claims that as the power of the sea curbs the sea, as physical excess turns upon itself, as deficiency balances success, so also in the realm of spiritual life, evil powers find their limit, and thus, according to an eternal law of nature, regulate the balance of life in spite of its ceaseless motion. On the basis of this principle that "balance rules the world," Mr. Orlando Smith builds up the fundamental verity of his world conception, which has become a religion to him. Progress is made by antagonism; nature's process is by test and trial, by unfolding, changing, ripping up, undoing, and redoing, and error dies in the struggle.

So far, every scientist, materialist, or one who accepts a purely dynamic view of the world, would agree with Mr. Smith, but he builds higher upon this foundation by saying that justice is incomplete in this present existence. Our life here is as a broken part of a broader life, and if death ends all, then the mass of mankind must live, toil, suffer, and die under a condition of hopeless injustice. Accordingly he arrives at three conclusions which are the fundamentals of his religious belief and constitute the essential meaning of his religion. These are: (1) That the soul is accountable for its action; (2) That the soul survives death of the body; (3) That there is a supreme power to right things.

Mr. Smith declares that both religion and science have been misinterpreted and perverted, but if properly understood, no school of thought denies religion except practical materialism, the doctrine that wrong rules the world; otherwise science and religion meet in all essential truths as to the meaning of life and death, of persistence of right and wrong, the uniformity of nature, etc.

We do not deny that Mr. Smith is right in insisting on the importance of the immortality of the soul in religious belief, but the difficulty is not so much that the soul persists after death, but how it persists. That the life of every man is as a broken part of a broader life is obvious, and the task devolves on the thinker to point out the whole of which it forms a part and in which it finds its completion, its comforting, and the fulfilment of its hopes. Mr. Smith leaves us doubtful as to very important details of his conviction. He says:

"It is a curious fact that the doctrine of the annihilation of the soul has not yet acquired a definite name, though its adherents include a number of learned men, capable in the expression of thought and in the coining of words. 'Materialism' is the word used, in the absence of a better, to name this doctrine, but the dictionaries do not justify that use. Haeckel, recognizing its namelessness, has recently invented the word 'thanatism'—in English, 'deathism'—a fit name for the belief in the extinction of the soul. I shall, however, use the word 'materialism,' which is better known."

The whole endeavor of Mr. Orlando Smith is to overcome the view called by himself "materialism" and by Haeckel "thanatism."

A MONTHLY MAGAZINE

oted to the Science of Religion, the Religion of Science, and the Extension of the Religious Parliament Idea

Editor: Dr. Paul Carus *Associates:* E. C. Hegeler. Mary Carus.

, XVIII. (no. 10) October, 1904.

CONTENTS:

CHICAGO

The Open Court Publishing Company

LONDON: Kegan Paul, Trench, Trübner & Co., Ltd.

Per copy, 10 cents (sixpence). Yearly, $1.00 (in the U. P. U., 5s. 6d.).

… XIV. No. 4. JULY, 190

THE MONIST

A QUARTERLY MAGAZINE

Devoted to the Philosophy of Science

…r: Dr. Paul Carus. Associates: { E. C. Hegele / Mary Carus.

CONTENTS:

CHICAGO:

…E OPEN COURT PUBLISHING C…

Price, 50 cts.; Yearly, $2.00.

LONDON: Kegan Paul, Trench, Trübner & Company, Limited.

In England and U. P. U., half a crown; Yearly, 9s 6d.

 Entered at the Chicago Post Office as Second-Class Ma…

Chinese Philosophy, Fiction, and Religion

CHINESE PHILOSOPHY: Being an Exposition of the Main Characteristic Features of Chinese Thought. By *Dr. Paul Carus.* Pp., 62. Numerous diagrams and native characters and illustrations. Price, paper, 25 cents (1s. 6d.).

"Valuable and of unquestioned reliability. The delineation of the philosophy that underlies the Chinese civilisation is so ably done in these pages that the reader cannot fail to appreciate the causes which produce Chinese conservatism."—*Toledo Blade.*

CHINESE FICTION. By the *Rev. George T. Candlin.* With illustrations from original Chinese works, specimen facsimile reproductions of texts, and translations of representative passages. Giving a clear and vivid *résumé* of Chinese romantic literature. Pp., 51. Paper, 15 cents (9d.).

"A list of 'fourteen of the most famous Chinese novels' is given. Many long quotations from plays, poems, and stories are given, and the pamphlet is a source of great pleasure. The pictures, too, are charming."—*The Chicago Times Herald.*

LAO-TZE'S TAO-TEH-KING 老子道德經 Chinese-English. With Introduction, Transliteration, and Notes. By *Dr. Paul Carus.* With a photogravure frontispiece of the traditional picture of Lao-Tze, specially drawn for the work by an eminent Japanese artist. Appropriately bound in yellow and blue, with gilt top. Pp., 345. Price, $3.00 (15s.).

Contains: (1) A philosophical, biographical, and historical introduction discussing Lao-Tze's system of metaphysics, its evolution, its relation to the philosophy of the world, Lao-Tze's life, and the literary history of his work; (2) Lao-Tze's *Tao-Teh-King* in the original Chinese; (3) an English translation; (4) the transliteration of the text, where every Chinese word with its English equivalent is given, with references in each case to a Chinese dictionary; (5) Notes and Comments; (6) Index.

"Extraordinarily interesting. Of great moment."—*The Outlook.*

"A truly remarkable achievement."—*The North-China Herald.*

"While of great importance to the serious student, it is usable and interesting to any one who cares at all for the thought and religions of the Orient."—*The New Unity.*

"Much labor has been put into this book. It will be a great addition to the knowledge which English readers have of one of the greatest of religious books and religious leaders."—*The Church Union.*

"It is a convenient volume through which to make such acquaintance with the Chinese language and Chinese thought as an American scholar must consider desirable in view of the present increased intercourse with the Oriental world."—*Reformed Church Review.*

"All that one could do to make the immortal 'Canon on Reason and Virtue' alluring to American readers has certainly been done by the author. The translation is faithful, preserving especially the characteristic terseness and ruggedness of style of the original, the type work is superb, the comments judicious, and the binding a bright yellow with blue and gilt and red trimmings."—*The Cumberland Presbyterian.*

THE OPEN COURT PUBLISHING CO., CHICAGO, 324 Dearborn St.

LONDON: Kegan Paul, Trench, Trübner & Co., Ltd.

Lightning Source UK Ltd.
Milton Keynes UK
UKHW011232310119
336488UK00006B/467/P

9 780331 00268